C0-AKU-037

Becoming a Woman
in the Age of Letters

Becoming a Woman in the Age of Letters

∽ DENA GOODMAN

Cornell University Press   *Ithaca and London*

Copyright © 2009 by Cornell University

All rights reserved. Except for brief quotations in a review, this book, or parts thereof, must not be reproduced in any form without permission in writing from the publisher. For information, address Cornell University Press, Sage House, 512 East State Street, Ithaca, New York 14850.

First published 2009 by Cornell University Press
First printing, Cornell Paperbacks, 2009

Printed in the United States of America

Library of Congress Cataloging-in-Publication Data

Goodman, Dena, 1952–
    Becoming a woman in the age of letters / Dena Goodman.
        p. cm.
    Includes bibliographical references and index.
    ISBN 978-0-8014-4761-7 (cloth : alk. paper)—
    ISBN 978-0-8014-7545-0 (pbk. : alk. paper)
    1. French letters—Women authors—History and criticism.   2. Letter writing, French—History—
18th century.   3. Women—France—Correspondence.   4. Women—France—Intellectual life—18th century.
5. Women—Education—France—History—18th century.   I. Title.

    PQ711G66 2009
    846'.5099287—dc22

                                                                                                2008049126

Cornell University Press strives to use environmentally responsible suppliers and materials to the fullest extent possible in the publishing of its books. Such materials include vegetable-based, low-VOC inks and acid-free papers that are recycled, totally chlorine-free, or partly composed of nonwood fibers. For further information, visit our website at www.cornellpress.cornell.edu.

Cloth printing   10 9 8 7 6 5 4 3 2 1
Paperback printing   10 9 8 7 6 5 4 3 2 1

CONTENTS

ACKNOWLEDGMENTS

Back in the last century I had the idea to write a little coffee-table book on the material culture of women's letter writing in eighteenth-century France. I imagined an extended essay with lavish illustrations. For a while Mary Sheriff and I were going to write it together, and the conversations we had about letters, images, and furniture over the course of a year or so were invaluable and wonderful. Without Mary's encouragement I would not have had the audacity to pursue my ideas into such unknown territory. Over the course of the next decade, the essay grew to a monograph and the pictures became more than mere illustrations. And although the heart of this book is still material culture, its overall subject has become more ambitious: how letter writing was inscribed into the meaning and practice of modern womanhood. It gives me great pleasure to acknowledge those people and institutions who helped me produce a bigger and better book than I had imagined.

I benefited from many conversations with friends and colleagues, but I remember especially those with Nadine Bérenguier, Carolyn Lougee Chappell, Michèle Cohen, Jay Cook, Natalie Zemon Davis, Madeleine Dobie, Elizabeth Goldsmith, Kate Jensen, Sheryl Kroen, Michael Kwass, Darline Levy, Peter Reill, Pierre Saint-Amand, and Sidonie Smith from whom I received direction at crucial moments or insights that stuck with me for years. Many other friends and colleagues suggested sources to investigate and sent me pictures and museum postcards of women and letters and writing desks. In particular, Jennifer Jones told me about the stationers' trade cards that I discuss in chapter 5; Jennifer Popiel extolled the riches of the Musée national de l'Education in Rouen, where I found a wealth of fascinating material. I thank them and hope that others will find in the richness of this book testimony to how much I valued their many suggestions.

Most of the research for this book was conducted over the course of many summers with support first from the Louisiana State University Council on Research and then from the Departments of History and Women's Studies at the University of Michigan. Most of the writing was accomplished in a variety of wonderfully collegial settings. With sabbatical support from LSU and a fellowship from the Voltaire Foundation, I spent fall 1997 at the University of Oxford as the Voltaire Fellow and visiting fellow of Linacre College; at the University of Michigan I was fortunate to spend 2003–4 at the Institute for the Humanities as A. Bartlett Giamatti Fellow; most glorious of all, with the support of a fellowship from the Guggenheim Foundation and a Michigan Humanities Award I finished the manuscript at the Camargo Foundation in Cassis, France. I am grateful especially for the opportunities these residencies afforded me to retreat from teaching to write and to emerge from writing to exchange ideas with my fellow fellows in formal seminars and informal conversations. In Cassis, I was sustained and assisted at key moments especially by Nicole Archambeau, Tom Broden, Christopher Butterfield, Karen Duval, Heiko Kalmbach, Susan Kinsolving, John McManus, and Laura McPhee. At Oxford, when I was just beginning to write, I was lucky enough to have many long, wonderful, conversations with Maxine Berg, Nicholas Cronk, Robin Jacoby, Sarah Knott, John Robertson, and Dror Wahrman, to all of whom I am grateful.

At the University of Michigan I received research assistance from Robert Kruckeberg and Jennifer Palmer who patiently downloaded, collated, and dated the letters of Catherine de Saint-Pierre from the working site of the Bernardin de Saint-Pierre Papers Project. Access to the site was generously given by the director of the project, Malcolm Cook, who was always willing to help puzzle out the letters themselves. Dominique Rouet, Conservateur at the Bibliothèque Municipale du Havre, graciously made the manuscripts of Catherine de Saint-Pierre's letters available to me for further study and photography. Jean Hébrard made a special trip to Rouen to introduce me to the staff and resources of the Musée national de l'Education, just one moment in an ongoing conversation we have had about the meaning, power, and practice of writing from which I have learned a great deal. Gilian Wilson and Charissa Bremer-David generously shared their immense knowledge of eighteenth-century French furniture and opened to me the resources of the J. Paul Getty Museum in Malibu and then Los Angeles, California.

The research for this book went beyond libraries, archives, and museums, thanks to French people whose care for their own family papers and history was matched only by their trust in letting an American researcher study them. I was fortunate to be able to consult and photograph the original manuscripts of Geneviève Randon de Malboissière's letters thanks to the generosity of M. and Mme Christian de Luppé, who opened their family archives and their home to me. I thank M. de Luppé for permission to reproduce the photographs of some of these letters and of the desk at which their recipient later sat. M. and Mme Hubert de Silvestre also welcomed me into their home and opened their family archives to me. I am deeply grateful for their hospitality, as well as for permission to reproduce the photograph I took of the little physionotrace of Sophie Silvestre with which this book ends.

A book with as many pictures as this one presents extraordinary challenges. I am grateful, first, to John Ackerman of Cornell University Press for understanding immediately the importance of the visual material and committing the press to produce a book that would do it justice. I am also grateful to the Office of the Vice-President for Research, the Women's Studies Department, and the History Department of the University of Michigan who came through with a generous subvention to support the publication of this ambitious visual program. And I could not possibly have secured all the photographs and the permissions to reproduce them without the assistance of Katie Hartsough Brion, to whom I owe many thanks. Thanks, too, to Lou Robinson, Senior Designer at Cornell University Press, whose good judgment, patience, and expertise were essential to the production of this handsome volume. At Michigan, Dawn Kapalla in the History Department and Jennifer McJunkin and Shelley Shock in Women's Studies provided amazing support in the preparation of both text and images. At Cornell University Press, Ange Romeo-Hall and Katy Meigs were supportive and expert editors.

More challenging even than collecting the images was learning how to interpret and write about the visual and material culture they represent. I am grateful to Mary Sheriff from whose example I learned what it means to think about a painting and to Mary Salzman and Susan Siegfried for continuing that education. Jennifer Palmer showed me that it was possible to take paintings seriously as art while still pursuing the questions we ask as historians, while Katie Hornstein helped me to see that no image speaks for itself. Mimi Hellman and Carolyn Sargentson became my guides and my inspiration in the world of furniture and Natacha Coquery, David Hancock, and Morag Martin in the world of goods. From them I learned how to move beyond discourses, representations, and practices and think about things and the meanings they hold. Laura Auricchio and Jessica Fripp were generous with their knowledge of and thoughts about Adélaïde Labille-Guiard, the painter who gave me my muse in her portrait of an unknown letter-writing woman.

Between 1996 and 2008, I presented the ideas and research that would become this book at conferences, colleges, and universities on two continents. In particular, the Western Society for French History and the American and International Societies for Eighteenth-Century Studies provided welcoming forums for the presentation of this work as it progressed and stimulating and supportive communities in which it was nurtured. I am grateful too to the many colleagues who invited me to present my work at their home institutions, encouraged me to continue it, and sharpened my ideas with their questions and comments: Steven Kaplan at Cornell University, Darline Levy at NYU, Madeleine Dobie at Tulane University, Caroline Ford at the University of British Columbia, David Sabean at UCLA, Anita Guerrini at UC Santa Barbara, Colin Jones and Maxine Berg at the University of Warwick, Amanda Vickery at the Institute for Historical Research (London), Nicholas Cronk at the University of Oxford, David Bell at Johns Hopkins University, Aurora Wolfgang for the Western Society for Eighteenth-Century Studies, Barbara Taylor and Sarah Knott for the Feminism and Enlightenment Project (London), Rebecca Messbarger at Washington University, Katie Scott at the Courtauld Institute, John Styles at the Victoria and Albert Museum, Kathleen Wellman at Southern Methodist University, Monica Bolufer at the Universidad Menéndez Pelayo (Valencia, Spain), Susannah Ottaway at Carleton College, Liliane Hilaire-Pérez at the Conservatoire National des Arts et Métiers (Paris), Dean Lahikainen at the Peabody Essex Museum (Salem, MA), Karin Wurst at Michigan State University, Peggy McCracken at the University of Michigan, Charlene Boyer-Lewis at Kalamazoo College, Barbara Benedict at Trinity College, Jean Hébrard, Christian Jouhaud, and Dinah Ribard at the Ecole des Hautes Etudes en Sciences Sociales (Paris), Nicole Pellegrin at the Ecole Normale Supérieure (Paris), and Gillian Dow at the Chawton House Library (UK).

Earlier versions of parts of this book were published in a variety of venues. The discussion of mother-daughter correspondences in chapter 2 was first presented at a conference and then published by the conference organizers in a volume of essays that emerged from it as "Le Rôle des mères dans l'éducation des pensionnaires au XVIIIe siècle," in *Femmes éducatrices au siècle des Lumières: discours et pratiques,* ed. Isabelle Brouard-Arends and Marie-Emanuelle Plagnol (Presses Universitaires de Rennes, 2007), 33–44. The discussion of spelling in chapter 3 appeared first in "*L'Ortografe des Dames*: Gender and Language in the Old Regime," *French Historical Studies* 25 (Spring 2002): 191–223. Much of the discussion of writing paper in chapter 5 appeared in "Why Is Writing Paper Blue? Colour and Fashion in Eighteenth Century Writing Paper," in *Les archives de l'invention: écrits, objets et images de l'activité inventive,* ed. Marie-Sophie Corcy, Christiane Douyère-Demeulenaere, and Liliane Hilaire-Perez (CNRS/Université de Toulouse-Le Mirail, 2006), 537–546. Chapter 6 also draws on work that was presented at conferences and then published as essays in books that emerged from them: "Furnishing Discourses: Readings of a Writing Desk in Eighteenth-Century France," in *Luxury in the Eighteenth Century: Debates, Desires and Delectable Goods,* ed. Maxine Berg and Elizabeth Eger (London: Palgrave, 2002), 71–88; and "The Secrétaire and the Integration of the Eighteenth-Century Self," in *Furnishing the Eighteenth Century: What Furniture Can Tell Us about Europe and America in the Eighteenth Century,* which I edited with Kathryn Norberg (New York: Routledge, 2006), 183–203. Chapter 7 appeared first as "Letter Writing and the Emergence of Gendered Subjectivity in Eighteenth-Century France," *Journal of Women's History* 17 (Summer 2005): 9–37. I thank all the editors for permission to republish this material here. I am grateful to them and the peer reviewers whose advice they solicited for the encouragement and criticism that helped to deepen and sharpen the analyses that eventually found their way into this book.

The most generous colleagues were those who read parts or all of the manuscript and gave me feedback that was sometimes difficult to swallow but always valuable. I thank them all. Martha Jones, Mary Kelley, and Carroll Smith-Rosenberg read the education chapters in the context of an informal writing group that was one of the thrills of being at the University of Michigan. Alden Gordon, Mary Sheriff, and Susan Siegfried gave me absolutely crucial readings of chapter 1; Suzanne Desan and Jeffrey Merrick gave me very helpful comments on earlier versions of chapters 8 and 9; and Elizabeth Wingrove gave me the benefit of her great analytic vision as I struggled with the conclusion, as well as an earlier version of chapter 7. Sarah Maza and Kathleen Wellman somehow found the time to read the entire manuscript and give me comments that were both critical and encouraging when I needed them most.

John Ackerman of Cornell University Press is a great editor and a great friend. In an academic world that is characterized by movement and flux, it is a pleasure and a privilege to thank him in print for the third time. There is no one with whom I would rather make books.

NOTE TO THE READER

In part 4 of this book I analyze in detail the letters of four women: Catherine de Saint-Pierre, Geneviève Randon de Malboissière, Marie-Jeanne Phlipon, and Anne Charlotte Sophie Silvestre. I also turn to their letters throughout the book for insight into epistolary culture and practice. Unless otherwise noted, all references to these letters are from the following sources:

Papiers de Bernardin de Saint-Pierre, Bibliothèque municipale du Havre, folder 142. I am grateful to Malcolm Cook for access to electronic copies of these letters, to appear in *Correspondance de Jacques Henri Bernardin de Saint-Pierre*, ed. Malcolm Cook, et al. (Electronic Enlightenment, Oxford University Press), http://www.e-enlightenment. org/eeBornDigital/eeBSP_e.php.

Lettres de Madame Roland, nouvelle série 1767–1780, ed. Claude Perroud with the collaboration of Marthe Conor, 2 vols. (Paris: Imprimerie Nationale, 1913). The originals are apparently now lost.

Une jeune fille au XVIIIe siècle: Lettres de Geneviève de Malboissière à Adélaïde Méliand 1761–1766, ed. Comte [Albert Marie Pierre] de Luppé (Paris: Edouard Champion, 1925). Manuscripts were consulted in the Archives de Beaurepaire, courtesy of M. Christian de Luppé.

Papiers Bonnard, Archives nationales 352 AP. Lettres du chevalier de Bonnard (1744–1784): Lettres de sa femme, Sophie Silvestre AN 352 AP 34; Mme de Bonnard née Silvestre, papiers personnels: Lettres du chevalier de Bonnard, son mari AN 352 AP 39.

All translations from the French are my own unless otherwise noted.

*Becoming a Woman
in the Age of Letters*

Introduction

In France in the eighteenth century, increasing numbers of women, from the wives and daughters of artisans and merchants to countesses and queens, became writers—not authors, and not mere signers of names, but writers of letters. How that happened, what it meant for individual women and the concept and practice of womanhood, and how French society responded to women as writers are the central concerns of this book.

Scholarship on women writers in the eighteenth century has expanded greatly in recent years, with important monographs on individual writers and studies of gendered modes of authorship.[1] I hope to contribute to this body of work, but my focus is elsewhere, not on "women writers," but on writing as a cultural practice in which growing numbers of women engaged outside of authorship; that is, as an everyday cultural practice of ordinary (literate) women. By focusing on writing rather than authorship, and on the writing that women who write do, rather than on women writers, I believe I can make more convincing claims about gender, writing, and modern subjectivity than have been advanced by those who study published authors. At the same time, I want to draw attention to the contribution of education and epistolary competence in creating a new class divide among women just as the old distinction between aristocrats and commoners was breaking down.

Letter writing is an ancient cultural practice, but in the seventeenth century it began to expand significantly with the spread of literacy; the development of state postal services and international postal unions; and the increased movement of people and goods through trade, travel, colonialism, and government service. Furthermore, as literary historians have shown, starting around 1660, French cultural theorists distinguished letters from other forms of writing and associated them specifically with elite women they called "ladies."[2] Whereas all writing had previously been considered primarily a male occupation, letter writing now entered the repertoire of cultural practices that these elite women were expected to master, even as it was assumed to flow effortlessly from their nature. No matter what the aspirations of parents for their daughters, instruction in letter writing would be necessary: it was part of the equipment of a modern woman and a primary means of social mobility.

Along with conversation, letter writing became one of the ways in which eighteenth-century elite women displayed and demonstrated their refinement, but it also shaped the way they established and sustained relationships with others. And it emerged as women's primary site of reflection and self-reflection; in letters women were able to articulate a gendered subjectivity at a time when gender expectations were changing and often contradictory.

As the elite broadened over the course of the eighteenth century, epistolarity became embedded in the material and social world of increasing numbers of women. Stationers set up shop in the fashionable precincts of Paris to attract their business; fashion merchants developed a line of small writing desks to serve their needs; writing surfaces proliferated in the rooms women inhabited. To explore this material world of letter writing I draw and expand on the growing body of work on the history of consumption. In contrast to most historians of consumption, however, I am interested in the material as it serves cultural practice and examine it through the lens of gender. I ask how the material culture of letter writing was transformed by a regendering of the practice it was meant to serve just when France's consumer economy was poised to take off. By looking at consumption through the lens of gender and in the service of cultural practice, I bring into focus fashionable new consumer goods as they were used as well as fabricated, marketed, sold, and purchased. In this way, I show how letter writing and consumption—two practices in which increasing numbers of women engaged for the first time in the eighteenth century, and which came to be identified with them, came to shape them as modern women.

Letter Writing, Autonomy, and the Female Subject

"More than any other single invention, writing has transformed human consciousness," declares the philosopher Walter Ong. In certain times and cultures, magical power has been ascribed to writing, but in all cultures writing is a form of power and a basis of social distinction.[3] Because it allows a person to withdraw into him or herself, writing also facilitates the reflection through which personal autonomy is attained, or at least experienced. It is one of the learned skills that allow individuals to determine and follow their own will, to live and act according to their own values, and that make up what Diana Meyers calls "autonomy competency." Indeed, Michel de Certeau considers writing the key practice through which individuals produce themselves as subjects.[4]

The ability to reflect on oneself and the world is central to all theories of autonomy. Charles Taylor, for example, argues that it is precisely this reflexivity that distinguishes modern conceptions of the self from those of the ancients. Steven Lukes notes that the degree of autonomy a person enjoys is in part a function of the self-consciousness that such reflection makes possible.[5] Reflection through writing is equally crucial to what feminist theorists call "relational autonomy": an understanding of autonomy that begins from the premise that all people are socially embedded and that selves are formed not against relationships with others but in the context of them.[6] Such a conception sees autonomy as a matter of degree, rather than an absolute or a condition of being, and sees each degree of autonomy as an achievement. Like individualist conceptions of autonomy, however, relational autonomy emphasizes both reflection and choice.[7] Writing helps individuals who are socially embedded to reflect on themselves, their relationships, their society, their world, and to make choices based on their own standards or values, even as they may acknowledge the limits placed on both their autonomy and their choices. These may be consumer choices, or the word choices that are made each time a sentence is constructed, or life choices such as whom to marry. For women in the eighteenth century, such choices were always constrained, and autonomy was always an achievement, always a matter of degree, and always relational. Writing letters and engaging in correspondence helped women to achieve moments and degrees of autonomy within the context of human relationships—from family and friendship to social and gender systems, systems that were becoming modern as they were themselves.[8]

Letter writing is a practice and a competence through which such an autonomous but relational subjectivity can develop. "Herein lies the paradox of correspondence," writes Brigitte Diaz, "that one addresses the other to find oneself. . . . In the climate of confidence of the pair or the network, the letter appears to women as a privileged mode of access to the self, conducive to engaging in a true 'culture of the self.'"[9] If the diary has been more often seen as the site of production of modern subjectivity, correspondence is the form of writing par excellence of the socially embedded modern subject, because, for the letter writer, unlike the self-absorbed diarist, other people exist as autonomous subjects like herself. Indeed, letters are like language itself: writing them not only allows us to focus on things, people, ourselves, in a way that we otherwise could not, it also brings us and our ideas into human relation. "Being a person cannot be understood simply as exercising a set of capacities I have as an individual," argues Charles Taylor. "On the contrary, I only acquire this capacity in conversation." As a conversation in writing, correspondence is dialogue with reflection. If, as Taylor concludes, we become persons as interlocutors, we become modern persons as correspondents.[10]

Marie-Claire Grassi, who has studied hundreds of letters written by aristocratic men and women between 1750 and 1850, concludes that in the eighteenth century "the letter became an everyday privileged site for the expression of the self."[11] Jürgen Habermas concurs. He recognizes letter writing as the dominant practice through which men and women of the eighteenth century both came to know themselves as individuals and to develop what he calls "human" relations with one another. As the intersubjectivity of letter writing oriented the new subject it constituted outward, the letter writer's addressee would become the author's public. The sharing, circulation, and publication of "private" letters was thus the first stage through which private persons entered into the new public sphere that was both discursive and intersubjective.[12]

Habermas calls the eighteenth century "the century of the letter," but he does not consider what it meant for women, who were routinely praised for their "natural talent" as letter writers and encouraged to develop it, to be denied full participation in this new public sphere for which letter writing prepared them.[13] In response, much feminist ink has been spilled explaining and decrying the exclusion of women from the modern public sphere.[14] However, there is more to modernity than the public and the political. Privateness, too, was novel in the eighteenth century; intimacy, we are told, was "invented" then. Philippe Ariès has argued that by 1700 the articulation of a truly public realm for the first time since the fall of Rome made it possible "to create a closed private preserve, or at any rate a private realm totally divorced from . . . public service and completely autonomous."[15] And as Habermas himself shows, what distinguished the new public sphere of the eighteenth century was the privateness of the individuals who constituted it. The very possibility of coming together with others to form a public was predicated on this prior sense of oneself as a private person, achieved through cultural practices such as letter writing that developed interiority and reflection.

Letter-writing women became conscious of themselves as gendered subjects in the gap between a common experience of privateness and the differential positions defined by gender in the public sphere. As Grassi observes, "for the woman, be she mother, wife, lover, or friend, the letter was the only means of expression at her disposal. . . . In her confidences, the woman speaks of the difficulty of being a woman in the eighteenth century."[16] For women, letter writing was not simply a form of recreation or a second-best alternative to public writing; it was a crucial step in developing a consciousness of themselves as gendered subjects in the modern world.

This modern world was larger than home, family, village; it was larger than France or even Europe, extending outward across the seas that had limited the vision and movement of Europeans for centuries. By the eighteenth century, transoceanic mobility, like writing, was one of the things that distinguished modern from premodern subjects. It contributed to a modern view of self and world. Women who crossed the Atlantic counted on letters to maintain their ties to family left behind, as well as to record their thoughts and observations of the New World they encountered.[17] Yet, as Grassi reminds us, "whether she be wife, friend, lover, the woman is almost always the one who stays home and who takes up with the other a discourse about absence."[18] How, then, did French women, the vast majority of whom never boarded a ship, develop the specifically modern consciousness associated with the openness and opportunities of this transoceanic world? For many of them, reading, sociability, and epistolary exchange were the means by which they became part of an early modern European world that was powered by the sea, even as their own mobility was bounded by it. Letters to and from absent others, but also letters exchanged with friends or family about the world beyond the limits of their own circumscribed mobility, could stretch those limits and bring women into that larger, modern world.

Women wrote oceans of letters in the eighteenth-century, but most of the ones that have been published are of only limited value in helping us to understand letter writing as it was practiced by "ordinary" women in their daily lives, or how it might have functioned in the articulation of their gendered subjectivity. Chosen for their ability to represent masculine ideals of femininity or to flatter male egos, these letters tell us less about women than they do about the men who published them. Indeed, many if not most women's letters that have been published since the eighteenth century are presented as models of a single feminine ideal: what the nineteenth-century critic Sainte-Beuve called the "loving woman," by which he meant the woman who loved one man passionately. The love letters of Julie de Lespinasse to the comte de Guibert, first published in 1809 but of enduring scholarly and popular interest, epitomize the kind of letters that have shaped our ideas of eighteenth-century women and the letters they wrote.[19] Popular epistolary fictions, from the *Lettres portuguaises* (1669) to *Les Liaisons dangereuses* (1782) reinforce the impression that when women wrote they wrote about love. The published letters of prominent women of court and salon sometimes defy this male construction and challenge male hegemony, but such letters lack the everydayness of correspondence as most women practiced it.[20]

For this book I have turned elsewhere—away from famous women and women of letters, and from love letters. I have sought out letters written by women for whom writing was a regular practice but for whom personal letters were their primary form of writing. The letters of four women in particular have attracted my sustained attention: Catherine de Saint-Pierre (1743–1804), Geneviève Randon de Malboissière (1746–66), Marie-Jeanne (Manon) Phlipon (1754–93), and Sophie Silvestre (1764–98). Each woman left a body of epistolary writing, her half of a correspondence undertaken over many years with a trusted friend or family member. Their letters suggest how engaging in correspondence helped them to arrive at an understanding of what it meant to be a woman, to confront and work through the choices that womanhood entailed, and to arrive at some degree of autonomy as women.

Catherine de Saint-Pierre was born in Le Havre and spent her life in port towns on the Normandy coast.[21] Her mother's family were upstanding citizens of Dieppe, merchants and ship captains in the Atlantic trade who served the town as churchwardens, militia officers, aldermen, and commercial court judges. Her father, the director of the Le Havre office of the royal messenger service, claimed (erroneously) descent from Eustache de Saint-Pierre, one of the famous "burghers of Calais" who became Normandy's greatest heroes for having saved their town from the besieging English during the Hundred Years' War. Catherine's mother died when she was a child, and her father died when she was twenty-three. By that time, her three brothers had all left home to make their fortunes. Bernardin, the eldest of the three, was an engineer turned writer who is best known for *Paul et Virginie*, the most popular novel ever published in France.[22] Between 1766 and her death in 1804, Catherine wrote him more than a hundred letters that he saved.

Catherine de Saint-Pierre lived a relatively long but unhappy life, marked by poverty and illness; Geneviève Randon de Malboissière's life was much happier, but cut tragically short.[23] Geneviève's paternal grandfather was a *capitoul* of Toulouse, a member of the municipal council whose position brought him and his male descendants a title of nobility. Along with his brothers and male cousins, Geneviève's father entered into the lucrative world of royal finance.[24] In the 1740s, when Geneviève was born, he was in charge of collecting taxes in Soissons, where he got to know the royal intendant, Charles-Blaise Méliand, whose daughter, Adélaïde (Adèle), was just a year older than Geneviève. In the 1760s, the two families, both of them wealthy and well placed, lived near each other in Paris, and the two girls became best friends and correspondents. Adélaïde's letters to Geneviève have not survived, but she saved nearly three hundred letters that Geneviève wrote to her between 1761 and 1766. Perhaps this is because in 1766, at the age of twenty, Geneviève de Malboissière died of measles, just a few months after the death of her fiancé and the marriage of her best friend. Educated at home by a battery of tutors, Geneviève was eulogized after her death by Friedrich Melchior Grimm, who wrote of her in his *Correspondance littéraire* that "she was already famous in Paris for her learning."[25]

The social position of Marie-Jeanne Phlipon was as humble as that of Catherine de Saint-Pierre, and her life ended even more tragically than that of Geneviève de Malboissière—under the blade of the guillotine. Manon, as she was called, grew up in the heart of Paris, where her father was a master engraver and her maternal grandfather a fashion merchant. Although educated primarily at home by tutors, she spent one year at the Parisian convent of the Dames de la Congrégation, where she became friends with two sisters from Amiens, Sophie and Henriette Cannet. Manon began to correspond regularly with Sophie in 1767, and later also wrote sometimes to Henriette. All told, there are more than 250 extant letters from Manon to the Cannet sisters, but only one or two of their responses have survived. The correspondence ended in 1780 with Manon's marriage to Jean-Marie Roland. Along with her husband, Manon Phlipon Roland became a leader of the Girondins in the early years of the French Revolution. In 1793, during the Terror, she was arrested and tried as a counterrevolutionary and traitor and executed later that year. During the six months she spent in prison Madame Roland wrote her memoirs, which were published posthumously.[26]

Anne Charlotte Sophie Silvestre was born in Versailles to an altogether different sort of family, one allied with the French monarchy rather than those who would overturn it. However, they were not themselves aristocrats but distinguished artists descended from the engraver Israël Silvestre (1621–91).[27] Sophie's father, Jacques-Augustin Silvestre, was drawing master for the royal children; he also held the honorific title of "dauphin's gun-carrier." Her maternal grandfather, François Férès, was reader and librarian for the comte de Provence, the king's brother who would rule after the French Revolution as Louis XVIII. But Sophie's mother died just a month after her birth, leaving behind the infant Sophie and her two-year-old brother. When Sophie was sixteen, she married Bernard de Bonnard, a minor nobleman from Burgundy who had made a career in the artillery and a reputation as a poet before landing a plum position in 1777 as tutor of the sons of the duc de Chartres (a member of the powerful Orléans branch of the royal family and the future Philippe Egalité).[28] Close to three hundred letters between husband and wife have been preserved, most of them written between December 1781 (two months after the birth of their first child) and July 1784, two months before Bonnard's untimely death from smallpox. Sophie did not remarry, and with help from her brother raised her two sons through the most difficult years of the French Revolution until her death in 1798.

None of these women or their letters was "typical." Typicality depends on an artificial construct of womanhood against which individual women are measured, and it is not my aim in this book to establish such a construct, which easily falls into stereotype. Indeed, the closer one looks at particular women and their letters, the more individual they become, the less typical they seem: to look for the typical is to lose the individual. My approach has been to seek out the individual but not the extraordinary, while listening for the resonances of each woman's experience and writing in that of her contemporaries. But letters, no matter how many one reads or how closely one reads them, can never disclose fully the meaning and practice of epistolarity as women lived it in the eighteenth century. I have thus also tried to situate the letters of these individual women within two frameworks: the educational theories and practices that shaped how young ladies were taught to become letter writers; and the consumer revolution that shaped the material world they entered as letter writers. And, although the practice of letter writing that interests me here is primarily private, I hope to show how it was embedded in larger fields of activity that expanded the meaning and the horizons of epistolary practice: the discursive field of literary history and the political field of monarchy and empire.

Women, Letters, and Literary History

Historians have traditionally pointed to the uprisings against the monarchy known as the Fronde (1648–53) as the moment when the nobility of France was finally pacified after a century of struggles that began with the French Wars of Religion and ended with the triumph of Louis XIV and the monarchy. For noble women, Joan DeJean has argued, this defeat led to a forced retreat from the public sphere of the pen.[29] For them, the novel and the letter were a sort of "court in exile," like that of one of the defeated *frondeuses*, Mademoiselle de Montpensier (1627–93). This granddaughter of Henri IV and cousin of Louis XIV dreamed of a new city of women whose language was that of inaction, of *repos*: "I want . . . every one of us to have a *cabinet*," she declared, "where we would learn . . . to delight in that *repos* that we will have chosen over the turbulent agitation of the court and the world."[30]

As power shifted in France from a weakened aristocracy to a triumphant monarchy, it also shifted from the sword to the pen. Even as Louis XIV's armies expanded and solidified France's borders and competed with European rivals to colonize Asia, Africa, and the Americas, the monarchy consolidated its power at home and abroad through administration and bureaucracy. But it was not just the state that embraced the pen and its power. Throughout France, literacy rates increased for both women and men, although it remained and grew stronger in the north than the south, and in urban areas rather than the countryside. In the century between 1690 and 1789, the percentage of women who signed their names on parish registers nearly doubled, from 14 to 27 percent. The percentage of male signers increased too, but not quite as much, from 29 to 48 percent. On the eve of the French Revolution, male literacy was still much higher than female literacy, but the gap was narrowing, especially among the elite.[31]

More women could read and write, but few of them were "writers," and those who were formed a modest fraction of the whole. Both the male academies and the female-dominated salons that had flourished since the seventeenth century fostered the development of what Alain Viala has called "the birth of the writer," by associating the man of letters with print publication, and print publication with men.[32] The population of France's Republic of Letters skyrocketed, to be dominated numerically by men of common birth. And while the number of women in the expanding population of writers increased too, they remained a minority even in the most "feminized" genre, the novel. Women authors published in other genres besides the novel (pedagogy and memoirs, for example), but in areas such as natural history, philosophy, and law their presence was barely felt—despite such luminaries as Newton's translator, Émilie du Châtelet.[33] Among women more than men, the gap between the ability to write and being a published writer or author grew, even as literacy rose over the course of the eighteenth century. The practice of letter writing expanded to fill that gap.

In literature and art, women were rarely figured as writers, and then only of letters. And the letters with which they were identified were less the newsy letters of Mme de Sévigné than the hopeless love letters written from the cloister by a fictional Portuguese nun and published anonymously by Gabriel-Joseph de Guilleragues in 1669 as *Lettres portugaises*. "Epistolary woman was a male creation," writes Katharine Jensen. "As a creature of emotion, woman was seen to take naturally to letter writing, her passion for a man overflowing spontaneously into writing to him about it." Jensen acknowledges that women were now encouraged to write, but she maintains that the ideal of Epistolary Woman, the limitation of women's writing to letters, and to letters about love in particular, undermined any positive effects of this encouragement. Trapped within epistolarity, they not only gave men free rein to conquer the great new expanse of the literary field, but were powerless to write themselves out of a self-defeating plot of love, seduction, and betrayal.[34]

I take a more optimistic view of the implications of women's association with letter writing because I believe (and I believe the following chapters show) that the power to write, once given, can never be fully controlled. Indeed, if the letter itself could not be contained within the boundaries of private, intimate discourse, neither could those who wrote them. In the eighteenth century who held the pens and what they did with them defined a whole series of power struggles that marked the rise of the public sphere and the modern world it would shape. The history of women, writing, and letters is part of this larger history.

Women were not told to exchange their pens for needles and distaffs, but they were scared away from the profession of writer and the increasingly powerful sphere of the printed word and actively encouraged to use their "natural" talent for epistolary expression. This encouragement came in many forms. Educators, pedagogues, and men of letters developed and promoted methods of teaching epistolary skills within a moral discourse of femininity that was meant to contain letter writing within marriage and motherhood. Fashion itself became a tool in the campaign to contain women's writing and limit their use of the pen to the letter, but also to contain it within the bounds of private communication and intimate expression. And, although this campaign was in many ways successful, the power of the letter to open up a world beyond the walls of the home, to connect minds as well as to express hearts, undermined its purpose.

Material Culture, Epistolarity, and Gender

The power of writing stems in part from its dual nature as both a material and an intellectual practice; it is neither mere transcription of words already formed nor the formation of those words in the mind alone. In order to traverse the cultural boundary between private and public and the physical distance marked by absence, the letter incorporates the mind, making the spiritual material. The material culture of epistolarity is the extension of the incorporation of the mind—the expression, communication, and preservation of thoughts and desires—which constitutes the letter itself. As Christine Haas declares, "the relationship between writing and the material world is both inextricable and profound. Indeed, writing is language made material."[35]

Just as a single letter is part of a correspondence, so is the material culture of epistolarity part of a system of commerce and trade. In eighteenth-century France, that system was centered in Paris, just as were the post and the fashion system. Like them, too, it spread European culture to the four corners of the world as it brought that world back to enrich the culture of Paris, France, and Europe. As the narrow world of France expanded through the conquests of Louis XIV and his successors—as well as through the improvements they made in the infrastructure of communication and transportation within the French hexagon—so too did the epistolary and material culture of Parisians at the center.[36] In place of the "natural" community of village or province, mediated communities were constructed of epistolary ties and material goods, communities bound by new values and the value of the new. The letter-writing woman was a modern woman—up to date, fashionable, furnishing her home according to her own taste. Because there was no tradition of female epistolarity, the practice of letter writing compelled her to enter the arena of the new, since only there could she find the tools she required.

Traditionally, writing was a masculine culture, its tools designed for masculine purposes and male bodies, often taboo for women to handle. In ancient and medieval times, men held the pens because composition and inscription were carried out by different people of different social status and power: the common scribe was directed by the noble composer as the hand was directed by the brain—and scribal work was men's work. With the integration of these two activities into a single practice, elites of both sexes took up pens, and writing became personal for the first time. There was, however, a gender lag. As late as the sixteenth century, the poet Madeleine des Roches worried that pens were being kept out of women's hands: "Our parents have the laudable custom, / In order to deprive us of the use of our wits, / Of keeping us locked up at home / And of handing us the spindle instead of the pen," she complained.[37] Until women overcame the cultural taboos against writing, no material culture was designed or built for them, and the equipment designed for men was off limits. But when letter writing became associated with and then embraced by elite women, it generated a material culture that came to represent the new tastes, fashions, and values of the age.

By 1662 Molière could ridicule the husband who tried to hold on to his wife by depriving her of the letter-writer's tools. The seventh of Arnolphe's eleven marriage maxims in *L'École des femmes* is quite clear on the subject: "Among her furnishings, she should not get bored, / There is no need for inkstand, ink, paper, or pens; / The husband, according to good customs / Should write all that is written in his home."[38] But the jealous man's efforts to keep pen and paper out of the hands of young Agnès fail immediately, as she manages to sneak a note to her lover by wrapping it around a rock and heaving it out a window at him.[39] By the eighteenth century, men were encouraging women not only to learn to write beautiful letters but to buy everything from lessons and spellers to decorated paper and elegant writing desks.

The regendering of letter writing became the impetus for the production, distribution, and consumption of a whole new array of goods. This was not simply because women's bodies are different from men's, or because men and women wear different clothes, but because gender itself is constructed. In the words of Joan Scott, gender is "a social category imposed on a sexed body."[40] It is not just sexed bodies that are gendered, however, but all that is material. Gender gives meaning to matter. The increased demand for, production of, and circulation of epistolary paraphernalia, along with the particular forms these objects took, represent not just the increased participation of women in the practice of letter writing but the acceptance by producers, merchants, and journalists of the legitimacy of this practice—in part, no doubt for their own personal gain. By becoming part of the fashion system, letter writing was legitimized as a female activity and promoted for commercial gain.[41]

The fashion system marked the shift from a cultural economy of stability to one of change, in which novelty and being "up to date" meant more than adhering to traditional practices and products. It was part of a shift in the generation of consumption from the court to the public, as taste and judgment came to be the province of urban tastemakers and individuality played a larger role than imitation or deference. The press took charge of diffusing consumption beyond the limits of the nobility and challenging female readers to develop their own taste under its informed guidance.[42]

Paper, pens, inkstands, and writing desks were produced and sold in the same quarters of Paris as fashionable clothing and fashionable books. These objects participated in the transformation of the productive economy to one centered on distribution, in which the mercer (*marchand mercier*), like the *marchande de modes* and the printer-bookseller, acted as the orchestrator and middleman between producer and consumer. The development of print media further facilitated fruitful interaction between producers and consumers of epistolary paraphernalia, just as it did between dressmakers and their clients, novelists and their readers. With advertising, a press, and a market, goods circulated faster and more broadly. The role of Paris was central, for as Daniel Roche observes, "here, producers and consumers, in the commercial relationship, shaped the new manners."[43] As the market in consumer goods expanded over the course of the eighteenth century, the practice of letter writing rode the crest of Paris's lead in the production of fashionable goods for an expanding female market.

Because both literacy and wealth were available only to an elite in the eighteenth century, the letter writer's tools were luxury goods in the same sense that books were luxury goods: they nourished the mind, not the body; they implied the availability of time freed from productive labor; they could be bound in luxurious materials; and they carried prestige and status. And, like novels in particular, objects associated with letter writing carried the gendered implications of femininity. But if letter writing was never a material necessity like feeding or clothing the body, it was not equivalent to decorating the body either: the writing desk was different from the dressing table or *toilette*, the furniture form to which it is most closely related, because it supported a cultural practice whose means were bodily but whose ends were spiritual, intellectual, psychological, and social. Over the course of the eighteenth century, writing tools and supplies became necessary to increasing numbers of women for whom letter writing was no mere luxury.[44]

In the eighteenth century, writers and critics tended to discuss the objects that filled the shops and furnished homes, not in terms of luxury and necessity, however, but in terms of fashion, taste, comfort, and, above all, utility. As the marquis de Condorcet quipped in a letter to his friend, Mme Suard: "Books about luxury are the most useless things in the world, after the fashion merchants."[45] Critics no longer saw excessive consumption as a legitimate way for the aristocracy to distinguish themselves from and display power to their laboring and producing inferiors, as had been the case throughout the Middle Ages and the Renaissance. Such opulent display of luxury was now considered bad taste at best, abuse of power at worst. In the age of Bernard Mandeville and Adam Smith, wealth and the things it could buy were validated, not as a privilege of a hereditary elite, but as signs of industry and social improvement. The consumer, however, remained suspect, and the fear of excess, of consumption that was not tied to industry and utility, remained suspect as well. Those who did not earn wealth threatened the system that validated it and the happiness of those who claimed to enjoy it legitimately.

With the rise of new practices of consumption in the eighteenth century and the proliferation of new goods to consume—what some historians call the "consumer revolution"—the marker of consumption began to shift from the status category of aristocracy to the gender category of women.[46] With this move, the moral and economic critique of aristocratic consumption and display came to rest on women and fashion. Consumption remained morally suspect (because unproductive), even as commerce and the commercial economy took on positive masculine associations.[47] By the nineteenth century, as Joan Scott has shown, the gendering of consumption as feminine was secured by the masculinizing of production in the heroic labor of the (masculine) working classes.[48] Where moralists had criticized aristocratic luxury, they now turned their attention to the frivolity and irresponsibility of the female consumer. The turning point can be seen in the vitriolic attacks on Marie Antoinette, begun in the 1780s but gaining heat in the revolutionary decade that followed, as both female consumer and decadent aristocrat whose extravagance bankrupted the state and starved the nation.[49]

At the same time, however, as Daniel Roche argues, fashion "defended happiness, glorified the feminine identified with the human in civilization and contributed to the victory of individualism." The triumph of fashion was the victory of feminine culture over brutish nature, of mind over body. Fashion undermined traditional society and culture by validating pleasure in this world and promoting "a new vision of life devoted to the minor arts" that liberated human beings through their mastery of nature.[50] In Roche's scheme, fashion was both the culmination of an Old Regime and Enlightenment world view in which women elevated men from brutishness to civility and a modern, liberating, force.[51] As letters dissolved the difference between the material and the spiritual, fashion brought them into harmony. No longer seeking redemption through the renunciation of worldly goods, men and women could attain a new sort of liberation by embracing both the material world of human invention and taste and the intellectual qualities behind it.

Another perspective is offered by Jean-Christophe Agnew, who looks at modern consumer culture in terms of longing and belonging—terms that could also describe the emotional matrix of epistolarity. Consumption, he suggests, is about making a home and becoming part of a community through the accumulation of goods.[52] If the moment of longing (epitomized by window shopping) is essentially an intimate or private moment set in the public sphere of the marketplace, that of belonging is a communal or public move effected through the consumption of objects for private or personal use. Letters, too, create a sense of longing and belonging. In Old Regime France they forged a connection between individuals separated by the centrifugal forces of state-building, travel, and colonial expansion. They enabled women to include distant friends and family in their community: family members such as Mme de Sévigné's daughter, separated from her mother in Brittany through her marriage to the governor of Provence; friends such as abbé Galiani, retained in the community of Parisian philosophes after returning to his native Naples through his correspondence with Mme d'Épinay.[53]

Michel de Certeau provides yet another perspective on consumption, one that is more political and less sentimental. Consumption, he says, "is devious, it is dispersed, but it insinuates itself everywhere, silently and almost invisibly, because it does not manifest itself through its own products, but rather through its *ways of using* the products imposed by a dominant economic order." What de Certeau calls "strategic" power lies with producers, but "tactical" power is claimed by consumers through the choices they make, the uses to which they put the objects they consume, and, above all, by the meanings they give them. "The tactics of consumption, the ingenious ways in which the weak make use of the strong, thus lend a political dimension to everyday practices," he concludes.[54] In the eighteenth century, letter writing too was an everyday practice through which the "weaker sex" claimed tactical power in the face of patriarchal strategies of writing and production.

Work, Leisure, and Gender

By the end of the eighteenth century, the distinction between nobles and nonnobles had lost much of its meaning and power in France, and wealth alone was enough to bring a man into the ranks of the elite. Men who grew wealthy in manufacturing, trade, or the colonies could distinguish themselves from others without bothering with a title of nobility, although many continued to buy them. Those who cared most about such titles were the poor nobles, for whom a title not only distinguished them from their neighbors but opened doors to careers in the military, their last preserve. Historians now tend to downplay the difference between nobles and commoners and to think instead in terms of an undifferentiated social and political elite in the years leading up to the French Revolution. At the time, social critics saw wealth eroding social order.[55]

Meanwhile, the female counterparts of these elite men became increasingly associated with leisure. Whereas men moved up in life by training for the professions, or by buying a royal office with administrative or judicial responsibilities, women who entered the elite or aspired to it made their claim through their ability to engage in leisure: in Paris they strolled in the gardens of the Tuileries or the Palais Royal and visited the shops along the rue Saint-Honoré; they entertained in the new domestic spaces of sociability—salons, dining rooms, and cabinets; they played table games like tric-trac and quadrille and read novels; they kept busy with decorative needlework projects, rather than darning socks or sewing shirts; they attended the theater; they traveled for pleasure and visited monuments and other attractions listed in guidebooks. As literature, art, and music became the terrain of male professionals, the artistic and literary production of women was contained within the realm of leisure. Unlike the achievements of men, their talents and skills were the mere "accomplishments" of ladies.[56]

Thus, as the line between work and leisure that had served to divide noble from nonnoble men for centuries faded, it was redeployed to articulate a gender divide *within* an expanding elite: men worked and produced; women engaged in leisure and consumed.[57] The gendered distinction between letters and other forms of writing mapped onto that between (feminine) leisure and (masculine) work. Letter writing and leisure came together on the same side of the gender divide that separated elite women from productive labor and figured them as mere consumers. For an illustration of how socially disruptive such a realignment of leisure from a status to a gender category could be, consider the story of a fashion merchant and his wife uncovered by Arlette Farge in the archives of the Paris police.[58]

The story revolves around the breakdown of the couple's marriage in the 1770s because the husband continued to believe that his wife should work beside him, as was traditional in the artisan household, while his wife asserted "that she would not work, that she had not been made for work, and that it was up to a man to look after a woman." Mme Montjean was not simply lazy: she fought her husband to engage in the leisure activities that she understood to be appropriate to her station and her sex: "She wanted to be by the window reading a book," her husband reported in utter frustration. One day when Montjean ran into her strolling in the Tuileries gardens with male friends, he noted pointedly that he had a hole in his sock; she refused to take the hint, however, so he gave up, declaring that he was going home to darn it himself. Mme Montjean also entertained friends in her home (with, her husband complained, his wine and food—but what food and drink in their home was not his?). And she wrote letters, using the family's servants and a *petit Savoyard* who lived downstairs to deliver them.

Both the Montjeans were fundamentally concerned with honor: she felt that work would lower and thus dishonor her; he worried about what people would think if they saw his wife strolling in public with rouge on her cheeks and a man who was not her husband on her arm. It is easy to condemn Mme Montjean for being frivolous and immoral—even criminal—and for forgetting her place in society and her responsibilities in the household. Certainly that's what her husband did in his lengthy complaint to the police. But what is more interesting is how this woman took social mobility into her own hands. At bottom, the problem was not the wife's behavior but the fact that she engaged in it independent of her husband and out of synch with his own. The leisured woman could be moral and respectable only within a family gender economy established by the husband in which he understood her leisure to demonstrate—not undercut—his honor. This situation, alas, Mme Montjean did not enjoy. And while other women of more elevated social status may not have encountered the same opposition, all women who embraced the new leisure ideal of femininity were vulnerable to the moral critique that went with it. Parents and educators thus tried to teach young ladies to engage in useful pursuits without, however, working. The practice of letter writing became central to the education of young ladies as it took its place in the new morality of leisured femininity. Like motherhood, and in conjunction with it, letter writing would become central to both the meaning and practice of womanhood among the expanding leisured elite.

What did it mean to become a woman in the age of letters, an age whose modernity, like the autonomy it valued, was a matter of degree? To answer this question, in part 1 I look at an extraordinary portrait of a letter-writing woman painted by Adéla-ïde Labille-Guiard in the 1780s. I read this painting at the intersection of two modes of representation: the many genre paintings through which French men created a passive, eroticized image of "epistolary woman," and portraits of male writers. From this analysis emerges a vision of a new, modern woman whose sensibility and maternal care are articulated through epistolary practice. In part 2 I turn to the question of epistolary education: how girls were transformed into young ladies through learning to write, and to write letters in particular. Through debates on female education, changing ideas and practices of femininity and motherhood, a burgeoning print culture, and the establishment of new educational institutions, I trace the meaning and experience of epistolary education and show its centrality to education for elite womanhood. In part 3 I explore the material culture of letter writing, from paper to inkstands and writing desks. Through this material world I show the modernity of the epistolary practice in which women engaged, as it intersected with the consumer revolution, the global economy, and practices of leisure and sociability that defined modernity in the eighteenth century. In the concluding section I turn to the letters written by Geneviève de Malboissière, Manon Phlipon, Catherine de Saint-Pierre, and Sophie Silvestre, both to track the development from girlhood to motherhood through letters and to see how, through corresponding with a trusted other, each woman came to be her own modern self.

PART I

Images

Picturing the Subject

I

Portrait of a Lady as Letter Writer

Thanks to a wealth of well-known Dutch and French paintings, it should not be hard to picture the letter-writing woman who is the subject of this book. And yet, in these paintings we do not see women struggling to achieve a measure of autonomy through writing; we do not see either the growing confidence or the moments of doubt that reflection through writing to another must have brought about. Indeed, if we are to believe the artists, in the eighteenth century women read letters, but they did not write them, and the letters they read were overwhelmingly about love. This is because the male artists who developed the letter theme in genre painting used their brushes to represent the ideal of "epistolary woman" they imagined. They triangulated women and letters with love (of men), turning a female cultural practice into a trope of male love and desire. Rather than representing modern women's agency and autonomy through writing, the letters in these paintings serve as placeholders for their absent others: the male painters and viewers outside the picture whose possession of women through love, they tell us, is never secure.

To disrupt the image of women and letters collectively painted by men for their own purposes, I would like bring into focus a counterimage: Adélaïde Labille-Guiard's *Portrait of a Woman* (see fig. 1.1). For as the images created by male "masters" continue to shape if not obscure our vision of eighteenth-century women, they also overshadow the lesser-known, less celebrated images created by the women who were their contemporaries, including Labille-Guiard, who was one of the premier portrait painters of her day.[1] When she took up the letter theme in this portrait of an unknown woman, she not only restored to her the agency of the pen but placed writing itself at the center of the modern vision of womanhood. This image is thus all the more striking because traditionally portraits of people writing were portraits of men of letters, not letter-writing women. With it Labille-Guiard reshapes both the visual trope of women

1.1. Adélaïde Labille-Guiard, *Portrait of a Woman* (ca. 1787). Oil on canvas, 100 × 81 cm. Musée des Beaux-Arts, Quimper. Photo: Luc Robin.

and letters elaborated in genre painting and reimagines writing as a feminine cultural practice.

It should be noted first that this is a large and impressive portrait, much more than a simple bust, even if not quite full length. What is most striking, of course, is that the subject is shown in the very act of writing a letter. Seated on a red velvet upholstered chair at a simple writing desk, she is fashionably dressed in the style of the late 1780s. Her dress of shimmering white silk has a *redingote*-styled bodice; around her neck and buttoned under the bodice is a *fichu* or scarf in a dotted lace; a matching butterfly cap sits atop her curled and powdered hair.[2] In her left hand she clutches a handkerchief, while in her right hand she holds a quill pen over the last word she has written. A second quill sits ready in an elegant neoclassical inkwell, and a stick of red sealing wax lies on the table. Although the woman is in the act of writing, she gazes directly at the viewer. She is not so much caught in the act as posed. There is no surprise in her gaze, no attempt to cover the words she writes, which, without too much difficulty, the viewer can read: "à mes enfants / je vous recommande / à l'amitié elle vous protegèra"—*to my children, I commend you to friendship, it will protect you.*

By harnessing letter writing to motherhood, Labille-Guiard produced a striking new vision of the modern woman. The fact that we do not know who the sitter is allows us to imagine through her image the many women who wrote letters in the eighteenth century and are the subjects of this book.

The Letter Theme in Dutch Genre Painting

The letter theme was central to the transformation of genre painting in the middle decades of the seventeenth century from scenes of the everyday life of common folk to that of elites, and especially of elite women. When French artists took up genre painting in the eighteenth century, the letter theme came with it, forming a line of continuity from Vermeer to Fragonard.[3] As most commentators have not failed to observe, in these pictures letters are associated overwhelmingly with love. "Love, then, is in the air in these letter pictures," writes Svetlana Alpers. "Or to be more precise, it is inscribed in the letters that are the center of attention." And yet the text of the letters is never legible. Alpers suggests that "we know the subject is love only by the attention to the epistolary surface."[4] But love can encompass a range of emotions from loss and longing to erotic desire, so the blank page must be filled in. The letter's illegible contents are inscribed in the painting as a whole, from the faces and bodies of writers, readers, maids, and messengers to the decorative elements of the rooms in which they are located.[5] The illegible letter is the puzzle at the center of the painting, which the rest of the elements must be used to decipher.

Already in the 1650s, Gerard ter Borch had the clever idea of painting two pendants, one of a man writing a letter, while the messenger waits to carry it to its destination, and the other of a woman responding, while the same messenger waits to carry the reply back to the man in the first picture.[6] In the 1660s Gabriel Metsu paired a painting in which a man writes a letter with another in which a woman reads it. Rather than representing the continuing drama of an ongoing and reciprocal relationship through the practice of correspondence, Metsu associated the initiatory action of writing with the man and the passive response of reading with the woman. Through the use of the pendant he shows us the absent other represented by the letter, but he turns the circularity and reciprocity of love and letters into a one-way street, a narrative in which through reading the woman is absorbed in the absent male other.

In a half-dozen letter paintings made between 1659 and 1671, Vermeer portrays women at each moment in the process of correspondence. Three paintings feature the same woman wearing the same striking yellow velvet jacket trimmed with ermine.[7] In the first one she looks up and straight at the viewer as she is caught in the act of writing. In the second, she is again interrupted, but this time by a maid with a letter who causes her to look away from us as she considers whether to accept it, or perhaps to wonder why a letter has arrived before she has answered the previous one. In both paintings the writing table at which the woman sits, covered or partially covered by the same blue cloth, is so far forward as to push out of the frame of the picture. In the third painting, by contrast, we see the same woman, but in the distance through an open doorway. She is again turned away from us, again interrupted by a maid with a letter, this time as she plays her cittern. The first painting isolates the act of writing from its epistolary context, the second assures us that the woman is engaged in correspondence, and the third goes even further, finding the woman in the back of the house where she is engaged in an entirely different pursuit, to insist with a letter that she return to the correspondence. It is as if the absent letter writer refuses to allow her to do anything but think of him. As Alejandro Vergaro points out, the theme of love resonates throughout this third painting in the musical imagery, reinforcing the love theme implied by the letter itself.[8]

In four of Vermeer's letter paintings, maps, open windows, and paintings within the paintings evoke the great world from which the letters come or into which they will go. The function of these openings, however, is not to send the viewer out into that world but to bring us back to the woman and her letter. For example, in *Woman Reading a Letter at the Open Window* we see an elegantly dressed woman engrossed in the letter she is reading (see fig. 1.2). We can see precisely where she is in the letter—more than half-way down the page she is holding—but not what she is reading. Similarly, although she is standing before an open window, a red curtain deliberately pulled away and draped over the glass to reveal the outside world, that world is not within the viewer's angle of vision. What we see is a woman so totally absorbed in what she is reading that she is unaware that she is being watched. As Alpers points out, whereas Metsu and others had created narrative tension by having female letter readers and writers surprised and spied on by men in their paintings, Vermeer himself takes the position of the voyeur and invites the viewer to share his perspective.[9] The intimacy of the letter's contents and the privacy of the woman absorbed in them are at the same time established and violated as, with the painter, we stand on the other side of the

1.2. Jan Vermeer, *Woman Reading a Letter at the Open Window* (1659). Oil on canvas, 83 × 64.5 cm. Gemaeldegalerie, Staatliche Kunstsammlungen, Dresden. Photo: Erich Lessing/Art Resource, New York.

curtain he has pulled back for us, watching the woman read. The letter draws us in as it draws her in, but it also draws her outward, through the open window, as it connects her to the absent writer whom she knows and we do not. The painter helps us to read the illegible letter, but its contents ultimately elude us: we can never know what goes on in the letter or inside the woman who reads it. At the same time that the letter stands in for the absent (male) writer, it also represents the (female) reader as elusive object of desire that can never be fully known or possessed.

The woman at the open window is alone with her letter and her thoughts of the person whom it conjures. However, a female servant or male messenger often figures in letter paintings, either delivering a letter or waiting for a response, as is the case with two of the paintings in the series with the woman in the yellow jacket. In another of Vermeer's letter paintings, *Lady Writing a Letter with Her Maid* (fig. 1.3), a maid stares out the window, either out of boredom or discretion, waiting for her mistress to finish the letter she is writing. On one level, the maid is the human counterpart of the letter that connects the woman we see with the man who is absent. But she also serves as a

1.3. Jan Vermeer, *Lady Writing a Letter with Her Maid* (ca. 1670–71). Oil on canvas, 71.1×58.4 cm. Courtesy of The National Gallery of Ireland. Photo: Bridgeman-Giraudon/Art Resource, New York.

marker of the social status of the woman even as she reminds us of the limited physical mobility such a woman enjoys. If the lady has the power of writing, the maid is the one who will move beyond the interior in which the lady waits for the return of the man to whom she writes. If the window represents for the lady the greater world in which that man moves about, for the maid it represents a temporary escape from the watchful eye of her mistress, the freedom of the street.[10]

Vermeer breaks the solitude of the central figure only with a discreet female servant who brings her mistress into better focus. However, female friends or confidants could also play a part in the painter's epistolary narrative, as in ter Borch's *The Letter Writer* (or *Curiosity*, as it has been known since the eighteenth century; fig. 1.4), in which one young woman grabs the back of the chair to look over the shoulder of another as she pens her letter; a third woman looks away, as if she is above the drama that is unfolding. Such scenes remind us that both love and letter writing were social practices, embedded in female networks of family and friends. The letter is not always simply the connection between two hearts, but between two worlds, that of women and that of men.[11]

1.4. Gerard ter Borch, *Curiosity* (ca. 1660). Oil on canvas, 76.2×62.2 cm. The Jules Bache Collection, 1949. The Metropolitan Museum of Art. Photo: © The Metropolitan Museum of Art, New York/Art Resource, New York.

The invention of the letter genre is testimony to the high rates of literacy in the seventeenth-century Netherlands, but literacy alone does not explain the linking of women, letters, and love in these paintings. It also reflects the popularity of French letter-writing manuals, especially Jean Puget de la Serre's *Le secrétaire à la mode*, first published in Paris in 1641 and reprinted nineteen times in Amsterdam alone between 1643 and 1664, as well as in Dutch translations.[12] In the seventeenth century, the French language became the lingua franca of European elites, and the French culture of court and salon was exported throughout Europe in civility books and letter-writing manuals. And yet, *Le secrétaire à la mode* was popular not because people were desperate to learn how to write a proper letter in the French style; rather, the sample letters that made up the bulk of Puget de la Serre's text provided both vignettes of *le monde* and narratives of love requited and spurned, of women pursued and men rebuffed with wit and charm. Puget de la Serre was the Ovid of *le monde*, an Ovid for the modern world in which women, too, learned the art of love. Indeed, while Ovid taught men how to pursue their goals in love as in war, with the letter as the primary weapon of love and the woman as fortress whose defenses had to broken down, Puget de la Serre presented love as a duel: he gave as much importance to the feminine parry that kept the exchange going as to the masculine thrust. For him, the model for love was the correspondence itself.[13]

Puget de la Serre's contemporary, Charles Cotin, went even further, declaring that in the *correspondance gallant* or the exchange of love letters, ladies wrote better than gentlemen did: "It is to these beautiful and lucky hands that the glory belongs to represent well the thoughts of the heart; it is to them that nature has given [the ability] to express without affectation and without art the feelings of nature."[14] It was to demonstrate and share their virtuosity in this regard that Cotin decided to publish "Diverses Lettres & Billets des Dames, avec quelques Réponses," in his *Oeuvres galantes* (1663). For Cotin, the epistolary art of love was a female art, so men had to learn it from women, as, he explained, he himself had in his youth. Whether Metsu, ter Borch, or Vermeer read Cotin is impossible to say, but their paintings of ladies writing as well as reading and receiving letters reflect this seventeenth-century idea that in matters of love, the epistolary art was a feminine art because ladies, unschooled in literary form but refined through upbringing and experience in *le monde*, gave pure and direct expression to the heart.[15]

For Puget de la Serre, as for the letter painters, the materiality of the letter was as important as its form and content. "Letters must be written *properly*," he asserted, "without anything crossed out, on fine paper (gilded and musked, if one wishes) and with good margins. Because, as it is with the action in a speech, so it is the same with the writing of a letter. It must not fatigue the eyes of the reader at all, but be so beautiful that he pauses with pleasure and considers it."[16] The surface of a letter, like the surface of a painting, mattered; like a painting, a letter should be beautiful as well as true. The character and morals of the writer were as evident in the letter as the face and clothed body of the subject were in a well-painted portrait or genre painting. The pleasure of reading a beautiful letter was matched by the pleasure of viewing a beautiful painting. No wonder the letter emerged as a central theme in genre paintings, and no wonder these paintings focused on ladies and love.

The Letter Painting in France

The letter theme was but one way in which genre painting was already gendered feminine when it was taken up by French painters in the eighteenth century. "An art that privileged detail, tactility, and coloristic effects was inevitably derided as 'feminine,'" explains Richard Rand, "as opposed to a 'masculine' art like history painting that foregrounded strong draftsmanship rather than distracting color, that abstracted and idealized its imagery rather than glorified the quotidian details of the everyday world." Eighteenth-century art critics came to associate genre painting with the "inner lives" of women, as much as with the ephemeral materiality with which they clothed and surrounded themselves.[17] The letter reduced that inner life to love.

The specifically modern temporality of genre painting was effected through situating figures and action in a setting that was most subject to fashion: the domestic interior of the urban house or apartment. In domestic feminine settings, letters contributed

1.5. François Boucher, *Woman Fastening Her Garter, with Her Maid (La Toilette)* (1742). Oil on canvas, 52.5×66.5 cm. © Museo Thyssen-Bornemisza, Madrid.

to the iconography of modernity. Typically, the scene is set in a lady's *cabinet* or boudoir, furnished in the latest style and strewn with fashionable objects, as in François Boucher's *Woman Fastening Her Garter, with Her Maid (La Toilette)* (fig. 1.5). We know we are in eighteenth-century Paris by the goods we see and the clothes in which the lady and her maid are dressed, just as we knew we were in mid-seventeenth-century Holland by the fashions worn by Vermeer's ladies and maids and the decorated rooms in which we found them, with their turkey carpets, checkerboard tiled floors, and rectilinear chairs. Indeed, genre scenes such as this one may owe something to the fashion press, which was known to accessorize the latest fashions with a letter, as in figure 1.6, a fashion plate from the 1770s.

In Boucher's painting, a letter is barely glimpsed among the profusion of delicate objects—a porcelain tea set on a small table, an embroidered fire screen, from which a lady's purse hangs casually, little cosmetics pots in various shapes on a dressing table surmounted by a fabric-framed mirror. At the center of the room and the picture is a

1.6. "Elegant young woman dressed in a long *polonaise....*" Engraved by Deny after a drawing by Desrais. Gallerie des modes et costumes (1779). Bibliothèque nationale de France.

woman in *négligé* fastening a pink satin garter around her outstretched leg. A maid with her back to us prepares to give her mistress a pretty lace cap. The letter is leaning open against a candlestick on the mantelpiece, next to a porcelain incense burner and matching porcelain bird. The red wax of the letter's broken seal catches the viewer's eye and suggests figuratively that the woman fastening her garter, perhaps in readiness to meet the author of the letter, is no virgin. The kitten playing with a ball of string between the woman's open legs confirms the suspicion.

The portrait peeking out from behind the Chinoiserie screen reminds us that this was the sort of space where portrait sitters lived and where they would proudly display their portraits as the fashionable, decorative objects they were. With her fashions, her furniture, her letter and its requisite paraphernalia, Labille-Guiard's letter writer would have been at home in such a space. Her portrait would have been read through the lens of more than a century of such paintings of fashionable elite women in their intimate spaces marked by letters and exuding love.

As Dutch genre painters drew on epistolary manuals for inspiration, the fictions played out in the salons and boudoirs of French genre painting were mediated by two literary genres that evolved from them: the novel and the *drame*. The *drame* (often called the *drame bourgeois*) was a new sort of play theorized and championed by Denis Diderot that was set in modern times and dramatized ordinary lives, in contrast to the trage-dies and comedies of French classicism that either exalted the noble or ridiculed the commoner.[18] The novel, too, was new in the eighteenth century, and its most popular form was epistolary.

As conventional as they may be, the story and the characters in genre painting are fictions of the artist's own making and thus can never be fully known. Because the stories that can be told are infinite, they cannot even be confined to the limits of a painter's intention; because each genre painting may tell many stories, the figures in it cannot be limited to a specific model, sitter, or text. Reading a genre painting requires us to enter imaginatively into the world the artist has created in order to construct a story that makes sense of the setting, characters, and actions.

1.7. Jean-Honoré Fragonard, *The Love Letter* (ca. 1770). Oil on canvas, 83.2 × 67 cm. The Jules Bache Col-lection, 1949 (49.7.49). The Metro-politan Museum of Art. Photo: © The Metropolitan Museum of Art, New York/Art Resource, New York.

Consider, for example, Fragonard's *The Love Letter* (fig. 1.7). Here we see a woman with a small dog perched behind her, leaning forward in her chair, perhaps to smell the bouquet of flowers she holds in her left hand. In her right hand she grasps the note that was tucked into the bouquet. Although her body leans away from us, her face is turned back, directly toward us, as she is caught in the act of accepting the bouquet and reading its accompanying note. We can almost but not quite make out the name on the note—indeed various hypotheses have been put forward to identify it, but the uncertainty remains. Deirdre Dawson suggests that the painting may have started out as a portrait, "but the inclusion of the love letter creates a narrative and anecdotal context which, from the spectator's point of view, makes the identity of the sitter insignificant. What interests us is the *story* generated by the flowers, the letter, and the sly little dog and his mistress, not the biographical facts behind the painting."[19] The woman faces us only because she has been surprised, not because she has chosen to have her portrait painted. And the note that both asks to be deciphered

1.8. Louis-Léopold Boilly, *The Sorrows of Love* (1790). Oil on canvas, 45 × 55 cm. By kind permission of the Trustees of the Wallace Collection, London.

and refuses to yield definitively to our efforts epitomizes the indeterminate narrative of genre painting that engages the viewer in a story that he or she is called upon to create.

As the century progressed, epistolary fictions became more widespread and more elaborate, moving from the single-voice narratives of Marivaux and Graffigny to the polyvocal novels of Rousseau and Laclos.[20] Late eighteenth-century letter paintings, such as Louis-Léopold Boilly's *The Sorrows of Love* (fig. 1.8), presented more complex narratives as well.

We are again in a lady's boudoir, with various bibelots and other fashionable paraphernalia strewn about the mantelpiece. A faithful little spaniel, like the one in Fragonard's *Love Letter*, peeks out from under a chair to the left, against which leans a guitar. The two central figures are a pair of fashionably dressed ladies. One is falling into the arms of the other as a result of a letter accompanied by a portrait, which have just been delivered. The maid has been pushed into the background, where she holds the portrait and the letter, waiting to be told what to do. Further back, at the far left, is the silhouette of the messenger who delivered the letter and the portrait; he has turned back to look at the two ladies, presumably after having heard the lady who is falling cry out. The association of the letter with the returned portrait; the lady, whose features we recognize in the portrait, falling back, distraught, into the arms of her friend; and the departing messenger spell out the narrative of the callous ending of an affair and its emotional impact on the woman who has been dumped. The friendship between the two ladies is represented as clearly as the love affair between the lady and the absent man who broke with her by means of the telltale letter and its portrait twin.[21] Even though no words are visible, the letter provides the key to the puzzle of the picture, and the rest of the painting the clues to the content of the letter. The clues are easily deciphered and the puzzle just as easily solved because the scene has been played out in so many plays and novels.

We have already seen how frequently servants, and especially maids, figured in Dutch letter paintings. There the maid played several roles: like the letter, she was the intermediary between the woman and the absent man, but she was also a marker of the elite social status of the central figure and, as her intermediary with the world outside, a reminder of the lady's limited mobility. In *The Sorrows of Love*, however, the servant is just a servant, useful only in spelling out the narrative. Perhaps by the end of the eighteenth century artists had realized that the letter alone was sufficient to mark the elite status of the woman pictured, since literacy, although not exclusive to the elite in the eighteenth century, was uneven among servants and especially rare among maids.[22] Furthermore, the skills necessary to write a letter and thus to participate in the cultural practice of correspondence—penmanship, spelling, grammar, and rhetoric—were among the accomplishments that distinguished young ladies from other girls. Even at a time when increasing numbers of girls as well as boys were taught to read, simply picturing a woman reading or writing a letter would identify her as a lady.

Eliminating the maid focuses the viewer's attention squarely on ladies and letters. Compare, for example, Fragonard's painting, simply called *The Letter* (fig. 1.9), with Vermeer's *Lady Writing a Letter with Her Maid* (fig. 1.3). Annie Leclerc, Jane Gallop, and Carolyn Steedman compel us to see that Vermeer's painting is as much about the relationship between the mistress and the maid as it is about the lady and the absent gentleman. Even if we do not go as far as to imagine that the addressee of the lady's letter is the maid (I find this possibility, suggested by Leclerc and endorsed by Gallop, far-fetched), we must still acknowledge that the maid is as important to the mistress as the absent male is.[23] In the end, it is the maid who is present and the male who is absent. The maid cannot simply be dismissed as instrumental to the relationship, or the letter would have to be dismissed for the same reason. If the letter matters, so does the maid. As the letter's contents remain opaque, so does the maid. The indeterminacy of the letter is paralleled in the autonomy of the maid, who is both the servant of the lady and a woman in her own right. What distinguishes them, what marks their difference, is the letter. Indeed, as Deidre Dawson points out, the exclusion of the servant from the text of the letter makes clear that the lady's relationship to the writer

1.9. Jean-Honoré Fragonard, *The Letter.* Oil on canvas, 38 × 30 cm. Private collection.

is entirely separate from her relationship to the maid.[24] It is the lady who is the intermediary between the two worlds represented by the man and the maid, one defined by social status, and the other by gender.

Fragonard refuses to let us even imagine the relationship between the mistress and the maid. In his painting there is only a lady wholly absorbed in her reading of a letter. Indeed, she is reading not just one letter, but a whole drawer full of letters. She is alone in her room with nothing but love letters that fill a drawer to which only she has the key. Her face, supported by the arm that rests on the drawer, is suffused with a gentle blush that shows her pleasure in the time she steals to reread one or maybe even all of these letters. There is no triangle here and no independent relationship between women, only a dyadic relationship between a lady and an absent gentleman that is renewed and reaffirmed with each new letter and each rereading. By eliminating the maid, the painter both essentializes woman as lady and makes her life and the meaning of her life contingent on that of the man whose letters absorb her.

The drawer full of letters is a reminder of the absent man's need to repeat his love for and claim upon the lady over time. It is a reminder that love is eternal only if it is constantly asserted. The indeterminacy of the letters we cannot read reminds us of the uncertainty of love, especially when the lover is absent. The painting is meant not to arouse but to reassure the viewer who can never be certain of his lady's love. The pleasure of the lady rereading the absent lover's letters relieves his anxiety, but, of course, it is only a fiction of the artist's imagination and wishful thinking. He will continue to write letters to assure her of his love, and the painter will continue to paint her reading them, to reassure him of hers. In the end, the letter painting tells us less about the everyday life or love of ladies than it does about the need for men to be secure in their possession of the women they claim through love: each letter is a reassertion of this claim, each painting a projection of its positive reception.

The flushed face of Fragonard's woman dreamily reading through a drawer full of love letters hints toward the erotic, but other painters did more than hint. As the implicit narratives of letter paintings were made more explicit over the course of the eighteenth century, the implicit erotics of love were also represented more explicitly. Key to this eroticization of the letter theme was the narrowing of the representation of epistolary practice to reading. Although in the seventeenth century Dutch artists had been almost equally interested in women writing, receiving, sending, and reading letters, the French genre painters who took up the theme of women and letters took no interest in the letter-writing woman. If letters are not simply present and already read—on the floor, on the mantelpiece, or spilling out of a drawer—they are generally being read. Roger Chartier has argued that in the eighteenth century the iconography of reading was strikingly gendered: unlike representations of men reading, pictures of women engaged in the same activity "reveal the power of an association between female reading and idleness, sensual pleasure, and secret intimacy."[25]

Chartier gives as an example Pierre-Antoine Baudouin's *Reading* (1765), in which a young woman has dropped from her left hand the book she is reading, to fall back into the caress of her upholstered chair, while her right hand seems to reach dreamily under her skirt.

Jean-Frédéric Schall took the letter theme in this same inevitable direction in *The Love Letter* (fig. 1.10). Here we see a woman reading a letter in virtually the same pose as Fragonard's dreamy reader in *The Letter*. We see her face in profile, as she leans her head on her hand and reads a letter propped up on a bunch of roses. This woman, however, is in *négligé*, or rather she is more out of it than in it. The letter absorbs her attention, but not ours: we are drawn instead to the white breast that faces us directly, as the sleeve of her gauzy covering slips down around her wrist. Because she is absorbed in her letter we are placed in the familiar position of the voyeur, of the man who, to assure himself that she is thinking of him, writes to her and then spies on her as she reads his letter. His pleasure lies not just in looking at her exposed sexual body but in watching her absorbed in him. Through the letter, the autoeroticism of Baudoin's reader is thus transferred to the voyeuristic viewer.

1.10. Jean-Frédéric Schall, *The Love Letter* (18th century). Oil on canvas, 33.2 × 26.8 cm. Inv. 1938F876. Musée Magnin, Dijon. Photo: Réunion des Musées Nationaux/Art Resource, New York.

1.11. Jean-Frédéric Schall, *The Beloved Portrait* (1783). Oil on panel, 29.5 × 22.8 cm. Private collection.

We see the same eroticization in highly narrative letter paintings, especially when the letter is paired with a miniature portrait—twin tokens of love and absence—as in another work by Schall, *The Beloved Portrait* (fig. 1.11). There is really no ambiguity here at all. The painter has presented us with a woman thinking only of her lover, whose portrait, held in her left hand, she kisses, while her right hand, which holds open his letter, has dropped to her lap, spread wide by her legs. The only thing left to the viewer's imagination is to enter into the pleasure evoked by the image. Since neither the face in the portrait nor the words of the letter are legible, it is his portrait she kisses, his letter that has raised the flush in her cheeks. The fact that the woman in the painting is fully dressed, from shoes and stockings to straw hat, activates the viewer's imagination even more, inviting him to undress her in his mind to enter fully into the scene.

Diderot has described for us the effect such a painting had on him as a viewer. He explains first that the painting he will describe (not this one, but a now lost painting by Greuze) has not been exhibited publicly and probably never will be. Here is how Diderot describes the scene in the picture:

Imagine a window overlooking the street. At this window a green curtain is half open; behind this curtain, a charming young girl, getting out of bed, and not having had the time to get dressed. She has just received a letter from her lover. This lover passes under her window, and she throws him a kiss in passing. It is impossible to paint for you the *volupté* of this scene.[26]

Diderot proceeds to do so, nonetheless, caressing each part of the girl's body with his words. He rests finally on her fingers, which carry him to her face: "And the voluptuous softness that reigns from the extremity of the fingers of her hand, and that one follows from there down the rest of her face. And as this softness overtakes you, and snakes its way through the spectator's veins as he watches it snake through her face! This is a painting to turn one's head, even yours which is so good."[27] The "voluptuousness" of the painting courses through the veins of the girl stimulated by the letter from her lover, and into those of Diderot, the spectator, the otherwise good "you." The erotic experience of viewing such a painting is stimulated by the girl who is stimulated by the letter. The painting becomes a site of private pleasure for its owner and his guests.

1.12a. François Boucher, *The School of Friendship* (1760). Oil on canvas, 64 × 80.5 cm. Staatliche Kunsthalle, Karlsruhe.

1.12b. François Boucher, *The School of Love* (1760). Oil on canvas, 64.5×81 cm. Staatliche Kunsthalle, Karlsruhe.

The closed circuit of the erotic letter painting is meant to produce pleasure in the (male) viewer, but also security. As he enters imaginatively into the picture, following the trail of the letter, the viewer is assured that this woman, alone with his letter, is his alone. Not just her body, but her every thought belongs to him. This same message comes through even in paintings in which two women are pictured, such as Boucher's *The School of Friendship*, when it is read alongside its pendant, *The School of Love* (figs. 1.12a and 1.12b), because the center of attention remains the letter of the absent male.

In *The School of Friendship* we see two young ladies in a rare pastoral setting. The brunette is reclining, propped up by the crossed legs of her blonde friend, and reading a letter, while the other girl listens and dreams. In *The School of Love*, we see the same blonde dreamer in a similar setting. This time, however, it is she who is reclining against the crossed legs of a young man, and there is no letter. Instead, the young lady holds against her stomach her flower crown, while in her other hand she holds a basket from which roses spill. The painting of the two lovers thus resolves the uncertainty at the heart of the *School of Friendship*: it reassures us that the content of the letter the two friends read together is the love of the absent male for one of them, lets us know which of the two beauties he has chosen, and then boasts that, in response to his letter, she has given herself to him. His letter achieves its end while cementing the friendship between the two girls, as we see in the merging together of their two bodies. The viewer is thus reassured that female friendship, far from threatening love, supports it.

In 1760, the same year in which Boucher painted these pictures, Rousseau made just such a close bond between two cousins who are best friends the basis of his epistolary novel *Julie, ou la nouvelle Héloïse*. As Rousseau himself later wrote in his *Confessions*, although the story was about love, it grew out of the friendship between the two girls.

> I imagined two girlfriends, rather than two male friends, because, if the example is more rare, it is also more charming. I endowed them with characters that were analogous but different; with two faces, not perfect, but to my taste, that were animated by benevolence and *sensibilité*. I made one brunette, the other blonde, one lively, the other gentle, one wise and the other weak, but of such a touching weakness that virtue seemed to triumph over it. I gave one of them a lover of whom the other was the dear friend, and even a bit more; but I admitted neither rivalry, nor quarrels, nor jealousy, because all painful feelings were costly for me to imagine, and because I did not want to tarnish this pleasant picture with anything that degraded nature.[28]

Rousseau claimed to have fashioned his novel out of the letters the blonde Julie and the brunette Claire wrote to each other, but in fact almost all the letters in the first two parts of the book are to and from Julie and her tutor, the unnamed lover. It is the female reader who takes the place of Claire, as she reads the letters exchanged between the two lovers, just as Boucher's brunette reads the letter her blonde friend has received from her lover. But it is the male reader who takes pleasure in reading Julie's letters to the unnamed lover as if they were written to him. Boucher's blonde "Julie," however, writes no letters, so the pleasure of the male viewer is different from that of Rousseau's male reader. It lies not in imagining himself the recipient of a woman's love letters but in the resolution of the uncertainty inherent in her receipt of his letters. In fact, Rousseau wrote a much more complex story than Boucher did, for in *Julie*, the exchange of love letters that culminates in the tutor's possession of Julie is only the prelude to the real drama, which revolves around their struggle between passion and virtue, love and duty. Boucher's story is merely the premise of Rousseau's, where the satisfaction it offers is shown to be the result of a merely pyrrhic victory.

The very need to reassure the lover-viewer that he is secure in his possession of his love suggests that such security was indeed elusive. In *The Love Letters* (fig. 1.13), Fragonard dealt with the problem by showing a young lady with her lover on one side of her, and his letters on the other. The lover looks up at the young lady's happy face as she rereads one of his letters, encircling her with his arms. It is unclear if her pleasure results from having his arms around her, from reading his words, or both. In any case,

1.13. Jean-Honoré Fragonard, *The Love Letters* (1771–72). Oil on canvas, 3.17 × 2.16 m. © The Frick Collection, New York.

these are two versions of the same thing, taking possession physically, or through words. One ought to be enough, but the painter reassures his viewer by duplicating the claim of the letter through the presence of its writer, just as other painters doubled the letter with the portrait. The maid may no longer be necessary to establish the social position of the lady, but the letter alone is never enough to establish the lover's claim. The presence of both letter and lover reminds us of the absence that always threatens possession and love and that a torrent of letters could never secure. They remind us of the uncertainty of love, of ladies, and of letters.

Philibert-Louis Debucourt thematizes the threat to possession most obviously, if least seriously, in *The Casement* (fig. 1.14), an etching that brings to the surface the tension and the subtext that create the drama and define the stakes in the letter painting.[29] Here we see an elegantly dressed young woman perched in a window casement reading a novel she holds in her right hand. Inside the room behind her, the elderly gentleman who is her husband or lover, has placed his hand possessively on her knee. What he does not see and we do is that in the garden outside the window a young man is kissing the young woman's outstretched left hand, with which she is handing him a letter. The old man looks adoringly and contentedly at the young woman seemingly absorbed in her reading, like a viewer looking at a painting of a woman reading.

1.14. Philibert-Louis Debucourt, *The Casement* (1791). First state, color etching. Bibliothèque nationale de France.

He is the owner of this *tableau vivant* or living picture of a young woman reading, with its erotic charge and reassurance of possession. But we know that the woman is not absorbed in her reading, that possession is not at all assured, and that, indeed, the old man is being cuckolded. And he is right there, with his hand on her knee, not at letter-writing distance. Rather than reasserting possession, the letter being passed from the young woman to the young man is the agent of her betrayal of the (present) man. The letter does not provide reassurance because it cannot resolve the uncertainty in love or ladies, the uncertainty that resides in letters as it resides in language itself.

The fact that we can never actually read the letters in these paintings should remind us that uncertainty is always at the heart of the letter painting, even when all the clues around the letter seem to resolve it. If love is always in the air, it is never pinned down, never secure. What the letter actually says is always uncertain. Indeed, even if we did know what it said, we could still never be certain of its sincerity, of the meaning of its words or the intention of its author, for the words of which letters are composed can never represent transparently and can never be entirely trusted. The *confiance* that defines the pact between writer and reader is always an act of faith, if not will.[30]

Genre Painting and Portraiture

Labille-Guiard's portrait of the letter writer tells a very different story than that of love, uncertainty, and reassurance that is the classic narrative of the letter painting. Nor does it simply give us the satiric inversion of this narrative, the story of misplaced confidence and betrayal. Indeed, it does not seem to concern an absent lover or husband at all. The letter, however, remains central to the modernity of Labille-Guiard's subject, her social status, and the implicit narrative. Because of this affinity we could say that at the heart of this painting, too, is uncertainty—generic uncertainty as it hovers between portrait and genre and that is captured in the uncertainty of the meaning of the letter at its center and the woman who writes it.

Labille-Guiard was not the first portrait painter to borrow freely from the conventions of genre painting. Consider, for example, Jean-Baptiste Santerre's very early eighteenth-century portrait of another unknown woman looking up from a letter (fig. 1.15). Santerre seems to have taken as the model for this composition one of the Dutch pendants of a woman engaged in an amorous correspondence. However, by having her face the viewer directly, as sitters in portraits generally do, the painter has transformed the modest Dutch genre figure into a seductive French woman.[31] Her beckoning finger implicates the viewer in this reading, taking him out of the voyeuristic shadows in which the Dutch painters had safely left him. And as the finger beckons the viewer, the letter beckons the reader. The absence of writing implements suggests that the authorship of the letter is immaterial; what matters are the man and the relationship it represents.

Fifty years later, François-Hubert Drouais modeled a family portrait on a typical French genre scene, François Boucher's *The Milliner (Morning)* (fig. 1.16).[32] In this

1.15. Jean-Baptiste Santerre, *Portrait of a Young Lady, Beckoning* (ca. 1703). Oil on canvas, 80.6 × 65.1 cm. Private collection. © Christie's Images Ltd. 2008.

painting, Boucher gives us another brief episode in an ordinary day of a fashionable lady: choosing a new bonnet among those offered by her milliner as she finishes her morning toilette. The furnishings of the elegant room include a little writing desk out of whose open drawer a letter, its red seal broken, has spilled onto the floor. Drouais set his *Family Portrait (April Fool's Day, 1756)* (fig. 1.17) in the same intimate space of a lady's boudoir. The scene is depicted in meticulous detail, from the clock on the wall above the husband's head, to the open gift box on the floor at the wife's feet, from which pink ribbon and striped silk, lace, and pearls spill out. Amid the cosmetics bottles, a powder puff stands up in its box on the dressing table. The time on the clock (11:17) not only tells us that it is late morning, but situates the portrait in real time, rather than in the timeless present of traditional portrait iconography.[33] Drouais used the setting to introduce a narrative into the portrait, capturing the moment when the husband, who has come into his wife's boudoir to see how she likes the gifts he has sent her, finds her putting the finishing touches on their young daughter's coiffure. In his hand he holds his wife's gift to him, a poem folded as letter.[34]

1.16. François Boucher, *The Milliner (Morning)* (1746). Oil on canvas, 64 × 53 cm. © The National Museum of Fine Arts, Stockholm.

1.17. François-Hubert Drouais, *Family Portrait (April Fool's Day, 1756)* (1756). Oil on canvas, 2.44 × 1.95 m. Samuel H. Kress Collection. Image courtesy of the Board of Trustees, National Gallery of Art, Washington, DC.

Both Santerre and Drouais infuse their portraits with the narrative imperative of genre painting. However, their narratives are limited by another imperative: likeness. Whereas genre depicts types of people and seeks its form of truth in the typicality of the situation or narrative in which they are placed, a portrait always depicts a specific, identifiable person and strives for a likeness of her. These are two very different forms of truthfulness or *vraisemblance* that require two different kinds of viewing.[35] However, if portraiture limits the narrative possibilities of genre painting, portraits that borrow setting and theme from genre painting also borrow from it the truthfulness of the everyday and the specificity of urban space and modern temporality that define it.

Like Santerre and Drouais, Labille-Guiard pushed the boundaries of portraiture toward genre painting in her portrait of the letter writer, but she also pushed them in the other direction, toward history painting, in her magisterial portrait of Louis XVI's aunt and her patron, Madame Adélaïde, exhibited at the salon of 1787 (fig. 1.18). A comparison of this portrait with that of the letter writer suggests some of the choices Labille-Guiard made in portraying her unknown subject as she did. Both portraits demonstrate Labille-Guiard's celebrated virtuosity in rendering the silks, velvets, and lace that clothed the elite and upholstered their furniture. Both present women whose erect posture and carriage, as well as their expressions, testify to their upbringing, as well as to their moral rectitude and seriousness of purpose. There is also a sadness in the expressions of both figures, highlighted by the handkerchief each woman clutches in her left hand, suggesting the tears she might have to wipe away. The portrait of Madame Adélaïde, however, comes close to a history painting, "not only because of its large scale, compositional and iconographic complexity," as Melissa Hyde observes, but also due to the explicitly political content of its narrative. It places the king's aunt in the same iconographic tradition as her mother (Louis XV's queen, Maria Leszczynska), while referring explicitly to both her parents and her brother (the former dauphin), all now dead, in the triple silhouette in an oval frame to which she gestures with her handkerchief. Even the space in which she is standing, with its marble floors and tall columns, places her in the halls of royal power.[36]

The intimate space in which the portrait of the letter writer is set, as well as the letter evoking friendship addressed to her children, tell a very different story. Moreover, Labille-Guiard was as deliberate in representing the letter writer as fashionable as she was in representing the king's aunt as unfashionable. Especially in the 1780s, when Marie Antoinette made fashion central to her personal and political agenda, the representation of clothing in portraiture was highly charged.[37] Madame Adélaïde, who disapproved of Marie-Antoinette and her taste, had no desire to be portrayed as a follower of fashion. In her portrait she is dressed conservatively in the *robe à la française* traditionally worn at court. By contrast, the letter writer is dressed in the latest fashions. For Labille-Guiard and her sitters, fashion gave meaning to clothes, a meaning that the letter writer embraced and Madame Adélaïde did not, for it positioned its wearer among those who looked forward rather than back, even as it situated its subject in the present. At the same time, the embrace of fashion positioned the portrait of

1.18. Adélaïde Labille-Guiard, *Madame Adélaïde de France* (1787). Oil on canvas, 2.71 × 1.95 m. Châteaux de Versailles et de Trianon. Photo: Réunion des Musées Nationaux/Art Resource, New York.

the letter writer within the conventions of genre painting, as its rejection positioned the portrait of Madame Adélaïde within the conventions of the state portrait and history painting.

If Labille-Guiard's letter writer is as fashionably dressed as any lady in a genre painting by Boucher or Fragonard, she differs from them in her carriage and the comportment it represents. Although there is as much softness in her limbs and features as in any of Boucher's women, there is also a straightness about her. She could lean back in her chair, but she does not. Instead, the angle of the chair back serves to emphasize the erectness of her back. If genre painting is about setting a scene, and history painting is about action and movement, portraiture is about carriage—how a lady holds herself, and thus how she comports herself. In the eighteenth century, a lady's carriage was a dimension of her general comportment, a result and representation of her upbringing and her morals. If the portrait painter revealed the character of the sitter in her face, she represented her upbringing in the carriage of her body.[38] Labille-Guiard's letter writer exercises a form of restraint, visible in her carriage, that could only be learned in *le monde*. It is the form of self-restraint that Norbert Elias has identified with the "civilizing process" that began in Europe in the sixteenth century; by the eighteenth century, it too was associated with ladies, who were considered to be its driving force.[39]

Portraiture and the Writing Subject

If it was the rare French artist who painted a woman engaged in letter writing in the eighteenth century, Labille-Guiard was not alone among the few women in their ranks who took up the subject. Élisabeth Vigée-Lebrun (1755–1842) and Anne Vallayer-Coster (1744–1818) also made portraits of letter-writing women, and both also told different stories in them from the ones told by their male contemporaries. In Vigée-Lebrun's portrait of the comtesse de Cérès (fig. 1.19), the subject is not writing, but she is actively engaged with a letter she has initiated—in this case, folding one she has just written—rather than passively reading or dropping one. Like Labille-Guiard's unknown subject, she is shown with the tools of the letter-writer's trade—a quill pen, a stick of sealing wax, and the corner of an inkwell. Like her as well, she is not absorbed in her work, as the letter readers of genre paintings are, but looks straight out at the viewer, commanding the viewer's attention. It is the letter-writing woman who is the center of attention, not the letter as stand-in or substitute for an absent (male) other who absorbs the attention of the subject and thus of the viewer.

In *Portrait of a Woman Writing and Her Daughter* (fig. 1.20), Vallayer-Coster portrays two women, a mother and her daughter. If the daughter lacks agency in this picture, the mother does not. The mother writes, but rather than being absorbed in her task, she looks at her daughter, who looks straight out at the viewer. The daughter's virginity (symbolized by the roses in her hand) is the mother's pride and possession, not the uncertain male possession in the typical letter painting. The object of her mother's gaze, she is thus shown to be the subject of her letter. The letter is perhaps the vehicle

1.19. Louise-Élisabeth Vigée-Lebrun, *Comtesse de Cérès* (1784). Oil on canvas, 93 × 75 cm. Toledo Museum of Art. Purchased with funds from the Libbey Endowment; gift of Edward Drummond Libbey, 1963.33.

of the daughter's marriage, the letter that seals the deal. If so, it represents not the absent male but the present daughter whose absence through marriage it anticipates.

In both these portraits we see ladies and letters, but the role of the letter is to illuminate the woman, rather than to make present an absent man. Although a man may well be part of the story of both paintings as the probable recipient of the letters, he and his anxiety are not the viewer's concern. Indeed, the portrait of the comtesse de Cérès could only contribute to such anxiety: as the subject hides what she has written from the viewer, she seems to be telling us that the letter is none of our business, that we are not its recipient. Rather than drawing us in and reassuring us, she pushes us away.

Like the women in the portraits by Vigée-Lebrun and Vallayer-Coster, Labille-Guiard's letter writer is not concerned with reassuring someone else but with the rightness of her own action. We may not know why she writes to her children, but she writes openly and frankly, expressing no surprise in our catching her in the act of writing. She sits ramrod straight in her chair in the knowledge that her action in writing this letter is as morally upright as it is appropriately feminine. Writing this letter is emblematic of her as a (modern) woman and mother.

1.20. Anne Vallayer-Coster, *Portrait of a Woman Writing and Her Daughter* (1775). Oil on canvas, 130.1 × 61.9 cm. The Bowes Museum, Durham, UK.

These three portraits by women artists are all the more striking because traditionally portraits of people writing were portraits of men of letters, not letter-writing women. As Peter Sutton notes, when a letter figured in a portrait it functioned as an " 'attribute' which merely advertised the sitter's status as a literate individual, *homo literatus*."[40] Such an emblematic use of the letter, however, like that of the genre painters who strewed letters on the furniture and floors of ladies' boudoirs, did not actually require the subject to be shown with pen in hand. Indeed, such manual labor would have been considered beneath the dignity of the sorts of men and women who generally had their portraits painted; throughout most of history, they would have employed others to transcribe by dictation the thoughts they composed.[41] However, like painters with their palettes and brushes, men of letters were often shown at work with the tools of their trade.

The portrait of Erasmus by Hans Holbein the Younger (fig. 1.21) is a distinguished example of a portrait of a man of letters writing. What may be surprising is that he is writing a letter. Not only is the paper on which Erasmus writes relatively small,

1.21. Hans Holbein the Younger, *Erasmus Writing* (ca. 1523). Oil on wood, 42 × 32 cm. Musée du Louvre, Paris. Photo: Erich Lessing/Art Resource, New York.

like letter paper, but it is already folded as a letter would be. Erasmus was the most admired of the humanist letter writers at a time when letters remained within the realm of learning and literature.[42] His letters, written in Latin and modeled on Cicero's, were a sign of his classical erudition and a reflection of his rhetorical training. "For all the authors of French letters published at this time," explains Roger Duchêne, "the letter was a literary genre, which presupposed that its author was cultivated and a trained writer. Barring extremely rare exceptions, this was not the case for women."[43]

As we have seen, however, in the 1660s, a "revolution" in gender and epistolarity had begun that would partition the territory of writing between masculine literature and feminine letters.[44] Thus, when Louis-Michel Van Loo painted a portrait of Denis Diderot writing a letter and called it *Denis Diderot, Writer* (fig. 1.22), it is perhaps not surprising that the writer protested that the painter had gotten him all wrong. The paper on which Diderot is shown writing is the same size as the letter to which it is a response, shown propped up on bundles of other letters. We know it is a letter not

1.22. Louis-Michel Van Loo, *Denis Diderot, Writer* (1767). Oil on canvas, 81 × 65 cm. Musée du Louvre, Paris. Photo: Erich Lessing/Art Resource, New York.

only by the size of the paper, but, as in Holbein's portrait of Erasmus, by the marks of the folds left after it has been opened. Van Loo's Diderot is practicing the art of correspondence, of which the bundles of letters on which the last one rests is a visual reminder.

While acknowledging that the portrait was "a fair likeness," Diderot protested that Van Loo had portrayed him as "pretty like a woman" in a dressing gown so luxurious as to "ruin the poor writer [*littérateur*]." Van Loo had given him "the air of an old coquette" and "the pose of a secretary of state and not of a philosopher." Addressing the portrait directly, Diderot exclaimed: "My pretty philosopher, you will always be for me a precious testament to the friendship of an artist, an excellent artist, a more excellent man. But what will my grandchildren say when they come to compare my sad works with this laughing, cute, effeminate, old coquette? My children, I warn you that this is not me."[45]

Mary Sheriff reads Fragonard's *portrait de fantaisie* of the philosopher (fig. 1.23), which the Louvre gives the same title as Van Loo's painting, as a response to Diderot's critique. In Sheriff's reading, Fragonard adjusted the "inspired writer pose" to make it

1.23. Jean-Honoré Fragonard, *Denis Diderot, Writer*. Oil on canvas, 81 × 65 cm. Musée du Louvre, Paris. Photo: Erich Lessing/Art Resource, New York.

more inward-looking and suggest "the self-absorption of philosophical reflection," while increasing the size of the forehead, where the philosopher's great genius resided.[46] There are other changes as well. Whereas Van Loo had represented Diderot with pen in hand, Fragonard showed him turning the pages of a large book, no doubt a folio volume of Diderot's life work, the *Encyclopédie*. Sheriff also suggests that Fragonard "focuses attention on the individual" by responding to Diderot's critique of the luxurious clothes in which Van Loo had outfitted the "poor writer."[47] But Fragonard did not really dress Diderot in less costly material, just less fashionable clothes. The velvet robe, lace cuffs, and medallion hanging from a gold chain are a far cry from sackcloth. Rather, these rich materials are notable because they are distinctly unfashionable. Not for the philosopher to be depicted in *négligé*, in a fashionable French silk dressing gown over a silk vest, the full lace cuffs of the shirt fairly dripping onto the surface of the desk. No, Fragonard's Diderot is dressed theatrically in a style reminiscent of another Holbein portrait, that of Erasmus's close friend Thomas More (fig. 1.24). Holbein's More, like Fragonard's Diderot, is not shown writing at all: More merely holds a letter in his hand as an emblem or attribute of the *homo literatus*; Diderot turns the pages of

1.24. Hans Holbein the Younger, *Portrait of Sir Thomas More* (1527). Oil on oak panel, 74.9 × 60.3 cm. © The Frick Collection, New York.

his great book. Whereas Van Loo had updated Holbein's portrait of Erasmus by dressing his subject according to contemporary fashion, Fragonard responded to the gender problem that such a reworking raised by taking a different Holbein humanist as a model, one associated not with letter writing (and religious tolerance) but with moral integrity and martyrdom. Fragonard's Diderot was not the writer of ambiguous gender but the man of integrity and a martyr: he was the editor of the *Encyclopédie* who dedicated himself to truth, nation, and humanity, and put his reputation in the hands of posterity.[48] This is how Diderot wanted to be remembered.

Why would Van Loo have represented a philosopher in such a way that he looks more like a fashionable lady than a deep thinker? He was probably not thinking of Diderot the editor of the *Encyclopédie*, but of Diderot the art and theater critic who promoted *sensibilité* in championing Greuze's moralistic genre painting and his own invention for the stage, the *drame*. Diderot himself referred to the subject of Van Loo's portrait as "le philosophe sensible."[49] In the *Encyclopédie*, the chevalier Louis de Jaucourt contrasted *sensibilité*, which he defined as "a tender and delicate disposition of the soul which makes it easy for it to be moved, and to be touched," with philosophical reflection. "Reflection can make the man of probity; but *sensibilité* makes the virtuous man," he asserted.[50] At the same time, however, the language of sensibilité was understood to make connections between individuals on a human level, it was "a system of signs aimed at connecting individual sensation and collective experience by making inner experience visible and insisting on its universal character."[51] It was the basis of a new kind of humanism. As reason was understood as common sense, sensibilité was understood as the common feelings that united individuals into a single humanity modeled, as Sarah Maza has argued, on a loving family.[52] As a philosopher and man of letters, Diderot was identified with both reason and sensibilité.

But sensibilité was the quality that was said to distinguish women's letters from those of men. In an essay on epistolary style, Jean-Baptiste Suard argued that the quality that most distinguished Mme de Sévigné's letters was "this spontaneous *sensibilité*, which is moved by everything, spreads over everything, receives with breathtaking speed different sorts of impressions."[53] Sévigné's letters stood as a model throughout the eighteenth century precisely because they seemed to be the purest expression of this natural feminine quality. As Suard himself noted, Mme de Maintenon's letters were full of "wit and reason," but their tone was "serious and uniform," and above all, they lacked sensibilité.[54] In other words, they were well written, but too masculine. If men were to attain their full humanity, they needed to be *sensible* as well as rational, but *sensibilité* was the expression of their feminine side. A painter who attempted to represent the philosopher as a modern humanist by showing his sensibilité ended up representing him as a modern letter-writing woman.[55]

Van Loo's failed portrait of Diderot was thus a perfect model for Labille-Guiard's portrait of a woman as letter writer. The proportions of the two portraits are the same, although Labille-Guiard's is 20 percent larger. Both figures are set before a plain background, both are dressed in fashionable silk and lace, both are seated at a simple desk, poised in the act of writing a letter. On the lady's desk there is only an inkwell and a stick of sealing wax; on Diderot's, an inkwell and a bell. When viewed in the context of Van Loo's *Diderot*, the sadness in the lady's eyes seems to express her sensibilité.

There are some differences between the two portraits, of course. The lady is writing a single letter to her children, whereas Diderot is engaged in a correspondence, responding to the most recent of many letters piled on his desk. His left hand reaches out toward the viewer with a gesture that seems to invite us in, across the desk that stands between him and us, whereas in her left hand the lady clutches a handkerchief (to which I will return shortly). Although the lady does not gesture to us in the same way, neither does her desk, turned ninety degrees and set at the left side of the picture, create a barrier between her and us that needs to be overcome. In this position it also allows us to read the words she has written. Indeed, her left arm crosses her body, discouraging the viewer from approaching it, while at the same time guiding us toward the letter she is writing. With the pen in her right hand she does not so much write as point to the words on the page that she has just written. Moreover, the light falling from right to left (over her left shoulder, that is) illuminates the words, whereas because Diderot is facing the other way, the light falling in the same direction (from right to left) obscures his letter, casting it in shadow.

These differences between the two portraits can be related to the gender of their subjects. Diderot's sensibilité is expressed as an act of friendship, suggested by the ongoing correspondence and the hand gesture—both of which call to mind the reciprocity of friendship—and acknowledged by Diderot when he called the portrait "a precious testament to the friendship of an artist, an excellent artist, a more excellent man."[56] Such friendship was prized in the classical and humanist traditions associated especially with Erasmus (and Thomas More). "Modeled on the familiar letters of the ancient Roman orator, Cicero, the humanist letter was conceived as a conversation between absent friends, relative equals who preferred to emphasize friendship rather than honor and rank," Jane Couchman and Anne Crabb remind us.[57] In the *Nouveau manuel épistolaire*, published the year that Labille-Guiard made her portrait of the letter-writing woman, the rubric "Friendship" included nineteen model letters, but none of them were written by women.[58] Van Loo represented Diderot as a writer in the tradition of Erasmus, for whom letters and literature, friendship and humanism, were noble masculine pursuits along a single continuum.

Labille-Guiard's portrait of the letter-writing woman alludes to friendship too, but in a very different way. It is not through the reciprocal practice of correspondence that friendship is invoked here, but in the advice that the mother gives to her children. Unlike friendship, maternal love is unidirectional, although it too calls forth a response in the dutiful and loving child. But mother and child are never equals, and a mother's letter is loaded with both responsibility and wisdom. Because motherhood is not structured by reciprocity, in the manner of friendship, or even love, there is but one letter in the picture. If the model for Van Loo's Diderot is Erasmus, the model for Labille-Guiard's letter writer must be Sévigné, whose hundreds of letters to her daughter were published in the eighteenth century without a single reply. This is the figure of maternal love in the form of letter writing.[59]

Compared to Sévigné's letters, however, the letter in Labille-Guiard's portrait is unspecific, despite the fact that the words are legible. It is addressed not to one specific child, as Sévigné's are, but to "mes enfants." As such it functions in the painting as a sign of maternal care, more than as the representation of a real letter. The advice she gives to her children is one sign of her care for them as a mother. But simply by writing to them the mother shows herself to be dutiful and caring. She is teaching them how to engage in correspondence, initiating them into the practice of epistolarity and thereby commending them to the friendship they will be able to practice through it. Through her letter, she is teaching them both the technology and the importance of friendship.

By taking the portrait of the writer as her model, rather than the epistolary woman of genre painting, Labille-Guiard found a new way to represent the new, modern woman, defined by her sensibilité and maternal love and idealized by Enlightenment men of letters such as Rousseau and Diderot.[60] In the late eighteenth century, maternal love, like sensibilité, was assumed to be a natural quality of women that, when cultivated, would motivate them to dedicate themselves to their children, and especially to the education of their daughters, which was their particular responsibility.[61] In Labille-Guiard's portrait, the act of letter writing puts sensibilité and maternal care into action, the text of the letter puts letter writing itself into words, and the handkerchief clutched in the lady's other hand—the hand that does not hold the pen— gives sensibilité and maternal love material form. For the portrait painter, letter and handkerchief are attributes of motherhood, as plans and drafting tools are attributes of the architect, and a brush and palette the attributes of a painter.

The handkerchief, however, like the letter, was not simply a sign of the eternal feminine but a material component of modern elite femininity. Items of refinement and luxury, handkerchiefs came into use among the European elite of both sexes in the sixteenth century. Norbert Elias considers the handkerchief (like the fork) to be one of the key indicators of what he calls "the civilizing process" whereby the elite distinguished themselves from others by controlling their bodies by, for example, blowing their noses into fine cloth, rather than into their hands.[62] In the sixteenth and seventeenth centuries court painters often portrayed aristocratic women with large lace-trimmed handkerchiefs in one hand as a mark of refinement and status.[63] However, as Stephanie Dickey notes, even as the handkerchief suggested refinement, in portraiture it alluded not to blowing the nose, which surely would have been inappropriate, but to wiping away tears. As Will Fisher argues, it was the "ideological work" of art that cemented the association of women and tears through the materiality of the handkerchief.[64]

Just as the letter theme had literary origins and theatrical parallels, by the eighteenth century the handkerchief, too, was a familiar stage prop, as weeping, both on stage and among the spectators, became a common fixture of tragedy and comedy alike.[65] In his theory of the *drame*, Diderot promoted weeping as a dramatic gesture of sensibilité that was more effective than mere words.[66] Pierre Gobert's late seventeenth-century *Portrait of a Young Actress* (Musée des Beaux-Arts, Rennes) shows her waving coquettishly to the audience with one hand and holding a large handkerchief in the other. In Jean-Antoine Watteau's *The French Comedians* (fig. 1.25), the large handkerchief makes legible both the unseen tears of the actress who weeps into it and the invisible words of the letter crumpled on the floor that has caused the crisis in the action. In genre paintings such as this one or Jean-Baptiste-Marie Pierre's *The Bad News* (1740, Musée Nissim de Camondo, Paris), handkerchiefs were paired with letters to convey the unhappy face of love. In portraits, however, where handkerchiefs were often paired with a consoling book, and sometimes with a miniature portrait of remembrance,

1.25. Jean-Antoine Watteau, *The French Comedians* (1720–21). Oil on canvas, 57.2 × 73 cm. The Jules Bache Collection, 1949 (49.7.54). The Metropolitan Museum of Art. Photo: © The Metropolitan Museum of Art, New York/Art Resource, New York.

they were attributes of sorrowful widows. In seventeenth-century Dutch portraiture, as Stephanie Dickey shows, the handkerchief "allud[ed] to the state or condition of sorrow," as well as to its remedy: consolation.[67] Similarly, in Labille-Guiard's portrait of the letter writer, the handkerchief may be a sign of a particular sorrow or loss (as it is in her portrait of Madame Adélaïde discussed above), but it also suggests the refined sensibilité of the sitter. "The personal composure of the sitter takes on a special poignancy when enacted in symbolic proximity to tears," Dickey writes of such portraits. "The demonstration of personal decorum—to which the handkerchief as fashion accessory already contributes—now encompasses not only polite deportment but also mastery of feeling."[68] In the eighteenth century feeling and refinement came together in a new way in the concept of sensibilité, materialized not in uncontrollable tears but in the handkerchief that was ready to wipe them away.

In the portraits of widows as in the genre paintings of wives and lovers, handkerchiefs and letters bring the absent male into the picture. They help not only to portray women in their relationship to men but to affirm the feelings women have for them—their undying love, their constancy even after the death of the husband. In Labille-Guiard's portrait of the letter writer, however, the letter, which is at the center of the picture, is addressed to the sitter's children. While the handkerchief may tell us that she is a widow, the letter she writes proclaims the centrality of motherhood to her identity and expands the meaning of the handkerchief to include the sensibilité of the caring mother conveyed by the letter itself. This association of the letter with motherhood is new. For example, in Drouais' family portrait discussed above (fig. 1.17), the child and the letter are unrelated; it is the husband who holds the letter, while the mother fixes the child's hair. Through the letter we see the woman as wife, through the child we see her as mother. In a similar family portrait by Greuze, the child pulls the mother away from her writing table, as the husband looks on.[69] In a family portrait of Camille and Lucile Desmoulins with their baby (fig. 1.26), Lucile and the baby in her arms actively distract and draw Camille away from the letter he is writing: the baby's hand turns his head toward them, while his wife's pulls his hand away from the paper. Only in Vallayer-Coster's portrait of the mother and daughter is the letter the mother writes related to the practice of motherhood. Labille-Guiard goes further, however, when she eliminates the child from the picture altogether and signifies modern motherhood only with a letter and a handkerchief.

As Carol Duncan has shown, "happy mothers" were a new and popular theme in French art and literature in the second half of the eighteenth century.[70] Not surprisingly, most artists who treated the theme of motherhood did so by representing beautiful young mothers with healthy, happy babies, sometimes sucking greedily at the breast. In these pictures, the baby is an attribute of motherhood, as a letter was an attribute of literacy or love, and the handkerchief of sorrow and consolation; without it, the subject would be just another eroticized woman. When Greuze showed a study for the central figure of his *The Beloved Mother* (1769) in the Salon of 1765, Diderot remarked on how erotic the woman looked without her children. "How can it be that

1.26. Studio of Jacques-Louis David, *Portrait of Camille Desmoulins, His Wife Lucile, and Their Son, Horace Camille* (ca. 1792). Oil on canvas, 1.000 × 1.230 m. Châteaux de Versailles et de Trianon. Photo: Réunion des Musées Nationaux/Art Resource, New York.

[in one setting] a character is decent, and that [in another] it ceases to be so?" he asked. In case the reader missed his point, Diderot went on to describe the woman as she appeared without the children. "This voluptuous mixture of pain and pleasure makes all honest women in the room lower their eyes and blush," whereas in the finished painting, "it would be the same attitude, the same eyes, the same neck, the same mixture of passions; and none of them would even notice." But it didn't really matter if, in their embarrassment, the ladies moved quickly past the provocative sketch. "The men," Diderot wrote, "are spending a long time in front of it."[71] His point was not that the sketch was for men and the painting of the woman surrounded by her children for women. From Diderot's perspective, both pictures appealed to the male viewer, one to his desire and the other to his soul. *The Beloved Mother*, he wrote, says to "every man who has a soul and feelings: Maintain your family in comfort; give your wife lots of children; give her as many of them as you can; give them only to her, and you will be certain to be happy at home."[72] If letter paintings were meant to reassure men that their love was reciprocated and their possession secure, the image of a mother surrounded by her children, her husband looking on with pride and satisfaction, would create an alternative, moral, sense of security. Remove the children, though, and the mother was just another object of male desire.

By representing motherhood with a letter instead of a child, Labille-Guiard steers well clear of the erotics of babies and breasts, even as she challenges the erotics of the letter by having her subject write rather than read. The mother she puts before us is not just serious and *sensible*, but active and thoughtful. Freed of the erotics of Rousseauian or Greuzian desire, we see the dignity and virtue of the good mother not in her breasts, but in her straight back. And we see motherhood not simply as an expression of bodily nature, but as a learned social, intellectual, and material practice. But this picture cannot really represent that practice in any direct or mimetic way; rather, the letter is meant to reflect on the woman represented in the picture—as all letters were said to reflect on the morals and character of their writers. If this sounds cold, the handkerchief reminds us that maternal care, like the letter, is an expression of sensibilité as well as reason.

Labille-Guiard's portrait of a lady as letter writer gives letter writing a central role in expressing a modern notion of womanhood, even as it is portrayed as motherhood. But there is a tension here, if not a contradiction, between the modern woman as *sensible* mother and as writing subject, between two ideals of the modern woman: as the woman whose vocation and dignity reside in motherhood, and the one who engages in the liberatory, sociable, and constitutive practice of writing. For writing as a practice cannot be limited to letter writing, just as letters cannot be limited to love or womanhood to motherhood. Women, writing, and letters always threaten to break out of any limits set for them by gender, or by other forms of power. That is why writing is a liberatory practice, even if and as it is a sociable one. By presenting us with a portrait of a lady as both letter writer and mother, Labille-Guiard has set out an ideal that resolves pictorially the dilemma faced by elite women in the second half of the eighteenth-century as they struggled between new, gendered ideals of subjectivity and motherhood to become modern women in a modern world. It is this portrait and the contradiction it seeks to resolve, rather than the many images of women and letters and love that proliferated in the eighteenth century, that we should keep before us as we consider the role and meaning of letter writing in the lives of eighteenth-century women.

PART II

Education

Designing an Education for Young Ladies

2

The skills to write not just a letter but an elegant letter, an appropriate letter, the kind of letter that was said to come naturally to women, had to be acquired. However, in the eighteenth century there was no established system of education and no standard method of instruction for girls. Indeed, the question of whether women should be educated, and if so, what they should be taught, was at the center of the *querelle des femmes* or debate about women that had been percolating throughout Europe at least since Christine de Pizan wrote *Le livre de la Cité de dames* at the beginning of the fifteenth century. By the 1760s, however, when the field of public discourse itself had expanded greatly through the growth of literacy and the explosion of print culture, the question had shifted from whether girls should be educated to how and what they should be taught—especially those subjects that had never seemed useful or appropriate for them before.[1] The question of how girls were to be trained to write letters was thus discussed within the larger framework of debates that stimulated a proliferation of new textbooks, courses, and schools designed to meet the growing demand for female education.

Pedagogy in the Public Sphere: Debates on Female Education

The final decades of the eighteenth century were awash with pamphlets, treatises, handbooks, and essay competitions on the subject of education. In October 1762, the year that the Jesuits were expelled from France and Rousseau published *Émile*, his popular treatise on education, the *Mercure de France* opened its review of Charles-Étienne Pesselier's *Lettres sur l'éducation* by noting that, "although we already have a great number of writings on this subject, and in the last instance, we have been given four Volumes that seem to embrace the most general system of Education," there was plenty more to say on the subject. Indeed, the *Mercure*'s editor believed that education was of such importance, especially in the current situation when it was unclear who would take over the many secondary schools for boys run by the Jesuits, "that it seems to invite everyone to concern themselves with it."[2]

Rousseau's treatment of female education in chapter 5 of *Émile* was one of the factors that stimulated interest in that subject—often by those who disagreed with him, such as his former friend and patron, Louise d'Épinay, who published her own treatise on female education, *Conversations d'Émilie*, in 1774.[3] An earlier respondent was Mlle d'Espinassy, who published *Essai sur l'éducation des demoiselles* just two years after the appearance of *Émile*. She considered Rousseau's portrait of Sophie, the girl he created for Émile, "truer in many respects" than Émile himself, and she found Rousseau's sketch of Sophie's education to reverberate with her own thoughts on how young ladies should be educated. "But he only touched upon this subject," she complained. Moreover, she noted, "he seems not to judge women capable of sustaining a certain education: they are only born, according to him, to bend constantly under the yoke of a husband. My way of thinking is very different; this will be seen in the course of this Work."[4]

The following year Claude Renaudot wrote a letter to the editor of the *Mercure* that called for more attention to the education of girls. "In the present moment, when all patriotic minds are occupied with perfecting education, may I be permitted to share with the Public some ideas that may make a contribution?" he asked. After noting the lack of attention devoted to education, despite its importance for the individual and for society as a whole, Renaudot turned to the question of female education in particular. "The little attention that one does pay to education, why is it turned exclusively to young men?" he asked. "Aren't Young Ladies capable of reflection, judgment, feeling?" And yet, he continued, young ladies were taught only to dance, sing, and play musical instruments. By the time abbé Pierre Fromageot published *Cours d'études des jeunes demoiselles* in 1772, his claim that "much has been written on the education of young men, and nothing on that of girls," was certainly an exaggeration, but the continuing disparity between the attention paid to male and female education was striking enough to justify the hyperbole.[5]

Things were, however, changing, both in the classroom and in the public sphere, where the purpose and importance of female education were at least being openly debated. In 1777 the Academy of Besançon offered a prize for the best essay on the subject: "How could the education of women contribute to making men better?" Five years later, the Academy of Châlons-sur-Marne launched a competition directly on the question: "What are the means of improving the education of women?" The following year, 1783, the Academy of Rouen asked the public to consider the proposition that "the little care given to the instruction of women, dedicated by their current education to laziness or frivolous occupations" was the "most immediate cause of the change in morality."[6] That same year, Mme d'Épinay and Mme de Genlis—who had the previous year published her major pedagogical work, *Adèle et Théodore*—were the finalists for the French Academy's first prize for "utility." Épinay won the prize, but Genlis went on to become the most prolific and influential writer on the education of girls right through the revolutionary decade and beyond. By 1786 the author of *Le Lycée de la jeunesse* could declare: "It is finally almost abolished among us, that gothic prejudice that condemned women to ignorance, to the obscurity that follows it, and to the fatigue of frivolous pleasures."[7] Indeed, ignorance was now considered a moral failing, of a piece with the luxury and moral laxity to which women were thought to be prone and that were responsible for the moral decline of society. Educating women was a moral imperative and a social and political necessity. Mothers were increasingly given the message that it was their duty to educate their daughters.

If earlier writers tended to contrast the needle with the pen to represent gender difference, by the second half of the eighteenth century most writers were placing both needle and pen in women's hands—as long as the pen did not stray far from the letter. "We see . . . young ladies who know the art of fashion, many dance gracefully, some have a passable knowledge of music; others, finally, have a lot of skill in handcrafts," wrote Jean-François Dumas in his essay for the Châlons-sur-Marne competition, "but we see few who have command of their language to even a mediocre degree, fewer still who write in a passable manner."[8] Educators designed curricula that included both needlework and grammar, and novelists created an ideal woman who plied the pen as well as the needle. In *Nouvelles lettres angloises* (1755), abbé Prévost's Miss Byron writes to her friend Miss Shelby about a new acquaintance who she hopes will become a friend:

> I have been told that she writes perfectly, and that she is [considered] a Sévigné on the basis of her correspondences. I flatter myself that one day I will be among that number; but I find that the pen and her reading have not caused her to neglect the exercise of her needle. She is for this even more respectable in my eyes, in that she is an example to produce against those who do not at all approve of learning in women; . . . I would not wish this quality to be the principal distinction of a woman whom I love; but when one has received talents, why not recognize them rather than leave them uncultivated. It seems to me, my dear, that after the essential virtues of my sex, which are modesty, docility, and attachment to the duties of religion and morality, it is no disgrace to have the mind a bit cultivated.[9]

While no one advocated that women remain ignorant, too much education was still thought to be dangerous. As Bernardin de Saint-Pierre noted in his submission to the Besançon prize competition, even if a girl were only given useful knowledge, her education might still be a cause of marital discord later on. "A girl might adopt principles opposed to those of her husband, she, who ought to consider herself less knowledgeable than he, and see things as he sees them." Even if a girl's education did not produce outright disagreement, one of the pleasures of marriage (for men) was threatened by an educated wife: "By this precocious enlightenment," he warned, "marriage loses the conversations so necessary to its long days; and conjugal love so much pleasant ignorance that is one of its great charms."[10]

Thus, at the same time that mothers were enjoined to educate their daughters, they were reassured that education would not in any way damage their marriage prospects or their ability to carry out their duties as wives and mothers by violating acceptable gender norms and turning them into monsters. As Marie-Claire Grassi notes, educational practice continued to rest on the assumption of a fundamental difference between the sexes and the belief that the role of education was to maintain the social order that rested upon it.[11] Girls themselves might see the value of education as maintaining emotional order, as Manon Phlipon did. When her friend Sophie expressed concern that she was studying too much, Manon responded: "You scold me for indulging myself too much in my studies: imagine, then, that without them, love would excite my imagination, possibly to madness. This is a necessary diversion. . . . I do not at all seek to become learned."[12]

Manon Phlipon's words echo the routine disclaimers made by all educators and educational reformers that they had no intention of turning girls into *savantes*. "Do not believe that in having your daughter learn all these things, you will turn her into a *fille savante*, something that is much dreaded, and to which a lot of ridicule has been inappropriately attached," Mlle d'Espinassy assured the mothers for whom she wrote her *Essai sur l'éducation des demoiselles*. "She will still be quite a long way from being learned, and will know precisely what is required to not be ignorant."[13] Mme de Miremont, whose *Traité de l'éducation des femmes et cours complet d'instruction* ran to seven volumes, agreed. "Women are doubtless not destined to pursue deep study," she admitted, "and I have never claimed to engage them in it. It is even more essential to straighten the mind than to ornament it."[14] Even Marie Le Masson Le Golft, who proudly declared her membership in various learned societies on the title page of her *Lettres relatives à l'éducation* (1788), declared that "the goal of education ought to be very far from forming academicians." Indeed, it was her belief that "although we have reason to cry out often against the too narrow limits within which the education of persons of our sex would be circumscribed, we must acknowledge that this education ought never to aim to form *femmes savantes*."[15] When, in the first year of the Revolution, Mme Mouret wrote in the first issue of her *Annales de l'éducation du sexe* that "when I speak of the need to enlighten the [female] Sex, I do not claim to produce ridiculously learned women," she was continuing this long tradition rather than breaking new ground.[16]

When Marie-Julie Cavaignac recalled her youth in the memoirs she wrote after the Revolution, she both downplayed her educational achievements and explained why she had no desire to build on them. Despite the fact that she had studied Latin and competed for and won several prizes for her accomplishments, she claimed that, thanks to her brother, they gave her no "vainglory" or any desire to "get a swelled head." "He showered me with mockery, called me little pedant [*savantesse*], Philaminte, Uranie [Molière's *femmes savantes*], in short, all those names that are given to pedantic and ridiculous women." Without his mockery, she wrote, she might well have come to deserve the epithets he gave her, when, in fact, it was "not my fault if I had been taught Latin." With her brother's help, she wrote gratefully, "I was ashamed of my learning instead of being vain about it, and I hid it like something wrong or ridiculous."[17]

Every writer on female education laid out a path between the Scylla of ignorance and the Charybdis of pedantry, but with few exceptions, no matter what the path, it excluded Latin and included writing. Indeed, one of the most conservative of them even advocated writing as a means to prevent girls from becoming too combative. "One must avoid long arguments: they are boring to the instructor, and render the child who engages in them argumentative," wrote comte Golowkin. To avoid this problem, he advocated having the student write down her answers whenever possible. While this would contribute to the development of the girl's writing style and stimulate her mind, the aim here, according to Golowkin, was "to give to the child's reason only the force necessary to follow directions."[18] In fact, learning to write well was the very antithesis of pedantry, as another commentator, Claude Renaudot, made clear.

> I do not claim ... that a Young Lady should know how to translate Greek and Latin; that she should occupy herself with measuring the distance of the stars, the depth of the earth, the immensity of the heavens. No: but I would like her to know her own language according to its principles; for her to speak and write with facility; for her to read methodically and fruitfully; for her to be able to identify the examples that she must follow and propose to those whom heaven has destined to her care.[19]

For Renaudot, instruction in the French language defined the path between ignorance and pedantry along which young ladies would grow into virtuous women and enlightened modern mothers. Key to such instruction were the grammatical and orthographic principles that were crucial to writing both fluently and correctly.

Pedagogues and other commentators did not suggest that epistolary competence take the place of the traditional *agréments* or accomplishments of young ladies; nor did they consider it a form of pedantry that might threaten either femininity or male authority. Indeed, as a manual and intellectual practice that could display both the grace and sensibility that were central to elite femininity while strengthening individual virtue and the moral order, letter writing could be said to epitomize the goals of female education as they were elaborated in the second half of the eighteenth century.[20]

Early Childhood Language Instruction:
The Governess Problem

In Mme d'Épinay's *Conversations d'Émilie*, the mother reprimands seven-year-old Émilie for claiming that she knows how to write when all she can do is form her letters—an accomplishment the mother compares with learning to tie one's shoes.[21] In fact, basic instruction in writing was part of the curriculum even of the *petites écoles* that had been giving day students in Paris and other cities a rudimentary education for free for over a century. Teaching orders like the Ursulines might have three or four hundred of these day students and only about thirty elite boarders.[22] Most elite girls, however, such as the fictional Émilie, learned these basic skills at home. But who was there to teach them? Mothers, who were often poorly educated themselves, and governesses, who were really just servants. In her memoirs, Mme Roland explained how two sisters, her grandmother and her great-aunt, fulfilled for her the different roles of tutor and governess during the year that she lived with them. "Widowed after a year of marriage," she explained, "[Mme Phlipon] had my father as an only and posthumous child; downturns in the trade in which she had been established having thrown her into misfortune, she had been forced to seek help from distant wealthy relatives, who preferred her to others for the education of their family." Mme Phlipon was thus put in charge of the education of their two children, a boy and a girl, until "a small inheritance guaranteed her independence." Mme Phlipon's sister Angélique never married. "This good girl, asthmatic and pious, pure as an angel, simple as a child, was the very humble servant of her elder sister," Mme Roland explained. "She became quite naturally my governess, at the same time that Mme Phlipon became my tutor [*institutrice*]."[23]

Both Marie Jeanne Riccoboni and Mme de Genlis complained that the "governess" was usually just a lady's maid who had grown too old to be useful to her mistress. "We, neglected by our fathers, too often regarded as useless beings, a burden, who comes to make off with a portion of the inheritance of a son, the sole object of vanity of a great family," wrote Riccoboni, "we are abandoned to the care of an old chambermaid, who passes from the toilette, where she has begun to displease, to the difficult job of clarifying our first ideas."[24] Not only were such women ignorant of academic subjects such as literature and history, wrote Genlis, "but they know neither their own language nor how to spell." To bring her point home, she asked her readers if they would trust the education of their sons to such persons. "Until we make the status of a Governess equivalent to that of a Tutor [*instituteur*]," she proclaimed, "persons worthy of occupying such a position will blush to accept it." In a footnote, she asked her readers if it was not "odious and ridiculous that in the same family *the Governess of the daughters* is not treated like *the Tutor of the sons?* One lives like the equal and friend of the parents; the other has as her society only servants; the one is at the table of the masters of the house; the other eats only in the pantry, etc."[25]

Advertisements for governesses in provincial newspapers show how little was expected of them, how much they resembled servants, and the ambiguity of their status within the household. "Seeking a governess who knows how to read and write, and with good lifestyle and morals. She will be given wages proportional to her knowhow," read one such ad. A more detailed ad in the same paper made clear that whereas the governess's status in the household would depend on her social origins and experience, her academic training and skills were those of a domestic servant.

> Seeking a governess who knows how to read and write well, to sew well, take care of linens and is on top of housekeeping, from 35 to 40 years old, with good references, as much for probity as for morals, with a respectable wardrobe. If she has been served at table where she has lived, she will have that; and in the event that she is from a passable family, and she has not before been in service, she will also have it; then rewards will take the place of wages.[26]

Women looking for work as governesses touted their skills and know-how, not their learning. "A person who speaks French, English, and Italian wishes a position as a Governess for one or several Young Ladies, either in a convent or in the home of their parents," wrote one such aspirant in the *Affiches de Paris*. "She knows how to mend lace and do all the fitting required by young Ladies."[27]

Six letters from one servant cum governess to her mistress are conserved in the French National Museum of Education. The servant, Bellette Dupuy, wrote from Paris to the marquise de Calvisson at her estate near Nîmes in the south of France. Here is how the first letter, dated 25 January 1768, opens:

> Madame,
> If I have waited so long to have the honor of writing to you [it is because] I have still been awaiting the arrival of mademoiselle your daughter in order to give you news. She is finally here in the best health. Moreover, madame, I do not have a secretary at my disposal and wanted to inform you about the move, which is completely done—everything is arranged well, so you can rest easy. Allow me, Madame, to repeat all my respect and attachment and deign to receive my [good] wishes for you, for monsieur the marquis, and your lovely family. I have been to the convent. The Calvisson girls are doing marvelously. I have been there five times in fact.[28]

The rest of letter reports primarily on purchases and other commissions made for the young ladies. The writing is disconnected because the letter has been dictated to a "secretary," who sends his regards at the end of the letter. The lack of punctuation and capitalization suggests that this secretary was not a professional writer, but another servant. In fact, each year Bellette seems to have turned to a different person to write her letters for her. When she sent her New Year's greetings to her mistress in January 1773, she began by apologizing, "If I knew how to write, I would have had the honor of writing to you already to wish you a happy new year." But the person she recruited to write down her greetings had a shaky hand (see fig. 2.1). Indeed, he notes at the end of the letter of 2 May 1773: "The secretary of this letter assures you of all his respect. He had a lot of trouble writing it. His hands tremble a lot."

Bellette Dupuy's letters report on the health of the young ladies and purchases made on their behalf, all the while assuring the marquise of both the loyalty of the servant and her conscientiousness in fulfilling her duties. While she was clearly given significant responsibility in accompanying the young ladies to Paris and remaining there for years as each of them completed her education under the tutelage of the nuns, Bellette Dupuy's own education did not extend far enough even to allow her to write the letters with which she showed her loyalty.[29]

Genlis and Riccoboni had little interest in or sympathy for the governesses, however. The issue for both of them was the lack of concern for daughters shown by parents, compared with the money and attention lavished on sons. "Everything is done for a paris le 7 janvier 1773

Madame

Si je scaurois ecrire jaurois eu lhonneur deja de vous ecrire
pour vous faire mon compliment sur la nouvelle année, vous
connoisse mon coeur, madame, et je me flatte que vous ne douté pas
de mon attachement, et datteste ma reconnoissance mes voeux sont
les mesmes pour m. r le marquis, et pour vos chers enfants
il a fait si mauvais temps depuis quelques jours que jay été privée
daller voir m. r votre fille mais je compte qu'elle se porte je la vois
ordinairement trois fois par mois madame l'abbesse en a un soin —
particulier, ce qui me tranquilise beaucoup
jassure mademoiselle de mas[s]illarguy de tout mon respect et luy —
souhaite mille bonheur
m. r Daune ma remis cent vingt livre, dont je vous remercie, et vous
suis parfaitement obligée
je suis tres inquiete dapprendre que vous ayes recu le paquet que je —
vous ai envoyé je vous prie de m'en donner des nouvelles parceque je
ferai les demarches necessaires pour le retrouver et pour le faire payer
je vous supplie madame de m'honorer toujours de votre amitié
je suis avec un tres profond respect

Madame

votre tres humble et tres
obeissante servante
Bellette Dupuy

2.1. Letter from Bellette Dupuy to the marquise de Calvisson, 7 January 1773. Musée national de l'Education—INRP—Rouen—France. Inv. 6.2.01/1979—12353—4.

them," complained Riccoboni, "ten years employed to give them wit, reason, to render them capable of seeing, feeling, judging; they have everything, the enjoyment of everything; the world seems to have been created for them alone." Girls, by contrast, were left to educate themselves. Riccoboni closed her essay with a passage supposedly quoted from the memoirs addressed to his two daughters by a caring father. "Is it possible," he asks, "that parents would dare to have such different views about creatures who are so similar, who impose on them decidedly the same obligations, and that the law of humanity, more holy than that of custom, ought to render equally dear!"[30]

New Approaches to Skills Acquisition: Writing as Play

Pierre Fresneau was another commentator who compared the attention lavished on the education of boys to the casualness with which their sisters were treated. "It is a glaring mistake and extremely prejudicial to the State, to thus neglect this half of the human race," he declared.[31] Fresneau, however, did more than complain: he was one of the innovative and entrepreneurial teachers who not only called for more serious attention to the education of girls but offered both services and products to support it. The father of a daughter who was his first pupil, he opened an "Academy for Children of Both Sexes" in Versailles, and then, in 1772, published his teaching method and the materials he developed for the benefit of the public. "The zeal of a Christian, a Father, and a Citizen, motivated me to apply myself to the search for a means of making it easier for Children to learn how to read," he explained, "in order to help these innocent little ones to avoid the pain, the reproaches, and the often unreasonable punishments that inevitably inspire in them a distaste for books and the study of all the sciences."[32]

Fresneau was not alone in believing that making learning fun was the key to success. In the eighteenth century, educational games and toys were marketed to both tutors and parents, who had to be convinced not only that the new pedagogies were effective but that they were worth the money. "The majority of Fathers and Mothers will find perhaps that I am proposing too much expense for facilitating the primary instruction of their Children," wrote Fresneau, "but I dare to maintain to them that they are not so tightfisted when it comes to puerile playthings, superfluous sweets, and frivolous finery; they will willingly spend a louis for any one of these useless things." Like many a modern educator, Fresneau urged parents to substitute educational games, "which amuse and instruct [children] pleasantly without effort," for toys that did nothing more than entertain.[33]

The most widely recommended educational game, and the one that probably encouraged the invention of others, was the Bureau typographique, or Printer's Desk invented by Louis Dumas in the early eighteenth century (see fig. 2.2). Soon endorsed by a commission of teachers, the Printer's Desk was designed to teach young children to read and spell phonetically and was used in its original or in modified form into the nineteenth century. Abbé Fromageot promoted it in his *Cours d'études*. For teachers who wanted their students to learn to spell "without disgust and without any trouble,

ORDRE DANS LEQUEL LES LETTRES SONT DISTRIBUÉES DANS LE BUREAU.

a	b	c	d	e	f	g	h	i	j
k	l	m	n	o	p	q	r	s	t
u	v	x	y	z	é accentués.	Léttres doubles.	Lettres accentués.	ponctuations.	chiffres.

A PARIS, chez J. G. MÉRIGOT, Libraire, *Rues Pavée et St. André, N°. 7.*

2.2. Printer's Desk invented by Louis Dumas (ca. 1808). Musée National de l'Education—INRP—Rouen—France. Inv. 3.4.03/1978–00113.

either for you or for them," Fromageot advised, "adopt the method of the Printer's Desk."[34] A complete set came in a wooden box divided into 180 cubbyholes designed to be used for an increasingly complex series of games. The simplest game used the metaphor of the post office: "The first desk ... for the use of a child of two to three years is simply a table like that where the postmen sort missive letters," Dumas explained. "The child is shown how to place each card next to the letter that corresponds to the one on that card."[35]

As Dominique Julia has shown, the new methods for teaching reading and spelling were taken up by the schools and tutors that catered to the urban elite who could afford both the teachers and the up-to-date materials they used, as well as being attracted to whatever was modern and new.[36] Mme de Miremont encouraged mothers to use this educational game to engage in play with their daughters. She recommended having the child use the letters to form her own words, out of which she could then build sentences.[37] Fromageot encouraged the use of Dumas' game in schools. He recommended breaking the class into small groups and giving each of them a few key words from the day's reading to spell with their letters. "To get the most out of this little exercise," he advised further:

> Never help the one who will compose [the word] yourself; but, if she makes a mistake, choose another to compose with her; finally, never get involved in the composition except in cases where they are really stuck, and when none of them has been able to succeed. Do not regard the time they spend on this as wasted. The more difficult it is for them to succeed, the better they will remember the word and its difficulty.

In order to "fix" the words and their correct spelling in the students' minds, Fromageot recommended that when they had finished the game, the girls write down the day's words in their notebooks, to be corrected later by their teacher.[38]

Fresneau advocated a cheaper, simplified version of the Printer's Desk that he had developed himself.[39] Other inventors developed card games that they claimed were at least as effective for teaching reading or spelling. One game was invented by a schoolmaster named Py Poulain de Launay and publicized by his son in a 1741 book touting his father's pedagogical method. It was made up of two decks of cards: one of twenty-five letter cards and the other of fifty syllable cards. After explaining how the card game could be used to supplement traditional instructional methods, the inventor's son made sure to note that this was precisely how one of the main teaching orders that ran schools for girls used his father's invention with young children from three to seven.[40]

Urbain Domergue, who identified himself on the title page of his *Grammaire françoise simplifiée, ou traité d'orthgraphe* (1778) as a professor of eloquence and "one of the fifty teachers of Lyon," invented a card game because he thought that the Printer's Desk required more patience than active children could handle and more expense than poor ones could afford.[41] His was a real game designed for two children to play together, and quite complicated, with elaborate rules and multiple hands. Scoring was complicated and depended on knowledge rather than speed. Not only did players have to spell words correctly ("The least spelling mistake renders the word void, and forces the one who made it to lose to her opponent as many tokens as the longer word has syllables"), but they had to identify the part of speech and "give one rule that has some relevance to this word." The winner was the player who managed to compose a difficult word (agreed on in advance) out of the cards discarded after each hand.[42] Domergue's game may well have been more interesting for older children, but I have found no other mention of it, so it seems unlikely that it caught on like the Printer's Desk or even Py Poulain de Launay's card game. Even if it never saw the light of day, however, it is testimony both to the inventiveness of teachers of writing and to the general enthusiasm for play as a part of education.

The Printer's Desk and the card games it inspired testify to the new interest in early childhood education. They also suggest that in the eyes of modern pedagogues such education differed little for boys and girls. It was only when girls and boys were separated, with boys sent off to attend *collèges* or the preparatory schools that might precede them, and girls continuing their education at home with their mothers and then often as boarders in convents, that education became truly and radically gendered.

Convent Education, Maternal Education

A Paris almanac for 1769 listed thirty-eight convents that took in young ladies as boarders in Paris and its suburbs; in 1776 another almanac listed forty-one. Fees ranged from a low of 150 livres to a high of 600, but tutors in most subjects were extra.[43] Martine Sonnet has collected data on the boarders at seven Parisian convents between 1704 and 1792. Her research shows that of 1,075 students, just over 35 percent spent less than a year in school, while another 23.5 percent spent between one and two years there. Thus, almost 60 percent of the students had less than two years of formal institutionalized schooling. If we consider only the data for the period after 1750, we find that the numbers do not change significantly: there is no suggestion of an increase of years attending this sort of school even as demand for education grew.[44] Manon Phlipon spent about a year at the convent of the Congregation of Notre-Dame, and she claims that it was her own idea to go there at all; her friends Sophie and Henriette Cannet were enrolled for only two years. Mlle Boirayon, whom we know only from her correspondence with her mother, spent eight months at a convent in Lyon, from June 1770 to February 1771.[45]

The formal education of elite girls was typically shorter than that of their male counterparts in part because women tended to marry younger than men (often before they left their teens), but also because parents generally believed that a few years of formal education was sufficient investment in their daughters, who had no need for a Latin education or training for a profession. Bernard Magné notes that the difference between boys' and girls' education was quantitative, not qualitative: girls were taught fewer subjects because they were seen as less capable.[46] At the same time, girls were only expected to be given a "smattering" of knowledge, rather than to explore a subject in depth. The formal education of girls was thus generally neither as extensive nor as intensive as that of their brothers.

As historians have long noted, much of the eighteenth-century discussion of female education was either directly or indirectly a critique of this type of convent education.[47] Even in her defense of convents, Mme de Genlis admitted how weak they were as schools. She distinguished first between the convents run by the teaching orders (the Ursulines and Filles Sainte-Marie) that actually took charge of instruction, and those that served the elite, and did not. There, she explained "the boarders are each in their own rooms and under the supervision of a Governess who is given to them, and the Nuns do not get involved at all in their education."[48] However, girls traditionally also had the opportunity to receive instruction in the accomplishments such as dancing and music that would make them attractive to prospective husbands and prove useful in their married lives. Increasingly, as the critique of female frivolity grew louder, these useful skills came to include those related to letter writing. The language education of boarders focused on the skills that would distinguish them from the day students and prepare them for a life in which letter writing was a significant and central occupation.

External masters were thus made available for lessons, not only in music and dancing, but penmanship, spelling, grammar, and rhetoric. Fees were collected by the institution over and above the *pension* and then paid to the tutors for their services on behalf of the parents. The quarterly accounts for Mlle Boirayon show that her mother paid 18 livres per month for three months of basic pension and an additional 16 livres a month for two months of instruction from a dancing master and 12 livres a month for the services of a writing master for the same period.[49] Thus, she paid more in masters' fees per month than she did for the pension itself. And writing masters competed with dancing and music masters for the fees of parents who considered formal education an investment. Advanced writing skills required many lessons, not all of which could be provided by a single tutor, and parents who could find the money for the basic pension might well consider playing the harpsichord a more valuable or useful skill than writing a letter. No wonder that one critic lashed out against the whole system and called for the nuns to become real teachers: "Parents, the nuns say, give our students all sorts of teachers," he wrote. "Yes, I would answer them, hidden teachers, who cost the parents a lot, who have to pay them by the hour, the month, the twelve lessons hastily given, without any fruit. But, I would say to them further, wouldn't it be much better still if you yourselves alone were their teachers, and if they became, in fact, your students rather than just your boarders?"[50]

In the end, however, it was not nuns or tutors but mothers who were held responsible for the education of young ladies. As Nadine Bérenguier has shown, a virtuous daughter was considered to be a valuable commodity that was confided to her mother for safekeeping until she could be passed on to a husband.[51] This "dangereux dépôt" needed to be invested to realize its full value. When formal education was understood in these terms—as a means of enhancing marriage prospects—the mother's responsibility to educate her daughter was not just a moral but a fiduciary trust. For those mothers who sent their daughters to a convent for a year or two, the fees were a calculated investment in their daughter's future. In fact, the brief period of convent education became the culmination of a larger educational program overseen by mothers. As Martine Sonnet notes, "this use of the convent to supplement a course of home instruction was considered advanced and enlightened."[52] The good mother educated her daughter at home according to the most modern methods and then continued to participate in and monitor her education through letters when she launched her into the world of women that would prepare her for marriage.

The Role of Mothers in Convent Education

In 1779 Mme de Miremont explained to her readers how her own treatise on female education differed from those of her predecessors: "These Ladies wrote for Children," she declared, "I would like to write for Mothers."[53] In the second half of the eighteenth century, elite women were admonished, encouraged, and inspired by pedagogues to take an active role in the education of their daughters. On this Rousseau, Épinay, and Genlis could agree. Scholars have tended to view this call for maternal education as the counterpart of the Enlightenment attack on convent education that emerged from its critique of religion. For Enlightenment men of letters, nuns were the perfect marker for the darkness and ignorance from which a modern, enlightened education would release women. If the purpose of educating young ladies was to prepare them for their lives as wives and mothers, nuns seemed the last people to whom to entrust them: "*Women* who have renounced the world before getting to know it are charged with teaching principles to those who are obliged to live in it," complained the author of one of the articles on women in the *Encyclopédie*.[54] However, improving female education was more complicated than simply removing girls from the clutches of nuns and turning them over to their enlightened mothers. Rather, many parents and pedagogues sought to integrate the convent experience into a larger plan of education under the direction of a conscientious mother. Through correspondence, the mother would remain involved in her daughter's education even as her daughter began to learn how to function on her own in the world. At the same time, she would learn through practice one of the most important skills she would need as an adult: how to write a letter and maintain a correspondence.

Since the seventeenth century, young people of both sexes had been told that the best way to perfect their language skills was through conversation and correspondence with Parisian ladies. Charles Cotin declared that it was from such women that he learned the epistolary art, "which they learned without even thinking by frequenting *le monde*."[55] This informal pedagogy associated with ladies was integrated into new formal pedagogies when pedagogues encouraged mothers to engage in correspondence with their daughters. Mlle Le Masson Le Golft, whose treatise on the education of girls took the form of a correspondence between herself and a concerned mother, acknowledged her own lesser social status when she declared that only the countess could teach her daughter the art of letter writing. Remarking modestly that her own letters could never be models of "the pleasant, light, spiritual, etc., style that characterizes those of our French ladies and in particular yours," she advised the countess "never to write except in the presence of [her daughter]. This is the most effective means of forming her judgment and her style."[56] Paule Constant observes that young ladies were not so much taught to write letters as formed into letter writers by frequent practice.[57] Their mothers were their practice partners.

Although a girl could certainly learn from watching her mother write letters, the year or two when she left home to board at a convent created the perfect opportunity to engage her in a pedagogical correspondence. Among the sample letters that the Chevalier de Prunay included in his *Grammaire des dames* (1777), was one from a grateful *pensionnaire* to her mother. "My very dear Mother," it opened, and then continued:

I am taking advantage of the lucky opportunity afforded by the person who is eager to take charge of this letter to render to you my duties and to have the honor to tell you that I could not be better here with the Reverend Mothers, where you have had the goodness to place me. These are very virtuous Ladies who take great care of my education, since, everyday, they have me read *The French Grammar* that you had the kindness to send me; all that I lack now is a *Spelling Dictionary*, to be able to write correctly the sentences that they have the goodness to dictate to me; and to compare the words that I'm not sure of, in order to be in a position, in a short time, to be able to Spell everything that I write. They wish absolutely that I possess the principles of my language, telling me that only in this way does a Young Lady announce her education.[58]

Prunay managed not only to put in a plug for his own book but to send a message to mothers in a letter ostensibly written by a daughter and presented as a model letter for young ladies. The message was clear: a good mother does not simply send her daughter off to school, she provides her with textbooks and engages her in correspondence so that she acquires a full command of the French language.

Mme Mouret wrote explicitly that her *Annales de l'éducation du sexe* should be as useful to mothers as to daughters. "Mothers will also be able to get something out of it," she explained, "to learn and become versed in the dignity of their origin, the importance and extent of their duties, and generally all the obligations that religion, nature, and the *patrie* impose on them."[59] But the message to mothers—like the message pedagogues sent to their daughters—was at least as much moral as it was practical. As Fromageot wrote in the preface to his course of study for young ladies, "Tender mother who wishes that your daughter be raised under your eyes, give her few precepts, but lots of good examples; this is the foundation of the best education. If even once she finds your actions in contradiction with the lessons that you give her, all is lost."[60]

Janet Altman has pointed out that with the publication of Mme de Sévigné's letters to her daughter in 1725, "the child returns as a possible reader and beneficiary of published correspondences."[61] So, we should add, does the mother. Whereas the first edition of the letters emphasized what they revealed about court gossip and historical events, the second edition and subsequent ones stressed the maternal love to which they were said to be testament. Editors also called attention to the situation that gave rise to this timeless expression of maternal love: the separation of mother and daughter. "This separation which was cruel for such a tender mother," wrote the editor of the 1726 edition, "gave rise to all the Letters that you will see hereafter."[62] The letters thus validated the mother, proving her virtue as a mother under the trial of separation from the daughter. For many elite eighteenth-century mothers, that trial came at the moment when they sent their daughters off to school. Writing regularly to her daughter would not only allow a mother to prove her love but also to prove, in writing, that she was a good mother.

For most young ladies in the eighteenth century, the sojourn at the convent (or at one of the private boarding schools that started to spring up in the 1770s) meant separation from their mother for the first time. Marie Roume de Saint-Laurent was nine years old when she entered Pentemont; Manon Phlipon was eleven when she went to board with the Dames de la Congrégation; Pierre Fresneau gave the typical age as ten.[63] "Until that time, just the idea of being separated from my mother made me burst into torrents of tears," Mme Roland recalled in her memoirs. And even though it was she who asked to be placed in a convent to prepare properly for her first communion, she left home weeping. "How I grasped that dear mother in my arms at the moment of separating from her for the first time! I was suffocating, I was penetrated, but I obeyed the voice of God, and I crossed the threshold of the cloister offering him with my tears the greatest sacrifice that I could make to him."[64] The separation must have been as hard for the mothers as it was for their daughters, as Mme de Sévigné's correspondence with her daughter suggests. Mme Roland's language of sacrifice mirrors Sévigné's when she tried (unsuccessfully) one year to give up writing to her daughter for Lent.[65]

In anthropological terms, the convent was a liminal institution through which girls entering puberty passed to emerge as young women ready for courtship and marriage. In the convent a girl would not only be protected from danger (that is, men) but would begin the process of separation from her birth family in preparation for marriage.[66] After this ritual separation, the child could be reintegrated into the community through marriage into another family as wife and then mother.[67] Epistolary skill was uniquely appropriate for mothers to teach their daughters during this period of separation because the correspondence through which it was taught was a thread that, once begun, would continue to be spun and strengthened throughout two lives that, having begun as one, would only grow more apart. If the convent experience was the rite of passage through which these lives would be separated, letter writing was the practice through which they would reconnect in a new way that acknowledged the pain and difficulty of separation.[68]

When Mme Boirayon of Annonay sent her daughter off to the Abbaye de Chazeaux in June 1770, she put herself and her daughter to the test of separation. In her letters, Mme Boirayon urged her daughter to apply herself to her studies and listen to her mentor (Mme de Saint-Hilaire), but she also impressed on her the importance of honesty, transparency, and *confiance*—the virtues most central to epistolarity itself. "I had the honor to write to madame de Saint-Hilaire, it is true, a bit testily, concerning you," Mme Boirayon admitted to her daughter, but then explained:

> with good reason, however, since you seem to me to have kept an affected and ungracious silence toward me and Mme Véron. I have made sense of this negligence as I understood it; such is the duty of a mother who wishes to shape a daughter for the best. If you see things as I do, in a positive light, far from frightening you and making you despair, as you say, concerning the disposition of my heart, you will conclude that you are dear to me and without drawing further conclusions you will render me justice in deserving mine; I wish for that to be your sole desire.[69]

If this letter seems cold to the modern eye (as it did to the historian who first pub-lished it in 1922), a letter written by Mme Boirayon's daughter in December 1770 sug-gests how much such a letter might be valued by its recipient. "Either you are ill or you wish to put my tenderness to the test," she wrote, "but if you could understand how you make me suffer you would surely take pity on the situation into which your silence puts me [. . .]. My good mother, do not forget me, remember, I pray you, my tenderness. You are all my happiness and my satisfaction. Give me the consolation of writing to me or of having someone write to me that you have not forgotten me en-tirely." Before the letter was sent, the daughter was rewarded with one not only reas-suring her of her mother's love but bearing the good news that she was planning to visit. "I am impatient to see you again," the daughter added on receiving this news, "I will consider this day the happiest of my life."[70] Whether her mother was indeed try-ing to test her patience, Mlle Boirayon was learning the importance of holding up one's end of a correspondence. She now knew how it felt to be at the other end of an "unpleasant silence."

If correspondence helped mothers and daughters to deal with the pain of separa-tion and the knowledge of its eventual permanence, it also gave mothers a continuing role in their daughters' education as they separated from them. Through correspon-dence, a mother could monitor the education her daughter was receiving and the child's progress. Mme Boirayon's letters are filled with advice and admonitions, begin-ning with one written soon after her daughter's departure that suggests both her hopes and her fears: "Fear God, my dear daughter, this is the beginning of all wisdom," she admonished. But also: "I am of the belief that if you wish to succeed in this project [of enriching your soul], you would frequent less the young ladies of your own age than those who are older than you. . . ." Mme Boirayon's greatest fear as well as her hope in sending her daughter off to school was clearly the influence of the other girls she would meet there. When she wrote to her daughter again, she expressed her satisfaction that "you are in the group around the niece of Madame the abbess and that the young ladies who accompany her are older than you." She further advised her to "choose among them to imitate those who are the most popular; these are the models to copy."[71]

In the convent girls learned how to socialize in a female world like the one in which they would spend much of the rest of their lives—a particularly crucial form of edu-cation for the upwardly mobile. The wrong sort of friends could undo all the hard work of a conscientious mother, but suitable friendships could last a lifetime and be-come an important support, both moral and social, in later years. The papers of Marie Roume de Saint-Laurent include a whole batch of letters from friends she met during her years in the Parisian convent of Pentemont. The first ones, from school-mates who had married and moved on, were addressed to Marie while she was still at Pentemont, but they continued after she too had left for married life in the provinces.[72] The schoolgirl friendships Manon Phlipon formed with Sophie and Henriette Can-net turned into a correspondence that, with the approval of both mothers, continued for more than a decade.[73] Moreover, a friend might introduce a young lady to a brother, a cousin, or a family friend with whom, through marriage, she could cement the bond of friendship while achieving social advancement. This is exactly what happened when, through an epistolary introduction from Sophie Cannet, the artisan's daughter Manon Phlipon met Jean-Marie Roland, a well-educated state functionary (and future revolutionary) whom she would eventually marry.[74]

Mme Boirayon also urged her daughter to apply herself to her studies: "You are at an age, my dear daughter, to know well the particular interest in profiting from the education that I am giving you," she wrote. "I exhort you by the friendship I have for you to apply yourself and give your complete attention to the kindness of your mistresses and the lessons of your masters. You will gather from them all the fruits and fulfill my greatest ambition. Learn to dress your hair, my dear daughter, this is a very necessary thing." As her last admonition suggests, Mme Boirayon's major concern was not with academic studies but with the important accomplishments for which the convents were known. "Learn these little crafts that sit so well with young ladies," she wrote; and then: "I am told that you are arriving late at the dancing master's. This is not the way to profit from the lessons he gives to the young ladies in the house where you are."[75]

The letters exchanged between Mme Boirayon and her daughter show that when abbé Reyre organized his *École des jeunes demoiselles, ou lettres d'une mère vertueuse à sa fille* around a correspondence between a girl away at convent school and her mother he was encouraging an existing practice rather than inventing a new one.[76] Both the subtitle and the epistolary form convey the centrality of the mother-daughter relationship to Reyre's program, whose aim was at least as much to educate the mother in her duties as it was to lay out a plan of studies for the daughter. In her first letter, the mother reassures young Émilie that by sending her away to school she is not giving over care for her education entirely to her mentor. "I am too jealous not to share it with her, to the extent that I can. Every moment that I am free from the concerns of business and courtesies I will use to write to you. That way I will fulfill my duty and soothe my heart."[77] The mother asks for her daughter's confidence—"write to me not as a mother, but as a friend from whom nothing is hidden." Because the daughter is as fictional as the mother, her response is predictably dutiful: "You can count ... on my docility in profiting from your lessons: count on my exactitude in writing to you, count, above all, on the heartfelt tenderness with which I embrace you."[78]

Having established openness and trust in her first letter and received a satisfactory response on that count, the mother then evaluates Émilie's letter on the level of technique and finds it sorely lacking. Behind the fictional mother, Reyre emphasizes the importance of letter writing as an accomplishment well worth the added expense of a tutor. Knowing that parents think of education as an investment, he has the mother explain why letter writing is a skill that needs to be taken seriously.

> But in exhorting you to write to me, I cannot let you remain ignorant of the fact that you have great need of improving your writing and learning a bit of spelling: I had to

guess at half your words. Mme de Barilliers, whom I had read your letter, was not able to decipher a single sentence. . . . I blushed with shame; and, in order to be exposed no longer to a similar unpleasantness, I have decided to give you a writing master. If you benefit from his lessons as I assume you will, you will soon have a correct and readable hand; and your letters will flatter my eyes just as much as they charm my heart.[79]

One can easily imagine the scene in the mother's salon in which the daughter's letter is read aloud and passed around with pride among friends and family. Learning to write the kind of letters that could be read aloud in company was necessary, since the daughter would be expected to write them for the rest of her life. As Sévigné's correspondence with her own married daughter suggests, growing up meant that a daughter could expect to be separated from friends and family when she married and joined her husband's household. In some cases, marriage itself might come to depend on epistolary ties. Think, for example, of the fictional Mme de Tourvel in *Les Liaisons dangereuses*, and of all the real women whose husbands, like hers, were on extended duty abroad as military officers or royal officials.[80] Consider also the many families torn apart or spread about through the force of empire or the lure of economic opportunity in the colonies.[81] The year or two away at school was seen as practice for the permanent separation that marriage (or the cloister) would bring, even as it allowed girls to establish new friendships that could only be sustained through correspondence. Letter writing had become necessary to the condition of being an elite woman in the eighteenth century,

"Your cousins, your aunts, your female friends and mine ask me endlessly for news of you, and it gives me real pleasure to give it to them," Émilie's mother tells her in Reyre's book. This little bit of flattery leads into a lesson on epistolary etiquette:

> I would like to be able to add that you mention them in your letters; and I can't since until now you have not said a word about them. This is, however, a kind of attention that you ought to pay, as much out of politeness as of recognition and friendship for those who are attached to you. Do not fail to do so the next time you write to me. Everyone will be charmed; but no one as much as I, because the compliments that you charge me to pass on to our relatives and friends will give me the occasion to speak about you more often.[82]

There was a difference between maintaining real ties and observing formalities, but a woman had to be able to do both, and the *École des jeunes demoiselles* taught girls the importance of this act of epistolary respect and sociability.

The *École des jeunes demoiselles* also taught mothers their responsibility. "In order that my efforts may be more effective, I pray you Madame, to add yours to them, and to write to Émilie as often as you possibly can," Mère Rosalie writes to Émilie's mother. As the mother flatters the daughter to motivate her, the mother superior uses the same technique with the mother. "In rendering her this service," she continues, "you will procure for her the sweetest satisfaction; for she loves your letters to madness, and every time she has read them to me, I have found that she was right."[83] Later she tells the mother that she has encouraged Émilie to reread the letters her mother writes her. "This is, in my view, one of the most useful kinds of reading that she can do, and if I did not fear to abuse the confidence that you have shown me in permitting Émilie to share them with me, I would make copies of them and compile them into a collection that I would entitle: *L'École des jeunes Demoiselles*."[84] The message is pretty clear: mothers are just as important to the education of their daughters as educators are, and the letters they write their daughters provide a model and a discourse that is both irreplaceable by and a necessary support to all the efforts of professional educators on their behalf.

Another mother who took seriously her responsibility to supervise her daughter's education through correspondence, even in the face of serious obstacles, was Mme Roume de Saint-Laurent (Rose de Gannes de la Chancellerie). She and her husband were coffee planters in the French colony of Grenada who, like other Creoles and colonists, sent their daughter back to France for her education. Marie was a boarder at the very prestigious and expensive convent of Pentemont in Paris from 1756, when the global conflict that would become known as the Seven Years' War began, until her delayed marriage in 1767 at the age of twenty-two—longer than her parents had hoped.[85] When the war ended in 1763, France had lost most of its colonies, including Grenada, to Spain or Britain.

Colonists faced blockades that not only kept them from selling their crops but cut off regular communications with the metropole. When Mme de Saint-Laurent managed to get a letter to the mother superior at Pentemont in 1760, she thanked her for hiring the necessary masters for her daughter in the absence of her parents and the uncertainty of payment: "Thank you madame for the two masters that you have had the goodness to procure for her on credit. If you think it appropriate to give her others by the same means, just until the peace or a suspension of fighting, her father consents to it."[86] When the war ended, however, coffee prices plummeted, and all unnecessary expenses had to be cut. "Your father counts among this number all your masters," Mme de Saint-Laurent wrote to her daughter in December 1763. "He says that if [by now] you haven't learned how to dance, play the harpsichord, and geography, you never will. And then he says that since this expense does not count for anything in your dowry, it's useless to continue it. So, my daughter, suspend all your masters; you can take them up again when you're married."[87] When a good marriage prospect was located a few years later, the intermediary who found him advised the abbess of Pentemont that "Mlle de Saint-Laurent would do well to resume the harpsichord immediately; it is a great resource in the country. At the same time she must learn how to set it up and tune it."[88]

The masters hired by Mme de Saint-Laurent did not, however, include a writing master. Perhaps the school provided one, or perhaps Mme de Saint-Laurent assumed that she took at least part of that charge on herself in corresponding with her daughter. One of the first letters she wrote to Marie suggests the pedagogical dimension of this regular writing practice.

> I am quite pleased that you are writing to me on a small piece of paper; but I would like you to speak to me about your masters, and to speak to me naturally, as if to your confessor: "I have been very exact in all my duties this week. I worked hard at my harpsichord; I danced very gracefully; I studied my music; every day I spend fifteen minutes studying geography and a half hour reading," although you may say to me more naturally: "I have been lazy this week; I'm practically worthless." Voilà, my dear daughter, the letters it would give me pleasure to receive from you. All those that you have written me until now are in the style of a six- or seven-year-old.[89]

Marie was probably eleven at the time. "You are too big and too reasonable, too spiritual, even, to limit yourself to asking for my news and assuring me of your respect.... This style is too serious and too contrary to the feelings I have for you. I forbid it," her mother continued.[90] The weekly letters were not to be an empty exercise, an exchange of pretty formalities copied from a letter-writing manual, but a real means of communication between daughter and mother based on trust. Engaging in a regular correspondence with her mother would teach Marie how to write not the kind of formal letters found in the epistolary manuals but those that, in addition to being informative, were expressions of the heart, cemented the bonds of family, friendship, and trust, and served as an important means of communication for women of her station. It was through letter writing that the mother taught her daughter how to leave childhood behind and become a woman.

A story told by the princesse de Ligne in the reminiscences she wrote of her years at the Abbaye-aux-Bois in the 1770s suggests how much the correspondence between mother and daughter signified. Hélène's best friend was one day told by a classmate, and loud enough so that everyone could hear: your mother "was locked up because she had an affair with an actor." Mlle de Choiseul denied it, of course, maintaining that her mother "lives in the provinces because she has a taste for it, at least that's what I've always been told." In private, however, the accusation worried her, and she decided to find out if it was true. When her aunt confirmed that "the misbehavior of her mother forced her family to place her in a convent," Mlle de Choiseul asked if she could write to her mother. "Madame de Gramont responded that she could not take it upon herself to give that permission, but that she would talk to her family about it."[91]

Clearly, all communication had been severed between mother and daughter. When asked earlier by her friend if she had any reason to believe the calumny about her mother was true, she had replied: "No, I just figured that my mother was an odd woman, who was not loved by her family, and that was why she chose to live in the provinces."[92] But perhaps the girl had suspected (but could not say) that her mother, like her friend Hélène's, was not in the country, but dead. That might explain why her first response on learning that her mother was disgraced was a desire to write to her—now she knew that she was in fact alive. In the end, of course, she might as well have been dead—at least until her daughter was released from the convent to marry. Then she would no longer be under the rule of silence imposed by a father who had decided to punish his wife not simply by having her locked up but by cutting off all communication between his wife and their daughter. Prohibiting the correspondence between mother and daughter was tantamount to breaking the maternal bond.

When mothers like Mme Boirayon and Mme de Saint-Laurent sent their daughters off to a convent, it was not because they were bad mothers but to begin the painful process of separation that would transform permanently their relationship to their daughters into one shaped by marriage and mediated by correspondence. Taking seriously the role prescribed for them by pedagogues such as Mme de Miremont, Mlle Le Masson Le Golft, and abbé Reyre, they did not abandon their daughters selfishly, carelessly, or maliciously to the machinations of evil and ignorant nuns. They monitored their daughters' education and continued to participate in it by conducting pedagogical correspondences with them. Through correspondence, these mothers transmitted social knowledge to their daughters and taught them one of the crucial skills they would need to navigate the world as adult women. In so doing they strengthened the maternal bond as separation began to weaken it and gave their daughters the means to create and maintain relationships throughout their lives.

New Schools for New Women

By the 1770s, entrepreneurial women with some education themselves were meeting increased demand for formal schooling by taking small groups of girls into their homes as boarders and offering a wide range of instruction, from basic literacy skills and home arts to a variety of academic and artistic subjects, all within a more or less moral and religious context. Like the convents, these private schools aimed to attract and produce "young ladies" who would go on to be wives and mothers. Instruction was neither rudimentary nor supplementary, and social advancement through education was still the underlying goal. Notices for these schools placed in the Parisian and provincial press show that learning to write was essential to the education of young ladies in these modern schools that were springing up throughout the country to serve the needs of the most modern parents and their daughters.

For pedagogues and reformers, as for the parents who enrolled their daughters in the new schools established to serve them, the future lay with a new kind of education that grew out of society rather than the cloister and that educated girls to be members of that society and the families of which it was composed. In these schools, writing was not an option but one of the basic skills taught, because no matter what the aspirations of parents for their female children, whether they hoped for a good marriage to a local merchant, tradesman, or professional, or had more ambitious goals that might bring their daughter into the wealthier realms of finance and trade or the higher world of the nobility or from one rung of nobility up to another, writing would be necessary. It was part of the equipment of a modern woman.

Whereas the academic curricula of the convents had developed out of basic religious instruction leading to the first communion, the new *maisons d'éducation* may have been modeled on the pensions in which masters prepared boys for entrance into the *collèges* or the university. In 1754 the *Journal du Citoyen* listed thirty-three such boarding schools in Paris with annual fees generally between 300 and 400 livres per year.[93] M. Coutier, whose establishment was on the rue de Picpus in the faubourg Saint-Antoine, charged annual fees of 450 livres for room, board, and basic instruction; additional itemized charges for paper, pens, haircuts, powder and pomade, hair ribbons, visits to the dentist, a confessor, and maintenance of the chapel brought the total for basic fees to 486 livres per year. Included in this basic pension was the cost of masters in "Reading and Writing, French and Latin, Arithmetic, History, and Geography," but additional fees were charged for instruction in drawing, mathematics, singing, violin, arms, dancing, and military exercises. These were calculated separately and by the month, so that "one can take or cancel them when one wishes."[94] Except for military exercises, the same subjects, taught either by external masters or by the owner or owners of the *maison d'éducation*, began to be offered to girls in the 1770s.

Another model for the new *maisons* may have been the Paris neighborhood schools that, unlike the charity schools for girls, charged modest fees. These schools also had smaller classes—no more than twenty students in a class, as opposed to fifty in the charity schools. Although anyone could attend them, the neighborhood schools attracted primarily the daughters of master artisans and tradesmen: those who could best afford the fees, but also those who could expect their daughters either to marry up or at least to marry someone who would need a wife who could read, write, and calculate to assist him in his business. A well-educated acquaintance of Manon Phlipon reached such a state of poor health and economic distress in 1778 that his wife applied for and received a permit to open such a school. "The husband will serve as writing master, will be able to find some female students for spelling and language, and, if he should die, would leave to his wife a trade that would pull her through," Manon explained to her friend Sophie Cannet. Because Manon was asking Sophie to stake her friends, we learn from her what was required:

> One must apply to the Cantor of the cathedral [of Notre Dame] to have the necessary permit in such a case; it is only given on the basis of unequivocal recommendations and sworn testimony of good morals and ability; . . . they have been promised the first vacant place. But this place is still a business that has to be purchased: two, three, four hundred livres.

In the end, it was determined that 250 livres would suffice for the permit, the business, and moving expenses.[95]

Unlike the neighborhood schools, the convents, and the *pensions* and *collèges* for boys, the new boarding schools for young ladies were entirely independent of the Church and, as far as I can tell, unlicensed and unregulated. In 1770 Mlle Ecambourt established the first one in Paris on the rue des Postes (today, rue Llhomond in the fifth arrondissment), in a neighborhood where there were already many convents that took in boarders. That February, she announced her Pension de jeunes Demoiselles to the readers of *L'Avantcoureur* and the *Affiches de Paris*. While her own training was in music, she would be assisted by specialist teachers [*maîtres*] for instruction in reading, writing, and reckoning. Her sister would teach the young ladies needlework. Parents who so wished could also have their daughters instructed in history and geography, following the method of a well-known geography text for beginners. Finally, parents were assured that "the moral and social virtues being necessarily the goal of any solid education, . . . the most scrupulous attention will be paid to fulfilling this duty."[96]

By 1784 Mlle Ecambourt had married and moved to the rue de Vaugirard, on the more elegant side of the Luxembourg Gardens; her school, now called the Maison pour l'Éducation des Jeunes Demoiselles, was distinguished by the patronage of Madame (the comtesse de Provence), the king's sister-in-law (see fig. 2.3). Meanwhile, others followed her lead. In an undated prospectus for a Musée de Jeunes Demoiselles, also on the rue de Vaugirard, C. d'Epery announced that he was taking over the

2.3. Invitation to "Exercise in the form of an entertainment" at the Maison pour l'Education des Jeunes Demoiselles, rue de Vaugirard, Paris, 30 August 1784. Bibliothèque nationale de France.

Musée des Demoiselles founded by his father-in-law, Pierre Fresneau.[97] This was no doubt the same Fresneau who had founded the Academy for Children of Both Sexes in Versailles and published the *ABC ou Jeu des lettres* in 1772. At the end of his book, Fresneau had announced his intention to "push his work further for the instruction of my Daughter and the majority of my Students, which is to say, that I am going to undertake a Course of Study for the female sex."[98] His goal, he said, "was to render [women] less frivolous and more capable of giving Children a solid education." Fresneau agreed with André-Joseph Panckoucke (whose *Études convenables aux demoiselles* he claimed to take as his guide) that women could achieve the same greatness as men if given the means and opportunity to do so. However, his aim was not quite to give them those means or opportunities. "If we owe to the efforts and ability of men the order and rules that preserve States," he explained, "we owe to the efforts, the economy, and the intelligence of women the order and rules that preserve and augment the property and well-being of families." Fresneau concluded that "it is thus in their interest that we get to work early to form their minds and hearts in applying them to studies and reading appropriate to their status."[99] The Musée des Demoiselles, with its rigorous academic program, would give young ladies the means and opportunity to become useful and important members of their society as women, which is to say, as wives and mothers. The modern education they received there would allow and encourage them to reach what was thought to be their full potential.

"C. d'Epery, seconded by a Wife who, for fifteen years, has not ceased to profess the Course of Education of her Father, will himself give the Lessons in Writing, Calculation, Grammar, Geography, and History; he seeks Students strong enough to continue on to the study of French Rhetoric and the Latin and Italian Languages," Fresneau's son-in-law announced in his prospectus for the new Musée. Other family members would draw on their expertise to offer additional subjects: Epery's father would teach singing, and his wife, Apolline, the piano. Additional masters, "of well-known reputation and morality," would be hired to offer lessons in harp, drawing, and dancing. "From this order of things," he assured the parents of potential students, "it comes about that the Students of the Musée have constantly near them four Masters always ready to enlighten them, facilitate their work, to make it as pleasant as it is useful by removing the thorns that may be strewn along their path." As in Mlle d'Ecambourt's Maison pour l'Éducation des Jeunes Demoiselles, students of the Musée would periodically demonstrate to their parents the progress they had made in public exercises. It went without saying, he added, "that Religion and Morality are at the foundation of every study in the Musée, and that all other useful and agreeable knowledge relates to them." Although d'Epery did not mention the fees he charged, he did note that instruction in writing and grammar were among the subjects included in the basic pension, but that French rhetoric, Latin, and Italian, were supplementary.

If anything, the French Revolution encouraged the proliferation of new schools, as the convents were closed, education was promoted by revolutionary leaders, and women as well as men took advantage of new opportunities to enter the field of education.

The education they offered differed little if at all from that of the prerevolutionary *maisons d'éducation*, with academic instruction linked to moral and religious purpose within a healthy atmosphere. For example, in an undated prospectus from the revolutionary decade, two women who identified themselves as Citoyennes Leroux and Ceyselle announced the opening of their Pension de Jeunes Demoiselles on the rue de Courcelles in the faubourg Honoré (previously, of course, the faubourg Saint-Honoré). After touting the beautiful location of their school "at the center of the most sought-after promenades" and amid "superb gardens," its fresh air, and generally healthy atmosphere, Leroux and Ceyselle listed the subjects they were prepared to teach: reading, writing, and arithmetic, of course, but also geography, history, French, Italian, and English. Nonacademic subjects included embroidery and other needle arts, the specialty of Citoyenne Ceysselle, and dancing, music, and drawing, for which external masters had been retained. Like M. d'Epery, the two revolutionary ladies assured parents that they considered the education of girls to be a moral endeavor as much as an academic one. "Morals being the strongest bond of society and the first element of happiness," they declared, "we are committed above all to instill in the hearts of the students the seeds of gentle, philanthropic, and religious morality." Perhaps adapting the new language of the Revolution to traditional gender ideology, they described their approach as combining "honest liberty" with "wise reserve." Fees were set at 530 francs for young girls, but for older ones according to their age and the lessons they received. "From every point of view," the ladies concluded, "this establishment deserves to hold the attention of fathers and mothers jealous to procure for their children a fruitful and distinguished education."[100]

The success of Mlle Ecambourt's enterprise can also be measured by how quickly and widely she was emulated in the provinces. By 1774 Dame Billiard was advertising her Pension et Maison d'Éducation Pour de Jeunes Demoiselles in the outskirts of the capital to the provincial readers of the *Affiches de Picardie*. Her large and beautiful home and gardens, she wrote, could accommodate up to thirty boarders, aged four and older, from Paris, the provinces, and abroad. Lessons would begin with religion for the youngest girls and continue with reading, writing, arithmetic, history, geography, "la fable" (by which she probably meant moral instruction by means of fables such as those of La Fontaine), and music, as they got older. Instruction in needlework would also be included. For young ladies from the provinces and abroad, "the greatest attention would be given to teaching them the purity of the French language." Fees were set at 500 livres per year.[101]

Demoiselle Cavillon did not advertise her fees, but she did claim that they were modest. This was, however, the only thing that was modest about her establishment. Her pension in Amiens was already up and running, with thirty students enrolled and room for many more when she announced it in the *Affiches de Picardie* in October 1775. "She can take up to a hundred," she declared, "because she is assisted by Madame her mother, who shares her responsibilities with the same attention and the same intelligence." Demoiselle Cavillon taught reading, writing, spelling, arithmetic, and good pronunciation, as well as "the principles of Religion." As to her qualifications, she was "full of talents and gentleness for raising children well. Those who wish to confide them to her will be perfectly content with the care she gives them and can rest assured that they will employ their time usefully. Her teaching method and the emulation she inspires in them, compel them to make rapid progress."[102]

Mme Deboeek's school in Château-Cambresis, by contrast, was for girls of modest means and equally modest intellectual goals. "Beyond reading, writing, arithmetic, civility, and good morals," she offered those who boarded in her home "everything that counts as a complete education for girls; such as knitting, embroidery, sewing, making and cutting all sorts of clothing, hairdressing, and all kinds of fashionable altera-tions." In lieu of academic qualifications, she identified herself as the wife of a master of several disciplines: "writing, languages, music, drawing, etc."[103]

Mlle Beaufort announced herself quite differently in the same paper. First, she claimed already to be a successful teacher, having for the past two years taught geog-raphy to the young ladies of Amiens. Now, "animated by the desire to make herself more and more useful to persons of her [own] sex," she had opened a boarding school "where she will teach reading, with a method simpler that those employed up to now; the principles of writing and the French language; history, geography, religion, and good morals." Mlle Beaufort let it be known that she considered the spirit as impor-tant as the mind; she reassured parents that "she proposes to give all her care to form-ing the hearts of the pupils confided to her, in teaching them in particular to know the beloved Author of nature; what they owe him, what they owe themselves and those who have brought them into this world."[104] Whereas Mme Deboeek assured parents of modest means and aspirations that their daughters would learn all the domestic skills needed to care for home and family, Mlle Beaufort appealed to parents who were more ambitious for their daughters by offering them the most modern academic education available while reassuring them that the young ladies would at the same time be taught how to be good girls and upstanding women.

Books like Fromageot's eight-volume *Cours d'études des jeunes demoiselles* and Miremont's *Traité de l'éducation des femmes, et cours complet d'instruction*, both published in the 1770s, were no doubt as useful to the women who opened these schools as to mothers and the tu-tors they hired. Fromageot's letter to the head mistress at the convent of Port Royal, included in his *Cours d'études*, might just as easily have been addressed to anyone want-ing to open a school for young ladies. In it he gave concrete instructions as to how to organize the girls into classes and detailed their lessons over the course of the week. Miremont did the same, as did Mme Mouret in the *Annales de l'education du sexe*, which she published serially in 1790. Many of the pedagogues also recommended textbooks for the various subjects to be taught. Miremont, for example, recommended the abbé Batteux's *Cours de Belles Lettres, ou Principes de la Littérature* for rhetoric.[105] For the study of grammar and spelling, Lanteires recommended Barthelmy's *Grammaire des dames* for students, and Wailly's *Grammaire* for their teachers.[106]

By the 1780s, newspapers throughout France were carrying advertisements for schools in the regions they served. These newspapers were an important part of the economic and cultural life of the provincial capitals of France in the 1770s and '80s.[107] While providing useful information, such as announcements of new businesses and notices of people seeking either employment or employees (such as the ads for governesses discussed above), the *Affiches* also entertained and instructed their readers with articles of cultural interest: announcements of local theater schedules and the meeting times of local literary and reading societies, as well as news concerning new books and periodicals. They also invited their readers to contribute their own thoughts on topics of local and national interest, such as the slave trade or education. They thus engaged their readers with the larger world of commerce and culture that was the pride of urban life. Their subscribers were the most modern segment of eighteenth-century society: eager to try new things, forward-looking and ambitious for themselves and their children. These were the big fish in the small ponds of provincial cities, who were well aware that provincialism could hinder upward mobility in the larger world centered in Paris and that a good education could make all the difference.

Advertisers often noted their Parisian training or Parisian goods or Parisian birth in order to sell their goods and services, and those offering to educate young ladies were no exception. Down-on-their-luck Parisians who were too well bred to identify themselves by name in a public venue such as a newspaper were exactly the sort of people, their ads suggested, to whom provincial parents should entrust their children. In October 1778, one such man placed an ad in the Bordeaux paper for himself and his wife: "A person from Paris, of a very upstanding family, having just suffered some bad luck that has destroyed his fortune, would like to find young people to whom he would teach the principles of Language, either French or Latin, as well as all that relates to proper usage and a distinguished education," it began. With no other credentials to present, this was a man whose cultural capital lay solely in the education his parents had given him, a capital he was now reduced to investing in the provincial market for education. His wife was in the same position. "The wife of this same person," the ad continued, "would also like to find young ladies whose education she would shape according to the plan desired by the parents. She can take charge not only of everything that concerns the French language and correct pronunciation, but also everything related to politeness, taste, and the tone of good society."[108]

Few of these ads tell us if instruction in writing went beyond simple penmanship, however. Demoiselle Cavillon did specify spelling among the subjects she taught, but I suspect that Dame Billiard's students, especially if they stayed in school for the complete course of study offered, were more likely to advance to spelling, grammar, and rhetoric or composition than were Mme Deboeek's. Nor, of course, should we assume that the schools lived up to the glowing terms of the descriptions by which they were promoted.

In 1785 Charles-Robert Gosselin expressed his astonishment at how much writing, as well as reading, was neglected in the new schools.[109] "What do all these so-called institutions amount to?" he asked.

If not to laying out a beautiful plan that no one follows, lovely apartments where the pupils are not lodged, spacious gardens that they don't enter even once a year. If one then examines the conduct of the two spouses [who are the] Teachers, one sees that the first, entirely occupied with receiving visitors and the fees that they bring him, scarcely knows the names of his so-called students, while the other, playing the lady, is at best involved in arranging the meals, whose principle morsels will end up on a private and well-served table for her and her friends, who contribute to furnishing the house with food by extolling far and wide the good Education that one receives there.[110]

If the schools that were springing up every day did not live up to their claims, the blame, according to Gosselin, lay with the state for not taking charge of education; and at least the men and women who were taking the initiative to educate the young were providing a better model than the priests and nuns into whose hands the state had left education for too long.

Twenty years earlier, Claude Renaudot had identified the main obstacle to female education not as the "barbaric" belief that "ignorance was the lot of the [female] sex," or the lack of parental desire to educate daughters, but the incompetence of those entrusted with the task. "For in order to teach a science of any kind, one must know it," he proclaimed. "One must be in a position to clarify a thousand circumstances that arise in the reading of a work; one must be able to respond positively to objections that a student might make; one must be able to teach the causes and the effects of a fact that comes up: if not, all the knowledge in the world is no more than words that mean nothing, that one learns and forgets at the same time."[111]

In the early days of the French Revolution, Mme Mouret criticized the *maisons* and *pensions* in the same terms:

> Today education is confided to People who teach what they do not know; who promise the public lots of attention to morals, and who have none themselves; who advertise, in the announcement of their establishment, disinterest, devotion to the happiness of families and the Patrie, and who are, however, basely interested and very indifferent at heart to the happiness of those confided to them. God forbid that I should claim that all the Masters and Mistresses of education are like that! There are some who are worthy of esteem; but they are not the majority. It is thus to multiply them that I believe that one could not do better than to confide this important job to those whom the Nation judges worthy of it, on the basis of legitimate references.[112]

Despite the women and men who opened the *maisons d'éducation* claiming the expertise that Renaudot demanded, the reality no doubt fell short of those claims. The very fact of the claims, however, suggests the kind of education parents sought for their daughters in the final decades of the eighteenth century, and that the demand for public education was as much a reflection of their desires as a reaction against the Catholic Church.

Education and Empire: Tackling the Problems
of Colonial Education

By the 1780s, Mlle Le Masson Le Golft could begin to address the problem of educating the young ladies growing up in France's most remote provinces, its colonies. Le
Masson Le Golft lived in the port city of Le Havre, where ships arrived from and
departed for the colonies all year round. "Born and raised in a seaport much frequented by the Creoles of both sexes," she wrote in a letter to the Cercle des Philadelphes, the literary society of Cap François in the colony of Saint-Domingue (now
Haiti), "I cannot be ignorant of how much they are capable of receiving a distinguished education." Mlle Le Masson Le Golft was in fact a corresponding member of
this distinguished colonial society, and in 1786 had sent the manuscript of her letter
on natural history to her colleagues there. The society's enthusiastic response (which
she included in the book she published two years later, along with her own letter to
her colleagues) encouraged her to tackle the problem that concerned its members most
immediately: the education of their daughters. Acknowledging that education in general was "very much neglected here," and expressing their belief that the Creoles could
accomplish anything if only they had the proper education, they enjoined Le Masson
Le Golft: "Spread, Mademoiselle, your ideas on this interesting subject; you will be
the benefactress of a good part of the New world."[113]

In the ensuing publication, Le Masson Le Golft's collegial correspondence with the
Cercle des Philadelphes framed her feminine correspondence on female education
with Madame la comtesse de.... After telling the countess of the interest that the
Americans took in her work, she explained that geography had finally been introduced into the curriculum of young ladies when it was realized that "it was ridiculous
that a well-educated person could not take any part in the great events of society, or
that she could do so without knowing what she was talking about."[114] To the gentlemen, she proposed that a school be established for Creole girls (that is, girls of European descent born in the colony), in order to educate them apart from the pernicious
influence of slaves. "You know ... how much the type of ignominy that injustice has
attached even to forced slavery influences the feelings, and how essential it is to distance one's children from minds that are low, timid, superstitious, so that they do not
give in to these vices and those that follow necessarily from them." This was exactly the
sort of criticism that had been launched against the servants who served as governesses
to French girls. To this typical critique, now transposed for the colony, Le Masson Le
Golft added the equally typical praise of elite women as moral and linguistic models:

> One must, on the contrary, procure for [children] the conversation of persons of great
> soul, elevated spirit, who, speaking with as much energy as dignity, can form their judg-
> ment, give them by their example elevation, nobility, and the happy habit of basing their
> feelings only on principles that are sure. By frequenting persons with a select education,
> one also acquires those graces, that exterior nobility, that purity of language, in a word,
> that urbanity that has always distinguished the French nation from so many others.[115]

In the colony, where all Europeans and Creoles had slaves and traditional social distinctions among white people no longer had salience, educated women, as long as they were white, free, and French, could fulfill the function of socializing and civilizing through language that had been the role of elite Frenchwomen since the seventeenth century. This was the new republic of empire and the new republican model of girls' education marked by race: all white girls could and should be educated, but apart from and exclusive of the slave girls who served them. Letter writing would now divide along this racial line.[116]

If slaves posed a danger to the education of Creole girls, so too did the books that managed to make their way across the sea. "I seem to see you shudder, Sirs, in thinking about that immense quantity of obscene and insidious books with which the colonies are inundated, under the specious name of agreeable or philosophic productions," she acknowledged, but then went on to remind her readers that "good readings, on the contrary, could contribute to the cultivation of the mind, the purity of morals, protection against false philosophy and the enemies of altar and throne, to form judgment, purify language, maintain the love of duty, politeness, courtesies, etc." Her own book, written in the form of a correspondence with a concerned mother, would, she hoped, "produce the effect that you expected."[117] Although even in the colonies, the question (at least for those of European descent) could no longer be whether, but only how, girls should be educated, the model centered on the relationship between mother and daughter was undermined by the need to remove Creole girls from a home corrupted by slavery. In this situation, the pedagogical correspondence between mother and daughter could only become more important.

The Education of Mimi and Mélanie

Until schools were established in the colonies, those who could afford to do so brought or sent their children back to France for their education. This is what Henry Paulin Panon Desbassayns, a Creole planter from the Indian Ocean colony of Île Bourbon (now Réunion), did. In 1780 he placed his three older sons in the royal military school in Sorèze, near Toulouse, but when it came time to educate his next younger sons and daughters, he decided to board them at private schools in Paris. To this end, he left home in December 1789 with four of his children: two girls (Mimi and Mélanie) and two boys (Joseph and Charles), as well as two slaves (François and Perpétue). Left behind in Île Bourbon were his wife and the two youngest children, Gertrude-Thérèse and Sophie.[118]

Mimi was eleven years old and Mélanie eight when they reached Paris in May 1790. The diary that Panon kept from their arrival in Paris until their hurried departure in September 1792, provides a window on the education of girls at the end of the eighteenth century. The day after their arrival, Panon noted that he was glad the girls said they wanted to go to school but that he was having trouble finding one for them. By contrast, he had already found a pension for Joseph and Charles—the well-publicized establishment of M. Coutier on the rue de Picpus where several of their friends from home were already enrolled.[119] Ten days later, he took Mimi and Mélanie to visit the convent of Saint-Joseph. "The nuns gave me some trouble about letting me enter," he wrote. "I told them that it was to see the premises of the convent and of the boarders, that if it worked for me, I would place my daughters there." The nuns gave way and let him in, but it was soon clear that the girls did not want to go to school there.[120] It was another week before something suitable was found. On 22 May, Mimi and Mélanie settled in with a Mme Moreau, who took in boarders at her home at no. 27 rue Popincourt, in what is now the eleventh arrondissment. Panon visited the girls several times over the course of the next couple of months and found them happy with Mme Moreau. However, on 22 July he decided to place them elsewhere. "They are fine and are being taken care of," he noted, "but I would like to push their education ahead with more frequent lessons. I don't have a long time to stay in France. I would like to take my two daughters back to Bourbon with me."[121]

The day before, Panon had checked out two *maisons d'éducation*, one of which was run by the author of the *Annales de l'éducation du sexe*, which she had just started publishing that spring. Panon noted approvingly that Mme Mouret was the author of an "education plan for the [fair] sex that she presented to the National Assembly," but he decided to keep looking. Another possibility was the Musée des Demoiselles—not, however, the one founded by Pierre Fresneau, which was located near the Luxembourg Gardens; this one was farther out, in the suburb of Chaillot. In the end, however, Panon chose to board the girls with M. and Mme Roze, who took in boarders in their home on the rue Copeau near the Jardin du Roi (now rue Lacépède and the Jardin des Plantes). He had taken a pair of cousins with him to observe the class that Mimi and Mélanie would join and was satisfied with what he saw.[122] The move was quickly accomplished, and by 26 July, the girls were settled in their new school. Mimi declared herself happy with the move because, she said, "we are very busy and that will get me to learn sooner so that we can return to see mama."[123]

Mimi and Mélanie stayed at the Roze school for a little over two years—not as long as their father would have liked, but long enough to take their first communion and to learn quite a bit. In November Panon attended a concert put on by the students to celebrate M. Roze's birthday. Although his own daughters had not been there long enough to be able to participate, he was satisfied with the performance of the other students, although somewhat bemused by their parents. "After what I have just seen," he wrote that evening, "I have considerable regrets for not having known about the *maison* of Mme Roze when I arrived in Paris. . . . Among the people, parents of the boarders, I noticed that there were aristocrats and democrats. All of them had the exaggerated air of people who do not know one another, who do not know where to place the others, or what they think. The young ladies in this pension seem to have good manners. They are very modest." In August 1792, less than a month before their departure from France, he attended another concert, and this time had the pleasure of watching his own children perform. "My daughters Mimi and Mélanie played the forte-piano and the harp. I was happy enough with them, inasmuch as they had lots of masters for different accomplishments. They didn't know anything before they were in this pension."[124]

Panon had himself to thank in large measure for the progress his daughters made. Not only had he moved them to a more rigorous school but he monitored their education closely and hired whatever masters he thought they needed to supplement the instruction the school provided. In January 1791 he noted that, "according to the arrangements I had made with M. and Mme Roze to accelerate the education of my daughters," he was paying them an extra 112 livres per month above the basic pension, bringing the total for each child to more than 2,200 livres per year. This was a lot, compared to what he was paying to board their brothers with a former Jesuit and his wife. With room and board, the basic cost for each boy was only 1,200 livres. And, although additional masters would still mean extra fees, the basic pension included instruction in reading, writing, Latin, and arithmetic.[125] For almost twice that amount, the girls received only room, board, and instruction in music and the French language.

The Roze school included music lessons because M. Roze was a music master. After about six months, Panon decided that there was too much emphasis on music and not enough on what mattered most—French language instruction. "These are not the talents that I want them to know well," he wrote, "in the little time that they have to remain in France; it's the principles of their language and French grammar." When he visited the girls again four days later, they reported that "they were beginning to analyze different verbs with [their language master] M. Coitan." The next week Panon observed their English and drawing lessons, and the following week, another lesson in French grammar with M. Coitan.[126]

Panon continued to observe his daughters' lessons over the course of the next year and a half. He enjoyed listening to the music lessons and was pleased that the girls were on track to take their first communion in the spring, but he was particularly attentive to their progress in grammar and spelling. On 21 May 1791, for example, he attended both piano and reading lessons. "They are beginning to play a little," he noted. More important, "they are beginning to read correctly a little." The following week, "they had their reading lesson in front of me and conjugated and analyzed [verbs]." Ten days later, he must have been with them for half the day. "I watched them have their English lesson," he wrote. "I can't see that they're making much progress." The piano lesson followed, and then spelling. "They wrote under dictation," he observed. "This is beginning to go a little better as to spelling."[127] By August, when he brought one of his older sons to visit his sisters, the improvement was marked. "Mme Roze showed his sisters' writing," their father recorded in his diary. "He was very satisfied with it. He asked them questions in English. He told me that they were beginning to understand it well. They are beginning to make fewer spelling mistakes," he concluded. "Their handwriting is beginning to take shape."[128]

As Mimi and Mélanie pursued their studies, they also wrote letters to their father, which gave him great pleasure, and to their mother, which Panon sent along with his own packets of letters going off to the colony. On 24 October 1790 he noted that Mélanie had written to him the day before and that he was "quite satisfied with her writing." Mélanie, who was now nine, explained that her sister, twelve-year-old Mimi, "had dictated the letter to her." In January, he again noted that he had received a letter from Mélanie, and in April he included letters from all his children to their mother in a packet he was sending home.[129]

It is not clear from his diary how long Panon had planned to stay in Paris, but events forced him to cut the visit short and make alternative plans to continue his children's education back home. Already in February 1791 (when, admittedly, the weather had him down) he noted that if it were not for the girls, he would leave immediately. "If I didn't have to continue the education of my two daughters, Mimi and Mélanie," he wrote, "I would leave very quickly for my country. I am always afraid that some unfortunate event will cause a war with the English." By November, when France had decided to send troops to put down the slave revolt in Saint-Domingue, he wrote, "I do not enjoy any pleasure here, it can only be that it is in the interest of my children that I stay here." Five weeks later things were looking even worse, and he started making plans to leave:

> I have decided that if war is declared in France, I will return with my daughters. This news of war worries me because of them, since they have not yet completed their education. I will have to leave. The maritime powers can also declare war on us, and then, how would I be able to go without running the risk of being taken, and with my two daughters? For the boys, that doesn't mean anything, but the girls . . ."[130]

But Panon did not mean to cut short his daughters' education: he was looking for a teacher (an *institutrice*) who would move back to the colony with them.[131]

In April France declared war on Austria, and as the Austrian troops approached, Panon made sure that Mimi and Mélanie profited from what time remained to them in the capital, beginning with seeing performances at the opera and the theater.[132] One summer morning they watched the abbé Sicard give a grammar lesson at the famous school he ran for the deaf and dumb, and then, after lunch at a restaurant in the Palais Royal, they made a trip to Chaillot to see the steam pumps that brought fresh water to Parisian households.[133] On 14 July, they took the ferry across the Seine to watch the annual festivities commemorating the Revolution. "We went to the Bastille, where they are supposed to be placing the first stone of the column that is to be put up there. We took the boulevards where there was a considerable crowd. All the troops arrived there. I am happy that my daughters saw all this." For balance, he took them to Val-de-Grâce the next day, where they saw, among other inspirational objects, the hearts of Louis XIV and Louis XV that were housed there.[134] Through these excursions, Mimi and Mélanie were getting the kind of education in French history that went beyond the books they might read at home and that would no doubt give them a stronger sense of their French identity.

Over the summer, the girls continued their lessons with M. Coitan, as their father went on a shopping spree for books, furniture, and all the other goods that could not be purchased back home. When he could, Panon looked in on his children's lessons. "I went to see my daughters take their lessons in dancing and writing from dictation," he noted a few days after the trip to Chaillot. A week later, he was back again after checking in on his sons. "Joseph and Charles were having their violin lesson," he noted. "Mimi and Mélanie [were] writing."[135]

As unrest grew in the capital, Panon was able to report that he had found a teacher to come home with them. It was not an *institutrice*, however, but a M. Prévost. Panon collected all four children and brought them back to his hotel, where they met their prospective teacher. Three days later he wrote to his wife that M. Prévost would be coming back with them to take charge of the education of not only Mimi and Mélanie, but of Joseph and Charles, their two younger sisters, Gertrude and Sophie, and the daughters of one of his relatives. Meanwhile, Panon set off with his children for more touristing: back to the Gobelins tapestry factory, and then on to Bicêtre, one of the most notorious prisons in Paris, and the Salpetrière, the general hospital where women were incarcerated and "reformed," Les Invalides veterans' hospital, the École Militaire, the "altar to the *patrie*" on the Champs de Mars, and the Abbey of Saint-Germain-des-Prés. These visits, focused on the less fortunate, were no doubt designed to teach the children the virtues of humility and charity and to awaken their sensibilité.[136]

"Paris at this moment is furiously worked up by the division caused by opinions. I am much afraid that the enemies of France will profit from our divisions and cause us great pains," Panon wrote on 7 August; the next day he added some slippers for his wife to the shipping crate that already held a harp and a piano for Mimi and Mélanie, and then he threw in a set of harp strings for a neighbor's wife from her husband, who was staying on in Paris.[137] Two nights later, "the tocsin sounded all night, and in the morning they sounded the general [alarm]." This was the storming of the Tuileries, the bloodiest of the revolutionary *journées*, when at least a hundred insurgents were killed and the royal family was forced to take refuge with the National Assembly. The long day ended with the suspension of all the king's powers. Emerging the next day, Panon was astonished at the corpses that littered the streets and the statues of kings that had been toppled. "The chateau of the Tuileries is completely devastated, the furniture shattered and broken, the mirrors, lamps, drapes, broken and torn, from the main apartment all the way to the kitchen. What it took centuries to build has been annihilated in one day." On the thirteenth he went to check up on his children and was relieved to find them all well. "All four of them saw me with great joy," he commented. Armed persons were roaming the streets, but that night, with the streets and all the houses lit up for security, all seemed calm enough.[138]

On 17 August, Panon told M. Prévost to be ready to depart at any time. The next day he noted approvingly that the tutor was taking piano-tuning lessons, since no one in the colony would know how to tune the piano they were bringing with them. On the twentieth, he requested passports for passage on a ship leaving Lorient for the Indian Ocean colonies on the fifteenth of the next month. While he waited for the passports to be approved by the municipal authorities, Panon combined last-minute errands with lessons for the girls that could have been drawn from the pages of the *Encyclopédie*: they visited a milliner to learn how hats were made (and get measured for three hats apiece), and, after booking seats for everyone on the coach to Lorient, they visited a print shop. "The master had the goodness to show us the whole print shop, and to explain it all very well to my daughters. They were printing the *Almanac* for 1793. I bought three copies." The passports arrived the next day.[139]

"I have really run around town taking care of my errands and those of my children," Panon wrote on the twenty-ninth. He had heard that there would be a house-to-house search for weapons that night to arm those who were defending the city against the enemy troops that were steadily advancing toward Paris. With a certain regret he decided to leave the hunting rifles he had ordered for himself and a neighbor with the gunsmith, despite the fact that he had already paid for them. This turned out to be a wise decision. The searches were indeed conducted that night, and many people were arrested for having guns in their possession. On the night of 2 September they were among the hundreds who were dragged from the prisons of Paris to be summarily executed in what would become known as the September Massacres.

"It's today that I'm supposed to leave in the coach with my two daughters, M. Prévost, and Perpétue to go to Lorient for the embarkation, and Mlle Coder, who is going with me to the Île de France," Panon began his diary entry for 2 September. "There is some movement in Paris," he continued. "M. Graffin, whom I've just seen, told me that he didn't believe I would be able to leave. He thought that the order was going to be given at the gates not to let anyone leave Paris." At noon, as the general alarm was sounding, he got word that they could go, but just as the horses were hitched to the carriage "a rider came and ordered the coaches not to leave." As they waited, "there was a bloody operation that the people wanted to carry out. They took themselves to the Abbaye and killed all the prisoners. Those who were there for debts were spared. The rest were killed within the hour. This operation was carried out in all the prisons. That's what is happening in Paris."[140]

All night the alarm was sounded and nobody slept. More disturbing, perhaps, was Panon's realization that he might well have been among the dead that day. "These last few days they have searched all the houses to find all the arms in Paris. It is said that a lot of people have been arrested. All those who were taken to the prisons met the same fate as the other prisoners."[141] At noon the next day they were again told that the coach was ready to leave, and at 1 p.m. they were on the road at last. A week later they were in Lorient and, after much nervous waiting, finally boarded ship for home nearly a month later, on 8 October 1792. Five days earlier, Charles and Joseph had arrived on the Paris coach, their teacher having fled Paris not long after Panon himself. The *Beauté* being already completely booked, they would follow the rest of the family home on the next ship out.[142]

The Parisian education of Mimi and Mélanie, begun in the early days of the French Revolution, was cut short by the escalation of violence that culminated in the Reign of Terror. Nevertheless, unlike the majority of girls who boarded at convents in the eighteenth century, they still received more than two years of serious instruction, including instruction and practice in the skills necessary to conduct a correspondence. And although Panon's diary ends with their departure from France, we must suppose that their studies continued under the tutelage of the intrepid M. Prévost. This education must have stood them in good stead in later years. Both girls grew up to marry men who would thrive under the Restoration and lived out their lives not in the colony but the metropole. In 1797, a month before her nineteenth birthday, Mimi married the future honorary president of the Royal Court of Saint-Denis, where she lived until her death in 1863. In 1799 Mélanie married a man who was to become a count and a peer of France under the Restoration and to serve as prime minister to both Louis XVIII and Charles X. She died in Toulouse in 1855, a year after her husband.[143] Such excellent marriages must have reflected not only the wealth and reputation of their family but also the education the young women had received, since it would surely have distinguished them in a colony wholly bereft of educational institutions. And, in a family that would scatter throughout France, leaving behind only one son—Charles—in the colony, one can only assume that their father's concern that they learn how to write paid off in many letters to siblings, parents, and friends across the decades.

Writing as Discipline 3

Instruction in Penmanship and Orthography

As it was the mother's responsibility to educate her daughter, the mother's reputation as well as the daughter's success rode on the daughter's ability to craft a letter that could be read aloud and passed around with pride. Whether at home, in a convent, or in one of the new schools that sprang up in the 1770s and '80s, when girls reached the age of nine or ten they were ready for advanced instruction in penmanship, spelling, and epistolary style. In this chapter I deal with how gender shaped the way girls were taught penmanship and spelling, and in chapter 4 I discuss issues of epistolary style.

Every eighteenth-century mother would sympathize with the mother in Reyre's *École des jeunes demoiselles,* who was embarrassed to show her daughter's poorly written and badly spelled letter to her friend. If a letter was a mode of communication, it was also a surrogate for the absent loved one and an object to be displayed as evidence of a girl's charms, accomplishments, and virtue.[1] Above all, it reflected on the writer as a social and moral being, as Jean Léonor Le Gallois de Grimarest noted in his treatise on letter writing published early in the eighteenth century: "We do not assure our reputation, until we arrange [our ideas] nobly and accurately on paper," he asserted. "Thus, I believe that it is not reasonably permitted to judge completely the merit of a person by their conversation: one must wait to decide until one has seen their letters." The judgment such a reading produced, moreover, was typically not very favorable. In Grimarest's experience, "the ignorance of a woman, or a courtier, is almost always noticed in their letters."[2] Several decades later Eléazar Mauvillon made the same point in his treatise on epistolary style: "A letter is a witness that testifies for or against its Author," he declared. "It is a sort of certificate of good or bad character."[3] André-Joseph Panckoucke applied this principle specifically to women in *Les Études convenables aux demoiselles,* first published in 1749 and reissued periodically right into the nineteenth century. "Nothing," he declared, "better assures the reputation of a lady than knowing how to arrange her thoughts on paper nobly and accurately. . . . Without this one sees only disorder, impoliteness, errors of language and construction, sterility, ignorance."[4]

It was not just what a woman wrote, or even how she expressed herself, that mattered; the material qualities of the letter were at least as important. Jean Lanteires was not alone in declaring that spelling was the "touchstone upon which, in general, people are disposed to appreciate the degree of education that any person, but above all a woman who moves in society, has received."[5] Père Gregoire Martin gave a litany of reasons for the importance of good handwriting, beginning with the most obvious: "Beautiful Writing pleases everyone," he explained, "it makes one sought after."[6] Innocuous as this statement may seem, it had particular salience for women, since it resonated with one of the central gender assumptions of the age, stated most bluntly by Rousseau in *Émile*, that "woman is made specially to please man."[7]

Although critics pointed out that women's desire to please made them superficial, frivolous, and unstable, few people thought they could or should change. All one could do was to convince young women that virtue—and good spelling and handwriting—would please those worthy of them. Instilling these values and skills was the purpose of a good education. A lady's letters had to be elegant, in part because the letter was seen as a reflection of the writer and in part because her letters needed to be pleasing to the reader, especially if that reader was a man. The best way to teach a young lady how to write such a letter was to read and respond to the letters she wrote: trying to please one's mother was good practice for pleasing a future husband.

When a daughter wrote to her mother, or a wife to her husband, she had to be prepared to be judged on all levels, especially because there was just as much at stake for the recipient as for the sender in a world in which letters were shared with a circle of intimates. As Panckoucke pointed out, a letter reflected on the person who received it as much as the one who wrote it: "One reads, with double pleasure, a letter composed with taste; esteem is added to friendship; one is honored by one's choice of a friend; one shows these letters to other people, who judge our own feelings and mind favorably by the lightness and delicacy of our correspondents."[8] If the correspondence between mother and daughter was meant, above all, to teach the girl how to conduct a correspondence, the first lesson was that since thoughts are materialized in letters rather than conveyed transparently, the letter was a means of displaying its writer and honoring its recipient. Letter writing was not to be taken lightly.[9] Concerned mothers hired professionals to tutor their daughters in the difficult but necessary skills that went into crafting a beautiful letter, and the professionals went out of their way to offer their services to this growing market fed by raised expectations, upward mobility, and gendered insecurity.

Penmanship: Disciplining the Body

The men and women who developed schools, curricula, and methods to teach penmanship to women and girls adapted them to fit their own conceptions of the social roles, minds, and bodies of women. Mlle d'Espinassy believed that girls should be taught to write immediately after they learned to read, "at the same time that the dancing master and singing master come." Instruction in these forms of bodily discipline would precede the academic education to begin at the age of twelve. Mme de Genlis, who, like Rousseau, believed that early childhood was for play and exploration, agreed that the physical skills should be taught before the academic subjects. And Fresneau advocated that young children should only be expected to write legibly. "Writing ought to follow as closely after reading as possible," he advised; "but at that age one should not put a lot of effort into the beauty of the letter, as long as the child has a light hand, not much more is needed." Penmanship could be taught when a child was older, twelve or fourteen, at which age she would learn in four months what a younger child could not learn in four years.[10] In practice, as Paule Constant notes, instruction in penmanship was typically one of the "final touches" in a young lady's education, "just before the entry into the world, when the young girl was being graced with her final talents."[11] No matter when it was taught, penmanship was classified among either the basic skills or the accomplishments, while grammar, spelling, and style (rhetoric) were among the academic subjects facilitated by reading. Penmanship required a discipline of the body, whereas grammar, spelling, and rhetoric required a discipline of the mind.

The disciplining of the female body was generally entrusted to male masters with an expertise that they guarded jealously. Three centuries earlier, printing had created more demand for the services of writing masters than there ever had been for mere copyists by stimulating the greatest increase in literacy Europe had ever seen. Masters in the guild of writers—*écrivains* properly speaking—drew on their expertise to teach the various hands that constituted penmanship: "the art of forming the characters of the alphabet of a language, assembling them, and composing with them words traced in a plain, clear, exact, distinct, elegant, and simple manner." They taught children not only how to write but "the great principles of the Art of Handwriting considered in all its perfection." A 1759 almanac listed *maître écrivains* under the heading, "Useful Education, common to young people of both sexes," and distinguished them from their rivals, the grammar school teachers, who taught only "the first elements of Handwriting." Louis-Sébastien Mercier was considerably more cynical and blunt: "They are masters of the art of handwriting, and not the art of writing," he declared.[12]

In order to maintain their privileged position in the expanding market conditions of the eighteenth century, the writing masters employed two conflicting approaches that reflected the inherent contradictions of the guild system. Even as they responded to growing demand by making writing easier to learn, they renewed their claims to expertise, or for writing itself as a highly skilled craft or even an art. Within the guild, traditionalists emphasized the difficulty of writing as a discipline, while others called for a new, simplified approach to penmanship. The writing masters were thus divided between those who saw the future in writing for others, and those who saw it in teaching others how to write.

The critics, however, were unanimous. Grimarest railed for ten pages about what he saw as a rampant misuse of the letter *y*, which he blamed on the writing masters' desire to show off their virtuosity.[13] Abbé Jaubert urged his readers to take charge of their own writing, rather than letting themselves be intimidated into thinking that they needed the services of a professional. "Truthfully, everyone is not obliged by necessity or status to write as well as a *maître Écrivain*," he argued in his *Dictionnaire raisonné universel des arts et metiers* (1773):

> At the least it would always be useful to write legibly; one would have less recourse to people one does not know, such as those writers who work in chambers, or who have small offices dispersed in several locations in each big city, with whom discretion is as rare as their style is sometimes extraordinary and ridiculous; who write letters for the public, draw up briefs and petitions, make copies, duplicates of accounts, and other similar writing that is almost always incorrect.[14]

Beyond the pomposity of the professional writer, with his elaborate and unnecessary flourishes, Jaubert's deeper concern had to do with trust: to entrust one's affairs to a professional writer meant depending on a stranger. In the past elites had in their service all sorts of men bound to them by mutual ties of fidelity—soldiers as well as secretaries; people were bound together by obligation and trust.[15] In the modern world of the eighteenth-century city, however, no such trust bound the professional writer to the person who paid for his services. Jaubert thus advised his readers to learn how to write properly rather than entrusting their correspondence to paid strangers whose professional expertise was, in fact, mostly superfluous and whose discretion could not be counted on. One did not need the skills of the professional writer, just the ability to write legibly.

As the practice of letter writing became personal and crossed gender lines, it also created a new class divide between those who could write for themselves and those who were forced to depend on the skills of others whom they paid to write for them. Public writers set up stalls in poor neighborhoods to serve those who could not afford to learn to write properly but who needed to function in a society where the written word was increasingly necessary. According to one observer in 1779, there were "hardly any streets that are modestly large where one does not find some small temporary stalls or shops occupied by public writers." He went on to explain that "these sorts of Secretaries are very useful to the people, to servants, and generally to those who do not know how to read or write."[16]

Although the public writer provided practical and necessary services for all sorts of women and men who needed to have legal documents or business or family letters written for them, when Pierre-Alexandre Wille chose the public writer for the subject of a popular print, he depicted him within the familiar terrain of women and love (see fig. 3.1). Here we see the writer penning a love letter for a pretty young maid (identifiable by her bucket and mop, resting at the entry to the stall). We know it is a love

3.1. Pierre-Alexandre Wille, *The Public Writer* (ca. 1783). Etching engraved by C. Guttenberg (Paris). 41.5 × 35.3 cm. Bibliothèque nationale de France.

letter because the scribe holds in his left hand a miniature portrait for the young woman to address as she dictates her letter. While the servant's mistress remains indoors, enjoying the privacy and security afforded by the ability to read and write her own letters, the freedom of the maid to go out into the street is shown here to entail a lack of privacy, as she is forced to share her most intimate thoughts and feelings with a stranger. "I have always believed," declared the lawyer Michel de Servan, in a 1784 essay defending every citizen's right to the privacy of his or her letters, "that my thoughts belonged to me, that they were my property even more than my purse."[17] But the maid in this picture has no such rights, as she is forced to share her thoughts with a stranger in order to convey them to her correspondent. Even worse, she is shown to be wanton, without virtue at all, as she gives her thoughts, herself, to the writer on the street. The education in letter writing that had come to distinguish women from each other along class lines, as Carolyn Steedman reminds us, took on a moral dimension, as only those who could write had the privacy and the power to be virtuous.[18] Teaching girls how to write was thus central to the process of transforming them into young ladies, with all the privileges as well as constraints that such status entailed.

The writing masters disdained the semiprofessionals who set up stalls in the markets to serve the poor and associated themselves rather with the elites whose teachers they would be.[19] In young ladies in particular they recognized a new class of consumers for their services. Serving this new market contributed to the shift in theoretical and pedagogical approaches to penmanship away from technically difficult hands and toward a simpler hand that was more easily readable and required less skill and fewer lessons. Indeed, it might not require any lessons at all. In 1770 Sieur Colon, an "Expert Écrivain" himself, announced in the pages of the periodical *L'Avantcoureur*, a "new paper prepared for learning how to write." "In the interest of perfecting the art of writing and making it easier to learn," the notice read, Sieur Colon "has invented a paper divided by rectangular and non-rectangular parallelograms, of different lengths and widths; these parallelograms are marked by numbers and letters, so that anyone can know and practice thereafter on ordinary paper the mechanism of writing."[20]

In general, however, the writing masters were not so professionally suicidal as to want to put themselves out of business entirely by encouraging people to teach themselves how to write. Rather, the progressives among them developed new modes of writing and writing instruction that were meant to be especially attractive to ladies and their daughters. Leading the charge was the syndic of the guild, M. d'Autrèpe.[21] In a treatise on handwriting published in 1759, d'Autrèpe accused the greatest of his predecessors of "painting" words rather than writing them. As Jean Hébrard points out, the implications of d'Autrèpe's critique were threefold: first, writing as it was taught was too slow; second, it was illegible because it was too elaborate, but mostly because the aim was to produce a masterpiece of writing, rather than a means of communication; and third, it was reduced to a mechanical art or, worse, an *art d'agrément*—a mere accomplishment—thereby reducing its practitioners either to mere technicians or to the men of dubious masculinity who taught young ladies dancing, music, or drawing.[22]

D'Autrèpe advocated a radical new pedagogical approach that would focus on the principles of writing and the movement of the hand in creating words, rather than rote copying to reproduce a beautiful object. "The action of writing is simple," he declared:

> Nature indicates it. Take a pen between your fingers; bend them, unbend them in a certain movement, following the configuration of the letter that you trace; move your right arm away from your body, to the degree that you approach the side of the paper where the line ends; that's what the action consists in. But writing well is always the same action directed toward the different objects that compose it, by the means appropriate to assisting the operations of nature or rectifying what is defective in them.[23]

The pen was simply an extension of the hand, and the point of rules was to facilitate the "practice of a methodical and natural liberty." If, as Hébrard explains, d'Autrèpe's predecessors wanted to discipline the body into a writing machine, he aimed to guide the body's natural gestures toward writing.[24]

Both approaches to handwriting—the old one that stressed disciplining the body to produce a beautiful object, and the new one that aimed to develop the body's natural grace to produce a legible script—were adopted by those who thought about how to teach writing to young ladies within the gender norms of the day. "When I speak of writing," explained Charles-Robert Gosselin in his 1785 *Plan d'éducation*, "I do not mean an imperfect and crude representation of the letters of the alphabet, such as one is ordinarily contented with, but a *peinture* done with all the precision and the grace of which a child is capable."[25] Jean-François Dumas, however, discounted the importance of *peinture* altogether. "The art of writing must not be considered simply as the art of painting," he noted in his 1783 essay on the means of perfecting the education of young ladies. Dumas believed that too much emphasis was placed on teaching girls to form their letters perfectly, and not enough on developing their facility in writing and their style.[26] Mme de Miremont took a moderate position between these two extremes, noting, like Jaubert, that, "it is not very useful for a Woman to *peindre* perfectly, but it is necessary to write quickly and legibly."[27] Mercier agreed. "It is necessary to know well how to draw one's letters," he wrote, "because poor handwriting resembles a stutter in speech; but a legible character is sufficient." Mercier was thinking in particular here about "great nobles, pretty women, authors," who, he said, were wrong to take pride in poor handwriting. At the same time, he thought that writing masters placed too much emphasis on a beautiful hand. "A little bit of clarity, that's really all that's appropriate," he concluded.[28]

In the boarding schools run by the Ursulines, young ladies first practiced "holding their pens gracefully with three fingers." After that, they progressed methodically from letters to syllables to words and then to whole lines. According to the order's regulations, the writing mistress was expected to guide the hand of each student, attending especially to those who struggled and correcting them. "In guiding the hand of her pupils, the mistress acted also as an orthopedist," observes Martine Sonnet. "She took care to straighten the back that curved." This physical education was complete when the student's hand was "sufficiently strengthened." Only at this point was she ready to move on to spelling.[29]

Physical rectitude went hand in hand with moral rectitude; the writing teacher was responsible for straightening the mind and the will as well as the body, or perhaps through the body, as the following examples of young ladies' copybooks suggest. The first is dated 1757 and is the work of twelve-year-old Marie Marguerite Émilie Lavoisier (see fig. 3.2). On this page Mlle Lavoisier has dutifully copied out several uplifting thoughts, but without any punctuation separating them, as they would have appeared in the models she copied. Here is a translation of the first few of them:

> Think little speak of everything doubt nothing
> Inhabit only the outside of his soul cultivate only the surface of his wit
> To express oneself well, have a pleasant turn of the imagination
> A light and delicate conversation
> Know how to please by making yourself esteemed

Penser peu parler de tout ne douter de rien n'habiter que les dehors

de son ame ne cultiver que la superficie de son esprit S'exprimer

heureusement avoir un tour d'imagination agreable une conversation

legere et delicate Savoir plaire sans se faire estimer, être né avec

le talent equivoque d'une conception prompte et par la se croire au des=

sus de la reflexion estimer toutes les sciences Voler d'objets en objets

sans en approfondir aucun, cueillir rapidement toutes

les fleurs sans jamais donner aux fruits le tems de parvenir a

maturité C'est une faible peinture de ce qu'il a plu a notre

siecle honorer du nom d'esprit. A A A A B B

B B B B B C C D D E E F F G G G

H I J J J L L O H M O S O

P P P P Q Q R R S S T U V V

X X Y Y Z Penser peu parler de tout

ne douter de rien n'habiter que les dehors de son ame ne

cultiver que la superficie de son esprit S'exprimer heureusement

avoir un tour d'imagination agreable, une conversation legere et delicate

Savoir plaire sans se faire estimer être né avec le talent equivoque

d'une conception prompte et par là se croire audessus de la reflexion

M Me Lavoisier M Me Lavoisier M Me L

3.2. Page of copybook of Marie Marguerite Emilie Lavoisier (1757). Musée national de l'Education—
INRP—Rouen—France. Inv. 3.4.02/1979—08840.

When she came to the end of her assignment, Mlle Lavoisier practiced her capital letters, and then she began again: "Think little speak of everything doubt nothing." In the spaces between the lines she or her teacher made corrections, adding a missing letter or repeating a word that had not been written well. At the bottom of the page (and of every right-hand page), she practiced signing her name.

The second young scholar was Mlle Vanlerberghe, who won the first prize in penmanship at Mme Dessault's school in 1803 (An XII of the French Republican Calendar). The cover of her copybook is embellished with flourishes and a swan that show off Mlle Vanlerberghe's skill at "painting" (see fig. 3.3a). The eight pages of writing that follow are beautifully embellished as well, and each features a different kind of text. For example, one page is copied from orders from the minister of war to a lieutenant general in the French Army (fig. 3.3b), but the name of the general is made-up nonsense whose purpose seems to be to show off the young lady's *M*'s and *S*'s: an alphabet graces the bottom of the page. If, as I suspect, the young lady was the daughter of Ignace-Joseph Vanlerberghe, one of the major provisioners of Napoleon's army, the model might have been provided by her father, or the copy meant to impress him.

Moral lessons, however, remain a staple of the copybook, as another handsome example of Mlle Vanlerberghe's handwriting shows (fig. 3.3c). Beautiful as this specimen is, with its flourish at the bottom that turns into a bird, the thought is somber: "Unfortunately, human nature is subject to evils of all sorts. No one is exempt, the rich no more than the poor." The point of such an exercise was not simply to teach a girl to move her pen gracefully over the page but to engrave such moral lessons into her heart and thus to form her character as she learned to form letters and words beautifully.

However, both mothers and masters were concerned that the physical demands of writing could deform a young lady's body—just as too much academic knowledge could deform the female spirit by turning a girl into a scholar. In the 1750s and '60s, the distinguished writing master Charles Paillasson promoted a new writing posture designed specifically for young ladies, in response, he claimed, to the concerns of mothers that a daughter's waistline might be compromised or her breathing impaired by the standard one (see figs. 3.4a and 3.4b). Requiring the writer to rest his weight on the left hand, this "standard" posture had been practiced for centuries without a thought to girls or women. Paillasson explained:

> My intention is not . . . to discredit [the method] that is generally used, but it will be agreed that it is much better for men, for whom nothing hinders their movement, than for young ladies who are subjected, from a tender age, to whalebones or other constraints. . . . I have tested the [method] that I have announced here several times, and have always met with success. Thus mothers who, in order to protect the waistline of their daughters, deprive the majority of them of a skill that will be useful to them in whatever situation they find themselves, will have nothing to fear, if the master charged to instruct them uses [this method].[30]

Collection
Edgard
FOURNIER
N° 1156

3.3a. Cover of copybook of Mlle Vanlerberghe the elder (2 Frimaire An XII). Musée national de l'Education—INRP—Rouen—France. Inv. 3.4.02/1979–10812–1.

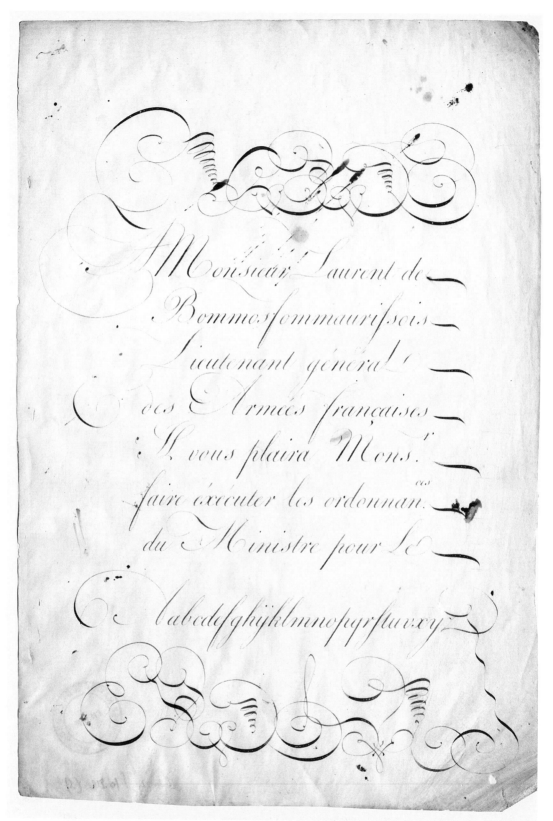

3.3b. Page of copybook of Mlle Vanlerberghe the elder (2 Frimaire An XII). Musée national de l'Education—INRP—Rouen—France. Inv. 3.4.02/1979–10812–1.

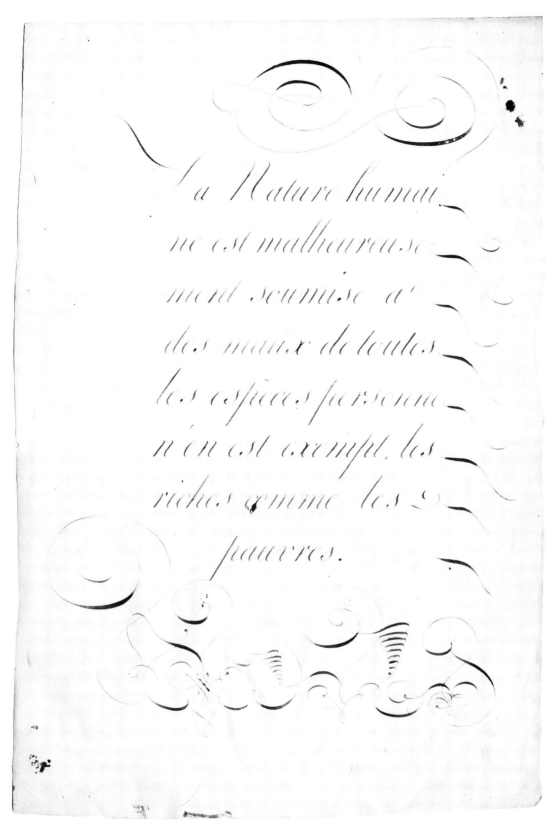

La Nature humaine est malheureusement soumise a' des maux de toutes les espèces personne n'en est exempt, les riches comme les pauvres.

3.3c. Page of copybook of Mlle Vanlerberghe the elder (2 Frimaire An XII). Musée national de l'Education—INRP—Rouen—France. Inv. 3.4.02/1979–10812–1.

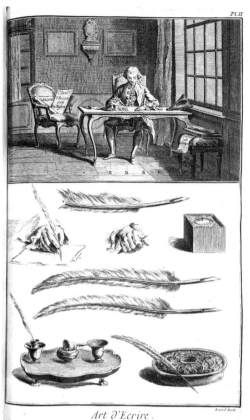

Art d'Ecrire.

3.4a. "De la position du corps pour écrire, & de la tenue de la plume." *Encyclopédie,* plates, vol.2, "Ecritures," plate II. Special Collections Library, University of Michigan.

Art d'Ecrire.

3.4b. "Sur la position des jeunes demoiselles pour écrire." *Encyclopédie,* plates, vol.2, "Ecritures," plate III. Special Collections Library, University of Michigan.

In 1766 the abbé de Petity endorsed Paillasson's gender-specific writing postures in his general textbook on the arts and sciences.[31] A few years later, Mme d'Épinay, who introduced penmanship in the second of the *Conversations d'Émilie*, seems to have adopted the Paillasson posture, too. Through the dialogue between mother and daughter, she makes two main points: first, that good handwriting depends on good posture; and second, that it requires patience and takes time to learn. When Émilie, who is nine, expresses a desire to be perfect, the mother tells her to begin by sitting up straight. "Have you written this afternoon while I had company?" she then asks. "Yes, Mama," Émilie replies, "but I don't dare show you my writing because it is so bad! ... such a scrawl!" "Ah," says the mother, "you had not yet made your resolution to be perfect! ... Look, your feet are already out of place, and your head...." Émilie, convinced that with her new resolution she will be able to write perfectly if simply given a second chance, asks if she can start over. The mother sits her down at the table, tells her how to hold her pen, and then her head. "Your writing is no more straight," she says. "Are you impatient? Be careful, impatience does not go with perfection.... I'm sorry, but this page is no better than the other." Émilie wants to try again, but this time she is told that she has studied enough for one day. "Everything takes time," the mother explains. "You must apply yourself in order to do a little bit less badly every day; but you cannot learn to write in one day."[32] Good handwriting required the disciplining of the body over time. The aim was straightness: a physical rectitude that was transferred from the body of the writer to the page she wrote through the correct posture, as well as the proper exercise of the pen.

In *Émile*, Rousseau had explained the "natural repugnance" of little girls to writing by comparing the writing posture with that of sewing. "As for holding a needle," he had declared confidently, "that's what they're always willing to learn." Although Rousseau's knowledge of little girls was limited to his own imagination, he went on to recount a story of a girl "who learned to write before she learned to read, and who began to write with the needle before writing with the pen." Her favorite letter, he tells us, was O. "She incessantly made O's large and small, O's of all sizes, O's inside one another, and always drawn backward." However, happening one day to see herself in a mirror while engaged in this activity, "and finding that this constrained posture was not graceful for her," she threw down her pen and refused to write any more, until the necessity of marking her laundry forced her to do with a needle what she would not do with the pen. "You can imagine the rest of her progress," he concluded.[33] The many images of girls and women plying their needles, their backs elegantly curved over the work that absorbs all their attention, contrast with the scarcity of images of women or girls sitting up straight or leaning on their left hand and writing, and suggest that Rousseau was not alone in finding the writing woman unattractive.[34]

The princesse de Ligne tells a very different story of O's in her account of her days as a boarder at an exclusive Parisian convent, the Abbaye-aux-Bois. She arrived there in 1772, when she was eight years old. "At that time I had a terrible aversion to writing well," she begins. "M. Charme was very unhappy with me and had assigned me to make nothing but O['s], which really bored me, and the whole class made fun of me, too, or said that I would never learn how to sign my name." She went on to explain, however, that she did not hate writing [*écriture*] at all: "To the contrary, I wrote my memoirs all day long, as was the fashion among the older girls in those days, and we wished to do the same. I thus scribbled away on paper all day, but this was a scrawl of which only I could understand anything, and far from benefiting me, it ruined my hand." Young Hélène loved to write, she just hated the discipline of penmanship, and it was that which she found difficult and resisted. Indeed, it was precisely this discipline that the writing master was expected to impose on the bodies of the girls entrusted to him, since, at eight years old, they already knew how to form their letters. Moreover, far from loving to make O's all day, Hélène was bored to tears. Eventually she submitted, but only after trying to get a friend to write her exercises for her and then, when caught lying about it, being forced to walk around all day with "ass's horns" on her head, and a sample of her own handwriting attached to her bottom as a tail.[35]

Although the princesse de Ligne acknowledged in her memoirs that, even at the time, she knew that the undisciplined scrawl was "ruining" her hand, it is hard not to be sympathetic with the little girl who loved to write and hated penmanship. And it's easy to see how d'Autrèpe and his followers were responding to a new generation of students for whom writing was a pleasure rather than a vocation. For young ladies in particular, d'Autrèpe's emphasis on the gracefulness of the writing body brought penmanship into the repertoire of skills their other masters were hired to teach them. It could become, as the abbé de Petity put it, "a choreography of the quill."[36] By emphasizing that writing had to be taught according to principles, however, rather than simply by copying examples, d'Autrèpe's approach also elevated handwriting to a science, rather than an art, and the master into an expert, rather than a technician or *petit maître*. The rest of French language instruction for young ladies would follow a similar path that elevated the master as it made writing more accessible and appropriate for the women they were being trained to become.

Writing for Sale: The Free Market in Writing Instruction

Maître écrivains taught only penmanship, but others without their technical expertise were eager to provide ladies and girls with instruction in spelling, grammar, and epistolary style via private lessons, books, and public courses, or as external masters hired by convents and, increasingly, *maisons d'éducation*. Victorine de Chastenay-Lanty recounts in her memoirs that at around the age of ten she and her brother were given a Latin master. Abbé Barême "was a gentle and pleasant man who gave lessons in history, grammar, and geography to ladies." Her mother had hired him for herself, but after a while he began to give the children lessons in these subjects as well.[37]

Baret de Villencour, who advertised in the *Mercure de France* in the 1770s, also offered his services to both children and adults. In 1783 we find his course on French elocution and spelling listed in the *Almanach du voyageur*, where visitors to Paris might look for information about educational services available in the capital.[38] Villencour noted that he taught "in Town and in the Convents or Boarding Schools for Ladies and Young Ladies," in addition to offering lessons in elocution and French spelling in his home to "persons of both sexes on different days." His qualifications included experience as a professor at the Bavarian court and the publication of a speech he had given on the subject of "Languages in general and the French Language in particular," which was available for purchase from the author.[39] In November 1777, he advised readers of the *Mercure* that he was about to open "a special Course on Epistolary Style" in the interim between sessions of his general course on French spelling and elocution. "The abridged Method that he has composed concerning this style cannot but be useful and agreeable to Ladies who wish to take lessons in their own homes," the advertisement declared.[40] Epistolary style not only formed part of the course he gave on elocution and spelling but was apparently a subject of interest to enough women that he could offer it separately to them. This was the only specialized course he offered, which suggests that letters were indeed what many women wanted to learn how to write properly and well.

From Villencour's ads we can also see the different venues in which a writing instructor taught: he might give private or group lessons in his own home, or take his services to an educational institution, either a convent or a *maison d'éducation*. A similar ad that appeared in 1778 in the local Bordeaux paper shows that these possibilities existed in the provinces as well:

> *Notice*: Sieur Dumarsais, Professor of the French language and of historical Geography, advises that, for the benefit of young persons of the female sex, he is going to give lessons in schools [*maisons*]: inquiries to M. Malavergne, *Écrivain*, rue des herbes, near the Salted-Fish; it is in the home of M. Malavergne that sieur Dumarsais, for the benefit of day students, gives a course in the French language, & above all Spelling, & a course in historical Geography; he is pleased to give full satisfaction in these two subjects.[41]

Dumarsais' ad shows him to be one of the progressive educators of the day who believed that advanced French language instruction belonged in the academic curriculum of young ladies, along with history, geography, and often the sciences. "Your daughter having reached the age of twelve is no longer a child," wrote Mlle d'Espinassy, "and should no longer be treated as such. . . . This is when a more serious study will begin." In place of dancing and music masters, the young lady would be given instructors in history, geography, drawing, and grammar. "She must study Grammar in order to know how to speak her language, which the majority of women mangle, thus taking away much of the pleasure [*agrémens*] of their conversation; and spelling, so that their writing is correct. The most pleasant style loses a lot by being badly spelled and badly punctuated, because it is more difficult to read."[42]

Everyone seemed to agree that spelling posed the greatest difficulties. Indeed, spelling was a contested subject within the history of the French language and French gender relations, and it was to spelling that most men who wanted to teach young ladies to write turned their attention. It is thus to spelling that we now turn as well.

L'Ortografe des Dames: The Problem of Spelling

Editors and historians since the nineteenth century have called attention to the poor spelling of eighteenth-century women, and especially *salonnières*, writers, and friends of the philosophes, as if to remind their readers that the gender gap central to the Republic of Letters was intellectual as well as social.[43] The editor of the salonnière Marie-Thérèse Geoffrin's correspondence with the Polish king Stanislas advises us in his preface that "it was not possible to preserve the constantly vicious spelling of Madame Geoffrin; it would have been an abusive exactitude and a fatiguing scrupulousness for the public. This multitude of errors would have given a tiresome aspect to the style and would not even have allowed for a good appreciation of the meaning."[44] In his magisterial history of the French language, Ferdinand Brunot provided "specimens" of women's poor spelling and noted that, when spelling is considered, "the distance is weak between a marquise de Verdelin, for example, and mother Levasseur, who served as J. J. Rousseau's secretary."[45] Poor spelling was the mark of intellectual inferiority, the counterweight to the material wealth and social and political superiority of the salonnière. Pointing it out redressed the balance between her and the men of letters who frequented her salon. It put ladies in their place.

And yet, according to traditional pedagogical theory and practice, spelling could not be part of a young lady's education. Because the principles of spelling were fundamentally etymological, it was assumed that they could not be understood without a knowledge of Latin—which girls were not taught because they were thought incapable of learning it or unwilling to put in the effort required to do so. Girls were thus taught to spell the way they were taught everything else—by example and through constant repetition and correction—except that spelling, it was believed, could not be taught that way. That's why most girls never really learned how to spell. Nevertheless, they learned as they could from printed models, just as they learned penmanship. This was possible at all because editors and printers took pains to "correct" the spelling of the women whose letters they published in letter-writing manuals and compendia. An orthographic norm was thus imposed on women's letters by the men who presented them as models to be emulated by young ladies. Mme de Sévigné's letters in particular thereby became the basis of a mixed-gender epistolary model, in which the woman's stylistic voice was materialized in a written form imposed on it by men of letters.

It is thus not surprising that in the second half of the eighteenth century, when both discussions of female education and the female practice of letter writing had become widespread, many men of letters and educators directed their efforts to figuring out ways to teach young ladies and their mothers how to transform and materialize their perfect speech into perfect writing through a mastery of rules that only men could teach them. Because spelling also raised perennial philosophical questions about the relationship between speech and writing, it was a domain that attracted men who wanted to make a mark in the Republic of Letters. Thus many men published books on French spelling and grammar, but to my knowledge, not a single woman did. Women's letters may have been held up as models for all to follow, but only men could teach the principles of writing that women, they claimed, required.

How did women spell in the eighteenth century? According to Marie-Claire Grassi, who studied 1,100 manuscript letters written by French nobles between 1700 and 1860, "the sex of the writer is, with geographic origin [rural or urban], the most determinant criterion of epistolary discourse." Grassi found that in the period from 1700 to 1770, more than 90 percent of the male letter writers she studied adhered to the orthographic norms of their day, while only 25 percent of the women did. By contrast, 37 percent of the women continued to write according to "archaic" practice. The remaining 38 percent of women's letters fell somewhere between these two poles. By 1820, however, 59 percent of women's letters adhered to the orthographic norms of the day, and by 1860, fully 86 percent did.[46] Statistically, then, women and men of the same social status did spell differently in the eighteenth century, but this distinction was in the process of disappearing at precisely that time, as the spread of education and literacy to (elite) women brought them into line with the orthographic norm.

Grassi inscribes the difference between the spelling of elite men and women into a progressive narrative in which women's practice was archaic and irrational and men's was both modern and normative. She not only embraces the *Encyclopédie*'s claim that orthography, properly speaking, does not include "the writing practice of uneducated people who . . . have no stable principle and leave everything to chance,"[47] but sees it as descriptive of the practice of the overwhelming majority of elite women. Here is an example Grassi gives of such an unprincipled female speller from 1732: "Linthéré qu ie prand monsieur en ce qui nous regarde ma fait pansé a un establissement qui celon moy nous scera tré convenable."[48] To the degree that the orthographic practice represented here is phonetic, however, it is hardly without principles. Nor is it simply archaic. Indeed, from the sixteenth century on, proponents of spelling reform argued that French orthography should be established on phonetic principles. And starting in the seventeenth century, they made their claims for phonetic reform in terms of a gendered understanding of language that idealized the phonetic principle as "l'ortografe des dames."

Latinacy, Spelling, and Gender

Spelling posed a problem because spoken French had developed farther away from its Latin origins than written French, which continued to hold on to traces of Latin in its grammar and orthography. There were basically two possible solutions to this problem: either students could be taught Latin so as to understand why French was written the way it was and learn to write it properly themselves, or written French could be brought into line with speech through spelling reform. Twelve years after the Académie française was established to "give certain rules to our language and to render it pure, eloquent, and capable of treating the arts and sciences,"[49] Claude Favre de Vaugelas provided the theory to support the second option when he declared that to "fix" the French language through rules of grammar or spelling would be to kill it. "Usage" alone could determine what was correct or incorrect, and usage would necessarily change over time. His goal, he wrote in *Remarques sur la langue françoise, utiles à ceux qui veulent bien parler et bien escrire* (1647), was simply to record the current state of the language.[50]

Vaugelas defined good usage as "the way of speaking of the healthiest part of the Court in conformity with the way of writing of the healthiest part of the authors of the time." He made a point of signaling the presence of women at court, "since women, ignorant of the usage of Latin, will give you a more naive and thus more authentic judgment."[51] Vaugelas considered the French language to be on the whole tilted toward the feminine pole of speech rather than the masculine pole of writing.[52] "The language of elegant conversation carried as much weight as that of fine writers," concludes Marc Fumaroli.[53]

Throughout the seventeenth century men of letters developed this theme. In 1672 Père Bouhours identified female speech as naive and natural—just like the French language itself—in contrast to masculine literary art. The speech of ladies, he explained, was more pure, since it was closer to the "sources" of the language. If the association of French with the king gave it its majesty and authority, its association with women made it the language "par excellence of affect and sensibility." French, he declared, was the "language of the heart."[54]

Men of letters associated with the Parisian salons were building on Vaugelas when they argued that French spelling should be reformed to bring it into conformity with speech. In *Le Grand dictionnaire des pretieuses* (1661), Antoine Baudeau de Somaize claimed that it was one of the salon women or "précieuses," Claristène, who announced one day "that a new Orthography must be devised, so that women may write as confidently and as correctly as men do." In Somaize's story, their male friend, Didamie, assures the three women present that this would be easy to do and offers to help them. Roxalie then establishes the principle on which they will operate: "Roxalie says that it must be done such that one could write the same as one speaks, & in order to execute this plan, Didamie takes a book, Claristène takes a pen, & Roxalie & Silenie get ready to decide what must be added or subtracted from words, in order to make usage easier and spelling more convenient." In short order the four friends work out the problem. Their solution is found in a list of words Somaize appended to the article, with both old and new spellings.[55]

The scene may be apocryphal and the characters fictional, but they nevertheless locate spelling reform efforts in the salon world.[56] And whether they invented the spelling Somaize associated with them, or merely adopted it happily as a systematic refinement of their conventional practice, the ladies did use this new phonetic orthography in the letters they wrote. "Mme de Sévigné, traditionally lampooned for her spelling and charged (quite wrongly) with ignorance and frivolity because of her spelling, deserves to be rehabilitated," writes Nina Catach; "she presents quite simply the traits of pronunciation and orthography of her day and her milieu, with a usage that is modernized and quite superior to the average manuscripts of the age." In short, her spelling was that advocated by the reformers.[57]

In 1668, seven years after Somaize published his dictionary, Louis de L'Esclache published *Les Véritables régles de l'ortografe francéze, ou l'Art d'aprandre an peu de tams à écrire côrectemant*.[58] L'Esclache was already well known for giving public courses designed to prepare Parisian women for salon life by teaching them subjects such as science and literature. Like Somaize, L'Esclache identified reform with the needs of elite women and himself as their champion. In his work, the battle lines were clearly drawn between the non-Latinate—identified with ladies of *le monde* and of wit—and the Latinate academic establishment:

> Those who do not know the Latin language and who have some wit, say that we ought to write as we speak: but certain scholars maintain that this method, as it causes us to lose the origins of words, prevents us from knowing their proper signification.
>
> It seems that the first, who do not have enough power to establish their opinion firmly, do not have enough authority to compel us to follow it. As the others cannot tolerate any damage to the Latin language or to the Greek, they hang on to their feelings with tremendous stubbornness.[59]

It was clearly the ladies whose writing practice derived directly from their speech and whom L'Esclache was opposing to the scholars concerned only with etymology. He would be the champion of the powerless ladies against the powerful academicians, whose authority was matched only by their stubbornness.

At the turn of the eighteenth century, the Académie française proclaimed both its independence from the court and its authority in the public sphere by asserting the priority of writing over speech. It asserted its legal privilege to judge in matters linguistic at the expense of ladies, who had been held up by Vaugelas and his followers as arbiters of taste because of their intimate and natural knowledge of the French language in its purity.[60] The academy now identified the French language with writing and devalued the spoken language as derivative and erratic, ungoverned and out of control. In the face of this natural force, the academicians fell back on their privileged access to history through their command of Latin.

In 1705, eleven years after the academy finally published its own dictionary, it sent forth its perpetual secretary to defend the old spelling against the reformers. François Séraphin Regnier Des Marais' *Traité de la grammaire françoise* was cast as a frontal assault on the reforms advocated by L'Esclache (although Regnier did not deign to name his adversary). In championing the old spelling, Regnier and the academy were not simply trying to conserve an old order in the face of inevitable and necessary change; they were severing a traditional alliance between women and men, speech and writing, which had been consecrated in the founding of their academy: they were declaring the independence of the Republic of Letters from both *la cour* and *le monde*.

By devaluing speech and denying its ability to set a standard of usage, Regnier implicitly challenged the legitimacy of women's contribution to shaping the French language. He also explicitly refused to consider relevant the reformers' desire to make French more accessible to "foreigners, women, and children."[61] Paris was now a major stop on the grand tour, L'Esclache had pointed out. With all the improvements and monuments that had made Paris a great city and a cosmopolitan center, the French now had an obligation to make visitors linguistically welcome: "The decoration that is added every day to Paris, the cleanliness of its streets, and the safety of walking there at night cause large numbers of foreigners to come there. As they will wish to learn our Language, we are in some sense obliged to facilitate the learning of it, and the best approach that we can take to arrive at this goal is to reduce our manner of writing to our manner of pronunciation."[62]

Regnier's response to this "argument from convenience," as he called it, was unequivocal: as foreigners must obey the laws of any country they visit, so must they accept the rules of any language they wish to learn.[63] As for children, they should learn to read as their fathers and grandfathers had learned. And women? "Where would we be in each Language . . . if because some women get confused in reading, we immediately had to remedy that by a universal change in Spelling?" he asked. "For those women who wish to instruct themselves by reading & to cultivate their minds, it is up to them to make use of the means that are available to everyone for the correct pronunciation of each letter."[64] Needless to say, Regnier did not address the question of female education.

In his response to Regnier's treatise, lawyer Nicolas Du Pont expressed the frustration of a public that had been waiting for the academy to reform spelling. Having read the *Traité*, Du Pont now realized that "these Gentlemen were a long way from entering into the spirit of that reform."[65] He then set out to refute Regnier's argument against reform, concluding that, "if it were possible . . . to produce an Orthography as accessible to children and women as to Scholars, it would . . . have to be advantageously received and included among those things that facilitate entry into the Arts and the Sciences."[66] In the voice of the obscure lawyer, the public called for greater access to the arts and sciences, while the academicians were busy erecting barricades to keep them out. Rather than guardians of a public trust, the forty Immortals who made up the academy were acting like a privileged *corps* with exclusive jurisdiction over the French language.[67] Reforming citizens like Du Pont wanted to spread written French as broadly as the spoken language, and so break down the orthographic barrier between writing and speech that the academy had erected out of the rubble of the old Latinate Respublica Litteraria.

When it came time for the academy to publish a second edition of its dictionary (it would appear in 1740), the pressure for change was overwhelming. Another one of the Immortals, abbé d'Olivet, was selected to determine what changes to authorize. "Preceded by usage, supported by opinion," writes Nina Catach, "d'Olivet thus realized a series of thoughtful reforms that mark a historical turning point and break strikingly with manuscript usage: one word in four was thus transformed."[68] D'Olivet and the academy were forced to concede because the printers and the men of letters whom they published had taken reform into their own ink-stained hands. In 1709 Père Buffier claimed that more than two-thirds of the books published in the previous ten years used the "new orthography"—and the works he named included those of more than half the current Immortals. In 1724 the abbé Castel de Saint-Pierre referred to the new spelling that "was getting established day by day."[69] Men of letters had reached consensus, and the authority of the academy would now simply back it to establish orthographic order after two centuries of anarchy, schism, and strife.

The men of letters were seconded by educational reformers like Louis Dumas, the inventor of the Printer's Desk, the game that taught children to spell phonetically. Dumas not only sang the praises of the abbé de Saint-Pierre's *Projet pour perfectioner l'ortgrafe des Langues de l'Europe* but employed a system of phonetic spelling of his own invention in his *Bibliothèque des enfans* (1733). Dumas explained how the game worked in Lockean terms, where what a child heard (the sound) and what she saw (the letter or syllable) corresponded exactly. "A child of three or four years, who knows by sight the shape of the letters and then by hearing the sound of simple or combined characters, will soon know how to write or print the sounds that one gives her with the cards," he explained.[70] By 1772 Pierre Fresneau could define "good usage" as "following the way of writing of good French Authors, and especially of the Académie française."[71]

The new orthographic order eroded the etymological foundations of the old spelling, but it also established the incontestable authority of the written over the spoken word, and thus of men of letters, who now claimed authority in all matters through their mastery of the written word. Thus, what may have been a defeat for the academy was a victory for the men of letters of the Enlightenment. In abandoning the old argument for phonetic spelling based on the need for writing to represent speech, they declared the independence of the written from the spoken word and their own independence from the ladies of the salons and *le monde*.

For Vaugelas language had been a set of social facts that it was his job to establish; he was a sociologist of language. The men of letters of the Enlightenment turned to the Jansenist authors of the Port-Royal Grammar for a different theory of language to underpin their claims. In contrast to Vaugelas, they were epistemologists of language who saw it as a tool for thinking. For them, French, like Latin, was primarily a means of representing ideas.[72] By the eighteenth century, most men of letters, inside and outside the academy, had come to think about French this way. The claims they made for the universality of French were associated with its ability to represent ideas; to do its work, it had to be fixed, stable, rational. One of the implications of this shift was to establish French in the image of Latin: fixed, grammatical, and based on the writing of men of letters rather than the speech of ladies.[73] The new orthography promoted by the philosophes was based on the *written* usage of contemporary men of letters (themselves) rather than the *spoken* usage of women of *le monde* and *la cour*. Their promotion of the "new spelling" reflected both their need to assert their authority through that of the written word and their assumed position as guardians of the French language. It was also embedded in the relationship they sought to establish between themselves and the reading public they often figured in their texts as an elite woman.

In the discourse of the seventeenth-century reformers, elite women had been cast as aesthetic judges because they were seen as the pure, uncorrupted other. The power associated with this role both gave rise to the spate of criticism that coalesced around the figure of the précieuse and was deployed by the reformers to fuel their arguments for phonetic spelling.[74] The philosophes, however, saw and presented *themselves* as uncorrupted through their Lockean epistemology, direct appeal to the public, and embrace of the French language. They staked their claims on the written word and its authority by appropriating the naive and natural female voice in their texts, even as they set out to conquer the academy, chair by chair.[75] No longer presenting female speech as a governing ideal outside of writing that the written word should follow, they absorbed the naturalness of female speech into their own writing and their own moderate practice of orthography. In Enlightenment texts, the purity born of ignorance that characterized women often coalesced around the naive heroine, who combined moral purity with intellectual foolishness.

Rousseau, who ventriloquized the female voice most successfully in his epistolary novel, *Julie, ou la nouvelle Héloïse*, appropriated it most thoroughly in his *Essai sur l'origine des langues* (1755–61). In the *Essai*, speech and writing play the roles assigned to women and men in the gender schemes of his other works, most notably *Julie* and *Émile*: speech is natural and expresses feelings, whereas writing is cold and rational and takes men away from nature. Rousseau gave primacy of origin to feminine speech over masculine writing and argued that writing removed language from its original purity. And yet, Rousseau asserted, "the art of writing does not at all depend on that of speaking."[76] Speech might be natural, pure, expressive, and historically prior to writing, but writing, no matter how inferior, was nonetheless independent of speech. It would neither be subject to speech nor model itself on it.

Jean-François Marmontel went even further in a speech he gave at a public session of the Académie française in 1785. His topic was "the authority of usage over language," and his purpose was to assert the freedom of writers in the face of that authority, which he considered illegitimate. To make his point, he compared natural language that was purely functional with modern speech, which he associated with all that the Enlightenment deemed feminine: fashion, luxury, the desire to please, accomplishments, nervousness, curiosity, uncertainty "in the search for its finery," and "the refinements and caprices of usage."[77] Much of Marmontel's speech took the form of a refutation of various arguments in defense of this "feminine" power of usage, the most compelling of which, he maintained, was that writing "like all the *arts d'agrément*" (like women themselves, he might have said) should seek to please the public, which was its final judge. Marmontel acknowledged that for certain works, such as plays and sermons, "whose success depends on the simultaneous emotion of the assembled public," this was true, but that all other writing, and especially that "judged by isolated and tranquil readers" who could depend on their own reason and taste, had no need to please. Indeed, writers, like readers, had to be free of the "power of opinion," he argued, if they wanted to write with a "noble frankness." How, he asked, could "the word follow the flight of thought, if though the one is free the other is burdened with chains?" Liberty, he declared, "is no less the first property [*bien*] of the arts than it is the first property of men."[78] If the vast majority of mediocre writers wanted to squabble among themselves within the constraints of usage, so be it, as long as "the small number of good minds and good writers" (numbered perhaps at forty?) on whom the "glory of an age" depended were free.[79] The glory of the nation depended on giving writers a masculine liberty, freed of the feminine constraint of "usage," once associated with the speech of women of the court and now with the caprice of public opinion.[80]

The written language was both the territory and the responsibility of men of letters. "The body of a nation alone has rights over the *spoken* language, and the writers have rights over the *written* language," declared Charles Pinot Duclos in his phonetically spelled *Remarques* on the Port-Royal Grammar. Writers, he went on, had an obligation to maintain their property, "to correct what they have corrupted."[81] They were thus doubly obliged to improve spelling: first, in their capacity as guardians of the written language; and second, as servants of the public with a responsibility to make knowledge as accessible as possible through writing. Duclos placed the history of writing in the center of the Enlightenment project: "This art serves equally to confound the lie and reveal the truth: if it has sometimes been dangerous, it is at least the repository of arms against error, that of religion and law."[82] For Duclos, writing could only tear away the veils of secrecy and superstition that masked truth if it was freed of the orthographic prejudice that kept it out of the hands of the public.[83] Duclos asserted the liberation of writing from speech so that men of letters could use their authority based on the written word to advocate further changes in the system of orthography that would make writing fully accessible to the public.

Voltaire, too, was able to endorse the *rationality* of phonetic spelling without, however, basing it on the *naturalness* of (female) speech.[84] In his view, writers were the "true masters of the language," because they were the ones who created it. Men of letters had to guard the French language against corruption, and the greatest threat to linguistic purity, it seemed, was now the (female) speech that, in the previous century, had been its redoubt. With Voltaire and his followers embracing French and rejecting Latin, writing was no longer in need of speech as a guarantee against barbarism and corruption. They would be its guardians; they would police the language that was their domain.

The *Encyclopédie* was the elaboration of this dual aim of, on the one hand, asserting the autonomy and authority of the written word and the men of letters whose "property" it was, and, on the other, the need to make the written word freely accessible so that it could function as an instrument of Enlightenment.[85] The article "Orthographe," however, echoes the conservative fears of Regnier more than the new confidence of Voltaire and Duclos. Its author, Nicolas Beauzée, endorsed Regnier's gendered argument against any reform based on speech and reasserted the importance of maintaining history through etymological spelling.[86] In the article "Néographisme," Beauzée continued his assault on phonetic reform while asserting the authority of men of letters.[87] Eventually, however, he renounced his retrograde stance. When he took up the subject again in 1789, he declared that it was now possible "to adopt, according to the characters legitimately authorized by usage, a simpler, tighter, more consistent orthographic system."[88] The last defender of the old spelling had been won over.

Noël-François de Wailly's *L'Orthographe des dames, ou l'orthographe fondée sur la bonne prononciation, démontrée la seule raisonnable, par une société des dames* (1782), in which the call for spelling reform is put into the mouths of ladies, would seem to be as retrograde as Beauzée's articles in the *Encyclopédie*, but in fact it is written in a modern key. Wailly was one of the most well-known writers on French grammar and spelling. The March 1763 ad in the *Mercure* for a new edition of the abridged version of his French grammar noted that it had been adopted for use by both the University of Paris and the royal École Militaire.[89] In Wailly's hands, the descendants of Somaize's précieuses spoke not from a position of natural linguistic authority but as mothers who needed to help their children and as humble representatives of the nation. They called on men of letters, whose authority they recognized, to make spelling available to all Frenchwomen and men by making it fully phonetic. "We beg of you, Sirs, to give us a reasoned, simple, uniform plan of orthography," they wrote. "Dedicated specifically to the study, to the perfection of our language and of our orthography, this learned company will render an important service to the nation, if by means of its reflections on language and orthography, it clarifies usage, directs it, perfects it. This labor seems to us truly worthy of the philosophers and grammarians who comprise this illustrious society."[90]

Wailly's ladies acknowledged that the men to whom they appealed might be afraid to look foolish in submitting writing to speech, but they challenged them to recast the question in terms of a new democratic politics: Why, they asked, was it reasonable to fault women for mispronouncing words whose spelling did not correspond to spoken usage, but not for misspelling those same words for the same reason?

> Why? It's that the laws of usage for pronunciation are within our reach. In fact, we have, like the scholars, organs for hearing and for making sounds. It's not the same with current orthography: based on a knowledge of several languages that no one has taught us, these laws are beyond our reach; and, as you have made sure, it is morally impossible for us to observe them. . . . A usage that is not within reach of the majority of those who must observe it is contrary to reason. It is an error, an abuse that must be corrected with alacrity.[91]

When Wailly placed the call for reform in the mouths of ladies, it was not to challenge the authority of men of letters but to petition them humbly for reform. "We have already said that the authors are the true legislators in this matter," the "ladies" wrote. "Use your rights Sirs; work to enlighten the nation more and more, to facilitate its acquisition of knowledge. Far from making you ridiculous, by putting within reach of everyone a knowledge as useful as orthography, you will render by this reform a signal service to the nation."[92]

In defending himself in the *Année Littéraire* against the charge that he, like so many reformers before him, was trying to "overturn the language" by imposing a new system on his own authority, Wailly reminded the Parisian academicians that his scheme was laid out by "Ladies" who were ever respectful of the men whose help they ardently sought. Quote upon quote emphasized the women's respect for the authority of men of letters ("You are our masters and our Judges") and its basis ("It is to the Tribunal of reason, we mean to say to yours, Sirs, that we bring our complaints about current spelling").[93] These were not *précieuses* wishing to create disorder in the Republic of Letters but *citoyennes avant la lettre* who asked only that the language of the nation be made accessible to them and those they represented.

Wailly's *Orthographe des dames* was a throwback, however, in that eighteenth-century *orthographes* and *grammaires des dames* were more likely to be pedagogical works whose authors were less concerned with the principles of orthography than with practical questions of how to teach it to the ladies who desperately needed their services. The change is evident in the preface to another *ortografe des dames*, this one published anonymously in 1766. "While this work is entitled *Ortografe des dames*," the author explained at the outset, "I do not however engage them to read it: it will surely bore them, and, despite this, I count on their suffrage, since it tries to give credit to their spelling, reduce it to principles, and persuade men to approximate it, as conforming more closely to pronunciation, the sole purpose of writing."[94] The author had to explain his outmoded purpose in his preface because in the 1760s most readers would assume that the book they had opened would not be an intervention in the spelling debates among men but a textbook aimed at women. By the latter half of the eighteenth century, the *Orthographe des dames* was not a treatise on spelling reform but a speller for ladies.

Spelling for Sale: Teaching Women to Spell Correctly

"It is a vain ostentation of erudition that has ruined spelling," Duclos had declared. "It is the *savans* and not the *philosophes* who have altered it. . . . The spelling of women, which the *savans* find so ridiculous, is, in many respects, less unreasonable than theirs. Some of them wish to learn the orthography of the *savans*; it would be better if the *savans* adopted a part of that of women, while correcting the defects of a half-education, that is, of the *savan*."[95] In suggesting that one could compare the orthography of *les savans* with *l'ortografe des dames*, Duclos meant to discredit the pedants more than promote the ladies. From the perspective of the new spelling, their orthography was no better than that of women—and possibly worse. It was from this confident perspective, and from their new position of authority, that Enlightenment men of letters and writing masters would develop new ways to teach women and girls how to spell correctly.

After 1740, when the new spelling was authorized by the academy, *l'ortografe des dames* no longer represented an orthographic ideal—the transparent transcription of a pure French unadulterated with barbaric Latinisms—but an anarchic reality outside the law: how women spelled was simply incorrect. Thus, Wailly's ladies begged the academy to reform spelling so that they could become good mothers and law-abiding citizens. Most men of letters and writing masters, however, saw the problem less politically: they simply told their female readers how embarrassing it was to write poorly and how badly it reflected on them to do so. By identifying poor spelling as a source of social embarrassment they encouraged women, and especially girls and their mothers, to be self-conscious about how they wrote and to experience a new sense of shame in it. Indeed, it was by invoking a fear of social embarrassment that pedagogues of all sorts could justify encouraging women to engage in a study that sounded like serious scholarship. "If I speak of studies for young ladies, do not think that I wish to overload them under the weight of labor, to apply them to [the study] of learned languages, make them pale over books, and tire them out with occupations that are too serious," Fromageot assured his readers. "Nothing of the sort enters into my views: I only assemble and arrange in a methodical order the different subjects about which it is shameful at a certain [social] rank not to be instructed."[96]

Men of letters and writing masters offered spelling lessons both in print and in person to solve the social problem they had identified, if not created. In July 1770, the *Avantcoureur* printed the following advertisement that first told women and girls that they should be embarrassed by their poor spelling, before offering to correct the problem:

It is not rare to see young people graced with agreeable talents, & who cannot write their own language correctly. One listens to them sing with pleasure, & one reads their writing with great difficulty & and with disgust. One fears to teach them a science that is ordinarily acquired only through long and painful diligence. A method that would shorten the study of this science & facilitate it cannot but be welcomed. M. MARTIN, former Navy writer, flatters himself that with his experience he can teach Ladies and Young Ladies French Orthography in the space of about four months, according to the aptitude of his subjects, with a daily lesson of one hour.... This Professor distributes at his address the *Prospectus* of a new theory of French Orthography, & proposes to publish soon all his observations and research on this interesting subject.[97]

M. Martin seems not to have published his book, but others appeared in the same vein. In January 1773, the *Mercure* announced a new *Traité d'Orthographe Françoise* with a commentary that identified women and girls as most in need of it—not only because they spelled badly, but because, it claimed, "it is even difficult to express oneself correctly in conversation if one is ignorant of the rules of Orthography." This was certainly a new twist, but the rest was predictable: "It is to this that the fair sex, primarily, does not pay enough attention. The treatise that we announce is very appropriate for remedying this difficulty by the very simple method that the author proposes."[98]

That year Manon Phlipon discovered that she had pushed the privileges of friendship too far when she used the same tone with her friend Sophie. "I have something to say to you about your spelling," she wrote sternly, and then continued:

> One would never imagine in reading your letters that you speak as correctly as you do, why does your writing not correspond to it? You are right not to take any trouble with me, but apparently you do not trouble yourself any more when you write to others, habit ought to carry it through, and that annoys me; when one knows one's language according to its principles, and one speaks well, one ought to write well too. I wish to see you perfect in everything.[99]

Manon went on to say that she did not expect an answer to her remarks, since "the body of your letters will bear witness to whether they please you or not." In fact, Sophie seems to have responded by refusing to subject the body of another letter to her friend's scrutiny. Manon's next letter ended: "Goodbye my tender friend, you are very much excused for not having responded to my last, it was really foolish."[100] The correspondence did continue for many years, but Manon kept to her role as friend and confidante. The job of improving a young lady's spelling belonged to men of letters and the mothers they enlisted to help them.[101]

Four years later, the *Mercure* announced, not in its section on new books, but in its social news, that "the chevalier de Prunay, captain of Grenadiers, had the honor to present to the Queen, Madame, Madame the comtesse d'Artois, Madame Élisabeth, Madame Adélaïde, and Madame Sophie of France a work of his composition dedicated to Madame the princesse de Lamballe, and entitled *Grammaire des dames*, to facilitate for young people knowledge of the principles of the French language and to give them the means of spelling correctly without any difficulty."[102] Since the sixteenth century it had been traditional to dedicate spellers to highborn women (as Regnier noted disparagingly in his *Traité*).[103] Prunay went even further by taking advantage of the press to publicize his dedication, just as merchants announced the endorsement of the queen and other members of the royal family to sell products from furniture to face creams.

In the preface to his book, Prunay both acknowledged the beauty of women's natural eloquence and stated his support for a reformed spelling based on it: "I hope that after having made clear the uselessness and the danger of conserving etymological letters in words in which they corrupt pronunciation, we will write, afterwards, as we speak, that is, as the Ladies speak at court and in the Capital."[104] But the chevalier also expressed his dismay at the poor command of grammar and spelling that deformed women's writing. His goal, after all, was not to praise women's speech, but to correct their writing.

> A Lady . . . gives a conversation all its pleasures by means of her wit, by the grace which she spreads over all that she says, by the fine and delicate expressions she uses; whereas when the same Lady expresses herself in writing, it seems that she is not the same person. Often she observes neither construction nor connection in the sentences, and the vivacity of her thoughts can no longer be seen except through an infinite number of mistakes in the most basic rules of spelling; such that what would have been so pleasant to listen to can only be read with difficulty.[105]

Making a larger social claim, Prunay went on to declare that if only women would learn to write properly, the French language would be "enriched beneath their pens," as the letters of Mme de Sévigné "and several other ladies" already attested.[106] Of course, this Sévigné was the printed version and not the practitioner of *l'ortografe des dames* promoted by the reformers of her day. By the time Prunay was writing, Sévigné had been classified as a woman and therefore "ignorant" of spelling (in the *Encyclopédie*'s terms). As Suzanne Necker noted in an unfinished *éloge* of Sévigné: "This woman, whose style was so pure, did not know how to spell."[107]

In Prunay's view, teaching ladies to spell would contribute to the patriotic and Enlightenment project of improving, rationalizing, and spreading the French language, but would it not also threaten French femininity? Generations of scholars had been telling women that learning to spell required both commitment and hard work that were contrary to their feminine nature, and a knowledge of Latin that, if it was not beyond their capacity, would turn them into monsters of erudition. With the new spelling, however, Latin was no longer a requirement, and therefore women were told, they could be taught to spell without endangering their femininity. Indeed, men like Prunay and Martin were now reassuring women that learning to spell was *easy* and cajoling them into *just trying*. "It was a question, then, of giving her the principles of the language, without boring her with the grammatical method and the barbaric terms that it employs," wrote Fromageot of his own experience in instructing a young lady in this thorny but necessary subject.[108] If, like Wailly (and the précieuses), they tried to suggest that the problem was spelling, not women, they were accused of being radicals who wanted to take the law into their own hands and overturn the social order. Thus, even as they presented themselves as innovators, men such as Pierre Fresneau took pains to assure their readers that they were not orthographic radicals. "Unlike so many others," he declared, he was not setting himself up as an "indiscreet reformer; I am not changing spelling at all."[109]

In 1785 abbé Louis Barthelemy took on the task of teaching young ladies to spell correctly in his *Grammaire des dames, ou Nouveau traité d'orthographe françoise*, which he dedicated to Mme de Genlis. He made clear in his preface the importance of correct spelling, while reassuring the concerned mothers who were his intended readers that he was not advocating serious scholarship for their daughters: "It is still not advisable to demand of a well-born person that she be a scholar," he further intoned. "Any display of erudition might even be called a crime: but the knowledge, for which there is no mercy given at all, is that of one's own language. In fact, the ignorance of its rules is excusable only among the people."[110] With orthography no longer a sign of Latinacy or erudition, it was on its way to becoming a marker of class; no woman who claimed a good birth and a good education could therefore afford to remain ignorant of it. Now it was not only possible but necessary that young ladies spell correctly. Fortunately, the abbé had made it easy for them by simplifying all the rules.

Barthelemy's second speller, *La Cantatrice grammairienne, ou l'art d'apprendre l'Orthographe française seul, sans le secours d'un Maître, par le moyen des Chansons érotiques, pastorales, villageoises, anacréontiques, &c. . . .*, used examples from love songs to make spelling simple and fun for the mature woman, who was advised to give her daughter the more age-appropriate *Grammaire des dames*. This libertine speller had a different dedicatee: not the moralizing educator, Mme de Genlis, but the poet and novelist Fanny de Beauharnais, author of, among other works, the epistolary novel *Lettres de Stéphanie, ou l'Héroïsme du sentiment* (1778); *L'Abailard supposé, ou le Sentiment à l'épreuve* (1780); and, the year before Barthelemy published *La Cantatrice grammairienne*, *Les Amans d'autrefois* (1787).[111] It also had a different tone and form, but the message was pretty much the same. "It is a constant truth that women possess more eminently than we the art of seizing contrasts . . . of replacing reasoning with an epigram and above all the talent of embellishing even their mistakes," the abbé began, thus reducing women's natural linguistic talent from speaking pure French to embellishing their mistakes in writing it.

> But however seductive the brush, which in their hands can often be regarded as a magic wand, if correct spelling does not accompany this enchanting pen, the effort it takes us to read them [i.e., women] will destroy forever the pleasure in it. . . . Spell, spell, we tell women constantly, if you want us to read you with all the interest that the freshness and luster of your brilliance inspire in us.[112]

Note that the emphasis here is on the impression poor spelling makes on the men who must decipher it. Granted, the abbé was using love songs as his hook for a certain kind of female reader and setting them to familiar tunes to make the lessons easy to learn, but the assumption that a woman's writing is a form of presentation of the self, and that the function of that self is to please others (especially men), was consistent with the more conventional spellers being produced by contemporaries such as Prunay and lies squarely within the paradigm of male Enlightenment discourse about women. But Barthelemy did not really blame women for spelling badly. Rather, he concurred with Boudier de Villemert's assessment in his *Ami des femmes* that *l'ortografe des dames* had its roots in the old prejudice that "condemned women as well as the nobility to a crass ignorance." Revising history, Boudier and Barthelemy now claimed that women intentionally spelled badly to avoid the ridicule attached to pedantry. "The ridicule cast upon pedantic learning had so discredited all knowledge, that many women made it a point of honor to mangle the words of their language," wrote Barthelemy citing Boudier.[113] The same men who discouraged women from becoming learned now accused them of foolishly taking that injunction too literally.

If Barthelemy tried to seduce female readers with love songs, others cast their dry subject in the pedagogical literary forms made popular by Enlightenment writers. In J. B. Roche's *Entretiens sur l'orthographe françoise*, for example, three gentlemen discuss the central issues of the debate on spelling reform. The English Milord represents the progressive foreigner who advocates the new spelling; the Comte is the conservative who defends both the old spelling and the study of ancient languages; and the Abbé is the teacher who will demonstrate that anyone can learn to spell French, if only they use his method.[114] When two ladies enter, the men volunteer to change the subject, but Sophie, the young lady, admits that orthography "is a science that I would very much like to know, and of which I understand nothing at all. I am so ignorant that, in order to express the most ordinary things, I write practically by chance. I can barely figure out myself what I meant to say. Often, for want of being able to spell the words that come into my mind, I am forced to use others that defigure all my thoughts."[115] Happily, the Abbé has devised a method of teaching spelling to those whose knowledge of languages is limited to French. "Myself, for example?" asks the Marquise. When the Abbé agrees to reveal his method to her, Sophie asks if she might listen in, since "you have announced your method in such a way as to give me some hope: perhaps it will not be entirely above my head." The Abbé then reveals his true purpose:

> I have fulfilled my goal, Mademoiselle, in inspiring in you the desire to acquire a science so fit to make the graces and the lightness of your spirit shine. I would have informed you of this already, but I feared boring you with the perspective of a study a bit too serious for your age. Be assured, Mademoiselle, that in all our conversations, I will make it a law not to say a word that will not be easy for you to understand with a bit of concentration.

So reassuring is the Abbé that even the Marquise wants to try, but she cries, "I am so lazy! How could I subject myself to a study that is so exacting of infinite details?" Don't worry, the Abbé tells her, she will have few rules to learn.[116]

A final concern is laid to rest when the Abbé casually mentions that once the ladies have learned the basics of French word construction, "we will seek in Latin and Greek the enlightenment that our language will have refused us." "Oh heavens," cries Sophie, "for me Latin! Greek!" "But, Sir," interjects the Marquise, "don't even think it." But the Abbé does. "Listen, Ladies. It is not a question of making a special study of these two beautiful languages: we will draw from them only a small number of words that serve as roots to an infinity of French words. As long as you are brave, I hope that before our return to the city, you will know all the parts of my method perfectly." Sophie then declares herself ready for the challenge: "I assure you, Sir, that you will have no cause at all to complain of my zeal and my application: I am too ashamed of the mistakes that I commit everyday."[117]

The mistakes made by Sophie and the Marquise were key to Roche's pedagogical method, as Élie Fréron noted approvingly in his review of the *Entretiens* in the *Année Littéraire*. Each dialogue begins with examples from the two ladies' homework based on the previous lesson where, of course, "there never fail to be some mistakes. The Abbé . . . uses these as the pretext for a review of the previous conversation."[118] Roche's dialogue told girls and women that to overcome the shame of poor spelling they would have to overcome their natural timidity and laziness. Whereas seventeenth-century commentators had praised ladies for the naturalness of their epistolary prose as an extension of their conversation, eighteenth-century successors such as Roche used the wedge driven between speech and writing to turn praise into admonition and polemic into pedagogy. The perceived differences between men and women no longer opened up possibilities of reform, ways of imagining a different way of doing things, as they had in the seventeenth century. More and more, they simply marked weaknesses or inadequacies of women relative to men that pedagogy was meant to address.

When Antoine Tournon published *Promenades de Clarisse et du Marquis de Valzé, ou Nouvelle méthode pour apprendre les principes de la langue et de l'Ortographe françaises à l'usage des Dames* (1784), the situation of a young lady who must learn to spell but is afraid to do so because she thinks, foolishly, that spelling is beyond her capacity was such a commonplace that it could become the premise of a quasi novel. In his review of the *Promenades*, Fréron quoted the opening paragraph that introduced the young and lovely Clarisse and the father who doted on her, and then commented sarcastically:

> Would you believe it Sir, if the title had not informed you? Would you believe it? That this is the beginning of a French Grammar? You have to admit, we live in a charming century. In the olden days there was nothing that curious ladies could use to learn the language but cold and austere grammars; the title alone of *Grammar* repulsed them; and so there were few ladies who dared even to approach it; but now *everything has changed*. First of all, this word, *Grammar*, that scarecrow of the sex, has been suppressed; & by a happy surprise, the pretty word *Promenade* has been substituted for it. . . . The promenade holds more attractions than grammar; & then, look at the art with which this promenade is offered. It's not a solitary promenade, but rather *the promenades of Clarisse & of the Marquis de Valzé*, & the title is suggestive. We suspect two lovers under the name of master and female student, & I bet we won't be wrong; it's the title of a novel at the head of a grammar.[119]

And, indeed, Fréron was right. On their arrival in Paris, Clarisse and her father meet the handsome Marquis who offers to teach the young English miss how to speak French properly. Although Clarisse wants to accept this honorable offer, "she had always heard that the principles of our language were difficult, & so much so, that very few Frenchwomen had the double advantage of speaking well and writing purely." So, Tournon explains, although "Miss wanted very much to know our language . . . she was afraid to study it." Valzé reassures her in the hopes of pleasing her. "He thus committed himself to present only principles that were clear, precise, & above all never boring."[120] The entire grammar, in fact, is embedded in a Rousseauian text that manages to combine the situation of Julie and Saint-Preux with the pedagogy of *Émile*. "Between us, Sir," Fréron confided to his reader, "I don't know if the grammar can continue through the twenty-fourth installment, because our Tutor strays off track a lot; I very much fear that the grammarian will give way to the lover, and that nothing will remain but the novel. . . . Don't you find, Sir, that this manner of indoctrination is reminiscent of that of the late *Abailard*?"[121] Tournon's "new method" for teaching grammar and spelling was really just the time-tested pretext for the teacher, following Abelard and Saint-Preux, to seduce his student. Its novelty was based on the idea that the way to win a young lady's heart was to offer to help her overcome the shame of spelling badly. Even as he encouraged his readers to overcome their female weakness, Tournon, like the other authors of spellers designed to teach girls and women to spell properly, affirmed social norms of feminine comportment as a "natural" hindrance to doing so.[122]

And women got the message. In 1773 Mme de Choiseul wrote to Mme du Deffand of her embarrassment that an academician with whom she wanted to raise a point of grammar should see her own writing: "I don't want him to find the spelling mistakes in a letter by a woman who has taken it into her head to reason about language," she explained.[123] Félicité Dupont, who worked for Mme de Genlis in the 1780s as under-governess for the daughters of the duc de Chartres, was also self-conscious about her poor spelling, and not without reason: her husband, Jacques-Pierre Brissot, criticized her for her spelling errors, driving her at times to write to him in English so as to avoid his criticism.[124]

As girls and women took up their pens to write the words that were supposed to flow naturally from their hearts in all sincerity and transparency, they were also conscious of how they looked and how their letters looked, and how they appeared to their readers through the letters they wrote. Indeed, before their inner beauty could shine through the letters they wrote, they had to be disciplined in mind and body. It was the job of educators and mothers to train them, and the privilege of men to tell them when they failed.

Epistolary Education 4

Learning to Be Natural

In the eighteenth century, a young lady lived in "a completely epistolary universe," observes Paule Constant.[1] The model letters in epistolary manuals were often artfully arranged to create mininarratives, and the epistolary novel itself derived in part from the letter-writing manual. And, as we have already seen, pedagogical treatises often took epistolary form. It is thus impossible to disentangle entirely the genres of pedagogical treatise, epistolary novel, and letter-writing manual, all of which taught young ladies how to do what their authors all claimed came to them naturally as women: writing letters, developing an appropriate epistolary style, and engaging in the practice of correspondence. Moreover, underlying all these treatises, novels, and manuals were common assumptions about gender and writing, letters and literature that shaped both the education and the epistolary practice of young ladies and the women they would become.

In this chapter I first trace how the letter-writing manual aimed at would-be social elites in the seventeenth century was transformed into a textbook aimed at young people, and especially young ladies, in the eighteenth century. I then look more closely at the gender ideology that underlay the distinction between letters and literature and the difficulties it raised for male writers and pedagogues who promoted their ability to teach young women to do what came to them naturally. For in their efforts to ground their difference from women in nature, men of letters created pedagogical difficulties for themselves and epistolary opportunities for the women whose masters they sought to be.

The Letter-Writing Manual

Historians have emphasized the multiple uses and readerships of letter-writing manuals or *secrétaires* in the seventeenth and eighteenth centuries. Carolyn Lougee has shown how upwardly mobile men of the seventeenth century turned to such manuals for assistance in moving into the world of the nobility. "Letters," she writes, "were as much a part of the quick curriculum in social refinement as were philosophy and speech."[2] Roger Chartier has encouraged us to look beyond the stated function of collections of model letters to other uses they may have served for unintended readers, such as the peasants who enjoyed archaic collections in the cheap editions of the *Bibliothèque bleue*. "To read a *secrétaire* might be to learn about the ordering of the social world, strictly translated into the formalities of the letter-writing code," he suggests. "Or it might mean penetrating a remote and 'exotic' universe, that of aristocratic ways; or again it might bring with it the pleasure of piecing together a plot from the series of letters furnished as examples for imitation."[3] Chartier is surely right to remind us that because *secrétaires* were texts, they were not simply used, but read, and that they succeeded (when they did) not simply because they presented good and useful models but because they did what good books do: they engaged their readers by creating stories and worlds and sometimes even characters.

Above all, those who wrote letter-writing manuals presented model letters that were meant to inculcate the values of the world they represented. In the seventeenth century these were the values of *honnêteté* and gallantry that permeated the cultures of court and salon. Parodies of such letter collections showed the fine line between the gallant and the libertine. The table of contents of *Le secretaire des demoiselles* (1704), for example, included letters for all occasions, just as the texts it parodied did—notably Puget de la Serre's *Le secrétaire de la Cour* (1634) and *Le secrétaire à la mode* (1640). In *Le secretaire des demoiselles*, these included a "Letter from a Friend to a man accused of having two wives," as well as a "Letter from a man to a Mistress whom he loves and who is marrying someone else out of self-interest," and, most intriguing, one "Concerning the gift of a pig's tongue."[4] Most of the letters were followed by a response, thus creating mininarratives or minidramas to engage the reader further.

Another variant on the genre was *La petite-poste dévalisée* by Jean Baptiste Artaud (1767). Artaud employed the sort of conceit that was by then standard in the epistolary novel—the packet of letters found by chance:

> Some young fools, in the wake of a debauch, enter a country tavern: beneath a wine-drenched table, one of them notices a package. He gathers it up, unties it, and what do you know, there's a bunch of letters on the tablecloth. The honorable thing to do never enters anyone's head; they laugh; they unseal; they read; and it's only after they've finished reading that someone notices by the stamp that this package must have been forgotten by some drunken postman. They look at each other ... what should they do? They can no longer return it to the [Post] Office. Burn them! ... They're amusing; they can amuse other people. Yes, says one of our eccentrics, we must have them printed, it's the only way left to get them to their destinations.[5]

Because the letters were random (not a correspondence, but a postman's bundle), they did not tell the story of a life or a relationship or a voyage, as a novel would.

However, *La petite-poste dévalisée* drew on the conceits of the epistolary novel to create a text that pushed the paradigm of the *secrétaire* beyond the realm of the court and polite society and would amuse more than teach. The book is literally a grab bag of letters, written by men and women, to men and women, of all classes and conditions.

Louis Philipon de la Madelaine's *Modèles de lettres sur différents sujets*, first published in 1761, also rejected the gallantry of the court and seventeenth-century notions of politeness and propriety or *bienséance*. As Janet Altman has pointed out, Philipon shifted the intended audience of the letter manual from adults to children, placing his book within the realm of pedagogy rather than advice literature for upwardly mobile adults.[6] Although he continued to provide model letters, Philipon divided them into chapters, each of which he opened with two or three pages explaining the *principles* of, for example, the letter of condolence or congratulation or thanks.[7] By introducing principles rather than simply providing models to be copied, Philipon was doing for letter-writing what d'Autrèpe had done for penmanship: claiming the status of a science for this traditional art, and the status of professional for the man who practiced and explained it.[8]

In his handbook for teachers, Jean Lanteires singled out Philipon's manual for praise. While he claimed not to approve of letter manuals in general, he did recommend, "for those who do not know it, a very good work, if there can be one in this genre; it is entitled: *Modele de Lettres sur différens sujets*."[9] When a new edition of Philipon's book was issued in 1804, it included a testimonial letter by the chemist Antoine-François de Fourquoy, who was at that time director-general of public instruction. Fourquoy declared that Philipon's book would be included "among the 1,500 volumes that ought to compose the library of a Lycée. This work, as useful as it is pleasant, is a true gift to the young people of our schools." Philipon himself went on to assure readers in his preface that his book "has nothing in common with the *Secrétaire de la Cour*, the *Art de la Correspondance*, the *Rhétorique épistolaire*, etc." In fact, he maintained, the repackaged *Manuel épistolaire à l'usage de la jeunesse* was "essentially a classic book: teachers, fathers, and mothers can put it in the hands of their children or their students without fear; it will be read by them with pleasure and success."[10]

Bernard de Bonnard had also distinguished this manual from others when he sent his young wife Sophie a copy of *Modèles de lettres sur différents sujets* in April 1783. "Prepare yourself, madame, to respond to your letters by yourself from now on," he chided her,

because, truthfully, it makes one shudder. At 18 and a half, a woman married for thirty-one months, the mother of Bonbon. I thought about this today and it spurred me to buy a book that has as its title model of letters on different subjects. This anthology is not the sort of trifle one might imagine. It is a collection of very pretty letters written by people who have had the highest reputations in this genre, Mme de Sévigné, the comte de Bussy Rabutin, Voltaire, and others.[11]

Since their marriage in September 1780, Sophie had been writing long, warm, newsy letters to her husband whenever they were apart, but she struggled to write the kind of letters included in the letter manuals. The year before, when Bernard was on a long visit to Burgundy where he had grown up, she suffered mightily trying to write little notes in response to those sent by his female relatives and friends who regretted that she was unable to join him on the trip, or who asked her to do little favors for them in the capital. "This morning I received a letter from Mme de Montbeillard," she wrote Bernard on 5 November 1782, "and I swear to you in secret that I am quite stuck about how to respond to her. If you were next to me I would not be without help, but my little stupidity must now appear in all its glory." Mme de Montbeillard had asked Sophie to buy something for her in Paris, which Sophie was happy to do; it was the letter in response to the request that was causing her so much grief. Bernard made it clear that Sophie must respond to this letter, but he also reassured her that she could do it. "You can't refuse [to respond to] the entreaties of my friends and their pretty letters," he told her, and then went on: "By the way, Mme Sophie, you will have to respond to them and all by yourself and that's so much the better, despite the bad mood that this will cause you. I bet you will not be as stupid as you think."[12]

This was exactly the sort of situation to which the authors of letter-writing manuals had been responding for more than a century. For example, Pierre Ortigue de Vaumorière noted that, whereas people learned to converse by conversing all the time,

> in writing only rarely and with a certain repugnance, the majority of men get stuck when they are obliged to take up the pen: Thus it is only with a lot of effort that we grasp the style that is appropriate for Letters. Experience demonstrates this every day: For a hundred people who speak well, one doesn't even find ten who write as well, even though it seems that one has only to put on paper what one wants to express.[13]

The *secrétaire* was designed to help people who spoke fluently in social situations to write just as easily, but it also served those who wrote easily to friends and family but were intimidated by the idea of writing formal letters to people they did not know.

Catherine de Saint-Pierre, who had little happiness in her life, found some in writing to her brother. But when she had to write a letter thanking someone who had intervened at Bernardin's request to secure her a pension, she too was paralyzed:

> If you think it appropriate that I write to the people whose protection you have secured me, give me some models, I beg you, because I cannot ignore my inability, [which is] that much greater since I don't know what it is I don't know. This alone disconcerts me and destroys my judgment. There is nothing but trouble that takes hold of me. I'm losing my head.[14]

When, the following year, Bernardin did send her a model, she thanked him profusely while apologizing for her inadequacy:

You have really helped me with the copy you've given me for your friend. You were right. I have lots of things to be humiliated about in my person and above all in my writing, for which I have always felt the disgrace in your sensitivity to this subject added to my own; but without being able to judge it myself, I cannot bring about any changes. To the contrary, this intimidates me to the point of making an impression on me right there. I would have believed myself able to put my thoughts on paper, but there is nothing which frightens me more, my will having no tolerance for my mistakes in continuing to predict or avoid them towards those persons to whom I am beholden; as to the others, I ask for their indispensable indulgence for our sex, whose education has not always permitted us to know more.[15]

Two years later, when Bernardin had become a celebrity author after the publication of his immensely popular novel, *Paul et Virginie*, he found not one but two patrons for his sister. This time he sent her a model letter of thanks with the good news, for which she was doubly grateful: "I cannot do better than to copy word for word that which your kindness had dictated to me for a model and which went out in the same post for M. Necker."[16]

Catherine often apologized to her brother for bothering him with her letters, but she did not feel the need to apologize for her style, her *écriture*, for writing like a woman. This awkwardness and embarrassment only appeared in reference to the formal letters of thanks she was required to write to her benefactors. Similarly, Manon Phlipon, who may well have written more letters and taken more pleasure in writing than any other young woman of her day, hated writing formal letters, although for her these were the empty formalities of New Year's greetings. As she wrote to her friend Sophie Cannet at the end of 1770: "You would laugh out loud if you saw me writing these letters of *bienséance* where one is forced to employ those insipid compliments that custom expects one to pronounce during the time it has allotted to them. I am not at the first line when I am dying of impatience to see the last."[17] Four years later, the task had not gotten any easier. "I'm sorry," she wrote to Sophie in the postscript to a long letter in December 1774, "I have to think about writing some New Year's letters that make me sick to my stomach."[18]

As soon as she received her copy of *Modèles de lettres sur différents sujets*, Sophie Silvestre sat down to write the letters she needed to write. "I suppose you have nothing to do, so I'm sending you the two pretty little letters I received and the responses that I've copied out expressly so that you can see them," she wrote her husband. "I hope you will tell me frankly what you think of them."[19] Bernard must have been pleased that she was taking his concerns and her epistolary responsibilities seriously at last and fell easily into the mode of a teacher correcting a student essay:

I am sending you back your letters and the responses you have written to them. That of Mme de M[ortemart] is more annoying than the other and surely cost you more trouble. I have underlined the repetitions, an awkward sentence, and some mistakes of spelling or language. There would be hardly any of these if you always remembered that you are a woman, and that this gender has its own distinctive character. A woman uses the letter $\underline{E}$ more than we do. For example, she is <u>touchée</u>, <u>fachée</u>, <u>sure</u>, etc. It is also important that she pay attention [*soit attentive*] in order to avoid these little mistakes that get by when she is distracted, above all when she knows so well how one ought to speak and write. These little blots aside, these two letters are very good, and when my good Sophie is willing, there will be no more blots on her style or in her words than in her actions.[20]

Although Bernard tried to distinguish between the informal letters she wrote to him and the formal ones she wrote to others, this distinction went only so far: all letters had to be free of spelling and grammatical mistakes, just as all actions had to be free of moral ones—the blots or stains that ruined a woman's reputation.

More than a year later, Sophie was still struggling with her correspondence. This time Bernard took a new tack in his encouragement mixed with admonition. If before he had emphasized her responsibilities as a woman and a wife, he now added those of a mother. "Poor Sophie, all of this is then so difficult to say . . . try . . . and you will do fine. In any case, remember to have your [sons] and your daughter start practicing early writing letters and notes of duty, propriety, or simple pleasantries."[21] The art of letter writing had to be mastered, not just because girls became women, but because daughters and wives became mothers.

Men of letters who produced letter-writing manuals in the second half of the eighteenth century saw a new market in the Manons, Catherines, and Sophies of their world—young women newly saddled (or soon to be so) with the responsibility to write formal letters, the expectation that they would perform this task well and teach it to their children, and the added burden of knowing that the letters they wrote would be read as a reflection of their character and upbringing. Rather than turning to a brother or a husband for a model letter, they could find one in a book. In turning their attention to this new market, advice givers provided more female models as well as models of a more modern and practical sort of letter: "Letter from a woman who requests time to pay the debts of her husband," for example, and "Letter from Mme de S. M. de T** to M. l'abbé de T** of the French Academy to request from him a catalog of his works."[22]

The line between the formal and the familiar letter was not always neatly drawn, however. One model letter of "absence" was "from a DAUGHTER to a MOTHER, who had come to see her in the city where she was." "However prepared I was for our separation," it began, "I felt the unhappiness of being far away no less. Why should we be apart when we get along so well together?"[23] A far cry from the witty *secrétaires* of the previous centuries, a manual such as this one could be usefully and safely given to a young boarder struggling to write her first letters home. Rather than encouraging his reader to delight in the voyeuristic indiscretion of reading other people's mail, as the author of *La petite-poste dévalisée* did explicitly and Puget de la Serre and his followers did implicitly, the author cautioned his young readers that their own letters might have unintended readers and thus unintended consequences. "Taste must direct style, and prudence conduct the pen," he intoned sternly. "People repent every day having said too much; but they repent even more having written too much, because spoken words are transitory, whereas written ones last. An intercepted letter has more than once furnished weapons against the person who wrote it in a moment of anger, or in the enthusiasm of a confidential friendship."[24]

The real difference between the familiar letters that a woman wrote willingly to a friend and the formal letters she was forced to write was the pleasure and satisfaction that only the first kind of writing gave her. As Manon Phlipon wrote to her friend Sophie Cannet in January 1773: "Thank heavens, I breathe, your turn has arrived; I am completely happy and completely relaxed to know that my pen will no longer move by necessity, by propriety, in the miserable land of compliments and the lie, but voluntarily and by love in that of truth and feeling."[25]

Mme de Miremont distinguished similarly among the types of letters that a young lady needed to learn how to write and maintained that, as with anything else, a woman would be more apt to write them if she became adept at doing so. "Business does not languish, duties are rendered, friendship is cultivated." But each type of letter required a different style. "For business, clarity and precision are needed; for duties, nobility and simplicity; for letters of friendship, naturalness, lightness, grace, and a bit of gaiety. The sweet expression of sentiment belongs much more to the heart than to the mind."[26] We should not be deceived, however: even this last sort of letter, the kind that young women like Sophie Silvestre and Manon Phlipon took pleasure in writing, was hardly the simple and natural expression of their hearts that theorists had been saying it was since the seventeenth century. For, as Walter Ong notes, "by contrast with natural, oral speech, writing is completely artificial. There is no way to write 'naturally.'"[27]

On Women and Letter Writing

Janet Altman sees a Rousseauian influence in Philipon de la Madelaine's emphasis on the naturalness of letter writing and its importance for friendship rather than relations of patronage, but as we have already noted, the identification of women as natural letter writers, and of letters written by women as models for all to follow, emerged in France more than a century before Rousseau's Saint-Preux praised Julie for the "simplicity" of her letters.[28] Since letters were seen as the extension in writing of conversation, and women were increasingly held up as models of civil conversation, it was only a matter of time before these same women—or their daughters—were being presented as model letter writers.[29]

As the spelling debates demonstrated, the speech of women of the court had become associated with the mother tongue in its purity because it was unadulterated with Latin, while at the same time removed from the baseness and variety of patois.[30] As a Latin education became the norm for elite boys, French was passed down through the female line. To learn their mother tongue, young men were urged to frequent salons and listen to the ladies who presided there.[31] Their salon education would complement the Latin education of the *collèges*.

Letter writing, however, fell somewhere between speech and writing. Defined as conversation with someone who is absent, it was ordinary language simply placed on the page; it was writing the way one speaks. The manuals themselves made this point repeatedly. The style of letters "ought to make its negligence felt and not differ at all from ordinary language," wrote Puget de la Serre.[32] "The precept to write as one speaks must still not be neglected; it is the most sure way of being understood by everybody," concurred Vaumorière.[33] Mauvillon taught similarly that "epistolary style should be lively, natural, and concise. Whatever type of Letter one writes, sentences, examples, comparisons, studied reasoning, and the other commonplaces of rhetoric must be avoided. Conversation does not demand so much preparation. Now, what is a Letter? Just a written conversation."[34] Philipon de la Madelaine himself brought out the old saw when he wrote that "letters used to be, just as they are today, a supplement to conversation, or rather a real enough conversation between persons who are absent."[35] If letters were simply conversation in another form, then they should not require the same kind of training as other forms of writing. Indeed, literary art had to be unlearned if the letter was to meet the standard of the natural. Women, who were not trained in such arts, were thus in the best position to write good letters.

Charles Cotin, who acknowledged his debt to the "women of quality" who had "polished [his] manners and cultivated [his] mind" in his youth, was the first to argue that such women wrote better letters than men did. While he did not declare that all women wrote great letters, Cotin did assert that the best letters were written by women. He explained this superiority as a result not of women's nature but of their social education, an education that was practical rather than intellectual and thus required no thought. He bowed to their "genius" in letter writing: "the art that they have learned, without thinking about it, in frequenting high society."[36]

In a second brief essay on the same subject, Cotin again contrasted the women whose letters he praised with "certain professional men of Letters who have nothing natural and free about them and who carry the scent of the Author with them in everything."[37] This authorial scent tainted letters that were supposed to speak from the heart; such letters were thus better written by women. "It is to these beautiful and happy hands that the glory belongs to represent the thoughts of the heart," he declared. "It is to them that nature has given the [ability] to express without affectation and without art the sentiments of nature." And if it was not sufficiently clear which sentiments he had in mind, he then addressed himself to his male reader to make the connection that is now so familiar to us between love, letters, and ladies:

> You know, Sir, that the beauties have only to make themselves visible to make themselves loved; I think similarly, that they have only to wish to write in order to write well. Without effort and without violence, everything that they desire comes to them, and they never desire anything but the most beautiful. Be it inspiration, be it chance, call the cause of these gallant Letters what you will, everything about them is natural and choice, everything is clear and intelligible.[38]

For Cotin, women's letters were love letters, and it was desire that spoke through them. These were the letters that men of letters wrote badly, because (male) reason and masculine art interfered with desire. This might be why you wanted men to govern, as the head governed the heart, but it was also why in matters of the heart and the letters that expressed them, women had a sort of genius. And just as masculine education strengthened reason, feminine education, the education of *le monde*, brought out the natural eloquence of women's hearts.

Indeed, even the most naive young lady became eloquent when she put pen to paper to transcribe the feelings of her heart, as Molière's Horace declared in *L'École des femmes*, published just one year before Cotin's collection of women's letters.

> All that her heart feels, her hand has known how to put down there:
> But in touching terms, and completely full of goodness,
> Of innocent tenderness, and ingenuousness.
> In short, in the manner that pure nature
> Expresses the first wound of Love.

This is how the smitten Horace describes the letter that Agnès, just emerged from a convent education intended to keep her both innocent and ignorant, has wrapped around a stone and thrown out her window to him.[39]

Men like Cotin were encouraged to finish their education by "polishing" their manners in the salons, while their female counterparts received a smattering of book learning to complete theirs. Indeed, the salon was a site of gendered educational exchange between men and women even as it was a site of sexual encounter. Letters embodied that exchange: whereas ladies may have been the teachers in the matters of the heart expressed in gallant correspondences, men of letters were dominant in the philosophical correspondences that were just as prevalent. But even this characterization is probably too dualistic: letters and correspondences between men and women could be and were both gallant and philosophic, the media for the expression of feelings and the exchange of ideas. Letters between friends could also combine ideas and feelings, as the letters of Manon Phlipon and Geneviève Malboissière discussed in chapter 7 make clear.

Cotin's praise of women's epistolary genius must be understood within a gendered dualism that associated women with feeling and men with reason and was supported by the different education of men and women. Salons and letters, conversation and epistolary writing, created the means of interaction between them in this Neoplatonic scheme of gender complementarity.[40] By the second half of the eighteenth century, a new binary distinction between two rhetorics, masculine oratorical eloquence and female epistolary eloquence, had replaced the simple contrast between feminine speech and masculine writing, just as it replaced the simple opposition between masculine pen and feminine needle. In the eighteenth century, men and women had their complementary modes of both speech and writing: conversation and correspondence for women; oratory and literature for men. The Academy's annual prize for the best *éloge* of a great man represented the interchangeability of masculine speech and writing, as the written eulogy was first crowned and then performed orally before an audience of academicians and the public. The man who won this prize more times than anyone else was Antoine-Léonard Thomas, who wrote in his 1773 *Essai sur les Éloges*: "I may be wrong, but it seems to me that a few lines that Madame de Sévigné has thrown haphazardly into her letters, without care, unplanned, and with the abandon of a sensitive soul, make us love M. de Turenne more and give a greater idea of his loss. There are words that say more than twenty pages, and facts that are beyond the art of all the orators."[41]

In the *Encyclopédie*, Jaucourt had also contrasted the rhetoric of men of letters with the epistolary style that, he claimed, came naturally to women. "Epistolary style is not in the least subject to the laws of oratorical discourse," he declared.

> There is a sort of negligence that pleases, just as there are women for whom it is quite becoming that they are completely unadorned. Such is elocution [that is] simple, pleasant, and touching, without looking to appear so; it disdains curling, pearls, diamonds, powder, rouge, and all that can be called makeup and foreign decoration. Cleanliness alone, joined to natural graces, suffices to make it pleasing.[42]

Jaucourt's flamboyant figures of speech, of course, were exactly what he meant by "all that can be called makeup." In describing epistolary style he drew the line between masculine and feminine writing, literature and letters, by employing the tools of the masculine man of letters rather than the feminine epistolarian. Of course, this meant that "masculine" writing was all dolled up with diamonds and rouge, but this was an implication Jaucourt did not pursue.

By the late eighteenth century, the superiority of feminine epistolary style had become a cliché throughout Europe. In *Letters to a Young Gentleman on His Setting Out for France* (1784) John Andrews advised his reader to complete his Continental education by finding a French lady and gentleman with whom to engage in correspondence. "Of the two correspondents I have recommended, let the fair one be the principal," he instructed. "Endeavor by all proper assiduity to engage her to be copious and frequent in her epistles: the benefit you will derive from it is more than I can here describe." However, it was not women of the court but "women of education," whom Andrews identified as "the most pleasing correspondents." It was these women whom he contrasted with "men of learning," thanks to the "ease and politeness in their manner of writing." And yet, paradoxical as it might seem to us, Andrews ascribed the superiority of educated women's letters to their *nature*. "The facility of their stile is genuine and unaffected, and is accompanied by those graces, which, whether on paper, or in their behaviour, women alone are mistresses of, and which carry more strength and conviction than all arguments," he concluded predictably.[43]

At least one eighteenth-century woman contested this gendered opposition between women's letters and men's literature. In a letter published in the *Mercure de France* and addressed to the novelist Anne-Louise Élie de Beaumont in response to her popular epistolary novel, *Lettres du marquis de Roselle*, this anonymous reader declared:

> In an age when it is barely acknowledged that we have a soul, and in which we are reduced to the needle and the spindle, you prove undeniably two truths: first, that that part that emanates from the divinity resides in us in a particular manner, and that it is accompanied by that delicacy of feelings, the pleasure of which is felt so deeply in your works; second, that the pen sits as well in the hands of a woman as in those of men; those little ingrates who are only too happy to come draw from our society that amenity and delicacy of expression that they will barely be able to acquire to the degree that they are found in the letters of the marquis de Roselle.[44]

In claiming female superiority in *sensibilité* and the "delicacy" of women's writing that results from it, the anonymous female author of this letter accepts the principle of difference and complementarity that was central to eighteenth-century gender thinking about letters and literature. But she finds that same delicacy in the published novels of Mme Élie de Beaumont and uses the Cartesian language of equality to praise them. She claims difference and the right to the pen in one breath, and draws no line between letters and literature. More radically, the author questions the very premise of male literary superiority by claiming the superiority of the letters of Mme Élie de Beaumont's male character, the marquis de Roselle, to those written by actual men. At a time when male writers such as Rousseau were attracting readers by "writing the female voice," this woman reader praised a female writer for the bold move of writing a male voice in order to challenge male literary supremacy without, however, denying women's natural talent for and supremacy in letter writing.[45]

Indeed, no one thought to challenge the idea that women were naturally talented in the epistolary domain. And yet eighteenth-century men of letters retained and even strengthened their position as the teachers of girls and women in the realm that they had ostensibly left to "the empire of women." If for most commentators the difference between letter writing and literary writing was the difference between nature and art, women and men, what could women possibly learn from men about writing letters, and on what basis could men possibly have the authority or expertise to teach them anything about it?

Pedagogues and Pedagogies: Teaching Women What They Already Know

"My Julie, how touching is the simplicity of your letter!" So reads the opening line of the letter Rousseau's fictional tutor writes concerning the course of study he has planned for his female student. "Your thoughts issue forth artlessly and effortlessly; they bear to the heart a delightful impression which a contrived style does not produce," he continues. Because Julie's natural morality is as pure as her epistolary style, it is she "who must determine our destinies." From that moment, the tutor proclaims, he will submit himself entirely to her will. However, he has come into Julie's life (and can only legitimately remain there) because her father has hired him to be her tutor, so he must design a plan of education for the girl whose taste and morality are superior to his own and who thus should be his teacher. Framing his employment as "duties" Julie has "imposed" on him, the tutor submits to the student's will by devising a course of study for her. He lays out a philosophy of education that disdains book learning as it seeks to nurture the heart rather than feed the head and that ends in tautology: "Let us therefore not go searching in books for principles and rules that we more surely find within ourselves," he concludes. Rejecting an education that would result in nothing but a vain "show of erudition," the tutor eliminates everything from his student's curriculum but "books of good taste and morality." These will provide the examples on the basis of which Julie's own taste and morals will be cultivated.[46] As Rousseau makes clear, however, it is Julie herself who is the true paragon of virtue, and her letters that are the model of taste. The tutor's letter, like his pedagogy, has come full circle. In matters of letters, as well as of love and morality, Julie becomes the teacher and the tutor she calls "St. Preux" the chastened pupil.

"Pray tell me, my dear friend, in what language or rather in what jargon is the narration in your last Letter?" Julie writes in her first response to Saint-Preux's letters from Paris. "What do you expect a poor Swiss woman to understand by these sublime figures?" Warming up to her theme, she continues her critique of his epistolary style:

> There is affectation and play in several of your letters. I am not referring to the vivid turn and vigorous phrases inspired by the force of sentiment; I refer to that prettiness of style which, being unnatural, comes spontaneously to no one, and is the mark of pretension in its user. . . . Did wit ever have time to manifest itself when we were alone together, and if the enchantment of a passionate conversation excludes it and prevents it from making an appearance, how could Letters, which absence always fills with a touch of bitterness and where the heart speaks more affectingly, ever tolerate it?[47]

Later in the letter Julie claims that this critique was more the doing of her cousin Claire than herself, but Julie often appeals to Claire's reason, as in the critical decision about whether to accept Milord Edward's offer to facilitate an elopement with Saint-Preux.[48] Since Claire has no will of her own, but only a desire to serve Julie and make her happy, her role in the novel is often simply to guide Julie's will when her own reason fails her. When Julie finds it difficult to criticize her lover, Claire does it for her.

Rousseau got around the problem of how a man could teach a woman how to write letters by writing the women who write the letters. This is what Elizabeth Goldsmith calls "writing the female voice," a practice, she points out, that acts to "*reduce* female scriptive authority rather than enhance it."[49] Authors of letter-writing manuals and pedagogues, however, could not always fall back on this sleight-of-hand that male novelists had been using since the seventeenth century. Perhaps abbé Pluche was right to devote little attention to the subject of letter writing, simply expressing his wish that by the age of ten or eleven a young lady would be "in a position to write as natu-rally as she speaks."[50] Others, however, were undaunted by the challenge. Philipon de la Madelaine, for example, explained the superior ease and negligence of women's let-ters as a result, "in part, of that softness in which they are raised, and that renders them more able to feel than to think; in part also of the fact that they seek less to write well, out of the conviction that we encourage, that in order to please, they have only to speak: and everyone knows that if one wishes to show one's wit, the great secret is not to have any."[51] At the same time, however, he made sure to let his readers know that one of the mistakes often made by those "with little experience in *le monde* . . . and which is no less contrary to this simplicity that I cannot recommend too highly" was a "low style." To remedy this problem, he advised "frequenting good company: I can't imagine a better school for forming an epistolary style."[52]

André-Joseph Panckoucke devoted a full section of his *Études convenables aux demoi-selles* to letter writing, although he did remark that "several ladies have succeeded per-fectly in this without knowing any rules of the art, and whose style and substance have pleased because they spoke according to beautiful nature, and did not seek to shine through wit."[53] Nevertheless, Panckoucke proceeded with the rules—not of style or substance, perhaps, but of form and function. These were rules designed not for the ceremonial letters of *les grands*, he made sure to point out, but "for those per-sons who have only a familiar and ordinary epistolary commerce." Even so, one of the first rules was that it was "impolite to *tutoyer* in letters." The others were really anti-rules. The familiar letter, he explained, "is an effusion, an outpouring of heartfelt feelings; it is a free and easy commerce of a friend writing to a friend, in which it suf-fices to observe the rules of common sense." The business letter was similarly natural: "Precision and clarity are the essential character of this genre of letters, for which we do not present a model, since every young lady who finds herself involved in com-merce will easily find the short and simple method of this sort of correspondence."[54]

It is worth noting that the first edition of Panckoucke's book was published in 1749; by the time this edition was published sixty years later, the rule against using the in-formal form of address no longer reflected usage. Manon Phlipon and Sophie Cannet were *tutoyant* in the 1770s, as was Sophie Silvestre in her letters to her husband in the 1780s. In the 1760s, however, Geneviève de Malboissière alternated between the two forms of address in the letters she wrote to her friend Adélaïde Méliand, although they are predominantly in the formal mode. In several letters she used both, as in this passage: "Your beautiful letter [*votre belle epitre*] was delivered to me yesterday, a moment before supper. If you knew [*Si tu savois*], my child, how I rushed through my meal in order to read it. After supper, I played a game of whist, and each time that we anted up, I took your letter [*ta lettre*] and read a bit of it and, finally, in adding them end to end, I finished by reading all of it."[55] The rules were clearly changing, but the printers who reissued the textbooks did not always keep them up to date. Panckoucke himself had died in 1753.

Another man who took it upon himself to teach young ladies how to write letters was Gabriel-Henri Gaillard, the author of the very successful *Rhétorique françoise, à l'usage des jeunes demoiselles*. "It would take boldness and even extravagance to claim to instruct Ladies in the beautiful art of speaking," Gaillard admitted. "Men who are a bit fair agree with good grace that the delicacy of thoughts, the happy choice of expressions, the lively and light ornaments of discourse are the attributes of this charming Sex, and that nature has liberally granted them, in this respect, that which for men is often the fruit of assiduous study and stubborn labor. . . . Their conversation, always pleasant, often even useful, is a type of Practical Rhetoric."[56] Gaillard went on to misquote the seventeenth-century poet Mme Deshoulières (Antoinette du Ligier de la Garde) to suggest that she shared his view that the best women's writing derived from their conversation and their ignorance of Latin: "Every day their pleasing ignorance, / To the shame of Greek and Latin, shows / How often is preferable / The usage of society to learning."[57] For women writers, Gaillard suggested, ignorance was a virtue. However, *Réflexions diverses* (1686), from which this verse is (mis)taken, is a meditation on the vanity of Man and the futility of learning. Its author, like all those who wrote eloquently of the folly of learning, was herself quite learned: private tutors had taught her Latin as well as modern languages, and the philosophy that underpins her poetry is indebted to her reading of the Roman philosopher Lucretius. She was elected to several academies and honored by the Académie française, where one of her poems was read aloud.[58] Gaillard, however, took Deshoulières to be recommending what all authors of conversation and letter manuals recommended—that men should frequent the society of ladies if they wanted to become polished rather than pedants. This interpretation not only ignores the long philosophical tradition in which the poem is embedded, but it is difficult to reconcile with the purpose of Gaillard's own book—to teach young ladies how to write. Indeed, a lesser poet than Mme Deshoulières highlighted exactly this difficulty in a poem he sent to the *Mercure de France* in 1787. Entitled "Couplets à Mme de . . . , en lui envoyant une Rhétorique Françoise" [Couplets to Mme de . . . , in sending her a French Rhetoric], it reads:

> All this pedantic knowledge
> Is nothing but a vain display;
> The secret of moving us
> Is in your language.
> You know how to render ingenious
> To the point of silencing us,
> And Love is in your beautiful eyes
> The God of eloquence.[59]

Paradox was one of the most common tropes in eighteenth-century poetry—or at least the kind sent in by readers to the *Mercure*. Sending Gaillard's *Rhétorique françoise* to a lady thus made an excellent subject for amusing couplets, but in their light, the gift itself must be seen as a defiance of logic. Aware of the seeming paradox of teaching ladies how to write, the author of the *Rhétorique françoise* presented himself as simply providing good models for girls to follow. Young women, he claimed, have a tendency to follow bad ones—novels in particular—rather than the defenders of good taste of bygone days.[60]

Jean-François Marmontel dealt harshly with Gaillard in his review of the *Rhétorique françoise*, calling into question the very purpose of such a book for young ladies by blowing apart the paradox at its heart:

> The author does not write for ladies at all. They have, he says, a natural rhetoric that supplies all the rules of the art; but young ladies need protection against the bad taste that reigns in novels. Ladies, whom he praises, have read novels and have not contracted the taste. Why should an essay on rhetoric that would have been useless to the mother be necessary for the daughter? Whatever he says, it is obvious that it is certainly not for the [fair] sex that he composed this work.

Marmontel went even further: the models Gaillard included, he declared, could only be useful for those who engaged in the kind of writing in which girls and women certainly did not engage:

> Conversation, epistolary style, and other similar genres, are the attributes of young ladies. In order to succeed in them, is there any need to know in detail the precepts that the author gives? Patru, Le Maître, etc., are the oratorical commonplaces for a lawyer, etc.; but can one propose them to a girl? When M. de Voltaire, whom he calls a *man of wit*, said *that it is only in imitating great models that one can become a model oneself*, he certainly was not talking to young ladies.[61]

Marmontel claimed (absurdly) that Gaillard recommended Voiture, Balzac, and Boursault as epistolary models for young ladies, but failed to mention Sévigné (whom Gaillard did in fact recommend).[62] And, in any case, Marmontel was simply refusing to take seriously Gaillard's claim that young women could become, not just good letter writers, but the Deshoulières of their time. The poet Deshoulières, however, could only serve as a model when her poetry was deformed to hide the learned poet behind the ignorant woman. Nonetheless, Gaillard went farther than Marmontel and most of his contemporaries in encouraging young women to become writers. "Should a misplaced shame, daughter of a ridiculous prejudice, deprive the Republic of Letters of the members who would honor it the most? Will we not see any more Daciers or Deshoulières? Aren't women allowed to think, to be pleasant, to have wit?" Gaillard blamed a misreading of Molière's *Femmes savantes* for the problem. "Molière wanted to make fun of the impertinence of Pedantry and to stop the progress of this vice that had extended through men to women. Could he anticipate that anyone would conclude bizarrely that it is shameful for women to have talents and cultivate them?"[63]

Even in encouraging women to aspire to become full-fledged members of the Republic of Letters, however, Gaillard never questioned the idea that they should write *as women*, which may explain why he rewrote Deshoulières in his own image of a woman writer. He saw his own role as giving girls appropriate (female) models so that they would write well *as women*. As Gaillard saw it, writing was one of the *talents* that young ladies should be cultivating. And just as the musical talents young ladies were encouraged to cultivate—singing, harpsichord, and harp playing—stemmed from their nature and natural charms, their natural linguistic talent for conversation would be nurtured in particular ways so that it would bloom in feminine writing. The role of the educator was to nurture and cultivate by providing appropriate models and dispelling prejudice.

Like Gaillard, Pierre-Joseph Boudier de Villemert saw the attack on *femmes savantes* as having gone too far. "Fortunately, we are no longer in those times when prejudice condemned women as well as the Nobility to a crass ignorance," he wrote in *L'Ami des femmes* (1758). "The ridicule cast upon pedantic learning had so discredited all knowledge that for a while several women made it an honor to mangle the words of their language."[64] Notwithstanding this dig at the précieuses, Boudier de Villemert, like Gaillard, went on to sing the praises of those he considered France's greatest women writers. "A woman can put together a library entirely of works by women," he declared. "The Villedieus, the Deshoulières, the Sévignés, the La Suzes, and a number of others challenge the genius of our greatest men. . . . The race of these superior women is not extinct: we still have Thalias for Comedy, Clios for History; and a flourishing Academy glorifies itself today by having in its bosom the elegant imitator [*imitatrice*] of Milton." Going beyond Gaillard, however, Boudier de Villemert recommended that women follow *only* female models, and only models such as these women provided. "It is in familiarizing themselves with such models that a spiritual woman can employ her leisure usefully and perfect in herself the fortunate gift of being able to express herself with nobility and ease," he declared.[65] Missing from Boudier de Villemert's recommended list were the distinguished translators of Homer and Newton. "If there are found among this sex some Daciers, some Du Châtelets," he warned, "these are rare examples, more to be admired than imitated." Boudier de Villemert also cautioned his female readers against following the model of Mme Guyon and other religious writers, whom he dubbed "théologiennes" and found more "shocking" than the libertine Ninon de Lenclos. No, the realm of women was "all that can awaken their curiosity and lend graces to the imagination," which, he asserted, "are more appropriate to them than to us: this field is vast enough that they can compete with us; they can even surpass us without humiliating us."[66]

Alongside the canon of women poets and novelists recommended as literary models was that of women letter writers, and above all Mme de Sévigné, for as Mauvillon declared most succinctly, "it will suffice to tell you that [her letters] are the best model that you could choose for the familiar style."[67] Women and girls were guided by a steady stream of print editions of women's letters, especially those of Sévigné. Indeed, as Marie-France Silver and Marie-Laure Girou Swiderski write, "It was undoubtedly difficult for a woman to write letters in the eighteenth century without thinking about the marquise."[68] How exactly to use such models, however, was not obvious. Mme de Miremont recommended the letters of Lambert, Maintenon, and Sévigné as models of epistolary style, but she made clear that they were not simply to be imitated. Young ladies should be exposed to these models as examples of "a pleasing negligence" that develops only "in the *bosom* of habit and familiarity." As she reminded her readers, "each person has her own style as [she has] her own imagination; and the best style is that in which one's character is found, because it is the most natural."[69] Miremont did not believe that one could or should write as one spoke, however, and she cited the naturalist Georges-Louis Leclerc, comte de Buffon, known for his style, to support her view. "'One must speak as one thinks and write as one feels,' says our Author. 'To write well, is to see well, think well, and feel well at the same time.'"[70]

For Manon Phlipon, the Sévigné to be emulated was not the devoted mother who wrote to her daughter but the trenchant observer of court life who sent news and gossip to her male friends and relatives. In 1776 Manon reassured her friend Henriette Cannet that "everyone cannot write like Mme de Sévigné, not only due to lack of a wit like hers, but because everyone is not, as she was, at the heart of the Court and brilliant social circles, that is to say, at the center where interesting anecdotes, pretty things, great affairs, important little nothings, happen; where the easy phrase, the friendly tone, finesse, the graces, are given to, are joined to, all that is done." One made letters out of the material life provided—the books one read, one's observations of the world in which one lived—but the rules that guided construction of the letter should be the same. "This is where order is necessary," Manon explained,

> first in one's ideas, then in one's communication and responses. Without it, one stifles one's thoughts into confusion or drowns them in the void; one speaks without answering, we misunderstand each other, we contradict each other, we hardly amuse ourselves; we do no more than forgive each other in silence. . . . I want us always to be ourselves, to unbosom ourselves freely; but in the matter of ideas and the communication of the mind, we must respond to each other exactly, make ourselves clear and precise.[71]

And yet if Sévigné could not imitated, she was a model and an influence even on Manon. In the memoirs she wrote many years later she acknowledged that in the early years of her correspondence with the Cannet sisters, "the letters of Mme de Sévigné would fix my taste."[72] The influence is evident in a letter she wrote to Henriette's sister Sophie in 1774, modeled on one of the most famous of Sévigné's—the one in which she breaks the news to her friend Coulanges about the forthcoming marriage of the king's sister, known simply as Mademoiselle, with the duc de Lauzun. Here is Sévigné:

> I am going to send you something that is the most astonishing, the most surprising, the most marvelous, the most miraculous, the most triumphant, the most stunning, the most unheard of, the most singular, the most extraordinary, the most incredible, the

most unforseen, the greatest, the smallest, the most rare, the most common, the most striking, the most secret until today, the most brilliant, the most worthy of envy . . . something, finally, that will take place on Sunday, when those who see it will think they've been blinded by it; something that will take place on Sunday, and that will perhaps not be over on Monday. I cannot resolve to say it; guess: I will give you three tries. Do you throw your tongue to the dogs? Well, then! I must tell you: M. de Lauzun is marrying on Sunday in the Louvre, guess who? I will give you four tries, I will give you ten tries, I will give you a hundred. . . . In the end I will have to tell you: he is marrying on Sunday, in the Louvre, with the King's permission, Mademoiselle, Mademoiselle de . . . Mademoiselle . . . guess the name: he is marrying, upon my word, Mademoiselle![73]

And here is Manon telling Sophie about a friend who is moving to Amiens. Although, as Manon knew, she could not begin to approach her exalted model, she could approximate the breathless drama of her style:

She is a young bride who leaves next Thursday for Amiens, where she will spend six months of the year; she said the other day that what would please her during her stay in Amiens, would be to find a good friend with whom she would have previously established an epistolary relationship; guess a little who this lady is? I will give you two tries, four tries, ten tries! Ah! Well! Do you throw your tongue to the dogs and your bonnet over the mills? She is, upon my word, guess . . . I have been charged to write to you to find out who is this Monsieur with the great name, of whom such great display is made; this is certainly woman's curiosity in which I indulge myself out of pure compliance. But finally, I must tell you that it is the elder Mlle Surugue.[74]

The allusion to Sévigné's style and figures of speech were an inside joke between schoolgirls. Since all young ladies would have read this most famous of Sévigné's letters, Manon could assume that her friend would catch it.

Manon was clearly not intimidated by the letters she read, but as she noted in her advice to Henriette, model letters could discourage a girl who thought she was supposed to write as well as Sévigné. Abbé Fromageot tackled this problem in his *Cours d'études* with a complex method that encouraged the student to use the model as a starting point for her own ideas, rather than simply copying it. "After having spent enough time looking at the rules and examples of all the genres of poetry, eloquence, and epistolary style," he writes, "I thought it was necessary to accustom her [his pupil] to representing her ideas by confiding them to paper." However, he continues, this new activity stumped the young girl at first "because her self-consciousness [*amour-propre*] got a little bit in the way. She wanted to write well, to cover the topics that were set for her, but she was willing to sacrifice what she had written to what she called the shame of not being able to approach her models." Fromageot had her find a topic in a passage in one of her books, read it over a couple of times, "and while her genius was aroused by this reading, she would write on the same topic." When she ran out of things to say, she would read over her work and compare it to what had inspired it, then rewrite her piece by removing anything that was not her own and improving anything she was not happy with, "in order to rework it again until everything came from her." After letting her writing sit for a while, she would come back to it, sometimes reworking it completely. "You can judge the progress she made by several letters that I will provide at the end of this work," Fromageot concluded, thereby suggesting his own student's letters as a new sort of model for his readers.[75]

Fromageot inverted the standard practice of providing model letters by asking the student to locate her model in her books, and then having her write a letter in her own words on the topic it treated. She would find her own voice by transforming print materials into letters, that is, into the feminine mode of writing that was appropriate to her and through which her own ideas could naturally develop and be expressed. Of course, this natural process required a familiarity with rules and models, self-critique, and hard work, but these were important things for a young lady to learn—diligence and self-criticism prevented the laziness and vanity that were among the natural vices of the female sex that education had to combat.

Fromageot built his method on the pedagogical practice of the extract. Since the Renaissance, boys had been taught to extract the best passages from their Latin readings in order to produce what the English called a "commonplace book." But it was not until the eighteenth century that French girls were encouraged to do so. Charles Rollin, the author of a popular history textbook, was the first to promote extracting as part of girls' education. According to Nicole Pellegrin, Rollin believed that extracting helped to "fix the ideas" girls learned through reading and to teach them how to write with "accuracy, precision, facility." He meant the production of extracts to be "a school of virtue" for girls, rather than a means of training future scholars and professionals. Rollin thus legitimized training girls in a (masculine) scholarly practice by redefining it as a (feminine) moral one.[76]

This is just the sort of definition of extracting that Mme d'Épinay gave in *Conversations d'Émilie*: "It is to take from a work that which interests you and leave out the rest. For example, in the one I am speaking of, I will transcribe everything that relates to the principles that you wish to engrave in your head and your heart, and I will leave out everything that is foreign [to them]. This is what is called to extract a work, to make an extract."[77] In the following conversation Émilie and her mother read together a manuscript "Extract of moral principles." When Émilie remarks that there is nothing new in it, that these are things they themselves say every day, her mother replies: "But that means nothing, if you are not convinced of the truth of these principles." The mother then advises Émilie to learn the extract by heart, "in order that you may be able to recall at every moment the principles that should direct your conduct." Émilie agrees with alacrity and asks if she may copy it out in order to learn the principles more quickly. Needless to say, the mother is happy to let her do so. "Go write them down," she says. "Here I go, Mama," Émilie cries, "and I won't stop until I have finished all of it." And so ends Épinay's treatise and Émilie's formal education.[78] Émilie would continue to learn, however, in a lifetime of reading and extracting and rereading that would shape her character and her actions. Like letter writing, extracting was meant to be a lifelong practice.

Mme de Miremont incorporated the art of the extract into her plan for educating future teachers:

> If from the first days of their studies one takes care to teach them the art of making extracts, of which one finds such good models in several Journals; if they amuse themselves by reading a few volumes of the Letters of Madame de Sévigné and the works of Madame de Lambert, if they have profited from the books of piety, morals, and history that will have been put in their hands, they will have a sufficient knowledge of what they should show to young people.[79]

For these young women, the extracts they prepared as students would serve them for the rest of their lives, not simply as a moral compass, but as a professional resource.

Pellegrin has found in the autobiographical works of several women writers evidence that after midcentury girls were indeed taught the art of the extract. Victorine de Chastenay-Lanty, for example, who was born in 1771, recalled that she was taught to make extracts when she about nine years old. "I then read the *Histoire de l'Angleterre* by Père d'Orléans and the *Révolutions romaines* by Vertot. My father urged me to give my extracts the form of letters; he responded to some of them, and were it not for that epoch during which so many papers disappeared, I would still have these dear responses."[80] Here is one case where Fromageot's method was put into practice. Like the mothers whom many of the new pedagogues tried to enlist in the project of educating their daughters, Victorine's father used the filial correspondence to monitor his daughter's education while encouraging her to practice writing and strengthening the bond between parent and child.

Geneviève de Malboissière and Adélaïde Méliand used the technique of extracting to construct catalogs of their natural history collections, and then they made copies of their catalogs for each other and exchanged them as gifts—or letters. "Here is my catalog," wrote Geneviève. "I think it would be best to copy your extracts into a sort of book that you will arrange according to the order you will have followed in yours, rather than leaving them on little loose sheets of paper. My pots are finally all labeled; all I have to do is to extract the history of each one of them, which is no small task."[81] In her memoirs, Mme Roland claimed to have been "inspired" to start making extracts as a way of "digesting" the works her mother read aloud to her in the evenings as she plied her needle—although it should be noted that one of the first books she mentioned extracting was Rollin. "As my first work in the morning I would put down on paper what had most struck me the evening before; then I would take up the book again in order to grasp the connections or to copy a passage that I wanted to have in its entirety. This taste became a habit, need, and passion." She then started extracting the books she read herself. "My father, having only a small library, which I had exhausted long before, I read borrowed or rented books; I could not bear the idea of returning them without having appropriated for myself what I considered the best parts."[82]

In fact, Manon Phlipon's correspondence and the journal she kept are rich with extracts. Among the poems, essays, stories, scattered thoughts, and a portrait of Sophie Cannet in Manon's journal are extracts from (among other works) Rousseau's *Discours sur l'inégalité*, Morelly's *Code de la nature*, the pseudo-Persian tales of Saadi, and abbé Nollet's *Leçons de physique expérimentale*.[83] In her letters to Sophie and Henriette, Manon sometimes included reworked extracts of the books she was reading, or used an extract as a springboard for her own thoughts—just as Fromageot taught his student to do. For example, she copied an ode by the English poet Alexander Pope into her notebook, and then into a letter to Sophie.[84] In another letter she wrote that she had just finished reading abbé Raynal's *Histoire des deux Indes*, which a friend had lent her. "I made a lot of extracts, following my custom for the books that I like." After commenting on the style, she went on to discuss the content of Raynal's eight-volume work and the impact that reading it had on her.

> Altogether, it presents a history that is universal, precise, instructive, noble, and well organized. This book is made to hasten the revolution that operates in minds, and it does honor to the philosophic century that produced it. It would change the way I think, if that change had not already occurred before I read it. I find in it the true principles of good morals and good legislation: the subordination of particular interests to the common good, the sole motive and basis of a good moral system and a wise administration.[85]

In the rest of the letter, Manon developed her own ideas stimulated by her reading and extracting of Raynal's work. In this, as in everything she did, Manon was self-conscious and deliberate. In a letter to Sophie in December 1778, she prefaced a discussion of Voltaire's *Dictionnaire philosophique*, which she had just read, with the following explanation: "One never learns anything when one simply reads, one must extract and transform, as it were, into one's own substance those things that one wishes to preserve, in penetrating their essence."[86] Extracting was not simply a rote exercise of copying, but a way of developing one's own ideas. Extracting the essence of what she read through the alchemy of writing was for Manon a process of incorporation that constituted the first step in the development of her own ideas. She came to own these ideas fully by sharing her extract with a friend. By explaining her thoughts in a letter, she became the teacher rather than the student, the active partner in intellectual as well as social exchange. She encouraged Sophie and Henriette to do the same.

A final example suggests how the art of the extract could expand the limits of the letter. In her manuscript memoirs, Mme de la Ferté-Imbault (the only daughter of the salonnière Mme Geoffrin) recounts how she came to begin writing extracts later in life. In 1765, when she was almost fifty years old and her own daughter was long dead, she befriended the young niece of a friend who was grieving the loss of her sister. "She took to moral [discourse] more than to devotion," Mme de la Ferté-Imbault explained, "and begged me to teach her philosophy. I found no other means than to extract from Seneca, Plutarch, Montaigne, and Mabillon the bits that had made the greatest impression on me in my youth, and of which the rest of my life had proven the truth, the enlightenment, the efficacy, against all the secondary causes, torments of my life."[87] Like Fromageot's pupil, and like Sophie Silvestre trying to write formal letters, she was, she says, "stuck," when she first began, "having never written except to my friends and for my own affairs." She showed her first short extract to a male friend, who told her she had done so well that she had to keep going. So did the young lady and her uncle. "Finally, I was so encouraged, and found myself so pleasurably occupied, that three years later I had managed to extract all of Seneca, Amyot's translation of Plutarch's *Lives*, and Montaigne, without getting tired, and without having to change my life at all." In the end, she had produced six volumes of extracts!

Mme de la Ferté-Imbault did not stop there, however. Word of her extracts spread, and copies began to circulate around Paris and Versailles. The comtesse de Marsan, a friend who was in charge of the education of the royal children, asked for copies for the princesses under her care.[88] Another friend, the philosophe Friedrich-Melchior Grimm, wrote to her from Saint Petersburg that the Empress Catherine also wanted a copy. "I spoke to [Catherine] about your extracts, your riches, the use that you have made of them. She began to drool. As she knows that you are always a bit recalcitrant at the first overture on any subject, she has ordered me to sound you out on the possibility of having a copy of these riches."[89] Mme de la Ferté-Imbault herself noted that Mme Necker also wanted a copy. A mutual friend had spoken to her about Mme de la Ferté-Imbault's "passion for the ancient and good philosophy, and of the quantity of volumes of extracts that I had made of Cicero, Seneca, and Plutarch. She wanted to read them, and at the onset of my mother's illness, in the month of January 1776, as she saw me often at my mother's, she asked me to lend her what I had made for princess Clothilde."[90] Suzanne Necker's daughter, Germaine, would have been ten years old at the time, just the right age to begin to appreciate them. Who knows how they may have influenced her development into the writer Germaine de Staël?

It is likely that Mme d'Épinay had a copy of at least one volume of Mme de la Ferté-Imbault's extracts when she was writing *Conversations d'Émilie*. In the sixteenth conversation of the 1782 edition, the mother gives Émilie "the notebooks of a woman I know of great merit." In them is "the extract of Plutarch's *Lives*, for the use of a young person who has really benefited from it. You know what an extract is, and you will understand that she has brought into focus the most remarkable traits of all the great and virtuous characters of antiquity." Épinay would have gotten the extracts as Catherine did, from Grimm, who was her lover.[91]

The person Mme de la Ferté-Imbault impressed most, however, was herself:

I was charmed by this production and at the same time so astonished, that I recalled Cicero's promises in his *Treatise on Old Age*, and I said to myself, *voilà*, the proof that he was right. These six children came out completely naturally because my mind, accustomed from an early hour to application and the love of these great authors, asked nothing more than to have something to do. All of a sudden the desire came to me to explain to myself the reasons that had been able to rouse and inspire in me at the age of 50, a gift that I had never felt. I am putting all my reflections in writing, and I will attach them to this history. This is my first production.[92]

In her fifties, the pleasure of writing had taken hold of this woman who had never before written anything but letters. It was through the process of writing extracts—of analyzing and explaining to young women the ideas of great men that meant something to her—that she was inspired to clarify and lay out her own ideas. She had found her voice. For this daughter of the greatest of the Enlightenment salonnières was inspired, she proclaimed, by the hope that by extracting the authors she admired, "this would quite simply form a contrast with the false and dangerous principles of the philosophers (who are called encyclopedists)." What is striking, of course, is that women at the heart of the Enlightenment—Épinay, Necker, and even Catherine—valued these extracts as much as their author and the governess of the French princesses did. Even the most enlightened mothers found in the classics moral principles appropriate for their daughters, and even the most conservative no longer thought it was sufficient to give their daughters the devotional literature that continued to be churned out by the presses. Mme de la Ferté-Imbault's extracts met the universal demand for moral literature written at a level that a young girl could understand. The letter-writing practice of young ladies and the women they would become was shaped as much by this moral content as it was by the stylistic model of Sévigné. But the practice of extracting, of appropriating the ideas of men of letters and putting them in one's own words, also shaped epistolary practice, as young ladies learned to write from the mind as well as the heart.

Conclusion: Taking Pride in a Well-Written Letter

Jean Lanteires' *Quelques avis aux institutrices de jeunes demoiselles* (1788) was the first book in French aimed explicitly at prospective teachers of young ladies. His chapter on letters and epistolary style covered a lot of familiar ground, but he also went into considerable detail about how teaching writing to girls should correspond to gender expectations. He made clear that young women (both teachers and their pupils) were not expected to write the way that men did who used this skill in their work or as if they were writing for the public. But this did not mean that they could be sloppy or careless in the letters they wrote. There was a minimum standard that all young women should meet, starting with physical presentation:

> In writing Letters, or more generally, the lines that they trace should be an equal distance apart, and the words separated from those that precede or follow them in such a way that they do not create any confusion. People with poor handwriting above all ought to adopt this method, since one senses how much handwriting that is mediocre would appear to better advantage if the eye were not busy separating the words and that it would peruse it with facility. Young girls, and even those who are older, also ought to take care to be more exact and more attentive in avoiding inkblots on their paper than they are ordinarily.[93]

Lanteires' frustration went beyond the written page to the entire material culture of letter writing. He complained that women only rarely kept their letters and other papers neatly and safely filed in portfolios. Instead, "they let them get crumpled up in their pockets, mixing them up with various other things that have no relation to them, or they just let them wander off into various pieces of furniture. Their secretary, their inkwell, if they have them, are in poor condition; their pens, their paper, and other objects necessary for writing clearly and without confusion, are in the greatest disorder." Losing patience altogether, he declared that women often "do not know either how to fold a letter according to received custom, or to address it in a way that is clear and distinct." At this point Lanteires backed off, apologizing for the harshness of his criticism. "My point," he said, "is not at all to humiliate my compatriots, but. . . ." He then went on patiently to explain the proper way to fold and seal a letter (the simplest, of course).[94]

This was a new voice in female pedagogy. Unlike Gaillard, Prunay, Barthelemy, Reyre, or the rest of the men of letters who first charmed and flattered their female readers and then tried to shame them into studying, Lanteires was stern and demanding. As far as he was concerned, the much-vaunted and studied *negligence* of feminine epistolary style was just that—negligence. "One is not severe enough about these things," he declared.

> People are foolish enough to count on the indulgence of others, and one does not receive it so often, or with such facility, as one likes to think. Finally, a young Lady, and women in general, ought never to excuse or justify the negligence with which they write by observing that they are addressing themselves to a girlfriend, or rather that *women are not expected to write well*; not only is this excuse frivolous, unfounded; but even more it becomes humiliating for the [female] sex that it wants to support.[95]

As far as style went, Lanteires recommended training the ear to recognize awkward language by reading aloud, but his foremost concern was clarity. "Never forget that the person to whom one writes asks for expressions that are more clear, in order to understand you, than you need to understand yourself," he reminded his readers.[96]

Like other writers, Lanteires distinguished between types of letters, but he followed Jaucourt, who wrote in the *Encyclopédie* that there were only two kinds of letters: philosophical letters, which treated literary subjects and were intended for publication; and familiar letters, which were exchanged between individuals.[97] Lanteires advised that young ladies not be given the first as models, since such letters "have a gravity that does not agree with them, something uncomfortable that announces the Author rather than the man." More worrying was the moral impact of such models. "I don't know if reading these great models would be of any help to a young Lady in forming her epistolary style; perhaps one would rather that they did not know about them; they might contract a false way of thinking concerning a lot of subjects with moral implications," he concluded.[98]

The line between letters and literature was clearly drawn along gender lines with a moral charge, but so was that between the formal and informal letters that a young lady needed to learn how to write. Like his contemporaries, Bernard de Bonnard and Manon Phlipon, Lanteires believed that for letters written in "friendship, confidence, and feeling" models were both unnecessary and inappropriate. "One looks only into one's heart, and, as Fénelon says, dips in one's pen."[99] At the same time, he acknowledged that model letters could be useful in other circumstances, and for them he recommended Philipon de la Madelaine's book, just as Bernard had recommended it to his wife Sophie. Like them, too, Lanteires held strongly that the studied "negligence" that was supposed to characterize familiar letters did not extend to spelling, handwriting, or inkblots, and that women should take care and pride in their writing, not because it was a sign of character, but because they should not set themselves lower standards just because they were female. If he accepted the gender ideology that defined men's and women's writing differently, he was adamant that women could and should write with pride and purpose within its constraints.

One young woman who did take pride in her letters, of course, was Manon Phlipon. In her memoirs she claimed that in her youth she saw the ability to write a good letter as representing the kind of merit that ought to be the basis of a person's value, rather than age or rank. "I could not hide the fact that I was worth more than Mlle d'Hannaches, whose forty years and genealogy did not give her the ability to write a letter that had common sense or was legible; I found the world very unjust and social institutions very extravagant."[100] Nevertheless, even in her teens, Manon understood the difficulties and contradictions of the woman letter writer in a way that her male peers never did. At times she was discouraged, at others she was angry, but most of the time she did write with her head held high and met the high standards she set for herself. We can see this in the regularity of her handwriting, the lack of blots on the page, the strength and clarity of the words she uses, and the passion of the voice that shines through them.[101]

PART III

The World of Goods

Supplying the Female Letter Writer

5

As young ladies grew into women, and letter writing became an integral part of their daily lives, furnishing them with supplies—pens, ink, paper, seals and sealing wax, desks and inkstands—became a commercial opportunity. The invention, promotion, and development of epistolary paraphernalia for women was a market response to the participation of the new and expanding group of literate women in the practice of letter writing; at the same time, porcelain inkstands, veneered writing desks, and decorated paper were also part of the expansion of the consumer economy through the creation, invention, importation, and marketing of new and existing goods as novel, fashionable, and useful.

The rhythm of fashion set the pace for a modern world in which letter-writing women participated as both consumers and correspondents. This was a world in which women were not the bearers of tradition or the keepers of the hearth but the bellwethers of change, the beacons of fashion, the proponents of taste. Because letter writing was a novelty for women, rather than a traditional practice, it required a new world of goods, of novelties, to support it. Whereas previous generations of elites may have looked back in time to establish their place in the world, the women who engaged in letter writing in the eighteenth century looked forward in search of novelty and outward to a world expanding through global commerce and colonialism, materialized in merchandise and communicated through retail trade, journalism, and epistolary exchange.

The new importance of letter writing in the lives of eighteenth-century women is perhaps most concretely demonstrated in the invention and proliferation of tables specifically designed for writing and storing letters. Starting in the 1740s, writing tables and desks were sold in fashionable shops in Paris and marketed to customers interested in the latest fashions. They were part of a profusion of small specialized tables that flooded the market and filled the apartments and townhouses of letter-writing women. Indeed, the writing desk was emblematic of the light furniture that helped to choreograph the sociability of the eighteenth century and articulate its spaces: small tables designed for games, needlework, intimate suppers, the *toilette*, and other sociable but intimate activities. But it was also a market response to rising consumer demand to meet the material needs of the letter-writing woman, as writing supplies were now integrated into and marketed in the emerging rhythms, spaces, and media of fashion.

If we use our imaginations to open the writing desk and look inside its various drawers and cubbyholes we will find paper and sometimes envelopes, as well as ink and the powder used to blot it. Tucked away in a locked drawer are letters the desk's owner has received and saved, secure, she thinks, from the prying eyes of servants, parents, or husband. We will also find quill pens and a penknife for preparing their nibs, and an inkwell filled with glossy black ink. There will be sticks or wafers of wax in different colors that will have to be stamped with a seal to close a letter with the writer's mark and prepare it for its journey to its intended recipient—and keep it safe from the prying eyes of unintended ones. The seal itself may be there too. If not, it is probably dangling from a chain pinned to the person of its owner, or in her pocket. All of these writing supplies could be purchased in the most fashionable shops in Paris.

If we close the desk now and go out to the shops, we may experience some of the excitement of being a woman of means in Europe's largest and most fashionable city in the throes of the consumer revolution. In search of paper, ink, and containers to hold them we will be surrounded by a dazzling array of goods from around the world that compete for our attention. The sheer variety is new, as slight changes in color, style, or technology multiply our choices. Quality remains important, but inventiveness is prized at least as much. Our letter-writing woman will have to enter the shops with both knowledge and acumen to make the fine discriminations known as "taste."

Into the Shops of the *Marchand-Merciers*

The merchants who formed the richest corps in Paris and propelled the market in consumer and luxury goods were members of the guild of *marchand-merciers*.[1] Incorporated in the fifteenth century to handle the increasing number of products that were either imported or fell between the provenance of the different guilds that produced finished goods, by the eighteenth century the mercers were tastemakers who specialized in the exotic and "enjolivement" or finishing. By 1769 almost half the mercers who dealt in furniture, jewelry, and fashionable clothing had set up shop on the rue Saint-Honoré.[2] At least two stationers, Flot and Des Lauriers, did business there, too, while many others were just across the river in the elegant residential neighborhood of Saint-Germain-des-Prés. By the second half of the eighteenth century, the rue Saint-Honoré had become the most fashionable shopping district of Paris. Its elegant shops and inviting cafés attracted ladies and gentlemen to enjoy a kind of sociable leisure that brought them out of their salons and into the world of commerce.

Although the shop sign Jean-Antoine Watteau painted for the mercer Gersaint in 1720 is well known today as one of the painter's masterpieces (see fig. 5.1), few are aware of the occasion for which it was commissioned: the decision to change the name of the shop from Le Grand Monarque to La Pagode. The renaming of Gersaint's shop marked not only a new era after the demise of Louis XIV, but a new approach to marketing that emphasized the fashionable, exotic, and cosmopolitan nature of the mercer's goods. As Andrew McClellan has shown, Watteau presents Gersaint's shop as a scene of elite leisure and sociability transposed from the fêtes galantes for which the artist was known.[3] On the left side, we are asked to follow an elegantly dressed lady over the threshold and into the shop, which is opened fully in front of us. With her, we watch as one man places a portrait bust of Louis XIV, the "Great Monarch" himself, in a packing case, while behind him an assistant dressed in Chinese-style cap and coat takes a mirror off the wall so that it can be sent packing with the king. Behind him is a clock in the now outmoded style of Louis XIV's favorite cabinetmaker, André-Charles Boulle. Old-fashioned portraits and religious history paintings on the walls await the same fate. As the lady, whose back is to us, looks down at the old king's face, her companion holds out his hand to her, urging her to move on and into the other side of the shop where more fashionable paintings and goods are on offer. As we follow his suggestion we see another fashionably dressed couple at the counter looking at a piece of jewelry being displayed for them by a female shop assistant; another couple examine a large round rococo canvas displayed for them on an easel by a man thought to be Gersaint himself, who is personally attending to these connoisseurs. On this side of the shop, where business is being transacted, the walls hold more fashionable

5.1. Jean-Antoine Watteau, *Gersaint's Shop Sign* (1720). Oil on canvas, 1.63 × 3.08 m. Charlottenburg Castle, Berlin. Photo: Scala/Art Resource, New York.

portraits and allegorical history paintings. A large mirror in an elaborate rococo frame hangs here, in contrast to the more sober ones on the left side of the shop, reflecting the difference in tone between the last years of the reign of the Great Monarch and the more upbeat and innovative ones of the regency of the duc d'Orléans, now in its fifth year.

Later, after the Seven Years' War, the mercers also stimulated and satisfied French Anglomania by selling goods ranging from English pins and steel buttons to pencils and pens in *magasins anglais* with names like Le Petit Dunkerque and Le Porte-Feuille Anglais.[4] Throughout the century, the mercers, who were the center of the fashion system, stressed their unique function as the local point of sale in a global economy: their métier was to introduce novelties into the Parisian market, to select and to decorate—taste was their basic commodity. As one mercer announced, "In his shop will be found things to satisfy the taste and knowledge of connoisseurs."[5]

The pleasure of fashion that the mercers sought to stimulate and satisfy should not be confused with the drive for social emulation that sociologists and historians have long invoked to explain the diffusion of taste and new consumer goods. While there is no point in denying social emulation as a possible motivation for consumption, it cannot alone account for the buying spree, product innovation, or marketing associated with the consumer revolution.[6] "The word 'Court' no longer imposes upon us as it did in the days of Louis XIV," wrote Louis-Sébastien Mercier in 1782. "The Court itself, which suspects this, does not dare to pronounce positively on a book, a play, a new masterpiece, a singular or extraordinary event: it waits for the decree of the capital."[7] Or as the Russian Grand Duchess Maria Feodorovna was reported to have said: "Doesn't fashion rule over kings themselves?" By the end of the eighteenth century the queen herself was being castigated as a slave of fashion.[8]

With the most fashionable shops on the rue Saint-Honoré catering to both ends of the market by selling goods in a broad price range, innovation and marketing designed to make fashion as capacious as possible, and luxury under attack by moralists of all stripes, the rich and powerful were compelled to embrace taste as a means of distinguishing themselves from more modest clients: simply heaping on the gold and silver no longer did the trick.[9] Indeed, sometimes taste was displayed by refusing to indulge in obvious luxury, as in the Parisian home of the marquise de La Rivière, which the baronne d'Oberkirch visited in 1782: "This house is less sumptuous than the others," she noted, "but it is prettier, in better taste perhaps; one senses the woman of quality everywhere, down to the least details. In this abode we see that gold is not everything."[10] Luxury had to be in good taste and within the parameters of fashion if its owner were to be admired rather than ridiculed, or worse—condemned as morally corrupt and socially pernicious. As Louis-Antoine Caraccioli told his readers: "If one means by luxury that massive sumptuosity that knows only how to gild and tinge with blue and spend profusely, the Europeans do not owe to the French the glory of having succeeded in this regard; if, on the contrary, it is a question of charm, of graciousness, of comforts, and even of magnificence, they are indebted both to the Parisians and to the Lyonnais. They commission them to furnish [their homes] and to clothe them, and never was a commission better executed."[11] With the help of the press, Parisian merchants promoted commerce by adopting taste as the fundamental criterion of fashion and subordinating luxury to it. They made fashion a function of knowledge rather than wealth, and gave power to those who carried the authority of taste.[12]

Trusting to the good offices of a respected merchant and the name of a well-known cabinetmaker assured the client that her purchase would testify to her refinement and good taste. In 1737 Mme du Châtelet ordered a combination writing box and sewing case from the Parisian mercer Hébert who invented the form and made it fashionable. The fittings were silver and the whole thing cost her a hefty 1,200 livres. Voltaire, who handled the order, wrote to one of his Paris agents: "I know very well that it would cost less to order the items separately from several artisans, but it would be less handsome and it would be a lot of trouble and the thing would not be completed as soon. Hébert is expensive, but he has taste." Two months later Mme du Châtelet's case was ready, and it must have pleased her; she later wrote in her *Réflexions sur le bonheur*: "It is certain that physical needs are the source of the pleasures of the senses, and I am persuaded that there are more pleasures in a modest fortune than in total abundance: a box, a porcelain, a new piece of furniture, are the true pleasures for me."[13]

A lady unsure of her taste might call on a decorator to assist her. In a supplement to the new edition of his *Dictionnaire raisonné universel des arts et metiers*, published in 1773, abbé Jaubert explained the role of this new taste professional: he adds "the delicacy of taste to the magnificence of the owner."[14] The woman who could not afford to hire a decorator could turn to the fashion press for guidance. In its inaugural issue of 1785, the *Cabinet des Modes* declared itself a "work that gives an exact and prompt knowledge, as much concerning new Clothes and Hairstyles for both sexes, as of new Furniture of all sorts . . . and generally of all that Fashion offers that is singular, agreeable, or interesting in all genres."[15] A woman who read the fashion press did not need to hire a decorator to make sure her purchases were tasteful or fashionable, and she could enter a shop already armed with the knowledge that the ability to read made available to all those with the leisure to use it.

Fashion also gave the eighteenth-century marketplace and its consumer a new temporality that was one of the distinctive features of the age—a counterpoint to the slow but regular rhythm of correspondence set by the regular comings and goings of the post and the frustrating but predictable delay between a sending a letter and receiving its reply. The accelerating pace of change based on novelty established fashion's basic tempo, but the rhythm of fashion was marked by several things: the changing of the seasons; the annual flurry of gift giving at the New Year; the periodicity of the periodical press (which accelerated over the course of the century, culminating in the daily newspapers of the Revolution); and the breathless announcements of novelties—the arrival of new merchants in town and new goods in the shops: new inventions, new discoveries, new products, new designs, new methods, new styles, new anything. Sometimes eighteenth-century merchants and tastemakers tied fashion to political and cultural events, thus riding the rhythm of the press that depended on both news-hungry readers and fashion-conscious shoppers.

The criterion of taste and the concept of fashion were crucial to the development of commerce and consumption. They allowed men of letters to condemn ostentation as bad taste, while allowing merchants to offer customers of widely diverging means a broad range of goods that all fell within the changing canons of approved taste and fashion. T. H. Breen, a historian of early America, sees in consumer choice a model for democracy: "In politics as well as religion, ordinary men and women were encouraged to make choices from among contending possibilities, to break out of traditional communities and patterns of behaviour, to rely upon their own reason in making decisions, in a word, to reconceptualize the whole social order."[16] Here is surely where the empowerment of consumption lay for many French women: in developing and learning to depend on their own judgment in making decisions about purchases their mothers would not even have contemplated. As much as reading the latest writings of the philosophes, shopping brought them out of the world of traditions passed down and into the modern one in which it was crucial to keep abreast of the new and to be able to use one's own reason, knowledge, and sensibility to make good choices. Each good choice made was the result of personal agency and strengthened the consumer's sense of personal autonomy. And it was not just the big purchases (most of which were probably not made by women anyway), but the accumulation of small ones, that contributed almost imperceptibly to the growing confidence of women who entered the urban marketplace.

Throwing herself into interior decoration might be a socially acceptable way for an elite woman to exercise choice and act on desire, as well as to develop and demonstrate her taste. "Take care to entertain without leaving your home," is the final advice Mme de Puisieux claims to have received as a young woman from an older mentor. Having earlier warned her that there was no such thing as an independent woman in France, "because we are not born to enjoy our freedom," she advised the young woman to "choose a cheerful house; furnish it with taste and propriety, such that everything in your home breathes of you. Have good books, instruments, good friends, pleasant company: I promise you that with these things, you will be happy."[17] The materialism with which women were increasingly charged was perhaps a function of their limited freedom and options, their limited means to exercise their minds and follow their hearts. It became, for this reason, one of their gendered paths to modernity.

The Pleasures of Shopping

Anna Craddock, an Englishwoman who visited Paris with her husband in 1784, noted their stroll among the fashionable shops in her travel diary for Saturday, 24 April: "We followed the rue Saint-Honoré; a long, broad street that would be perfect if it had sidewalks for the pedestrian. It is bordered by lovely shops of all sorts. I relaxed in a pastry shop where I regaled myself with excellent cakes, while Mr. Craddock went into a café."[18] On a return visit to Paris in 1785, the Craddocks headed to the Palais Royal, which the duc de Chartres had just turned into a highly fashionable locale, with shops and cafés in the ground floor arcades and, in the upper stories, larger retail showrooms and meeting places for private clubs.

The Palais Royal was an extension of rue Saint-Honoré for the profit of its noble owner. Designed for and patronized by an elite clientele, it was a planned and controlled site of commercial leisure—the premier shopping mall of its day. Louis-Sébastien Mercier called it "a unique point on the globe" and noted that others called it "the capital of Paris" because "everything is found there."[19] The *Almanach du voyageur* was equally enthusiastic: "The ground floor forms a covered gallery, pierced around the garden by 180 arcades, on each of which there is a streetlight. The back of these galleries is occupied by shops where all sorts of Merchants, different kinds of spectacles, and games, are established."[20] In 1787 an anonymous writer blamed the Palais Royal for seducing customers away from an older shopping district that represented the prefashion values of the honest merchant. "The last farewell of the Quai des Gêvres to the good city of Paris" was an attack on fashion and the modern morals it represented, in which the abandoned street complained: "I was no longer tolerable, it must be admitted, since the Palais-Royal has been transformed into a delicious salon, since every talent finds its theater there, each grace its niche, every folly its sleighbell."[21]

One observer compared the galleries on the ground floor of the Palais Royal to a nonstop fair for young people of both sexes. "What difference does it make to those out for a stroll if the merchants are good or bad? No one goes there to buy things," he noted.[22] Mercier explained why: rents were high, and prices consequently triple or quadruple what they would be elsewhere. Nevertheless, he wrote, "there seems to reign here an attraction that draws money from every pocket, above all those of foreigners, who go nuts over this collection of varied pleasures."[23] Frances Anne Crewe, with her husband and brother in tow, headed straight for the Palais Royal on her first day of sightseeing in Paris. "Mr. Crewe, my Brother Charles and I, walked some time this Morning in the Palais Royalle Gardens—The scene there is the busiest and most entertaining I ever saw—There are shops of every kind, and in short, it is full of Shews and Sights which give it the Appearance of a large Fair—One may go up Stairs and down Stairs, or under the Piazzas, or into the Gardens: All is a Scene of Gaiety and Business, and Chearfullness!"[24] Indeed, even though she intended, she wrote, to see all the sights of Paris, except for Versailles and the Sèvres porcelain factory, both of which were beyond the city walls, the Palais Royal was the only one she visited during her two-month stay in the French capital.

Mrs. Craddock was also impressed by the Palais Royal: "All around it had opened a great number of lovely shops, some restaurants, some cafés, which make the square quite lively and one of the most charming spots to hang out." Looking for a good seat from which to watch a parade, Mr. Craddock checked out one of the cafés. Seeing ladies inside, he motioned his wife to follow him. "He drank coffee, I chocolate, and

I saw, not only gentlemen, but many ladies doing as I did. I remarked very particularly one who seemed to belong to good society...Three ladies came in after her: they asked for chocolate and, while one read the paper, the two others played dominos as did, for that matter, several of the customers."[25] Mrs. Craddock had reason to be surprised: although the Palais Royal continued to be a well-known locale for prostitutes, it was now one of the rare public spaces in which respectable and nonrespectable women mixed. Mercier remarked on this novelty several times in a book that is obsessed with producing a moral taxonomy of modern women. "There [are found] whores, courtesans, duchesses, and honest women; and no one confuses them," he declared.[26]

The idea of a commercial public space that sought to attract anyone with money to spend—women as well as men, without regard for social or moral status—was both novel and disturbing, especially when "pleasures for sale" could and did describe both *bijoux* in the shops and sex on offer.[27] But what disturbed Mercier fascinated others; not only the Craddocks, but Henry Paulin Panon Desbassayns, the planter from Île Bourbon who brought his young daughters Mimi and Mélanie to Paris for their education in 1790. Panon already knew the Palais Royal from an earlier visit. In June 1785, he wrote in his diary: "We strolled by the Palais Royal, we ate waffles and macaroons and left there at ten o'clock. It can be quite amusing to see the quantity of whores who come in as soon as night falls. You can recognize almost all of them by their look. This Palace is a place where you can find everything you might desire. There is an astonishing number of people of every condition."[28]

As we have already seen, Panon was a dedicated tourist. As the French Revolution was heating up, he took Mimi and Mélanie to all the sites he had visited five years earlier. Indeed, he visited every attraction of the capital mentioned in the guidebooks and almanacs, and he concluded with them that the Palais Royal, which he "never tired of examining," was a "perpetual fair. Here you find everything that you could desire. You have to see it to believe it. There is only one Paris in the world. One could add to that 'and only one Palais Royal.'"[29] The hotel where Panon stayed in 1785 was right on the rue Saint-Honoré, not far from the Palais Royal, and strolling there at all times of the day was one of his great pleasures. For Panon, shopgirls, the goods they sold, and the prostitutes who sold themselves, were all part of the charm of the place that was like no other on earth. One evening he brought his very respectable female cousins to the Palais Royal to enjoy with him its pleasures—the crowd, the whores, the shops, the spectacle, and the glitter:

> There was a big crowd. A beautiful evening. We sat in an alley, we occupied ourselves with watching all these hookers. You have to see it to believe it; they have neither honor nor modesty. They carry themselves decently because if the Swiss [guards] noticed any indecency, it would not be good for them. In this same Palais Royal, a store has just opened under the name of <u>Prix fixe.</u> The price of each thing is written on a card beneath it. There is no haggling. We were there at night, everything was beautiful and sparkled.[30]

Panon Desbassayns was not the only traveler who found magic in the way the Palais Royal was lit up at night. A young French visitor named François Cognel recalled: "We left at nine o'clock in order to enjoy the brilliant sight offered by the Palais-Royal, illuminated not only by a streetlight between each arcade, but by the quantity of lamps with which the shops are lighted; these make the richness apparent, and form a striking contrast with the dark paths under the chestnut trees."[31] If the dark paths facilitated the commerce of the prostitutes, the bright lights made shopping, like whoring, an evening activity, but more respectable, because bathed in light.

New commercial spaces such as the Palais Royal, which combined shopping with other forms of entertainment, reflected new attitudes toward consumption that transformed Paris into a commercial mecca in the second half of the eighteenth century and attracted both women and men into the streets and the shops.[32] Whereas elite customers traditionally depended on suppliers to come to their homes to transact business in private (as in Boucher's *The Milliner*, fig. 1.16), they were now lured into the marketplace by the sociable and commercial pleasures it offered. Appropriately accompanied, ladies in search of inkstands, writing paper, and goose quills could surely be seen strolling in this public space where goods from around the globe called out to them.

Parisian weeklies such as the *Feuille nécessaire* and its successor, the *Avantcoureur*, served as venues for free commercial publicity for the mercers, amid cultural news of all sorts. For the journalist, ads were an easy source of copy that attracted readers by mirroring and supporting the commercial and leisured sociability of fashionable shops and cafés. Not surprisingly, then, the newspapers, magazines and other periodicals that featured these ads could be found in the most fashionable Parisian locales and "in nearly all the cafés"—as visitors learned by reading the *Almanach du voyageur*.[33]

The *Avantcoureur* informed its readers of a wide range of fashions and novelties, from new plays to new medical remedies and scientific discoveries, and including inventions and new commercial products offered for sale, such as the "new paper prepared for learning how to write" announced on 2 April 1770.[34] Charles Granchez regularly listed shipments of new goods arriving at his shop, Le Petit Dunkerque, in the columns of the *Avantcoureur*. The rhythm of fashion was conveyed in his regular listings of new items, such as the "steel pens as flexible as goose quills," which the public learned of in July 1770. Some advertising copy was targeted specifically at a female market, such as news of new cosmetics and, on 18 May 1772, news that "economical steel pens from England designed for writing" were available in a shop just up the street from Le Petit Dunkerque. These pens, the notice reads, "never get dull and always form the same character of writing. They are for this reason very suitable for people, for ladies in particular, who are not in the habit or do not wish to take the trouble to cut their nibs. As these steel nibs are fitted into ordinary quills they are just as light and easy to use."[35]

The busiest shopping season for fashionable goods was at New Year's, when gifts were traditionally exchanged. Frances Anne Crewe was surprised to find the French so caught up in this holiday practice when she arrived in Paris on 26 December 1786. On 2 January she wrote in her diary: "Every one who came here last Night talked of Ettrennes, that is of the Presents which People had made to each other on Account of it's being New Year's Day; for this Custom is so general that they all complain of it's being abolished; and indeed I should think It must occasion a vast deal of mutual Trouble."[36] John Andrews, another English visitor, got into the swing of holiday shopping and advised his reader of where to find the best shops, especially if he had female friends or relatives back home expecting souvenirs. "During the latter days of the year, on the last especially, be sure to repair to the Palais marchand," he wrote in *Letters to a Young Gentleman on his Setting out for France* (1784); "you will there find a world of those things which the philosopher of old congratulated himself for not wanting. But that philosopher did not live at Paris, nor probably much in the female circle: if he had, it is highly probable, that however he might have affected to slight these things on his own account, he would quickly have found them useful in obtaining and preserving the good graces of his fair acquaintance." Andrews described the Palais Marchand, a grand shop on the rue Saint-Honoré, as "a repertory of all those ornaments and decorations, that constitute so capital a part of the wants and desires of womankind."[37]

Trouble for consumers was business for shopkeepers, who advertised heavily in the run up to the new year. Readers of the *Feuille nécessaire* were encouraged to forego the traditional (and inexpensive) gift of flowers for something more original, if just as ephemeral, from the mercer's shop. On 31 December 1759, the editor ran the following notice under the heading *Étrennes*: "There is an infinity of pretty bagatelles that can be offered as presents to people who would not accept substantial gifts. Such are all the little novelties that are found chez Sieur *Chervain*, Merchant, at the large shop, rue Tiquetonne; these are of the sort to be distributed and received without any more consequence than the flowers that they imitate." Chervain was pleased to offer an array of trinkets made of Chinese wicker, including an inkstand in the shape of an exotic bird. The reader was assured that the proprietor "has had his shop suitably furnished and decorated to receive persons of distinction who do him the honor of visiting him during the New Year's season."[38]

In December 1771, the *Affiches de Paris* commented on the degree to which the most mundane items were now subject to fashion in a notice for "Peruvian seals"—a novelty item available at the shop of its inventor in the heart of the Marais. These novelty seals were handsomely enameled, could be purchased by the dozen or half-dozen, and created a different kind of impression than the traditional coat of arms. Rather than asserting the dignity of the letter writer's station, these seals were engraved with "gallant symbols for love, friendship, gratitude, filial tenderness, greetings of all sorts, New Year's, birthdays, weddings, etc. There are [seals] for military valor and for other traits." They came attractively packaged "in an envelope, as much to create a pleasant surprise for the person who opens it, as to protect them from any friction that might damage them, even though [they are] quite solid." The inventor was marketing his seals both as a gift item for the New Year and to those who might want to use them to seal their own New Year's greetings to friends and family.[39]

Two things are particularly noteworthy about this new product. First, it would have appealed especially to those modern persons whose sense of identity was not bound up with that of their family—especially those whose families were nothing to brag about and had no coat of arms. Although Mercier was in general a critic of fashion, he would certainly have preferred the "Peruvian seals" to a popular alternative—those with fake coats of arms:

> Our vanity is pretty laughable, but never as much as when we try to create imaginary ancestors for ourselves, and after having nourished ourselves with this sort of nonsense, come to puff ourselves up with a pride equal to our credulity. Of all the petty things of which the human spirit is capable, this seems to be the most miserable and the most ridiculous.
> Out of a hundred letters, whose seal is engraved with a coat of arms, ninety-nine have a fake seal.[40]

Nonetheless, in 1787 Louis-Mayeul Chaudon advised in his *Nouveau manuel épistolaire* against using seals that included "galant or funny emblems" when writing to those "who deserve our respect or consideration." Chaudon reinforced his opposition to gallant seals in one of the sample letters that made up most of his book. Under the category "Gifts" he included the following letter: "Letter to M. l'abbé de ***, in sending him a Seal: Here it is, my dear FRIEND, this seal that you wanted so much. May it seal for a long time the secrets of friendship! I have had it made with a monogram, where our two names are intertwined, just as our hearts are joined. I did not think it possible to engrave it with the emblems you proposed: true attachment must be accompanied by simple ornaments. Our names should suffice. &c. &c."[41]

Also significant is the fact that the novelty seals were given a name that was both exotic and referred to a popular epistolary novel, Françoise de Graffigny's *Lettres d'une Peruvienne*. The seals, with their little greetings, were a far cry from the complex Peruvian technology of knotting ribbons or strings, by means of which Graffigny's heroine wrote to her fiancé before learning to use the European technologies of pen and paper, but the point here was surely to give a new French product an exotic reference with fashionable epistolary associations.[42]

The Peruvian seals were the novelty item of a season, but, from the 1750s on, mercers teamed with gold, lacquer, and enamel workers to produce and sell a whole variety of little containers (*étuis* and *nécessaires*), including those designed to hold sealing wax, and others that held ink, metal pen nibs and holders, and served as "pocket écritoires" (see figs. 5.2a and 5.2b). Made by the same craftsmen and sold in the same shops were similarly decorated snuffboxes, boxes to hold beauty marks or *mouches*, and little sewing kits. These were the expensive trinkets that tempted foreigners and Parisians alike, and which could serve as tokens of love or friendship, especially when ornamented with a miniature portrait. Less expensive versions were available, too. The

5.2a. Container thought to be designed for holding sealing wax (Paris, 1767–68) by Jean-Joseph Barrière. Gold and enamel. Waddesdon, The Rothschild Collection (The National Trust). 2815 (stolen). © The National Trust, Waddesdon Manor.

Musée Grobet-Labadié (Marseille) has a collection of small boxes and cases decorated in colorful straw marquetry that held toilette, needlework, and writing supplies (see fig. 5.3). In gold and enamel, *vernis martin*, or humble straw, such an array of little boxes created an aesthetically harmonious material world in which letter writing joined the two other domestic pursuits associated with ladies: needlework and the *toilette*.

At Le Petit Dunkerque, Granchez made sure to place a special ad every December in the *Avantcoureur* with gift ideas from his shop. In December 1769, for example, his notice called attention to the "innumerable objects for the New Year with which French and foreign industry has enriched the shop of sieur Granchez this year." Among these were "figures in imported porcelain; paper for writing without ink using any sort of metal except iron and steel; memory tablets for writing at night without light." Three years later, Granchez's December listing featured "Secretaries in a Chinese taste, decorated with paintings and bronzes," that, although quite new and valuable, were moderately priced.[43] Mercier noted that Le Petit Dunkerque was so mobbed during the first week of January that the proprietor had to hire a guard to maintain

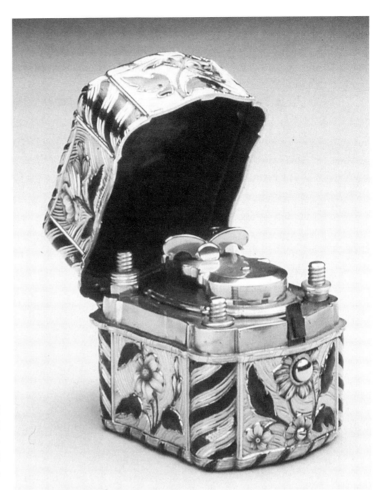

5.2b. Container with inkpot and pen (1750–52) by Julien Berthe. Gold and enamel. Waddesdon, The Rothschild Collection (The National Trust). 2766 (stolen). © The National Trust, Waddesdon Manor.

5.3. Collection of straw boxes and containers (18th–19th century). Musée Grobet-Labadié, Marseille.

order among all those who wanted to hear their friends say, on opening their gift: "It's from Le Petit Dunkerque!"[44]

Le Petit Dunkerque opened in 1767 on the quai de Conti, just across the river from the rue Saint-Honoré at the foot of the Pont Neuf and the beginning of the rue Dauphine. Granchez had opened his first shop, the Perle d'Orient, in the town of Dunkirk, a city that thrived on the transchannel trade with England.[45] Now he was bringing both English products and English marketing techniques—attractive shop design with plate glass windows and aggressive advertising in the metropolitan press—to Paris, where Le Petit Dunkerque would become the most celebrated commercial establishment.

The baronne d'Oberkirch, who visited Le Petit Dunkerque on several trips to Paris in the 1780s, suggested that its appeal was the same as that of the goods it sold: "Nothing is as pretty and brilliant as this shop, filled with *bijoux* and golden trinkets."[46] Mercier completed the picture by making the connection back to the homes in which these purchases would be displayed: "The *bijoux* of Le Petit Dunkerque seem to be in harmony today with our little apartments, our pretty furniture, our clothes and our hairstyles," he concluded. "There are thus in everything hidden rapports, which have their origin and their connection."[47]

In 1773 an anonymous poet commemorated a visit to Le Petit Dunkerque by the dauphine, Marie-Antoinette, with verses that compared the beauty of the client with that of the goods found in the shop:

> In order to charm our DAUPHINE
> In your [shop] are found together
> From both England and China
> The most finely embellished *bijoux*:
> But the day that this Beauty
> Came to choose with her own hand
> No, nothing as rare as She
> Was in your shop.[48]

Through this unified aesthetic, domestic interiors, shops, and the fashionably dressed and coiffed ladies who moved between them became part of a single world. Inkstands, letter paper, and writing tables were elements of this world, and the correspondence conducted with them was one of the key means of expanding it, replicating in reverse the journeys made by products that found their way to the shops and cafés of Paris.

Shops and cafés may have offered different pleasures to the urban elite, but the role of the shopkeeper and café owner were very much the same: both made available for local consumption exotic novelties in an atmosphere that promoted mixed-gender sociability and blurred the line between noble and commoner. Carolyn Sargentson has noted the similarity between the interior of Le Petit Dunkerque and the equally fashionable Café Militaire. Both featured the mirrors, mahogany, and gilding that characterized the salons where noncommercial sociability was practiced and which they studiously imitated. Indeed, Mercier referred to cafés as "mirrored salons."[49] Andrew

McClellan argues that Gersaint was the first mercer to claim for himself the identity of a gentleman and for his shop that of a refined sociable space, modeled on the salon and the collector's *cabinet*. The sign that Watteau painted to hang outside and represent Gersaint's shop presents, in McClellan's words, "an image of sociability centered on art" and its proprietor as "the purveyor of the good life."[50]

Unlike the salon, however, the shop and café were public and commercial spaces that made claims to taste—to its formation, commodification, and consumption— and were open to all respectable ladies and gentlemen, such as those anonymous couples inspecting the merchandise on Watteau's shop sign. Shops and cafés were less intimate but also less exclusive than the salons to which one needed an invitation for dinner or supper or a private chamber music concert, and the polite conversation that accompanied it. Like books, periodicals, and public courses and clubs, shops and cafés spread polite (and sometimes Enlightened) sociability beyond the walls of salons and into the commercial public sphere. Like letter writing, strolling among the shops of the Palais Royal or along the rue Saint-Honoré was one way in which a lady could expand her horizons. The purchases she made on such an expedition allowed her not only to exercise her taste and participate in the culture of fashion but to bring the most distant and exotic lands into her own home and then to tranship them by means of her correspondence with distant friends and family members.

The latest goods and news of their arrival in far-flung provinces also traveled from the capital, so that women in the provinces did not have to make the trip to Paris themselves. "Everything that comes to Paris is not meant to stay there," wrote Mercier. "Materials arrive in order to be worked; then they depart, embellished by that exquisite taste that gives them a new form." Carters operating out of a central office in Paris trucked merchandise, packages, and furniture to provincial cities, facilitating distribution to local merchants.[51] Local merchants established relationships with their Parisian colleagues, who shipped them goods in the latest style. The records of Mme Blakey, the proprietor of the *magasin anglais* on the rue des Prouvaires in Paris, reveal that a substantial part of her business was with clients in the provinces and the colonies.[52]

The press spread the word of Parisian fashion far and wide, so that over time the difference between Parisian and provincial taste was precisely that—time. The purpose of the press was to narrow the temporal and thus the spatial gap between Paris and the provinces. Beginning in the 1740s, Parisian magazines such as the *Avantcoureur* and, in the 1780s, those devoted exclusively to fashion such as the *Cabinet des Modes* brought foreign, colonial, and provincial readers information about the latest fashions, including fashions in epistolary furniture and furnishings. A sampling of the provincial *affiches* shows that they too carried notices of interest to fashion-conscious letter writers. On 1 January 1778, for example, Sieur Tessa placed a notice in Bordeaux's local paper advising readers that he had "every sort of *bijouterie* and *mercerie* in the latest taste" in stock for New Year's, including inkstands and "leather portfolios, equipped with scissors & penknives," which had just arrived from London. The upholsterer Lapoujade ran several ads that year listing "all sorts of furniture in the latest taste."[53]

New businesses also announced themselves in the local papers, conveying news from the capital in another form. "Sieur Poirier of Paris, Student of the first Valet-de-Chambre-Upholsterer ordinary of the King," read an announcement printed in the *Affiches de Provence* in September 1778, "offers his talents to the public for all sorts of furniture in the latest taste."[54] That same year "le sieur *Louis Simon*, painter, who has worked for several Princes & Gentlemen of the Court," advised readers of the *Affiches de Bourdeaux* of his skill in "the art of imitating Asian lacquers." He offered to apply his talents to "all types of furniture," including secretaries.[55] Sieur Monville, "newly arrived in this City," informed readers of the same paper that he made and sold "all sorts of handiwork out of cardboard, such as dressing tables, secretaries, *nécessaires*, lecterns fitted with inkwell and powderbox."[56]

Fashionable writing supplies could also be ordered directly from Paris through agents who undertook commissions for those who were unable to visit the capital themselves. One Sieur Sarazin, known, he said, as *Saladin*, announced in the *Affiches de Picardie* that he made trips to Paris from his home in Amiens twice a month and offered his services in making small purchases for provincial clients.[57] Chaudon included among his model letters one to "a Paris correspondent," in which the writer, somewhere in the neighborhood of Orléans, apologized for asking him to do her yet another favor before launching into a long list of items she would like him to purchase on her behalf, including "a writing table, 32 inches by 21, in walnut, with the top covered in leather; an inkstand in the side drawer."[58] Fashion intermediaries, from purchasing agents to journalists, merchants, and craftsmen, connected provincial ladies to the capital and thus to the larger world through fashion and commerce.

Fashionable Inkstands

In Watteau's shop sign, the Chinese assistant who crates up the old to make way for the new both signals the new name of the shop and figures the vast quantities of Asian goods that were taking Europe by storm. Serving initially as ballast for ships returning from the East, the crates of porcelain arriving at Atlantic ports from China and Japan propelled the taste for all things Asian known as "chinoiserie," from tea cups and incense burners to folding fans and porcelain *magots*.[59] By midcentury, chinoiserie defined the mercers' trade as it transformed both the interiors and the daily lives of the women who were its major purchasers. But the mercers did not just sell Asian objects to European customers; over time, design and *enjolivement* became increasingly significant aspects of the mercer's trade. This might entail having lacquered chests imported from Japan and China knocked down for the cabinetmakers to make into decorative trays or boxes, or veneered onto the frames of writing tables or secretaries. Through such "design by assembly," as Carolyn Sargentson has noted, "the mercers created new types of goods and integrated oriental objects into the Parisian registers of fashion and taste."[60]

Holding pride of place in the trade card François Boucher designed for Gersaint twenty years after Watteau painted his shop sign is an example of the mercer's hybrid

5.4. François Boucher, trade card of Edme Gersaint (1740). Bibliothèque nationale de France.

art: a cabinet veneered with a Japanese lacquer panel and finished with fine French hinges (see fig. 5.4). The text of the card emphasizes the exotic origins of Gersaint's wares: "At the Pagoda. Gersaint, Merchant-Jeweler on the Notre-Dame Bridge sells all sorts of hardware, new and in [the latest] taste, jewelry, mirrors, cabinet paintings, *pagodes*, Japanese lacquer and porcelains, shells and other natural history items, stones, agates, and in general, all curious and foreign merchandise." Inkstands, which sat on a table or desk and held the letter writer's necessities sold by the stationers—ink, powder or sand to dry it, pens, sealing wax and candles to melt it, and a bell to call a servant—were the sort of thing that inspired mercers like Gersaint to the heights of "design by assembly." They had come into use in the sixteenth century, when writing had become first a noble and then a gentlemanly practice. Until the eighteenth century, the finest ones were crafted out of precious metals, some by the leading sculptors of the day.[61] With the simultaneous development of letter writing as a female practice, and the import and manufacture of porcelain and faience in Europe, inkstands were transformed.

One design featured three Chinese porcelain cups set into delicate gilt bronze holders and then laid out on a French lacquer tray—just like the tea set that figures among the goods shown on Gersaint's trade card. At the rear are three chinoiserie figures in white porcelain and a two-branched candelabra in gilt bronze (see fig. 5.5).[62]

5.5. Chinese porcelain inkstand with French mounts on tray of *vernis martin* (Kangxi, early 1700s; France, ca. 1750). 20.3 × 35.6 × 26.7 cm. Collection of the J. Paul Getty Museum, Los Angeles, California. 76.DF.12.

A more elaborate version in Chinese style but German porcelain has been described as "a scene in a Chinese garden" (see fig. 5.6). Here three porcelain cups with ormolu mounts and covers are again set on a lacquer tray; mounted at the rear is a gilt screen laced with porcelain flowers on gilded vines; at the center of the screen are a female Chinese figure with a small clock at her left and a child on her right; two candleholders float from the bottom of the screen. Sargentson considers the clock the epitome of the mercer's creative role in the design of fashionable goods.[63]

The figures known as *pagodes* or *magots* that are incorporated into these inkstands were popular collectibles from the late seventeenth century through the middle decades of the eighteenth, when chinoiserie was at the height of fashion. Indeed, *pagodes* and *magots* were the epitome of fashion (and bad taste) for those like Denis Diderot and Louis-Sébastien Mercier who criticized it.[64] They are littered throughout the rococo profusion of goods for sale in the trade card Boucher designed for Gersaint. Boucher furnished the settings of the genre scenes he painted in the 1740s with just such trinkets (see figs. 1.5 and 1.16). For the painter, such objects were signs of modern taste and femininity. For the women who owned them, they were also emissaries of a distant world that expanded her horizons even as they filled and decorated the spaces in which she lived.

Sometimes *pagodes* and *magots* were simply sold as knickknacks, to sit on a shelf or the top of a commode, as we see them in Boucher's genre paintings and trade card, but the mercers also fashioned them into useful items, from potpourris and incense burners to candelabra and, as we have seen, inkstands. The most popular *magot* was the *hotei*—a laughing Buddha with a big belly that at least one mercer found convenient for an inkstand (see fig. 5.7): here the *hotei* is made of French porcelain from Chantilly and set in a bronze mount; between his legs is a globe that opens to reveal the inkwell, pounce-pot, and other epistolary needs.[65]

5.6. Chinoiserie inkstand (Louis XV period). Meissen porcelain on a lacquer tray with gilt bronze mounts. *Connaissance des Arts* 72 (February 1958). Photo: CDA archives/akg–images.

Like the belly of the Buddha, the globe was a convenient shape to contain ink and powder, while serving also as an icon of the global reach of epistolarity. The most famous *écritoire à globes* is a model made at Sèvres around 1765 (see fig. 5.8): the inkpot is in a terrestrial globe, and the pounce-pot is in a celestial one. This inkstand seems to have been made for Mme Adélaïde; another, now in the Residenzmuseum (Munich), belonged to the Electress Elizabeth of Bavaria.[66]

The production of porcelain inkstands was driven by the expansion of letter writing to the ladies who bought porcelain tea, coffee, and chocolate sets and decorated their rooms with figurines and other decorative objects made of Chinese or European porcelain. Enameled tin or *tôle*, which was invented by the English to imitate both porcelain and lacquer, expanded the market for such items. In 1770 the *Avantcoureur* announced that a *vernis sur tôle* factory was now producing in Paris inkstands and other goods "of tested strength," which "joined to the advantage of a price well below that of silver and porcelain a more agreeable look due both to the variety of finishes and the beauty of the designs." These were fashionable modern goods, characterized by "utility, taste, and decoration in imitation of silver and porcelain following the newest and best chosen models."[67] Mme Blakey sold a wide array of goods decorated with *tôle* plaques in her *magasin anglais*, including inkstands.[68] Pierre Verlet reports on an inkstand in "enameled tôle with gilt bronze mounts" in a private collection that bears

5.7. Inkstand of soft-paste porcelain from Chantilly in the form of a *hotei*. Former collection of F. H. Fitzhenry. Hôtel Drouot, 13–16 December 1909.

5.8. Inkstand (1758). Possibly by Charles-Nicolas Dodin. Sèvres porcelain. Inv. C488. By kind permission of the Trustees of the Wallace Collection, London.

the mark of Le Petit Dunkerque.[69] The simple inkwell in Labille-Guiard's portrait of the letter writer seems to be made of *tôle*; perhaps it too was purchased at Le Petit Dunkerque.

However, one did not have to be one of the well-to-do customers of the mercers on the rue Saint-Honoré to own a fashionable inkstand or inkwell. Factories throughout the French provinces produced such useful items in the latest taste out of the tin-glazed earthenware known as faience, a material that was considerably cheaper than porcelain. Faience might not be as fine or set in ormolu mounts, but the inkstands and inkwells fashioned out of it had rococo curves, "Chinese" figures, and the colorful (often floral) patterns on white backgrounds that distinguished Chinese porcelain and its European imitations. Like porcelain, faience took off in France in response to the import of Asian porcelain in the seventeenth century. In Paris, it was sold by both the mercers and members of the guild of *fayenciers*.[70] A factory at Nevers, which had been established by Italians in the sixteenth century was the first to transform Italian into French faience by way of chinoiserie. Soon there were faience factories in every French province. In the 1740s, a new firing technique already in use in Germany and Holland permitted the development of polychrome ware (and, in particular, the use of reds), for which Strasbourg and Marseille became particularly well known. French faience came into its own in the second half of the eighteenth century, as pottery became fashionable for the first time by responding to cosmopolitan influences and meeting and creating demand with new technologies and design innovation.[71] French faience factories produced the whole panoply of goods that the porcelain factories were crafting for the wealthiest consumers, helping to make Asian-influenced ceramics the primary material of modern practices of sociability, individuality, and taste.

Two faience inkstands from Lunéville in eastern France are all rococo curves and include candleholders in their practical designs;[72] the decorations on one from Lyon look remarkably like the floral silks for which that city was known (fig 5.9). An inkstand made in Sinceny (in Picardy, northeast of Paris) in the middle of the eighteenth century takes the form of a writing stand and is elaborately decorated in chinoiserie (fig. 5.10). A similar inkstand made in Rouen is decorated in the Moorish style (fig. 5.11).

The design that most reflected gendered notions of female letter writing, however, was the inkwell in the shape of a heart. As painters insisted on associating women, letters, and love, so too did the faience factories. Today heart-shaped inkwells can be found in museum collections throughout France. An example in the Musée du Nouveau Monde in La Rochelle is typical, with a hole pierced through the center of the flower decorating each point of the heart to hold quills, and a large opening in the center for ink (fig. 5.12). The center hole in a similar bichrome model in the Musée de Louviers in Normandy is fitted with a candleholder, to facilitate both writing and sealing a letter. Another version, in Quimper's Musée de la Faïence, is made of enameled terra

5.9. Inkstand (second half of the 18th century). Faience of Lyon and gilt bronze. Musée des Tissus et des Arts décoratifs, Lyon. MAD 1262. Photo: Pierre Verrier.

5.10. Inkstand (mid-18th century). Faience of Sinceny. Musée du Louvre, Paris. Inv. OA3835. Photo: Réunion des Musées Nationaux/Art Resource, New York.

5.11. Inkstand with Moorish decoration. Faience of Rouen. Musée Lambinet, Versailles.

cotta from a local factory and has three openings into which a pen could be dipped, rather than one, and a candleholder at the top of the heart. Small and inexpensive, inkwells such as these may have been given as gifts or tokens of love or friendship from one correspondent to another. Such a practice is suggested by a heart-shaped inkwell made of enameled terra cotta from the Eure (fig. 5.13). The name "Jean Guinces" incised into the clay is surrounded by little hearts. Perhaps it was meant to function as a miniature does in a genre painting, to remind the woman of the man to whom she is supposed to be writing. What more appropriate gift from a man to his lover or wife on his departure?

With the use of faience and porcelain fashioned into hearts and decorated with flowers and chinoiserie, such mundane items as inkwells were introduced into the world of the women for whom fashion and taste were important and writing was central for the first time. Bringing epistolary goods such as these into harmony with the gendered norms of taste and comportment that shaped women's lives made them not only fashionable but feminized; that is, they were made acceptable and even attractive for women to own, handle, and display.

5.12. Heart-shaped inkwell. Faience. Collection Musée d'Orbigny-Bernon, La Rochelle.

5.13. Heart-shaped inkwell (18th century). Enamelled terra cotta. Eure. Musée National de Céramique, Sèvres. Inv. MNC10300. Photo: Réunion des Musées Nationaux/ Art Resource, New York.

At the Stationer's

The smallest of the purchases made in the fashionable shops were the most mundane items stocked by stationers—quills, ink, pounce, sealing wax, and paper. Such goods were traditionally sold in the Latin Quarter and near the law courts for the convenience of the students, clerks, notaries, and lawyers who primarily bought them; now, however, stationers were setting up shop in the faubourg Saint-Germain, where ladies and gentlemen lived and shopped, and just across the Pont Neuf from the rue Saint-Honoré. Stepping outside Le Petit Dunkerque at the foot of the bridge, a customer would find herself within a block or two of the most fashionable stationers, whose shops were located up the rue Dauphine to the carrefour de Bussy and in neighboring streets such as the rue de Bussy and the rue de Seine.[73]

Fashionable stationers not only located their shops in neighborhoods patronized by ladies and gentlemen, they also placed themselves under signs meant to attract a fashionable clientele. Some placed themselves under signs that evoked faraway places and illustrated their trade cards with exotic images. The printed trade cards were distributed by the stationers and pasted into the ledgers, notebooks, and portfolios they sold. Those that have been preserved give us a glimpse, not only of the variety of goods the stationers offered the letter writer, but how they marketed them to the fashionable writing public.[74]

On the rue Betizy, Niodot sold his wares Au Grand Empereur, while Larcher placed himself À la Teste Noire. Two trade cards for Larcher show both the importance and the fantasy quality of the exotic as advertising (see figs. 5.14a and 5.14b). One sports the head of an African, while the other, which is dated 1756, is ornamented with the head of a man in a feather-crested turban, denoting some unspecified Orient. The paper goods sold in the stationers' shops had little connection to Africa or the Orient, but as we have seen, mercers typically used exotic references to sell their wares.[75] More squarely within the discourse of letter writing was Louis Boullanger's shop on the rue de la Truanderie, which he placed Au Puits d'Amour, that is, at the fountain of love (see fig. 5.15).

But as paper was the stationers' stock in trade, several of them chose to place themselves under signs that referred to specific types of small format writing paper, appropriate for the kind of letters ladies wrote: Blanchard, À la Couronne d'Or; Blanché,

5.14a. Trade card of Larcher, "À la Teste Noire." Bibliothèque national de France. Est Li 4G.2 fol.

5.14b. Trade card of Larcher, "À la Teste Noire" (1756).
Bibliothèque national de France. Est Li 4G.2 fol.

RUE DE LA TRUANDERIE,

A droite, en entrant par la rue S. Denis,

AU PUITS D'AMOUR.

LOUIS BOULLANGER, Marchand à Paris,
Vend toutes sortes de Papiers fins tant de France que
de Hollande, pour l'Ecriture, pour l'Impreſſion & le Deſſein,
de toutes grandeurs : toutes sortes de Regiſtres pour les
Marchands, Banquiers, & tout ce qui concerne la four-
niture des Bureaux : Cartes de toutes grandeurs : Plomb pour
la Chaſſe ; il vend auſſi la bonne Encre double & luiſante :
le tout en gros & en détail, & à juſte prix. A PARIS.

5.15. Trade card of Louis Boullanger,
"Au Puits d'Amour." Archives de
Paris. D43Z.2.

Au Griffon; Le Testu, À la Petite Romaine; Des Lauriers, À l'Enfant Jésus (see fig. 5.16).[76]
In the 1780s, the *Encyclopédie méthodique* listed fifteen varieties of writing paper, differen-
tiated by size and usage, all of which could be made by different manufacturers and
marked by a variety of watermarks. But the variety of paper sold in the shops far ex-

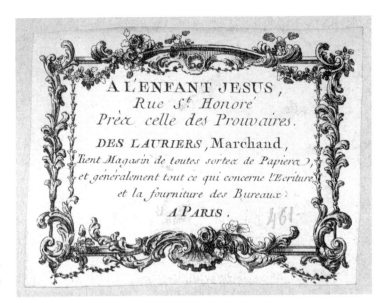

5.16. Trade card of Des Lauriers, "À l'Enfant Jésus." Archives de Paris. D43Z.2.

ceeded the sizes and grades designated by manufacturers, and indicates the importance of fashion in the developing and marketing of paper products as much as size and quality.

Among the dozens of items the stationer Jollivet advertised for sale on one of his trade cards was "letter paper, gilded or nongilded in several sizes" and, on another, "some very nice Dutch paper, very fine, and others, beaten, washed, cut, gilded, glazed, *satiné*, prepared in all sizes, for writing and drawing well" (see fig. 5.17). Langlois, whose paper goods ranged from "all the beautiful wallpapers appropriate for decorating Ladies' Boudoirs" to the paper and scissors for the fashionable activity of *découpage*, brought his huge list of goods to an end with "all sorts of blank writing paper, from France as well as Holland, and for letters, gilt-edged and with vignette, very fine sealing wax . . . sealing wafers in all colors; all sorts of pens, cut and uncut, powders of gold and boxwood, toothpicks, double and glossy ink. All at a fair price" (see fig. 5.18).

Drying one's ink with gold powder was surely one way to make a letter more elegant, especially a letter written on gilt-edged paper. Sealing wax also offered a range of possibilities. At the Porte-Feuille Anglais both ink and sealing wax came in "all colors." Niodot, who advertised himself as "Stationer and Manufacturer of Spanish [Sealing] Wax," notified the public that he "sold wholesale and retail the true Spanish Wax, red, black, green, brilliant, in all colors, ambered and musked."

In 1746 Louis Racine brought his daughter in the provinces up to speed on the latest in Parisian letter-writing fashions. "[Ladies] are writing on paper of every color, with inks of every color," he announced. "This one, which is mourning paper, is no longer in fashion, because they were using it a month ago. The two letters that follow are on papers so fashionable that the merchant was sold out of them."[77] One of these, according to the editor of Racine's correspondence, "is decorated with colorful vignettes; at the top is a fashionably dressed lady, to replace the word *madame*, and at the end, to

A L'IMAGE N DAME
Ruë de Bussi vis a vis
l'Hôtel Imperial Faubourg
St Germain.
A PARIS.

JOLLIVET, *Marchand ordinaire du Roi et de M.*
la D'auphine, vend de très beau papier de Hollande très
fin, et autres, batu, lavé, coupé, doré, glacé, satiné, préparé
de toutes grandeur, pour bien écrire et dessiner, de toutes
sortes de Papier de Musique, d'excellentes plumes de
Hollande, et des mieux taillées, Encre de la Chine, de la
plus belle Cire d'Espagne de toute couleur, des Canifs de
toutes façons, des registres de toutes grandeurs, des porte-
feuilles de Maroquin rouge, et noir, des plus à la mode
fermants à clef, et d'autres manière, des tablettes de
Maroquin des plus nouvelles, garnies d'argent, des écritoirt
de toutes grandeurs, garnies d'argent fermtes à clef et decouvte
pour mettre sur des Bureaux; des Cachets, porte crayons, et com-
pas d'argt. Couteaux d'ivoir, et la Veritble encre double et luisante
et des Marchandises des plus nouvelles et à juste prix.

5.17. Trade card of Jollivet, "À l'Image de Notre Dame." Bibliothèque nationale de France. Est Li 4G.1 fol.

À LA RENOMMÉE,

Rue S. Jacques, vis-à-vis la Fontaine S. Severin, à Paris.

LANGLOIS, Marchand, vend & achete toutes sortes d'Estampes tant anciennes que modernes, des plus habiles Graveurs d'Italie, de France, de Flandre, d'Allemagne, d'Hollande, les met en Quadre doré, uni & façonné, rouge & noir, sous de beaux verres blancs, & les belles Estampes en maniere noire pour peindre sous verre ; vend & achete toutes sortes de beaux Tableaux des plus habiles Peintres, fait venir & vend les belles & grandes feuilles des Indes & de la Chine, tant à fleurs, oiseaux, que personnages, pour garnir toutes sortes de Cabinets & Paravents; les colle de la derniere propreté sur les chassis ; fait & vend aussi tous les beaux papiers peints propres à garnir les Cabinets de toilettes des Dames, & les fait coller sur place; vend les papiers en vrai marbre pour les cheminées, les papiers fins en façon de bois de pallissandres, violettes, bois de nœuds & d'écailles, les beaux papiers d'Allemagne à fleurs d'or & d'argent, les feuilles d'or & d'argent fin unies & matelées pour modeler; les beaux papiers unis en cendrebleu couleur de feu, verdeaux, & généralement toutes autres couleurs; les cartons dorés pour les reliquaires, les belles & véritables découpures d'Allemagne, & les bons ciseaux du même endroit pour les découper, comme aussi les découpures du dernier goût pour les bois de toilettes & de quadrilles ; toutes sortes de grandes découpures tant Françoises que Chinoises, en couleurs, & camayeux pour les dessus de portes, paravents, dessus & devant de cheminées, & panneaux de Cabinets accompagnés de leurs bordures, les papiers en façon de dentelles pour garnir les rayons de lingeries, avec le grand papier bleu d'Hollande pour les coller dessus, les Images de velin de Flandre, tant en blanc qu'en couleurs, des Canons pour dire la Messe de toutes sortes de grandeurs; vend toutes sortes de papiers blancs à écrire, tant de France que d'Hollande & à lettre, dorés sur tranche & à vignettes, cire d'Espagne très-fine & à graveur, pains à cacheter de toutes couleurs; toutes sortes de plumes taillées & non taillées, poudre d'or & de buis, curedents, encre double & luisante. Le tout à juste prix.

De l'Imprimerie de GISSEY, rue de la vieille Bouclerie à l'Arbre de Jessé.

replace that of *servant*, one finds a handsome gentleman making a deep bow."[78] A letter from the duchesse d'Aiguillon to the scientist Maupertuis, probably from around the same time, is written on paper that is similar. Where the greeting should be there is a gentleman with a sword; where the closing should be there is the gentleman again, and then below him and to the right, a lady with a fan. The duchess has written her compliments next to the gentleman and signed her name under the lady. Another of the duchess's letters to Maupertuis was written on paper bordered with pink flowers, and two others were on paper with solid borders of robin's egg blue. Since they are not addressed, it is likely they were sent in matching envelopes.[79]

In 1759 the *Feuille nécessaire* carried a notice for fashionable writing paper from the stationer Flot, located right on the rue Saint-Honoré: "The desire to please has carried the taste for ornament to things that would seem the least susceptible to it," the notice read. "Several years ago someone thought to place a vignette on the border of notepaper; but now these borders have been enriched again. One can find these papers in all sizes, cut-out, painted, and gilded very carefully along the edges, the envelopes trimmed and painted in miniature."[80]

At the Porte-Feuille Anglais on the rue Dauphine, Salmon sold paper and envelopes decorated with spangles [*paillettes*] and vignettes, as well as "white envelopes ready-made for all formats of writing paper, morning notes, visiting cards." On the rue Saint-Martin writing paper was available from Ybert with printed borders and vignettes "in all colors." Perhaps that is where Geneviève de Malboissière bought the decorated paper on which she wrote her New Year's greetings in January 1764. She used one last sheet of this pretty paper for a letter she wrote to her friend Adèle on the eighth (fig. 5.19). Twenty years later, Bernard de Bonnard sent his wife Sophie a letter in which he enclosed two tiny envelopes, each of which also contained a tiny letter (figs. 5.20a and 5.20b). Both paper and envelopes are bordered with a pink design; the edges of the paper are gilded, as is the ink he used to write on it.[81]

The stationer Dubois (also at Le Renommée, like Langlois, see fig. 5.18), noted that "his trade also includes a shop that deals in perfumes, gloves, and mittens of all colors, all sorts of Fans, all sorts of Powders, and fine scents" (see fig. 5.21). The elaborate engraving that forms the frame for this text shows a fan next to a bottle of ink and a quill, and another fan near a deck of cards. If fashion plates are any indication, folding fans such as these were exclusively used by women and were the most common fashionable accessory.[82] The broadening of the stationer's wares to include fashionable goods of all sorts suggests how letter writing and the women who engaged in it were brought into the fashion market by those who supplied them.

"Owning and using fashionably coloured objects was a visual acknowledgement of participation in the social culture of the period," writes Sarah Lowengard.[83] The stationers who enticed women into their shops with the rainbow of colors, the sheen and sparkle, even the scents of inks, powders, and sealing wax, were like the merchants of old who brought the sensory delights of the distant East to those who could otherwise only read or hear about them. It was one of the hallmarks of the

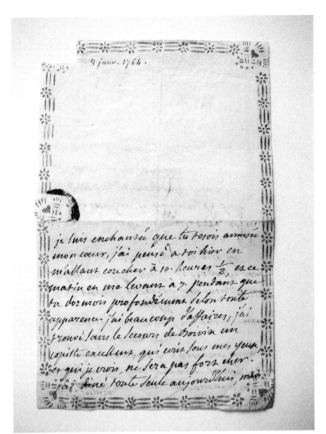

5.19. Geneviève Randon de Malboissière to Adélaïde Méliand, 8 January [1764]. Archives de Beaurepaire. Courtesy of M. Christian de Luppé.

5.20a. Letters from Bernard de Bonnard to Sophie Silvestre, 4 December [1783], in decorated envelopes. Document held in the Archives nationales, Paris. Photo: Atelier photographique des Archives nationales. 352 AP 39.

5.20b. Letter from Bernard de Bonnard to Sophie Silvestre, 4 December [1783]. Document held in the Archives nationales, Paris. Photo: Atelier photographique des Archives nationales. 352 AP 39.

consumer revolution of the eighteenth century to make widely available in permanent shops (rather than transient markets) the riot of colors, tastes, and smells that had previously been available only to the privileged few. Now, a woman of even modest means could walk into a stationer's shop on any day and regale her senses. Moreover, ladies who purchased decorated paper, scented or colored wax, glossy ink, or gold powder would be able to send their correspondents letters that breathed of the Parisian marketplace where the most fashionable goods that delighted all the senses were available. Things had surely come full circle when, in 1789, a fictional visitor from the East could write to a friend back home that a Frenchman would use "flowered paper, delicate as satin, with gilded edges" when writing from Paris, "in order that his letter have the imprint of the capital."[84] Once returned home, a real visitor—more likely to be from the French provinces than the Far East—could turn her letters into sensory postcards of her Paris sojourn and keep alive her own memories of it every time she wrote to a friend.

QUO FAMA VOCAT

Vires acquirit eundo.

A LA RENOMMÉE

Magasin de Papiers au coin des rues Montorgueil
et du Bout du Monde, au bas
des Petits carreaux.
A PARIS.

DUBOIS,

Marchand, Mercier Vend toutes sortes de beau et bon Papier
d'Hollande, et autres, Battu, Lavé pour le Dessin, et la Musique; Cire
d'Espagne très fine, La véritable Encre Double, et luisante, Plummes
d'Hollande, Ecritoires en Maroquin garni fermants a Clef. et Géné-
-ralement tout ce qui concerne les Bureaux des Finances et
autres, et son Commerce. Tient aussi Magasin de Parfumerie, Gants,
et Mitaines de toutes couleurs, toutes sortes d'Eventails, toutes
sortes de Poudres, et Odeurs fines. Tient aussi toutes
sortes de petite Mercerie. Le tout
à juste Prix.

5.21. Trade card of Dubois, "A la Renommée." Archives de Paris. D43Z.2.

Fine Writing Paper: Dutch Ingenuity
Meets French Fashion

Of course, the vast majority of letters were written on plain white paper. But even such apparently ordinary paper could be fashionable, especially because, for all its apparent simplicity, paper was economically the most important commodity used by letter writers.

Pierre Claude Reynard has argued that the tremendous diversification of paper in the eighteenth century was a response to uneven quality as production levels increased, rather than a result of the entrepreneurial spirit to broaden markets through design innovation and the cheapening of output that have generally been seen as characteristic of the consumer revolution.[85] Paper manufacturers did not make small batches of different grades of paper; rather, they sorted the paper they produced by quality and gave each grade a name. The result, as Reynard notes, was that consumers entering the stationer's shop "expected a vast array of papers of differing quality rather than a limited range of perfect sheets." This proliferation of choices transferred some of what Reynard calls the "quality burden" onto customers, who had to develop an eye and a touch in order to exercise discernment in making their purchases.[86] The lady who entered the stationer's shop looking for writing paper had to have practical knowledge to buy the right type of paper for her purposes, acumen to discern quality, taste to recognize elegance, and fashion knowledge to make sure that her purchase was in style.

In the eighteenth century, it was generally agreed that the ideal writing paper was the whitest, thinnest paper that would sustain the action of a sharp quill and fold without tearing—a paper whose fine grain would guide the pen and whose finish would hold the brightest ink without blurring or absorbing it. The blackness of the best ink set off the whiteness of the finest paper.[87] The smooth surface of fine writing paper allowed the writer's pen to glide over it gracefully; that grace would be apparent to the reader in the elegant hand in which words were formed. As postage was calculated on number of sheets, not weight, thinness should be seen as an aesthetic rather than an economic value, one that was shared by many fashionable goods of the eighteenth century. Thick incrustations of precious metals were no longer a sign of good taste: the thinnest veneers on light-weight furniture (such as the desks on which letters were written); the thinnest porcelain tea sets; and at the end of the century, the thinnest gauze for dresses, were all signs of fashion and taste. The aesthetic value—lightness—complemented and supported the cultural value—grace; gracefulness in turn meant not overturning desks, tripping over skirts, spilling one's tea, or blotting or tearing holes in one's letters. It meant being able to negotiate a material world that was fragile and delicately balanced.[88]

Scientists and inventors looked for new ways to achieve black ink and white paper. Traditionally, the way to achieve whiteness was to use the whitest linens and then to clean them rigorously. Because the rags were the manufacturer's greatest expense, really white paper was a luxury.[89] In 1777 the *Almanach sous-verre* was thus pleased to announce the discovery of a plant (probably a variety of cotton) that could be used for making paper. Its virtues were softness, fineness, and whiteness. "It is believed," the *Almanach* reported, "that by mixing it with old linens, one can make a paper that is white and glossy."[90] It thus may come as a surprise that in 1791 this same almanac reported the discovery by a M. de la Vieville of Marseille of a process to make paper blue, rather than white: "*Azured blue of paper.* Discovery of a means of imitating the azured blue that the Dutch give to their paper. After a number of instructive attempts, we have just succeeded in composing a liquor that gives paper this nuance that is so sought after."[91]

Why would anyone want to produce blue writing paper? The answer to this question begins with Dutch ingenuity, but it ends with French fashion. In the early eighteenth century, the Dutch invented a wind-driven paper mill and a new process of pulping rags that revolutionized the paper industry and allowed them to dominate the rapidly expanding market for fine writing and printing paper. The Dutch triumph was at the expense of the French, who were the main exporters of paper until the 1720s. As Joseph de Lalande explained in a treatise he wrote for the French Academy of Sciences in 1761, "About a century ago, all of Europe drew from France the greatest and best part of its paper; but whether because this art was neglected among us, or because the efforts of the Dutch were more successful than ours, in the end they have come to enjoy the largest trade in it."[92]

Everyone agreed that the Dutch enjoyed this supremacy because their paper was superior to the finest French product. One of the Montgolfier brothers backed his claim that the paper they produced in their Annonay mill was "the handsomest paper of the kingdom" by declaring, "We have even frequently equaled the paper of Holland if we haven't surpassed it."[93] Jean-Baptiste Réveillon once claimed that the only glory he sought after wresting the wallpaper market from the English was to do the same to the Dutch in the matter of writing paper—but that triumph was to elude him.[94]

In 1766 Diderot switched from French paper to Dutch paper for his letters. That same year French papermakers admitted privately to selling their paper domestically under false foreign names in order to attract customers; by 1789 one of the most prominent among them was advertising his letter papers openly under Dutch names; and as late as 1814 the Netherlands was forced to prohibit the importation of paper bearing false Dutch watermarks. In 1782 a papermaker from Rouen, who was seeking industry protection from the French state, realized that the paper on which the controller general of finances had responded to his plea was Dutch: "You yourself, Monsieur, in your *Cabinet*, with your own hand, you honor foreign manufactures with your suffrage and your preference," he complained.[95]

After repeated failures by French manufacturers to produce paper using the Dutch mill, the government resorted to industrial espionage: in 1768 the Bureau de commerce sent an inspector on a tour of Dutch mills to learn their secrets. The results of

Inspector Desmarest's investigation were made public in two reports he presented to the Academy of Sciences and distributed to all French paper manufacturers.[96] Desmarest explained Dutch superiority with a narrative that began dubiously with French Huguenots bringing papermaking to the Netherlands in the 1690s, where they were forced to adapt French technology to local conditions. This meant shifting from water power to wind power and developing a new industrial process that produced paper of rough and uneven grain. This problem forced them to develop new processes of sizing and finishing, which resulted in a better glaze, finer grain, smoother paper, and thus the overall finer quality of their paper.[97] They were now able to produce fine paper that lacked only one of the qualities of the ideal: whiteness.

Modern scholars have determined that to solve this problem the Dutch manufacturers added the mineral smaltine, a type of cobalt, to whiten their paper; they can date the introduction of the secret ingredient precisely to 1746, when the regular exploitation of mines in Saxony that produced it began.[98] They have thus confirmed in a precise manner what eighteenth-century consumers observed in the stationers' shops of Paris: that Dutch paper was a little bluish. Lalande did not know precisely what the Dutch were adding to their pulp to give it the blue tint, but he believed that they added it because the salt they used in their production process caused the paper to yellow quickly. "In order to disguise this defect," he explained, "the Dutch came up with the idea of putting blue in their beaters, and today one sees more than ever this bluish tint in their papers: it is not simply a milky white as it used to be, it's an azured white, or rather a pale blue."[99] By the 1760s the Dutch had turned that defect into a distinction: the faint blue tinge was now a pale blue, and it was the blueness that allowed customers to recognize Dutch paper. In a time of untrustworthy watermarks, the distinctive *bleuâtre* of true Dutch paper was its only trustworthy and recognizable mark. As this tint came to be valued as a mark of distinction, it became an object of emulation among inventors as much as the papermaking process of which it was a by-product.

By the time the *Encyclopédie méthodique* came out in the 1780s, Desmarest (who wrote the article on papermaking for it) had to revise the definition of good writing paper given in the original *Encyclopédie*. "The foundation of this paper will be white, or rather it will give the hint of a very light blue, which adds to the brightness of the natural white. . . . In indicating the qualities that are essential to writing paper, I have indicated the qualities of Dutch paper," he noted.[100] French consumers now expected fine writing paper to meet Dutch standards, and these included a blue tint. By 1782 a manufacturer in Provence was producing "a lovely azured paper" and selling it as Dutch paper. A 1788 report on the state of French industry by the intendant of Champagne claimed that a manufacturer in Troyes had managed to imitate fine blue Dutch writing paper so successfully as to have stolen away the monopoly on it.[101] Three years later there was M. de la Vieville in Marseille claiming to have discovered the process by which to achieve the azured blue of Dutch paper.

In order to protect the French paper industry, Louis XV had issued an *arrêt de Conseil* in 1771 that detailed the many attempts by the crown to help the manufacturers since Louis XIV had first tried to implement protectionist trade policies on their behalf in 1697. Once again the king was forced to decree a ban on the exportation (and smuggling) of everything from rags to horses' hooves, raw materials whose scarcity was seen by the paper manufacturers as the cause of the high costs that kept them from being competitive. He upped the penalties for smuggling, prohibited the establishment of paper mills within four leagues of the coast or the frontier, and in a complementary *arrêt* issued the same day, imposed new duties on imported paper. Whereas, before, all paper had been taxed at the same rate, the new duties were graduated according to the quality of the paper, hitting writing paper hardest.[102] And yet Dutch paper continued to be preferred and purchased by those who could afford it.

As the state increased import duties on writing paper to satisfy the manufacturers, Parisian stationers such as Louis Boullanger at Le Puits d'Amour diplomatically assured their customers that they carried "all sorts of fine papers, French as well as Dutch," and all "at a fair price." The premium consumers paid for Dutch paper, however, was steep. The *Almanach parisien* for 1776 advised its readers that common writing paper could be had in packs of twenty-five sheets for 8 sous. Ordinary letter paper cost only a bit more: six sheets for 2 sous. Six sheets of Dutch letter paper, however, was sold at 3 sous, or a premium of 50 percent.[103] The willingness to pay this premium cannot be explained entirely by superior quality. Furthermore, the fashion and taste that shaped consumer choice in the eighteenth century were associated, not with the sort of patriotism that French manufacturers tried to summon, but with the exoticism and cosmopolitanism fostered by Parisian merchants.

"The beauty of fine papers from Holland, and possibly their high price, have always made the French wish to be able to imitate them," Lalande had declared in the 1760s. Abbé Jaubert concurred in his 1773 *Dictionnaire des arts et metiers*. He claimed that the French tried to imitate Dutch paper because they liked the way it looked: "because of its beauty and its lovely color."[104] Because the paleness of blue writing paper had all the delicacy an eighteenth-century sensibility could hope for, it contributed to the subtext of a fashionable letter: the refinement and taste of the woman who sent it. Fine Dutch paper and the quality of the handwriting it supported would reinforce the good impression a lady's letter was supposed to make, and especially its "lightness and delicacy."[105]

As more and more women threw themselves into their correspondence, they did not simply take up paper that was ready-to-hand; rather, writing paper was transformed as women began to use it. The fierce competition between French and Dutch manufacturers for the market in writing paper, and the French zeal to imitate the properties of Dutch paper that made it desirable, suggest the impact of women's letter writing on the commercial economy of the eighteenth century. At the same time, the creation and development of writing supplies within a gendered discourse and market reinforced women's association with letter writing and contributed to the legitimization of writing in women's lives, even as it encouraged the participation of women as agents in the growing consumer economy, its discourses, spaces, and practices. Through their participation in these modern practices of consumption and communication, women did not just become modern: they participated in the modern world in the making.

The Writing Desk

Furniture of the Modern Self

6

Letter writing connected elite Parisian women to the world beyond their homes—whether they were strolling through a world of imported and exotic goods in the fashionable shops of the rue Saint-Honoré and the Palais Royal, or writing to distant friends or family on Dutch paper at a desk veneered in West Indian woods shaped into marquetry designs of Chinese tea ware. Provincial ladies, too, were connected to the capital and the world for which it served as clearinghouse and entrepôt when they read about fashionable writing paper in a Parisian magazine or bought imported goods from fashionable Parisian merchants on trips to the capital or through corresponding or traveling agents. Local merchants touted their Parisian wares, and Parisian-trained craftsmen set up shop in provincial capitals, where their fashion knowledge was as valuable a commodity as their skills.

But letter writing was also a solitary practice that demanded privacy, even if women did not always achieve it. As Annik Pardailhé-Galabrun has shown, the growth of privacy in the eighteenth century was made possible by the multiplication and diffusion of specialized rooms in the Parisian home. Defined by the dictionary of the Académie française as "a place of retreat in which to work, or to converse privately, or to keep papers, books, or hang pictures, or other precious things," the *cabinet* was one of these new private spaces that proliferated in modern houses. "The presence of wall hangings, curtains, a day bed or comfortable armchairs contributed to creating a refuge for relaxation and privacy within these lodgings that were otherwise open on all sides and not conducive to isolation," explains Pardailhé-Galabrun.[1] Henry Havard maintains that the popularity of the cabinet, its fashionableness, began with the précieuses, women known for their writing.[2]

Along with architects, merchants and craftsmen created the material world in which women could develop a new subjectivity and autonomy through letter writing. If paper and ink were the simplest and most ephemeral of writing equipment, the desk, located typically in the cabinet, was the most substantial and complex. The most obvious function of a writing desk was to provide a surface on which to write, which is why desks are considered a form of table. But it also provided storage for writing supplies, and sometimes a ledge on which to place a candle. Indeed, over time, designers of writing desks began to incorporate many of the functions of the inkstand into the desk itself. The most distinctive feature of the writing desk, however, was the locked drawer in which letters received could be securely stored. The locked drawer signifies the importance of privacy to epistolary practice, but it also reminds us that to write letters was to engage in correspondence, that letter writing was an intersubjective communicative practice.

We can learn a great deal about the lives of letter-writing women by examining the writing desks that survive in museums and by reading the wide variety of eighteenth-century texts in which such furniture plays a role. Before considering these material and textual sources, however, let us turn to more mundane ones: the daybooks of a Parisian merchant and the inventories of several well-furnished eighteenth-century houses. In them, we will be able to follow epistolary furniture from the shops in which it was purchased into the homes in which it was used. Afterward, we will look more closely at individual pieces, examining their surfaces, opening their drawers, and placing them within the human and feminine context in which they took on meaning.

Daybooks and Inventories: Epistolary Furniture from Shop to Home

Daybooks of mercers, cabinetmakers, and upholsterers track goods at the point of sale; inventories of large houses and estates suggest where they went when they left the shop. However, the descriptions in daybooks and inventories are not sufficiently detailed for us always to know what kind of desk was purchased, or even what kind of table. Desks and writing tables came in all shapes and sizes, from the small ones that women and men used for writing personal letters to the large ones that men, and particularly professionals and royal officials, used for their work. The sales price or notarial valuation is helpful, but ormolu mounts or porcelain plaques could easily run up the value of even the smallest writing desk. Nevertheless, daybooks and inventories are a good place to start if we want to understand how those who made and sold furniture responded to the entry of women into the corps of letter writers.[3]

The surviving daybooks of the mercer Lazare Duvaux, which cover the years 1748 to 1759, give us a glimpse of the daily trade in the fashionable new furniture of letter writing on the rue Saint-Honoré. Since most purchases were made on credit, Duvaux, like other merchants, listed each one as it was made, with the name of the purchaser, a brief description of the purchase, and the price (noting later when payment was made or, occasionally, if the item was returned for credit).[4] Duvaux's clients were a mixed elite of noble and nonnoble women and men, but they included especially the financial elite who were renting or buying the big Parisian *hôtels* and wanted to furnish them in the latest fashion. Of the approximately 160 women who bought something from

Duvaux in the years covered by his daybooks, 31 bought at least one writing table or desk, and 5 more who did not buy desks made other writing-related purchases of items such as inkstands or engraved seals. Duvaux's female clients included the queen, the dauphine, the royal princesses, and the king's sister. Mme d'Épinay visited his shop three times, once coming home with a combination secretary–fire screen that cost 60 livres. It was made of cherrywood and fitted with an inkstand and a leather writing surface; the screen was of fashionable India paper.[5] Duvaux's best client, however, was Mme de Pompadour. Over the course of these eleven years, she visited the shop almost five hundred times and bought some seventy writing tables, large and small.

There is, of course, no way of knowing for whom the many purchases of writing desks—by women or men—were made. Even Mme de Pompadour could not have used all seventy of the desks she purchased from Lazare Duvaux! Indeed, the four large writing tables she purchased on 3 June 1752, were destined for the king's apartment in her château de Crécy.[6] But at least we know that women frequented the shop and, while there, included purchases related to letter writing among the other fashionable items with which they would furnish their homes. For example, on one visit, in addition to a writing table veneered in satinwood, with several drawers, ormolu mounts on the feet, keyholes, and pulls, and copper fittings with valves (96 livres), the comtesse d'Egmont purchased seven pieces of blue and white porcelain (60 livres) and a fountain in Chinese porcelain with gilt bronze decoration (36 livres). The following year her daughter-in-law bought three cups of Vincennes porcelain for 10, 12, and 24 livres and a writing table veneered in violetwood with silvered fittings for 72 livres. Five months later, Mme de Beaumont bought a chandelier of Bohemian crystal (440 livres), a cord of assorted Grenada silk (31 livres), seven yards of bell cord of the same silk, with their tassels (12 livres), and a writing table veneered in a mosaic of tulipwood with a bronze molding around the edge and ormolu decorations (240 livres). One last example: in May 1756, the marquise de La Ferrière bought two desks—a small secretary in tulipwood veneered with flowers of kingwood, garnished with decorations gilded in ormolu (432 livres); and a writing table with a writing slide and lectern and silvered fittings (96 livres). At the same time, she also purchased two crystal lanterns (60 livres), six cups and saucers of blue and white Vincennes porcelain (60 livres for the set), a sugar bowl (15 livres), and a Chinese tray (12 livres).[7]

Lazare Duvaux's daybooks demonstrate that from the beginning a broad range of women could find a desk to fit their budget as well as their taste, even at the most fashionable shops. The writing tables described above sold for 72 to 432 livres, but the full range was from a low of 48 livres to a high of over a thousand.[8] Nor did price always reflect wealth and status. In 1752, Mme de Pompadour bought two writing desks veneered in Japanese lacquer for 560 livres; three years later, she had Duvaux veneer one for her in Chinese lacquer for only 48 livres.[9] And while Mme de Pompadour was the purchaser of the most expensive desks, she also bought a dozen one day for 50 livres apiece; the king's sister bought one of the 48 livre desks. That same day she paid 132 livres for a pair of ormolu sconces, which should remind us that a writing table was hardly the most expensive purchase a woman would make in a shop such as Lazare Duvaux's.[10] The day the duchesse de Lauraguais bought a writing table for 184 livres (including an extra 28 livres for a silver pot for the inkstand) she also bought a set of two silver potpourris with ormolu decorations for 240 livres.[11]

In January 1756, Duvaux noted that Mme de Voigny had bought a writing table from him veneered in tulipwood for 144 livres and also sold back an "ancienne table" for which he paid her 120.[12] Barter, refashioning, and making trade-ins were common practices, as Natacha Coquery has shown in her study of the daybooks of the upholsterer Mathurin Law, who also did business on the rue Saint-Honoré. Law's clientele was much broader than Duvaux's, ranging from artisans and other merchants who lived or worked in the neighborhood to members of the legal professions and high aristocrats. Coquery has found many entries for goods returned, exchanged, and, a speciality of the upholsterers, rented for as short as a day or as long as a few months.[13] Like the dresses and hats being sold by the *marchandes de mode*, writing tables were not major investments or the purchases of a lifetime; they were useful goods in the latest taste that could be refashioned or replaced when tastes changed. Indeed, Pierre Verlet notes that small tables such as these were generally priced fairly low, so as to "encourage people to get rid of them without regret in order to replace them with more modern ones."[14]

The pattern of purchases from Lazare Duvaux is also worth noting. Mme de Pompadour was not the only woman to buy more than one desk at a time: one day Mme Rémond bought seven writing tables of different sizes, all of them fitted with locking drawers, inkwells, and leather-covered writing slides, for 132 livres apiece.[15] Nor was Mme de Pompadour the only repeat customer. The duchesse de Mazarin visited Duvaux's shop seventeen times; on three of these visits she bought writing tables, each one of which cost between 200 and 250 livres. Mme Rouillé also made seventeen visits, during five of which she bought writing tables, ranging from 72 to 288 livres apiece. Three days after she bought a cabinet-style secretary for 288 livres in December 1754, she returned for an inkstand of black and gold lacquer with gilt hinges and silver fittings for 192 livres. In January she was back again, this time for two small tables: a writing table and another table matching it but not fitted out for writing.[16]

Some of these desks may have been purchased as gifts, or for different residences of the purchaser, but inventories of houses drawn up in the 1770s show that writing tables were scattered throughout houses where several people lived, suggesting that they were understood to be personal furniture. In the most elaborate houses, where individuals had apartments rather than rooms, they could have more than one desk in their own private space. Whereas the multitude of chairs in eighteenth-century homes facilitated the sociability that was the primary form of leisure, the multitude of writing desks reflected the individuality that developed at the same time.[17] Letters were often read aloud to a group of family or friends seated in a salon or around a dining table, but they were written (ideally) on tables that were the personal furniture of the letter writer. After all, the locked drawer distinguished the writing desk from most other tables as much as the leather or velvet-covered surface did.

If we look more closely at these inventories, we will find writing tables in rooms associated with a single person, and only rarely more than one per room. The notarial inventory drawn up in 1771, after the death of the sculptor Jacques Verbeckt, included the furnishings of two houses in which he had been living with several adult daughters and a son. On the ground floor of the main house the notary found six writing tables or desks. One was in Verbeckt's own bedroom, and another was in the room of his eldest daughter. Upstairs were four more desks and writing tables, all in bedrooms or cabinets overlooking the garden. In the second house were two more secretaries and a small desk, one of which (in a room next to the kitchen) was no doubt used by the cook to keep the kitchen accounts. The total value of these thirteen desks and tables along with eleven chairs of various sorts and some other items valued with them was estimated at less than 275 livres.[18]

An inventory probably drawn up by the property manager of the vast château de Montgeoffroy in 1775 also walks us through the rooms of the house, although it does not provide a valuation or detailed description of their contents. Still, it is interesting because the owners had recently gone to Paris to buy everything to furnish their newly remodeled home. "The maréchale seems to have had the chateau furnished all at once through massive purchases in Paris," explains Pierre Verlet, who published the inventory: "fragments of accounts, still preserved at Montgeoffroy, retain the traces of substantial payments [she] made on this occasion."[19] There were many, many tables at Montgeoffroy, but only a few are identified as writing tables or desks. Indeed, there is only one bureau, and that is in the marechal's cabinet. There are, however, five *tables en secrétaire*. Mme Herault had one in her bedroom, while Mme de Sechelles had two: one in her bedroom and another in her cabinet. The three others were in bedrooms of un-named people: one man, one woman, and one described as belonging to a man and a woman. And it is possible that some of the other tables—such as the small table veneered in rosewood in the marechal's bedroom, or any of the plain wooden tables found in the rooms of chambermaids and valets—were also used for writing letters. Indeed, everyone living in the house seems to have had a table, and those whose names were worth mentioning all had tables designed specifically for writing.

A final inventory drawn up in 1779 takes us through an even grander house, the Palais de Bourbon, bought by the prince de Condé in 1768 (today the home of the president of the National Assembly). Verlet has published the inventory of only the three principal apartments, those of the prince himself, and those of his son and daughter-in-law, the duc and duchesse de Bourbon. In all there were seventeen secretaries and writing tables distributed among studies, bedrooms, salons, music rooms, wardrobes, and antechambers in the three great apartments; a couple were in hallways, two were built into the paneling of the house. Two of the secretaries were in the duchess's apartment: one in the antechamber belonging to her valets, and the other in her own bedroom, between the fireplace and the door to the music room. One was made up in old lacquer framed in tulipwood, and the other was decorated with landscapes and satin-wood; both were cabinet style, with marble tops and ormolu mounts. Also in the duchess's bedroom was a writing table veneered in marquetry with a green leather writing surface framed with a design in gold and sporting ormolu mounts. Four more small writing tables were scattered throughout her apartment: two in the music room (one of which was mounted with Sèvres porcelain plaques) and two more of simple beechwood in the two rooms of her wardrobe, presumably for the use of her maids. In all, seven of the seventeen writing desks were in the duchess's apartment.[20]

The daybooks of one of the most elegant shops in Paris and inventories of the wealthy and extremely wealthy can tell us about only a few of the desks used by the many women who wrote letters in the eighteenth century. But they do at least suggest a few things to keep in mind as we look more closely at the writing tables and desks themselves. First, the writing desk could be very fashionable furniture, but it was not necessarily luxurious, and certainly not rare. Second, even a very expensive writing desk was not a major purchase in relation to other sorts of furniture or furnishings that a woman might buy. Third, the writing desk was personal furniture bought by women as well as men and kept in the private space of a bedroom, *cabinet*, or private apartment.

Desks and the Material World
of the Letter-Writing Woman

In a book on the design of private houses published in 1737, the architect Jacques-François Blondel skipped over bedrooms and other private spaces because, he explained, "in bedrooms and other rooms that do not make up the *appartements de parade* people generally make do with whatever furniture they've got."[21] A decade later, however, these rooms were being filled and refilled with new light, fashionable furniture. By the 1780s, Louis-Sébastien Mercier could declare that "the wonders of architecture are, in Paris, in the interior of houses. Wise and ingenious divisions economize the property, multiply it and give it new and precious comforts. . . . Our small apartments are turned and distributed like round and polished scallop shells, and one lives with light and pleasure in spaces hitherto lost and awkwardly gloomy."[22] The writing table or desk was part of this array of light, movable furniture that reflected new values of comfort, elegance, amenity, and utility.[23]

Pierre Verlet emphasizes the elegance of the lightweight furniture that graced the newly articulated *appartements de société* and *appartements privés* and was "more responsive to the caprices of fashion and generally less ornate."[24] Mimi Hellman has shown how, with their carefully delimited functions—chairs for conversing, eavesdropping, and reading; tables for gambling, doing makeup, and letter writing—these pieces prescribed an intricate dance of civility and sociability among their users.[25] Pierre Devinoy captures the cultural shift marked by changes in furniture over the course of a century when he writes: "The *grand siècle* remained *on its feet*, its civility was centered around bowing; the eighteenth century was *seated*, chatting, the women embroidering, cutting out images [for *découpage*], braiding, the colonels doing needlepoint, everyone drinking coffee, and putting down objects that were in their way everywhere: small furniture with shelves multiplied."[26] Letter writing fit neatly into this busy new, seated world.

The table or desk designed especially for letter writing that was introduced into the growing array of small, mobile furniture in the 1740s was a typical product of the mercers: exotic in its surface materials and the idiom of its decoration, but of French construction and design for the French and European market.[27] At the intersection of fashion, function, and taste, such desks were modern, not only in the aesthetics of their design, but in the new technologies and materials they employed. The ingenuity of cabinetmakers and mercers went into complicating the simple design of the table, both to hide and protect the writing function beneath a veneered surface, and to make the writing desk better able to serve the complex practice of epistolarity. The result was a novelty that was functional, fulfilled an unmet and growing consumer need, and helped integrate letter writing into the material world of the woman who owned and used it. The writing desk was not simply an object of display but one of the props that contributed to shaping the life and sensibility of a modern, urban elite woman. Letter writing, that "choreography of the quill," was one way in which she performed her femininity as a matter not only of grace and elegance but of leisure. The writing desk was meant to facilitate this performance as it facilitated the writing of an elegant letter.[28]

The variations in style, decoration, and design of writing desks went well beyond the stylistic shifts by which furniture historians have traditionally associated the shape of a leg with the reign of a king. From the outset, writing desks were designed and marketed in a remarkable array of shapes, styles, and veneers. The fall-front secretary was probably the earliest style (see fig. 6.1). Many others soon followed, from simple tables to elaborately engineered mechanical desks whose tops flipped up, slid back, or rose via a spring mechanism at the turn of a key (see figs. 6.2 and 6.3).[29] No matter what the style, all these pieces had three common features that defined them as writing desks: a writing surface, a locking drawer, and small size. Typically, they also had a drawer fitted with an inkstand. As the daybooks of Lazare Duvaux document, it was the mercer who added this finishing touch, completing the transformation of a simple table into a writing desk by incorporating the inkstand into one of the drawers.[30]

The multitude of forms and the engineering of the clockwork mechanisms within them are testimony to the inventiveness of Parisian mercers and cabinetmakers, but also to the women and men who bought them for their novelty, and to the fashion market within which they were developed. If the stunning veneers of lacquer, wood marquetry, and porcelain that cover their surfaces are more often seen today as the zenith of traditional craftsmanship, they also demonstrate how the modern fashion economy stimulated innovation in an expanding market.

6.1. Fall-front secretary in Japanese lacquer (1745–49) by Jacques Dubois. Sotheby's New York, 6 May 1977, lot 176b.

6.2. Oval writing table (ca. 1770) by Roger Vandercruse, known as La Croix. 74.7 × 48.5 × 39.5 cm. Documentation Galerie Perrin, Paris.

6.3. Mechanical writing table (ca. 1760) by Jean-François Oeben. 68.3 × 72.3 × 34.7 cm. Bequeathed by John Jones. V&A Images/Victoria and Albert Museum, no. 1095–1882.

Surfaces: The Art of the Ébéniste

The dynamics of product innovation and marketing are apparent on the very surface of the desk, in the wood marquetry, lacquer, and porcelain veneers that have made French cabinetry of this period deservedly famous. All these veneers were new in the eighteenth century, and all of them brought traces of distant and exotic lands into the domestic interiors of French women who followed fashion and exercised taste.

French cabinetmakers or *ébénistes* had used the Italian craft of marquetry veneering since at least the sixteenth century to hide carcasses of common wood (oak or even pine) and not particularly notable construction. The great innovation of the eighteenth century was to substitute exotic Caribbean hardwoods for the more expensive precious metals, stones, ivory, and mother-of-pearl.[31] The American woods could be sliced more thinly and worked more intricately than native European woods because of their firmness and close grain; they also came in a breathtaking array of colors unlike anything coming out of European forests, and in colorful contrast as well to the black ebony that had been coming in from Africa, Madagascar, and India.[32] America, wrote the author of the *Dictionnaire du citoyen* (1762), "can be regarded as the wealth of Europeans." Among the various products it furnished Europe, from gold, silver, and diamonds to sugar, coffee, tobacco, and cotton, were "woods for marquetry and construction."[33] These included the dark "amaranth wood" or purplewood from Dutch Guiana, which contrasted nicely with the golden *bois de Cayenne* or the pale yellow *bois de citron* from Saint-Domingue. In the 1740s, pinkish-yellow tulipwood from Brazil came into use; by 1750 it had become the most popular ground for floral marquetry. By the 1760s, the use of mahogany from Cuba was widespread, and during the years of Louis XVI's reign demand for it increased. The 1780s saw the introduction of pale yellow satinwood from the Antilles, which contrasted well with the dark red mahogany.[34]

Wood marquetry was considerably cheaper to produce than either Italian pietra dura (hard-stone) or the ebony-based *ébénisterie* that came to be known as "Boulle marquetry" after Louis XIV's cabinetmaker André-Charles Boulle.[35] Wood marquetry, however, required different skills and technology—specifically, the ability to slice wood thinly and jigsaw it into curved pieces. Thin veneers were not simply a tour de force of craftsmanship, they were also a significant means of lowering the cost of materials, and in the eighteenth century, materials, not labor, determined the price of finished goods: the thinner the veneer, the cheaper the desk was to produce—no matter how great the skill of the craftsman or how many hours of labor it took him to produce it.[36] The cutting of these leaves of exotic woods into small, intricate shapes was the most demanding part of the cabinetmaker's job, and as the veneers got thinner, the likelihood of ruining a piece of expensive wood with the jigsaw increased.[37] Technology could help: in 1772, the *Avantcoureur* published the description of a new spring-driven jigsaw that was less prone to break the wood being sawed.[38] When cabinetmakers reached the limits of their saws, however, they cut costs by avoiding imported woods whenever possible. This could be done by dying domestic hardwoods such as maple to cover large surfaces that did not require fine cutting. Dying also allowed them to create colors that did not exist in nature—such as the green that was crucial to floral marquetry.[39]

As wood marquetry became fashionable and innovation brought down the cost of materials, the demand for skilled woodworkers increased in Paris (and London), where demand was high enough and guild restrictions were minimal enough to support specialists in cutting and veneering.[40] Not just the wood, then, but the craftsmen were imported, mostly from the Low Countries and Germany. The names of the most well-known "French" cabinetmakers of the eighteenth century are largely Flemish, Dutch, or German: Criard from Brussels, van Risenburgh from Gröningen, Vandercruse from the Netherlands, Molitor from Luxembourg, Oeben from Heinsberg near Aix-la-Chapelle and the Dutch border, Cramer and Weisweiler from the Rhineland, Riesener and Roentgen from Westphalia.[41]

The number of cabinetmakers multiplied especially in the faubourg Saint-Antoine, where foreigners and labor costs were unencumbered by guild restrictions, direct sales to the public avoided the mercer's markup, and those without the polish, means, or credit of the elite were more welcome as customers.[42] In 1776 the *Almanach parisien* directed those looking to buy furniture to the faubourg Saint-Antoine, and the same year the *Almanach du dauphin* suggested several reputable furniture and cabinetmakers in the neighborhood, most of whom, like Fromageot on the grande rue du faubourg Saint-Antoine and Bondin on the rue Traversière, "ship to the Provinces and Abroad."[43] Several years later, however, Mercier counseled his readers otherwise: "I don't know how this neighborhood survives," he wrote. "Furniture is sold there from one end to the other; and the poor who live there have no furniture at all. People from the countryside are responsible for three-quarters of the purchases; and, in general what gets delivered to them is only the discards of this merchandise, or what is most crude in this branch of commerce."[44] Elsewhere, Mercier attacked the poor quality of used furniture sold by the upholsterers in the faubourg: "They'll sell you a secretary that comes unglued three weeks later," he warned.[45] The quality of all the furniture for sale in the faubourg was not as poor as Mercier claimed, but it is nonetheless true that the guilds had little means of exercising traditional quality controls in this neighborhood protected from their supervision. After the guild reforms of the 1770s, however, the system of quality control was breaking down everywhere, and all consumers had to be more informed and more savvy, whether they shopped at the fashionable shops on the rue Saint-Honoré or at the showrooms of the cabinetmakers in the faubourg Saint-Antoine.[46]

The records of Nicolas Petit (1732–91) show not only the success it was possible to enjoy in the furniture business but also the range of work that one successful cabinetmaker produced and of clients that he served.[47] Petit came to Paris from the provinces between 1746 and 1753, trained as a cabinetmaker, and by 1755 was working as a nonguild craftsman [artisan libre] in the faubourg Saint-Antoine. In 1758 he married a young woman in the neighborhood with good connections and a substantial dowry, and in 1761 was received into the guild as a master cabinetmaker. Although the long illness and subsequent death of his wife only four years later put a strain on his finances, in 1766 Petit remarried, this time attracting an even bigger dowry, no doubt reflecting his enhanced status and his success in the trade. The couple soon rented a large apartment with a private entrance and an excellent location on the grande rue du faubourg Saint-Antoine that allowed Petit to expand his business to include direct sales. When he renewed the lease in 1780, he took over most of the building and, in 1789, all of it, subletting rooms when business slowed. In the 1780s, as his business prospered, he was also elected to important positions within the guild. At his death in 1791, the furniture in his workshops, storerooms, and showrooms was appraised at more than 26,000 livres; his personal fortune included clothing and silver valued at over 8,000 livres. At peak times, he employed at least twenty people in the cabinet shop and the salesrooms.

At the beginning of his career, Petit worked strictly as an ébéniste, veneering the carcasses produced by menuisiers or furniture makers, and then when he was done, turning them over to merchants to sell them; eventually he took over the work of both furniture maker and merchant by producing complete pieces in his own workshop and selling them in his own showroom. The inventory of goods at his death included not only the exotic woods used for veneering but the common woods for building frames, the bronze mounts used to ornament legs and feet, the molded bronze decorations for keyhole escutcheons, the pulls and knobs for drawers and writing slides, and marble tops. As to sales, at the time of his death, Petit had no fewer than nine shops, including one on the ground floor with street access. There, and in the large showrooms on the upper floors of his building, Petit had almost seven hundred pieces of furniture on display, from a worktable valued at 5 livres to a large rolltop desk at 900; the median value was 38 livres. As his biographer notes, Petit "seems to have made it a point of honor to offer his clients choice in diversity."[48]

Among the stock inventoried in 1791 were fifty drop-leaf desks, eighteen rolltop desks, two fall-front desks, and five hybrid desks, for a total of seventy-five secretaries, or about 10 percent of the total inventory. More than 40 percent of the total (289), however, was made up of "small tables," of which eighteen were described as writing tables, seven as *bonheurs-du-jour* or "tiered," and three as "three-way tables," which generally designated a table that combined the writing function with two others. In all, over one hundred of the seven hundred pieces in the inventory were designed for writing, ranging from large rolltops to small secretaries and writing tables. Most were not veneered in fine marquetry; their fashionability, like their utility, lay in their forms and function.

The diversity of Petit's wares lay not only in the types of furniture available but in their quality and price: from small pieces with simple floral marquetry to elaborate ones rich in ormolu and veneered in Japanese lacquer or elaborate marquetry designs (see figs. 6.4a and 6.4b). From the beginning of his career, Petit produced for a broad market. Before he had his own salesroom, he sold his work mostly through colleagues in the faubourg, but he also had two dealers on the rue Saint-Honoré. Later he sold some of his finer pieces to upscale upholsterers in the Marais and Saint-Germain-des-Prés, as well as to Nicolas-René Dubuisson, cabinetmaker to the king at Versailles. Through these intermediaries he reached a wealthy clientele, both noble and nonnoble. When the patron of an aspiring actress had her Paris apartment lavishly furnished in 1787, for example, a Petit bonheur-du-jour was supplied by one of the many professionals (upholsterers, mercers, mirror dealers) responsible for the decoration.[49] By the time of Petit's death he had also sold his work directly to two hundred individual clients, of whom about 40 percent were noble. Among them were Geneviève de Malboissière's cousin and first love, Pierre-Paul Randon de Lucenay, as well as Bernard de Bonnard's two employers: the duc de Chartres (although by then he had acceded to his father's title, duc d'Orléans) and the duc d'Harcourt, the royal governor of Normandy.[50]

Nicolas Petit was a successful cabinetmaker and merchant, not because he had the patronage of the queen or Mme de Pompadour like Lazare Duvaux, but because he aggressively marketed his work to a broad clientele that included a substantial minority of nobles, from a prince of the blood to an army officer with roots in the tax-farming nouveau riche. The majority of his direct clients, at least, were non-noble, which may reflect his decision to open showrooms to sell his work directly in the faubourg, while also placing it with dealers in fashionable and elegant neighborhoods.

Unlike Nicolas Petit, those cabinetmakers who catered to the most exclusive clientele, such as Jean-François Oeben, Jean-Henri Riesener, and Adam Weisweiler, produced signature designs in expensive materials that would make all their work

6.4a. Small writing table (ca. 1765) by Nicolas Petit. 68 × 33 × 26 cm. Documentation Galerie Perrin, Paris.

recognizable and expensive, and that would carry prestige without violating the canons of taste that made it fashionable. Oeben became known for his cube and floral marquetry, as well as his mechanical tables (see fig. 6.3), and Weisweiler for ornate giltbronze mounts in classical motifs (see fig. 6.5). Wood marquetry also allowed cabinetmakers to decorate writing tables with images such as Chinese vases, teapots, inkwells, and novels that situated epistolary practice within both modern, intimate sociability and the larger world that women could become part of through correspondence and commerce (see fig. 6.6). Other marquetry designs also integrated the writing table aesthetically into the world of elite women. As we have already seen (fig. 6.4b), cabinetmakers employed the same design vocabulary of rococo and chinoiserie as fashionable painters such as Boucher, sometimes even using their designs. The exotic marquetry landscape of Petit's secretary echoed those painted on imported porcelains and their European imitations.

A mechanical table from about 1760 attributed to Oeben provides another example of shared decorative vocabulary (fig. 6.7). Like the faience inkstand from Lyon (fig. 5.9),

6.4b. Upright fall-front secretary by Nicolas Petit. Decorated with marquetry of Chinese figures after Boucher on a landscape background. Galerie Gismondi, Paris.

it is veneered with a floral design drawn from the Indian calicoes and French silks used for both dresses and upholstery that were fashionable at that time, as shown in François-Hubert Drouais's 1763–64 portrait of Mme de Pompadour (fig. 6.8).[51]

Lacquer veneers brought the exotic Far East into the homes of letter-writing women even more directly—even if by 1745 it was virtually impossible to import Japanese lacquer into France as a result of a Dutch monopoly on trade with Japan. By then, however, the Chinese were producing their own lacquer for the European market.[52] A couple of fall-front desks made around 1745 are decorated with the exotic landscapes of Asia, one in Japanese lacquer (fig. 6.1), and the other in the less expensive Chinese version (fig. 6.9). By the 1750s, French lacquer made *chinoiserie* accessible to a broad market on a huge range of wooden goods from carriages to writing desks and decorative boxes (see fig. 6.10).[53] "Old" lacquer from Japan now became a sign of the most refined taste, and in the mercers' shops, where pieces veneered in French, Chinese, and Japanese lacquer stood side by side, customers learned to practice the discrimination that would define connoisseurship. As the Martin brothers, who developed French lacquer, brought down its price and increased its availability, the mercers taught their elite clients to value Japanese lacquer even more, both for its rarity and for its quality—apparent only to the true connoisseur.[54]

6.5. Writing table in Japanese lacquer (1784) by Adam Weisweiler. 73.7 × 81.2 × 45.2 cm. Sold by the mercer Daguerre to the garde-meuble for 3,260 livres and used by Marie Antoinette in her cabinet at Saint-Cloud. Musée du Louvre, Paris. Inv. OA 5509. Photo. © Réunion des Musées Nationaux/Art Resource, New York.

6.6. Bonheur-du-jour (ca. 1770) attributed to André-Charles Topino. 1.01 × 0.677 × 0.435 m. Musée Cognac-Jay, Paris. Inv. J380. Top view showing marquetry of teaware and epistolary motifs. Photo: Roger-Viollet.

6.7. Mechanical table (ca. 1760) attributed to Jean-François Oeben. 67 × 70 × 35 cm. Musée Cognac-Jay, Paris. Inv. J 373. Photo: Roger-Viollet.

6.8. François-Hubert Drouais, *Madame de Pompadour at Her Tambour Frame* (1763–64). Oil on canvas, 2.17 × 1.56 m. Inv. NG6440. © The National Gallery, London.

6.9. Fall-front desk veneered in red and gold Chinese lacquer by Guillaume Schwingkens. Louis XV period. 85 × 67 × 41.2 cm. Galerie Gismondi, Paris.

For those who made no pretensions to connoisseurship, there was inexpensive tôle, which could be made to imitate either lacquer or porcelain—even though it could not be mistaken for either one—as in the handsome little rolltop desk made by Claude-Charles Saunier shown in figure 6.11. As we have already seen, porcelain was the primary material by means of which mercers brought Asia into the private spaces of letter-writing women. Saunier was but one of several cabinetmakers who covered the surfaces of epistolary furniture not only with tôle but with expensive porcelain plaques. In the 1770s, the mercers Simon-Philippe Poirier and Dominique Daguerre ordered hundreds of such plaques from the Sèvres factory and had them mounted by cabinetmakers on a whole range of goods, from inkstands to writing tables and including jewel cases, worktables, and *cabarets*. These porcelain veneers brought whole suites of furniture into aesthetic harmony with the many porcelain objects that fashionable women used every day, such as tea, chocolate, or coffee services, or those with which they decorated their rooms, such as flowerpots, incense burners, and figurines of all sorts, including the ubiquitous *magots* and *pagodes*.[55] A particularly lavish example, shown in figure 6.12, is one of Martin Carlin's signature pieces, a writing table purchased from Poirier by Mme du Barry (Pompadour's successor as Louis XV's mistress) for 5,500 livres.[56]

6.10. Fall-front desk in French lacquer with chinoiserie decoration (ca. 1750). 97 × 94 × 47 cm. Galerie des Laques, Paris.

6.11. Claude-Charles Saunier, rolltop desk paneled in tôle, lacquered in imitation of Japanese lacquer according to a technique perfected by Samousseau in 1767. Sotheby's London, 24 November 1978, lot 184.

6.12. Writing table (ca. 1772) by Martin Carlin. 73 × 63 × 36 cm. Mounted with Sèvres porcelain plaques by Dodin (1771). Gulbenkian Museum, Lisbon. Inv. 2267.

6.13. Desk with straw marquetry, France(1750–75).97.2 × 76.2 × 44.5 cm. © The Cleveland Museum of Art. Gift of Grace Rainey Rogers in memory of her father, William J. Rainey. 1942.40.

More modest versions of the secretary or writing table can often be found in provincial museums in France and abroad. Consider, for example, the secretary shown in figure 6.13, which is veneered in marquetry not of exotic woods but straw. Straw, which never appears in the marquetry of the most elite Parisian cabinetmakers, was a fashionable material for all sorts of objects, as the collection of small boxes shown in figure 5.3 reminds us. If porcelain plaques brought the writing desk into harmony with the other furnishings in the spaces of the wealthiest ladies, straw marquetry was equally effective for coordinating pieces in the interiors of their more modest sisters.

Beneath the Surface: Form and Function

The writing desk was not a whimsical or rare furniture design but the basic variation on the simple table from which all other small tables followed. Thus, in his treatise on furniture making, André Jacob Roubo first discussed writing tables before moving on to other small tables. He concluded his discussion with the remark that "there are an infinite number of Tables of all sorts, all shapes and sizes, whose details I will not go into here, in view of the fact that they are often simply the work of the caprice of a few Workers, or of those who employ them; moreover, these sorts of Tables differ little from those I have described, whose use is more generally received, and on the basis of which one can invent whatever form one judges appropriate."[57] The differences among the various tables were indeed minor. If the stand that popped up was covered with velvet or leather, it was a writing surface; if it was veneered in marquetry or lacquer (as in fig. 6.5), it was meant to support a book. If a mirror took the place of the lectern or the writing surface and the drawers were filled with cosmetics, it was a dressing table.[58] Most common were the pieces that combined multiple functions, often in clever ways: for example, the table shown in figure 6.14 made by Jean-François Leleu. With the turn of a key the top slides back and the writing compartment, with its leather covered surface, comes forward. When the writing surface is raised on its hinges to access the shallow drawer beneath it in which paper and letters could be stored, the mirror on its inner face appears. The deep drawers on both sides would hold cosmetics.

The need to adapt the simple table to the practice of letter writing meant putting a lot of features into a single piece of furniture that had to remain small, for no matter what the design, the veneer, or the style of the writing desk, its function and its size—with its writing surface in particular too small for anything but the small sheets of paper used for personal correspondence—defined it. There was a practicality to the small size: a small writing table could be kept against a wall when not in use, and then placed (by a servant) close to a window or other light source when it was needed. In private rooms, a bed might be the only piece of furniture that remained stationary—dressing tables (*toilettes*), work tables (*chiffonnières*), night tables, candle stands (*guéridons*)—were all lightweight furniture designed to be moved about easily.[59]

6.14. Combined dressing and writing table (ca. 1764–75) by Jean-François Leleu. 70.5 × 55.8 × 39.3 cm. Widener Collection. Inv. 1942.9.422. Image courtesy of the Board of Trustees, National Gallery of Art, Washington, DC.

Most of the fashionable desks hid their writing surfaces in one way or another: in slides that had to be pulled out to be used or behind tops that had to be unlocked and rolled back or flipped down. The desk shown in figure 6.12 is an example of one popular design, which fitted a lid onto the locking center drawer: when the drawer was opened the lid, covered with fabric or leather, served as a writing surface; letters received could be kept safe in the drawer beneath the writing slide. The right side of the same drawer might be fitted with the inkstand, as in this example; or writing supplies might be found in an unlocked side drawer that pulled out from the right and could be accessed easily by a servant to replenish them. An identical piece, but without the unique and expensive porcelain plaques, is shown in figure 6.15. When the writing surface is pulled forward, the top slides back. Another writing table with the same form (and in the same museum) operates differently, however (see fig. 6.16). In this example, instead of a locked drawer at the front covered by a writing surface, there is a simple writing slide that pulls forward; the inkstand is in the side drawer.

6.15. Work and writing table (ca. 1770) by Martin Carlin. 73.8 × 79.6 × 46.1 cm. Widener Collection. Inv. 1942.9.425. Image courtesy of the Board of Trustees, National Gallery of Art, Washington, DC.

6.16. Writing table (ca. 1780) by Jean-Henri Riesener. 78.9 × 81.9 × 49.5 cm. Widener Collection. 1942.9.409. Image courtesy of the Board of Trustees, National Gallery of Art, Washington, DC.

The writing desk known as the bonheur-du-jour was distinctively different from these other tables and epitomized the fashion trade in furniture. A joint creation of enterprising mercers and cabinetmakers, it came in the full range of shapes, styles, veneers, and prices. Above all, it was eminently practical for serving the letter writer's needs: like other writing tables, its writing surface was supplemented by a drawer fitted with an inkstand, but there was an additional set of locked drawers and pigeonholes for letters received, blank paper, and other epistolary needs, and a shelf to hold candles for light and to melt sealing wax. Another shelf might hold a few small books or a natural history collection. The raised back that contained the pigeonholes, shelves, and drawers created a space of privacy even if the bonheur-du-jour was placed in the middle of a room.

André-Charles Topino, who chose motifs of epistolary paraphernalia for one rather boxy bonheur-du-jour (fig. 6.6), decorated a pair of oval ones with marquetry images of tea ware (fig. 6.17). Carlin mounted seventeen Sèvres porcelain plaques with delicate floral designs (supplied by Poirier) on at least eleven low, sleek bonheurs-du-jour, some with casters on their feet to facilitate moving them into place (see fig. 6.18).[60] Louis Moreau employed straight legs, classical motifs, and a screen that looks like a set of books by fashionable writers (Molière, Piron, Dorat, and Voltaire) on a shelf; the screen rolls back to reveal the drawers and cubbyholes within (fig. 6.19). Moreau complicated the design further by backing the writing surface with a mirror so that the desk could double as a dressing table, and he employed an elaborate locking mechanism to hide the inside drawers behind panels with a turn of the key.[61] Like other

6.17. Two oval bonheurs-du-jour with chinoiserie teaware motifs (1775) by André-Charles Topino. Sotheby's London, 23 June 1985.

6.18. Bonheur-du-jour mounted with Sèvres porcelain plaques (ca. 1768) by Martin Carlin. 82.5 × 65.7 × 40.6 cm. The Metropolitan Museum of Art. Gift of Samuel H. Kress Foundation, 1958 (58.75.48). Image © The Metropolitan Museum of Art.

6.19. Bonheur-du-jour (ca. 1778–80) attributed to Louis Moreau. 1.048 × 0.91 × 0.562 m. Musée Cognac-Jay, Paris. Inv. J 384. Photo: Roger-Viollet.

6.20. Bonheur-du-jour (France, Louis XV period). 101 × 47 cm. Veneered with mahogany, tulipwood, walnut, and straw. Inv. GL 922. Musée Grobet-Labadié, Marseille.

forms, the bonheur-du-jour could be made without the expensive gilding and marquetry for more modest clients and by craftsmen outside the capital who served a local market. Consider, for example, the simple bonheur-du-jour by an unknown maker shown in figure 6.20: Although the cabinetmaker did use mahogany and tulipwood for the marquetry, he also used native walnut and straw. The result is simple but just as functional and fashionable as the products of the great Parisian workshops.

Geneviève Souchal calls the bonheur-du-jour "one of the most graceful inventions of a century abounding in such inventions," but who is responsible for this invention is less clear. Alexandre Pradère gives the mercers full credit, while John Whitehead claims only that they provided customers with the variety of small tables for letter-writing that they demanded, including the bonheur-du-jour. Verlet assures us that, although a cabinetmaker may have invented the design, the mercers were responsible for popularizing it with the catchy name that evoked novelty, fashion, and a comfortable happiness. What is clear is that if any desk was designed especially for the female letter-writing market, it was this one.[62]

If desks designed especially to meet the letter-writer's needs demonstrate the significance of this new market, pieces designed to serve two or three functions contributed to the integration of letter writing into women's daily lives. Consider the combination fire screen and writing table that Mme d'Épinay bought from Lazare Duvaux, or the table with a mirror on the back of the writing surface and writing supplies in one drawer, beauty supplies in another. Consider a games table that could also function as a writing table. Especially popular were tables such as the ones shown in figures 21 and 22 that held all the equipment for both writing and needlework. Both of these pieces belonged to Marie-Antoinette, but she is said to have given the first one away as a gift to the wife of an English diplomat in 1786 after the successful conclusion of a treaty.[63] Note that in both designs the drawer that holds letters and writing surface locks, while the basket that holds the needlework is open.

Supplementing furniture designed to meet the letter writer's several needs, either alone or in combination with other functions, were the writing slides that were being built into virtually every piece of lightweight personal furniture used by ladies: worktables, dressing tables, jewel cases, and fire screens, such as the one

6.21. Work table set with a Sèvres porcelain plaque (ca. 1775) by Martin Carlin. 77 × 42 × 36.8 cm (plaque diameter). Bequeathed by John Jones. V&A Images/Victoria and Albert Museum, no. 1058–1882.

6.22. Trough-style work table (*chiffonnière en auge*) (1788) by Jean-Henri Riesener. 78 × 77 × 35 cm. Inv. 347. Les Arts Décoratifs— Musée Nissim de Camondo, Paris. Photo: Les Arts Décoratifs/Jean Tholance. All rights reserved.

pictured in the gouache by Nicolas Lavreince shown in figure 6.23. Roubo wrote that beneath the mirror of the dressing table "is placed a small writing Table, about a foot long, which slides out horizontally, and that one pulls out when one wants to use it."[64] Thus was letter writing integrated materially into the daily lives of eighteenth-century ladies.

Additional material evidence of the growing importance of letter writing in women's lives can be found in tables that were converted from one use to another in the eighteenth century. In July 1751, Louis XV's sister had a cedar inkstand installed in the drawer of a table; in April 1757, the dauphine had a drawer in the bookcase in her cabinet fitted with a velvet-covered writing slide and an inkstand with three silver pots.[65] The Musée Cognac-Jay has a worktable built around 1755 that was converted into a writing table later in the century. The right-hand compartment of the center drawer was fitted with an inkstand; at the same time a sliding shelf with a leather-covered writing surface on one side, which could also be raised to serve as a reading stand, was installed over the drawer's central compartment.[66]

6.23. Nicolas Lavreince, *The Novel*. Gouache on paper. Musée Cognac-Jay, Paris. Inv. J0153. Photo: Roger-Viollet.

Writing Desk or Ladies' Desk?

If writing was central to the material culture of ladies in the eighteenth century, writing desks were not, however, their exclusive property. Gentlemen, too, were expected to write graceful, elegant letters, and they too used small writing desks when engaged in writing such letters to friends or family. The marquis de Vaudreuil had himself painted seated at a writing desk piled high with various attributes of leisure: a violin, a journal, and letters and pens spilling out of the open drawer (fig. 6.24). The intimate setting is indicated by the dog lying at his feet and the fireplace with a chinoiserie jar on the mantelpiece. Although the marquis is sitting up straight, the chair in which he is seated is designed for reclining, not for work.

Marquetry designs provide further evidence that gentlemen owned and used writing desks. For example, the marquetry of the desk shown in figure 6.25 suggests that it may have been made for an officer retired from the field of battle. The top features the scene from Virgil's *Aeneid* of Aeneas bearing his father, Anchises, from a fallen Troy; on the front drawer beneath the writing slide is a trophy composed of arms (fig. 6.25b). Another desk is decorated with marquetry depicting a country scene, with sheep and cows in the foreground, the master surveying his property at the left, and in the background on the right, a chateau (fig. 6.26). Most striking is the portrait

6.24. Alexandre Roslin, *Portrait of the Marquis de Vaudreuil* (ca. 1765). Oil on canvas, 2.12 × 1.55 m. The writing table is decorated with fish-scale marquetry typical of Oeben's work. Courtesy of The National Gallery of Ireland. Inv. NGI.1824. Photo: © The National Gallery of Ireland.

6.25a. "Anchises" writing table (French, Louis XV period) by David Roentgen (top view). V&A Images/Victoria and Albert Museum, no. 381–1874.

6.25b. "Anchises" writing table (French, Louis XV period) by David Roentgen (front view of drawer). V&A Images/Victoria and Albert Museum, no. 381–1874.

6.26. Writing desk with a female head medallion set in pastoral landscape marquetry (1770–75) by François Bayer (top view). Bequeathed by John Jones. V&A Images/Victoria and Albert Museum, no. 1065–1882.

medallion of a lady inset above this scene, a reminder, perhaps, of the lady to whom the owner of the property would write upon this desk.

The small writing desk was associated with ladies, not because it was used exclusively by them, but because it supported the kind of writing they were encouraged and expected to do. This was the only desk a lady should have, and few ladies had any other. A gentleman, however, generally enjoyed the use of a *bureau plat* when engaged not in the leisure of writing familiar letters but in the work of the pen. The bureau plat was a man's desk because it was a working space. Defined in the *Encyclopédie méthodique* as a "large [table] designed for the labor of writing or study,"[67] a bureau was standard office furniture for men engaged in a variety of professions, from the lawyer meeting clients and crafting briefs to the man of affairs or the royal official to the man of letters who needed to spread out his books and papers. It was designed to impress and was central to the furnishing of libraries and the various sorts of cabinets that architects designated as masculine spaces.[68] Government ministers, men of letters, and professional men typically had their portraits painted next to the corner of such

6.27. Anonymous, *Portrait of an Architect*. Oil on canvas, 40.5 × 32.5 cm. Musée Magnin, Dijon. Photo: Réunion des Musées Nationaux/Art Resource, New York.

an impressive desk, as an anonymous architect did some time in the second half of the eighteenth century (see fig. 6.27). Although he is dressed informally in a dressing gown, the architect is seated in a desk chair upholstered in leather and next to an impressive desk with ormolu mounts. He is at home in his *cabinet de travail*. Architectural plans and drafting instruments that identify him by his profession cover the desk. The folio volumes standing on the large desk reinforce the masculinity of the self-presentation.

Small feminized versions of the bureau plat reinforce rather than call into question the masculinity of the form. The reduced size, rounded corners, and porcelain plaques mounted on the bureau plat shown in figure 6.28 make it impossible to mistake it for a man's office furniture while bringing it into stylistic conformity with the other small porcelain-mounted furniture that decorated the bedroom of its owner: the Russian grand duchess Maria Feodorovna.[69]

In principle, no woman had a *cabinet de travail* or owned a bureau because working women were not admitted into the ranks of professionals, and ladies were not expected to engage in work. In practice, there was no such thing as a *femme avocat*, and, as we have already seen, a *femme savante*, *femme de lettres*, or *femme auteur* was considered an "exceptional" woman, if not an aberration or a monster.[70]

6.28. Bureau plat set with fourteen Sèvres porcelain plaques (ca. 1778–1784) by Martin Carlin. 77 × 131 × 62 cm. Collection of the J. Paul Getty Museum, Los Angeles, California. 83.DA.385.

Thus, when Maurice Quentin de La Tour portrayed Madame de Pompadour seated next to a large bureau plat, on which stand a globe, architectural drawings, and several large tomes, including Montesquieu's *De l'Esprit des lois* and a volume of the *Encylopédie*, he drew the wrath of the critics, who accused him of portraying the king's mistress as a *femme philosophe*, too serious, too masculine (see fig. 6.29).[71] When François Boucher painted Pompadour the following year, he produced a very different effect by drawing freely on the visual language of the letter painting (see fig. 6.30). In Boucher's portrait, Pompadour leans back into the soft cushions of a chaise longue, like the female readers with whom we are familiar from genre paintings. Like them, she has let the small book she is reading—a novel, no doubt—fall into her lap. A large volume, like the ones in the La Tour portrait, lies forgotten on the floor under the writing desk at her side, the bookcase out of which it has been drawn closed and cast in shadow. By contrast, the small writing desk (like the gilt-bronze ornamented leg of the bureau plat in the La Tour portrait) is brightly lit, every detail of its design and craftsmanship visible. Indeed, it is so well rendered that it is assumed to represent one of the little tables made by Vanrisemburgh that Pompadour bought from Lazare Duvaux (fig. 6.4a is similar).[72] An envelope with a broken seal lying on the desk reiterates the erotic message of the roses at Pompadour's feet and on top of more forgotten volumes on the little shelf between the legs of the desk. The drawer of the desk, like its owner, is open and available, a quill standing provocatively at attention in the inkwell fitted into the drawer.[73]

An early twentieth-century art historian praised Boucher for the way he captured the everyday life of his subject who, according to his narrative, had just finished penning the letter that lies unsealed on the little desk: "Everything is arranged as usual so that the marquise is surrounded by the familiar setting of her life," he enthused.[74]

6.29. Maurice-Quentin de La Tour, *Portrait of the Marquise de Pompadour* (1755). Pastel, 1.75 × 1.28 m. Musée du Louvre, Paris. Réunion des Musées Nationaux/Art Resource, New York.

6.30. François Boucher, *The Marquise de Pompadour* (1756). Oil on canvas, 2.10 × 1.57 m. Bayerische Staats-gemäldesammlungen, Alte Pinakothek, Munich. (D.-Leihgabe. Hypo-Vereinsbank).

Boucher's portrait is perceived as documentary because Boucher has reinforced the critic's gendered assumptions about women, letters, and love. However, the accuracy of representation of the writing desk, the inkstand, the pen, the candle, the sealing wax, and the letter cannot fool us into thinking that Boucher has simply shown us Mme de Pompadour as she was, any more than he showed us the women in his genre paintings as they were in their simple everydayness. And even though La Tour too represented books, fashion, and furniture in exquisitely accurate detail, by presenting Pompadour in a different idiom—that of the man of law, letters, administration, or affairs—he opened himself to the critique of misrepresenting his subject by violating the gender order. Large and small books, large and small desks, made all the difference.

In a much quoted passage from her memoirs, Mme de Genlis claimed that she was the first woman in France to own a bureau, for which she was, she said, "much criticized." She quoted a long poem her brother sent her at the time that makes clear both the association of such a desk with men and the work they do and the absurdity, in her brother's view, of even imagining a woman behind it. It simply does not belong in her room.

> That an old notary in a long coat,
> With a pale and long face,
> Dries out before a bureau,
> That's his duty, that's what he does;
> But that this furniture of the bar
> That this dark and sad bureau
> Is found in your rooms, my Thémire,
> I cannot help but say,
> Ought to make you angry,
> Since a bureau is not made for you.
> No, this is not at all its place.

Genlis's brother ends his poem on an even stronger note, pleading with her to distance herself, not just from the desk, but from the "labors of study" that will cost her the feminine beauty that is the source of (female) happiness. "Get away from that desk," he cries. "The vain labors of study/ When one is loveable and pretty, / Are not worth the sweet repose they cost." A desk is only acceptable, he concludes, for "writing to one's love."[75] He does not suggest that *writing* is an inappropriate activity for her but that her writing ought to be limited to love letters, and that for such writing, a large masculine bureau is not only unnecessary but inadvisable, since it takes away from her feminine charms—and, by extension perhaps, from the charm of her letters.

Fortunately for Genlis, her husband, who gave her the desk, was not concerned to limit her writing to love letters. Not so fortunate were Suzanne Necker and her daughter, Germaine. Mme Necker was one of the foremost salonnières in Enlightenment Paris, but she limited her writing to a private journal (which included essays that she never tried to publish) and correspondence, both of which could be accommodated by a small writing desk.[76] Her daughter, whose education she personally supervised, grew up to be the novelist, historian, and critic, Germaine de Staël. Germaine's cousin, Albertine Necker de Saussure, claimed that Germaine, taking her cue from her mother, placated her father by limiting not her writing but the surface on which she wrote:

> As M. Necker had forbidden his wife to write, out of fear of being annoyed by the idea of interrupting her on entering her room, Mlle Necker, who did not wish to bring upon herself such a prohibition, got used to writing, as it were, on the wing; such that, seeing her always standing, or leaning against a corner of the mantelpiece, her father could not imagine that he was interrupting anything serious.

According to her cousin, the great writer "so respected this little weakness" of her father's that it was "only long after she lost him that she had in her room the least setup for writing." Germaine de Staël adapted her writing practice to her father's prejudices by accepting the gender economy of furniture of her day, but only until his death and her own public success as a writer. "Finally, after *Corinne* made a big splash abroad," her cousin recalled, "she said to me: 'I really want a big table, it seems to me that I now have the right to one.'"[77] The experience of the Necker family sheds light not only on the place of furniture in the gender economy of the eighteenth century but on how some women managed to accomplish great things on small surfaces.

The *Secrétaire* and the Gendered Writing Self

Between the bureau plat and the small writing table was the *secrétaire*, which could be either small or large, mobile or stationary. In his treatise on furniture making, Roubo divided writing tables into two types, which he identified first as "the large and the small." However, he went on to clarify his categories rather differently: by large tables he meant "desks of all sorts, closed and not closed, at which several people can work together." The small writing tables were those "appropriate to a single person," and thus included all the secretaries, regardless of their dimensions.[78] What distinguished the secretary from other types of desks was that, large or small, it was personal furniture, meant to accommodate only one person. The secretary, and the small secretary in particular—of which the bonheur-du-jour is the prime but not the only example—was designed to support not only epistolary writing but the epistolary self.

Unlike the simple writing table, the secretary extends vertically above the level of the writing surface both to contain drawers, cubbyholes, or shelves (thus complicating the flatness of the table) and to provide some measure of privacy to the writer. A comparison of seventy-three secretaries made between about 1740 and 1789 by at least twenty different cabinetmakers shows that they ranged in height from just under one meter to just over a meter and a half.[79] Only fifteen (19%) are more than a half meter in depth, and only one is more than a meter deep. The average secretary thus stands relatively flat against a wall, and those that are not too tall could easily be moved out to the center of a room or near a window to catch the light. (The finished veneers on their backs show that they were meant to be placed in the center of a room, either temporarily or permanently). If we compare the secretaries by width, the dimension that would relate most closely to the number of persons for whom a piece was designed, we find that thirty-seven, or just over half, are less than one meter wide—which would seem about right for one person. Only eight (about 10%) are more than one and half meters wide, and all but one of these very large secretaries are rolltop desks designed to accommodate multiple writers with writing slides that pull out from the sides when needed. These are comparable in width to the large bureaux plats, and, in fact, look like bureaux plats with tops.[80]

Between 1748 and 1757, Lazare Duvaux sold fourteen pieces identified as secretaries, or in the form of secretaries, to ten women. Not surprisingly, Mme de Pompadour bought four of them, but the comtesse de Marsan bought two: one for 258 livres that was veneered in floral satinwood with ormolu fittings, silvered pots for the inkstand, and blue velvet upholstery on the writing slide; and another "small secretary," also veneered in satinwood, four years later for 360 livres. But Mme d'Épinay only paid 60 livres for her fire screen done up as a secretary, and Mme Camuset paid only 36 livres for a base in lacquered wood for a "Chinese secretary," which Duvaux had repaired for her as well. The repairs, it should be noted, were to the mirror frame and the wood marquetry of the "toilette," so this was a combination piece. The marquise de Gontaut bought a secretary in the form of a bookcase, whereas Mme Rouillé's was a fall-front model with a marble top. Several, but not all, of the secretaries purchased by women were identified as "small," and one bought by the dauphine was only "30 inches." Even though it was small, it was not cheap: with gilt bronze mounts and tulipwood marquetry, it cost 672 livres, plus another 24 livres to have it delivered to her at Versailles.[81]

Despite the brisk business merchants and cabinetmakers did in secretaries from midcentury on, not until 1798 did the dictionary of the Académie française give as one of its definitions of *secrétaire* "a desk where one writes and where one keeps papers." Every other definition referred to a person, principally "someone whose job is to make and write letters, dispatches for his master, for the person on whom he is dependant." And despite the fact that secretaries were described and illustrated in the pages of the *Encyclopédie*—in Roubo's article on furniture and in the article on veneering—the *Encyclopédie* too defined the *secrétaire* exclusively as a person who helps someone with their letters.[82] The dictionaries thus failed to track one of the most significant transformations of the eighteenth century: the transformation of the secretary from a person to a piece of furniture.

The shift from secretary (the person) to secretary (the desk) reflected a fundamental change in the practice of writing that entailed a change in both its social meaning and its psychological significance. The creation of the secretary signaled a new authorial need for a personal surface on which to write, as private persons shifted from dictating their letters to a confidential secretary to penning them themselves. What had been two fundamentally different kinds of actions—a noble intellectual or spiritual act of composition and a base mechanical or physical act of inscription—carried out by people of different social status was now integrated into a single practice carried out by a single individual. The transformation of the secretary allowed writing to become fully personal—the expression of one's being or self—by eliminating for the composer the mediation of a servile human being and at the same time empowering the scribe to use his skill and his tools to his own ends rather than someone else's.[83]

Roland Barthes has noted that in ancient Rome writing was considered so base an activity that free men did not write; they dictated their thoughts to slaves.[84] And Lesley Smith has shown that the distinction between composition and copying explains the dearth of medieval images of women writing, at a time when nobles of both sexes composed texts. Since copying—the manual art of writing—was merely scribal, and scribal work was servile men's work, how could a woman writer be depicted? Women who composed texts (noble, spiritual women such Héloïse) could not be represented penning them. Those few women who were depicted in the act of writing were engaged in an act of spiritual dictation, acting humbly as inspired scribe for a male deity or saint and revealing visually their own lack of authority.[85] The dearth of images of women writing thus reflects not medieval views of women's intellectual abilities but the gender distribution of labor mapped onto the division of writing into two discrete social practices, one base and the other noble.

By the eighteenth century, however, writing was practiced and understood quite differently. The old division of labor between composing and copying obtained only in the realm of professional writing, where male secretaries toiled away for male bosses at vast bureaux.[86] As the secretary was taking on new meaning as a piece of personal furniture, the bureau followed a different trajectory: first from a surface used for business ("a Counter or table on which money is counted, or on which papers are put") to a more complicated piece of furniture that included storage of business papers ("a kind of table with several drawers and shelves, where one keeps papers"). It was then expanded to signify those agencies associated with paperwork (offices or bureaus), and then to the place where such work was conducted—the office. Most of the *Encyclopédie*'s definitions, for example, begin: "This is a place. . . ."[87] The expansion of business, trade, and government bureaucracy meant increased demand for secretaries to produce the full panoply of documents that kept the gears of state, society, economy, and empire turning. The etymological transformations of *bureau* and *secrétaire* thus reflect a new political division of writing, between documents produced by men to support the expanding work of law, the economy, and the state, and personal correspondence between individuals in their capacity as private persons that supported the growth of the individual and challenged the authority of the state.[88]

As the portraits of Diderot and Labille-Guiard's letter-writing woman discussed in chapter 1 suggested, the gender division of labor now mapped onto this new division of writing: as public and professional writing was masculinized, personal writing was feminized. Yet even the king, who still did not deign to pen his own letters, made a claim to doing so: when he employed a secretary it was not simply to transcribe his words but to counterfeit his hand.[89]

All noble hearts and minds were encouraged to express themselves and create social bonds through the writing of letters, and most French elites no longer saw the pen as a base tool but as a noble instrument, like the sword or the embroidery needle.

To assist the growing corps of letter writers, printers and men of letters churned out manuals on how to write letters, and agendas in which to keep track of their own appointments, finances, and thoughts, and dubbed them all *secrétaires*.[90] Furniture makers and dealers gave the same name to the desk that increasing numbers of both women and men now needed as they penned their own letters and kept track of their personal affairs. This is why Roubo classified all secretaries, large or small, with the small writing tables. As a piece of furniture designed to enable the individual to confide his or her self and secrets to paper and thence to a trusted and complicit other, the secretary was essential to the production of intersubjective intimacy and a new, modern self.

In the ARTFL-FRANTEXT database of French literature, the first reference to a secretary as a piece of furniture is in a letter Diderot wrote to his friend Sophie Volland in October 1759. On his return from a trip he had gone directly to see her, but she wasn't home. He left her a message, to which she must have replied that she had sent him one in care of a friend, where she expected him to have gone first. Incredulous, he replied, "[In your place] I would have left the letter on my secretary, and I would have said to myself: tomorrow it will be two weeks that she has not seen the person she loves; she has suffered, she has desired, she is worried. Her first moment will be for me."[91] Here the secretary is used by a friend (or lover) to write a personal letter [*billet*] to his or her counterpart. It is significant that Diderot imagines himself in Volland's situation, and her in his, and in both cases, the writer has his or her own secretary on which to write the letter. In addition, in suggesting that Volland should have left the letter to him on her secretary, Diderot implies that it is her personal space, one that she might share with him, her correspondent and friend, but which is understood to be hers. Because we know that Sophie Volland lived with her mother and sister, and that her relationship with Diderot was not a secret from them (Diderot addressed them in many of his letters to Volland, expecting her to share them with her family), the designation of the secretary as the appropriate spot to leave a letter for him invokes privacy as personal space, but does not suggest secrecy.

Secrecy is suggested in a letter Diderot wrote to Volland three years later, which turns up as the second documented reference to the secretary as a desk in the ARTFL-FRANTEXT database. Here it appears in an anecdote about Montesquieu and Lord Chesterfield. In order to prove his point that Frenchmen have no common sense and Englishmen do have wit, Diderot wrote, Chesterfield sent a mysterious stranger to warn Montesquieu that he would be arrested at any moment for his subversive writings. "The state inquisitors are fully aware of your conduct, you are being spied on, you are being followed, note is made of all your projects, they have no doubt that you are writing," he confided ominously. "Look, sir, if in fact you have written, consider that a line written innocently, but misinterpreted, could cost you your life." As Diderot recounted the story, Montesquieu immediately panicked: "His first movement was to run quickly to his secretary, take out all the papers, and throw them in the fire."[92] This anecdote represents the secretary as the working space of the man of letters, but more significantly as a storage space for important personal papers. Although there is an element of secrecy here, it is precisely the question of the security of the secretary that is called into question. Had Montesquieu believed that the secretary was secure from the intrusions of the state, he would not have felt compelled to remove his manuscripts from it and burn them.

Michel-Jean Sedaine was the first writer to use a secretary as a theatrical prop. In *Le Philosophe sans le savoir* (1765), the cabinet, furnished with "a secretary along one side, on which are papers and boxes," sets the scene for the family drama that will unfold.[93] As Mark Ledbury has noted, the setting is "simultaneously an intimate family sphere, a place of business, and a hive of celebratory activity as the family gears up for Vanderk's daughter's marriage."[94] It has long been argued that *Le Philosophe sans le savoir* was the first play consciously based on the new dramatic principles laid out by Diderot in *Entretiens sur le fils naturel*, and that the main character (the owner of the secretary) was modeled after the title character in Diderot's *Le Père de famille*. Ledbury maintains that Diderot in fact collaborated with Sedaine in writing this play. Regardless of who took the lead, Diderot loved the play. The day after the premiere he wrote to a friend: "Yes, my friend, yes, this is true taste, this is domestic truth, this is the room, these are the actions and the words of upstanding people."[95]

These different associations of the secretary—with both writing and storage; women and men; the person of the writer and the modern, intimate family; and privacy, secrecy, and limited security—distinguish it from the bureau. As we have seen, what distinguished the bureau physically from the secretary was its almost uniformly large size and flatness (which easily accommodated the traditional writing posture), and the location of its functional parts. On the bureau, leather was mounted right on the surface of the desk for everyone to see, and drawers were clearly visible, even if they required a key to open them. In the secretary, by contrast, the writing surface, drawers, and other storage spaces were all hidden inside the desk, often secured by a lock. The variety of secretaries lies most notably in the ways in which they open— via fall fronts, roll tops, cabinet doors, and so forth. The bureau proclaimed itself to any visitor as a desk; the secretary did not. As Carolyn Sargentson observes, the owner of a secretary could choose to share as much or as little of what went on within it.[96]

The secretary was, in general, much smaller than the bureau, and its limited surface almost required the new upright posture designed for ladies. It had but a single writing surface, and its body framed that of the writer. The back of the secretary both prevented others from seeing what was being written and closed the writer off from others, creating the sense of privacy that personal letters required. The secretary was personal furniture, like a dressing table, and was often found in the same personal spaces as dressing tables, jewel cases, and work tables. When veneered in the latest style, the secretary fit in beautifully with these other accouterments of the fashionable lady.

If we return to the ARTFL-FRANTEXT database, we learn that secretaries were always identified as personal furniture. That is, whether it belonged to a man or a woman, every secretary is referred to either as *my secretary* or *his* or *her secretary*. For example, in Louvet de Couvray's popular novel *Une année dans la vie du chevalier de Faublas* (1787), Faublas writes: "I sat down at my secretary. I wrote a first letter, which I tore up; I wrote a second, full of cross-outs, that had to be corrected."[97] Similarly, a character in Loaisel de Tréogate's *Ainsi finissent les grandes passions* (1788), says: "Without knowing what I was looking for, Eugenie's letters fell into my hands; I tossed them away indignantly, as monuments of lies and perfidy. I got up furious; I walked with great strides; I came to sit down at my secretary; I picked up a book, a pen, some papers, one after another, and none of this had the power to calm me down."[98]

Most important, the secretary provided hidden locked storage for letters and other valuables. When the wife of the cabinetmaker Bernard Molitor died in 1796, the notary found silver cutlery, three watches, and the family jewels in her secretary.[99] Increased sociability in the home meant more people coming and going; apartment living in a crowded city increased the risk of break-ins as well as fire; increased wealth meant that there was more to steal, while endemic poverty meant there was always the temptation to do so. As Mercier mused, "Love, ambition, and politics place their secrets under steel bands, the puzzle [*le jeu*] of which demands to be studied; and the artist, foreseeing at the same time the action of fire and that of violence, has deployed rather extensive knowledge to guarantee fragile papers from this double attack." He concluded that if the locksmith "is the guarantor of public security, he is not that of its happiness: his ingenuity testifies to that of the thief and the robber."[100]

The lock and key secured the identification of the secretary with its owner and were meant to protect the privacy of the owner's life and self, more even than her property. For documents, and especially letters written and received, contained the owner's thoughts, dreams, and desires, as well as evidence of actions and relationships; disclosing letters, even those written to the owner, was tantamount to baring his or her soul. The secrecy of the secretary is, at bottom, the privacy of letter writing itself, as it had come to be understood by the second half of the eighteenth century.[101]

When scribes wrote letters for their mistresses and masters, the desk was not (could not be) a place of security and privacy: the scribe was. By combining the functions of writing surface and secure storage, the secretary reflected the need and ability of modern writers to articulate their thoughts and feelings on paper and thence to confide them only to a trusted other who was an equal rather than a subordinate. So too, it should be noted, did the seal. Originally used like a signature to authenticate the authorship of a letter or document penned by a scribe, the seal was now meant to secure the thoughts confided to the letter from messengers, postmen, and other third parties through whose hands the letter must pass on its journey from writer to addressee.[102] Like the secretary upon which letters were written and in which papers were secured under lock and key, the seal was the materialization of the owner's self. Locks were as much evidence of breaches of privacy as they were of other sorts of thefts, just as the seal of a letter that was meant to protect the privacy of the communication within it could always be violated.

Because the secretary was so closely associated with a single person, and in particular with his or her private thoughts, it could represent its owner in the symbolic economy of fiction; plots could turn and character could be disclosed simply by violating its privacy. As the repository of the owner's most valued thoughts, actions, and desires, the secretary was a stand-in for its owner; violating a woman's secretary was thus a metaphor for rape. In genre paintings, leaving the drawer open with its key dangling in the lock and letters spilling out suggested the loss of virginity or the promiscuity of its owner. But as the repository of confidences like the confidential secretary it replaced, the secretary also represented the threat of betrayal. Novelists took full advantage of the secretary's dramatic potential by casting it both as a surrogate for the master and as the servant it displaced. Because a locking secretary was always a declaration of the autonomy of its owner, who effectively declares at least some part of him or herself beyond the power of another, the secretaries of wives and daughters were always a challenge to authority and potential sites of family dramas.

In Mme d'Épinay's unfinished roman à clef, *Histoire de Madame de Montbrillant* (1770), the eponymous heroine decides to spend the last of the money her father-in-law gave her as a wedding gift, only to find it missing from her secretary. Since it is locked, she knows that the only person who could have taken the money is her debauched husband, who has a key. She asks both him and his servant if he took the money, but they both deny it. She consults her mother who agrees that the lock has not been forced and thus that M. de Montbrillant must be the culprit.[103] The episode is revealing. First, although the theft is a violation of trust, the fact that the husband has a key to his wife's secretary shows that if there ever was any trust, it only went one way. Second, the secretary may well have been the only secure storage the wife had, since she locked her money in it, and not just her papers. And third, within the novel's plot, the husband's deed and his deception following it pretty much sum up his character and the plight of his wife, as he gambles away whatever he does not spend on mistresses. The secretary plays a central role in the marital drama.

Orest Ranum has noted that Samuel Pepys once gave his wife a cabinet that he had received as a gift—but only "after carefully examining the operation of its secret drawers." "Did possession of furniture that could be locked really mean that privacy had increased?" Ranum asks. "Pepys's wife could keep no secrets from prying Samuel's eyes."[104] Ruth Plaut Weinreb notes that Épinay's husband "deceived her almost immediately following their wedding, and gambled, and kept mistresses and squandered the family fortunes," just as Montbrillant did. Both author and character sought legal separation as their only recourse.[105] Whether M. d'Épinay did indeed use his own key to his wife's secretary to rob her, the episode figures well the problem of a woman's privacy, indeed of respect for her personal integrity within marriage and the patriarchal household: the husband's forced entry into the secretary to violate its integrity and steal the valuables within figures the husband's violation of the wife and her trust.

As private spaces, private property, and private thoughts were claimed by individual women, anxieties about violations of privacy began to run through the letters that they carefully sealed and then sent by the most trusted route they knew. When they received letters in return, they sought private spaces in which to read them and then locked them carefully in their desks.[106] Only when a desk's owner was alone or with a trusted friend or servant would hidden places be revealed. Later in Épinay's novel, Mme de Montbrillant explains how her dying sister-in-law entrusted her with the key to her secretary after the doctors had left and they were alone together.

> A sharp pain struck her head; she let out a cry, asking me suddenly for her pockets. It took me a minute to find them; she searched them for a long time without really knowing what she was doing; in the end she pulled out a key and repeated several times: "This is the key, this is the one . . ." She could not finish, and these were the last words she spoke. She lost consciousness again, and at five o'clock in the evening, she was no more.[107]

As the shock of the death hit her, Mme de Montbrillant remembered the key and realized that she must use it to find and destroy "whatever papers" Mme de Ménil might have locked away. "I went to her secretary, in which I had often seen her lock up letters from the chevalier after having read them. It was precisely this key that she had given me. I had but an instant; I took every bit of writing I could find and threw all of it into the fire." After making sure that every scrap burned, Mme de Montbrillant took the key to Mme de Ménil's husband, having done her duty to protect the reputation of her friend.[108]

Small secretaries contained personal correspondence, including but not limited to love letters and the records of extramarital affairs; large ones contained legal documents and family papers. In her memoirs, Mme de Genlis recalls the moment when the purchaser of her late father-in-law's "large secretary" came upon a spring mechanism that, when released, "revealed a little nook, in which we saw a portfolio of blue velvet, with gold embroidery. The portfolio was opened, and in it was found the will that named M. de Genlis the residual heir."[109] Secretaries represented and facilitated the privacy of both individuals and families, but sometimes they guarded their secrets too well. M. de Genlis's father would have done better to entrust the secret of his secretary to his son.

The plot of Choderlos de Laclos' *Les Liaisons dangereuses* (1782) turns on the discovery of the heroine's hidden love letters. Laclos, the writer who most exploited the potential of the epistolary novel, introduced the secretary in the opening letter of *Les Liaisons dangereuses*. Cécile Volanges, fifteen years old and recently returned to her mother's house from her convent boarding school, sits down to write a letter to her friend Sophie Carnay:

> You see, my good friend, [that] I am keeping my word to you, and that bonnets and pompons do not take up all my time; there is some left for you. . . . Mama has consulted me about everything; she treats me much less like a schoolgirl than she used to. I have my own chambermaid; I have a bedroom and a cabinet to myself, and I am writing to you on a very pretty Secretary, to which I have been given the key, and in which I can hide whatever I wish.[110]

Needless to say, Cécile's sense of security is entirely false. With the help of the devious Mme de Merteuil, she enters into an illicit correspondence with the handsome young chevalier de Danceny, carefully saving all of his letters in the locked drawer of her secretary. To advance her own plot, Merteuil later betrays Cécile by telling her mother of the correspondence. Mme de Volanges promptly demands the key to her daughter's secretary. "I pretended not to be able to find it," Cécile later recounted, "but in the end I had to obey." When, at the end of the novel, Cécile flees back to the true safety of the convent, her mother searches her room for clues. "I went through her armoires, her secretary; I found everything where it belonged and all her clothes, save the dress she left in. She had not even taken the little bit of money that she had in her room." Like Mme de Montbrillant Cécile had learned the hard way that a lock and key mean very little when one is a daughter or a wife. But it was not just the security of the secretary that was an illusion; there was also the freedom of letter writing, which she had exercised with innocent abandon. In the end, Cécile left behind everything she had described in that first letter to Sophie—including especially the freedom and the privacy falsely promised by the secretary.

Whether a secretary did indeed hold within it secrets that its owner wished to conceal from others, its very existence suggested the existence of such secrets. Because the functions of the secretary were concealed, the locked secretary could provoke anxiety on the part of those who did not have access to its hidden spaces, as women's bodies have always provoked such anxiety on the part of men. The theme of the locked desk, and especially of the secret drawer in a woman's secretary containing the letters that document a secret affair, has remained a theme in French literature into the twentieth century and parallels the letter theme in genre painting that bespeaks the same anxiety. In particular, writers have used the bonheur-du-jour to tell tales of family secrets and their revelation through the discovery of hidden compartments.[111] For twentieth-century fiction writers, secretaries are the furniture of nostalgia, whose secrets may go back centuries. They are the closets in which ancient skeletons lie waiting to be released by the writer who, through his art, is able to spring the lock and find the hidden compartment, with its secret stories waiting to be told.

For the historian, however, who looks at the secretary not from the point of view of the man who cannot open it but of the woman who holds the key, it is the furniture of the modern self. It represents the transformation of the secretary from servant to material extension of the writer's body, and of writing into the direct expression of the self in communication with a trusted other. For the woman who owned and used it to write and store her letters, as well as the materials necessary to produce them, the secretary contributed to the reintegration of mind and body and thus to the integrity and expression of the self that we know as modern.

PART IV

Letters

7

Coming of Age

Young Ladies, Privacy, and Epistolary Practice

The tragic plot of Laclos' *Les Liaisons dangereuses* follows inexorably from the fateful decision to entrust a naive young woman with the tools of the letter writer and the privacy necessary to use them effectively. The same conclusion could be drawn from Rousseau's *Julie, ou la nouvelle Héloïse*. But how else did young ladies become women except through writing letters? The tools they were given and the epistolary practice into which they were initiated during their convent years were crucial to that rite of passage by which they were prepared to enter the world and become the wives and mothers that, they were told, was their destiny. The inevitability of this plot, in which letter writing is the means of a young woman's downfall, is challenged in a novel that presents a very different trajectory for its naive young heroine: Françoise de Graffigny's *Lettres d'une Peruvienne*, published more than a decade before Rousseau's. It is challenged even more powerfully by the examples of two young women, Geneviève de Malboissière and Manon Phlipon, who embraced the practice of epistolarity in the 1760s and '70s and used it to confide in a trusted girlfriend. Unlike Cécile and Julie, these young women were not simply pawns in games played by self-interested adults. Rather, they were subjects struggling for autonomy through reflection and communication facilitated by the related practices of reading, conversation, and letter writing.

Zilia: Coming to Writing and Womanhood

Like *Les Liaisons dangereuses*, *Lettres d'une peruvienne* takes the story of an innocent young virgin—in this case a Peruvian princess abducted by the Spaniards on the eve of her wedding day—and follows her through an education in the ways of the world. But Zilia is no Cécile, and Graffigny's world is not that of Laclos. Moreover, we view that world not through the interplay of letters orchestrated by a male author but from Zilia's perspective alone: through her letters we see not only the France of the mid-eighteenth century but also her own development from a lovesick girl to a mature and autonomous woman. Like Montesquieu's Persian Usbek, with whom she has often been compared,[1] Zilia comes to know herself through her encounter with an alien culture which is, however, familiar to her readers. For her, too, letter writing makes possible the reflections in which she engages and which are central to the epistolary novel, as Marivaux suggests in the preface to his own epistolary novel, *La Vie de Marianne* (1731–41). Reflection, he argues, contributes to verisimilitude by countering the force of the narrative that propels the novel forward. Marianne's "long [and] such frequent reflections," moreover, were only possible because she "was retired from the world, a situation that renders the spirit serious and philosophical."[2]

Usbek, too, had retired from the world—first from the Persian court to France, and then from the bustle of Paris to a friend's country estate—in order to reflect on his life and the social and political system of which he was a part. For a woman, however, retreat meant, not only retreat from the public world of town or court, but from marriage as well. Zilia's decision not to marry, with which the novel ends, puts her in the literary tradition of Mme de Lafayette's Princesse de Clèves and the historical tradition of Mme de Sévigné, who also chose to maintain the independence conferred by widowhood rather than remarry. Mlle de Montpensier, the seventeenth-century princess who dreamed of a city of women in which each would enjoy *repos* in her own cabinet, once wrote: "Besides being a state conducive to putting the events of one's life in order, retirement gives one the spare time necessary to put this past onto paper."[3] In her retirement, Graffigny's Zilia turns her private writing into a text for the reading public. "It would be unnecessary to indicate that the first letters have been translated by Zilia herself," Graffigny tells us in her preface. She goes on to explain that "we owe this translation to Zilia's leisure in her retreat."[4] This retreat and the text it enables are achieved through means both epistolary and material. The voice we hear is that of the hard-won autonomy of a female subject.

Zilia's opening letter, however, is as naive as Cécile's. It establishes Zilia's dependence on her Peruvian fiancé (who is also, by Inca custom, her brother) and the distance she has to travel to achieve an autonomous sense of self. "Aza, my dear Aza!" she exclaims. "Like a morning mist the cries of your tender Zilia rise up and have dissipated before reaching you. In vain do I call to you for help, in vain do I wait for you to come and break the bonds of my enslavement."[5] How then does Zilia achieve the autonomy that rings clear in her final letter to the French suitor whose love she rejects in favor of a friendship that will enrich her independent life rather than end it? "You fear needlessly that solitude might damage my health," she writes. "Believe me, Déterville, solitude never becomes dangerous save on account of idleness. Always occupied, I will know how to fashion new pleasures from all that habit renders insipid."[6]

Letter writing is central to the epistolary heroine's existence. For the first half of the novel, however, Zilia has only *quipus* with which to "write."[7] According to Graffigny, the *quipus* were not really a form of writing because they were a mnemonic device rather than a means of expressing words or ideas, or of constructing sentences, narratives, arguments. Thus, when Zilia passes her last *quipus* through her fingers, she uses them to cry to Aza that she is losing him, losing her last link to him. "These knots, which seem to me to be a line of communication linking my heart to yours, are already nothing more than the sad objects of my regret. Illusion is deserting me, replaced by the awful truth: my wandering thoughts, lost in the immense void of absence, will henceforth be reduced to nothing with the same speed as time."[8] Fortunately, Déterville, the French nobleman who has rescued her from her Spanish captors, fallen in love with her, and brought her home to Paris has given her a tutor to instruct her in French and "in the method used here to give a kind of existence to thought." "This is done," she explains, "by drawing with a feather little figures called *letters* on a thin, white material they call *paper*."[9] For Zilia, coming to writing implies a loss of traditional ties to family, culture, and the man she loves, but it is also associated with lost illusions.

The *quipus* are identified with illusion on several levels: the illusion of Aza's love; the illusion that, wherever Zilia is, she is still within his domain, since the sun that defines it continues to shine on her; the illusion that she is experiencing only a disruption of her life as a Peruvian princess, a temporary adventure within the parameters of her Peruvian life that can be recalled and expressed through the knotting of the *quipus*. Letter XVIII marks Zilia's awakening; written French is the means by which the veil is removed. "I am still barely able to form these figures that I rush to make the interpreters of my tenderness," she admits. However, she is already feeling the effects of writing. "I feel myself being brought back to life by this tender occupation. Restored to myself, I feel as if I am beginning to live again."[10] Through writing Zilia is able to recognize and thus to experience her selfhood, but she finds herself in a very different world. "Alas," she writes, "how grievous has it been for me knowing the [language] I now use, how deceptive the hope that led me to learn it! As I gained understanding of it, a new universe presented itself to my eyes. Objects took another form, and each clarification revealed to me a new misfortune. Everything—my mind, my heart, my eyes—everything led me astray."[11]

Eventually Zilia will be reunited with Aza, only to learn that he no longer loves her, has betrayed her, and wishes to be released from his vows. She releases him, accepts the return of her letters, and thinks her life is over. However, after a seemly period of grief and despair that brings her near death, she regroups with the aid of books and solitude. "Reading at first with effort," she writes Déterville, "I find that imperceptively new ideas form around the horrible truth buried at the bottom of my heart and in the end offer some respite from my sorrow."[12] It is at this point and armed with these "new ideas" that Zilia confounds Déterville's hopes, based on his own cultural assumptions—assumptions that he shares with Graffigny's (male) readers. His illusions of marrying her are destroyed when she explains that, although French "notions of decency" may not "allow a person of [her] age the independence and solitude in which [she] now live[s]," she remains unconvinced that marriage is the only virtuous course. "Shall I admit it?" she asks. "Freedom's great sweetness enters my imagination at times, and I listen to it attentively. Surrounded by pleasant objects, I try to savor the orderliness that is their charm."[13]

What are these pleasant objects and what have they to do with freedom? Zilia's last letters are written from the little house Déterville had purchased for her out of the sale of part of the Inca treasure stolen by the Spanish that he had restored to her. Zilia was herself the prize of the Spanish booty, and the golden chair sold off by Déterville to buy the house was for her the embodiment of Aza.[14] Without consulting Zilia, Déterville chose this particular piece of her property to sell in order to buy the house, furnish it, and provide her also with a nest egg—a chest full of French money.

The house was meant to be a home for the reunited lovers—with Aza there, Zilia would no longer need the chair to represent him. In the end, however, she was left with neither Aza nor the chair, and the house became her refuge from the world and from marriage, the nest egg the basis of her freedom. Her property gave her the economic independence that allowed her to defy convention—to stand outside marriage and achieve the autonomy denied French women. (This property was only "hers" because it had been stolen by the Spanish in the first place. It was the treasure of the Incas, but only Zilia was there to make a claim on it: the prize became possessor; the object became subject.)

A whole set of transformations occur, moreover, when the chair that was Aza is turned into the house that will be Zilia's. It is a change of the same magnitude as the shift from *quipus* to writing. The *quipus* had bound Zilia to Aza and to the illusion of her need for him; with writing she was able, not only to discard old illusions and break through the confines of her Peruvian worldview, but also to establish a sense of her own selfhood through reflection on the world around her. The golden chair had been an object of devotion, the centerpiece of her worship of Aza, to whom the *quipus* had bound her. Through writing she began to define a new relationship between herself and others, herself and the world; within her own four walls she is able to continue that process of definition and self-definition. Most significantly, she turns her letters to Aza into a text aimed at a public: she unties the knots by engaging in the form of reflection made possible by writing for a public.

Earlier, Zilia had criticized the French for "turn[ing] their backs on those solid, pleasant objects produced in abundance by France itself, [and] instead extracting from all parts of the world and at great expense the fragile, useless furnishings that decorate their houses."[15] But she never mentions her own desk—whether it is a solid masculine bureau or a fragile little secretary veneered in exotic woods imported from the Caribbean and fabricated by craftsmen brought to France by the lure of wealthy patrons and consumers. At least we know that it is not useless, a mere luxury, for she must write her book on it. And we know where it must be located: in a small cabinet that affords her the privacy she needs.

All the rooms of her new house charm Zilia, but the one that arrests her is a library filled with books. She is only able to tear herself away from it when she is reminded of a golden key she had been given by Déterville, and which opens a door leading from this room into a cabinet. Its walls are covered with pictures, mirrors, and pictures that are mirrors. "In a thousand places on this paneling were representations of our Virgins wearing the same attire I had when I arrived in France. It was even said that they resembled me," Zilia remarks with delight.[16] The mirrors remind us not only that the cabinet is a site of reflection, but also of Zilia's first day in France when she was startled to see in the first house she entered "a young person dressed in the manner of a Virgin of the Sun," and who turned out, of course, to be her own reflection. "My amazement held me transfixed, eyes locked onto that shadow," she explained at the time. When Déterville stood beside her, and his reflection appeared next to hers, she began to comprehend both her error and the phenomenon of the mirror. "These marvels disturb the mind and offend reason," she wrote, and wondered if she had better fear or love a people responsible for them.[17] In the end she does neither, but rather finds a common humanity with those whose virtues make them worthy of her friendship. From her cabinet, in which she can reflect on both them and herself—as a woman, as a Peruvian princess, as she sees herself, and as she is portrayed by (French) others—she is able to extend such friendship, because she has constructed, through writing and through the acquisition of objects that both reflect her and provide a retreat from family and the world, a self defined by a set of values independent of both French and Peruvian cultures and materialized in her own private space, her cabinet.

For Geneviève de Malboissière and Manon Phlipon, too, the cabinet was a space of friendship, study, reflection, and writing. For them, as for Zilia, letter writing made possible what Walter Ong calls an "increasingly articulate introspectivity," as they explored both self and world, "opening the psyche . . . not only to the external objective world quite distinct from itself, but also to the interior self against whom the objective world is set."[18] Through the practice of letter writing and in the spaces of privacy, Geneviève and Manon articulated a gendered subjectivity by which they understood themselves both as individuals and as women and struggled with the cultural contradictions they had to confront as gendered subjects. Reading their letters gives us more than a window into their selves; it allows us to see how those selves were constructed intersubjectively through letter writing, and the role that gender and gender consciousness played in that construction.

Geneviève: The Uses of Privacy

Between 1761 and 1766, Geneviève Randon de Malboissière corresponded regularly with Adélaïde Méliand, her friend and confidante. Their fathers, who had known each other through royal service in the provinces, now lived in style in the heart of Paris: the Méliands on the rue des Blancs-Manteaux and the Malboissières just around the corner on the old rue de Paradis (now part of the rue des Francs-Bourgeois, where the Archives nationales stands).[19] Despite this proximity, the girls were generally allowed to visit each other only once a week, before or after Sunday mass.[20] In the summers even these visits became impossible, as one or both of the girls were taken to the country for lengthy vacations. Between visits, they wrote to each other, sometimes long letters, but often just little notes, such as two that Geneviève scribbled on playing cards in January 1765, enclosing them in envelopes no doubt left over from sending the obligatory New Year's greetings to relatives and less intimate friends (figs. 7.1a and 7.1b).

Correspondence nurtured and sustained a friendship that lasted until Geneviève's death from measles at the age of twenty. Although Adèle's letters are lost, nearly three hundred of Geneviève's letters to her survive, the first letter written when she was fifteen and Adèle was a year older; more than three-quarters of them were written over the course of two years, 1764 and 1765 (see fig. 7.2). The correspondence between

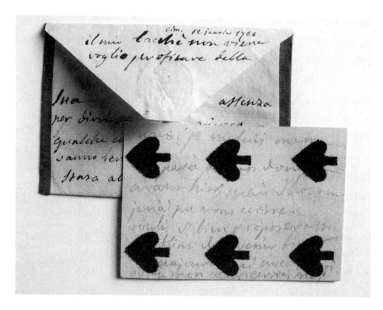

7.1a. Letter from Geneviève Randon de Malboissière to Adélaïde Méliand, 11 January [17]64 [65]. Archives de Beaurepaire. Courtesy of M. Christian de Luppé.

7.1b. Letter from Geneviève Randon de Malboissière to Adélaïde Méliand, 12 [13] J[anuary 17]64 [65]. Archives de Beaurepaire. Courtesy of M. Christian de Luppé.

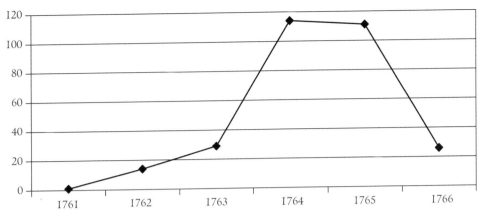

7.2. Geneviève Randon de Malboissière's letters to Adélaïde Méliand by year.

Geneviève and Adèle was an everyday affair, carried out for the most part on plain Dutch writing paper, often on half sheets of paper, or even scraps, when they were in town and could send their letters frequently and without postage via servants or messengers, on full sheets filled with writing when one girl was away from Paris and they had to use the postal service (see figs. 7.3 and 7.4).[21]

Geneviève wrote most of her letters to Adèle in the small world of her cabinet. There Geneviève met with her tutors for lessons in various languages, drawing, and mathematics. She also maintained a natural history collection in her cabinet and spent some of her time labeling, arranging, and cataloguing the items in it.[22] She read avidly, both at the direction of her tutors and to keep up with new works that were the talk of the town, including epistolary texts such as *Lettres et observations à une dame de province sur le siège de Calais* (1765) and Claude Joseph Dorat's *Lettre de Zeila, jeune sauvage, esclave à Constantinople à Valcourt, officier Français* (1764).[23] The cabinet was also where Geneviève wrote: poems and plays, translations of Latin and German verse, and, of course, letters.[24]

Geneviève left her cabinet to make forays out into the world of her parents' house twice a day for dinner and supper, and to spend a few hours after dinner in the salon with company, or to visit her mother in her own rooms, when her mother was ill. She also went regularly to the theater (the letters are filled with her reviews of the plays she saw), less regularly for an afternoon or evening promenade or on other excursions or visits. On Sundays she attended mass and sometimes went to Adèle's for breakfast. In the winter of 1764, she attended a natural history course three times a week.[25] But she spent the majority of her time within the walls of her cabinet, where she developed a sense of herself through the integrated practices of friendly sociability, reading, and writing.

Ownership of her room gave Geneviève privacy, and privacy gave her ownership of her self. The cabinet was private in the sense that it was Geneviève's own space, the space of her developing sense of self and the intersubjective discursive practices (letter

7.3. Letter from Geneviève Randon de Malboissière to Adélaïde Méliand, 20 November [1764]. Archives de Beaurepaire. Courtesy of M. Christian de Luppé.

a hanneucourt ce 16 juin 1764
a midy

En verité ma chere petite, il faut
qu'il y ait une bien Singuliere
Simpathie entre nous Jean —
puisque cette Simpathie Se fait
Sentir de 10. Lieues a la ronde.
jeudy vous aves commencé votre
lettre a midy, a la même heure
j'etois contente parce que je causois
avec vous, mais vous ne recevrés
la mienne qu'aujourd'huy a 2.
heures parce qu'elle n'a pû partir
qu'hier. je vous recevrois a
present mon enfant, vous etes
aimable, vous pensés souvenir a
moi vous n'etes plus 3. jours —
entiers Sans m'écrire, aussi vous
aimaige bien tendrement.

7.4. Letter from Geneviève Randon de Malboissière to Adélaïde Méliand, from Hanneucourt, 16 June 1764. Archives de Beaurepaire. Courtesy of M. Christian de Luppé.

writing, reading, and conversation) through which that self was articulated, but it was not isolation from others or communion with God. During the week there was a steady stream of tutors, as well as hairdressers, tailors, servants, and her governess, Mlle Jaillé; on Sundays, the visits of Adèle. Rather, the cabinet was a space that was hers to invite others into. Privacy was thus not aloneness but control over who could enter and the power to remove oneself from the power of others. This shared privacy was inscribed in letter writing as a dialogic practice, but the privacy of the cabinet also allowed her to engage in the critical practices (book and theater reviews, for example) out of which her modern subjectivity would also develop. It also allowed Geneviève to reflect on, share, and make sense of her life as she met the challenges of young womanhood.

The time Geneviève spent writing to Adèle was often stolen from other pursuits that dragged her away from her books, her writing, her studies, and her friend, so she often took advantage of her morning *toilette* to read or to write letters. "Good-bye, my dear child," she ended one letter, "[The hairdresser] is leaving, I am waiting for M. Huber [her German tutor]; I have to brush off my powder and put on a dress." And another day: "Good-bye, my child, my *toilette* is finished; I'm waiting for my mathematics teacher. We have people for dinner and in a little while a rehearsal."[26] However, morning was not the only time when Geneviève wrote to her friend; indeed, she wrote to her at all times of day and often noted both the time and the place. "Good evening, my dear child," she wrote on one warm summer evening in 1762. "I am in my little *cabinet*; there was such a terrible wind today that it carried away my inkstand and all my papers. I was forced to close the window."[27] This evocation of the cabinet would have helped Adèle to call up a concrete image of her friend as she read her words.

The privacy of the cabinet made it suitable not only for solitary contemplation and study but for friendship: it was a gathering place for friendly conversation, a place to write letters that solidified and demonstrated friendship, and a place where the tokens of friendship could be kept, enjoyed, and displayed. "As for me," Geneviève wrote one day, "I am very sensibly in my little cabinet, occupied with reading and thinking of you."[28] In January 1764, the two friends had exchanged allegorical busts as New Year's gifts: as Flore stood in for Geneviève in Adèle's cabinet, the bust of Hébé that presided over Geneviève's cabinet reminded her of Adèle (see fig. 7.5). In April Geneviève ended a letter by asking Adèle to kiss the bust of Flore for her. As a further keepsake and reminder, Geneviève later sent her friend a sketch portrait of herself done by her drawing master; she called it "the eternal pledge of our friendship."[29] The girls also exchanged birds, flowers, plants, and other objects, which then surrounded them as they wrote to each other. "Your mignonettes have given me the greatest pleasure," Geneviève wrote on 2 June 1764. "They are charming, they smell wonderful. I have put them above the fireplace in my cabinet where they have a very pretty effect." The following year she sent her friend a piece of lacewood from the Antilles for her natural history collection, and at the same time asked Adèle to send her Lady Mary Wortley Montagu's letters from Constantinople, first published in French the year before.[30]

7.5. Jean-Baptiste Lemoyne, *Geneviève-Françoise Randon de Malboissière* (1768). Marble. The Metropolitan Museum of Art. The Jules Bache Collection, 1949 (49.7.73). Image © The Metropolitan Museum of Art. This bust was commissioned by the father of Geneviève's dead fiancé after her death. The garland of roses suggests an allusion to the allegorical bust of Flore, now lost.

Books were often exchanged between the girls, either as gifts or as loans. Geneviève's letters are filled with comments on the books she was reading, often noting that she was sending her copy along to her friend.[31] There is a glimpse of the pleasure she took in surrounding herself with books in a letter she wrote on 16 May 1764: "Someone has just brought me thirteen Greek and Latin volumes from the Jesuit library," she wrote. "I'm enjoying arranging them." For Geneviève, for whom friendship was as important as study, the book may not have been the only "companion of choice in a new kind of intimacy," as Roger Chartier has written, but it was certainly one of them.[32]

Toward the end of each week, the girls fixed the place and time of their Sunday visit, anticipating the transformation of the cabinet from private study to intimate salon, where the conversation would be accompanied by and interspersed with other activities, such as drinking chocolate or coffee.[33] As in the sociability of the salon, written materials of various sorts were interjected into the conversation of the cabinet. On one Thursday in 1763, for example, Geneviève asked Adèle for advice about how to respond to a letter she had received from the philosopher David Hume, a friend of her parents. "I'll read it to you on Sunday," she promised.[34]

For Geneviève and Adèle, correspondence and cabinet were confidential spaces in which freedom and transparency were protected by privacy. In their letters, Italian usually functioned as a secret language, mostly when they needed to talk about matters of the heart: "You can write to me freely in Italian," Geneviève once wrote (in Italian), "but in French what anyone could read."[35] The privacy of the cabinet made it suitable for saying those things that could not be trusted even to a letter. When Geneviève's first romance began, she wrote to Adèle that she would tell her all about it when they met on Sunday.[36] Later, struggling to overcome her disappointment at not being received at court, Geneviève declared how much better were the conversations she and Adèle had in their cabinets. "Be very sure, my friend, that we are much happier than they are. . . . Between ourselves, we know no dissimulation."[37]

When summer came, the two girls were removed from the familiar spaces of their town lives and separated from each other for weeks on end; their letters only got longer and deeper. Before Geneviève's departure one year she sent all Adèle's letters back to her for safekeeping, and with them a blank book. "I command you, whenever you are alone in your cabinet, to put in it during my absence all your ideas, whatever they may be," she ordered. "I expect to find it filled with good follies."[38] Once arrived in the country, Geneviève's command became a plea, tinged with the sadness of separation: "I would hope that on these holidays, when you are in the habit of seeing me, you will write to compensate me for not being able to embrace you," she wrote.[39] A month later she expressed her frustration at being so far away: "I don't see you during the week, even when you're in Paris," she reflected. "But at any moment I can send over to your house, I can write to you or receive your letters; in the end, it's enough consolation to know that nothing separates us except the walls and the street. I know that, if we had the time, you could come to my house, and I to yours. But when there are leagues between us, this hope is stolen from me."[40] What remained was their correspondence. When they left their Parisian cabinets behind, they reestablished themselves in borrowed rooms, such as those Geneviève described in her first letter from Bourdonné, where she was visiting that September in 1764 (see fig. 7.6).

> I am in a very large and rather pretty room. . . . For furniture, I have a commode, a mantelpiece, a chaise longue that was once blue and white damask, six tapestry chairs, two armchairs, a crucifix, the portrait of the father and mother of our host [*chatelain*]. I have a view over the lake and across the park; but my *cabinet de toilette* is delicious. . . . There are two narrow windows, of which one is on the north side and looks out over the main part of the moat and a charming landscape. It is furnished in blue and white chintz, has a fireplace and a small mirror; that's where Mlle Jaillé sleeps.[41]

Geneviève was most pleased with the cabinet not only because of its view but for its coziness and modern décor, suggested by the blue and white chintz and the mirror.[42] This was where she looked forward to spending many happy hours reading, writing, and gazing out the window. Unexpectedly, the cabinet also became the site of romance when her cousin Pierre-Paul-Louis Randon de Lucenay entered this space of friendship and reflection. He disrupted her quiet life with the urgency and passions of romantic love that increasingly filled her letters to Adèle. Here is how Geneviève

7.6. Château de Bourdonné, Seine-et-Oise, France.

reported the opening scene of their affair: "A pleasant adventure befell us yesterday morning. Just before dinner he came in to see me, Mlle Jaillé was in the small cabinet, I was reading next to my table; he came over to me, took my hand in the usual way and kissed it. I, quite naturally, came forward to kiss him, his first movement was also to approach me; there was a split second of reflection, and then immediately we jumped back, both of us blushing and laughing."[43]

By the next week, Lucenay was coming to her rooms every evening: "We play, we laugh, we write, with difficulty, a page an hour." As she noted the hours passing in her letter ("Can you believe it, my heart, we thought it was scarcely 7:00, the boy looks at his watch, it's 8:30."), she was finally able to report that her "scoundrel has left, for the hunt" and that she would now "take advantage of his absence" to write to her friend at her ease.[44] A week later, however, Lucenay was there again, distracting her from her letter and her friend; she declared it a "miracle" when he left her alone long enough for her to write two pages. Soon, he was constantly at her side. "I see him at almost every moment," she wrote. "At 8:00 he is in my room, assisting at my *toilette*, powdering me, putting on my slippers, attaching my bracelets, fastening my necklace, putting on my rings; on the promenade, he always gives me his arm. In the evening, when Mlle Jaillé comes to fetch me for bed, he comes upstairs with me, takes everything off that he had put on me in the morning, and, as soon as my hair is done, he goes; every day it's the same."[45] When they returned to Paris, Lucenay continued to visit and correspond with Geneviève; when she broke with him a year later, however, she burned all his letters.[46]

But let us not get too sentimental or idealistic about a young woman's privacy in the eighteenth century. We have already seen how the locked drawers of the secretary were as much an invitation to the violation of such privacy as a guarantee of it. Geneviève's letters reveal the other side of the coin of privacy: a sense of enclosure. Unlike Lucenay and other young men her age, Geneviève could not come and go as she pleased. Whereas she could certainly roam the house in which she lived fairly freely, she was not free to visit him or even to venture out into the street alone. Her cabinet was a retreat from *le monde*, but it was also a gilded cage, a secure space in which she was protected from the dangers that threatened every young lady as she approached marriage age. Letter writing, like reading, required the privacy of the cabinet, but it also constituted a form of freedom from its constraints, as it allowed Geneviève to reflect on her life experiences and to articulate and express her ideas and feelings. Through reading and writing she was able to escape the confines of the parental home and achieve a limited freedom. And although, like Laclos' Cécile, she experimented with that freedom by writing secretly to her beau, Lucenay, this was a trivial sort of freedom compared to that embodied in her long correspondence with her friend Adèle.

Geneviève's limited mobility should be understood in the context of a world in which men roamed more freely and widely than ever before. We have already seen how the products of that mobility, in the form of Chinese porcelains and furniture veneered in exotic woods and lacquers, lured ladies into shops and came to fill the interiors of their homes. The seas, however, and the places to which they gave access, were overwhelmingly the world of men. Mastering the seas allowed European men to act on a larger stage—politically, economically, and personally; it allowed them to master other people and other lands, through conquest, the slave trade, and economic exploitation and domination. For most French women, however, the sea defined a limit, a boundary. Of course, most French men never set foot on a ship, but every man who did entered a world that the women of his family and his acquaintance, for the most part, did not. These men thus left one world, bounded by the sea, which they shared with female family and friends, for another, powered by that same sea, which they did not.

For their female counterparts, there were letters, books, and visitors. Many of the books Geneviève read took her across the seas in her imagination: in addition to those that took her to the Orient, such as Lady Mary Wortley Montagu's letters from Constantinople, she read popular novels and plays set in the Atlantic world, including *Robinson Crusoe* and *Gulliver's Travels*. When Geneviève wrote to Adèle about these books, she was engaging in a form of travel writing. When she wrote about an emissary from that world who had stepped right into her salon, she was narrating herself into the kind of popular *histoire* that freely crossed the line between fact and fiction.

"You made a big mistake in not staying a little longer [on Sunday]," Geneviève wrote triumphantly on 11 July 1764. "Just after you left, the prince came to pay me a visit." She was referring to a young man making the rounds of Parisian salons as the Prince of Angola. He had appeared at Geneviève's door with a copy of a statement he had just made to the Paris police, defending himself against the charge that he was a fraud. "Everything he says in it appears very credible to me," she wrote, "and I would have great difficulty believing that he is an imposter. I would be crushed if he were."[47] The young man had arrived in Paris several weeks before with a tale of having been sent by his father the king to arrange a trade treaty with France. The hapless prince, however, had made the mistake of leaving Africa aboard an English slave ship that had been captured by French pirates who stripped him of his considerable funds and left him in the French colony of Martinique. Having eventually made his way to Europe on a Danish vessel, he was now the toast of Paris, riding about in his own carriage, with two French lackeys and a secretary. His French was excellent because, he said, he had been raised in Paris in the retinue of the comte d'Argenson. All of this was reported in the press.[48]

The prince had apparently won over not only Geneviève but many ladies who were pleased to entertain him in their salons. One can only wonder what questions they asked him, what stories he told, and how a mysterious black man gained entry into the best houses of the capital—the capital of a large empire driven by the labor of African slaves. In the end (that is, before the end of the month), the young man was arrested— and beyond that there is no trace of what happened to him. But Geneviève refused to believe that he was a fraud. Although Argenson denied any acquaintance with him, she had heard that someone else "clearly recalled having petted in the Bois de Boulogne three little Negro princes raised by M. d'Argenson, among whom was this one."[49] At a time when slaves brought to France from the colonies were sometimes able to sue successfully for their freedom on the grounds that they were now on free soil, we can assume that free men of color in the capital were more likely to be former slaves than African princes. But at a time when it was fashionable for European aristocrats to keep about them as signs of wealth and power small African slave boys dressed in fine livery, it might be hard to tell a slave from a prince.[50] Indeed, there was no reason that a prince could not become a slave in real life. Finally, at a time when European literature and art tended to romanticize and exoticize the colonies, and when a fashionable Parisian stationer just a few blocks from Adèle's house advertised his shop under the sign À la Teste Noire, perhaps it is not surprising that this self-styled prince should captivate women like Geneviève, whose experience of the Atlantic world was shaped by commerce, novels, and plays. In fact, the plot of one such play, *Les Avantures curieuses et intéressantes d'Oronoko, prince afriquain* (a recent translation and adaptation of Aphra Behn's popular English novel of 1688) bore a striking resemblance to the story of this Prince of Angola.[51] Behn called her novel a "history" and maintained, as Geneviève could in her letters to Adèle, "I was myself an Eye-Witness, to a great part, of what you will find here set down; and what I cou'd not be Witness of, I receiv'd from the Mouth of the chief Actor in this History."[52]

A year after the exit of the Prince of Angola, another intriguing visitor appeared in Geneviève's salon: a young Peruvian, suspiciously called the "marquis de Magdonaldo." Geneviève recounted for Adèle the complicated story of this young man's life, just as she had that of the African prince. Unlike the prince, the Peruvian was well-educated and spoke several languages. As Déterville had taught Zilia French, he insisted on teaching Geneviève the rudiments of his language. "Yes, I love you," Zilia had repeated, over and over, not knowing what she said. Receiving the same lesson from her young Peruvian, Geneviève already knew the game. "I know enough in this language," Geneviève told Adèle, "to say: *ñuca llullu sçungu, mon tendre coeur* [my tender heart]." After explaining how to pronounce the three Peruvian words she announced: "You can congratulate yourself, my heart, for knowing three words in the language of Aza." Nevertheless, Adèle was now skeptical. "The young Peruvian of whom I spoke to you cannot be an adventurer," Geneviève reassured her, "since M. de la Condamine lived with all his relatives in Quito and was there at his birth."[53] And in this case, at least, she was not deceived.

For Geneviève, the Atlantic world was a space shaped primarily by her reading of works of the imagination that spoke to the heart, but she entered it critically, evaluating the facts and testimony presented to her, as eighteenth-century authors like Graffigny taught her to do. If she did not accept the judgment that the Prince of Angola was a fraud, it was not because she was a naive reader who followed only her heart but because she found good reasons to doubt Argenson's testimony. As to the young Peruvian, the trope of the "tutor of love" was much too familiar for any reader to miss or fall for. Graffigny herself had provided the critical perspective. The lesson of her novel lay in the way that Zilia learned through writing to free herself from love and transform her experience into critical narrative. Writing letters to a friend gave Geneviève the opportunity and the power to do exactly that.

For Geneviève de Malboissière, reading and letter writing provided a kind of freedom that she otherwise lacked because of her gender: within the private space of her cabinet she could roam the world unchaperoned through books, narrate her life and adventures, and communicate confidentially with the friend who, though she lived just a few blocks away, could be seen only once a week at best. She achieved this freedom, of course, with the material assistance of the postal service and the servants of both the Malboissière and Méliand households.[54] The limited freedom she achieved through letter writing was mediated by and dependent on these services. But it was also a function of the reflection in which she was able to engage in the space and through the practices of privacy. In her cabinet and her correspondence, Geneviève could reflect on what she read and heard, and could articulate her own thoughts in regard to it. Although Geneviève read a lot and wrote other things besides letters—plays, poetry, extracts—her correspondence with Adèle was the main practice through which she developed and articulated this particular sense of privateness as both personal freedom and autonomy (power over oneself), achieved through reflection.[55]

Manon: Letter Writing and the Gendered Subject

Geneviève de Malboissière and Adélaïde Méliand belonged to families that were recently ennobled and very rich but nonetheless socially distant from the rarefied and stultifying atmosphere of the court and the high nobility; the families of Manon Phlipon and Sophie Cannet were even more modest. Manon's father was a master engraver and her maternal grandfather a *marchand-mercier*; in 1780 she would marry Jean-Marie Roland and with him become a leading figure in the early years of the

French Revolution, until her death by guillotine in 1793. During the years of her correspondence with Sophie, Manon lived with her family in an apartment attached to her father's workshop on the rue de l'Horloge in the center of Paris. Sophie's family was richer and more important, but they lived in provincial Amiens, where her father was a local functionary and a captain in the militia. By the time Sophie was born, he had moved his family into the lowest ranks of the nobility by purchasing a royal office. After he died, Sophie's mother sent her and her sister Henriette to a convent in Paris to prepare for their first communion, where they would meet Manon in 1765. By the end of 1767, all three girls had returned home, and by 1770, when Manon was sixteen and Sophie eighteen, they were corresponding regularly. As Mme Roland explained many years later in her memoirs, the correspondence was meant to take the place of the daily confidences the two girls had shared in the convent. At first she simply returned to the convent for weekly visits; "but these visits were a poor substitute for the daily conversation and confidences of friendship," she discovered. The visits tapered off, "and I made up for them with letters, the commerce of which was established primarily with Sophie; the origin of my taste for writing, and one of the causes which, by force of habit, had increased my facility for it."[56]

While only one or two of Sophie's letters remain, we have more than 250 of Manon's. The pattern of Manon's letter writing (see fig. 7.7) was strikingly similar to that of Geneviève (see fig. 7.3), with a gradual rise to a peak year (1776) and then a steep decline (Geneviève peaked at eighteen; Manon at twenty-two). However, Manon's letters were less frequent than Geneviève's; over the course of ten years she wrote approximately the same number of letters to Sophie that Geneviève wrote to Adèle in half that time, at most one a week. But all of Manon's letters were long; she generally covered every bit of her paper with ink.[57] Unlike Geneviève, who could exchange several notes in a single day with Adèle via servants scurrying back and forth between their two houses, Manon's correspondence with Sophie was timed to the rhythm of the postal service and, with one exception, unmediated by visits. For Manon and Sophie, the correspondence was virtually the entire space of friendship.

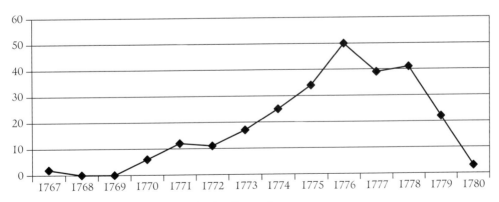

7.7. Marie-Jeanne Phlipon's letters to Sophie Cannet by year.

Despite differences in wealth, status, and milieu, Geneviève and Manon had a great deal in common. They were both serious students, in love with books and curious about everything. They were also devoted friends and dedicated correspondents whose letters were filled with expressions of both their undying devotion and their critical reflections on what they were reading, seeing, and doing. And, despite the modesty of the Phlipon household, Manon's life, even more than Geneviève's, was centered in the room she referred to variously as her *chambre, cabinet,* or *cellule.* In October 1770, for example, she opened a letter to Sophie: "Hello then, my dear friend, here I am alone and tranquil in my little room, pen in hand, calm and tenderness in my heart, deliciously occupied in writing to you, in painting for you my thoughts, expressing to you my feelings; I cannot tell you how many charms this situation has for me."[58] In her letters, Manon emphasized the quietness of her life and her taste for retreat and contemplation. To maintain her calm at the center of the Parisian storm, she spent every morning in her "little cabinet on the banks of the Seine," where she could not only be alone but do what she wanted. "I take up my pen, I think, I dream, and I write; I study and I make notes," she explained. "This keeps me busy and sustains me in embellishing my life; I really think that it's my vocation," she declared.[59]

When circumstances prevented her from writing for a whole week, Manon expressed her amazement at having survived. At the same time, she realized that writing required time and the freedom to use it. Once, when she did not receive a response by the next post, she broke the rules of correspondence and wrote again anyway, acknowledging that "you must be enough the mistress of your time as I am of mine . . . to pour out your heart to that of a friend without having anything new to tell her."[60] For Manon, as for Geneviève, letter writing was more than a medium for exchanging news; it was a necessary means of self-awareness and self-expression. Writing, she thought, was when she was most herself.[61]

For Manon, friendship, too, was primarily a function of writing. Whereas Geneviève and Adèle had many Sunday mornings together, in fourteen years Manon and Sophie saw each other only during one three-month period in 1775, when Sophie came to Paris on an extended visit with her mother and sister. Manon thus came to see letter writing as the matrix and medium of friendship: through correspondence friendship developed as friends became self-aware, reasoning individuals. As Manon maintained in a letter to Sophie a few months before her friend's projected visit, their friendship might well have floundered had they both lived in the same city: "Returned to the bosom of our families, enclosed within their societies, we would not have been very free to cultivate assiduously our relationship." Moreover, she continued, writing shaped both the quality of their friendship and the persons they had become through it: "In finding between us a distance that could not be crossed easily, the need to write to each other made itself felt almost at the moment when we began to care about each other: the need to satisfy it put the imagination in play, forced ideas to hatch and feelings to be expressed." Felt needs led to "general and moral reflections because they are a good resource in such a case," she concluded, and then went on to elaborate an epistemology of epistolarity that was indebted to Lockean empiricism. "We had to reason and to describe, consequently to observe and reflect," she reasoned. "Thus it was that our efforts, mandated in some way by circumstances, caused new faculties to develop in us."[62] Years later, Mme Roland remembered the pleasure of this epistolary education: "I learned to reflect more by communicating my reflections," she recalled. "I studied with more ardor because I found pleasure in sharing what I had learned, and I observed with more attention because I took pleasure in describing."[63]

During Sophie's visit, the two young women had spent every possible moment together and written very little. Two weeks after her departure, Manon's only consolation was the cabinet: "Since you left, I'm hardly busy at all. I would like to see [Henriette], however I cannot take it upon myself to go out, to leave my dear cabinet."[64] Her cabinet, she explained, was "the place in the house where I have the most privacy; it is where you enjoyed yourself sometimes, it is the repository of my thoughts; it is the place, finally, where I always write to you, where I converse with the illustrious dead whose works instruct and amuse me."[65]

Above all, the cabinet was a space of reflection and self-reflection, activities Manon considered central to her very being. "Knowledge of ourselves is, without hesitation, the most useful science," she declared in December 1771. She took up the theme again several years later: "It is in solitude that the mind develops, the soul becomes calm, the passions are stilled."[66] Manon believed that developing the mind and reflecting on oneself were important for all human beings, but especially for her. "Rousseau says that the man who reflects is a depraved animal," she had observed in a letter probably written in February 1774. "In that case, of all the animals of my species I am the one who has arrived at the highest degree of depravity, because reflection has become necessary to me to the point of my not being able to do without it." Writing and reflection had become, she said, as necessary as her daily bread.[67]

In all the years they corresponded, Sophie managed only that one visit to Paris, and Manon never got to Amiens, less than 150 kilometers away. For Manon, as for Geneviève, reading and letter writing were the practices through which she could break through the constraints of daily life, including her very limited mobility. In May 1772, Manon described her reading as travels through space and time, and a letter from Sophie as a quick stop in Amiens, whence she returned home to take up her pen.[68] Meanwhile, Sophie's brother traveled back and forth between the two cities in the course of his business, often carrying letters between his sister and her friend.[69] But Nicolas Cannet de Sélincourt was far from Manon's only visitor. In 1772 she wrote to Sophie: "My normal society is confined to a narrow circle of three or four relatives and more or less the same number of friends, of whom the majority also see only a few people; nevertheless, it happens often enough that, visiting some of them, I find myself in a much larger social group; as to conversation, like you, I only enjoy that of which history, the sciences, and news are the main topic."[70]

Moreover, the correspondence between Paris and Amiens shows that Manon and Sophie were hardly cut off from the doings of a French world that extended well beyond the range of their own circumscribed mobility. Indeed, their correspondence was a circuit through which information about and experiences of more distant friends and visitors flowed in both directions. In their letters, the young women both shared and reflected together on what they learned about this world that they knew only second hand. In 1773, for example, Sophie passed on news from a girlfriend who had written to her from her new home in the French Antilles. "I should not be surprised that your friend was homesick," Manon responded, if

> it is she who is partly responsible for the household chores and overseeing the Negroes. It would seem flattering for the ego to see oneself surrounded by slaves to whom one has but to command, and to enjoy the privileges of king and legislator; but looked at another way, it is even more tiring to be responsible for the conduct of people who, for the most part, are as brutish as animals and almost entirely incapable of reflection and of the principles of common morality.... It seems to me that the religion and delicacy of your friend cannot adapt to these customs, unless it is the case that, staying with her brother and not getting involved in anything, she is a simple observer of these things.[71]

A couple of months later Sophie's friend wrote to her about the corrupt morals of colonial society. Again, Manon was not surprised: the young woman's observations agreed with what Manon had learned from other sources. She was surprised to learn, however, that by coincidence Sophie's friend was living in Guadeloupe, where a good friend of her parents was serving in the artillery. She asked Sophie to pass along her compliments to him via her friend.[72] Sophie's letters about her friend's experience in Guadeloupe also spurred Manon to report on a visitor of her own who had just returned from the colonies: "a fine Gascon who made his fortune through his own industry."[73]

In fact, from her letters we learn that Manon knew quite a few people who either lived or had lived abroad in France's colonies. There was, for example, Pahin de la Blancherie, a Rousseau-inspired young man of letters who, after finishing his studies, took off for America. In 1770, three years after his return to France at the ripe old age of seventeen, he met Manon at a concert and proceeded to court her. When, a couple of years later, Sophie asked Manon if she was familiar with a poet from the Antilles named Léonard, whom she had just met, Manon replied. "I don't believe I have ever heard his name mentioned, nor any that resembles it; I only know a certain Pahin de la Blancherie who has been to the Islands, like your M. Léonard, and who, like him, has amused himself by writing poetry." She then ticked off everyone else she knew who might fit the description, but was forced to conclude that "the other people of my acquaintance who are in the Islands surely do not write poetry; I know that they are too busy with their business affairs for that and anyway, their genius does not go in that direction."[74]

At the other end of the French empire was Demontchéry, a young man who had gone to India to make his fortune and maintained hopes of coming back to Paris one day and marrying Manon. "I have spoken to you, I believe, of a character who is in Pondicherry," Manon wrote to Sophie in January 1776; "he has written to my father on every possible occasion, and we have news of him as often as he is able [to send it] of a rather distant land." The most recent letter had been delivered personally by a friend of the young man's, who was introduced in the letter as "a deputy of the Council of Pondicherry (where he occupies a distinguished position), coming here to the Court on colonial business."[75] This was Joseph-Charles de Saintelette, a man who had begun his career in Louisiana, ended it in India, and would soon return home to France permanently to retire.[76]

Months later, Saintelette turned up in Manon's salon as she was transcribing for Sophie and her sister Henriette her copious notes on a book she had just finished reading: Cornelius de Pauw's *Recherches philosophiques sur les Américains*.[77] Manon's notes included her thoughts on such matters as the moral ideas and ferocity of the Indians, and she was thrilled to have her own informant to interrogate on these matters. "This is how I was reasoning with myself concerning the different parts of M. de P.'s work," she wrote,

> when M. de S. L. came to see me. You can judge what a joy that was! Here was an observer to consult. For fourteen years M. de S. L. had been director of the fur trade in Louisiana and west of the Mississippi; less concerned with trade than with philosophy, he selected to the best of his ability the traders whom he sent to the savages to give them rifles, hardware, etc. . . . all these miseries that they love and they receive in exchange for furs, etc.; he listened to their reports, compared them, verified them, and sometimes had savages brought to him. I asked him if it was true that they were beardless, weak, extremely limited mentally, that they mistreated their wives, etc.; here is what I learned. . . .[78]

And then she explained how the visitor contradicted de Pauw on every point. She meticulously recorded everything she had learned from Saintelette in "several conversations," and left it to her friends to comment on this wealth of new information. Two weeks later she wrote to Sophie that Saintelette was visiting three or four times a week, and that she often steered the conversation toward America. "I have several anecdotes that I will pass along to you in due course," she wrote, and then went on to share what she had learned so far about Amerindian women, and then about the differences between animals on the two continents. Eventually, the conversation turned to France's premier colony, Saint-Domingue, which Saintelette had not visited, but about which he had information to pass on from others he had met in his work and travels. This led Manon to her own reading about Saint-Domingue, and then to other books she was reading. "I swear," she concluded, "that physics, natural history, would right now be the objects of study that would most pique my curiosity; these are the true bases of knowledge, but, but! . . . why am I a woman?"[79]

The following year, when she was feeling down and found it difficult to concentrate, Manon took to playing music and reading geography to distract herself. "I travel and I feel all right," she explained to Sophie and Henriette.

> I make everyone I meet contribute. I found myself with a military engineer who has arrived from Corsica and is on his way to Gorée, where he has just been named governor. This is a small island off the coast of Guinea, which serves us as some sort of entrepôt for the Africa trade, of which the slave trade is the main part. To the question, among many others, that I posed to him concerning the island itself, what it produces, and what he plans to do there: "I see nothing," he responded, "except an abundant crop of laurels to reap if the English attack me, and the minister gives me money to have fortifications built."

Manon expressed her frustration with the glib engineer to her friends. "I worked hard at trying to learn about the state of Corsica, the customs of its natives, etc., but it is so difficult to have a sustained conversation in ordinary societies, that I was unable to draw much enlightenment from him."[80]

Much as she took pleasure in reading, writing, and conversation, Manon was frustrated by her inability to cross the oceans and learn for herself, a limitation that she ascribed to her gender. When her visitor knew no more than she did, or when his interests were crass and material rather than intellectual, all she could do was continue to read and to hope that some other man would stumble into her life to supplement her own book learning with his first-hand experience. Through her correspondence she would pass that knowledge along to Sophie and Henriette who, in turn, would share with her what they learned from the letters and conversations that passed through their own provincial salon. Books, letters, and visitors expanded their horizons and their knowledge, but at the same time they made apparent the limits to mobility and direct experience imposed by their gender.

"Readers are travelers," writes Michel de Certeau. "They move across lands belonging to someone else, like nomads poaching their way across fields they did not write, despoiling the wealth of Egypt to enjoy it themselves."[81] By contrast, he continues, "writing accumulates, stocks up, resists time by the establishment of a place." For Manon, that place was the self she was in the process of constructing, but the materials out of which she constructed it were drawn from her vast reading and her deep reflection. The intersubjective space of the correspondence was her construction site, a safe space where a self oriented toward others could be constructed.

"The most dangerous time for persons of our sex is that which elapses between the ages of fifteen and thirty, sometimes earlier, sometimes later, but principally during the first years of adolescence," Manon declared when she was seventeen. "It is in this critical moment that the passions develop and act so much more effectively than the prudence of experience, which can no longer stand up to them. There is no age when we reflect less, ordinarily, and there is none when it is more necessary."[82] Her correspondence with Sophie Cannet fits neatly within this critical period, from the age of sixteen until her marriage at twenty-six. Manon was extraordinary in that she rose to the challenge of adolescence by dedicating herself to writing and reflection so that they became her passion, but reflection and writing, especially to a trusted confidante, are typical of adolescent girls once they have the skills and the means to engage in them. We need only look at the popularity of diary keeping in nineteenth-century America, or Geneviève's letters to Adèle in the eighteenth. Or, of course, the female confidantes who are as important to the epistolary novel as its lovers—Rousseau's Julie and Claire, for example, or Samuel Richardson's Clarissa and Anna Howe. Personal writing of this sort is one of the hallmarks of modern female adolescence.[83]

Confidentiality became an issue for Manon (as it had for Geneviève), when she found herself needing to write to her friend about things she could not tell her mother.[84] While the correspondence with Sophie had begun in all transparency and with the approval of the mothers of both girls, over time, as Manon realized, it had opened up a space for her to think and to say things that she could not tell her parents. From 1773 on, the letters themselves are filled with cautions to Sophie not to respond except in a very general way to the confidences expressed in them, or to do so in a way that anybody might read.[85]

By 1775 Manon was hiding as much as she was revealing. "For a long time I have wanted to converse with you with an open heart about all those little nothings to which friendship gives so much importance," she opened her first letter of that year. "But this is a satisfaction that I can rarely enjoy. It's not that I ever say anything in my letters that I don't believe, only that I don't put in everything that I think." This confession was stimulated by a conversation that had troubled her a few days earlier. "A certain gentleman maintained that between friends there are things that a third person does not and ought not to know," she reported. Manon's mother had disagreed. "Mama remained persuaded that two girlfriends could not have anything to say that a beloved mother, as she knows herself to be, could not or even ought not to know." Manon had wisely kept her own counsel during this conversation, but she found herself unhappy and somewhat confused that she could not in fact confide in her mother, although she found some consolation in confiding this, too, to her friend—if, indeed, she was confiding in her. "I write this to you without knowing when you will have it," she wrote, perplexed.

> I hesitate even in conducting my pen, I am afraid that a sudden and unanticipated glance might come and discover what it traces, because our apartment is so unpleasantly arranged that one cannot take a step without it being known. . . . My greatest difficulty is to send [this letter] to the post office, because I don't like to take advantage mysteriously of the servant, I hate the hidden services that one receives from these people. . . . I must then wait to go out alone, but for me that's as rare as it is for a young Spanish girl.[86]

Manon may have been dramatizing here, caught up in the romance of sneaking out of the house to post her letter, but her concern for confidentiality, expressed so frequently, was surely real.

This was, not coincidentally, the same letter in which Manon told Sophie about a match being arranged for her by the good sisters in their old convent—a match that Manon dreaded. She was stalling for time, but she knew that eventually she would have to deal with it, with him, and with her parents. For the moment, though, she just let her feelings go in a long poem that was more rant than art. "Ah! Cursed be the verbiage / That I am deafened with every day! / I want to repudiate love, / And marriage even more," she began. By the fourteenth stanza she had lost none of her initial defiance: "I will keep my liberty! / I know the imposture of destiny: / I will fly to where nature/ Shows me some happiness."[87]

Manon's need was not just to write and reflect but to write to a female friend of her own age with whom she could reflect on the dilemmas she confronted as a young woman: that is, as a gendered being who was beginning to differentiate herself from her family and from her mother in particular. The practice of letter writing, learned perhaps through a correspondence with her own mother during the year she spent at the convent, was crucial to this differentiation and its articulation. Manon's dilemmas included a contest between religious faith and the new Enlightenment philosophy; underlying it was the question of how to lead a moral life as a woman: through devotion to God, through motherhood, or through the public service open only to men. In practice, this meant wondering and worrying about whom she would marry, or if she should marry at all—a dilemma we will explore in the next chapter. On a deeper level, as she expressed it in the poem quoted above, Manon struggled with the conflict between marriage and personal freedom.

Manon articulated what Geneviève only suggested—that writing to a confidante helped her to work through the dilemmas she faced as a young woman of her time and social status. Yet there are hints of this consciousness even in Geneviève's letters. When she was fifteen—just the age Manon identified as the beginning of the dangerous years—Geneviève, too, expressed skepticism about marriage: "There's good reason to marry us off young," she wrote, "since I think that, if one waited until one were older, one would be hard-pressed to resolve to take up an engagement in which one could be morally sure (oh, excuse me, I forgot the almost) that one risked one's happiness and one's liberty." She came to this conclusion, she explained, after having watched a married couple in a neighboring box at the theater, the young wife looking very sad, the husband humming a nasty tune. "Why do these scoundrels of men, who sometimes have everything they need to be happy, thus seek to make us miserable?" she asked Adèle. "Why, for example," she continued, "would I want to get married? Happy as I am, I desire nothing." Whereas a suitor could be charming, a husband, she observed, was quite a different beast: "Brusque, scolding, argumentative, miserly, with no respect [he] shows you all his faults and imagines that, since you are united with him, you must, as an obedient slave, bend without complaint to the yoke with which it pleases him to weigh you down."[88]

Like Manon, Geneviève compared her perfect friendship with Adèle to the dubious attractions of marriage and assured her friend with equal passion of her constancy: no matter what happened, they would be friends for life.[89] Amid the whirl of parties, suitors, and the theater that would come to occupy so much of her time, she too needed the privacy of her cabinet and the occasions for reflection that it afforded: "Good-bye, my child," she ended one letter, "I am going to read my Burlamaqui, he's the most honest and the most virtuous of men. If you [only] knew how content one is to find oneself in what one reads, and to find a moment sometimes to commune with one's interior. My little one, it's in the wake of all these conversations that I feel even more vividly the pleasure of loving you."[90]

As both Geneviève and Manon realized, writing to a friend allowed a young woman to develop her thoughts and her mind; it allowed her to develop and articulate an individual self. At the same time, through writing, concerns about marriage, men, and loss of freedom and friendship sometimes led to more general reflections on the condition of women in society. Where Manon differed from Geneviève was in pushing her reflections on men and marriage farther, so as to approach what Brigitte Diaz has called feminism *avant la lettre*.[91]

In October 1775, Manon tried to reconcile her aspirations to be useful to society with the limits that society placed on her as a woman. Women, she conceded, could never attain greatness. "Our sex bars us from such an aspiration in depriving us of the means of raising ourselves to it," she told Sophie. "Made to be unknown, it is in the depths of obscurity that we must live out and finish our days, more peaceful than brilliant." It was not fame or fortune that Manon regretted, however, but the ability to engage in the moral action of public service. Without it, how was she to become a moral being, a truly useful member of society? "If it is impossible for us to enlighten men, to work for the happiness of the greatest number, to really serve society," she concluded, "at least we shall work to form in ourselves the most enlightened, best intentioned members of it." Self-cultivation could be turned to good use should marriage give her the opportunity to raise children, and, she wrote, "make men of them," but this was clearly a second-best means of attaining a moral life. And even this possibility was beyond her control. Manon consoled herself and her friend with the reminder that even if marriage and thus motherhood continued to elude them, they were still contributing to the good of society by studying, reflecting, and writing (to each other). "In perfecting ourselves," Manon declared, "we will acquire self-esteem: this is a possession too sweet to neglect to acquire, it is the first source of happiness."[92]

Through letter writing, Manon not only worked out her ideas but came to understand herself (that is, to construct herself) as a moral subject and a woman. Through writing, she developed what Habermas has identified as the novel sense of privateness necessary to agency in the modern public sphere. But she also learned the limits of agency in that sphere imposed by attitudes toward gender; in her worst moments she wondered if there was any point in cultivating the self when that self could not fulfill its moral purpose. In one letter, she compared herself to a plant dying in a desert.[93] And one winter evening in 1776, Manon poured out her love for retreat and reflection as regret for being born a woman in eighteenth-century France. "I long for retreat and for solid study," she wrote.

> I want to nourish my heart in cultivating my mind.... In truth, I am really bored with being a woman: I need another soul, or another sex, or another century. I should have been born a Spartan or Roman woman, or at least a French man. As such, I would choose as my *patrie* the republic of letters, or one of those republics where one can be a man and obey only the laws.... I am like those animals in burning Africa who, transported to our menageries, are forcibly enclosed in a space that barely contains them, their faculties designed to be deployed in a happy climate, with the vigor of a nature strong and free.[94]

Manon Phlipon's letters articulate the gap between the novel sense of privateness that eighteenth-century women not only could but were encouraged to develop through the practice of letter writing, and the gendered possibility of moral agency in the public sphere as Manon understood it. The paradox of womanhood, as Manon lived and expressed it, was to find true freedom only in the restrained space of the cabinet. She found solace and meaning and even happiness in the practices of privacy, but these same practices led her to understand that for her they were a dead end, a tautology, leading nowhere but deeper inside the self or, at best, around the endless circle of correspondence between friends. Worse still, the very practice of reflection that she maintained was the source of all happiness, and especially her own, was really a masculine practice, and, as such, an illusory vocation for her. Who, she seemed to be saying, was she kidding?

And yet, Manon's letters also show us how writing itself could be a form of agency, a form of freedom that she learned to value in its contrast to the constraints of her life as a woman. Indeed, writing could stiffen her resolve to go out and fight the battles life sent her. As she closed a letter to Sophie on 1 July 1777: "I did well to write to you; sleep has fled, my heart is refreshed, time has passed sweetly; with you I've regained my courage and my gaiety; I'm going to return to combat, the enemies are at the gate."[95]

Geneviève de Malboissière, it must be said, never carried the gendered logic of privacy this far. But then, her life had a very different shape. Although she was untroubled by concerns about money or family conflicts over a suitable match, her life was cut off at the height of her happiness by the sudden death of her fiancé, followed only a few months later by her own. And, in any case, women are not all alike. What we learn from reading the letters of Manon Phlipon and Geneviève de Malboissière is that despite their differences in wealth and status and the other cards life dealt them, they both came to understand themselves as subjects and as women in the space of privacy, and through the epistolary practice they engaged in during the many hours they spent there. In cabinets of their own they both retreated from the world in order to reflect on it, and, to the best of their ability, they escaped the bounds of that world to experience a form of freedom that they learned to value in its contrast to the constraints of their lives as women. Writing to a friend helped them both to articulate their feelings and to analyze the reasons for them. Manon's longer and deeper reflection, her troubled soul, and her greater articulation of the complexities and contradictions of being both a woman and a private person, only cast greater light on Geneviève and the many other young women who spent their happiest hours writing to a best friend in cabinets of their own. It is among these women that a modern gendered subjectivity surely emerged.

Epistolary Reasoning

Writing about Marriage

8

Enlightenment writers made women's life choices around marriage a central theme in the stories they told. If Françoise de Graffigny challenged readers to imagine a woman choosing not to marry, male novelists crafted their stories around the virtuous young woman torn by the conflict between nature and culture, duty and desire. Men of letters who had nothing to offer women but their hearts promoted the idea that marriage should be based on free choice and love, and that love was by definition opposed to interest and thus to duty. They pitted meritorious young men like themselves against cruel parents who thwarted love in favor of cold economic and lineage interests. And they appealed to their female reading public to validate them not only as writers but as men, by following their hearts and recognizing their true merit without regard for rank or fortune. Love was to women, according to Diderot, as literary fame was to men of letters: "If you hear a woman speak ill of love, and a man of letters deprecate public consideration; you will say that the charms of the first have passed, and of the other that he is losing his talent."[1] Feminine love and masculine merit were hopelessly intertwined.

Merry Wiesner notes that in early modern Europe "marriage was the clearest mark of social adulthood for both women and men."[2] In the eighteenth century, however, it took on additional meaning and value for women alone. As Enlightenment men of letters helped all men to claim the right to a place in the world and the rewards that went with it based on their individual talents, skills, and effort, they limited the achievement of happiness for women exclusively within marriage and motherhood. Not only would men alone be valued and rewarded for their achievements, but the reward that would bring them the most happiness would be their heart's desire: the wife they earned through their own merit. Women were thus portrayed as the objects of male desire, rather than as willing, desiring subjects in their own right. Their merit, which would make them the worthy objects of such desire, was moral. Their social usefulness lay in raising children and creating a well-ordered haven out of the home. The ambition to achieve anything else (especially in competition with men) would "desex" them—that is, it would turn them into men.[3] For women, then, marriage choice was really the only kind of choice they could make.

At the same time that they encouraged women to find happiness and personal fulfillment in marriage and motherhood, men of the Enlightenment attacked the traditional alternative to marriage: religious vocations. For these new men, as Mita Choudhury notes, nuns were "the antithesis of the maternal ideal."[4] In *La Religieuse* (1760), for example, Diderot portrayed the convent as a site of misery and sexual perversion and the extension of the dysfunctional family based on interest rather than love. He called the convent "the sewer into which society's waste is thrown."[5] The discrediting of religious vocations left women with no way outside of marriage to create a meaningful life. The "spinster" too was a failure and a parasite, and by definition unhappy and unfulfilled—the secular sister of the discredited nun.[6] The field was thus cleared for marriage and motherhood as the only means by which women could be fulfilled, both as women and as human beings.

And yet, women were expected to achieve marital happiness within a structure defined by the inequality of the partners. The educational system that fostered merit reserved places in the schools and universities for men alone. Property law made married women economically dependent on their husbands, even as it made it difficult for single women to support themselves. Laws that punished women but not men for extramarital sex placed the fulfillment of desire squarely within marriage only for them.[7] For women, marriage meant loss of freedom, equality, and human dignity. How then were they to choose the path to happiness through marriage?

Nonetheless, choice was central to new ideas about freedom and marriage for both women and men. The crusade for companionate marriage, or marriage based on the love and the free choice of the partners, was one of the central campaigns of the Enlightenment against tradition and patriarchal authority. In *Lettres persanes*, Montesquieu equated forced marriage with what he called "oriental despotism," the antithesis of modern Western liberty.[8] Indeed, in the West, arranged marriage remains synonymous with forced marriage, the very definition of unfreedom, while the triumph of the nuclear family based on the freely joined companionate couple over the lineage family with its strategies and interests remains one of the pillars of our understanding of social progress as the rise of the individual. Although historians may disagree as to exactly how large a role love may have played in traditional marriage, no one doubts that the modern idea of happiness can result only from a marriage based on the free choice of individuals following their hearts.[9]

Lettres persanes ends in tragedy when Usbek learns that his favorite wife has chosen liberty by choosing death. "How could you have thought that I was credulous enough to imagine that I was brought into this World only to adore your whims?" Roxane asks him in the final letter of the novel. "That, while you allow yourself everything, you would have the right to thwart all my desires? No! I have been able to live in servitude, but I have always been free: I have rewritten your laws according to those of Nature, and my spirit has always held to independence."[10] Like Graffigny's Zilia, Montesquieu's Roxane chooses freedom over marriage, but she finds her freedom only in death; her declaration of independence is a suicide note.

Rousseau's most famous epistolary heroine also takes her own life. But in *Julie, ou la nouvelle Héloïse*, the tragic ending is only the final resolution of the heroine's struggle between love and duty that drives the novel in letters that seemingly flow directly from her heart to the printed page. When, early in the novel, she is forced to choose between eloping with her lover and marrying the man chosen for her by her father, Julie agonizes in a letter written to her cousin and best friend Claire: "Obedience and faith dictate opposite duties to me. Shall I follow my heart's penchant? Who is to be preferred of a lover or a father? Alas, by harkening to love or nature, I cannot avoid casting one or the other into despair; by sacrificing myself to duty I cannot avoid committing a crime, and whatever choice I make, I must die both unhappy and guilty." Realizing that happiness is out of the question (and predicting her own fictional fate), Julie decides to obey her parents because, she says, "it will be less cruel to lament in my misfortune than to have caused theirs."[11] Whereas Molière had resolved this same problem in *L'École des femmes* by revealing at the last moment that the father's choice was also, by happy coincidence, the son's, Rousseau refused the mechanism of fortune, and, like Montesquieu, found escape only in the death of his heroine.[12]

For a modern reader, Julie's recourse to an argument for filial duty to the father who beats her hard enough to cause a miscarriage may not be a convincing alternative to the argument from the heart and nature. We root for love to win out and happiness to be thereby achieved. It is, however, too easy to say, as Milord Edward does in Rousseau's novel, that if individuals could just follow their hearts, all would be well. "Let rank be regulated by merit, and the union of hearts by their choice," he declared. "That is the true social order."[13] The opposition between arranged marriage and love matches, between a family's head and an individual's heart, does not adequately take account of either the complexities posed for young women by the prospect of marriage or the intellectual work they did in contributing to marriage decisions.[14]

For the women who took up their pens to write about marriage choices, there was never a clear path from the heart to happiness, as Graffigny made clear in *Lettres d'une peruvienne*. Nor were women unconcerned about or oblivious to the matters of "interest" that novelists and historians have traditionally associated with families and fathers. Indeed, to assume that they were is to limit women to the realm of feeling and deny the importance and utility of their reason in what was certainly the most important decision of their lives. By the same token, to take the letters crafted by male novelists in their name as representations of "women's writing" is to mistake male desire for female practice; it is to substitute Epistolary Woman for all the women who engaged in correspondence.

Writing created a space for women to lay out the issues, options, and dilemmas about which they had to reason and on which their future happiness depended. Unlike the "women's" letters of male-authored epistolary fictions, the letters and novels written by women were not the direct expression of the heart but the site of epistolary reasoning by means of which they and their characters worked through the complex problems that choosing a life through marriage posed. What made these women modern was not the freedom to follow their hearts into marriage but the reasoning they used to sort through the possible paths to happiness through marriage with which life presented them.

We have already seen that reasoning at work in Graffigny's *Lettres d'une peruvienne*. In *Lettres de Lausanne* (1785), Isabelle de Charrière challenges the assumption that arranged marriages are inherently bad. In her first letter, Charrière's protagonist calls her cousin "romanesque"—literally "novelistic"—for complaining that she had no say in her daughter's marriage: "A son-in-law of middling merit, but whom your daughter has married without repugnance: a marriage that you yourself regard as advantageous, but about which you were scarcely consulted! What difference does that make? What does it matter to you? Your husband, his relatives, and the conformity of fortunes have taken care of everything. So much the better."[15] And the marriage itself? The writer makes clear that there is no way to predict whether the marriage will be happy based on how it was contracted. From her maternal perspective, marital happiness is a different subject entirely (indeed, later in the novel she suggests that motherhood brings the only rewards in marriage).[16] She then declares that it is she who has more to complain about, since, lacking the wealth and family connections of her cousin, she will have to put her own daughter on public display to attract a suitable husband.

> My poor Cécile, what will become of her? She turned seventeen last spring. It has been absolutely necessary to take her out into the world to display her to the world; to let the young men who might think about her look at her. . . . Think about her! What a ridiculous expression in this context! Who would think about a girl whose mother is still young and who would have after the death of this mother 26,000 French francs. Our income, my daughter's and mine, is 1,500 French francs. As you can see very well, if someone marries her, it will not be as a result of thinking, but of seeing her. It is thus necessary to put her on display.[17]

In this scenario, love leads to marriage only if the gentleman decides to "purchase" the goods put on display before him. The rest of the novel recounts the complicated game of mother and daughter in a social world in which gentlemen are happy to enjoy the charms of young ladies who then fall in love with them, but whom they have no intention of marrying. Unlike Rousseau's Julie who struggles between love of a man and duty to her parents, Charrière's young lady and her mother present a united front in a campaign to turn a young man's love into a marriage proposal, but the novel ends in uncertainty, as the mother plays her last card and hopes for the best. Unlike Rousseau's Saint-Preux, mother and daughter have no Ovidian strategy modeled on the art of war; they are "tactical" actors (to use Michel de Certeau's term), who must employ a tactical intelligence in their everyday struggles because they are the "others" of power, from which they are excluded.[18] It is they who must do the thinking, because the young men are just looking.

Katharine Jensen argues that by constructing their own epistolary novels, women such as Graffigny and Charrière reappropriated the female love letter and infused letter writing with the power of writing itself.[19] But literature was not the only mode by which women could defy the limits of Epistolary Woman. Indeed, as the literary terrain became increasingly contested over the course of the eighteenth century, the private space of letter writing became the major site in which women enjoyed the freedom to exercise the power of the pen. As the love letter moved to the center of the novel, women's epistolary practice expanded to become a mirror image of the literary field claimed by men, a field in which women could engage in philosophical and religious reflection, social commentary, and narrative. Whereas male-authored fictions presented Epistolary Woman as a "creature of emotion" who "was seen to take naturally to letter writing, her passion for a man overflowing spontaneously into writing to him about it," the letters of eighteenth-century women reveal them as reasoning beings for whom epistolarity facilitated reflection, especially about men and marriage.[20]

Manon Phlipon, whom we have already met, and Catherine de Saint-Pierre, sister of the novelist Bernardin de Saint-Pierre, were very different women who had one thing in common: they both worried and reflected and struggled over the question of whom and how and if they should marry, and neither did so in a paradigmatic way that opposed their hearts to their fathers' heads, their desire to family interests. One woman married and the other did not, but both used the correspondence with a trusted other to work through the complex issues raised by the marriage proposals they received over the course of several years. Their letters show us women as subjects using their letters and their reason to approach matters that generations of writers had tried to convince them were simply matters of the heart.

Catherine: Weighing the Pros and Cons

Almost everything we know about Catherine de Saint-Pierre we learn from the 131 letters she wrote to her brother Bernardin between 1766, shortly after their father died, and her own death in 1804. They suggest that, while she may not have been typical of Frenchwomen of her age, she was surely not exceptional or extraordinary. Her education in a local convent and her ability to engage in correspondence were typical of women of her class and urban milieu, although not, of course, of French women in general. Neither were her economic distress and chronic poor health exceptional in the eighteenth century, nor the fact that she was orphaned at twenty-three. These conditions did, however, create particular difficulties that all women did not have to overcome; hers was a particularly difficult situation.

What most distinguished Catherine from her female contemporaries was the fact that she never married. In the eighteenth century only about 10 percent of women in France remained unmarried by the time they were fifty (thus, effectively their whole lives), as Catherine did. Granted, the number of unmarried women was rising and was already double the proportion of unmarried men. In addition, the average flattens out the fact that urban women like Catherine were more likely to remain unmarried than the rural women who made up the vast majority of the female population. Nevertheless, it was still the case that marriage remained the norm for all women as for men.[21]

An analysis of Catherine de Saint-Pierre's marriage opportunities and the ways in which she presented and analyzed them in her letters thus cannot tell us how "women" thought in the eighteenth century. Catherine's letters do, however, allow us to enter into the head of a woman, a place that both novelists and historians have tended to suggest was empty when it came to marriage decisions, or at least overwhelmed by the passions of the heart. The particular reasoning in which Catherine engaged is thus less important historically than the evidence that she used her epistolary skill to reason complexly and that she did so not in a vacuum, but in a social, familial context. In so doing, she did not submerge herself in the family; rather, she articulated herself as a thinking, willing agent in this context and when faced with the question of marriage. As Natalie Davis has argued, in early modern France, "virtually all the occasions for talking or writing about the self involved a relationship," and the most important, or at least the most common of these, was the family or lineage."[22] Catherine de Saint-Pierre's correspondence with her brother provided her with not just the occasion, but the medium for such an articulation of her self.

Catherine de Saint-Pierre lived her whole life in port towns in Normandy, never straying far from the sea but, like Manon Phlipon and Geneviève de Malboissière, never crossing it either. Her letters show us how she figured in a family whose very identity and livelihood were rooted in the Atlantic world, and how, through correspondence, she maintained family ties that were essential for her selfhood and her life. Her epistolary practice and reasoning about marriage were meant to strengthen those ties, weakened across time and space, even as they allowed her to articulate her own voice, feelings, and ideas.

All three of Catherine's brothers went to sea, leaving her behind pretty much to fend for herself. Dominique was a ship captain and Joseph a soldier; both spent time in France's colonies and were involved in the slave trade. The eldest brother, Bernardin, went off to Martinique with one of his ship captain uncles at the age of twelve.[23] He returned to complete his schooling, but almost twenty years later, after traveling across Europe, from Germany to Malta, Russia, and Poland, he shipped out again: this time for France's Indian Ocean colonies as an infantry captain in the royal engineering corps. When he returned to Paris in 1771, it was with thick journals that would become the raw material for essays on nature that would launch him in the Republic of Letters; when his sentimental novel, *Paul et Virginie*, appeared in 1788, he became one of its stars.

In 1766, when Catherine's correspondence with Bernardin began, both their parents were dead (the mother had died years before), Joseph and Dominique were far away, and she was twenty-three years old, in poor health, and living for the time being at the Ursuline convent in Honfleur, where she had boarded in her youth.[24] Bernardin had just returned home briefly in the hope, he told his patron, of "pulling together the debris of my inheritance that will help me to prepare my fortune to come." But there was not much of an inheritance to claim; Bernardin sold it off for six louis and returned to Paris. Six months later, he was on a ship to Île de France (now Mauritius) as a member of the royal engineering corps.

While Catherine's own movements were limited to seaports along a short piece of the Normandy coast, her family ties expanded her world. Indeed, transoceanic mobility defined the very conditions of her life, for it left her alone in a seaport with the abandoned wives and widows who made up her female kin; it also gave rise to the correspondence that both gave her an important role in her family and tells us about her life. As the one immobile sibling, she was the central node in a family communications system that extended at times from the Indian Ocean to America, Ireland, and the slave coast of Africa. In her letters to Bernardin, Catherine reported on news of her other brothers when she had it, either directly from them or indirectly from other relatives. In January 1769, for example, she reported that, much to her chagrin, her brother Dominique had married "precipitously" the daughter of a local sea captain and was about to set out to sea again.[25] Catherine's new sister-in-law was left behind in Dieppe with (eventually) a couple of children and power of attorney for her husband and his brother. The brother, Joseph, had joined the army that policed the colonies; over time he got involved with the slave trade, the American Revolution, and some shady dealings that landed him in the Bastille in 1779.[26]

Catherine did not write to Bernardin only to convey news of others, however. Between 1766 and 1788 she recorded five marriage proposals, three of which she described in detail. It is in her discussion of these proposals that we see her epistolary reasoning at work, as she sorted through the issues they raised and tried to compel her brother to meet his responsibilities to her as head of the family. The first proposal came from a man she described only as a surgeon and pharmacist. She received the second proposal on New Year's Day 1773, from a "gentleman glassmaker." A second glassmaker proposed the following year and was quickly dismissed. Then nothing until 1786, when a widower, newly returned from Guadeloupe to retire on his family property, offered Catherine his hand in marriage. The last proposal came in 1788. It was from a widowed merchant who offered her not exactly marriage but a "celibate status," in which she would fulfill all the responsibilities of a wife and mother except those of the conjugal bed. There is no way of knowing if there were other proposals.

As we examine the letters that Catherine wrote to her brother about these proposals, we need to keep in mind that their existence is a function of his absence, and that much of what shapes them is her desire, as much as his, that he should take up the role of father for her. Had her father been alive, or had Bernardin lived in Le Havre or Dieppe rather than Paris, proposals of marriage would have been made to him directly (and she probably would have been living under his roof). With her brother's absence, it was up to Catherine to receive the proposals herself and relay them to Bernardin so that he could play the paternal role that he had accepted at his father's death, and to which the correspondence is testimony. It was up to Catherine to gather information about the suitor, his family, and his finances so that Bernardin could make a good decision on her behalf. She tried to present each suitor's proposal as fairly and completely as she could, but she also contributed her own calculations and made sure to point out the strengths, weaknesses, and risks of each as she saw them. Paradoxically, then, in empowering her brother to act for her as a father, Catherine took responsibility for herself and exercised her own powers of reason and judgment. At the same time, the more fully Bernardin shouldered this responsibility, the less she felt able to make her own decisions, both in light of the impact of her life on his, and out of gratitude for what she saw as his kindness and generosity. Rather than deferring meekly to Bernardin's new authority as head of the family, Catherine gave deference in exchange for the responsibility Bernardin was willing to shoulder in regard to her well-being. Her deference to him was a matter of her own choosing and even of her own creation.

Catherine's first mention of a proposal of marriage came in response to an unexpected expression of interest in her from Bernardin in October 1766. Rather than challenging his new authority over her since the death of their father ten months earlier, Catherine cautiously welcomed her brother's interest in her. Whereas the first three letters she wrote him had been brief, in this fourth one she poured out her troubles and concerns at Bernardin's prodding. Having told him about her poor health, her retreat to a convent for lack of other options, and her money problems, she then continued: "Since you still seem to be interested in me, I will tell you that a proposal has been presented to me, which I received from his family and himself, all of whom have moved away from this area." The suitor was a surgeon and pharmacist whose assets added up to 1,600 livres. Catherine gave her brother no further information, holding back until he proved that his interest in her was serious. "I will not tell you what my feelings are today, being very happy to know yours on this occasion in order to see what interest you really want to take in me by the response that you give me."[27] Although we do not have Bernardin's response to this or any of Catherine's letters (nor do we know if he even responded), we do know that Catherine shared four more proposals with her brother over the course of their correspondence.

As Bernardin came to take increasing responsibility for her welfare, Catherine came to see herself as a burden on him and to view decisions about her future in terms of their impact on him as well as herself. She deferred to his opinion more than his authority and tried, for the most part, to keep her feelings to herself. By 1773, when she received another proposal of marriage, she was both more forthcoming and more aggressive in requesting Bernardin's help. She reminded him not only of how much she appreciated his assistance, both material and moral, but how much she now counted on him. "Having taken care of my misfortune like a second father, you have allowed me to avoid the greatest disgraces when everything overwhelmed me." Now, she continued, she felt that she could not "reject the opportunities that might present themselves for marriage," since they might be useful to him or "at least, out of fear of [my] becoming a burden to you." She then laid out the proposal and the additional information she was able to gather about the suitor, and engaged in her own calculation of the pros and cons, before assuring him again that her main concern was his welfare, not hers: "You will see then that I have no desire at all to get married, but rather not to harm your fortune."[28] Did Catherine want to marry? Her economic and emotional dependence on Bernardin make it impossible to know. What we can say, however, is that it is in her calculations, which factored Bernardin into the equation, rather than in declarations of love or defiance, that we find Catherine's agency.

By showing how complex these calculations could be, I want to challenge the assumption that marital choice for women was simply a matter of following their hearts. However, I do not want to suggest that Catherine was simply a cold, hard, calculating machine, or that she made her calculations in a vacuum. If we are to reject the caricature of fathers coldly making marriage decisions for their daughters and daughters simply consulting their own hearts, it would be equally foolish to suggest that women such as Catherine consulted only themselves and their narrow, individualistic interests. If her calculations entailed consulting her brains and her imagination as well as her heart, they also involved consultations with trusted others. Indeed, the existence of this correspondence is testimony to the role that Catherine's brother played in the decision-making process, or at least the role she wanted him to play in it. The final decision, moreover, was only one point in a longer process of finding, presenting, evaluating, and negotiating with a suitor that involved friends and relations as well. In thinking about how women used their epistolary skills to reason about marriage, we need to place them within the social world in which they operated as human beings rather than machines.

Like her contemporaries, Catherine understood singleness and marriage as different *états* (status or situations) for women. Like other *états*, singleness and marriage had legal meaning in the Old Regime: they were understood differently before the law and carried with them different privileges, just as noble and commoner did. The title "madame" was thus not simply honorific (or sexist) but legal as well.[29] Catherine thus framed her discussion of marriage, not in terms of finding a husband, or of hoping or waiting for one to come along, or even of comparing different suitors, but in terms of exchanging one *état* for another, and she was only willing to do so if she saw in the acceptance of a particular marriage proposal an improvement in her life.

Catherine also used the term *état* to refer to her life situation in general. For example, in 1767, she used it figuratively to say that she forgot her own troubles in thinking about her brother Joseph. "I leave my situation often to occupy myself with our poor gendarme, who is at the height of misfortune."[30] As to her other brother, Dominique, she did not want to let him know about her "current situation," because, as she said, "the poverty of some should not crush the others." Finally, *état* could mean social status, and Catherine was very concerned with maintaining it as well. While upward social mobility was possible, downward social mobility was more likely. If a woman's *état* was married, single, or religious, a man's *état* was his profession, trade, or nobility. Marriage changed a woman's status not only by transforming her from *mademoiselle* to *madame* but also because through it she adopted the status of her husband in exchange for that of her father. A future husband's status thus determined both her social position and her economic prospects.

Thus Catherine did not weigh the proposals she received against each other but against her personal status quo. With each of the three proposals she discussed in depth, she considered a whole range of issues that together created an image of what her life would be like if she decided to accept it. What would she give up in trading her current life for the one proposed to her? Where would she live and in what conditions? What would be expected of her, and what could she expect in return? How secure would she be financially? What would happen to her as a person in becoming the wife of the man proposed to her as a husband? What would be the nature of the family and the household that she would join?

For women, more than for men, a marriage delineated the contours of a life, and it was that life that Catherine tried to imagine for herself each time a suitor came forward. In each case she gave voice to fears as well as hopes and expectations in imagining herself in this marriage for life. The fundamental test that each proposal had to withstand was this: Would entering into this marriage make my life better than it is now? The answer lay not simply in her woman's heart but in the details of the proposals she received and analyzed; arriving at a decision each time required calculation, extrapolation, and imagination.

Economic Calculations

Although we are told that property, income, financial prospects, and security were the exclusive concerns of parents, Catherine's letters show how seriously she took these matters. Because her own financial position was so precarious and she had no dowry to offer, her primary concern had to be whether or not the proposed marriage would place her in a better or a worse position economically—she simply could not afford to accept an offer that would pull her down into misery. Her calculations went beyond simply adding and subtracting assets and debts to calculating risks based on investment strategies and life expectancy.

"It is a question of a gentleman glassmaker who proposed to me on New Year's Day," Catherine wrote to Bernardin in 1773, when she was approaching thirty. "He is said to be twenty-one years old, with 200 livres of investment income, his work at 3 livres 10 sols per day, the hope of a better job, that is to say at double [the salary], 7 livres, when they are working." The work, however, was seasonal: for four months of the year the glassmakers were on "vacation" at no pay, and every sixteen to eighteen months they were out of work for six full months while the furnace was rebuilt. Also to be considered was the state of the workers' health: "I forgot to tell you that during the time when they are working, they are fed, but this job that he has is, in addition, bad for the health. As young as he is, he seems to me, by his own admission, in very uneven health. This takes a toll on the temperament. It's necessary to interrupt work in order to get well and rarely do they live to an old age. They retire before they reach forty."[31] While the income and prospects might have looked good on paper, Catherine had to factor in the lost work days and the short life expectancy of her suitor. While other factors (such as the discrepancy in their ages) concerned her as well, she urged Bernardin to remember her own financial situation, combine it with that of the young glassmaker, and understand that although she was not looking to make her fortune, she "did at least fear misery."[32]

More than ten years later, Catherine received another proposal that required complex financial analysis; two long letters were required to explain the situation and Catherine's thinking about it. The suitor was a widower who had just returned to Normandy after spending twenty-five years in the French colony of Guadeloupe. A hurricane had wiped out most of the fortune he had made, and most of his wife's money went to her son from her previous marriage. Eustache Morin had returned home to live on a modest income from property he had inherited near Honfleur. He had invested his share of the 10,000 livres realized from the sale of his wife's house in Guadeloupe in *pacotille*: cheap goods that ship's officers and ordinary sailors were allowed to carry on board to trade (for slaves or other goods) for their own profit. He had been making repairs on his family property in order to make it habitable and was looking for a wife to join him in this new phase of his life. A friend of Catherine's from her convent days in Honfleur had sung her praises to him and his to her and arranged an interview.[33]

Catherine saw this marriage as her best chance to escape both the humiliations and the economic distress of her current situation as a boarder in the Hôtel-Dieu, Dieppe's charity hospital. "I reiterate the news of a proposal announced by my friend from Honfleur, which I mentioned in my last, intimately persuaded as she is of the type of happiness that can settle my future," she wrote to Bernardin. Although Morin's fortune was small, it would come to Catherine or to her children if she were to have any.[34] A widower with neither siblings nor children was rare and held out the possibility of economic security after his death. The only encumbrance in this case was a five-year-old mulatto boy, whom Morin had purchased in Guadeloupe and brought back to France with him. To Catherine, he acknowledged the child as his son, the result of a liaison with a slave woman. Morin had placed him with his tenant farmer who, for 60 livres a year, would raise him and send him to the village school. At fourteen, the child would be emancipated, with the choice to return to Guadeloupe with a trade or remain in France as a servant. In either case, his father's financial responsibility would have been met.[35]

Social Status and Respectability

Catherine was also concerned about the social status of her suitors. Since marriage meant taking on the status of her husband, she could only maintain her precarious hold on respectability through marriage to a man whose status was at least equal to her own. She may have been virtually destitute, but she was what the Old Regime called a *bourgeoise*, a daughter of the urban elite, with a convent education that prepared her for a life of useful idleness rather than manual labor. Two of her brothers were educated to be engineers, and the third was a ship captain. They had all been brought up to believe that they were descended from one of the most illustrious families of Normandy. Catherine's first letters to Bernardin included reports about her fruitless efforts to find some evidence of nobility in their family so that he could claim eligibility for a commission in the army.[36]

Although for novelists considerations of rank were obstacles to good marriages, for Catherine rank was a nonissue because all her offers came through social and familial networks that were the fabric of her social milieu. In particular, she was indebted to her female cousins in Dieppe (that is, on her mother's side of the family) and her female friends from her convent in Honfleur for at least two of the proposals she received, and for counsel in regard to all of them. She never entertained an offer from anyone who was not well matched to her in rank, even if, like Catherine herself, most of her suitors were in some economic distress. The surgeon was "from a good family," and Eustache Morin was connected to "some of the oldest and best families of Honfleur."[37] The widower with eight children, a man who had studied law and then been taken into the substantial wholesale trade of his wife's family, was characterized as "upstanding, although of humble origin." His father, it seems, was a mere butcher. "But today, holding the rank of wholesale merchant, like the higher merchants, who, I am assured are, for the most part, only men of fortune who are no better born. It is thought that his [fortune] will be made within ten years."[38]

The "gentlemen glassmakers" were engaged in manual labor, but they had a unique status in Old Regime France, where nobles were legally prohibited from such work. By royal decree, however, certain noble families had been given the privilege to engage in glassmaking. In the eighteenth century some of them had been given the exclusive privilege to supply window glass to Paris and Versailles. Catherine's suitor, as she noted, was a member of one of the four Norman families who enjoyed this privilege.[39] She assured Bernardin that the alliance was "honorable," even as she noted that "it would seduce someone who did not have the experience of misfortune."[40]

The marriage of the glassmaker's sister to a gentleman "who has never known any other status" was also meant to be reassuring; Catherine would be marrying into a family that had maintained its respectable status, despite misfortune.[41] This was, of course, exactly what Catherine herself constantly struggled to do. As she had written to Bernardin back in 1767, when she saw she would have to leave the convent in Honfleur, "I will leave here as late as I can. It will only be after I have spent my forces and my efforts, and perhaps against some of my good breeding. For the public, whom I have no desire to inform, will not fail to attribute this change to lack of stability. Thus I do not wish to lay down my arms until I've fought a good fight, having no other resource."[42] Maintaining one's status in the face of adversity meant caring about public opinion, but it was not out of vanity that Catherine or the glassmaker struggled to do so. This sort of respectability was a crucial aspect of what Pierre Bourdieu calls "social capital," or the advantages that accrue from one's place within a social network and that cannot simply be reduced to economic resources or class.[43] It was also crucial to Catherine's sense of self and self-respect.

Catherine was concerned about maintaining her respectability and the reputation of her family in the face not only of her own poverty but also of questionable behavior on the part of her brothers Dominique and Joseph. She wrote often of her own disgrace and that of others.[44] With every proposal she received, she expressed her concern that word of it might "leak out" before a decision was made, and thus embarrass her if it fell through. A responsible male head of family was proper, and having Bernardin fill that role helped both her respectability and her credibility in dealing with her suitors and their seconds. As she urged Bernardin, when faced with the glassmaker's proposal: "Decide, or rather, come, if at all possible; confer about all this with the interested parties. People could only praise the deference that I would show you. And that [would be] even more salient, inasmuch as the family does not know about it."[45] Catherine would be in a stronger position with her brother representing her than she would be alone. His authority placed her properly within a respectable family and made her less vulnerable to those who thought they were dealing with a woman without allies.

What is perhaps most surprising is that Catherine seems to have seen poverty and loss of social standing as a greater humiliation than remaining single. Although historians have emphasized the precarious social position of "women without masters," and the social stigma attached to failure to marry, Catherine never ascribed her humiliations to her single status.[46] Nor did she weigh the social advantages of being married into her calculations. While it is certainly true, as Cécile Dauphin has noted, that Enlightenment ideology held that woman's vocation was to marry and have children, that this was her very nature, Catherine expressed no concern at all about fulfilling such a destiny.[47] Remaining single would have been perfectly respectable, if only she had had enough income to support herself. It was because her "revenue is so limited as to attract disgrace wherever I go," she told Bernardin in 1770, that she had moved into the Hôtel-Dieu, where she was forced to "submit to the shock" of being cloistered again.[48] That shock, however, was preferable to the disgrace of living in poverty outside the convent walls.

Beyond the Couple: Siblings, Children, and In-Laws

A solid financial basis and social status were the minimum requirements for establishing a household through marriage, but people came into play as well. Children from previous marriages, mothers-in-law, siblings, and members of one's own family often had to be considered, so Catherine had to learn as much as possible about the suitor's family and any encumbrances it might entail. Eustache Morin's lack of siblings and legitimate children was a point in his favor, not only for economic reasons, but because it meant that Catherine would not be brought into a family fraught with tensions or asked to take on the responsibilities of a family already formed. Sometimes, however, the situation of the suitor mirrored her own. The gentleman glassmaker, for example, was, like Catherine, an orphan, and, like Catherine's brothers, he had a sister to worry about. Catherine learned that his mother had been widowed when the children were young and then scraped along on a modest income:

> This lady finished her life as an invalid for several years, which left her with some debts. This young man, they say, made every effort to maintain the status of this family, which was in real misery, as to linens as much as to the necessities of life, always maintaining its rank. She finally died after languishing for three or four years, a good year ago. Since then he married his sister, who is younger than he, to a gentleman who is involved in hunting.[49]

Although he was only twenty years old, the glassmaker had already proved himself to be a responsible head of his family. His mother's illness and his support of her and his sister helped to explain the weakness of the young man's economic position, but also to reassure a future wife that his property and future income were now unencumbered, while showing him to be responsible beyond his years.

Catherine could only compare this brother with her own. When her father died, her brothers were scattered to the winds, and she retreated to the convent in Honfleur, where the nuns took her in for the modest fee she could afford because she had been one of their boarders as a girl. By the following year, however, she was forced to leave: the Ursulines were now demanding the full pension, and another woman who could pay it wanted her room.[50] Bernardin sent her some money to help out that fall, but at the end of the year, when the rates went up again, he was about to depart for the colonies and could do nothing for her.[51] Catherine did not hear from him again for more than a year, so when her situation became truly impossible, she looked to her next brother, Dominique. He promised that when he returned from his latest voyage the two of them would set up house together; he even asked her to rent a house for them in his name. Meanwhile, Catherine accepted the offer of a family friend named Dubosc to stay with him and his new wife until her brother returned, but only on condition that "he allow me to pay him for my room and board, as at the convent, although modestly, in accordance with my income. Otherwise I would not at all consider myself at liberty in his home."[52]

Prudently, Catherine did not take out a lease on a house, out of concern, she explained, for her brother Dominique's finances: "In my view, a household would have weakened the fortune of my brother, who is just beginning to achieve some comfort. Out of fear of undermining his well-being, I stayed in the convent for the good of the cause." Dominique did return, but instead of setting up house with his sister, he married "quickly" and without consulting her. "He let me know eight days before the publication of the banns. . . . It's a marriage that won't benefit either of them, as I understand it." While assuring his sister of his friendship, Dominique then announced his intention to depart again, this time for the slave coast of Guinea, no doubt, according to Catherine, to make some quick money, "having married in advance."

Catherine had been betrayed by Dominique, her other brothers were out of the country, and, it turned out, there had been a misunderstanding with M. Dubosc: he too expected her to pay more than the modest amount she could afford.[53] For Catherine, paying rent was symbolic: she knew she couldn't afford to pay for her keep, but she did not intend to be reduced either to someone who had to earn her living or to a household dependent—a servant in all but name. After an unpleasant exchange of words, Catherine fled to another temporary haven with her next closest male relative. But when her uncle realized that Catherine's brother Dominique was not going to contribute to her maintenance, he, too, kicked her out. "I had to find an asylum," Catherine explained, "which I soon fixed at the Hôtel-Dieu, where there are a few boarders in the interior of the house." She may as well have stayed in Honfleur with the Ursulines, who at least had some feelings for her, she realized, since the fees were exactly the same. She had counted on Dominique, but now he did not even respond to the letters her uncle sent him. "I know that he is completely occupied with his new family and also his career," she wrote, "which will succeed only if he supplies it with funds. He has gotten married before building his house; that will make life very hard for him."[54] In contrast to her own brothers, seeking their fortunes at sea, marrying, and leaving her behind to fend for herself, the glassmaker took care of his sister before setting up his own household. And he had just bought the little house in which he proposed to establish it.[55]

Siblings could and did have an impact on a marriage, but the most delicate and complicated issues to consider had to do with children from a first marriage. Young children needed to be raised, and grandparents and other relatives of the deceased parent might well get involved to protect the interests even of adult children. Catherine was quite aware of what could happen to children. Her letters to Bernardin began shortly after the death of her father and concerned the children's attempts to claim their inheritance from their stepmother. In fact, it was the death of her father that sent Catherine into the tailspin from which she struggled to emerge: no place to live, a paltry income, no one to look out for her. It is hard to know why Catherine moved out of her stepmother's house on the death of her father, but when she took temporary refuge with her uncle in Dieppe, she said she had "no other choice."[56]

When widowers approached her, Catherine had to consider the impact of a second marriage on children from the previous marriage, as well as her own position in a family that was already formed. Eustache Morin had reassured her on this point when he stipulated that his illegitimate child would have no claims beyond maintenance until his fourteenth year, and that Catherine and any children she might have would be the sole claimants upon his death. His first wife, of course, had made sure that the bulk of her fortune would go to her own son when she remarried, thus leaving Morin with little when she died.

When a second widower approached Catherine two years after the match with Morin fell through, the situation and the terms were quite different. "I have been offered a celibate position," Catherine explained:

In truth, [it is] a lot of work, but rewarding, a thirty-eight-year-old father of a family, newly widowed by an unexpected accident in childbirth. This separation has attracted public attention, as much because of the youth of this woman as for the utility of all her virtues for the good of her household [and] its wholesale trade, of which she ran the office. Even more, for the care of a small family, four sons and four daughters, of whom the eldest is said to be twelve years old; three are said to be at nurse.[57]

Despite the widower's dire need for assistance, his wife's family, on which his business depended, did not want him to remarry, out of fear that a second wife and family might cut into the interests of their grandchildren. He tried to convince them that it was for the sake of the children that he wanted to marry. When this plea failed, he asked around to see if anyone could find him someone "who could fill the functions of a mother of a family and mistress of the household, for the government of his housekeeping interests and the well-being of his fortune, renouncing any intention to marry again, making assurances that he would give all the consideration in his power to her who would render his plight less overwhelming by becoming the adoptive mother of his [children]."[58] Catherine's female relations in Dieppe proposed her for the position.

This "celibate status" would not give Catherine the economic security of a marriage, or the social status of a married woman, or, of course, the possible pleasures of the marriage bed or happiness of motherhood. As she told Bernardin, however, there were definite advantages to the situation. For one, she would no longer have to pay for her room and board, the cost of which had just been raised yet again. Moreover, she wrote, she hardly needed to remind her brother of "the other disgraces of poverty, in a community that cares only about wealth, where I have aged miserably." Catherine was forty-four years old when she wrote this and had suffered the miseries and indignities of boarding with the sisters of the Hôtel-Dieu for almost eighteen years.[59] Taking up the widower's offer would mean a lot of hard work, but it would free her from a situation that was becoming both economically untenable and psychologically intolerable. Changing her status, however, might have further economic implications, which she brought up on a separate sheet inserted in her letter to Bernardin, with the caution that he should not communicate the contents of her letter to anyone. Bernardin was in the process of applying for a royal pension for his sister. Would it be possible, she asked, to avoid mentioning her change of address, should she join the widower's household? It would no doubt look suspicious (or at least less meritorious) if she were domiciled not in the Hôtel-Dieu but in the home of a prosperous widower, whatever her actual status there would be.

Catherine's final, and perhaps strongest, consideration was that taking up this new position might relieve her own brother of the burden of taking care of her. She reminded Bernardin of the sacrifices he was making to supplement her income and how much it pained her to have to accept his money. "If this change in status takes place," she told him, "my own income will be devoted to my support, which my efforts at economizing have made me neglect, and I would like for the gifts you have sacrificed to me to serve as my acknowledgment of your economizing. If I had my way, they would be offered to you as just tribute for you to dispose of as I would myself." Catherine reiterated this point in a postscript. "You should not refuse because of the pleasure that I would feel. Compare it to those that you have felt in helping me, if this can enter into your calculations. And me, from my perspective, should I arrive at some recourse of comfort to improve my situation by my own economies, perhaps one day I would be able to be useful to you, without being a burden to you. Your books have penetrated me on this subject."[60]

Catherine had just received her copy of the final volume of Bernardin's *Études de la nature*, which included *Paul et Virginie*, his great novel of love between brother and sister. "For me," she had written at the beginning of the letter, "penetrated by its content, your Virginie and your Arcadia oppress the heart. In places that are personal to you, I did not have enough tears, suffocations, a painful situation that cannot be expressed. But even to the point of melancholy, you offer pleasures."[61] These were the pleasures that Catherine wanted to offer Bernardin, pleasures that would emerge from her own sadness and sacrifice. Accepting the merchant's proposition would not bring her marital happiness, but it would allow her to make a sacrifice that would give her pleasure in returning the many favors she had received over almost two decades. In considering the merchant's proposition, she thought most about its implications for her brother.

Imagining a Life

As we have seen, economic considerations, social status, and concerns about other family members could not be entirely separated; each obviously had an impact on the other. By the same token, when Catherine tried to imagine what her life would be like if she accepted a proposal made to her, she did not ignore these other considerations, but rather tried to fill in the picture, of which the proposal gave only a rough sketch. She took all the bits of information she could gather—from a personal interview, from intermediaries, from friends and relatives in the community—to create for herself and Bernardin an image of what her life would be like.

The closest Catherine came to expressing her vision of a good husband was not in response to a proposal of marriage but to Bernardin's request that she describe to him some friends she was visiting in the summer of 1781. "In singing the praises of the different qualities that characterize my friend," she wrote, "I cannot sing those of her husband better than in telling you that I would consider myself only too happy if providence had destined for me a husband who had his qualities."[62] What those qualities were, though, she failed to say. When it came to discussing the men who proposed to her, only suggestions of their character or what she thought of them peek through. After meeting Eustache Morin, for example, she noted that, although he was "short for a man and not handsome, forty-eight years old [but] appearing older," he had "a twinkle in his eye. I see common sense and an honest air, speaking well [enough] to appear anywhere."[63] In discussing the merchant, Catherine emphasized his love for his children and noted that "he has touched deeply" the mothers of the town.[64] Of the glassmaker she could only say that, concerning his conduct, he's a young man, but I don't know anything directly disagreeable about him."[65]

Catherine tended to worry when she imagined her married life with one of these men. "Think of me at the head of a small country household far from the church," she pleaded after laying out the glassmaker's proposal. "Winter and summer, taking the roads, such as they are. Not a single person to see. The place is deserted. The garden in place of vegetables and fish. A husband whom one sees on Sunday, being a league from the place where he works, they only have Sundays to come home." Saint-Saire, where he had just bought the house with its garden and room for a cow, was an inland village about halfway between Dieppe and Rouen, only thirty kilometers away on today's roads, but culturally a world apart from the seaports where Catherine and all her friends and family had always lived.[66] Catherine asked Bernardin to consider the material difficulties she would suffer on top of the loneliness:

> A house ready to furnish, or at least having only the bare necessities of an unfurnished house. No linens or so few that he cannot tell me how many pairs of sheets. All this is important when one marries because our mothers make every effort to furnish us with them [linens], foreseeing children who will then destroy them. If, as it is said, some debts . . . if some other unknown details surface, it seems to me that, to start a family, these are a lot of encumbrances.[67]

Life with the glassmaker looked bleak, and Catherine pointed out all the negatives. By contrast, life with Eustache Morin was more tempting, and Catherine felt herself obliged to emphasize the positives, especially since her friend, who had arranged the match, was pushing her hard to accept it. She urged Catherine to choose this "rustic retreat under a small roof that [Morin] says is pleasant," and volunteered to go look at it herself. Since Morin proposed to leave the house and his entire modest fortune to her in his will, Catherine could expect to live out her life there. She begged Bernardin to help her decide what to do, indeed, to decide for her:

> You see two futures for me, and this is the moment of truth. If you are opposed, that will be my law. If you are in favor, I will regard your applause as a paternal benediction that will allow me to overcome the perplexity with which this position weighs me down. I will regard it as a destiny that would continue forever your tender friendship that I cherish with silent tears. My hope would be to see you in my little retreat.[68]

Despite the attractions of Morin's offer and her increasing desperation to get away from the mean-spirited sisters at the Hôtel-Dieu, Catherine turned this proposal down. We do not know what Bernardin may have written in response to her plea for a decision, but in two subsequent letters, Catherine reassured him that she did not blame him. She reminded him that it was only his encouragement "to overcome my fears" that had pushed her to agree to the interview her friend had wanted to arrange. "I was afraid," Catherine confessed. "Seeing him, I calmed down, but the government of a household established on a mediocre fortune in part [invested] at sea, another illness, children, or any other servitude that comes with this *état*"—her thoughts trailed off.[69] She admitted that she regretted "the honest man and the rustic life," but less for the happiness they promised than because they would have "delivered me again, doubtless forever, from my asylum where I do not cease to be a stranger."[70] Things did get worse for Catherine at the Hôtel-Dieu after she turned down Morin's proposal, but the marriage was still, according to her calculations and Bernardin's, a bad risk. It is, of course, impossible to know if she made the right choice, but it was a choice that she acknowledged to be her own in letters written in her own hand (see fig. 8.1).

Making Decisions: Calculation and Consultation

The context in which Catherine was being asked to make such a decision was particularly hard for someone who did not assume that any marriage was better than no marriage. There was no courtship or other means to get to know her suitor personally, no parents at hand to look out for her interests, and inadequate financial means to take an economic risk on a marriage without strong foundations. She was always under pressure from suitors, as well as well-meaning friends and relatives, and had to decide within a time frame that was absurdly short. We should not be surprised if Catherine lacked confidence in her own ability to choose the right path or chose not to depend entirely on her own reason. In each case, she learned what she could, weighed the pros and cons, and used her imagination to envision what her life would be like if she accepted. Then she turned to Bernardin for help, asking him to take the final decision out of her hands.

Not surprisingly, the first thing Catherine said about the prospect of taking over the role of wife and mother for the widowed merchant with eight children was that it would be "in truth, very hard work." She was concerned about the merchant's youth, as she had been about the glassmaker's. "His few years made an impression on me, in the fear that he still has some youth about him. But already several wrinkles, which in me are a prelude to others, joined to my maintenance, which the years will only make more serious, make me consider the pros and cons, and I do not want to deliberate without knowing your feelings." Catherine was so concerned to consider this proposal dispassionately that she told the widower not to bring his children around to meet her. "I opposed all this, which would have touched my heart and broken our secret, essential to keep until a decision [is made], for which they do not want to grant me any delay."[71]

Catherine reached out to Bernardin at least in part because she was under pressure from her female cousins, who tried to convince her that she was being called to do God's work. "For this past month I have been presented with this work of humanity, to which are attached ideas about Providence. They certainly expected the whirlwind of reflections that I've had, that have overwhelmed me, without however, anyone blaming me. But they persist." Her cousins knew she would consult her brother and, according to Catherine, "fear that I would prejudice you against the object in question."[72] Perhaps, after so many years, they suspected that Catherine was using Bernardin as an

93   36

Mon cher frere et amy

ma derniere lettre toute[s] confiante ment a a'titée une
semblable de votre part vos reflections sont pu ajouter
aux mienes qui déja ma cablois de leur propre pois
mais ce qui fesoit mon rigoureus[e] conbat etoit
la néssesitée de me délivrer des disgrasse journalière
a'nuelle que me procure la pension la plus basse
et même seule de ce jenre dans la maison que j'abite
ou au moindre contredit on me repro[che] les chausse
ordinaire on suprime chaque jour tanpis pour celle
qui ne peuse supleé par leur revenu aux objets
esensiels on a'non cas augue ment tation de pension
jénérale dont je fais consp avec l'abandon ou
l'on est lors que l'on subit des maladie il i a
en an pu dans ce temps cy une pierre double tierse
cautidiene une tase de bouillon en vingt quatre heure
etoit plus que mon besoin ma convalescence de mendoit
des égard apres plus d'un mois a'titée dans cet état
je né prouve des dépausitre que insensibilitée
rpe sones dont j[e p]u dispauser je nay plus m[rs] blondel
il i a des a'née sa peste n'a pu se repauser nous nous
portons des regres mutuel c'est trop vous dire pour an
a'me sensible sillacer donc

8.1. Letter from Catherine de Saint-Pierre to Bernardin de Saint-Pierre, 26 May 1786. Bibliothèque municipale du Havre, MS 142.

excuse to turn down proposals that she, for her own reasons, did not want to accept. In part, at least, they were probably right. In the letter she wrote after laying out the glassmaker's proposal, Catherine had said of it only, "with regard to my marriage, my reflections agree with yours. There is nothing to it and will be nothing to it." After turning down Morin's proposal she had written similarly, "Your worthy reflections on the marriage about which I consulted you were precisely my own."[73] Catherine also came to count on the delay that consulting her brother necessarily entailed and the opportunity that it afforded her to lay out for herself the pros and cons of each proposal. When we look at the terms she was given, this should not surprise us.

The glassmaker had made his proposal to Catherine on New Year's Day 1773. "I requested a month," she wrote," which I had difficulty obtaining. And yet the letter to Bernardin was dated 15 January, half-way through the allotted month. Perhaps it took Catherine two weeks to gather the information she needed; perhaps she realized only after two weeks that she could not make this tough decision herself. "I must have a response," she concluded after laying out everything she knew, and "it will be yours that determines my own. Do not delay. Within twelve days I owe mine, for which he is very impatient. I regard you as my father and I expect from your zeal a response that will bring to a close this matter, which must not leak out."[74]

The pressure on Catherine was even greater when her old school friend set up the interview with the widower from Guadeloupe. "I have been asked to allow M. Eustache Morin to come greet me," she explained on 20 April 1786. "This would be an acceptance on my part, after which the contract and the marriage would follow immediately." Her friend proposed to accompany Morin and, after the interview, to whisk Catherine away to her new country home, where she and Morin would be married. "I swear to you," Catherine told Bernardin, "that whatever desire and need I have to settle my future, I have never been so afraid of such haste." She refused to go along with this plan on the grounds that she was not given "the leisure to reflect on it."[75] Ten days later, Catherine wrote again and again invoked her friend who was pushing her to accept Morin's offer. "I remind you of the news of a proposal announced by this friend from Honfleur, which I mentioned in my last, intimately persuaded as she is of her happiness in settling my future." Again, Catherine asked her brother to help her make a decision. In the meantime, she would ask God for help, too. "Put me within reach of responding immediately, because the days are numbered. I want to have a mass said and to take communion during the interval of your response. Let it be decisive, do not send it back to me, because I am incapable. It is you who are my support, who will make me overcome my weakness."[76]

Seven months later, when Catherine tried again to explain to Bernardin that although she regretted the decision she made, she did not blame him, she pointed out that her calculations had been different from his. While she had evaluated the proposal in the same way as he had, she had also compared the life it offered with the one she had: "Your worthy reflections on the marriage about which I consulted you were precisely my own, which proved to me more and more the true friendship that causes everything to be felt and foreseen, but with this unfortunate difference, that on my side I was more than penetrated with the daily and revolting problems of my situation." She asked him to put himself in her shoes: "Picture for yourself my position, where I had to decide between these two extremes." It was this impossible choice that paralyzed her. "Not having wished to act according to my own lights," she explained, "I had a mass said, where I received my God, while I waited for your response, which was to make me think about the consequences."[77] Bernardin had helped her to evaluate Morin's offer on its own merits, something she had been unable to do because, from her perspective, it was above all an escape route from her daily miseries. But whose perspective was better? Bernardin's "objective" one or Catherine's experiential, subjective one? "I had no sooner finished [writing] this refusal, when it seems that heaven took up arms against me," Catherine continued. "My friend, who was displeased, quarreled with me, the Convent, which knew nothing about it, made me suffer what it had for a long time threatened: the augmentation of pensions."[78]

There is no question that Catherine's life got worse, but does this mean that she made the wrong decision or that she was unduly "persuaded" by Bernardin, to borrow a phrase from Jane Austen? What is clear is that the options before her were not those posed by Austen to the heroine of *Persuasion*: between following her own heart or following the practical, rational counsels of her family. Catherine's heart was not at issue here, and it gave her no counsel. And her own calculations were as practical and rational as her brother's; they were just different because they factored in her present situation in a way that his could not. And although it is true that Catherine never married, she did in the last years of her life manage a solution that in 1786 she could only suggest as an impossible way out: renting a room in town and living there on her own income. The family with whom she now boarded were in-laws of one of her maternal cousins. The woman was the "respectable mother of a family," whose husband, a merchant, was paralyzed. The cousin, who was at sea more than he was home, lived right next door with his wife and young children.[79] With the income Bernardin had secured for her from the crown, a small legacy from her maternal uncle, and the modest income she had inherited from her father, Catherine was now able to live out her days on her own terms, as a respectable, independent woman.

Unlike Montesquieu's Roxane, Rousseau's Julie, or countless other heroines of eighteenth-century novels, Catherine did not choose death as the road to freedom, as the only possible alternative to an *état* forced on her. She refused both risky marriages and the cloister to find herself, on the eve of the French Revolution, more like Graffigny's Zilia: happy at last because she had escaped economic misery and maintained both her *état* and her freedom, which is to say, her dignity as a human being and a woman.

Manon (Again): Using Rousseauian Reason

Manon Phlipon, too, faced multiple marriage proposals, but her reasoning about them differed from that of Catherine de Saint-Pierre. Like the philosophes she admired, Manon believed that marital happiness depended on compatibility and that compatibility could only be achieved through the free choice of the individuals concerned. In fact, despite Manon's later denials, her marriage to Jean-Marie Roland was a love match freely chosen by both parties and arranged by no one but themselves. How could it have been otherwise, when Manon herself wrote in a letter to Sophie when she was twenty-two: "Oh liberty! Idol of strong souls, nourishment of the virtues, never will I immolate myself to vile interests, to the conventions of prejudices!"[80] Despite the bravado of these words, however, Manon struggled just as much as Catherine did when faced with concrete proposals of marriage. Indeed, it was generally in the face of such proposals, and in working out her response to them, that Manon Phlipon developed her reasoned positions not only on marriage but on freedom, social responsibility, and gender. Her correspondence was the site of this practical reason and its medium.

Manon was seventeen when she received her first marriage proposal. It came from a twice-widowed merchant jeweler in her neighborhood who was also twice her age. In letters she wrote to Sophie Cannet as the negotiations progressed, Manon shared everything she was able to learn about the gentleman, whom she met, by arrangement, at the home of a relative. After the meeting, her parents made clear that they thought this was a good match but that the decision was hers: "They do not demand anything of me," Manon wrote to Sophie. "Wishing to make me happy, they leave me free to accept or not."[81] The decision may have been hers, but she was asked to make it based on a single meeting whose purpose was to find out simply if she found the gentleman "repugnant." But Manon refused to act on the basis of a visceral response, because, as she explained to her parents, "I don't care about looks at all, only character, feelings, and the [gentleman's] way of thinking can be relevant to my decision." The jeweler then proposed a second visit in which he would reveal these interior qualities for her approval.[82] Now what should she do?

To Sophie, Manon explained that she wanted to do her "duty," but it was not at all clear to her what that duty was. The question was not simply whether she found the proposed match acceptable (that is, not repugnant). She was not sure that marriage was even the right path for her:

> Concerned solely with the desire to accomplish the will of divine Providence in all things, and particularly in this important situation, on which I am convinced that my eternal happiness or unhappiness depends, I find myself completely indifferent regarding every sort of status, equally ready to marry, to enter into religion, or to remain as I am, having no other will than to do what is most pleasing to God in taking the path that He has decided for all eternity that I should take to him.[83]

The problem was not choosing between duty and desire but figuring out what her duty and desire were; she knew neither God's will nor her own.

If Manon was perplexed about what her destiny in life was, she refused simply to wait passively to be told. Nor did she accept the proposition, as she put it, that "there are three things in life, of which getting married is one, that one must do without reflection."[84] It was precisely on marriage that she reflected most during this period of her life, and on reflection she concluded that "marriage is ordinarily the most bizarre thing in the world: we are united to each other by the most sacred ties, we swear a tender, sincere, unshakeable love, to whom? To a man whom we often know only superficially, and whom one is often pained to find little worthy of the sentiments that duty obliges us to feel toward him." Most people, she concluded, would never marry if they really thought about it.[85]

No longer seeking an answer in religion, Manon was struggling to reason through the question of whom to marry. She sought, above all, to reconcile the desires of her parents with her own. When she wrote to Sophie shortly before her twentieth birthday that "reflection has become necessary for me to the point that I cannot do without it," it was in a letter in which she admitted how difficult it would be to find that rare person who suited her, and even more difficult for such a man to suit her parents as well: she was looking for someone with whom she was personally compatible, she explained, while they were more concerned with finding someone whose *état* was compatible with hers.[86]

The real problem, however, was not her parents, who, she admitted, "cherish me, with whom I live happily and satisfied, and who would never impose their will on me absolutely."[87] Rather, it was the disparity between her economic situation and her aspirations. As an only child of parents who loved her and wanted only for her to be happy, she could hardly sacrifice herself and her happiness to some mistaken idea of duty. Nor could she marry a poor man for love because, as she explained, "I am not poor enough to accept a man who has nothing, nor rich enough to make his fortune." More troubling, she realized that the kind of man she was looking for—one who shared her Rousseauian family values—was unlikely to emerge from the social and economic milieu from which her suitors came: "The modesty of my property does not allow me to extend my aspirations far, which leaves them trapped within a class where, apparently, they will not find anyone who can fulfill them."[88] Apparently, the Rousseauian dream was not available to a woman of her class.

But Manon was not about to run off with the first Saint-Preux who knocked at her heart. Just two months earlier, she had met just such a person—Claude-Mammès Pahin de la Blancherie, the young poet she had mentioned to Sophie who had gone off to America at fifteen to seek his fortune. When Manon met him in 1773, she was nineteen and he was twenty. Back in France for three years already, he was completing work on his first book, the proofs of which he later brought her, perhaps as proof of his love, like a trophy from a knight to his fair maid. "He's from a good family," Manon wrote Sophie, "and is destined for the magistracy; but due to the state of his affairs, he cannot set up a household for three or four years. No matter! His imagination has certainly been blinded by the *Émile*; he thought he had found his Sophie and wanted to stake his claim to her."[89]

Manon clearly found La Blancherie attractive, but his youth, poverty, and unsettled future made marriage to him a pipe dream. "However," she told Sophie, "all jokes aside, from what I have been able to learn about him as a person, he seems to me to have a true and honest heart, lots of love for the arts and sciences, wit, and knowledge. Really, if he were established in his career, older, and with a more seasoned head, a little more solidity, he would not have displeased me."[90] Six months later she was more enthusiastic. "I am still discovering new rapports in our ways of thinking; his soul would seem to be the expression of my own: this is precisely what I need. I find in him a lot of feeling, as much education; wit, knowledge, gentleness, religion, and even birth, to which I do not have the right to aspire."[91]

If Manon had found her duty unclear when faced with her first suitor, she was equally unready now simply to "follow her heart." Even when, in January 1776, she tried to cast herself as a Rousseauian heroine by writing La Blancherie a letter declaring her impossible love and having her maid pass it to him on the stairs, her good sense told her that she could not marry a man who was unable to support himself, let alone her, and she refused to consider the kind of clandestine and disreputable existence that marriage without her father's consent would entail. She declared herself willing to wait for La Blancherie to establish himself in a career, but she did not even contemplate simply following her heart and worrying about her parents and her material interests later. Rather, she would remain true to him forever, and she assumed that he would of course remain true to her.[92]

Two weeks later Manon reassured Sophie that she never actually said she loved La Blancherie and she agreed that "no real engagement, in the normal sense, attaches me to D.L.B." She also admitted that she was perhaps expecting more of the young man than he could deliver in the way of constancy. By April she was conceding that "in D.L.B. I don't find a superior merit, but precisely the one who is right for me; he's not a genius, but he has a soul that is pure, simple, noble, great, and worthy of me."[93] In June, however, she ran into him in the Luxembourg Gardens with another woman and a feather in his hat that, in her opinion, violated all his claims to simple Rousseauian values. "Oh! You would not believe how much this awful feather has tormented me," she wailed. "I have turned it over in every direction in order to square it with his philosophy, with his taste for simplicity, with that way of thinking that made me love him: I have exhausted myself in this sad research." Even worse, her companion recognized La Blancherie as someone who, she said, "used to see some rich and lively young ladies from whose home he was asked to leave because he had been bragging that he was going to marry one of them." Manon claimed to be skeptical of this story, but still, she said, she was "starting to believe that it might be possible that I had regarded him as more worthy than in fact he is."[94]

By July the bubble had burst. "I spoke about him with the person through whom I met him; I did not find that anyone esteems him very highly," she reported. The best she could say was that La Blancherie was "still a man whom I wish well more than others, but he is not the one whom I would accept as a husband. I am coming back to the position I used to hold that the encounter of two souls that resemble each other, of two lovers united by virtue and pleasures is the Elysian Fields of the poets, the chimera of young, sensitive, and honest hearts, the winning ticket of the lottery of happiness that is drawn scarcely once a century. I have lost all hope."[95] With all her belief in marriage as "it ought to be contracted," she told Sophie, she was convinced that she would not achieve it. "The people proposed to me are not compatible with my *état* [or] my fortune; circumstances prohibit me from having any other hopes, and [even] if I were richer, I do not see myself finding anyone to my taste in the next class up. I am thus firmly persuaded that celibacy will remain my lot, and I feel myself capable of being happy with it."[96]

As each new suitor presented himself, Manon's frustration grew. The one who caused her the most agony, perhaps, was a man she described as "capable of making a woman happy, by the goodness of his heart and the evenness of his character, if, however, a certain compatibility of mind and way of seeing things were not just as necessary for the happiness of a union whose fruits require caring for them together." In other words, the fellow was rich and kind, but not too bright, and Manon had no intention of playing both mother and father to her children.[97] As she had observed a few years earlier, interviewing suitors was similar to interviewing prospective tutors for one's son.[98]

Manon's father, meanwhile, refused to play the role his daughter had assigned to him. For a while, she later claimed, he displayed a "charming docility," allowing his daughter to draft the letters in which her other suitors were summarily rejected. "I had fun playing papa," she admitted. "I treated my own interests with all the seriousness that the matter deserved and in the end for myself, in the style and wisdom of paternity."[99] At the same time, Phlipon had banned La Blancherie from his house, humiliating and angering Manon, but also allowing her to play the Rousseauian heroine. Drawing his character from a different sort of novel, however, Manon's father lost interest in his work, let his business go down the drain, and proceeded to fritter away his fortune, his late wife's dowry, and his daughter's, on debauchery and mistresses.[100] With a true air of defiance, Manon declared: "Never will I give either my hand or my heart [to someone] simply in order to have what is called an *état* and pull myself out of [financial] embarrassment, if I should ever be in it. Well-founded esteem, delicacy, and feeling will conduct me to the altar, or I won't go there at all."[101] Finally, as her father became increasingly irresponsible, Manon became more committed to what she considered her duty as a daughter and he considered her stubbornness. As she sacrificed herself to him, taking over the household duties, he stopped talking to her, stayed out later and later, and continued to spend money and resent her. She retaliated by spying on him: disguising herself as a servant and following him to the home of his mistress and confronting him with his treachery. He wanted her out of the house, but she refused to desert him.[102]

There was more to the story, however, than Manon was telling Sophie. The same week in which she wrote her fatal letter to La Blancherie, declaring (or not declaring) her love for him, she met another man who impressed her even more, but who seemed way out of her league. Jean-Marie Roland was twenty years her senior: forty-two years old to Manon's twenty-two. If not quite noble, he was from a well-respected land-owning family in the Lyonnais, and he too was an aspiring man of letters, the author of articles and reports on manufacturing that he planned to present to the Academy of Sciences and publish in the *Encyclopédie méthodique*. He was a friend of Sophie's family in Amiens and rumored to be interested in Sophie's sister Henriette. But when he went to Paris in January 1776, Sophie entrusted him with a letter to her friend, a standard means of introduction. After delivering it, Roland stayed for an hour and half chatting with Manon and her father. He asked if he might call again, and Manon agreed, she reported, "wholeheartedly."[103] Manon's father was as impressed and flattered by the attention of this distinguished man as Manon was. Far from banning him from his house, he encouraged the visits, during which his accomplished daughter discussed with this rather serious man all the ancient and modern authors whose works they both admired. When Roland left for a tour of Italy in August, he confided the manuscripts of his own works to Manon and promised to return with an account of his voyage.[104] And then he kissed her, in full view of witnesses. Manon did not tell Sophie any of this, although she continued to write to her just as before. In September she mentioned her esteem for Roland briefly, but claimed still to be comparing every prospective suitor with La Blancherie.[105] By my count, there were eleven of these suitors between August 1776, when Roland left for Italy, and January 1780 when, at last, Manon married him.

The twists and turns of Roland's courtship of Manon are too complicated to detail here. The letters they exchanged, however, prove that despite Manon's later denials (in the memoirs she wrote in prison during the Terror) there was real passion between them. He declared his love to her in April 1779, and after only a brief hesitation, she assured him that she loved him too.[106] Within days she was writing to him: "What are you doing right now, my friend? Are you thinking of me, who loves you, who writes to you, who wants to forget with you all the boring little tasks that I've just finished?"[107] She also declared to him in true Rousseauian fashion that she was "ready to do her duty against [her] heart, if that [should be] necessary."[108] Her father had finally risen to the occasion and refused to allow her to marry Roland because he thought that Roland had insulted him and his family. Roland returned the favor by taking Phlipon's refusal as an insult to him and his family. Manon refused to marry Roland without her father's consent. Fortunately for all of them, Manon, Roland, and her father finally managed to agree on a marriage that they all wanted but that was foundering on the pride of all three.

The premarital tensions between Manon and Roland had to do with their very different social status and class—his wealth, profession, and land; her poverty and artisan upbringing. Roland was genuinely nervous that his family would disown him for marrying her, but he was afraid to tell her of his fears and afraid to tell his family (especially his mother) that he wanted to marry her. His mother's blessing meant as much to him as Manon's father's did to her. This marriage was a very daring move into uncharted territory for both of them. You can tell from reading Roland's letters to Manon that acknowledging his love for her was the hardest and scariest thing he had ever done. This was love, not reason.

The marriage of Manon Phlipon and Jean-Marie Roland did not turn out very well. In her memoirs Manon denied that she ever loved him. "His gravity, his morals, his habits, all dedicated to work, made me think of him as a person without a sex, as it were, or like a philosopher, who existed only through his reason," she claimed. When he declared his love, she said, "I advised M. Roland, as a third party would have, to dissuade him from thinking of me. He persisted, I was touched, and I consented to let him take the necessary steps with my father." After recounting her own version of the ups and downs of the subsequent courtship, she came to the marriage itself:

> Married in the full seriousness of reason, I found nothing to draw me away from it; I devoted myself to it with a fullness more enthusiastic than calculated. By thinking only about the happiness of my partner, I noticed that something was missing in my own; I never ceased for a single second to see in my husband one of the most estimable men who existed, and to whom it was an honor to belong; but I often felt that there was missing between us a sense of parity, that the ascendancy of a dominant character, joined to that of twenty years seniority, was too much.

In the end, she concluded, "I cherish my husband as a sensitive daughter adores a virtuous father to whom she would sacrifice even her lover; but I have found the man who could be that lover, and, while remaining faithful to my duty, my artlessness has not been able to hide these feelings that I subordinated to it."[109] Needless to say, Roland was jealous. When Manon declared that she was sacrificing herself to him, he became even angrier. They were miserable until the French Revolution martyred them both.

Neither marriage nor motherhood brought Manon Phlipon the happiness she had worked so hard to attain through her own free choice of a man she found not only compatible but admirable. This inescapable conclusion no doubt surprised Manon and may surprise modern readers, too, since our ideas of love and marriage, like hers, continue to be shaped by the ideas purveyed first by men of letters like Rousseau. To understand what happened, we need to turn our attention away from how the marriage was contracted and toward the terms of companionate marriage as Rousseau theorized it. For the lack of "parity" or equality that Manon complained of was integral to the script for companionate marriage that Rousseau had written in both *Émile* and *Julie*: the husband was supposed to be the master and the wife his dutiful second. At the same time that Rousseau (in the voice of Sophie's father) asserted that "it is up to the spouses to match themselves," he also noted (in his own voice) that "if [Sophie] had only to find someone to help satisfy youthful needs, the choice would soon be made. But a master for the whole of life is not so easy to choose."[110]

The basic principle on which companionate marriage was to be established, according to Rousseau, was that of gender difference: "One ought to be active and strong," he explained, "the other passive and weak. One must necessarily will and be able; it suffices that the other put up little resistance." From this principle it followed, according to Rousseau, "that woman is made specially to please man." Rousseau then translated these differences into the language of power: "[Man's] merit is in his power," he explained. "He pleases by the sole fact of his strength. This is not the law of love, I agree. But it is that of nature, prior to love itself." It thus followed, not only that "woman is made to please," but also that she is made "to be subjugated" to man.[111]

In her letters to her own friend Sophie, Manon wrote that she wanted to find a man to whom she would be able to subordinate herself, but that she thought this might be impossible. She accepted the terms of the Rousseauian bargain in principle, but in practice she saw the difficulty, if not the impossibility, of choosing a master to whom to submit herself. "I hate my sex and its dependence," she wrote after discouraging one suitor. "This last poisons the duties that I would find delicious to fulfill, if I imposed them on myself by choice. It is sweet to obey the one we love, but it is terrible to put oneself out of necessity in the position of having to love someone under penalty of law."[112] Six months later she reiterated her commitment to the principle of wifely obedience. "I am intimately convinced that the role and the duty of a wife is obedience and devotion," she asserted. "I would find it delicious to immolate myself to the happiness of a person I hold dear, but I could not stand even the idea of taking as master someone who is no better than I am; I have said it often, I want my chief and guide to be my equal in feelings, my superior in enlightenment."[113]

At nineteen, Manon had distanced herself from the young women her age who thought only of snaring a husband. Sophie had conjured up for her "this image of an army of girls, lined up, armed, dressed in their uniforms, ready to march in review before their judges." What shocked her, she told Sophie, was the "servitude that these chains of opinion present, with which people voluntarily enslave themselves." Such slavery went against her very nature, she declared: "A noble pride makes me revolted by this idea, and I am seized by indignation when the truth has been established by the cowardice of so many. Must one sell shamefully one's liberty, in seeming to put it in irons?" she asked.[114] A week later Manon drew on the heroic language of the Romans she read and admired to remind herself that her parents loved her and would never ask her to "immolate" herself on her "liberty" by marrying someone against her will.[115] In a world full of young women who marched willingly into bondage, Manon and Sophie were able through their correspondence to reinforce each other in their shared commitment to defend their natural freedom.

By the time she was twenty-two, Manon could bolster the ancients with the Rousseau who, in the *Discours sur l'inégalité* (1754), had called liberty "the most noble of human faculties."[116] In the following years she struggled to figure out a way to maintain the freedom with which she knew she was endowed as a human being, while also finding a path to a virtuous life (and possibly happiness) through marriage. How could she be both free and married? How could she marry and still retain sovereignty over her own person? At the same time, how could she, as a woman, embark on a life of social utility and thus virtue, if not through marriage and motherhood? When it seemed that she had to choose between marriage and liberty, she declared: "I belong to me, and so I will remain."[117] She used the language of liberty also to express her frustration, bordering on rage, at the central conundrum of her life as a woman. After railing about being born a woman and comparing herself to a caged animal, she cried: "Oh liberty! Idol of strong souls, food for the virtues, you are for me but a name!"[118]

Like Catherine de Saint-Pierre, Manon's central concern was dependency. If freedom was the human condition, dependency through marriage was the female condition. Unlike Catherine, however, Manon saw dignity in work. The daughter of an artisan, she declared that she would choose humble labor over a marriage in which she would be forced to subject herself to a husband who was beneath her in soul, sensibility, and intellect. For her, human dignity was more important than social status. "When I should have no way to feed myself in remaining single, I would rather become a servant, if necessary, than to deliver myself up to a man whose soul was common and low." In fact, she saw such a marriage as a form of servitude so absolute that even a convent looked preferable. "Yes, nonbeliever as I am, despite the contempt with which I regard the monastic life and the pity I feel for its victims, groaning in the shadow of the cloister, it would take little . . . a nothing . . . to make me embrace it," she declared. Feeling herself "chained in a thousand ways," the cloister appeared to her as a form of suicide, of death, but voluntary death. Such a sacrifice seemed to her "less harsh even than that of my hand and my heart to an . . . ordinary man." And if Sophie objected that this was crazy, that marriage *was* voluntary, she responded, "No! It is not true that one is always free; there is an inflexible necessity, formed by the chain of circumstances, that yells at us, that carries us along: one must groan as I do under the iron yoke, and know how to distinguish all these chains, in order to know and understand their empire."[119]

In the end, Manon chose freedom through marriage, but only after rejecting many proposals that she saw only as servitude. "The cruel shackles of necessity will not constrain my will in the most important action of my life," she declared. "I belong to myself; I can remain so, and only give myself away by a feeling whose choice has been approved by reason. I feel the full price of a liberty that I am allowed to keep and that I was on the point of sacrificing to painful considerations."[120]

One might ask why Manon did not reject marriage altogether, but that would be to miss the paradox that her age, and Rousseau in particular, presented to women like her—offering them freedom as human beings, but happiness, purpose, and value only as wives and mothers.[121] When we consider that by the mid-eighteenth century, marriage was understood more as a contract than a sacrament, we might turn to another of Rousseau's contributions, his theory of the social contract, to see how Manon might have understood freedom through marriage.[122] "What man loses by the social contract is his natural liberty and an unlimited right to everything that tempts him and that he can attain," Rousseau asserted. "What he gains is civil liberty and the property of all that he possesses." But security of one's property was not the only advantage in accepting the bargain implicit in the social contract; there was also "moral liberty, which renders the man truly master of himself, because the impulse of appetite alone is slavery, and obedience to the law that one prescribes to oneself is liberty."[123] Manon could convince herself that in choosing a husband she would achieve this form of autonomy.

My point here is not that Manon thought herself in need of mastery or self-mastery to save herself from the slavery of desire, but that she could find in Rousseau both a way to assert her natural liberty as self-sovereignty, autonomy, and free will *and* a reason to enter into a social (marriage) contract through which she would attain civil and moral liberty. Manon translated Rousseauian and classical republican ideas of liberty in gendered terms that allowed her to understand marriage as a matter of trading her natural liberty for a higher, civil and moral liberty, but only if her husband, like the general will, was more rational than she. In doing so, however, she conflated what the political theorist Carole Pateman has called the "sexual contract" with the social contract.[124]

Through experience, however, Manon discovered that for women freedom and companionate marriage were incommensurate because a master cannot be freely chosen, and that marital happiness depended not on the free choice of a partner but on accepting subordination to one's husband and master. When she finally found someone whom she believed to be her intellectual superior and married him, she discovered that such superiority did not justify the power he exercised over her. The freedom and equality that underlay the marriage contract did not justify the loss of freedom and equality within the marriage so contracted.

By putting the focus on marriage choice Rousseau diverted the critical gaze of the Enlightenment from marriage itself, leaving in place the patriarchal structure whereby women continued to be subordinated to the men they married. Diderot assumed likewise that for a woman the problem was not the patriarchal structure of marriage but lack of love that made patriarchal power unbearable.[125] Isabelle de Charrière came to understand the fallacy, not to mention the masculine self-interest, in such reasoning. In her first publication, a short story called "Le Noble" (1762), written when she was just twenty-two, she told the story of a young woman who overcame her father's prejudices to marry the man she loved—a young man with a modest pedigree, but lots of merit. While her father looked to the past, she looked to the future, choosing to found her happiness on a love match with a man who had earned her love through his own merit. By 1784, however, the year before she published *Lettres de Lausanne*, Charrière had lost her illusions about the power of love and the utility of choice. In *Lettres de Mistress Henley*, another of her short epistolary novels, a young wife soon realizes that she made a terrible mistake in choosing to marry a man who matched the rational Rousseauian ideal. "This place is like its master," she writes of the country house to which her new husband takes her, "everything is too perfect; there is nothing to change, nothing that requires my participation or attention." She has everything that should make her happy—except power and agency:

I contemplate and admire this world that is so full, so alive. I lose myself in this vast whole that is so wonderful, I do not say so wise, for I am too ignorant: I know not its ends, I know neither its means nor its purpose, I do not know why the voracious spider is entitled to so many gnats; but I watch, and hours pass during which I have not thought even once about myself or my childish sufferings.[126]

Unlike Graffigny's Zilia, who is empowered by having a room of her own, a private space for friendship and personal reflection, Mistress Henley is expected simply to fulfill her role by occupying the same space as generations of women before her. "The walls of my room were hung by sections," Mistress Henley writes. "Dark green velvet separated panels of needlepoint done by Mr. Henley's grandmother. Heavy armchairs that were very hard to move but very good for sleeping, embroidered in the same hand, bordered in the same velvet, were, along with a very firm settee, all my room had by way of furniture." When her husband complains about the damage her cat is doing to the upholstery, invoking his mother and his grandmother, Mistress Henley replies: "They would doubtless say . . . that I must use my furniture as it suits me, as indeed they themselves did, and that I should not be a stranger even in my own room."

By enlisting the mother and grandmother to her own side, Mistress Henley suggests that the conflict here is not generational but gendered: these women would understand her need for furnishings that reflect her own taste and her own times. Mr. Henley, however, will have none of this: " 'My first wife,' replied Mr. Henley, 'liked these furnishings.' " What could Mistress Henley say? After her husband leaves, she simply takes action: "He had told me I was the mistress; I had the armchairs taken to the parlor, the settee to a storage room. I ordered a lackey to take down the portrait of the first Mrs. Henley, which was opposite my bed." She replaces the settee with light, fashionable, and comfortable wicker chairs and waits for her husband to come home. When he does, it is he who is now speechless. Reasserting his authority, "he came up to my room without a word, and wrote to London for the finest India wallpaper, the most elegant armchairs and brocaded muslin for the curtains." Mistress Henley is left in a miserable state of self-doubt: his (rational) authority or her (unrecognizable) reason, which should be her guide? "Was I wrong, my dear friend, other than formally?" she writes. "Have old things more merit than new? And do those who are reputed to be reasonable do anything other, most of the time, than gravely maintain their prejudices and tastes against prejudices and tastes more forcefully expressed?"[127]

Like Manon, Charrière's Mistress Henley thought long and hard about marriage, turning down many suitors before she chose the man who was "reasonable, knowledgeable, judicious, perfectly even-tempered," because he promised "an altogether reasonable and sublime happiness such as angels must applaud."[128] Manon, of course, had thought she was in love—was in love—but like Mistress Henley, like Rousseau, she thought that her happiness would be based on her own virtue, her respect for the man she married, and their shared values. Like Mistress Henley, she found that she had married a tyrant, a man "who held so firmly to his opinions that it took me a long time to find the confidence to contradict him."[129]

When a woman entered into marriage in the eighteenth century, whether by means of an arrangement worked out by her relatives, or through her own initiative, she gave up her liberty and submitted herself to a her husband for life. Just as it always had, her happiness depended, not on how that marriage was contracted, but on how the man she married exercised the power he now held over her, and her own willingness to accept that power as legitimate. Ironically and perhaps tragically, it seems that the woman who most firmly embraced the principles of liberty and equality and tried to achieve them in her choice of a marriage partner was the one least able to submit to the power of a husband and thus to achieve the happiness held out to all human beings by the philosophers of the Enlightenment. This is where her epistolary reasoning brought her.

Marriage, Motherhood, and the Letter-Writing Woman

9

Letter writing did not end with marriage, even if marriage seems to have tested if not broken the epistolary bonds of friendship. Geneviève de Malboissière, bereft at the sudden death of her fiancé in October 1765, was hit with a second blow when her friend Adèle married in January of the following year. Although Geneviève continued to write to her friend, the infrequency of the letters and Geneviève's pleas in them for a response make it clear that Adèle was no longer as free to respond.[1] And, despite her avowals of eternal friendship, Manon Phlipon's letters to Sophie Cannet stopped abruptly with her marriage to Roland. In her memoirs, she blamed her husband. "Roland had wished, at the beginning of our marriage, that I see little of my good friends; I bent to his wishes and did not take up the liberty to frequent them more until time had inspired in my husband enough confidence to eliminate his concerns about competition for my affection."[2] At the time, however, she explained the priority of her husband over her friend as a duty that she took up willingly, using the same reasoning that had convinced her that she could marry and remain free, as long as she found the right man. "Single and free, I was above all a frank and devoted friend, always loving and sincere," she wrote to Sophie twelve days after the wedding; "today I am a wife, this relationship takes priority, and you are but in second place. My confidant, my friend, my guide, and my support are found at my side; duty [and] inclination are united and mingled together."[3]

As Anne Vincent-Buffault notes, Manon Phlipon, not only rearranged "the hierarchy of [her] affections" when she married Roland, she also adopted his friendships, which meant in practice that she entered into correspondence with his friends.[4] Marriage tested girlhood friendships by subordinating them to both love and patriarchy, but it was the condition for which the epistolary education a young lady had received was designed. Indeed, from the perspective of marriage, girlhood correspondences, with either a mother or a friend, were simply practice for the epistolary responsibilities that

9.1. Anne-Louis Girodet de Roussy-Trioson, *Angélique-Adélaïde de Méliand, marquise de la Grange* (1809). Oil on canvas. Galerie Massol, Paris. Photo: SCEI-Édition.

came with womanhood. As we have seen, those responsibilities included corresponding with an extended family, sending and receiving formal requests, thank you notes, invitations that facilitated both sociability and patronage, and corresponding with children as they left the nest for school and eventually for families of their own.

The letters that Geneviève de Malboissière wrote to Adélaïde Méliand were discovered after Adèle's death by her grandson, who found them mixed up with the letters he had himself written to her many years later.[5] Indeed, the family archives contain many letters that Adèle, now the marquise de la Grange, wrote to family and friends throughout her long marriage. In the portrait that Anne-Louis Girodet made of her in 1809, she is shown holding the letter in which she learned of the battle in which one of her sons was wounded (see fig. 9.1). In Beaurepaire, the country house from which Adèle wrote to Geneviève in September 1763, and which became her home after she married its owner two years later, is a little bonheur-du-jour at which one can imagine she wrote those many letters (see fig. 9.2). Indeed, one of the first expenses recorded in the personal account book she started keeping when she got married was 21 livres "for Monsieur's bureau and my secrétaire.[6]

9.2. Bonheur-du-jour attributed to Claude-Charles Saunier. Château de Beaurepaire. Courtesy of M. Christian de Luppé.

Another young woman who threw herself into letter writing with her marriage was Sophie Silvestre, whose letters to her husband suggest the range of her epistolary responsibilities. The correspondence between husband and wife shows both how one woman took up these new responsibilities that came with womanhood through marriage, and how that marriage itself came to be mediated through correspondence. Most important, in her letters we see a young woman's confidence and sense of self emerge through writing in the context of a marriage that was both patriarchal and companionate, that is to say, modern. They show us a young woman gaining a sense of self and self-confidence through the practice of writing and the experience of motherhood.

Sophie: Portrait of a Modern Letter-Writing Woman

If Sophie Silvestre corresponded with a trusted girlfriend before her marriage, the letters are now lost. In any case, unlike the other young women whose letters we have read, Sophie married quite young, at sixteen—at around the same age that Laclos' fictional Cécile Volanges emerged from her convent in anticipation of her marriage and that Manon Phlipon received her first marriage proposal. Their correspondences were in large part a function of the new uncertainties and pressures that marriageability placed on them and trace the years between marriageablity and marriage itself. Geneviève de Malboissière's letters trace these same years, although they end tragically in death rather than marriage. For Sophie Silvestre, marriage followed directly on marriageability, so it is unlikely she could have engaged in such a correspondence. To learn that her marriage was entirely arranged, the very antithesis of a love match, and how it came about, we must turn to the correspondence between the man she married and his older brother. Like Manon Phlipon and Catherine de Saint-Pierre, Bernard de Bonnard, too, calculated in his letters, but his position was quite different from those of the women whose letters we have read.

When Bernard de Bonnard accepted his new post as tutor to the sons of the duc de Chartres in December 1777, he calculated that within three years he would be able to pay off all his debts and live quite well. The duke was paying him 5,000 livres a year, with another 10,000 set aside to reimburse him for living expenses, as well as free lodging in the Palais Royal (the duke's domain in the heart of Paris that he would soon transform into the shopping and leisure center described in chapter 5).[7] Marriage, too, entered into Bernard's calculations, as he explained to his brother: "If my debts were paid off, I would have taken great pleasure in being of some small service to you, because then I would be rich. In any case, they will be soon and I will be rich as soon as I get married, if, that is, I ever marry."[8] Like Catherine de Saint-Pierre, Bernard thus considered first how each prospective match would help him to achieve his goal of economic well-being. In September 1779, for example, he updated his brother on a proposition that had looked promising but turned out to be disappointing. "[It] could not take place, even in principle, in light of information I have been given by people who seem to be well informed. They say that the fortune is zero or negative. The mother has a lot of debts and is not as she would have seemed. The daughter is in very poor health."[9] The following July, however, the Silvestre match was proposed and Bernard leaped at the opportunity. "I will tell you only that it is now a question for me of a very advantageous marriage that is now being offered to me, just when others have been proposed," he told his brother. "But this one deserves all preference. One hundred thousand écus at least guaranteed, an interesting person, and a lot of support if necessary. Five to six thousand pounds in *rente* (investment income) right away."[10]

Five days later, Bernard went to Versailles to meet Sophie's father and grandfather over dinner and, as he put it, "see the young person."[11] After the dinner, Bernard sent his brother a quick update, assuring him that things continued to look good. "Yesterday I saw M. Ferès and the Sylvestre family. The young lady is fine, very fine," he noted.[12] Three days later, Bernard filled his brother in on the details about the family and the young lady. "The parents have fallen all over me," he reported. "It's just a question now of obtaining a dowry." This he was promised as a gift from the duc de Chartres. "I imagine everything will go well now," Bernard explained happily. At this point he also thought fit to describe the young lady he would be marrying: he noted first her age, and then that "she is better than not bad, even pretty, and very well put together, raised well, full of talents, and it is said that she is bright and beyond all that both her natural and acquired reason are well beyond her age. This is what pleases me the most, since reason is necessary in a household." Just as important as these personal traits were Sophie's family and their connections:

> From the name of Mlle Sylvestre you see that she is the great-niece of the abbé Bouchu, the daughter of the drawing master of the royal children, Knight of Saint Michel and a good gentleman besides; granddaughter of M. Ferès, a man of merit and wit, first valet de chambre, reader, librarian, and loved especially by Monsieur, the king's brother [the comte de Provence].[13]

On August 3, Bernard was able to report that the duc de Chartres had committed to the dowry of 1,000 ecus in *rente*, and that the articles of marriage would be drawn up the following Monday.[14] The marriage contract was signed on August 30, and the wedding held September 12. The priest who performed the ceremony declared his satisfaction in "blessing at this time one of those happy marriages, truly written in heaven, before being contracted on earth."[15] From start to finish, the whole business was wrapped up in less than two months.

Because Bernard was an adult male, he represented his own interests and those of his family; because Sophie was both a minor and female, her interests were represented by her father and grandfather, who conducted the negotiations on her behalf. While she may have been consulted, we have no record of her opinions; instead, there is Bernard's comment that "a lively desire to please her parents" was one of her virtues.[16] Nevertheless, although it is true that Bernard was more than twice Sophie's age, he was surely an attractive suitor: no property or wealth of his own to speak of, but accomplished as both a soldier and a poet, with a solid title of nobility and a very good salary and position within the highest patronage networks of France, and by all accounts responsible, *sensible*, and handsome (see fig. 9.3). Bernard's age may also have been a plus: he was old enough to have sown his wild oats (which, in fact, he had) and to be established in his career, yet he was still young enough that his bride could expect him to be a father to their children for many years to come. Sophie's trousseau included diamonds from Monsieur and Madame, and other jewelry and lace from her parents. Bernard sent her a gift basket made up by Rose Bertin, the queen's dressmaker and the most fashionable *marchande de modes* in Paris. As he explained to his brother, "all the reason in the world will not prevent a young woman from loving pretty finery a lot. That's in the order [of things]." Among the trinkets included in the basket was a seal for her letters.[17]

Bernard seems to have been charmed, or at least pleased, with Sophie and to have found in her all the requirements of a good wife. Four days after the marriage contract was signed, he described her in these terms: "I believe above all that the young person will be a very lovable wife for me, very respectable and truly charming. She has common sense, wit, a good soul, talents, the habit of being busy, and a lively desire to please her parents, by whom she is adored."[18] He might just as easily have been describing one of Rousseau's heroines. What Sophie thought or felt we do not know.

9.3. *Bernard de Bonnard.* Engraved by Nicolas de Launay after a miniature by Antoine Vestier. Bibliothèque nationale de France.

Sophie Silvestre and Bernard de Bonnard were married in Paris on 12 September 1780. Thirteen months later, on 9 October 1781, their first child was baptized in the parish of Saint Eustache. The only record of the first year of the marriage is Bernard's personal journal and a few scattered notes he wrote to Sophie at times when they were separated for a few days. She apparently wrote him little notes as well, but he did not save them. In December 1781, however, they were apart more than they were together, she in Versailles with her family, he forced to stay in Paris to tend to sick children and a sick friend—and they wrote to each other almost daily, carefully saving the letters they received. Writing to each other regularly and saving each other's letters to reread would soon become central to their marriage.

In January, the duc de Chartres informed Bernard that he had decided to turn the education of his sons over to Mme de Genlis, who was already directing the education of his daughters. Bonnard could either work for her or resign. He chose to resign. As Dominique Julia observes:

> For Bernard de Bonnard, the humiliation was total. The material advantages agreed to by the prince did not compensate him for the loss of his hopes, particularly the consideration that he could expect, after fifteen years of good and loyal service...."I also love glory," he told the comtesse de Genlis, in his last interview with her, "what will I do with my freedom? It amounts to going into early retirement at thirty-seven. I would thus no longer be a person useful to society."[19]

But Mme de Genlis had made it impossible for him to continue. Not only did she make clear that his duty would be simply to follow her orders ("In an important education, as in any great enterprise, authority must lie in one place only"), but she forced him to choose between his career and his family. She would be moving the children to the château de Saint-Leu for eight months of the year; accommodations would be available for Bernard, but not for his wife or their son. With great regret but no hesitation, Bernard chose his own family over the children to whom he had planned to dedicate the next fifteen years of his professional life.[20]

When the news broke of the appointment of Mme de Genlis, the public vilified her, suggesting dire consequences for the nation should one of her charges become king (they were in the line of succession), and predicting great things for their former tutor. "The public traces my route and announces the highest destiny for me," Bernard told his brother. "People mention Versailles to me; the Princes, the Dauphin."[21] In fact, however, Bernard had lost not just his position but the favor of his patron, on which such important posts depended. As a sign of that favor, the duc and duchesse de Chartres had promised to serve as godparents for Bonnard's child, but with the loss of it, they never fulfilled their promise and the baby was never christened. In their letters, his parents simply called him "Bonbon."[22]

While he waited in vain for a post in which he could still achieve glory, Bernard accepted the offer from an old friend and patron, the duc d'Harcourt, to accompany him on his annual tours of inspection of Normandy, of which he was the royal governor.[23]

For the next two summers, Sophie returned with Bonbon to stay with her parents in Versailles while Bernard went to Normandy. They wrote to each other by every post, three times a week, and saved every letter. During these summer months, their marriage was entirely epistolary. Or, as Bernard wrote to Sophie in June 1782: "We cannot see each other: let us each think about the other; we cannot speak to each other; let us write. Isn't writing a language? . . . in the end, let us submit to necessity and seize the resources that it leaves us. These resources are pleasures for our souls, for our spirits, for us."[24] Sophie said she would try. "How I love to see you, desire your return," she responded.

> And what pleasure I take in rereading <u>the one I love so much</u>, words that make my happiness on reading them, so long as I do not have that of hearing them from the mouth of the one who is so dear to me. Yes, dear friend, I will be happy and calm when you are near me, but not before. Give me a little bit of your reasoning, and then I will be able to stand, with a little less pain, your long absence, and make the best of the circumstances.[25]

Two days later she responded to his next letter: "I have received all your letters, dear friend, and the last one always has the most appeal for me. It has left your hands not so long ago, your most recent sentiments are in it, and while these are always the same, I love the confirmation of them, they are so tender, so sweet, my heart feels them, shares them so well, that I cry with pleasure in reading your letter and in writing to you."[26]

The marriage between Sophie and Bernard may not have been a love match, but the letters they exchanged as husband and wife were every bit love letters.[27] And we should not be surprised that Sophie wrote hers so well: after all, for more than a century men had been praising women for their natural ability to express love through their letters, encouraging them and giving them confidence, as well as models in epistolary manuals and novels. Even as her evident pleasure in writing to her husband grew, however, Sophie continued to struggle with the rest of her correspondence. One day, for example, she apologized to Bernard that she had only a moment left to write to him; she had finally sat down and written with considerable difficulty the letter to his sister-in-law that he had been nagging her to write. She was writing to him now because, as she explained, "I did not want to get up from my secretary without saying a little something to you."[28]

In chapter 4 we saw how Sophie resisted taking on this responsibility, even as her letters to her husband became longer and freer. By the spring of 1783, Bernard seems to have lost patience with Sophie's attempts to get out of writing the kind of formal letters that required the discipline that made the task onerous. "The two little letters that I received are charming," she had written him from Versailles, "but no less of a burden to respond to for all that. I would send them to you if I were sure that you would receive my letter."[29] It was in response to this attempt to get him to write her letters for her that Bernard sent Sophie Philipon de la Madelaine's *Modèles de lettres sur différents sujets* with the admonition that it was about time she learned to take care of her correspondence, since she was, after all, "18 and a half, a woman married for thirty-one months, the mother of Bonbon."[30] Despite the fact that Bonbon had just come down with the measles, she dutifully wrote the two letters and sent them to her husband for his critique and approval.[31]

Between caring for a sick child, a temperamental father, and grandparents, Sophie was expected to cultivate relationships that would maintain good kin relations and further her husband's foundering career. Sophie's correspondence was material to her family's future because both kinship and patronage had economic implications that would benefit her and her children. There could be a lot riding on such letters. Having grown up in a family whose success and position depended on the patronage of members of the royal family (to which her own marriage was testimony), Sophie must have known this. And yet she persisted in using the language of friendship to describe the "charming" letters she did not want to answer. "Have I done wrong, my good friend? Not to have responded to all your good friends," she had asked the previous fall at the end of their struggle over her letters to his kin in Burgundy. "They only wrote me little notes and I counted strongly on you to respond to them in my name."[32] "Yes, Madame Sophie, you have done wrong," he replied. "One responds to a letter with a letter and to a note with a note."[33] But Bernard also found it difficult to separate feelings from duties: his feelings for his wife and his duty to guide, teach, and correct her. Having scolded her he went on to say, "My Sophie, here I am closer to you and on the route that leads me to you. I am writing to you before your image, because my sister has taken care to have it placed in my room. Just now I scolded your image and now I caress it. I am just; you deserve both."[34]

Sophie and Bernard lived in a world that was shaped by both the old system of kin and patronage and the new discourse of family values associated with Rousseau. Their letters reflect both worlds, often uneasily, and as such represent well the practice of epistolarity at the end of the Old Regime. When faced with adversity, Bernard worked the patronage networks that had allowed him to make his way in the world as a fatherless, virtually penniless provincial noble, providing him with the education and contacts that he then used to full advantage. He was an Old Regime success story, and he wanted Sophie to understand the importance of her letters to whatever future happiness they would enjoy through the benefits of further patronage and the generosity of kin, such as the two elderly cousins—a widow and her unmarried daughter—who wanted to meet her and Bonbon and might leave them a handsome legacy.[35] But Bernard was also a devoted follower of Rousseau, and he was as concerned to impress these new values on his young wife, too, in the interest of another form of happiness he imagined for them. It is impossible to know if Sophie also brought these values to the marriage, but in her letters she embraced them.

"Monsieur and Madame, whom M. Ferès has informed about the coming marriage, seemed satisfied with it," Bernard had written to his brother in August 1780, "and have had the goodness to tell him that they have heard good things about me, that they wished to meet me, and that they promised me the same kindness that they have for him."[36] In other words, Bernard could expect to receive preferment and other rewards from the new patrons in the royal family into whose network he was marrying. In the same letter Bernard told his brother about a little mix-up they would have to sort out: apparently both of them had ordered sets of Rousseau's complete works, but in different formats, and the orders had gotten confused.[37] Rousseau had, of course, benefited from all sorts of patronage, but in the 1760s he became famous for refusing to accept it as much as for his sentimental works *Julie* and *Émile*.[38] Rousseau's readers admired him for his much-publicized rejection of the patronage system, but, like Bernard, they generally saw no need to emulate him.

Nine months later, on 19 May 1781, when Sophie was pregnant with Bonbon, Bernard noted in his diary: "lovely evening spent with my Sophie. We read *Émile*." They continued their reading over the next two days with Rousseau's "advice to mothers who wish to breastfeed." "What a tender interest attracts both of us to this reading," Bernard exclaimed, "happy moments."[39] He noted Sophie's difficulties with the pregnancy, but also that "we will continue to read *Émile*. My wife claims that she doesn't understand very well except with me." On June 7, he noted "a delicious reading of *Émile*." And again on the tenth, "*Émile* with Sophie." After that, however, Sophie's morning sickness, exacerbated by a summer heat wave, took over. He walked and read, while "dear Sophie has a case of nerves. Her involuntary tears would afflict me more if I did not know that the cause is her condition." The next day she was still crying; later in the week Bernard noted her "tender *sensibilité*." By the nineteenth, however, they were reading *Émile* again. On the twenty-fifth, they had come to the last chapter, in which Rousseau laid out the requirements for and painted a picture of the perfect wife for Émile: "I am reading *Sophie* with Sophie," Bernard wrote, and then, "a walk. My spirit is calm." Finally, on 13 July he wrote: "I am finishing with Sophie the beautiful work of Rousseau, the *Émile*. The portrait of their marriage and their happiness makes us feel the charm of our position and moistened our eyes with a few tears that are very sweet to shed. How happy I am right now! Sophie loves me and I am going to be a father."[40]

Two years later, with their future very much up in the air, and as he struggled to remain positive about his career prospects while she struggled with a sick child, demanding parents and grandparents, and little notes to write, and both of them worried about money, Bernard wrote Sophie a letter from the château de Boulay, south of Paris near Fontainebleau, where he had gone to get away for a few days. The letter consisted mostly of what he called "a long idyll on the happiness of living in the country" (see fig. 9.4).[41] Sophie responded that it did not seem so long to her. "I have read it and reread it many times and the more I read it the keener was my desire to enjoy the happiness that you painted for me so well and for which you know I have so much of a taste."[42] The paper of this letter is indeed softer and the creases deeper than the others, as if it has been opened and read and folded up again many times. Unlike the other letters, which have been folded in half, this one is folded in quarters, perhaps to

au château du Boulay par Nemours
ce 16 avril 1783.

nous ne sommes partis qu'à onze heures passées, ma chère Sophie, et arrivés qu'à 7 h. ½ du soir. ça été une grande joye de nous voir. j'ai bien soupé, bien dormi. mon rhume, ma toux, mes douleurs errantes ont disparu; le vent les a sans doute emportées sur le chemin; bref, je me porte à merveille. la journée a été superbe; j'ai beaucoup promené; le parc est vaste et bien entendu. la verdure nouvelle, les rossignols, la solitude animée des champs, le parfum des violettes, les arbres déjà tout couverts de feuilles, le silence des bois... tout cela porte avec soi un calme, un intérêt, une joye, un bonheur que mon âme sait bien sentir. oh ma Sophie, quand aurons nous donc une petite terre, une habitation champêtre à nous appartenante où nous pussions vivre

352 AP 39

9.4. Letter from Bernard de Bonnard to Sophie Silvestre, 16 April 1783. Document held in the Archives nationales, Paris. Photo: Atelier photographique des Archives nationales. 352 AP 39.

keep it in a pocket or a special place. I imagine that after Bernard died, Sophie returned to it often to remember him and console herself, reading the words and touching the paper that, as she put it, had passed from his heart and hands to hers. His dreams for the future became the *quipus* that bound her to the past.

The future that Bernard imagined for them both and that Sophie embraced was framed as a promenade and a reverie, the forms of Rousseau's final works. "The day has been superb," Bernard began. "I have walked a lot; the park is vast and well maintained. The new grass, the nightingales, the living solitude of the fields, the scent of violets, the trees already covered with leaves, the silence of the woods."[43] This was not the first time that Bernard had fallen into such a reverie about their future while walking in a park. In the English garden at Harcourt the previous summer, he rested at the temple erected to Ovid's loving old couple Baucis and Philemon, "on that hill that M. d'Harcourt had so artfully arranged," with "the story of their private lives, the altar to Jupiter, their hut, and even the two oak trees into which they were transformed." Such gardens, from Ermenonville, where Rousseau was buried, to Marie-Antoinette's at the Petit Trianon, were inspired by the park in Rousseau's *Julie*.[44] "The other day, sitting at this post, I dreamed of Sophie," Bernard wrote. "I wished for her and for me a life and an end like that of those upstanding and virtuous spouses."[45] Two days later, he again imagined himself with Bonbon and Sophie, "good, sweet, *sensible*, reasonable." He would always owe his happiness to her, he said, which made him even happier. But was it really his Sophie that he imagined, or Rousseau's? In Bernard's imagination, the two merged seamlessly into one perfect woman.

> To see my Sophie grow in virtues, in perfections, worthy mother of the family, estimable wife, deserve and obtain a [good] reputation, have wit without pretension, instruction without pedantry, reason without partisanship, severity for herself and indulgence for others, to see my Sophie honored, esteemed, happy, conserving the timid graces, the modest gaiety of her present age, truly the mother of her children.
>
> This is what my imagination paints for me in all my solitary meditations, in all my conversations with myself, it is Sophie everywhere, Sophie as she is, as she will be, Sophie loving me today, Sophie loving me forever.
>
> I am thus ashamed to kneel before your image and say to you: Oh, my Sophie, how happy you make me! And how I honor and love you![46]

Sophie was happy to be loved and promised to learn La Fontaine's version of the fable of Baucis and Philemon, as Bernard had requested. "I will have so much pleasure in reciting it to you, but all that pleasure is reserved for me for four months and in our poor little lodging which will be the most beautiful in the world and will have for me all the adornments that are possible."[47] She responded enthusiastically to the second letter as well, but cautioned Bernard that she was hardly the paragon he imagined. "Your Sophie loves you," she assured him, "and her entire ambition is to love you forever and to be loved equally, but, dear friend, your Sophie is not so perfect." How did she see herself? "I have a *sensible* and tender heart, and there are all my perfections and almost all my faults. Do not kneel before my image, but love it and you will make me happy in loving the original a little bit more."[48]

Bernard's imagination, however, fueled by Rousseau, helped him to cope with a disappointing reality. The "long idyll" he sent Sophie the following spring was a vision of a different kind of life and a different kind of happiness than the one he had been working toward for decades:

> Oh, my Sophie, when will we then have a little piece of land, a country house that belongs to us, in which we would be able to live peacefully practically ignored during seven months of the year, enjoying nature and ourselves, busy with our children, dividing our leisure between study, working the fields, the pleasure of being useful to the good folk close by to where we live, and that of cultivating fruitfully our small property![49]

Bernard projected his imaginary Sophie, traced now on the template of Rousseau's Julie, into this imaginary future: "I see you already taking charge of all the details inside the house, spending your time in the farmyard, having cows, beehives, a pigeon cote, directing a little pharmacy with which you would help the poor sick people whom you would visit, creating a little domain of charity, being happy at last through the good that you would do, the simplicity of your manners, nature, and love."[50] Bernard's dream was a literary fantasy, but it was also a shared moral vision that reached the height of its popularity among French elites in the final decades of the eighteenth century.[51] And, indeed, even Bernard realized that to live it they would have to go back to the capital to recharge themselves every winter, with people, arts, culture, and "to cultivate the protectors of our children and reap new means of happiness for our dear countryside, to which we would return with the spring."[52]

Out of the shambles of his career, Bernard was trying to forge a modern vision of the future beyond personal glory, a vision that sought to balance the Rousseauian pastoral with urban culture and political reality. To this end, he was checking out country properties for sale, right up until his death the following year. Indeed, just a week before he had fallen into his reverie Sophie had mentioned a property that a friend of theirs had found, only a day's ride from Paris. "It seems to me that the description of it is lovely," she wrote. "I hope that the reality is the same and that it might suit us." Money, however, was tight, and remained so.[53] More than a year later Bernard was still looking for that corner of paradise for his growing family. "I have just seen at a short half-league from here, a rather pretty little house with vines, a large garden, a vast pond, and a very precious setting," he wrote from the duc de Mortemart's chateau at Everly in June 1784.[54] Two days later he was on his way to check out another house for sale in the neighborhood. Sophie, however, was firmly grounded in economic reality: "No country house," she replied. "My good friend, we must still renounce it for some time, at least this year."[55]

As he concluded his idyll, Bernard thought twice about what he would be giving up in embracing it; what Sophie might have to lose, or how she might have to change, did not enter his mind, since as he saw her, she was defined not by what she might accomplish but by her virtuous and *sensible* being.

> Oh, Sophie, this is the true life of the sage, the life of the happy man, of the *sensible* and virtuous woman. This is the one that agrees with us. I hope that in 18 months or two years, our dreams of happiness will be realized. I have seen men, courts, the world; I have bought this experience and, since I have it, I do not repent having paid a bit dear for it; the passions no longer torment me; my ambitious career is probably over. We will love each other, we have a son; this son will perhaps have a sister and brothers; let us return to ourselves, live with ourselves, enjoy the real goods that are so close to us. Let us dare to be happy.

Was Bernard trying to convince Sophie that the Rousseauian path was the right one to take and not just the expedient one? Or was he trying to convince himself? After daring her and perhaps himself to embrace it, he hesitated, retreated, expressed his doubts, and suggested a more moderate position. "In truth," he admitted, "the more I dream about this, the more I fear that events will pull me back into that great theater that I have left. Whatever may happen, let us establish our retreat and take up residence there in advance. It is the only way to not wish to leave it or to feel the pleasure of returning to it."[56]

If he was not quite ready to abandon his dreams of glory, Bernard would continue to reach for Rousseauian happiness; either way, however, his Sophie, surrounded by her children, helping the poor, would be at the center of his vision for the future, a future he had to believe she wanted as much as he did, "because everything that I feel, everything that I think in this vein, my Sophie feels and thinks too, and it is without doubt this conformity, so sweet and so dear, that holds me to my opinion, that gives my sentiment a charm that I do not seek to deny myself and that everything ceaselessly recalls for me."[57] When Eustache Morin presented Catherine de Saint-Pierre with a similar vision in his proposal to share a simple life with him in the country, she evaluated it critically; Sophie Silvestre was only too happy to share in her husband's dreams, however unrealistic they may have been.

Sophie's letters, however, were more than simple responses to her husband's, although it was he who encouraged her to write the long letters in which she narrated the ups and downs of her daily life. It is in these narratives, generated by his desire for her, and to make up for his absence from her, that we see Sophie learning the pleasure of writing that Geneviève de Malboissière and Manon Phlipon had discovered through correspondence with a girlfriend. Like Catherine de Saint-Pierre, Sophie needed to be encouraged to write, to know that her thoughts and feelings were welcome and valued before she could take up the pen for herself as well as for the man to whom she addressed her letters. But she also needed to gain the experience on the basis of which she could write with authority. By the time Bernard sent her his long idyll in April 1783, she could encourage him by responding with pleasure in a sentence or two, and then fill up the rest of her letter with her own life and concerns.

"I have several more events that have happened that I have written to you about [before] and that I must recount to you," she declared, the most important of which was Bonbon's recovery from his bout of measles.

First, your Bonbon is much better. He will be purged tomorrow and I hope that you will find us in Paris if we do not receive any other orders. He has not had a fever for two or three days, and his natural gaiety and appetite are really back. He will not have taken from this illness anything but a little more mischievousness, but you will help us to correct this. You surely see that it is not today that I will respond to your letter from this morning. Pardon me, I find it excellent, but our Bonbon has been ill and is still weak.[58]

The next update was on the health of her grandfather, who was still suffering from a cold, spitting blood, and as a cautionary measure had been bled the night before. To add to her troubles, because of Bonbon's measles, they were not allowed to visit him. "Imagine," she wrote, "that in the avenue I kissed his hand, not daring to hug him, he in his carriage coming to get news of our Bonbon, and that he said to my brother that he didn't know if he had made a mistake in letting me get so close to him. He is in an inconceivably bad mood." She then reported on the death of a friend in Paris and "another piece of news that is not so sad"—that a servant she was happy to see go had quit. This brought Sophie to the end of her news. She closed by reminding Bernard playfully to tell her exactly when she could expect him, since "as you know, Sir, a husband must always be announced," and sending all the requisite regards to his friends and from her family. She ended with "a big kiss from Bonbon" and from herself: "Your Sophie thanks you for all your tenderness that is so dear to her and assures you that if she had the wit to express everything in her heart for you she would tell you, if it were possible, even more."[59]

This was a typical letter and apparently a typical day for Sophie, most of it taken up with family and illness, and a stark contrast to Bernard's country idyll. Sometimes, however, Sophie had a major event to report, and this she did with great enthusiasm, using as a model, perhaps, the letters of Sévigné that would have been central to her education. Indeed, she told her stories so well that she disarmed her husband, especially when he was trying to instill in her the importance of "perfecting" herself to become the woman and the wife he imagined her to be. Two events and Sophie's accounts of them illustrate how she could use her narrative skill and her position as a Rousseauian mother to triumph in the subtle power struggles that run through the correspondence.

The first event took place on 1 July 1782. Here is how Sophie broke the news:

I have only half an hour this evening, dear friend, and I'm using it to chat with you and respond to your pretty and charming letter. Your son, your Bonbon, is even more charming than ever, despite some difficulties caused by his teeth. He has said <u>mama</u> and more than once. Imagine all the joy I felt when I heard him say this word. I'm always afraid that I'm fooling myself. I listen to him with the attention of a mother who has heard herself named for the first time. That says it all because I can't imagine anything sweeter right now.[60]

And then she went on to recount exactly how it happened, and how she tried to get him to say "papa," too, but failed. So with regret, but elated and exhausted, Sophie closed her letter: "Good night, dear friend. I won't send my letter today. I still have a lot of things to tell you. It's nine o'clock, which forces me to leave you and I don't expect to be able to write to you again this evening. Goodnight again dear friend. Sleep well. I kiss you for the son, for the fathers, brother, girlfriend, and above all for your Sophie, who encloses here tenderness, love, and friendship."[61]

It was just the day before that Bernard had been lost in his reverie in the English garden at Harcourt, but Sophie had not yet received the letter in which he shared with her his vision of them growing old together like Baucis and Philemon. The letters they exchanged over the course of the next week show how his imagination and her experience fed each other, but how differently the two of them approached both writing and the world. He, after all, was a man of letters and a poet, as well as a teacher; she was not yet eighteen years old, and Bonbon provided her with new experiences and a new sense of herself every day. Just as Sophie's response to Bernard's visions was to remind him that she was not the paragon he imagined, Bernard's response to Sophie's letter recounting the momentous news of Bonbon's first word was a flight of visionary imagination and moralizing.

In the same letter in which she cautioned Bernard that she was hardly the paragon he imagined, and that her only virtue was a good heart, Sophie also told him he would really get a kick out of Bonbon, "if you saw him already starting to walk around very prettily. He runs in his *panier* [baby walker]."[62] As Sophie sent Bernard this additional news of Bonbon's accomplishments he was receiving the news of the first. His response was enthusiastic, but it flew quickly into the realm of the Rousseauian imaginary. "Honor and glory to the charming Bonbon," he declared.

> He laughs, he thinks, he talks; and the first word that he spoke was <u>Mama</u>. That this word may always be dear and sacred to him; he can only distinguish his mother right now, and that is a lot for him. May he know her soon, that he may love her as soon as he is able to feel, as soon as he knows how to love. May he love her with tenderness, respect, gratitude. May he become good like her, sweet, sensitive, reasonable, worthy of the esteem of men and the love of women. May he please everyone, while loving only one person and being loved by her whom he will love.[63]

As Sophie charted the events she observed at the center of her life, Bernard dreamed and imagined a happy future around an idealized Sophie and Bonbon. While not directly challenging the narratives Bernard spun, narratives in which he used the power of language to shape and mold Sophie into his Rousseauian ideal, Sophie countered them with her stories of everyday life, grounded in her own experience, and which projected her and her family into a more restrained future. If, as Michael Mascuch argues, the modern self is, "figuratively speaking, a producer and consumer of stories about himself and which place the self at the center of the system of relations, discursive and otherwise," then surely Sophie was asserting and articulating such a self in her letters.[64]

The second event, which occurred less than a month later, while perhaps not quite as momentous, also concerned Bonbon. Sophie recounted it in the context of an ongoing struggle that had to do, perhaps predictably, with spelling. The struggle had begun with the correspondence itself, in December 1781. "Madame Sophie . . . you are very kind, I love you dearly, your letters are charming despite the little mistakes in spelling, and it's a happy moment for me when I receive one," Bernard had begun one of his letters that first Christmas season they were apart.[65] When he received no response to this gentle hint, Bernard sent her what he called "a little sheet of reproaches and insults," which he advised her to open in private and show to no one. "It seemed to me to be a very private bit of pedantry," he explained. "But I thought that you would not hate the author. He's an old man who's always going on, preaching [that one should pay] attention, nagging, remonstrating, and who is, however, at heart, a decent enough man. But he's nuts for the best; he sees perfection everywhere; he wants people to be all that they can be; that they do whatever they are capable of; et cetera." And then to withdraw the sting further he closed by noting that "if he ever had a wife and child I can't emphasize enough how insufferable he would become."[66]

Bernard was used to dealing with children, and he dealt with his seventeen-year-old wife in much the same way—with a combination of cajoling and stern lectures, much like the authors of the grammars and spellers aimed at young ladies just like her. But he worried that perhaps he had gone too far this time. "Do you forgive me for my little pedantries of yesterday?" he wrote the next day. "I thank the old man for his lessons," she replied. "They will always please his Sophie. She will ask him sometimes, however, for [his] indulgence."[67] The next day when she had not received a letter from him and thought he might be angry with her she brought up the subject of his "little pedantries" again. "Everything that comes from my good friend always pleases me, even when he scolds me," she reassured him. At the same time, she again asked for his indulgence. The letter she had written him the day before "was so long, and I was so rushed that really it would be on your conscience not to have some indulgence for your poor idiot of a Sophie."[68] Bernard had no choice but to reassure her in turn: "I won't scold you," he wrote, "even though you provoke me; but don't count on this being out of gentleness of character; no, there isn't any of that."[69] And there the matter rested for that year. They continued to exchange letters for a few more days, until Sophie came back to Paris on New Year's Eve.

The following summer, when Bernard was in Normandy, he was concerned that in his absence Sophie was not attending to her studies. He recommended that she read abbé Millot (probably *Éléments de l'histoire de France*, the fifth edition of which appeared in 1782) and La Fontaine's fables; that she continue to work on her drawing and practice the harpsichord; and he suggested "a bit of spelling when you write quickly." He was not overly concerned, he said, but he was thinking of their children: "Oh Sophie, how many things you will teach our son and above all his sisters, for he really must have sisters."[70] In her reply, Sophie said she was not so sure about producing sisters for Bonbon but that she had taken up Millot the day before and "would need a few more days perhaps to get back to her other studies."[71] Not a word about her spelling, and no noticeable change either. A few weeks later, Bernard brought up the subject again. "I kiss you as I love you. Your letters are charming. All that's missing is a bit more correcting of the spelling."[72]

Sophie must have tried to pay more attention to her spelling after this, but sometimes she just got carried away with what she was writing. On 26 July, for example, she was in a hurry, but she had to whip off a quick letter, both in response to one of Bernard's and to tell him of Bonbon's latest discovery.

> Speaking of Bonbon, I have to tell you a little story about him that will surely astonish you. This morning I forbade him from touching his little business, since I must tell you everything. He didn't listen to me at all. I gave him a little swat, he looked at me and began to laugh and then took up his little game again. I gave him another, and as he did not realize who was the stronger, he caught my hand and made as if he wanted to bite it. I withdrew my hand and having no other way to avenge himself, he began to spit through his nose as hard as he could. You see, dear friend, that your son already has character and that he holds fast to all his little desires.

Having written this, Sophie looked over her handiwork and realized that in telling her story she had forgotten to pay attention to her grammar and spelling. "Pardon, dear friend," she wrote, "how badly written my letter is, but on rereading the errors of your son I see that I made a mistake throughout the sentence, which I have tried to fix as best I could."[73] He could either continue to read her letters for her errors, she implied, if that was more important to him, or to learn about Bonbon's.

In telling this story Sophie not only disarmed Bernard but reset the priorities of value. For more than a century, men of letters had been telling women like Sophie that these little faults of language were their downfall; now she was writing back, refusing to be embarrassed or humiliated, and letting her reader/husband know that she was more interested in her child than her spelling, and that perhaps he should be too. Perhaps Bernard was right when, in his reply, he told Sophie that in her standoff with Bonbon she should have let him know that she was "the stronger" by giving him one firm slap; nevertheless, she had already shown that she knew how to assert her authority where it really mattered: in the battles with her husband, not her child.[74]

In October Sophie noted that she was reading her husband's journals in which he had documented the education of the young princes.[75] By November she was presenting her own theories of child rearing, respectfully but with confidence, backed by her experience as an engaged mother who was observing her child. "Our Bonbon is well as always, however he is becoming ever more charming," she wrote.

He has an intelligence that surprises me. He becomes more willful each day, but it cannot be otherwise; right now he conceives only of his own will and his power and does not have enough reason to know that of others. I think you will agree with me, it seems to me that it is better to concede to him at present as much as one can, rather than to oppose him at each instant. Which only makes him more obstinate because in the end one gives in to his cries what one should have accorded him before.[76]

Sophie acknowledged that Bernard might not "find [her] reasoning sound," so she offered additional support for her position: "It is that, as my child is presently in the hands of several servants, each of whom does as she thinks fit, and who, I think, do not know how to maintain a just proportion of will that is required for a child of this age." Bonbon thus learned to hold out for what he wanted when it was important to him. Not surprisingly, after boldly striding into Bernard's territory as the expert on child rearing, Sophie then finished by "asking a thousand pardons for my narration, good friend, and by telling you that I think I am better able to feel than to explain myself."[77]

Bernard replied first to the form and then to the content of her letter: "The things that I read [in your letter] seem to me so lovable that I cannot even be severe about the inaccuracy of the spelling, which comes only from the little attention [given to it]. I tell myself: her pen flows under the dictation of her heart. She lets it run; if she were writing to other people rather than me, she would not make any of these mistakes."[78] But this was hardly Sophie's heart speaking, it was her mind based on her observation and experience, and Bernard's "indulgent" response was simply a retreat to the comfortable tropes about women, letters, and love. He was right, though, that Sophie's mistakes were a result of lack of attention on her part; she was paying attention to Bonbon and the various servants who interacted with him and trying to understand both what was going on and how best to raise him. She had more important things than spelling on her mind.

Considering the fact that Bernard seemed to think that Sophie's words flowed directly from her heart, it is perhaps not surprising that he did not take her ideas very seriously. "I took great pleasure in reading the good reasons that you gave me for not opposing Bonbon," he wrote, and then suggested (punning, perhaps, on her name), that her reasoning was a bit "sophistic," before moving quickly on to other topics.[79] She, however, would not just let the matter drop. Her real point, which he did not seem to get, was that Bonbon was a wonderful and interesting child and that his father should be home and paying attention to him, rather than away and worrying about her spelling. "I thank you for having very much wished to condescend a little to the simple reasons that I gave you about shaping the will of our Bonbon," she wrote, which must have gotten his attention. "It is impossible to be more intelligent than he is at his age. You will surely find him even more changed for the better when you come. He is nice, gay, caressing, and has the prettiest little manners possible. He has a vivacity that always astonishes me and I don't know where he gets it. He puts a finesse

9.5. Letter from Sophie Silvestre to Bernard de Bonnard, 4 July 1783. Document held in the Archives nationales, Paris. Photo: Atelier photographique des Archives nationales. 352 AP 34.

in all his little manners that is astonishing. In sum, our Bonbon is charming and everyone thinks so."[80]

Of course, Bernard was not included in this "everyone," because he was in Burgundy, extending his stay with his old friends and relatives, rather than coming home to his new family, the one about which he waxed eloquent in his letters but seemed not to be in a hurry to rejoin. To encourage him, Sophie told another little Bonbon story, the moral of which was pretty obvious. "This morning I asked him where his mama was and he pointed to his heart for me. I asked if someone had taught him that and was assured that no one had, and that he had made it up all by himself. Tell me then, if this is not charming." How could Bernard disagree? But Sophie was not finished with her story. "I am sorry to tell you," she continued, "that I asked him the same question for Papa and that he looked all around him without responding. But it's your fault. You are always far away from him and when you are near you don't want him to love you since you don't ever talk to him or caress him. However, he kisses many of your letters and asks for you even more."[81] Bernard never really answered this letter; instead, he came home.

When Bernard left for Normandy the following summer, the correspondence started up again. By then, Bonbon too missed his father and looked forward to the letters he wrote. "He read the first one, kissed it, and gave it to me to kiss and read too," Sophie wrote happily. "I told him that it was from papa and I assure you that he understood me very well. The fact is, that he seems to take almost as much pleasure as your Sophie does, and you will easily understand all that she felt in reading you."[82] Ten days later Sophie reported that Bonbon "kisses your letters as soon as he sees them, says that they are from papa, that papa has gone to dada, and that mama writes to papa." And even as she had to confess that she was reading very little, and had not yet taken up drawing again (but was resolved to do so on Monday), she made graphically clear that what stood between her and the studies Bernard continued to encourage her to pursue was Bonbon. "Bonbon loves papa with all his heart and gives him a thousand pretty little hugs," the little boy had added to his mother's letter—with her guidance, of course (see fig. 9.5).[83] Bernard must have been charmed, but he was not deterred. "You have delayed so long applying yourself again to drawing. Think, then, that you must teach Bonbon the first principles of it and form him. And this little girl, if she arrives, isn't it you from whom she will learn these talents?"[84] Sophie, however, had her own ideas about how to raise a child, ideas that she developed in her letters to her husband and that she demonstrated in guiding Bonbon's small hand to form words on a page.

Coda: The Education of Bonbon and Augustin

On 13 September 1784, Bernard de Bonnard died from the smallpox he contracted by attending Bonbon during his inoculation. Bonbon, who was just a few weeks shy of his third birthday, came through fine. Sophie was inconsolable, crying over her husband's death "as if it were an irreparable loss."[85] At twenty she was now a widow with two small children: Bonbon and his brother, Augustin, who had been born that March. The three of them went to live with her father in Versailles—which is where they were when the French Revolution began in 1789.

Throughout the Revolution, Sophie attended to the education of her sons. From 1790 to 1792, Bonbon was enrolled in a *maison d'éducation* in Picpus, just outside of Paris. Augustin joined him there in 1791.[86] In 1792 the whole household left Versailles for Jacques-Augustin Silvestre's apartment in the Galleries du Louvre, where artists who enjoyed royal patronage were housed; Silvestres had lived there since 1668.[87] In April, Sophie, her father, and the two children left Paris for the relative safety of Montferrat, a country house she owned outside the village of Courtacon, in the neighborhood where Bernard was checking out property in the summer of 1784. This was perhaps the house that Bernard had dreamed of, but Sophie's stay there during the Reign of Terror could hardly have been idyllic. Nevertheless, the inventory of the contents of the house taken at Sophie's death suggests that it was there that she attended personally to the education of her sons. In a small room on the ground floor, the notary inventoried a bookcase containing four volumes of the *Journal d'éducation*, the works of Mme de Genlis in thirteen volumes, abbé Pluche's *Spectacle de la Nature* and *Histoire du Ciel*, the works of Gessner and Plutarch, a compendium of "oriental literature," an *Encyclopédie littéraire*; Roziers' eight-volume *Dictionnaire d'agriculture*, and five volumes of the *Journal des Dames*. There was lots of history, too: Henault's *Histoire de France*, as well as Dufresnoy's *Principes de l'histoire* and Robin's *Histoire ancienne*. Finally, of course, there were the letters of Mme de Sévigné in ten small volumes.[88]

On a trip back to Paris with the two boys in August 1794, just days after the fall of Robespierre, Sophie went to the establishment of Gilles-Louis Chrétien on the rue Saint-Honoré to have a portrait done with his fashionable invention, the physionotrace, which historians now call the precursor of photography (see fig. 9.6). For only 36 livres, Sophie would have purchased a dozen engraved prints, based on a drawing that took less than five minutes to produce.[89] Sophie was still six months shy of her thirtieth birthday when she sat for this portrait. It shows a woman with hair cropped fashionably short under a simple but pretty cotton bonnet trimmed with lace and bows. She is dressed in the simple style of the revolutionary woman, with a redingotestyle jacket and a plain white scarf or *fichu* modestly covering her bosom. But her head is held high, her chin up, as she looks into an uncertain future.

In 1797, with the family reinstalled in Paris, Bonbon entered the new École Polytechnique; he also attended the zoology lectures of Jean-Baptiste Lamarck at the Jardin des Plantes.[90] In March of the following year Augustin was studying at the Musée Central des Arts (as the Louvre was then known) under the tutelage of the history painter, Jean-Baptiste Regnault.[91] In August Sophie was issued a passport to travel back to Courtacon, but she returned quickly to Paris. Soon after she left, Augustin had fallen ill. He died on 12 September 1798, and ten days later, so did Sophie, leaving behind her son, Bonbon, who was almost seventeen. Three days later, Bonbon went with his uncle and his grandfather to see the local notary. There he had himself registered

9.6. *Anne-Charlotte-Sophie de Silvestre (Mme de Bonnard)* (physionotrace portrait, [1794]). Drawing by Fouquet, engraved by Gilles-Louis Chrétien. 6 × 6 cm. Courtesy of M. Hubert de Silvestre.

officially as "Augustin-Henry Bonnard."[92] Under that name, the child who had figured so prominently in his mother's life and letters would go on to a successful career as an inspector of mines and a member of the Academy of Sciences. He would become the mayor of the little town of Courtacon where his family had waited out the worst years of the Revolution.[93] And throughout his life he would write hundreds of letters—to his aunts and uncles, his school friends, and his scientific and professional colleagues.[94] His mother would surely have been proud of him.

Re-imagining the Letter-writing Woman

To these bit and pieces of traces of Sophie Silvestre and her children gathered in the archives, I would add one more, the result of a reverie rather than research. I like to imagine that Labille-Guiard's portrait of a woman pausing to look up as she writes a letter to her children is a portrait of Sophie Silvestre, who once said of herself, "I have a *sensible* and tender heart, and there are all my perfections and almost all my faults. Do not kneel before my image, but love it and you will make me happy in loving the original a little bit more."[95] Labille-Guiard's portrait is not an image before which a man should kneel, an image of an idealized mother, surrounded by her children. There is a specificity to the portrait that we have already noted, in its modern dress and decor, its lack of erotic or allegorical symbols. Instead, there are the tools of the letter writer, and the woman calmly and confidently using them. The freshness of the sitter's complexion under the powdered locks might suggest a young widow in her twenties, but with the full maturity of a woman married seven years before, and, for the past three years, responsible for raising her two sons—one of whom she had already begun to teach how to write through her correspondence with his father. The seriousness, if not sadness, in the eyes of Labille-Guiard's sitter, might reflect the seriousness of the burden of raising those children as well as the sadness at the loss of their father. The handkerchief in her hand suggests not just her widowhood but the continued presence of Bernard in her life. For she would have been thinking of him as well as them as she sat down to write her letter.

"Continual tears are the testimonies of a perfect love," Puget de la Serre had written in the *Secretaire à la mode*. But Bonnard himself was a believer in friendship even more than love. "I give thanks to the friendship to which I owe so much," he wrote in his journal one day after reading Rousseau, Marcus Aurelius, and his own account books, in which he found "the history of my life from 1763 to 1780."[96] The following year, surrounded by old friends and family in Burgundy, but missing Sophie and Bonbon, he addressed his one-year-old son directly: "Oh Bonbon, be good, be just, you will be honored. Be capable of friendship, love, and you will be loved." And then to Sophie he wrote: "Breathe this into his gentle and tender soul, inspire our dear son with your *sensibilité*; let us love him for himself, let us not spoil him, let us make him a good man."[97] When in August 1783 he received his first written greetings from Bonbon, Bernard saw behind them the woman he wanted and imagined Sophie to be: the woman whose happiness and fulfillment came through the duties of motherhood and the pleasures of friendship.

> Sophie, here you are obliged to teach our son to write, or rather to continue your lessons with him. How many things you will have to teach him. I am persuaded, my dear friend, that this idea of the duties of a good mother presents itself to you often, that it will accustom you insensibly to distribute your time, to organize your days, to occupy yourself usefully and agreeably in order to become useful, agreeable, essential to your children. I am quite certain that nothing agrees more with your heart; for you were born to be happy by means of virtue, through the sweet feelings of duties fulfilled, of friendship shared.[98]

In his last letter to Sophie, written just a year later, Bernard included his final gift to her, a poem celebrating their name days and their friendship: "On this day that brings me my *fête* and yours / These flowers are a tribute to good friendship; / I have received from you the first half / And my heart consecrates to you the other."[99] Bernard, whose own father had died when he was young, credited his success and happiness to the friends who had helped and sustained him throughout his life. Sometimes it was manifested as patronage, sometimes through the institution of freemasonry, but always idealized and constantly invoked in his journal, his poems, and his correspondence. If the woman in Labille-Guiard's portrait is Sophie Silvestre, then the words of the letter—"I commend you to friendship, it will protect you"—would be both hers and his, the father's legacy to the children, but written in the mother's firm hand.

This could be a portrait of Sophie Silvestre, but it could be a portrait of many women. Indeed, if the letter in the painting is more suggestive than real (addressed to "my children," rather than one person by name), the portrait should perhaps be said to represent the act of reflection in the practice of letter writing, the practice through which a woman and a mother reflects on the world and her experience in it in order to frame her thoughts and express her feelings. Sophie Silvestre was just such a modern woman, but so were Manon Roland and Catherine de Saint-Pierre; and so would have been Geneviève de Malboissière, had she lived to enjoy her womanhood. For all of them, and many other women like them, letter writing was not just a burden or a formality, it was a practice by means of which they came to know themselves through interaction with another and came to realize the authority that resided in those selves, the authority of the writer.

Conclusion

The debates in recent years about whether the French Revolution was "good" for women—that is, whether women lost more than they gained as a result of the social and political upheavals that began in 1789—tend to overlook the significant changes that began in the decades before 1789 and continued right through the revolutionary decade. As I have tried to show here, the theoretical groundwork that associated women with letter writing in the seventeenth century began to shape women's lives in the second half of the eighteenth century when the education of women became a matter of public concern, female consumers became a market to be taken seriously, and motherhood began to be viewed as a vocation and a career. At the same time, France itself was changing as a result of Enlightenment ideas and practices, France's political development as a bureaucratic state, and its overseas expansion through commerce, trade, and colonization. For all these reasons, girls who game to womanhood in Paris and other urban centers in the decades before 1789 do not fit easily the tired caricatures of the decadent Old Regime aristocrat or the new, virtuous republican mother.

The women who emerged at the forefront of French society in the 1780s were the product of an education that gave them new tools and new values, whether they were the daughters of old aristocrats, new nobles, colonial planters, provincial bourgeois, or Parisian artisans. Some did not survive the Revolution, but those who did were the best equipped to succeed in the world that emerged from it. Whether in the metropole, the colonies, or the countries that harbored émigrés, their education would have practical value even as it distinguished them from their mothers and grandmothers, their male peers to whom they would be subordinate, and their female contemporaries to whom they would be superior. These were "ladies" who came to know themselves as modern subjects through practices of writing that were both classed and gendered.

The ability to write facilitated a modern gender consciousness that would allow some women to speak publicly as women and on behalf of women, even as it drove a wedge between them and the illiterate others for whom they spoke. At the other end of the social spectrum, the same feminists who wrote publicly on behalf of women's rights and equality often sought to distance themselves from "ladies" and their epistolary writing. In 1792 Mary Wollstonecraft championed the rights of women, but she called ladies "weak, artificial beings" who "undermine the very foundation of virtue, and spread corruption through the whole mass of society" because their education tended "to render them vain and helpless."[1] Everything they had been taught to develop and value in themselves—"susceptibility of heart, delicacy of sentiment, and refinement of taste"—made them only objects of pity that turned quickly to contempt. In the interests of women, Wollstonecraft indicted the modern education that turned girls into ladies by giving them only a "smattering of accomplishments" and limiting their desires to marriage.[2]

Wollstonecraft was of course right to show how women were being damned with faint praise and how the inequality of the gender system rested on women embracing qualities that reinforced their dependency and weakness. But she also gave that system a bit too much credit and ladies too little. What I have tried to show in this book is how elite women developed both autonomy and gender consciousness through the education they received, not in spite of it. Their education was certainly different from that of their husbands and brothers, but it was a modern education nonetheless, one meant to prepare them for a world in which families were dispersed, accomplishments competed successfully with birth, social mobility was assumed, and motherhood was a career.[3] If pedagogues and men of letters constantly reminded girls and women of their natural laziness, foolishness, and weakness of character, they also developed rhetorical and pedagogical approaches that would enable them to learn how to write, spell, and think for themselves. Letter writing was meant to contain women's writing, but it was as expansive as the group of letter writers themselves, growing to meet the demands placed on it and the possibilities it held out. As we have seen, women burst open the seams of epistolary theory, refashioning the epistolary material into texts that allowed their minds to roam freely. In the letters they thus fashioned they could be critics, poets, historians, philosophers, and child psychologists.

And yet Wollstonecraft was as concerned to distance her writing from letters as she was from the ladies who wrote them. "I shall be employed about things, not words!" she exclaimed. "And, anxious to render my sex more respectable members of society, I shall try to avoid that flowery diction which has slided from essays into novels, and from novels into familiar letters and conversations."[4] As she did not want to confuse women with ladies, Wollstonecraft did not want her readers to confuse her serious work with the frivolous writing ladies did.

When Simone de Beauvoir took up the cause of women a hundred and fifty years later, she sought to distance herself from these same women and the letters and novels they wrote. "Woman's situation disposes her to seek salvation in literature and art," Beauvoir declared in *Le Deuxième sexe*:

> In order to create a world different from that in which she never succeeds in realizing herself, she needs to *express herself*. It is thus understood that she is a chatterer and a scribbler; she unburdens herself in conversations, in letters, in diaries. With just a bit of ambition there she is writing her memoirs, transforming her life into a novel, breathing her feelings into poems.[5]

Like Wollstonecraft, Beauvoir disdained this modern woman who had been taught not to take herself or her writing seriously, dismissing her writing as mere scribbles—as letters, not literature.

Torn between the blank canvas and the mirror in which she admired herself, Beauvoir's modern woman outfitted herself with brushes to play at art, pen and paper to play at writing: "Seated before her secretary, ruminating on vague stories, the woman assures herself of a peaceful alibi in imagining that she is a writer: but one must eventually trace signs on the blank page, and they must have meaning in the eyes of another." For Beauvoir, the secretary was not the furniture of the modern self but the lady's desk it had become in the nineteenth century. For her, the other who mattered was the critical (male) eye rather than the sympathetic (female) ear. Echoing unwittingly the pedagogues who admonished girls to try harder and learn from their mistakes, she complained that "the least criticism discourages [women]; they do not realize that mistakes can open the road to progress."[6]

The woman writer had remained forever an "amateur," according to Beauvoir, and forever the same:

> Rather than grasping words as an interpersonal relationship, an appeal to the other, she sees them as the direct revelation of her sensibility; it seems to her that to choose, to cross out, is to repudiate a part of her very self; she doesn't want to sacrifice anything because she is at once happy with who she *is* and does not aspire to become someone else.[7]

Beauvoir thus acknowledged the importance of writing for women's sense of self, but only to critique women's writing as a form of complacency, of vanity even, because they used it not to change but to validate themselves. But if women saw themselves in the letters they wrote it was because others looked for them there. Letters were seen as a reflection of the self, but they were also the most "interpersonal" form of writing. Because all their writing was an expansion of epistolary practice or incorporated within it, letter-writing women were taught to think of words precisely as "interpersonal relationships" and to choose them always with a thought to the other who would read them. Far from being a form of complacency, in the late eighteenth century epistolarity was perhaps the most important medium of women's aspirations. Unlike conversation, correspondence allowed them to retreat to a space of privacy in which to reflect, and from which they could, as Manon Phlipon so eloquently wrote, launch themselves through time and space beyond the limits of their daily lives. The epistolary matrix of women's writing presupposed a reader as the very pretext for writing and shaped the sort of subjects they would become through it.

For Beauvoir, however, women's letters were simply the outpouring of feeling, as male theorists had claimed they were since the seventeenth century. They were not literature, and certainly not the result of critical reflection that philosophy required. "A woman could never have become Kafka," she declared, not because of her biology, but because of her upbringing, her education, her economic and legal status, her very psychology, all of which defined her "situation" as a modern woman. The problem was not a lack of originality, of genius, but of discipline, hard work, and critical reflection. "Accustomed to laziness, having never experienced in her life the austere necessity of discipline, she will not be capable of a sustained and persevering effort, she will not be forced to acquire a solid technique," Beauvoir complained.[8]

Women's originality, according to Beauvoir, was a "bizarre genius" that was simply recorded in "their life, their conversation, their correspondence." They could "transmit" it in these ways, but they could not create art: "If they try to write, they feel themselves crushed by the universe of culture because it is the universe of men; they can only mumble."[9] Beauvoir recognized that women remained outside the gates of literature erected in the seventeenth century and reinforced by the philosophes of the Enlightenment, but in that recognition she accepted uncritically the idea that letter writing was mere transcription, the natural record of the female heart. In the eloquence of women's letters she heard only mumbling.

What we hear in Beauvoir's critique of women as mere letter writers is the echo of those eighteenth-century mothers, teachers, and men of letters who told girls and women that they could never be real writers, and then urged them to sit up straight and try a little harder, to work on their spelling and take pride in themselves and the letters they wrote. If this monitory discourse stayed well within the bounds of the modern gender ideology that was emerging in the eighteenth century, it still created a space for women to seize the power of the pen. Beauvoir was right to challenge that ideology but wrong to disparage the writing that women did. Taking letters seriously as the writing of the modern self sheds light on a path to autonomy and to an understanding of it that is rooted in the experience of women (and men) whose lives are intertwined with those of others. It was because such a path was hidden from Beauvoir that she believed that as a woman she could be emancipated only by "assimilating herself" to men.[10] Embracing the seventeenth-century distinction between writing and letter writing blinded her to the possibility of seeing in women's epistolary practice the emergence of a modern subjectivity that did not have to be the same as that of their male contemporaries to give them a measure of autonomy.

Because they were oriented toward another, letters created the connections through which women's modern gendered subjectivity could carry them beyond the constrained immediacy of their daily lives. For women, the world of letters and the world of goods had this very important power in common of expanding their horizons and creating a space of freedom. To make a consumer choice is to assert one's own authority in matters of knowledge, taste, and experience; to choose one's words and put them on the page for others to read, consider, and respond to is to assert the authority of the author. Through the intellectual, emotional, social, and material practice of epistolarity, eighteenth-century women did both in a way that exploited gendered norms rather than challenged them. For much as pedagogues and men of letters tried to contain women's writing materially and morally by limiting it to the small format of letter paper and the limited readership of the letter's addressee, in teaching and encouraging women to write letters they authorized them to write. And the power of writing can never be contained.

Beauvoir's own materialism made her fatalistic about the life trajectories of the women she saw around her, especially in the stark comparisons she made to the freedoms and opportunities enjoyed by their brothers.

> Whether he be ambitious, absent-minded, or timid, it is toward an open future that the boy is launched; he will be a sailor or an engineer, he will stay in the country or he will leave for the city; he will see the world, he will become rich; he feels himself free in the face of a future in which unknown opportunities await him. The little girl will be wife, mother, grandmother; she will keep house exactly as her mother does, she will raise children as she was raised; she is twelve years old and already her story is written in heaven.[11]

The story Beauvoir tells begins like that of Catherine de Saint-Pierre, with her sailor and engineer brothers crossing the seas in search of opportunity and fortune; but Catherine did not in fact repeat the lives of her mother and her grandmother—not only because she did not marry or bear children as they did, but because she had to negotiate a changing world and had new epistolary tools with which to do so. Her letters show how she struggled to think through the options she did have, and how in the end she managed to take charge of her life. Through letter writing Catherine not only became part of the larger world in which her brothers moved; she was also able to reflect on herself and her "situation" in words that she chose and directed toward another. Her life was not determined by the materiality of her female body. Her misery was gendered, but it was her own.

In this book I have taken a different approach to the materiality of women and the past without, however, endorsing a new deterministic materialism. Exploring the material world of letter writing has shown how the material is gendered and how it changes over time in response to changes in the discourses and practices of gender. Letter writing has not only provided a lens through which to view the material world of eighteenth-century women; it has also shown how that world was constructed to serve the new needs of a new sort of woman who was coming into being. If letter writing was not by itself constitutive of modern womanhood, studying it has allowed us to follow girls into the spaces—interior, pedagogical, public, and psychological—in which they were formed into women in new ways that were material as well as discursive.

Sixty years of feminist scholarship since Beauvoir declared boldly that "one is not born a woman; one becomes one,"[12] have only deepened our understanding of how women are constructed socially and culturally. They have also helped us to read women's writing more sympathetically than Beauvoir did and to understand better the women whose writing we read. It is a measure of the distance between her time and ours that our own standing as writers and scholars is not threatened by that of the letter writers considered here. Not just this book, but the many other works of scholarship on women writers and letter writers on which I have drawn are testimony to the institutional status and respect that women have achieved in the academy in the past sixty years. This change in our situation has made it possible, not just to escape, but to analyze critically the masculine discourse about women, letters, and writing in which Simone de Beauvoir herself was trapped, and to see more clearly the women that discourse has overshadowed if not supplanted. It has allowed us to look for modern subjectivity in the world women inhabited and the words they chose to use, rather than assuming that the only path to modernity is the one forged by men. This, at least, has been my aim in this book: to paint a new picture of the modern letter-writing woman who took shape in France in the eighteenth century, taking as my guides the women artists and writers who struggled in their own day to bring these women and their world to life.

NOTES

Introduction

1. See, e.g., Joan Hinde Stewart, *Gynographs: French Novels by Women of the Late Eighteenth Century* (Lincoln: University of Nebraska Press, 1993); Carla Hesse, *The Other Enlightenment: How French Women Became Modern* (Princeton: Princeton University Press, 2001); Aurora Wolfgang, *Gender and Voice in the French Novel, 1730–1782* (Burlington, VT: Ashgate, 2004).

2. Elizabeth C. Goldsmith, "Authority, Authenticity, and the Publication of Letters by Women," in *Writing the Female Voice: Essays on Epistolary Literature*, ed. Elizabeth C. Goldsmith (Boston: Northeastern University Press, 1989), 46–59; Katharine A. Jensen, "Male Models of Female Epistolarity; or, How to Write Like a Woman in Seventeenth-Century France," in *Writing the Female Voice*, 25–45.

3. Walter J. Ong, *Orality and Literacy: The Technologizing of the Word* (London: Methuen, 1982), 78, 93; Henri-Jean Martin, *The History and Power of Writing*, trans. Lydia G. Cochrane (Chicago: University of Chicago Press, 1994); Roland Barthes, "Variations sur l'écriture," in *Oeuvres complètes*, ed. Éric Marty (Paris: Le Seuil, 2002), 4:271, 294–95; Roger Chartier, "The Practical Impact of Writing," in *A History of Private Life*, vol. 3, *Passions of the Renaissance*, ed. Roger Chartier, trans. Arthur Goldhammer (Cambridge: Harvard University Press), 122–24.

4. Diana T. Meyers, *Self, Society, and Personal Choice* (New York: Columbia University Press, 1989); Michel de Certeau, *The Practice of Everyday Life*, trans. Steven Rendall (Berkeley: University of California Press, 1984), 134; see also Barthes, "Variations sur l'écriture," 293.

5. Charles Taylor, *Sources of the Self: The Making of Modern Identity* (Cambridge: Harvard University Press, 1989), 174–75; Steven Lukes, *Individualism* (Oxford: Basil Blackwell, 1973), 128. See also Jerrold Seigel, *The Idea of the Self: Thought and Experience in Western Europe since the Seventeenth Century* (Cambridge: Cambridge University Press, 2005), 10.

6. Catriona Mackenzie and Natalie Stoljar, "Introduction: Autonomy Refigured," in *Relational Autonomy: Feminist Perspectives on Autonomy, Agency, and the Social Self*, ed. Catriona Mackenzie and Natalie Stoljar (New York: Oxford University Press, 2000), 18, 4. Even in the sixteenth century "embeddedness did not preclude self-discovery, but rather prompted it." Natalie Zemon Davis, "Boundaries and the Sense of Self in Sixteenth-Century France," in *Reconstructing Individualism: Autonomy, Individuality, and the Self in Western Thought*, ed. Thomas C. Heller, Morton Sosna, and David E. Wellbery (Stanford: Stanford University Press, 1986), 63.

7. Marilyn Friedman, "Autonomy, Social Disruption, and Women," in *Relational Autonomy*, 37.

8. Recent works on the topic of writing and modern subjectivity include: Hassan Melehy, *Writing Cogito: Montaigne, Descartes, and the Institution of the Modern Subject* (Albany: State University Press of New York, 1997); Michael Mascuch, *Origins of the Individualist Self: Autobiography and Self-Identity in England, 1591–1791* (Cambridge: Polity Press, 1997); Roy Porter, ed., *Rewriting the Self: Histories from the Renaissance to the Present* (London: Routledge, 1997).

9. Brigitte Diaz, "Avant-Propos," in *L'épistolaire au féminin: Correspondances de femmes XVIIIe–XXe siècle*, ed.

Brigitte Diaz and Jürgen Siess (Caen: Presses Universitaires de Caen, 2006), 9. Her reference is to Michel Foucault, *Histoire de la sexualité*, vol. 3, *Le souci de soi* (Paris: Gallimard, 1995), 181.

10. Charles Taylor, "The Person," in *The Category of the Person: Anthropology, Philosophy, History*, ed. Michael Carrithers, et al. (Cambridge: Cambridge University Press, 1985), 272–76. On the diary, see Alain Girard, *Le journal intime* (Paris: Presses Universitaires de France, 1963).

11. Marie-Claire Grassi, "Naissance de l'intimité épistolaire (1780–1830)," *Littérales* 17 (1995): 74; see also her major study, *L'art de la lettre au temps de "La nouvelle Héloïse" et du Romantisme* (Geneva: Slatkine, 1994).

12. Jürgen Habermas, *The Structural Transformation of the Public Sphere: An Inquiry into a Category of Bourgeois Society*, trans. Thomas Burger with Frederick Lawrence (Cambridge: MIT Press, 1989), 43, 49–51. Jean-Marie Goulemot elaborates on this point, arguing that the eighteenth century invented intimacy by publicizing it. "Tensions et contradictions de l'intime dans la pratique des Lumières," *Littérales* 17 (1995): 15.

13. Habermas, *Structural Transformation*, 48.

14. See esp. Joan B. Landes, *Women and the Public Sphere in the Age of the French Revolution* (Ithaca: Cornell University Press, 1988); Nancy Fraser, "Rethinking the Public Sphere: A Contribution to the Critique of Actually Existing Democracy," in *Habermas and the Public Sphere*, ed. Craig Calhoun (Cambridge: MIT Press, 1992), 109–42; Johanna Meehan, ed., *Feminists Read Habermas* (London: Routledge, 1995); Joan B. Landes, ed., *Feminism, the Public, and the Private* (New York: Oxford University Press, 1998). See also Habermas's response in "Further Reflections on the Public Sphere," and "Concluding Remarks," in *Habermas and the Public Sphere*, 421–79.

15. Goulemot, "Tensions et contradictions," 13; Philippe Ariès, introduction to *Passions of the Renaissance*, 10.

16. Grassi, "Naissance de l'intimité épistolaire," 74; see also Marie-France Silver and Marie-Laure Girou Swiderski, introduction to *Femmes en toutes lettres: Les épistolières du XVIIIe siècle*, ed. Marie-France Silver and Marie-Laure Girou Swiderski (Oxford: Voltaire Foundation, 2000), 5.

17. See, e.g., Marie-Madeleine Hachard, *Relation du voyage des dames religieuses ursulines de Rouen à la Nouvelle Orléans, parties de France le 22 février 1727 et arrivez à la Louisiane le 23 juillet de la même année* (Rouen, 1728); Natalie Zemon Davis, *Women on the Margins: Three Seventeenth-Century Lives* (Cambridge: Harvard University Press, 1995); and Jane E. Harrison, *Until Next Year: Letter Writing and the Mails in the Canadas, 1640–1830* (Waterloo, ON: Wilfrid Laurier University Press, 1997).

18. Marie-Claire Grassi, "Quand les épouses parlent d'amour . . . ," in *Femmes en toutes lettres*, 239.

19. C. A. Sainte-Beuve, ed., *Letters of Mlle de Lespinasse*, trans. Katharine Prescott Wormeley (Boston: Hardy, Pratt & Co., 1903); Janet Gurkin Altman, "Women's Letters in the Public Sphere," in *Going Public: Women and Publishing in Early Modern France*, ed. Elizabeth C. Goldsmith and Dena Goodman (Ithaca: Cornell University Press, 1995), 99–115; Goldsmith, *Writing the Female Voice*; Katharine Ann Jensen, *Writing Love: Letters, Women, and the Novel in France, 1605–1776* (Carbondale: Southern Illinois University Press, 1995).

20. E.g., Evelyne Lever, ed., *Correspondance de Marie-Antoinette* (Paris: Tallandier, 2005); English Showalter, et al., eds., *Correspondance de Madame de Graffigny* (Oxford: Voltaire Foundation, 1985–); Isabelle Vissière and Jean-Louis Vissière, eds., *Cher Voltaire: La correspondance de Madame Du Deffand avec Voltaire* (Paris: Des Femmes, 1987).

21. For biographical information, see Maurice Souriau, *Bernardin de Saint-Pierre d'après ces manuscrits* (Paris: Société Française d'Imprimerie et de Librairie, 1905); Lieve Spaas, *Lettres de Catherine de Saint-Pierre à son frère Bernardin* (Paris: L'Harmattan, 1996).

22. Malcolm Cook, *Bernardin de Saint-Pierre: A Life of Culture* (Oxford: Legenda, 2006).

23. For biographical information, see editor's introduction to *Une jeune fille au XVIIIe siècle: Lettres de Geneviève de Malboissière à Adélaïde Méliand 1761–1766*, ed. Comte [Albert Marie Pierre] de Luppé (Paris: Edouard Champion, 1925), vi–ix.

24. See Guy Chaussinand-Nogaret, *Gens de finance au XVIIIe siècle* (Brussels: Complexe, 1993).

25. [Friedrich Melchior Grimm], *Correspondance littéraire, philosophique et critique de Grimm et de Diderot, depuis 1753 jusqu'en 1790* (Paris: Furne and Ladrange, 1829), 5:143–44, 1 September 1766.

26. There are many biographies and studies of Madame Roland, the best known of which in English remains Gita May's *Madame Roland and the Age of Revolution* (New York: Columbia University Press, 1970). I have depended on the editor's "Notices sommaires," in *Lettres de Madame Roland, nouvelle série 1767–1780*, ed. Claude Perroud, with the collaboration of Marthe Conor (Paris: Imprimerie Nationale, 1913), 1:xix–l; and Marie-Jeanne Roland, *Mémoires de Madame Roland*, ed. Paul de Roux (Paris: Mercure de France, 1986).

27. On the Silvestre family, see Edouard de Silvestre, *Renseignements sur quelques peintres et graveurs des XVIIe et XVIIIe siècles* (Paris: Mme Vve. Bouchard-Huzard, 1868); and http://israel.silvestre.free.fr/index.php (accessed 2 August 2006).

28. On Bonnard, see Dominique Julia, "Bernard de Bonnard, gouverneur des princes d'Orléans et son *Journal d'éducation* (1778–1782)," *Mélanges de l'École française de Rome, Italie et Méditerranée* 109 (1997): 383–464; Simone Gougeaud-Arnaudeau, *La vie du chevalier de Bonnard*

1744–1784, ou le bonheur de la raison (Paris: L'Harmattan, 2005).

29. Joan DeJean, *Tender Geographies: Women and the Origins of the Novel in France* (New York: Columbia University Press, 1991), 36.

30. Ibid., 43–66.

31. Chartier, "Practical Impact of Writing," 113.

32. Alain Viala, *Naissance de l'écrivain: Sociologie de la littérature à l'âge classique* (Paris: Minuit, 1985); Erica Harth, *Cartesian Women: Versions and Subversions of Rational Discourse in the Old Regime* (Ithaca: Cornell University Press, 1992), chap. 1.

33. On female authors, see Wolfgang, *Gender and Voice*, 1–16. For numbers of writers in the eighteenth century, see Robert Darnton, "The Literary Facts of Life in Eighteenth-Century France," in *The French Revolution and the Creation of Modern Political Culture*, vol. 1, *The Political Culture of the Old Regime*, ed. Keith Michael Baker (Oxford: Pergamon Press, 1987), 261–91. However, Darnton's statistics account for only fourteen female authors in 1757 and only forty-nine by 1784. These figures amount to 2% of the total, as male authors increased in numbers from 854 to 1,344 (see fig. 5, p. 274). Darnton's numbers have been accepted and built on by Hesse in *The Other Enlightenment* and challenged by Wolfgang. On Châtelet, see Judith P. Zinsser, *La Dame d'Esprit: A Biography of the Marquise Du Châtelet* (New York: Viking, 2006).

34. Jensen, *Writing Love*, 2–3.

35. Christine Haas, *Writing Technologies: Studies on the Materiality of Literacy* (Mahwah, NJ: Lawrence Erlbaum Associates, 1996), 3.

36. On the history of the postal service, see Eugène Vaillé, *Histoire générale des postes françaises* (Paris: Presses Universitaires de France, 1947); Roger Duchêne, *Comme une lettre à la poste: Les progrès de l'écriture personnelle sous Louis XIV* (Paris: Fayard, 2006).

37. "Ode 1," *Les Oeuvres de Mes-Dames des Roches de Poetiers mere et fille*, 2nd ed. (Paris, 1629), 2, quoted and translated by Tilde Sankovitch in "Inventing Authority of Origin: The Difficult Enterprise," in *Women in the Middle Ages and the Renaissance: Literary and Historical Perspectives*, ed. Mary Beth Rose (Syracuse, NY: Syracuse University Press, 1986), 231.

38. Molière, *L'École des femmes* (London, 1732), act 3, scene 2.

39. Ibid., act 3, scene 4.

40. Joan Wallach Scott, "Gender: A Useful Category of Historical Analysis," in *Gender and the Politics of History* (New York: Columbia University Press, 1988), 32.

41. Daniel Roche, *The Culture of Clothing: Dress and Fashion in the Ancien Regime*, trans. Jean Birrell (Cambridge: Cambridge University Press, 1994); Jennifer M. Jones, *Sexing "La Mode": Gender, Fashion and Commercial Culture in Old Regime France* (Oxford: Berg, 2004), 4.

42. Ibid., 179–210.

43. Roche, *Culture of Clothing*, 262.

44. For a similar argument, see Colin Jones and Rebecca Spang, "Sans-Culottes, *Sans Café, Sans Tabac*: Shifting Realms of Necessity and Luxury in Eighteenth-Century France," in *Consumers and Luxury: Consumer Culture in Europe 1650–1850*, ed. Maxine Berg and Helen Clifford (Manchester, UK: Manchester University Press, 1999), 37–62.

45. Marie Jean Antoine Nicolas de Caritat, marquis de Condorcet to Mme Amélie Suard, [1780], in *Correspondance inédite de Condorcet et Madame Suard, 1771–1791*, ed. Elisabeth Badinter (Paris: Fayard, 1988), 211.

46. On the consumer revolution, see Neil McKendrick, John Brewer, and J. H. Plumb, *The Birth of a Consumer Society: The Commercialization of Eighteenth-Century England* (Bloomington: Indiana University Press, 1982); John Brewer and Roy Porter, eds., *Consumption and the World of Goods* (London: Routledge, 1993); Daniel Roche, *A History of Everyday Things: The Birth of Consumption in France, 1600–1800*, trans. Brian Pearce (Cambridge: Cambridge University Press, 2000); Berg and Clifford, *Consumers and Luxury*; John Styles and Amanda Vickery, eds., *Gender, Taste, and Material Culture in Britain and North America, 1780–1830* (New Haven: Yale Center for British Art and Paul Mellon Centre for Studies in British Art, 2006).

47. Amanda Vickery, "Women and the World of Goods: A Lancashire Consumer and Her Possessions, 1751–81," in *Consumption and the World of Goods*, 274; Jennifer M. Jones, "Repackaging Rousseau: Femininity and Fashion in Old Regime France," *French Historical Studies* 18 (Fall 1994): 960; Daniel Roche, *France in the Enlightenment*, trans. Arthur Goldhammer (Cambridge: Harvard University Press, 1998), 554–55, and *Culture of Clothing*; Styles and Vickery, introduction to *Gender, Taste, and Material Culture*, 1–34.

48. Joan Wallach Scott, "Women in the Making of the English Working Class," in *Gender and the Politics of History*.

49. Dena Goodman, ed., *Marie-Antoinette: Writings on the Body of a Queen* (New York: Routledge, 2003).

50. Roche, *Culture of Clothing*, 493–94.

51. Sylvana Tomaselli, "The Enlightenment Debate on Women," *History Workshop Journal* 20 (1985): 101–24; Dena Goodman, *The Republic of Letters: A Cultural History of the French Enlightenment* (Ithaca: Cornell University Press, 1994), 3–7.

52. Jean-Christophe Agnew, "Coming Up for Air: Consumer Culture in Historical Perspective," in *Consumption and the World of Goods*, 30.

53. Ferdinando Galiani and Louise d'Épinay, *Correspondance*, ed. Daniel Maggetti with Georges Dulac (Paris: Desjonquères, 1992).

54. De Certeau, *Practice of Everyday Life*, xii–xiii, xvii, xix.

55. Sarah Maza, "Luxury, Morality, and Social Change: Why There Was No Middle-Class Consciousness in Prerevolutionary France," *Journal of Modern History* 69 (June 1997): 199–229. See also Guy Chaussinand-Nogaret, *The French Nobility in the Eighteenth Century: From Feudalism to Enlightenment*, trans. William Doyle (Cambridge: Cambridge University Press, 1985); and Jay M. Smith, *The Culture of Merit: Nobility, Royal Service, and the Making of Absolute Monarchy in France, 1600–1789* (Ann Arbor: University of Michigan Press, 1996).

56. This phenomenon has been studied most in the visual arts. See, e.g., Whitney Chadwick, "Amateurs and Academics," in *Women, Art, and Society* (New York: Thames and Hudson, 2002), 139–74; Ann Bermingham, *Learning to Draw: Studies in the Cultural History of a Polite and Useful Art* (New Haven: Yale University Press, 2000).

57. Despite the claims of revolutionaries in 1789 that the aristocracy were simply parasites on society, noblemen were increasingly involved in and important to the economy in the eighteenth century. At the same time, work itself was being redefined to include the expanded intellectual labor that had been the province of the clergy in the medieval world. See Chaussinand-Nogaret, *French Nobility in the Eighteenth Century*, esp. chap. 5, "The Nobility and Capitalism."

58. Arlette Farge, *Fragile Lives: Violence, Power, and Solidarity in Eighteenth-Century Paris*, trans. Carol Shelton (Cambridge: Harvard University Press, 1993), 83–99.

1. Picturing the Subject

1. Anne-Marie Passez, *Adélaïde Labille-Guiard: Biographie et catalogue raisonné* (Paris: Arts et Métiers Graphiques, 1973); Laura Auricchio, *Portraits of Impropriety: Adélaïde Labille-Guiard and the Careers of Professional Women Artists in Late Eighteenth-Century Paris*, (Ann Arbor: UMI, 2000); Kathleen Nicholson, "Labille-Guiard (née Labille), Adélaïde," Grove Art Online. Oxford University Press, http://www.groveart.com.proxy.lib.umich.edu/ (accessed 24 January 2007); Laura Auricchio, with the collaboration of Sandrine Lely, "Adélaïde Labille-Guiard," SIEFAR, http://www.siefar.org/ (accessed 10 February 2007).

2. Aileen Ribeiro, *The Art of Dress: Fashion in England and France 1750 to 1820* (New Haven: Yale University Press, 1995), 67, 70.

3. Richard Rand, "Love, Domesticity, and the Evolution of Genre Painting in Eighteenth-Century France," in *Intimate Encounters: Love and Domesticity in Eighteenth-Century France*, ed. Richard Rand, with the assistance of Juliette M. Bianco (Princeton: Princeton University Press, 1997), 3; Jean Leymarie, *The Spirit of the Letter in Painting*, trans. James Emmons (n.p.: Hallmark Cards and Albert Skira, 1961); Peter C. Sutton, *Love Letters: Dutch Genre Paintings in the Age of Vermeer* (London:

Frances Lincoln, 2003). My own search of books, databases, and museum collections in Europe and the United States has yielded more than a hundred genre images of women and letters painted in France in the eighteenth century.

4. Svetlana Alpers, *The Art of Describing: Dutch Art in the Seventeenth Century* (Chicago: University of Chicago Press, 1983), 194, 196.

5. Robert Druce, "The Vanishing Reader: The Changing Role of Letters in Paintings," *Word and Image* 4 (1988): 178.

6. Peter C. Sutton, "Love Letters: Dutch Genre Paintings in the Age of Vermeer," in *Love Letters*, 19.

7. The three paintings are: *A Lady Writing* (ca. 1665–66), National Gallery of Art, Washington, DC; *Mistress and Maid* (ca. 1666–67), The Frick Collection, New York; *The Love Letter* (ca. 1667–70), Rijksmuseum, Amsterdam.

8. Alejandro Vergara, *Vermeer and the Dutch Interior* (Madrid: Museo Nacional del Prado, 2003), 257. http://essentialvermeer.20m.com/cat_about/love.htm (accessed 2 February 2007).

9. Alpers, *Art of Describing*, 202.

10. On the significance of the maid in these paintings, see Jane Gallop, "Annie Leclerc Writing a Letter, with Vermeer," *October* 33 (Summer 1985): 103–17; and Carolyn Steedman, "A Woman Writing a Letter," in *Epistolary Selves: Letters and Letter-Writers, 1600–1945*, ed. Rebecca Earle (Aldershot, UK: Ashgate, 1999), 111–33.

11. Carroll Smith-Rosenberg, "The Female World of Love and Ritual: Relations between Women in Nineteenth-Century America," in *Disorderly Conduct: Visions of Gender in Victorian America* (Oxford: Oxford University Press, 1985), 53–76.

12. Sutton, "Love Letters," 33–38; Ann Jensen Adams, "Disciplining the Hand, Disciplining the Heart: Letter-Writing Paintings and Practices in Seventeenth-Century Holland," in *Love Letters*, 63–76; Leymarie, *Spirit of the Letter*, 15–16. It is, of course, pointless to try to determine a simple causal sequence among text, image, and social practice. As Alpers remarks, "there is indeed a question as to whether the pictures document social behavior—the activities of a society actually engaged in the writing and reading of letters—or illustrate the literary fictions created in the manuals." Alpers, *Art of Describing*, 193–94.

13. Maurice Daumas, "Manuels épistolaires et identité sociale, XVIe–XVIIIe siècles," *Revue d'histoire moderne et contemporaine* 40 (October–December 1993): 539.

14. [Charles] Cotin, "Diverses Lettres & Billets des Dames, avec quelques Réponses," and "Sur le mesme sujet. A un de mes illustres Amis," in *Oeuvres galantes de Mr Cotin, tant en vers qu'en prose* (Paris, 1665), vi.

15. I discuss this complex gender politics of language and nature in chapters 3 and 4.

16. Jean Puget de la Serre, *Le secretaire à la mode, augmenté d'une instrucion d'escrire des lettres; cy devant non imprimée* (Amsterdam, 1645), 48.

17. Rand, "Love, Domesticity, and the Evolution of Genre Painting," 8–9.

18. See Sarah Maza, "Luxury, Morality, and Social Change: Why There Was No Middle-Class Consciousness in Prerevolutionary France," *Journal of Modern History* 69 (June 1997): 224–28; Mark Ledbury, "Intimate Dramas: Genre Painting and the New Theater in Eighteenth-Century France," in *Intimate Encounters*, 49–68.

19. Deidre Dawson, "Visual Image and Verbal Text: Reflections on the Letter in Seventeenth- and Eighteenth-Century Painting," *Recherches sémiotiques/ Semiotic Inquiry* 12 (1992): 174. Mary Sheriff notes that Fragonard's painting *The Swing* "also stretches the boundaries of the portrait by transforming it into a scene whose narrative components conceal its identification with that genre." Mary D. Sheriff, "Invention, Resemblance, and Fragonard's *Portraits de Fantaisie*," *Art Bulletin* 69 (March 1987): 86. Both *The Swing* and *The Love Letter* were painted during the period when Fragonard was engaged in painting what are now called his *portraits de fantaisie* (1767–72) and when, as Sheriff argues, he was interrogating the very category of portraiture.

20. Deidre Dawson, "La lettre dans la vie et l'oeuvre de Fragonard (1732–1806)," in *La lettre au XVIIIe siècle et ses avatars*, ed. Georges Bérubé and Marie-France Silver (Toronto: Le Gref, 1996), 327–45; Leymarie, *Spirit of the Letter*, 59. Montesquieu invented the polyvocal form of the epistolary narrative in the *Lettres persanes* (1723), but it was not until after the international success of Samuel Richardson's *Pamela* (1741), and especially *Clarissa* (1748), that it became the dominant form of the novel in France as in England.

21. Susan Siegfried, "Femininity and the Hybridity of Genre Painting," in *French Genre Painting in the Eighteenth Century*, ed. Philip Conisbee (Washington, DC: CASVA Publications, National Gallery of Art, 2007), 29–30; Jennifer Milam, "Matronage and the Direction of Sisterhood: Portraits of Madame Adélaïde," in *Women, Art, and the Politics of Identity in Eighteenth-Century Europe*, ed. Melissa Hyde and Jennifer Milam (Burlington, VT: Ashgate, 2003), 119.

22. Roger Chartier, "The Practical Impact of Writing," in *A History of Private Life*, vol. 3, *Passions of the Renaissance*, ed. Roger Chartier, trans. Arthur Goldhammer (Cambridge: Harvard University Press, 1989), 143; Sean Takats, "Domestic Expertise: Literacy and Numeracy in the Eighteenth-Century Kitchen," *Proceedings of the Western Society for French History* 32 (2004): 46–64. http://hdl.handle.net/2027/spo.0642292.0032.004 (accessed 13 February 2007).

23. Gallop, "Annie Leclerc Writing a Letter," 111.

24. Dawson, "Visual Image and Verbal Text," 169.

25. Chartier, "Practical Impact of Writing," 147.

26. Denis Diderot, "Salon de 1765," in *Oeuvres complètes*, ed. Jules Assézat and Maurice Tourneux (Paris: Garnier, 1875–77), 10:415.

27. Ibid., 416.

28. Jean-Jacques Rousseau, *Les Confessions* (Paris: Charpentier, 1869), 420–21.

29. A similar scene is enacted in reverse in Nicolas Delaunay's print *Le Billet Doux* after a gouache by Nicolas Lavreince, in which a lady is so absorbed in her reading that she doesn't notice that the gentleman who attends her is also reaching back to the other, younger, lady in the room, who eagerly takes a folded letter from his outstretched hand.

30. On the importance of *confiance* in letter writing, see Janet Gurkin Altman, *Epistolarity: Approaches to a Form* (Columbus: Ohio State University Press, 1982). On the centrality of uncertainty to painting itself, see Siegfried, "Femininity and the Hybridity of Genre Painting"; and Mary D. Sheriff, "The Cradle Is Empty: Élisabeth Vigée-Lebrun, Marie-Antoinette, and the Problem of Intention," in *Women, Art, and the Politics of Identity*, 164–87.

31. Genre painters crossed the same line by turning their figures outward to face the viewer, as François Boucher did in a 1743 painting, now in the Frick Collection, New York, which used to be known as *Portrait of Madame Boucher* but which is now considered to be a genre painting and has been renamed *A Lady on Her Day Bed*. See Siegfried, "Femininity and the Hybridity of Genre Painting," 18. On this painting, see also Colin B. Bailey, catalog entry for Boucher, *Presumed Portrait of Madame Boucher* (1743), in *The Age of Watteau, Chardin, and Fragonard: Masterpieces of French Genre Painting*, ed. Colin B. Bailey (New Haven: Yale University Press, 2003), 224.

32. See Rand, "Love, Domesticity, and the Evolution of Genre Painting," 3–4.

33. On Jean-François de Troy's use of the clock as a narrative element in his genre painting *The Garter* (1724), see Mary Salzman, "Decoration and Enlightened Spectatorship," in *Furnishing the Eighteenth Century: What Furniture Can Tell Us about the European and American Past*, ed. Dena Goodman and Kathryn Norberg (New York: Routledge, 2006), 158–59.

34. In a letter to her husband, Sophie Silvestre describes a similar scene on her name day: "[I'm sorry] that you were not here today, you would have wished me a happy name day like all my good relatives, who surely thought about it more than I did. I was quite surprised on going into my room to see my dressing table decorated with flowers. I was presented with a pretty hat and a very pleasant letter with verses. All this made and given by my brother. Your Bonbon [who

was nine months old] arrived to bring me a bouquet and kissed me with his ordinary grace." Sophie Silvestre to Bernard de Bonnard, 26 July [1782].

35. On Diderot's notion of likeness as the "truth" of portraiture, see Sheriff, "Invention, Resemblance, and Fragonard's *Portraits de Fantaisie*," 80.

36. Melissa Hyde, "Under the Sign of Minerva: Adélaïde Labille-Guiard's Portrait of Madame Adélaïde," in *Women, Art, and the Politics of Identity*, 141–43; see also Milam, "Matronage and the Direction of Sisterhood," 115–38; Heidi A. Strobel, "Royal 'Matronage' of Women Artists in the Late-18th Century," *Women's Art Journal* 26 (Fall 2005/Winter 2006): 3–9.

37. See Mary D. Sheriff, "The Portrait of the Queen," in *Marie-Antoinette: Writings on the Body of a Queen*, ed. Dena Goodman (New York: Routledge, 2003), 45–71; and Caroline Weber, *Queen of Fashion: What Marie Antoinette Wore to the Revolution* (New York: Henry Holt, 2006).

38. Diana Donald, "Characters and Caricatures," in *Reynolds*, ed. Nicholas Penny (New York: Harry N. Abrams, 1986), 357.

39. Norbert Elias, *The Civilizing Process*, vol. 1, *The History of Manners*, trans. Edmund Jephcott (New York: Pantheon Books, 1978); Sylvana Tomaselli, "The Enlightenment Debate on Women," *History Workshop Journal* 20 (1985): 101–24; Carolyn C. Lougee, *"Le Paradis des Femmes": Women, Salons, and Social Stratification in Seventeenth-Century France* (Princeton: Princeton University Press, 1976); Dena Goodman, *The Republic of Letters: A Cultural History of the French Enlightenment* (Ithaca: Cornell University Press, 1994), 90–135.

40. Sutton, "Love Letters," 15.

41. Lesley Smith, "Scriba Femina: Medieval Depictions of Women Writing," in *Women and the Book: Assessing the Visual Evidence*, ed. Lesley Smith and Jane H. M. Taylor (London: British Library and University of Toronto Press, 1997), 21–44.

42. Jane Couchman and Ann Crabb, "Form and Persuasion in Women's Letters, 1400–1700," in *Women's Letters across Europe, 1400–1700*, ed. Jane Couchman and Ann Crabb (Burlington, VT: Ashgate, 2004), 8.

43. Roger Duchêne, "The Letter: Men's Genre/Women's Practice," trans. Donna Kuizenga and Suzanne W. Drolet, in *Women Writers in Pre-Revolutionary France: Strategies of Emancipation*, ed. Colette H. Winn and Donna Kuizenga (New York: Garland Publishing, 1997), 318–19.

44. Duchêne, "Letter," 322.

45. Denis Diderot, "Salon de 1767," in *Oeuvres complètes*, 11:20–23.

46. Sheriff, "Invention, Resemblance, and Fragonard's *Portraits de Fantaisie*," 82. As she notes in a later version of this article, there is no evidence that Fragonard had read Diderot's comments, but it is likely that

his ideas circulated around the world of writers and artists that both inhabited. Mary D. Sheriff, *Fragonard: Art and Eroticism* (Chicago: University of Chicago Press, 1990), 245n32, 246n2.

47. Sheriff, "Invention, Resemblance, and Fragonard's *Portraits de Fantaisie*," 82.

48. The Fragonard "portrait" is dated to around 1769, four years after volume 8 of the *Encyclopédie* appeared. Volume 8 was the first to be published after a silence of many years, when Diderot had taken the outlawed project underground. It opened with a foreword in which Diderot presented himself as a martyr to the cause of humanity. See Jacques Proust, *Diderot et l'Encyclopédie*, 3rd ed. (Paris: Albin Michel, 1995); Goodman, *Republic of Letters*, 34–52.

49. Diderot, "Salon de 1767," 21. On the importance of *sensibilité* in the Enlightenment, see Anne C. Vila, *Enlightenment and Pathology: Sensibility in the Literature and Medicine of Eighteenth-Century France* (Baltimore: Johns Hopkins University Press, 1998); and Jessica Riskin, *Science in the Age of Sensibility: The Sentimental Empiricists of the French Enlightenment* (Chicago: University of Chicago Press, 2002).

50. Chevalier Louis de Jaucourt, "Sensibilité (morale)," in *Encyclopédie, ou Dictionnaire raisonné des sciences, des arts et des métiers*, ed. Denis Diderot and Jean le Rond d'Alembert (Paris, 1751–1765), 15: 52.

51. Maza, "Luxury, Morality, and Social Change," 227.

52. Ibid.

53. Jean-Baptiste Suard, "Du Style épistolaire et de Madame de Sévigné," in *Lettres de Mme de Sévigné* (Paris: Firmin Didot frères, 1851), iv. Suard's career as a man of letters began in the 1750s, but this text seems to have first appeared in 1810 in *Lettres choisies de Mmes de Sévigné, de Grignan, de Simiane et de Maintenon* (Paris: Bossange et Masson, 1810).

54. Ibid.

55. Maurice Quentin de La Tour apparently committed the same error in reverse when he portrayed Mme de Pompadour at a large desk laden with a globe and folio volumes of philosophic works, including a volume of the *Encyclopédie*. "One might say that M. de la Tour was proposing to paint the portrait of a philosophe," complained one critic. "Doesn't he know that the distraction and array of details and attributes must be avoided when one wants to represent a beautiful woman?" Quoted in Nicholson, "Ideology of Feminine 'Virtue,'" 57. I discuss this portrait in chapter 6 (fig. 6.29).

56. Diderot, "Salon de 1767," 21.

57. Couchman and Crabb, "Form and Persuasion in Women's Letters," 8. On the gendering of friendship, see Anne Vincent-Buffault, *L'exercice de l'amitié: Pour une histoire des pratiques amicales aux XVIIIe et XIXe siècles* (Paris: Le Seuil, 1995), 185–247.

58. [Louis-Mayeul Chaudon], *Nouveau manuel épisto-laire* (Caen, 1787).

59. There are no contemporary portraits of Mme de Sévigné writing to her daughter, since she did not become famous for the letters she wrote to her until they were published, thirty years after her death. On the publication of Mme de Sévigné's letters, see Marie-France Silver and Marie-Laure Girou Swiderski, introduction to *Femmes en toutes lettres: Les épistolières du XVIIIe siècle*, ed. Marie-France Silver and Marie-Laure Girou Swiderski (Oxford: Voltaire Foundation, 2000), 1–3.

60. See Lieselotte Steinbrügge, *The Moral Sex: Woman's Nature in the French Enlightenment*, trans. Pamela E. Selwyn (New York: Oxford University Press, 1995).

61. See chapter 2.

62. Elias, *Civilizing Process*, 1:143–52; see also Alain Montandon, "Places et rôles des mouchoirs dans les pratiques de la politesse," in *Le mouchoir dans tous ses états*, ed. Jean-Joseph Chevalier, Elisabeth Loir-Mongazon, and Nicole Pellegrin (Cholet: Association des amis du Musée du textile choletais, 2000), 187–92.

63. Joanna Woodall, introduction to *Portraiture: Facing the Subject*, ed. Woodall (Manchester, UK: Manchester University Press, 1997), 2; J. Levillier, "The Handkerchief in History," *The Connoisseur* 96 (1935): 274–79.

64. Will Fisher, "Handkerchiefs and Early Modern Ideologies of Gender," *Shakespeare Studies* 28 (2000): 205.

65. André Blanc, "Sur quelques effets de mouchoirs au théâtre sous l'Ancien Régime: de l'accessoire de scène à l'objet fétiche," in *Le mouchoir dans tous ses états*, 247–54.

66. Stephanie S. Dickey, " 'Met een wenende ziel … doch droge ogen': Women Holding Handkerchiefs in Seventeenth-Century Dutch Portraits," *Nederlands Kunsthistorisch Jaarboek/Netherlands Yearbook for History of Art* 46 (1995): 337. On Diderot, see Maza, "Luxury, Morality, and Social Change," 224.

67. Dickey, " 'Met een wenende ziel … doch droge ogen,' " 340.

68. Ibid.

69. Jean-Baptiste Greuze, *The Happy Family* (mid-1760s). The Hermitage, St. Petersburg. http://www.hermitagemuseum.org/ (accessed 6 June 2008).

70. Carol Duncan, "Happy Mothers and Other New Ideas in French Art," *Art Bulletin* 55 (December 1973): 570–83.

71. Diderot, "Salon de 1765," 352; see also Duncan, "Happy Mothers," 572.

72. Diderot, "Salon de 1765," 354.

2. Designing an Education for Young Ladies

1. See Roger Chartier and Dominique Julia, "L'éducation des filles," in Roger Chartier, Dominique Julia, and Marie-Madeleine Compère, *L'éducation en France du XVIe au XVIIIe siècle* (Paris: CDU/SEDES, 1976), 231. Martine Sonnet notes that between 1760 and 1790, 161 works were published on education in France, compared to only 51 between 1715 and 1759. However, she does not specify how many of these dealt with female education. Sonnet, "A Daughter to Educate," trans. Arthur Goldhammer, in *A History of Women*, vol. 3, *Renaissance and Enlightenment Paradoxes*, ed. Natalie Zemon Davis and Arlette Farge (Cambridge: Harvard University Press, 1993), 108. See also Comte [Albert] de Luppé, *Les jeunes filles à la fin du XVIIIe siècle* (Paris: E. Champion, 1925), 18–20.

2. *Mercure de France* (October 1762): 88–89. That same month, the *Mercure* listed the recent publication of two additional works on education: [Henri Griffet], *Lettre à M. D.*** sur le livre intitulé "Émile ou De l'éducation" par Jean-Jacques Rousseau* (Amsterdam and Paris, 1762); and Colomb, *Plan d'Éducation publique, pour ce qui regarde la partie des Études* ([Paris], 1762).

3. On the relationship between the works of Rousseau and Épinay, see Rosena Davison, introduction to [Louise] d'Épinay, *Les Conversations d'Émilie* (Oxford: Voltaire Foundation, 1996), 10–15. On female responses to Rousseau's educational theories more generally, see Jean Bloch, *Rousseauism and Education in Eighteenth-Century France* (Oxford: Voltaire Foundation, 1995), 215–22; Jean Bloch, "The Eighteenth Century: Women Writing, Women Learning," in *A History of Women's Writing in France*, ed. Sonya Stephens (Cambridge: Cambridge University Press, 2000), 92–101.

4. [Mlle d'Espinassy], *Essai sur l'éducation des demoiselles* (Paris, 1764), 4–6.

5. Claude Renaudot, "Lettre à M. de La Place sur l'éducation," *Mercure de France* (July 1765): 113–15; Abbé [Pierre] Fromageot, *Cours d'études des jeunes demoiselles* (Paris, 1772–75), 1:v.

6. On the Rouen and Châlons competitions, see [Antoine-François] Delandine, *Couronnes académiques, ou Recueil des prix proposés par les sociétés savantes, avec les noms de ceux qui les ont obtenus, des concurrens distingués, des auteurs qui ont écrit sur les mêmes sujets, le titre & le lieu de l'impression de leurs ouvrages* (Paris, 1787), items no. 530 and no. 901. Pierre-Ambroise-François Choderlos de Laclos, the future author of *Les Liaisons dangereuses*, competed for the Châlons prize, but it was won by Jean-François Dumas, a lawyer from Lons-le-Saunier. His essay was published as *Discours sur cette question: Quels sont les moyens de perfectionner l'éducation des jeunes demoiselles? Proposé & couronné en 1783 par l'académie des sciences, arts & belles-lettres de Châlons sur Marne* (Neuchâtel, 1783). Another entrant was Charles-Robert Gosselin, who later published *Plan d'éducation; en réponse aux académies de Marseille et Châlons* (Amsterdam, 1785). Both Manon Phlipon and Jacques-Henri Bernardin de Saint-Pierre wrote essays for the

Besançon competition. See Marie-Jeanne Roland, "Comment l'éducation des femmes pourrait contribuer à rendre les hommes meilleurs," in *Une éducation bourgeoise au XVIIIe siècle*, ed. Christiane Lalloué (Paris: Union générale d'éditions, 1964), 159–81; Jacques-Henri Bernardin de Saint-Pierre, "Discours sur cette question: Comment l'éducation des femmes pourrait contribuer à rendre les hommes meilleurs? Pour rendre les hommes bons, il faut les rendre heureux," in *Oeuvres complètes*, ed. Louis Aimé-Martin (Paris: P. Dupont, 1826), 113–63.

7. Moustalon, *Le Lycée de la jeunesse, ou les études réparées; Nouveau Cours d'Instruction à l'usage des Jeunes Gens de l'un & de l'autre Sexe, & particulièrement de ceux dont les Études ont été interrompues ou négligées* (Paris, 1786), 1:3. See also Renaudot, "Lettre à M. de La Place," 116.

8. Dumas, *Discours sur cette question*, 55.

9. Abbé [Antoine François] Prévost, *Nouvelles lettres angloises* (Amsterdam and Paris, 1784), 115–16.

10. Saint-Pierre, "Discours sur cette question," 134.

11. Marie-Claire Grassi, *L'art de la lettre au temps de "La nouvelle Héloïse" et du Romantisme* (Geneva: Slatkine, 1994), 131.

12. Marie-Jeanne Phlipon to Sophie Cannet, 27 March 1776; see also Phlipon to Cannet, 16 August 1773: "I trace parallels, I raise perpendiculars, I describe polygons; finally, here I am a semi-geometer, but secretly, because I respect opinion, and take care not to make myself a scholar."

13. Espinassy, *Essai sur l'éducation des demoiselles*, 41–42.

14. [Anne d'Aubourg de la Bove, comtesse de Miremont], *Traité de l'éducation des femmes, et cours complet d'instruction* (Paris, 1779), 1:120.

15. [Marie] Le Masson Le Golft, *Lettres relatives a l'éducation* (Paris, 1788), 158–59, 24–25.

16. Mme Mouret, *Annales de l'éducation du sexe, ou Journal des demoiselles* (Paris, 1790), no.1, p. 16; see also 153–54n7.

17. [Marie-Julie Cavaignac], *Les mémoires d'une inconnue, publiés sur le manuscrit original, 1780–1816*, 2nd ed. (Paris: Plon, Nourrit et Cie, 1894), 49. On emulation, see Laura Auricchio, "The Laws of *Bienséance* and the Gendering of Emulation in Eighteenth-Century French Art Education," *Eighteenth-Century Studies* 36 (Winter 2003): 231–40.

18. [Comte Golowkin], *Mes idées sur l'éducation du sexe; ou précis d'un plan d'éducation pour ma fille* (London, 1778), 22–23.

19. Renaudot, "Lettre à M. de La Place," 115–16.

20. Nancy Armstrong argues similarly that female education in Britain in the eighteenth century was an education in femininity and that a moral critique emerged from this new idea. Armstrong, *Desire and Domestic Fiction: A Political History of the Novel* (New York: Oxford University Press, 1987), 19–20.

21. Louise-Florence Pétronille Tardieu d'Esclavelles, Marquise d'Épinay, *Conversations d'Émilie* (Leipzig, 1774), 272.

22. Philippe Annaert, *Les collèges au féminin, les Ursulines: Enseignement et vie consacrée aux XVIIe et XVIIIe siècles* (Namur, Belgium: Vie Consacrée, 1992), 173. Annaert notes that a few large houses (in Lille and Tournai) took in more than a hundred boarders. Martine Sonnet notes that while in theory day students were taught writing as well as reading in practice this was not always, or perhaps even usually, the case. Sonnet, *L'éducation des filles au temps des Lumières* (Paris: Le Cerf, 1987), 240–42.

23. Marie-Jeanne Roland, *Mémoires de Madame Roland*, ed. Paul de Roux (Paris: Mercure de France, 1986), 233.

24. Madame [Marie Jeanne de Heurles Laboras de Mézières] Riccoboni, "L'Abeille," in *Oeuvres complètes* (Paris: Volland aîné, 1809), 1:65–66.

25. Mme de Brulart, ci-devant Mme de Sillery, [Stéphanie-Félicité du Crest de Genlis], *Discours sur la suppression des couvens de religieuses, et sur l'éducation publique des femmes* (Paris, 1790), 13–15 and note. The *Encyclopédie*, which treats governesses only in relation to elite boys, contrasts this first teacher with the tutor or *gouverneur* who takes over from her, as the boy "passes into the hands of men." We learn that it is up to the *gouverneur* to repair the damage done by the *gouvernante*, who has spoiled the child by giving into his whims rather than disciplining him. "Gouvernante," and "Gouverneur d'un jeune homme," in *Encyclopédie ou Dictionnaire raisonné des sciences, des arts, et des métiers*, ed. Denis Diderot and Jean Le Rond d'Alembert (Paris, 1751–65), 7:783–88, 792. Both articles were written by André Lefebvre (1718–68), who was trained as a lawyer but began working as a private tutor in Paris in the 1740s. See Frank A. Kafker and Serena L. Kafker, *The Encyclopedists as Individuals: A Biographical Dictionary of the Authors of the "Encyclopédie"* (Oxford: Voltaire Foundation, 1988), 201–2.

26. *Annonces, affiches et avis divers de Picardie, Artois, Soissonnois et Pays-Bas françois* (*Affiches de Picardie*), 30 January 1773, no. 5; 19 June 1773, no. 25.

27. *Annonces, affiches et avis divers [Paris]* (*Affiches de Paris*), 27 September 1769, 156. Some women offered their educational services jumbled in with a host of others that might find a market. For example, the forty-year-old childless widow, Mme Hodiber, sought a position "raising children," including giving them basic instruction in reading, writing, and politeness. She also offered her services as a housekeeper. *Recueil des Annonces, affiches et avis divers pour la ville de Bordeaux* (*Affiches de Bordeaux*), 20 August 1778, no. 34.

28. Letter from Bellette Dupuy to the marquise de Calvisson, 25 January 1768. Musée national de

l'Education—INRP—Rouen (hereafter cited as MNE), inv. 1979–12353. The other letters are dated 3 January 1769, 6 June 1772, 7 January 1773, 2 May 1773, and 11 October 1775.

29. Five of the six letters are written in the same hand and signed in another. The letter of 6 June 1772 is written in a different, rather elegant hand, but the spelling is more phonetic and erratic. The person who wrote it also signed it simply "Dupuy." This scribe may have been another female servant.

30. Riccoboni, "L'Abeille," 74.

31. Pierre Fresneau, *ABC ou Jeu des lettres de l'académie des enfants, et recueil de leurs études* (Paris, 1772), 236. The book was also available from the author at "the Academy of Children of Both Sexes" in Versailles.

32. Ibid., 203.

33. Ibid., 231.

34. Fromageot, *Cours d'études*, 1:lxxi–lxxii.

35. Louis Dumas, *La Bibliotèque des enfans, ou les Premiers élémens des lettres, contenant le sistème du bureau tipografique, le nouvel A B C latin, le nouvel A B C françois, l'essai d'un rudiment pratique de la langue latine, l'introduction générale à la langue françoise . . . à l'usage de Mgr le Dauphin . . .* (Paris, 1732–33), 24–25. Quoted in Dominique Julia, "Livres de classe et usages pédagogiques," in *Histoire de l'édition française*, vol. 2, *Le livre triomphant (1660–1830)*, ed. Henri-Jean Martin and Roger Chartier (Paris: Promodis, 1984), 473–74; see also Sonnet, *L'éducation des filles*, 246.

36. Julia, "Livres de classe et usages pédagogiques," 476–77.

37. Miremont, *Traité de l'éducation*, 14.

38. Fromageot, *Cours d'études*, 1:lxxii–lxxiv.

39. Fresneau, *ABC ou Jeu des lettres*, 204, 210.

40. Py Poulain de Launay, *Méthode pour apprendre à lire le français et le latin par un système si aisé et si naturel qu'on y fait plus de progrès en trois mois qu'en trois ans par la méthode ancienne et ordinaire* (Paris, 1741), 156; cited in Sonnet, *L'éducation des filles*, 246–47.

41. Urbain Domergue, *Grammaire françoise simplifiée, ou traité d'orthographe, . . . Ouvrage destiné a l'instruction des jeunes personnes de l'un et de l'autre sexe* (Lyon, 1778), 3–4n3.

42. Ibid., 276–79. See also [Claude-Louis] Berthaud, *La Théorie et la pratique du Nouveau Quadrille des enfans, ou d'une Nouvelle Méthode pour apprendre à lire, par le moyen de 160 figures, dont les objets familiers aux enfans servent à imprimer, en très peu de tems, dans leur mémoire, tous les sons et toutes les syllabes de la langue . . .* (Paris, 1744), discussed in Julia, "Livres de classe et usages pédagogiques," 474; and Abbé [Louis-Édouard-Camille] Gaultier, *Jeu de grammaire, ou méthode pour apprendre, d'une manière facile et agréable, les principes de la langue françoise* (Paris, 1787).

43. [Roze de Chantoiseau], *Essai sur l'Almanach général d'indication d'adresse personnelle et domicile fixe des six corps, arts et métiers* (Paris, 1769); *Almanach du dauphin* (Paris, 1776),

s.v., "PENSIONS CONVENTUELLES pour les Dames et Demoiselles."

44. Sonnet, *L'éducation des filles*, table 19.

45. H. Mollière, "Le Dossier d'une pensionnaire à l'abbaye de Chazeaux," *Bulletin historique du diocèse de Lyon* (April 1922): 51–56.

46. Bernard Magné, "Éducation des femmes et féminisme chez Poullain de la Barre (1647–1723)," in *Le XVIIe siècle et l'éducation: Colloque de Marseille* (Marseille: n. p., 1971), 116.

47. For critiques of convent education, see Luppé, *Les Jeunes filles à la fin du XVIIIe siècle*, 35–45; and, e.g., Saint-Pierre, "Discours sur cette question," 127–31; Miremont, *Traité de l'éducation des femmes*, xxvi–xxvii.

48. Genlis, *Discours sur la suppression des couvens*, 13.

49. There were incidental costs as well: a couple of pounds of coffee, for example, and a coffee pot and cup for about 3 livres, a catechism for 16 sols, and another livre or so for candles, etc. Mollière, "Dossier d'une pensionnaire," 56. These figures seem reasonable, but they are not entirely clear from Mollière's transcription, since he notes 2 livres 65 sols for the two pounds of coffee, for example, when a livre was equivalent to 20 sols. The only way I can arrive at his total of 184 livres 9 sols for the quarter is to assume that he means the 18, 16, and 12 livres to be per month and to assume that he miscalculates the sols at 2 to the livre rather than 20. There is no indication in the article as to the current whereabouts of the manuscript, which the author describes simply as "among a lot of old papers acquired at a sale held at Lyon a few years before the war."

50. [Nicolas Adam], *Essai en forme de mémoire sur l'éducation de la jeunesse* (Paris, 1787), 15; quoted in Luppé, *Les Jeunes filles à la fin du XVIIIe siècle*, 42.

51. Nadine Bérenguier, *L'infortune des alliances: Contrat, mariage et fiction au dix-huitième siècle*, Studies on Voltaire and the Eighteenth Century 329 (Oxford: Voltaire Foundation, 1995), esp. chap. 1. "Let us pause here a moment, so that mothers should consider with fear the extent of the vigilance that is imposed upon them," wrote Mme Roland in her memoirs. "Everything conspires against the tender deposits that are confided to them, and the conservation of their integrity results only from a rare prudence." Roland, *Mémoires*, 221.

52. Sonnet, "Daughter to Educate," 113; Grassi, *L'art de la lettre*, 58.

53. Miremont, *Traité de l'éducation*, 1:iv. Miremont also reassured her readers that she was not proposing "that you immolate yourselves for the health of the next generation" (vi–vii). The predecessors she acknowledged were Jeanne-Marie Leprince de Beaumont (1711–80), author of the *Magasin des enfants* and the *Magasin des adolescentes*, and the marquise de Lambert (Anne-Thérèse de Marguenat de Courcelles) (1647–1733), widely known

for her *Avis d'une mère à sa fille*, as well as her *Avis d'une mère à son fils*.

54. [Joseph François Edouard] Desmahis, "Femme (morale)," in *Encyclopédie*, 6:472. See Mita Choudhury, *Convents and Nuns in Eighteenth-Century French Politics and Culture* (Ithaca: Cornell University Press, 2004); Luppé, *Les Jeunes filles à la fin du XVIIIe siècle*, 35–45.

55. Charles Cotin, "Diverses Lettres & Billets des Dames, avec quelques Réponses," in *Oeuvres galantes de Mr Cotin, tant en vers qu'en prose* (Paris, 1665), v.

56. Le Masson Le Golft, *Lettres relatives a l'éducation*, 123–24.

57. Constant, *Un Monde à l'usage des demoiselles*, 293–95. I am focusing on mother-daughter correspondences, but parents also corresponded with sons, and fathers with daughters. See [Gregoire Martin], *Lettres instructives et curieuses sur l'éducation de la jeunesse. Ouvrage utile aux Pères de Famille, & nécessaire aux Précepteurs* (Paris, 1761), 42; Grassi, *L'art de la lettre*, 58; Deidre Dawson, "'Chère Maman': Lettres de deux des derniers 'élèves du roi' au collège militaire de Tournon à l'époque de la Révolution, 1786–1791," Colloque du 28 Mai 2005, *Revue du Vivarais* (2005): 195–218; Philippe Marchand, "La part maternelle dans l'éducation des garçons au XVIIIe siècle," in *Femmes éducatrices au Siècle des Lumières*, ed. Isabelle Brouard-Arends and Marie-Emanuelle Plagnol-Diéval (Rennes: Presses Universitaires de Rennes, 2007), 45–61.

58. Chevalier de Prunay, *Grammaire des dames, où l'on trouvera des principes sûrs & faciles, pour apprendre à Orthographier correctement la Langue française, avec les moyens de connaître les expressions provinciales, de les éviter, & de prévenir, chez les jeunes Demoiselles, l'habitude d'une prononciacion vicieuse* (Paris, 1777), 42–43.

59. Mouret, *Annales de l'éducation du sexe*, 10–11.

60. Fromageot, *Cours d'études des jeunes demoiselles*, 1:xiv.

61. Janet Gurkin Altman, "The Letter Book as a Literary Institution, 1539–1789: Toward a Cultural History of Published Correspondences in France," *Yale French Studies* 71, *Men/Women of Letters*, ed. Charles A. Porter (1986): 57.

62. Aimé-Nicolas Bussy-Rabutin, quoted in Altman, "Letter Book," 55.

63. Fresneau, *ABC ou Jeu des lettres*, 209.

64. Roland, *Mémoires*, 222–23.

65. See Larry Wolff, "Religious Devotion and Maternal Sentiment in Early Modern Lent: From the Letters of Madame de Sévigné to the Sermons of Père Bourdaloue," *French Historical Studies* 18 (Autumn 1993): 359–95; see also Katharine Ann Jensen, "Mother-Daughter Mirroring in Madame de Sévigné's Letters: Identity Confusion and the Lure of Intimacy," *L'Esprit Créateur* 44 (Spring 2004): 108–20.

66. Elizabeth Rapley, *A Social History of the Cloister: Daily Life in the Teaching Monasteries of the Old Regime* (Montreal: McGill–Queen's University Press, 2001), 235.

67. On the concept of liminality, see Arnold van Gennep, *The Rites of Passage*, trans. Monika B. Vizedom and Gabrielle L. Caffee (Chicago: University of Chicago Press, 1960), 10–11.

68. Walter Ong sees the teaching of Latin to boys as a similar rite of passage: "For well over a thousand years, [Latin] was sex-linked, a language written and spoken only by males, learned outside the home in a tribal setting which was in effect a male puberty rite setting, complete with physical punishment and other kinds of deliberately imposed hardships." Walter J. Ong, *Orality and Literacy: The Technologizing of the Word* (London: Methuen, 1982), 113. For young people of both sexes these complementary rites of passage through language and writing enhanced gender difference and strengthened gender solidarity in preparation for marriage.

69. Mme Boirayon to Mlle Boirayon, undated, in Mollière, "Dossier d'une pensionnaire," 53.

70. Mlle Boirayon to Mme Boirayon, 1 December 1770, in ibid., 53–54.

71. Mme Boirayon to Mlle Boirayon, 1 July 1770, 23 July 1770, in ibid., 51–52. Mme de Genlis sent this same message in *Adèle et Théodore*. On entering the convent, Adèle immediately gets seduced by the wrong sort of friend, but fortunately her mother is with her to make sure that she learns her lesson and never makes the same mistake. See Stéphanie-Félicité du Crest de Genlis, *Adèle et Théodore ou lettres sur l'éducation*, ed. Isabelle Brouard-Arends (Rennes: Presses Universitaires de Rennes, 2006), 525–29. In this epistolary text, Genlis is apparently unwilling to count on letters as a means of maternal education.

72. Papiers Desjours de Mazille, Archives nationales (hereafter cited as AN) T 1496/4.

73. Roland, *Mémoires*, 247–48. On the control and monitoring of correspondence within the convent, see Sonnet, *L'éducation des filles*, 249–50.

74. See Marie-Jeanne Phlipon to Sophie Cannet, 11 January 1776.

75. Mme Boirayon to Mlle Boirayon, 12 August 1770, and undated, in Mollière, "Dossier d'une pensionnaire," 52–53.

76. Abbé Joseph Reyre, *L'école des jeunes demoiselles, ou lettres d'une mère vertueuse à sa fille*, 2nd ed. (Paris, 1786).

77. Ibid., 1:4–5.

78. Ibid., 1:5, 1:8.

79. Ibid., 1:25.

80. See also the analysis of the correspondence of the Lamothe family in Christine Adams, *A Taste for Comfort and Status: A Bourgeois Family in Eighteenth-Century France* (University Park: Pennsylvania State University Press, 2000); and Grassi, *L'art de la lettre*, 329–42.

81. On the importance of letter writing by spouses separated by the Atlantic for years at time, see Jennifer

Lynn Palmer, "Atlantic Crossings: Slavery, Race, Gender, and the Construction of Families in Eighteenth-Century La Rochelle," (PhD diss., University of Michigan, 2008).

82. Reyre, *École des jeunes demoiselles*, 1:78–79.

83. Ibid., 207.

84. Ibid., 253.

85. In 1769 one almanac gave the fees at Pentemont as the highest in the city at 600–800 livres, with the average for the thirty-eight schools listed at 426. Roze de Chantoiseau, *Essai sur l'Almanach général*. In 1776 the *Almanach parisien* noted that most charged between 300 and 400. By 1783 the *Almanach du voyageur* showed that Pentemont's fees had been reduced to 500–600, the same as those of the Abbaye-aux-Bois and the Abbaye de Port-Royal. None were listed as more expensive. For a complete listing of all the convent schools in Paris in 1760, see Sonnet, *L'éducation des filles*, 291–308. See also her figure 7, which shows that the fees at Pentemont were indeed the highest in Paris in the years covered (1760 to 1789).

86. Mme Rose de Gannes de la Chancellerie de Saint-Laurent to Mme de Béthisy de Mézières, mother superior of the Convent of Pentemont (Paris), 12 September 1760, AN T 1496/4.

87. Mme de Saint-Laurent to Marie Roume de Saint-Laurent, 17 December 1763, AN T 1496/4. Parts of this letter and other letters in this correspondence are published as an appendix in Luppé, *Les Jeunes filles à la fin du XVIIIe siècle*, 218–19.

88. Abbé Lallement to Mme de Mézières (end of 1766 or beginning of 1767), AN T 1496/4.

89. Mme de Saint-Laurent to Marie Roume de Saint-Laurent, undated [probably 1756], AN T 1496/4.

90. Ibid.

91. Quoted in Lucien Perey [Clara Adèle Luce Herpin], *Histoire d'une grande dame au XVIIIe siècle: La Princesse Hélène de Ligne* (Paris: Calmann Lévy, 1887), 128–29, 133–34.

92. Quoted in ibid., 130.

93. "Maîtres de Pension," in *Journal du Citoyen* (The Hague, 1754), 163–65.

94. *État de conditions & effets nécessaires à la Pension de M. Coutier...* (printed prospectus, n.d.). MNE inv. 2.1.01/79306 (1 et 2).

95. Marie-Jeanne Phlipon to Sophie Cannet, 24 February 1778; 15 March 1778.

96. *L'Avantcoureur* 8 (19 February 1770): 118–19. The geography text is Étienne André Philippe de Prétot, *Essai de géographie pour les commençans, divisé en trois parties* (Paris, 1744). The editor of the *Affiches de Paris* called the Maison d'Éducation pour les jeunes Demoiselles "one of the best establishments of its kind that we know." *Affiches de Paris*, 15 May 1771, 79.

97. *Musée de Jeunes Demoiselles*. (printed prospectus, n.d.). MNE inv. 2.1.01/81069 (13).

98. Fresneau, *ABC ou Jeu des lettres*, 231–32.

99. Ibid., 232–33.

100. *Pension de Jeunes Demoiselles* (printed prospectus, n.d.). MNE inv. 2.1.01/81069 (14).

101. *Affiches de Picardie*, 23 July 1774, no. 30.

102. Ibid., 7 October 1775, no. 40.

103. *Affiches de Picardie*, 28 August 1773, no. 35 (supplement).

104. Ibid., 5 February 1774, no. 6. See also the advertisement for Dame Poirier in *Affiches de Bordeaux*, 16 July 1778, no. 29.

105. Miremont, *Traité de l'éducation des femmes*, 234.

106. J[ean] Lanteires, *Quelques avis aux institutrices de jeunes demoiselles, sur les différens objets qui influent essentiellement sur leur bonheur & leur succès; & sur les Études auxquelles elles doivent se livrer. Suivis de quelques idées générales sur l'Éducation, l'instruction des jeunes Filles; & d'un Dictionnaire de plusieurs mots employés dans les Belles-Lettres & en Littérature* (Lausanne, 1788), 93, 216–17. The reference is to Noël-François de Wailly, *Grammaire françoise* (Paris, 1754).

107. See Colin Jones, "The Great Chain of Buying: Medical Advertisement, the Bourgeois Public Sphere, and the Origins of the French Revolution," *American Historical Review* 101 (February 1996): 13–40; Stephen Auerbach, "'Encourager le Commerce et Répandre les Lumières': The Press, the Provinces, and the Origins of the Revolution in France, 1750–1789," (PhD diss., Louisiana State University, 2001).

108. *Affiches de Bordeaux*, 22 October 1778, no. 43; see also 12 November 1778, no. 46; 3 December 1778, no. 49; *Affiches de Picardie*, 11 September 1773, no. 37.

109. Gosselin, *Plan d'éducation*, 73.

110. Ibid., 60–61.

111. Renaudot, "Lettre à M. de La Place," 113–18.

112. Mouret, *Annales de l'éducation du sexe*, no. 2, 55–56.

113. Le Masson Le Golft, *Lettres relatives a l'éducation*, xiii–xiv.

114. Ibid., 95–96.

115. Ibid., 148–49, 153–55.

116. Le Masson Le Golft does not raise the question of the position of free women of color or of the mixed-race children of white planters. The categories she uses (Creoles and slaves) do not admit of these real complexities. Race is an implicit rather than an explicit dividing line here. On how language about race and slavery changed over the course of the eighteenth century, see Sue Peabody, *There Are No Slaves in France: The Political Culture of Race and Slavery in the Old Regime* (New York: Oxford University Press, 1996).

117. Le Masson Le Golft, *Lettres relatives a l'éducation*, 163.

118. Marie-Hélène Bourquin-Simonin, "Le Journal de M. Panon Desbassayns," in Henry Paulin Panon Desbassayns, *Voyage à Paris pendant la révolution, 1790–1792: Journal inédit d'un habitant de l'Île Bourbon*, ed. Jean-Claude

Guillermin des Sagettes and Marie-Hélène Bourquin-Simonin (Paris: Librairie Académique Perrin, 1985), 17–26.

119. Panon Desbassayns, *Voyage à Paris pendant la révolution*, 7 May 1790.

120. Ibid., 16 May 1790.

121. Ibid., 22 July 1790; see also 25 July 1790: "My daughters Mimi and Mélanie have been placed as boarders with M. and Mme Roze, who have a *maison d'éducation* that seems good to me in every respect. It was a bother to remove them from Mme Moreau's, but I think they would have taken longer to finish their education there. They were very well at Mme Moreau's, they put on weight during the time they stayed there"; and 31 July 1790: "I would like to be with my two daughters in the Île Bourbon, my country, where I think it is peaceful. The education of my children must be completed for me to return."

122. Ibid., 21 July 1790; 23 July 1790; 24 July 1790.

123. Ibid., 27 July 1790.

124. Ibid., 3 November 1790; 18 August 1792.

125. Ibid., 3 December 1790; 18 January 1791; 26 February 1791; see also 15 November 1790.

126. Ibid., 2 February 1791; 6 February 1791; 14 February 1791; 20 February 1791; 3 April 1791. The editor of the diary notes that Panon always spelled "grammaire française" "grand-mère français" (see 117n). A page of Panon's diary is reproduced on the last page of the book and confirms that his spelling was thoroughly phonetic. If he practiced the "orthographe des dames," which I discuss in the next chapter, he was committed to making sure that Mimi and Mélanie would not.

127. Ibid., 21 May 1791; 26 May 1791; 8 June 1791.

128. Ibid., 5 August 1791.

129. Ibid., 24 October 1790; 29 January 1791; 2 April 1791.

130. Ibid., 4 February 1791; 19 November 1791; 24 December 1791.

131. Ibid., 24 December 1791.

132. Ibid., 18 December 1791; 3 January 1792; 19 January 1792.

133. Ibid., 6 July 1792.

134. Ibid., 14 July 1792; 15 July 1792.

135. Ibid., 10 July 1792; 17 July 1792.

136. Ibid., 1 August 1792; 4 August 1792.

137. Ibid., 7–8 August 1792.

138. Ibid., 10–13 August 1792.

139. Ibid., 16–18 August 1792; 20–25 August 1792.

140. Ibid., 2 September 1792.

141. Ibid.

142. Ibid., 3 September 1792; 10 September 1792; 18 September 1792; 3 October 1792; 8 October 1792.

143. Bourquin-Simonin, "Journal de M. Panon Desbassayns," 18–20.

3. *Writing as Discipline*

1. See Orest Ranum, "The Refuges of Intimacy," in *A History of Private Life*, vol. 3, *Passions of the Renaissance*, ed. Roger Chartier and Philippe Ariès (Cambridge: Harvard University Press, 1989), 246.

2. [Jean Léonor Le Gallois] de Grimarest, *Traité sur la maniere d'écrire des lettres et sur le ceremonial: Avec un Discours sur ce qu'on appelle usage dans la Langue Françoise* (Paris, 1735), 1–3. The first edition of this work was published in 1709; Grimarest died in 1713.

3. Eléazar Mauvillon, *Traité général du stile, avec un traité particulier du stile épistolaire* (Amsterdam, 1750), 255.

4. [André Joseph Panckoucke], *Les Études convenables aux demoiselles, contenant la Grammaire, la Poésie, la Rhétorique, le Commerce de Lettres, la Chronologie, la Géographie, l'Histoire, la Fable héroïque, la Fable morale, les Règles de la Bienséance, et un court Traité d'Arithmétique* (Paris: Les Libraires Associés, An XI), 1:155. The first edition was published in Lille in 1749.

5. J[ean] Lanteires, *Quelques avis aux institutrices de jeunes demoiselles, sur les différens objets qui influent essentiellement sur leur bonheur & leur succès; & sur les Études auxquelles elles doivent se livrer. Suivis de quelques idées générales sur l'Education, l'instruction des jeunes Filles; & d'un Dictionnaire de plusieurs mots employés dans les Belles-Lettres & en Littérature* (Lausanne, 1788), 94.

6. [Gregoire Martin], *Lettres instructives et curieuses sur l'éducation de la jeunesse. Ouvrage utile aux Peres de Famille, & nécessaire aux Précepteurs* (Paris, 1761), 27–28.

7. Jean-Jacques Rousseau, *Émile ou de l'éducation* (Paris: Garnier-Flammarion, 1966), 466. See also Anne Thérèse de Marguenat de Courcelles, marquise de Lambert, "*Avis d'une mère à sa fille*," in *Oeuvres*, ed. Robert Granderoute (Paris: Honoré Champion, 1990), 104, 130; [Pierre-Joseph Boudier de Villemert], *L'Ami des femmes* (Hamburg, 1758), 185; "Femme (morale)," in *Encyclopédie, ou dictionnaire raisonné des sciences, des arts, et des métiers*, ed. Denis Diderot and Jean Le Rond d'Alembert (Paris, 1751–65), 6:473; and Jacques-Henri Bernardin de Saint-Pierre, "Discours sur cette question: Comment l'éducation des femmes pourrait contribuer à rendre les hommes meilleurs? Pour rendre les hommes bons, il faut les rendre heureux," in *Oeuvres complètes*, ed. Louis Aimé-Martin (Paris: P. Dupont, 1826), 153.

8. Panckoucke, *Les Études convenables aux demoiselles*, 1:163.

9. See Mauvillon, *Traité général du stile*, 257.

10. Pierre Fresneau, *ABC ou Jeu des lettres de l'académie des enfants, et recueil de leurs études* (Paris, 1772), 216.

11. [Mlle d'Espinassy], *Essai sur l'éducation des demoiselles* (Paris, 1764), 18; Stéphanie-Félicité du Crest de Genlis, *Adèle et Théodore ou lettres sur l'éducation*, ed. Isabelle Brouard-Arends (Rennes: Presses Universitaires de Rennes, 2006), 66–67; Paule Constant, *Un monde à*

l'usage des demoiselles (Paris: Gallimard, 1987), 275; Martine Sonnet, *L'éducation des filles au temps des Lumières* (Paris: Le Cerf, 1987), 240–51.

12. *Almanach du dauphin* (Paris, 1776), s.v., "Écrivains." [Roze de Chantoiseau], *Essai sur l'Almanach général d'indication d'adresse personnelle et domicile fixe des six corps, arts et métiers* (Paris, 1769) lists 144 members of the writer's guild doing business in Paris in 1769; Abbé [Pierre] Jaubert, *Dictionnaire raisonné universel des arts et metiers*, (Paris, 1773), 2:92; de Jeze, *État ou tableau de la Ville de Paris considérée relativement au nécessaire, à l'utile, à l'agréable et à l'administration* (Paris, 1759), 1:177; Louis-Sébastien Mercier, *Tableau de Paris*, ed. Jean-Claude Bonnet (Paris: Mercure de France, 1994), chap. 314: "Maîtres écrivains," 1:828. See also Alfred Franklin, *Dictionnaire historique des arts, métiers et professions exercés dans Paris depuis le treizième siècle* (Paris: H. Welter, 1906), 284; Jean Hébrard, "Des écritures exemplaires: L'art du maître-écrivain en France entre XVIe et XVIIIe siècle," *Mélanges de l'École française de Rome, Italie et Méditerranée*, 107 (1995): 473–523.

13. Grimarest, *Traité sur la maniere d'écrire des lettres*, 193–202.

14. Jaubert, *Dictionnaire raisonné*, 2:97; see also Mercier, *Tableau de Paris*, chap. 84: "Les écrivains des Charniers-Innocents," 1:215–16.

15. Roland Mousnier, "Les fidélités et les clientèles en France aux XVIe, XVIIe et XVIIIe siècles," *Histoire sociale* 15 (1982): 35–46; Yves Durand, ed., *Hommage à Roland Mousnier: Clientèles et fidélités en Europe à l'époque moderne* (Paris: Presses Universitaires de France, 1981).

16. [Pierre-Thomas-Nicolas] Hurtaut, *Dictionnaire historique de la ville de Paris et ses environs* (Paris, 1779; rpt: Geneva: Minkoff, 1973), 1:707.

17. Antoine-Joseph-Michel de Servan, "Commentaire sur un passage du livre de M. Necker, ou éclaircissements demandés à messieurs les commis des postes, préposés à décacheter les lettres," in *Oeuvres choisies de Servan*, ed. X. de Portets (Paris: Didot l'aîné, 1822), 2:474.

18. Carolyn Steedman, "A Woman Writing a Letter," in *Epistolary Selves: Letters and Letter-Writers, 1600–1945*, ed. Rebecca Earle (Brookfield, VT: Ashgate, 1999), 111–33.

19. See Christine Métayer, *Au tombeau des secrets: Les écrivains publics du Paris populaire, Cimetière des Saints-Innocents, XVIe–XVIIIe siècle* (Paris: Albin Michel, 2000).

20. *L'Avantcoureur, Feuille Hebdomadaire, où sont annoncés les objets particuliers des Sciences, de la Littérature, des arts, des Métiers, de l'Industrie, des Spectacles, & les Nouveautés en tout genre* 4 (2 April 1770): 214.

21. Hébrard, "Des écritures exemplaires," 517. The treatise is d'Autrepe, *Traité sur les principes de l'art d'écrire, et ceux de l'écriture* (Paris, 1759).

22. Hébrard, "Des écritures exemplaires," 515.

23. Quoted in ibid.," 521.

24. Ibid., 520–21.

25. Gosselin, *Plan d'éducation*, 73.

26. Dumas, *Discours sur cette question*, 53–55n, 93–94.

27. [Anne d'Aubourg de la Bove, comtesse de Miremont], *Traité de l'éducation des femmes, et cours complet d'instruction* (Paris, 1779) 1:47.

28. Mercier, *Tableau de Paris*, chap. 314: "Maîtres écrivains," 1:828.

29. Sonnet, *L'éducation des filles*, 247–49; quotes from *Réglemens des religieuses ursulines de la congrégation de Paris* (Paris, 1705). Sonnet contrasts this individualized instruction with that given to poor girls in charity schools, which singled out the most promising and gave the rest only minimal instruction. Instruction here was not otherwise individualized, and students were expected simply to copy from common examples that could be reused, rather than having the teacher demonstrate the formation of letters and words at each girl's side.

30. *Encyclopédie*, plates, vol. 2, "Écritures." Paillasson later published the sixteen plates and accompanying text as *L'art d'écrire réduit a des démonstrations vraies et faciles: Avec des explications claires, pour le dictionnaire des arts* (Paris, 1763).

31. Jean Raymond de Petity, *Bibliothèque des artistes et des amateurs, ou, Tablettes analytiques, et méthodiques, sur les sciences et les beaux arts: dédié au roi: ouvrage utile à l'instruction de la jeunesse, à l'usage des personnes de tout âge & de tout état ...* (Paris, 1766), 2:1:286 bis.

32. Louise-Florence Pétronille Tardieu d'Esclavelles, Marquise d'Épinay, *Conversations d'Émilie* (Leipzig, 1774), 33–36.

33. Rousseau, *Émile*, 479, 480–81.

34. On women and needlework, see Nicole Pellegrin, "Les vertus de 'l'ouvrage': Recherches sur la féminisation des travaux d'aiguille (XVIe–XVIIIe siècles)," *Revue d'histoire moderne et contemporaine* 46 (October–December 1999): 747–69.

35. Quoted in Lucien Perey [Clara Adèle Luce Herpin], *Histoire d'une grande dame au XVIIIe siècle: La Princesse Hélène de Ligne* (Paris: Calmann Lévy, 1887), 33–34. In the Ursuline schools in the seventeenth century "the young ladies traced the letters *o* and *i* 'as the foundation of all the others,' then the *a, u, m, n*, 'not changing their letters until they knew how to form the first ones well.'" Constant, *Un monde à l'usage des demoiselles*, 277–78.

36. Quoted in ibid., 277.

37. Victorine de Chastenay-Lanty, *Mémoires, 1771–1815*, ed. Guy Chaussinand-Nogaret (Paris: Perrin, 1987), 35.

38. [Thierry], *Almanach du voyageur à Paris* (Paris, 1783), 156–60. On public courses listed in the *Almanach*, see Michael R. Lynn, *Popular Science and Public Opinion in*

Eighteenth-Century France (Manchester, UK: Manchester University Press, 2006).

39. Thierry, *Almanach du voyageur*, 159. The following ad appeared in the *Mercure de France* (January 1777), 1:208: "*Course on Elocution and French Spelling.* The complete course on Elocution and French Spelling of M. Devillencour, formerly Professor at the Court of Bavaria, continues with success, rue Bétizy, near the rue Tirechappe, at the shop of the Princes, where one should speak to the Porter." There is no record of the lessons ever having been published, but the speech was. Baret de Villencour, *Discours public sur les langues en général, et sur la langue françoise en particulier. Suivi de notes instructives* (Paris, 1780). Villencour used the sheet between the title page and the preface of his book to plug his course. He had a new address, and in addition to his course on elocution and spelling, he now offered "Lessons in town, and shows to Ladies and Young Ladies in a short period of time, a French Rhetoric, the study of which is as simple as it is agreeable." He also noted that he had two books in press, a treatise on spelling and *Elémens raisonnés de la Langue Françoise*, but there is no record that either of these ever appeared.

40. *Mercure de France*, November 1777, 179.

41. *Affiches de Bordeaux*, 23 April 1778, no. 17.

42. Espinassy, *Essai sur l'éducation des demoiselles*, 36–37, 38–39. See also Miremont, *Traité de l'éducation des femmes*, 70–71.

43. See Dena Goodman, *The Republic of Letters: A Cultural History of the French Enlightenment* (Ithaca: Cornell University Press, 1994).

44. Charles de Moüy, *Correspondance inédite du roi Stanislas-Auguste Poniatowski et de Madame Geoffrin (1764–1777)* (Paris: Plon, 1875), ii–iii.

45. Ferdinand Brunot, ed., *Histoire de la langue française des origines à 1900* (Paris: Armand Colin, 1966), 7:176–78, 6:2:925.

46. Marie-Claire Grassi, *L'art de la lettre au temps de "La nouvelle Héloïse" et du Romantisme* (Geneva: Slatkine, 1994), 123–31.

47. Quoted in ibid., 123.

48. Ibid.

49. "Statuts et règlements de l'Académie Française," in [Paul] Pellison-[Fontanier] and Abbé [Pierre-Joseph] d'Olivet, *Histoire de l'Académie française*, ed. Charles-Louis Livet (Geneva: Slatkine Reprints, 1989), 1:493.

50. See Marc Fumaroli, "L'apologétique de la langue française classique," *Rhetorica* 2 (Summer 1984): 142–43.

51. Quoted in Alexis François, *La Grammaire du purisme et l'Académie Française au XVIIIe siècle* (Paris: Société Nouvelle de Librairie et d'Édition, 1905), 127.

52. L.-F. Flûtre, "Du rôle des femmes dans l'élaboration des *Remarques* de Vaugelas," *Neophilologus* 38 (1954): 241–48.

53. Fumaroli, "Apologétique," 144.

54. Ibid., 155–59; see also Katharine Ann Jensen, *Writing Love: Letters, Women, and the Novel in France, 1605–1776* (Carbondale: Southern Illinois University Press, 1995), 18–19.

55. Antoine Baudeau de Somaize, *Le Grand dictionnaire des pretieuses* (Geneva: Slatkine Reprints, 1972), s.v., "Ortographe."

56. Brunot, *Histoire de la langue française*, 1:97–98; Wendy Ayres-Bennett, "Le rôle des femmes dans l'élaboration des idées linguistiques au XVIIe siècle en France," in *Histoire, épistémologie, langage*, 16, *La grammaire des dames*, ed. Wendy Ayres-Bennett (1994), 45.

57. Nina Catach, *L'Orthographe*, (Paris: Presses Universitaires de France, 1988), 33n1.

58. See also [Antoine] Lartigaut, *Les progrès de la véritable ortografe ou l'ortografe franceze fondée sur ses principes confirmée par démonstracions* (Paris, 1669); and the same text under a new title, *Les Principes infallibles et les regles asurées de la juste prononciacion de nôtre langue* (Paris, 1670).

59. Loüis de L'Esclache, *Les Véritables régles de l'ortografe francéze, ou l'art d'aprandre an peu de tams à écrire côrectemant* (Paris, 1668), 4.

60. Ayres-Bennett, "Rôle des femmes," 47.

61. [François Séraphin] Regnier Des Marais, *Traité de la grammaire françoise* (Paris, 1705), 76. The linking of women and foreigners can be seen in the title of Abbé Girard's *L'Ortografe française sans équivoques & dans sés Principes naturels: ou L'Art d'écrire notre langue selon les loix de la Raison & de l'Usage; d'une manière aisée pour lés Dames, comode pour lés Étrangers, instructive pour lés Provinciaux, & nécessaire pour exprimer & distinguer toutes lés diférances de la Prononciacion* (Paris, 1716).

62. L'Esclache, *Véritables régles*, 9–10.

63. Regnier Des Marais, *Traité*, 103.

64. Ibid., 102.

65. [Nicolas] Du Pont, *Examen critique du "Traité d'orthographe de M. l'abbé Regnier Desmarais . . . avec les principes fondementaux de l'art d'écrire* (Paris, 1713), 2–3.

66. Ibid., 34.

67. This is exactly how Brunot interprets Regnier: "Not even once . . . is the least desire shown to bring into orthographic chaos a bit of clarity and logic. . . . Certain members were visibly not at all upset that spelling had become so difficult." Rather than fulfilling their Cartesian mission to effect rational democratic reform, this "aristocracy," as he calls the academicians, defended an archaic and irrational linguistic order solely in order to maintain their own power. (*Histoire de la langue française*, 4:1:109–10).

68. Catach, *L'Orthographe*, 35–37, and the table on 44. Ambroise Firmin-Didot estimates that nearly 5,000 of the 18,000 words contained in the first edition were modified in the second. Firmin-Didot, *Observations sur l'orthographe ou ortografie française suivies d'une Histoire de la*

réforme orthographique depuis le XVe siècle à nos jours (Paris: Ambroise Firmin-Didot, 1868), 13.

69. Liselotte Biedermann-Pasques, *Les grands courants orthographiques au XVIIe siècle et la formation de l'orthographe moderne: Impacts matériels, interférences phoniques, théories et pratiques (1606–1736)* (Tübingen: Max Niemeyer, 1992), 53. The texts she cites are: Claude Buffier, *Grammaire françoise sur un plan nouveau*; and Abbé de Saint-Pierre, *Projet pour perfectioner l'ortografe des langues d'Europe*.

70. Quoted in Dominique Julia, "Livres de classe et usages pédagogiques," in *Histoire de l'édition française*, vol. 2, *Le livre triomphant (1660–1830)*, ed. Henri-Jean Martin and Roger Chartier (Paris: Promodis, 1984), 473.

71. Fresneau, *ABC ou Jeu des lettres*, 60–61.

72. Fumaroli, "Apologétique," 145. Antoine Arnauld and Claude Lancelot, *Grammaire générale et raisonnée, contenant les fondemens de l'art de parler expliquez d'une manière claire et naturelle . . . et plusieurs remarques nouvelles sur la langue françoise* (Paris, 1660).

73. Fumaroli, "Apologétique," 161.

74. See Domna C. Stanton, "The Fiction of *Préciosité* and the Fear of Women," *Yale French Studies* 62 (1981): 107–34.

75. François Albert-Buisson, *Les Quarante au temps des Lumières* (Paris: Fayard, 1960).

76. Jean-Jacques Rousseau, "Essai sur l'origine des langues," ed. Charles Porset (Bordeaux: Guy Ducros, 1970), 67, 61. On Rousseau, see Lieselotte Steinbrügge, *The Moral Sex: Woman's Nature in the French Enlightenment*, trans. Pamela E. Selwyn (New York: Oxford University Press, 1995), 54–82.

77. Jean-François Marmontel, "De l'autorité de l'usage sur la langue," Discours lu dans la séance publique de l'Académie française, le 16 juin 1785, in *Oeuvres complètes* (Paris, 1819–20; rpt. Geneva: Slatkine, 1968), 7:1:89.

78. Ibid., 102.

79. Ibid., 104.

80. Marmontel used this same language of masculine liberty to assert the independence of men of letters from the authority of salonnières. See Goodman, *Republic of Letters*, 107–9. His argument here also mirrors his position in the contemporary debates on theater seating discussed by Jeffrey S. Ravel in "Seating the Public: Spheres and Loathing in the Paris Theaters, 1777–1788," *French Historical Studies* 18 (1993): 173–210. Marmontel's figuring of public opinion as feminine and capricious, needing to be pleased, was at odds with that promoted by others at the time, who imagined it as a rational tribunal. On this point, see Jürgen Habermas, *The Structural Transformation of the Public Sphere: An Inquiry into a Category of Bourgeois Society*, trans. Thomas Burger with Frederick Lawrence (Cambridge: MIT Press, 1989), 89–102; and Keith Michael Baker,

Inventing the French Revolution (Cambridge: Cambridge University Press, 1990), 167–99.

81. Charles Pinot Duclos, *Remarques sur la grammaire générale et raisonnée*, in *Oeuvres complètes* (Paris, 1756), 9:38.

82. Ibid., 41.

83. Ibid., 43.

84. Quoted in François, *Grammaire du purisme*, 140–41.

85. Diderot contributed his own two cents to the spelling debates in his article, "Encyclopédie." In seeming seriousness he laid out a plan to bring spelling into conformity with speech that required the development of a "descriptive alphabet," in which each letter corresponded to a single sound. The analysis of the production of each sound by the human body, and the further correlation of each word, now translated into the descriptive alphabet, with its Latin or Greek root. Thus would the living language be "fixed" by tying it to the body and to unchanging dead languages. Diderot acknowledged that his own encyclopedia was fatally flawed for not having undertaken the massive effort such a project required. He suggested that the Académie française, which he had derided a few pages before for never completing anything, was the appropriate body to take it on. Denis Diderot, "Encyclopédie," in *Encyclopédie*, 5:637–40.

86. "Orthographe," in *Encyclopédie*, 11:669. Beauzée's language echoes that of the discourse on women in the *Encyclopédie* more generally. See Lieselotte Steinbrügge, "Qui peut définir les femmes? L'idée de la 'nature féminine' au siècle des Lumières," *Dix-huitième siècle* 26 (1994): 333–48; and her *Moral Sex*, 21–34. On Beauzée, see Frank A. Kafker with Serena L. Kafker, *The Encyclopedists as Individuals: A Biographical Dictionary of the Authors of the "Encyclopédie"* (Oxford: Voltaire Foundation, 1988): 26–29.

87. "Néographisme," in *Encyclopédie*, 11:94.

88. Quoted in Firmin-Didot, *Observations*, 297.

89. *Mercure de France*, March 1763, 95.

90. [Noel-François de Wailly], *L'Orthographe des dames, ou l'Orthographe fondée sur la bonne prononciation, démontrée la seule raisonnable, par une Société de Dames* (Paris, 1782), 1, 9, 36–37.

91. Ibid., 37–38.

92. Ibid., 41.

93. "Lettre de M. de Wailly, au Rédacteur de l'Année Littéraire," *Année Littéraire* (1783): 201, 209–11.

94. *Ortografe des dames, pour aprandre a ècrire et a lire corectemant en tres peu de tems* (Nancy, 1766), 1. This book is written entirely in the phonetic spelling its author was promoting.

95. Duclos, *Remarques*, 38.

96. Fromageot, *Cours d'études des jeunes demoiselles*, 1:xx.

97. *L'Avantcoureur* 28 (9 July 1770): 439.

98. *Mercure de France*, January 1773, part 2, 127–28.

99. Marie-Jeanne Phlipon to Sophie Cannet, 23 April 1773.

100. Phlipon to Cannet, 21 May 1773.

101. Geneviève de Malboissière once sent a grammar to her friend Adèle, but in a very different spirit. Rather than criticizing Adèle's writing, Geneviève was doing her a friendly service in sending her books from Paris to help her to while away the time in the country. Playing on the double meaning of *temps*, which means both tense and time, she noted: "The grammar is very good; read above all *l'usage des temps*, that's what is most useful to you at the present time." Geneviève de Malboissière to Adélaïde Méliand, [26 August 1762].

102. *Mercure de France*, January 1777, part 2, 208–9.

103. Regnier Des Marais, *Traité*, 83–84.

104. Prunay, *Grammaire des dames*, xv–xvi. The antiphilosophe Élie-Catherine Fréron tore Prunay apart for his attempt to bring spelling into line with speech. "The principle is true," he wrote, "but it proves, in general, that we will never have a good orthography; because it is clear that this reform would produce a universal upheaval, and would render useless, or very disagreeable to read, all the printed books we have, either in French or in Latin." *Année Littéraire* (1776), Letter II, 28.

105. Prunay, *Grammaire des dames*, xviii. See also Lanteires, *Quelques avis aux institutrices*: "What good would it do a Teacher to think with precision, to express herself with grace, purity, and ease, if when she wishes to make her thoughts known to a person who is far away, she cannot communicate them without offering him unformed characters, assembled without order, without method; in the end, with that confusion for which women imagine, very incorrectly, that men will indulge them" (102); he expands on this point in his chapter on letter writing, 213.

106. Prunay, *Grammaire des dames*, xxxii–xxxiii. Fréron wrote a scathing review in the *Année Littéraire*, which ended: "We have so many good books on French Grammar...that it is astonishing that M. *de Prunai* has not made at least a more tolerable compilation. However, this work, mediocre as it is, has been received favorably by M. *de Voltaire*, who disdains none of the literary homages rendered him." Not surprisingly, Fréron accused Prunay of pandering to his female readers in order to enlist them as the main force in a campaign to "make a happy revolution in our orthography." *Année Littéraire* (1776), Letter II, 29–30, 38.

107. [Suzanne Curchod Necker], *Mélanges extraits des manuscrits de Mme Necker*, ed. Jacques Necker (Paris, 1798), 3:409–10.

108. Fromageot, *Cours d'études des jeunes demoiselles*, 1:xlvii–xlviii.

109. Fresneau, *ABC ou Jeu des lettres*, 205.

110. Abbé [Louis] Barthelemy, *Grammaire des dames, ou Nouveau traité d'orthographe françoise, réduite aux regles les plus simples, & justifiée par des morceaux choisis de Poésie, d'Histoire, &c.* (Geneva, 1785), v.

111. On Fanny de Beauharnais, see the entry on her by Morgane Guillemet in *Dictionnaire des femmes de l'Ancienne France*, http://www.siefar.org/ (accessed 7 March 2007).

112. Abbé [Louis] Barthelemy, *La Cantatrice grammairienne, ou l'art d'apprendre l'Orthographe française seul, sans le secours d'un Maître, par le moyen des Chansons érotiques, pastorales, villageoises, anacréontiques, &c. . . . Ouvrage destiné aux Dames* (Geneva and Paris, 1788), viii–ix.

113. Ibid., x, note.

114. J. B. Roche, *Entretiens sur l'orthographe françoise, et autres objets analogues* (Nantes, 1777), 2–4.

115. Ibid., 6–7.

116. Ibid., 9–10.

117. Ibid., 11.

118. *Année Littéraire* (1778), Letter VI, 137.

119. Ibid. (1785), Letter VI, 123–25.

120. [Antoine Tournon], *Promenades de Clarisse et du Marquis de Valzé, ou Nouvelle méthode pour apprendre les principes de la langue et de l'Ortographe françaises à l'usage des Dames* (Paris, 1784), 1:4–6.

121. *Année Littéraire* (1785), Letter VI, 129–30.

122. On the female body as hindrance, see Iris Marion Young, *Throwing Like a Girl and Other Essays in Feminist Philosophy and Social Theory* (Bloomington: Indiana University Press, 1990), 146–47.

123. Mme de Choiseul to Mme du Deffand, 22 November 1773; quoted in Brunot, *Histoire de la langue française*, 6:2:928n.

124. See Leonore Loft, "'Un des ces esprits aieriens descendu sur la terre': Félicité Dupont and the Paradox of Sensibility," in *Femmes Savantes et Femmes d'Esprit: Women Intellectuals of the French Eighteenth Century*, ed. Roland Bonnel and Catherine Rubinger (New York: Peter Lang, 1994), 299.

4. Epistolary Education

1. Paule Constant, *Un monde à l'usage des demoiselles* (Paris: Gallimard, 1987), 295.

2. Carolyn C. Lougee, *"Le Paradis des Femmes": Women, Salons, and Social Stratification in Seventeenth-Century France* (Princeton: Princeton University Press, 1976), 54. Konstantin Dierks sees letter manuals operating in much the same way in late eighteenth-century England and America for a broader class of women and men. "The Familiar Letter and Social Refinement in America, 1750–1800," in *Letter Writing as a Social Practice*, ed. David Barton and Nigel Hall (Amsterdam: John Benjamins, 2000), 31.

3. Roger Chartier, "Introduction: An Ordinary Kind of Writing," in Roger Chartier, Alain Boureau, and Cécile Dauphin, *Correspondence: Models of Letter-*

Writing from the Middle Ages to the Nineteenth Century, trans. Christopher Woodall (Cambridge: Polity, 1997), 5.

4. *Le secretaire des demoiselles; contenant des Billets Galans, avec leur réponses sur divers sujets* (The Hague, 1704).

5. [Jean Baptiste Artaud], *La Petite-Poste dévalisée* (Amsterdam, 1767), "Avertissement," n.p.

6. Janet Gurkin Altman, "The Letter Book as a Literary Institution, 1539–1789: Toward a Cultural History of Published Correspondences in France," *Yale French Studies* 71, *Men/Women of Letters*, ed. Charles A. Porter (1986): 57.

7. Louis Philipon de la Madelaine, *Modèles de lettres sur différents sujets* (Lyon, 1761).

8. On the process of professionalization in the eighteenth century, see Sean Takats, "Corrupting Cooks: Expertise and Domestic Service in Eighteenth-Century France," (PhD diss., University of Michigan, 2005).

9. J[ean] Lanteires, *Quelques avis aux institutrices de jeunes demoiselles, sur les différens objets qui influent essentiellement sur leur bonheur & leur succès; & sur les Études auxquelles elles doivent se livrer. Suivis de quelques idées générales sur l'Éducation, l'instruction des jeunes Filles; & d'un Dictionnaire de plusieurs mots employés dans les Belles-Lettres & en Littérature* (Lausanne, 1788), 221.

10. Louis Philipon de la Madelaine, *Manuel épistolaire à l'usage de la jeunesse ou instructions générales et particulières sur les divers genres de Correspondance; suivies d'exemples puisés dans nos meilleurs Écrivains*, 2nd ed. (Paris: Imprimerie de Brasseur Ainé, An XIII), n.p. and v–vii.

11. Bernard de Bonnard to Sophie Silvestre, 14 April [1783].

12. Bonnard to Silvestre, 9 November [1782].

13. [Pierre Ortigue] de Vaumorière, *Lettres sur toutes sortes de sujets: avec des avis sur la manière de les écrire et des réponses sur chaque espece de lettres*, 4th ed. (Paris, 1706), ii–iii.

14. Catherine de Saint-Pierre to Bernardin de Saint-Pierre, 24 December 1785, 142 (A82–83).

15. Catherine de Saint-Pierre to Bernardin de Saint-Pierre, 13 May 1787, 142 (A16–17). See also letter of 22 December 1787, 142 (A20–21).

16. Catherine de Saint-Pierre to Bernardin de Saint-Pierre, 25 February 1789, 142 (A22–23).

17. Marie-Jeanne Phlipon to Sophie Cannet, [29–30 December 1770].

18. Phlipon to Cannet, 20 December 1774. She had made the same complaint in her letter of 2 January 1773.

19. Sophie Silvestre to Bernard de Bonnard, 16 April 1783.

20. Bonnard to Silvestre, 20 April [1783].

21. Bonnard to Silvestre, 26 May [1784].

22. [Louis-Mayeul Chaudon], *Nouveau manuel épistolaire* (Caen, 1787), "Lettres de demande," no. 24, 40. On the increased inclusion of letters by women in the manuals published after 1760, see Janet Gurkin Alt-man, "Women's Letters in the Public Sphere," in *Going Public: Women and Publishing in Early Modern France*, ed. Elizabeth C. Goldsmith and Dena Goodman (Ithaca: Cornell University Press, 1995), 111–15.

23. Chaudon, *Nouveau manuel épistolaire*, "Lettres d'absence," no. 3.

24. Ibid., 1:xxi.

25. Phlipon to Cannet, 2 January 1773.

26. [Anne d'Aubourg de la Bove, comtesse de Miremont], *Traité de l'éducation des femmes, et cours complet d'instruction* (Paris, 1779), 234.

27. Walter J. Ong, *Orality and Literacy: The Technologizing of the Word* (London: Methuen, 1982), 81.

28. Altman, "Letter Book," 57–58; Jean-Jacques Rousseau, *Julie, or the New Heloise: Letters of Two Lovers Who Live in a Small Town at the Foot of the Alps*, trans. Philip Stewart and Jean Vaché (Hanover, NH: University Press of New England, 1997), 45.

29. Roger Duchêne, "Le mythe de l'épistolière: Mme de Sévigné," in *L'épistolarité à travers les siècles: Geste de communication et/ou d'écriture*, ed. Mireille Bossis (Stuttgart: Franz Steiner, 1990), 13.

30. Altman, "Letter Book," 30.

31. See Elizabeth C. Goldsmith, *Exclusive Conversations: The Art of Interaction in Seventeenth-Century France* (Philadelphia: University of Pennsylvania Press, 1988), 20; Lougee, *Paradis des Femmes*, 52–54.

32. [Jean] Puget de la Serre, *Le secretaire à la mode, augmenté d'une instrucion d'escrire des lettres; cy devant non imprimée* (Amsterdam, 1645), 45.

33. Vaumorière, *Lettres sur toutes sortes de sujets*, vi–vii.

34. Eléazar Mauvillon, *Traité général du stile, avec un traité particulier du stile épistolaire* (Amsterdam, 1750), 258. Several scholars examine this unexamined premise in *Art de la lettre/Art de la conversation à l'époque classique en France*, ed. Bernard Bray and Christoph Strosetzki (Paris: Klincksieck, 1995). The differences emerge as more striking than the similarities.

35. Philipon de la Madelaine, *Modèles de lettres sur différents sujets*, 5. See also Louise-Florence Pétronille Tardieu d'Esclavelles, Marquise d'Épinay, *Conversations d'Émilie* (Leipzig, 1774), 244, in which the mother defines *écriture*—not just letter writing—the same way for Émilie.

36. [Charles] Cotin, "Diverses Lettres & Billets des Dames, avec quelques Réponses," in *Oeuvres galantes de Mr Cotin, tant en vers qu'en prose* (Paris, 1665), iv–v.

37. [Charles] Cotin, "Sur le mesme sujet. À un de mes illustres Amis," in *Oeuvres galantes*, v–vi.

38. Ibid., vi.

39. Molière, *L'École des femmes* (London, 1732), act 3, scene 4.

40. On Neoplatonism in the salons, see Lougee, *Paradis des Femmes*, 34–40.

41. Antoine-Léonard Thomas, *Essai sur les Éloges*, in *Oeuvres complètes* (Paris: Firmin Didot, 1822), 2:78.

42. *Encyclopédie, ou dictionnaire raisonné des sciences, des arts, et des métiers*, ed. Denis Diderot and Jean Le Rond d'Alembert (Paris, 1751–65), 15:553.

43. John Andrews, *Letters to a Young Gentleman on his Setting Out for France: Containing a Survey of Paris, and a Review of French Literature; with Rules and Directions for Travellers, and Various Observations and Anecdotes Relating to the Subject* (London, 1784), 565–66.

44. "Lettre à Madame Élie de Beaumont, à Paris, le 10 août 1765," *Mercure de France* (September 1765), 125–26. The letter is unsigned, but the author claims the female sex. *Lettres du marquis de Roselle* had been published the previous year.

45. Elizabeth C. Goldsmith, ed., *Writing the Female Voice: Essays on Epistolary Literature* (Boston: Northeastern University Press, 1989).

46. Rousseau, *Julie*, part 1, letter 12, 45–49. In fact, the "education" that Saint-Preux gives Julie only threatens the natural simplicity of her letters, as she remarks down the road: "There was a time, my gentle friend, when our Letters were easy and charming; the sentiment that dictated them flowed with an elegant simplicity; it required neither art nor coloration, and its purity was its only ornament. That happy time is no more: alas! it cannot return." Part 1, letter 32, 83.

47. Ibid., part 2, letter 15, 195–97.

48. Ibid., letter 4, 164–65; and Claire's reply, which follows it.

49. Elizabeth C. Goldsmith, "Authority, Authenticity, and the Publication of Letters by Women," in *Writing the Female Voice*, 48.

50. Quoted in René Grevet, "L'éducation des filles vue par l'abbé Pluche dans son *Spectacle de la Nature* (1746)," in *L'éducation des femmes en Europe et en Amérique du Nord de la Renaissance à 1848: Réalités et représentations*, ed. Guyonne Leduc (Paris: L'Harmattan, 1997), 201.

51. Philipon de la Madelaine, *Modèles de lettres sur différents sujets*, 43–44.

52. Ibid., 13–14.

53. [André-Joseph Panckoucke], *Les Études convenables aux demoiselles, contenant la Grammaire, la Poésie, la Rhétorique, le Commerce de Lettres, la Chronologie, la Géographie, l'Histoire, la Fable héroïque, la Fable morale, les Règles de la Bienséance, et un court Traité d'Arithmétique* (Paris: Les Libraires Associés, An XI), 1:155.

54. Ibid., 156, 157, 162, 169.

55. Geneviève de Malboissière to Adélaïde Méliand, 16 June 1764.

56. [Gabriel-Henri Gaillard], *Rhétorique françoise à l'usage des jeunes demoiselles*, 2nd ed. (Paris, 1748), i.

57. Ibid., i–ii.

58. John J. Conley, *The Suspicion of Virtue: Women Philosophers in Neoclassical France* (Ithaca: Cornell University Press, 2002), 45–74. The verse Gaillard misquotes is from *Réflexions diverses*, verse XVI, reprinted as appendix B in Conley, *Suspicion of Virtue*, 179. See also Frédéric Lachèvre, "Madame Deshoulières," in *Les Derniers libertins* (Paris, 1924; rpt. Geneva: Slatkine, 1968), 25–63.

59. M. Morel, "Couplets à Mme de . . . , en lui envoyant une Rhétorique Françoise," *Mercure de France*, 29 September 1787, 196.

60. Gaillard, *Rhétorique françoise*, ii–iv.

61. Jean-François Marmontel, "L'Observateur littéraire," in *Oeuvres complètes* (Paris, 1819–20; rpt. Geneva: Slatkine, 1968), 7:308–9.

62. Ibid., 309–10.

63. Gaillard, *Rhétorique françoise*, ii–iv.

64. [Pierre-Joseph Boudier de Villemert], *L'Ami des femmes* (Hamburg, 1758), 38.

65. Ibid., 61–62. The "imitator of Milton" was Marie-Anne Lepage, Mme du Boccage, a poet and translator of Milton, Pope, and others. Notable among her poetry is *La Columbiade, ou la Foi portée au Nouveau Monde*, the first poetic celebration of Columbus. She was a member of several Italian and provincial academies. Mme de Villedieu was Marie-Catherine Hortense Desjardins (1640?–83), a prolific author whose most notable work is the six-volume autobiographical fiction, *Les Mémoires de la vie de Henriette-Sylvie de Molière* (Paris, 1672–74). Twelve volumes of her complete works were published in 1720–21. On Villedieu, see Elizabeth C. Goldsmith, *Publishing Women's Life Stories in France, 1647–1720: From Voice to Print* (Burlington, VT: Ashgate, 2001), chap. 5. Henriette de Coligny, comtesse de la Suze (1618–73) was a poet and salonnière associated with Cotin, among other poets and academicians of the day. La Suze was one of the women writers (along with Madeleine de Scudéry and Deshoulières) who were figured as the three graces in Louis Garnier's 1718 sculpture, *The French Parnassus*, an engraving of which was made in 1723. See Roger Chartier, "The Man of Letters," trans. Lydia Cochrane, in *Enlightenment Portraits*, ed. Michel Vovelle (Chicago: University of Chicago Press, 1997), 178–79. For biographical information on these and other French women writers of the period, see Fortunée Briquet, *Dictionnaire historique, biographique et littéraire des Françaises et étrangères naturalisées en France* (1804), http://siefar.org (21 September 2008).

66. Boudier de Villemert, *Ami des femmes*, 27–30.

67. Mauvillon, *Traité général du stile*, 364. On the importance of Sévigné as a model, see Constant, *Un monde à l'usage des demoiselles*, 295–96; Goldsmith, "Authority, Authenticity, and the Publication of Letters by Women," 51–52; and (in England) Stella Tillyard, *Aristocrats: Caroline, Emily, Louisa and Sarah Lennox 1740–1832* (London: Chatto and Windus, 1994), 94–96. On the publication history of Sévigné's letters, see Fritz Nies,

Gattungspoetik und Publikumsstrucktur: Sur Geschichte des Sévignébriefe (Munich: Wilhelm Fink, 1972).

68. Marie-France Silver and Marie-Laure Girou Swiderski, introduction to *Femmes en toutes lettres: Les épistolières du XVIIIe siècle*, ed. Marie-France Silver and Marie-Laure Girou Swiderski, (Oxford: Voltaire Foundation, 2000), 1–2.

69. Miremont, *Traité de l'éducation*, 235–36.

70. Ibid., 236.

71. Phlipon to Cannet, 4 September [1776].

72. Marie-Jeanne Roland, *Mémoires de Madame Roland*, ed. Paul de Roux (Paris: Mercure de France, 1986), 239.

73. Marie de Rabutin-Chantal, marquise de Sévigné, to Philippe Emmanuel, marquis de Coulanges, [15 December 1670], in Sévigné, *Selected Letters*, trans. Leonard Tancock (Harmondsworth, UK: Penguin, 1982), 61.

74. Phlipon to Cannet, 4 November 1774.

75. Abbé [Pierre] Fromageot, *Cours d'études des jeunes demoiselles* (Paris, 1772–75), 1:l–li.

76. Nicole Pellegrin, "Lire avec des plumes ou l'art—féminin?—de l'extrait à la fin du XVIIIe siècle," in *Lectrices d'Ancien Régime*, ed. Isabelle Brouard-Arends (Rennes: Presses Universitaires de Rennes, 2003), 119–20. Both Victorine de Chastenay-Lanty and Marie-Julie Cavignac remembered reading Rollin when they were girls in the 1780s. Victorine de Chastenay-Lanty, *Mémoires, 1771–1815*, ed. Guy Chaussinand-Nogaret (Paris: Plon, 1896; rpt. Paris: Librairie Académique Perrin, 1987), 223; [Marie-Julie Cavignac], *Les Mémoires d'une inconnue, publiés sur le manuscrit original, 1780–1816* (Paris: Plon, Nourrit et Cie, 1894), 24–25. On the use of extracts by male writers, see Élisabeth Décultot, ed., *Lire, copier, écrire: Les bibliothèques manuscrites et leurs usages au XVIIIe siècle* (Paris: CNRS Éditions, 2003), especially, her introduction, "L'art de l'extrait: Définition, évolution, enjeux," 7–28; Ann Blair, "Reading Strategies for Coping with Information Overload ca. 1550–1700," *Journal of the History of Ideas* 64 (January 2003): 19–23.

77. Épinay, *Conversations d'Émilie*, 331.

78. Ibid., 428–30. Épinay published a new edition in 1782 that expanded the dialogues from twelve to twenty and ended on a very different note. Placing her hands on her daughter's head, the mother says: "Receive, my dear daughter, the benediction of your father and your mother. You who are so often for us the subject of anxiety and fears, may you also be the constant subject of our joy and our satisfaction, as you are of our wishes and our solicitude." Épinay, *Conversations d'Émilie*, ed. Rosena Davison (Oxford: Voltaire Foundation, 1996), 406. Davison notes that the "imperative and didactic tone" of the first edition was considerably softened in the second and that the author claimed in her preface that it was her granddaughter, the inspiration for the first edition, who had helped to change the tone in the second. Introduction, 41–42.

79. Miremont, *Traité de l'éducation*, 79.

80. Chastenay-Lanty, *Mémoires*, 22–23.

81. Malboissière to Méliand, 15 May [1765].

82. Roland, *Mémoires*, 245.

83. Papiers Roland, VII: Notes et papiers divers de Mme Roland, Bibliothèque nationale de France (hereafter cited as BNF), NAF 6244, mf 6057; Papiers Roland, II, NAF 9533.

84. Phlipon to Cannet, 18 May 1772; BNF NAF 6244, fol. 217.

85. Phlipon to Cannet, 5 December 1775.

86. Ibid., 12 December 1778.

87. Marie-Thérèse Geoffrin, marquise de la Ferté-Imbault, "Extraits des voiages que ma raison a été obligé de faire pour triompher des devoirs les plus pénibles et les plus variés. Fait en 1773." Fonds d'Etampes-Valençay-Geoffrin, AN 508 AP 23–38. I remain grateful to the late comtesse de Bruce and her son, Charles Edouard de Bruce, who allowed me to study these papers many years ago when they were still in private hands. See my "Filial Rebellion in the Salon: Madame Geoffrin and Her Daughter," *French Historical Studies* 16 (Spring 1989): 38–39. An earlier study of Mme de la Ferté-Imbault, which I only discovered later, notes that three small volumes of her extracts of Malebranche composed in 1769 for the duchesse de Rohan-Chabot are in the Bibliothèque de l'Arsenal in Paris (MSS. 2787–2789). See Constantin Photiadès, *La Reine des Lanturelus: Marie-Thérèse Geoffrin, Marquise de la Ferté-Imbault (1715–1791)* (Paris: Plon, 1928), iv.

88. Suzanne Necker to Mme de la Ferté-Imbault (undated letter); Grimm to Mme de la Ferté-Imbault, 25 April 1776: both in AN 508 AP 23–38. On Mme de la Ferté-Imbault's friendship with the comtesse de Marsan, see Photiadès, *Reine des Lanturelus*, 138–47. Grimm was one of the original members of the Order of Lanturelus that Mme de la Ferté-Imbault founded in her salon in 1771—the same year that she became officially associated with the education of the princesses. See "Annales pour le moins aussi curieuses que celles de Tacite," AN 508 AP 23–38; and Photiadès, *Reine des Lanturelus*, 152–53.

89. Friedrich-Melchior Grimm to Mme de la Ferté-Imbault, 25 April 17[?], AN 508 AP 23–38.

90. "Anecdotes sur M. et Mme Necker," 10 June 1780, AN 508 AP 23–38.

91. Épinay, *Conversations d'Émilie*, ed. Davison, 338–39. Davison identifies the author of the extract as Mme de Lambert, but she does not give the basis for this ascription. Not only had Mme de Lambert died in 1733 when the future Mme d'Épinay was seven years old, but Épinay had good reason not to mention the name of Mme de la Ferté-Imbault if she was indeed the "woman of great merit" to whom she referred. Grimm and Épinay were at the heart of the group of philosophes associated

with the *Encyclopédie* and the salon of Mme de la Ferté-Imbault's mother, Mme Geoffrin.

92. La Ferté-Imbault, "Extraits des voiages."

93. Lanteires, *Quelques avis aux institutrices*, 214.

94. Ibid., 222–23, 227.

95. Ibid., 215.

96. Ibid.

97. Jaucourt, "Style (Gramm. Rhétoriq. Eloq. Bel let.)," in *Encyclopédie*, 15:553; Lanteires, *Quelques avis aux institutrices*, 218–19.

98. Ibid., 220.

99. Ibid., 220–21.

100. Roland, *Mémoires*, 246.

101. See Marie-Jeanne Phlipon to Sophie Cannet, 23 January 1776, in BNF NAF 9533.

5. Supplying the Female Letter Writer

1. Carolyn Sargentson, *Merchants and Luxury Markets: The Marchands Merciers of Eighteenth-Century Paris* (London: Victoria and Albert Museum with the J. Paul Getty Museum, 1996). See also Pierre Verlet, "Le commerce des objets d'art et les marchands merciers à Paris au XVIIIe siècle," *Annales ESC* 13 (January–March 1958): 10–29; and Cissie Fairchilds, "The Production and Marketing of Populuxe Goods in Eighteenth-Century Paris," in *Consumption and the World of Goods*, ed. John Brewer and Roy Porter (London: Routledge, 1993), 228–48.

2. Sargentson, *Merchants and Luxury Markets*, 18–23; and [Roze de Chantoiseau], *Essai sur l'Almanach général d'indication d'adresse personnelle et domicile fixe, des six corps, arts et métiers* (Paris, 1769), list of "Merciers, Jouailliers, Bijoutiers, Quincailliers, Marchands de Modes, de toiles de dentelle, dorures, soyeries, &c. de la ville et faux-bourgs de Paris," n.p. See also Robert Hénard, *La rue Saint-Honoré*, vol. 1, *Des origines à la Révolution* (Paris: Émile Paul, 1908).

3. Andrew McClellan, "Watteau's Dealer: Gersaint and the Marketing of Art in Eighteenth-Century Paris," *Art Bulletin* 78 (September 1996), 439–53; Andrew McClellan, "Edme Gersaint and the Marketing of Art in Eighteenth-Century Paris," *Eighteenth-Century Studies* 29 (Winter 1996): 218–21.

4. Sargentson, *Merchants and Luxury Markets*, 113–42.

5. *L'Avantcoureur, Feuille Hebdomadaire, où sont annoncés les objets particuliers des Sciences, de la Littérature, des arts, des Métiers, de l'Industrie, des Spectacles, & les Nouveautés en tout genre* 20 (15 May 1769), 311–12.

6. See Michael Kwass, "Big Hair: A Wig History of Consumption in Eighteenth-Century France," *American Historical Review* 111 (June 2006): 641–44; Dena Goodman, "Furnishing Discourses: Readings of a Writing Desk in Eighteenth-Century France," in *Luxury in the Eighteenth Century: Debates, Desires and Delectable*

Goods, ed. Maxine Berg and Elizabeth Eger (Basingstoke, UK: Palgrave Macmillan, 2003), 71–88, esp. 72.

7. Louis-Sébastien Mercier, *Tableau de Paris*, ed. Jean-Claude Bonnet (Paris: Mercure de France, 1994), chap. 347: "De la Cour," 1:953.

8. *Mémoires de la Baronne d'Oberkirch sur la cour de Louis XVI et la société française avant 1789*, ed. Suzanne Burkard (Paris: Mercure de France, 1989), 164; Pierre Saint-Amand, "Adorning Marie Antoinette," *Eighteenth-Century Life* 15 (November 1991): 19–34.

9. On the eighteenth-century luxury debates, see John Sekora, *Luxury: The Concept in Western Thought, Eden to Smollett* (Baltimore: Johns Hopkins University Press, 1977); Daniel Roche, *France in the Enlightenment*, trans. Arthur Goldhammer (Cambridge: Harvard University Press, 1998), 561–74; Sarah Maza, "Luxury, Morality, and Social Change: Why There Was No Middle-Class Consciousness in Prerevolutionary France," *Journal of Modern History* 69 (June 1997): 199–229; Berg and Eger, *Luxury in the Eighteenth Century*; Kwass, "Big Hair."

10. Oberkirch, *Mémoires*, 213.

11. Louis-Antoine Caraccioli, *Paris, le modèle des nations étrangères, ou l'Europe françoise* (Venice and Paris, 1777), 119.

12. Sargentson, *Merchants and Luxury Markets*, 145; Jennifer M. Jones, "Repackaging Rousseau: Femininity and Fashion in Old Regime France," *French Historical Studies* 18 (Fall 1994): 947. In her discussion of the rococo, Reed Benhamou emphasizes that in matters of taste, authority is always unstable and subject to contestation. Benhamou, "Furniture Production in 18th-Century France: An Interactive Process," *European Studies Journal* 1 (1984): 49.

13. Hénard, *Rue Saint-Honoré*, 1:433–34; Gabrielle-Émilie de Breteuil, marquise du Châtelet, *Les Réflexions sur le bonheur*, in *Lettres inédites de Madame la Marquise du Chastelet à M. le Comte d'Argental* (Paris: Xhrouet, 1806), 363.

14. Abbé [Pierre] Jaubert, *Dictionnaire raisonné universel des arts et metiers* (Paris, 1773), 4:473. One decorator who published a portfolio of his designs declared it "useful to Artists and to Persons who wish to decorate with taste." [Richard de] La Londe, *Oeuvres diverses* (Paris, 1788–96), n.p.

15. *Cabinet des Modes/Magasin des modes nouvelles, françaises et anglaises* (Paris, 1785–90). See also the francophone *Journal [des Luxus und] der Moden*, ed. F. J. Bertuch and G. M. Kraus (Weimar, 1786–99), which features many plates of fashionable furniture, including a fall-front secretary and a rolltop desk (in 1787).

16. T. H. Breen, "The Meanings of Things: Interpreting the Consumer Economy in the Eighteenth Century," in *Consumption and the World of Goods*, 249–60, quotes 256–57.

17. [Madeleine de Puisieux], *Conseils à une amie* (n.p., 1749), 131–32, 187–88.

18. [Anna Francesca Craddock], *Journal de Madame Cradock: Voyage en France (1783–1786)*, ed. and trans. O. Delphin Balleyguier (Paris: Perrin, 1896), 18–19.

19. Mercier, *Tableau de Paris*, chap. 820: "Palais-Royal," 2:930–31.

20. [Luc Vincent] Thiery, *Almanach du voyageur a Paris, contenant une description sommaire, mais exacte, de tous les monumens, chef-d'oeuvres des arts, etablissemens utiles, & autres objets de curiosité que renferme cette capitale: ouvrage utile aux citoyens, & indispensable pour l'étranger* (Paris, 1786), 293–94, 356–59, quote 357. See also *Almanach du Palais royal, utile aux voyageurs, pour l'année 1786* (Paris, 1786), 183; [Mayeur de Saint-Paul], *Tableau du nouveau Palais-Royal* (Paris, 1788).

21. [Jacques de La Vallée], *Les Derniers adieux du Quai de Gêvres à la bonne ville de Paris* (London [Paris], 1787), 5.

22. *Tableau du nouveau Palais-Royal*, 2:38–42.

23. Mercier, *Tableau de Paris*, chap. 821: "Suite du Palais-Royal," 2:937–38.

24. *An English Lady in Paris: The Diary of Frances Anne Crewe, 1786*, ed. Michael Allen (St. Leonards, UK: Oxford-Stockley Publications, 2006), 67–69.

25. Craddock, *Journal*, entry for 18 October 1785, 318–19. See also [John Charles Villiers, Earl of Clarendon], *A Tour through Part of France, Containing a Description of Paris, Cherbourg, and Ermenonville, with a Rhapsody, Composed at the Tomb of Rousseau. In a Series of Letters* (London, 1789), 92–93; Oberkirch, *Mémoires*, 312–13, 354, 400.

26. Mercier, *Tableau de Paris*, chap. 162: "Palais-Royal," 1:381

27. Ibid., chap. 820: "Palais-Royal," 2:931; chap. 821: "Suite du Palais-Royal," 2:941–42.

28. Henry Paulin Panon Desbassayns, *Petit Journal des Epoques pour Servir a ma Mémoire (1784–1786)*, ed. Annie Lafforgue with Christelle de Villele and Jean Barbier (Saint-Gilles-les-Hauts: Musée historique, 1990), 51. Panon bought Mercier's eight-volume *Tableau de Paris* during his visit to Paris. When he left, he shipped it home along with a four-volume *Dictionnaire de Paris*, a one-volume *Paris miniature*, and two volumes of *Géographe parisien*. (See appendix 17 to *Petit journal*, 381–82.)

29. Ibid., 309. Gilles Chabaud has calculated that the number of editions of Parisian guidebooks multiplied almost thirtyfold between 1601 and 1830—from 4 to 114—with the biggest jump occurring in the period 1751–70. Chabaud, "Les Guides de Paris: Une littérature de l'accueil?" in *La ville promise: Mobilité et accueil à Paris (fin XVIIe–début XIXe siècle)*, ed. Daniel Roche (Paris: Fayard, 2000), 77–108, data 79–81.

30. Panon Desbassayns, *Petit Journal*, 216, 223. On the prix fixe store, see Olivier Dautresme, "Une Boutique de luxe dans un centre commercial à la mode: L'exemple du 'magasin d'effets précieux à prix fixe' au Palais-Royal à la fin du XVIIIe siècle," in *La boutique et la ville: Commerces, commerçants, espaces et clientèles, XVIe–XXe siècle*, ed. Natacha Coquery (Tours: Publications

de l'Université François Rabelais, 2000), 223–47. For a description of the shop, see *Almanach du Palais royal*, 155–56.

31. François Cognel, *La Vie parisienne sous Louis XVI* (1787), quoted in Claire Walsh, "Shopping et tourisme: L'attrait des boutiques parisiennes au XVIIIe siècle," in *La boutique et la ville*, 236.

32. For predecessors to the Palais Royal, see *L'Avantcoureur* 23 (5 June 1769), 359–60; *Annonces, affiches et avis divers (Affiches de Paris)* (7 August 1771), 128; [de Gaigne], *Almanach de l'Étranger pour l'année 1771* (Paris, 1771); *Almanach parisien en faveur des étrangers et des personnes curieuses...* (Paris, 1776), 58–60; Thiery, *Almanach du voyageur* (1781), 42; Mercier, *Tableau de Paris*, chap. 214: "Colisée," 1:536.

33. Thiery, *Almanach du voyageur* (1786), 251.

34. *L'Avantcoureur* (2 April 1770).

35. "A selection of these can be found *chez* Sr Fontaine, Marchand Bijoutier in Paris, rue Dauphine, carrefour de Bussy, at the Royal Medallion; price 1 liv. 10 sols each pen." Despite the niche marketing, steel pens never caught on in the eighteenth century. See John Grand-Carteret, *Papeterie & papetiers de l'ancien temps* (Paris: Georges Putois, Maître Marchand-Papetier, 1913), 86.

36. *An English Lady in Paris*, 81.

37. John Andrews, *Letters to a Young Gentleman on His Setting Out for France: Containing a Survey of Paris, and a Review of French Literature; with Rules and Directions for Travellers, and Various Observations and Anecdotes Relating to the Subject* (London, 1784), 542–44. See also *Almanach parisien* (1776), 206–7: "Works of Porcelain: Chinese *Pagodes*, Vases, Flowerpots, Cups, & other ornaments for Mantelpieces and *Cabinets*. These can be found in large numbers at the Palais-Marchand, rue Saint-Honoré, near the Oratoire, etc. There is nothing less fixed than the price of these sorts of things: in general, they are expensive."

38. *La Feuille nécessaire* 47 (31 December 1759): 743–44.

39. *Affiches de Paris* (18 December 1771), 203–4. On the use of enamel to coat seals of common steel to keep it from rusting and make them fashionably attractive, see Henry René d'Allemagne, *Les Accessoires du costume et du mobilier depuis le treizième jusqu'au milieu du dixneuvième siècle* (Paris: Schemit, 1928), 1:77, 196–97.

40. Mercier, *Tableau de Paris*, chap. 468: "Cachets," 1:1293–94.

41. [Louis-Mayeul Chaudon], *Nouveau manuel épistolaire* (Caen, 1787), 1:xvi, and example 18. In general, Chaudon believed that one ought to use a seal engraved with one's coat of arms—"as long as one is not in a position not to have a coat of arms. But who doesn't have one today?"

42. The editor of the *Affiches* noted that "the Inventor associates this invention with the *Quipos* of the Peruvian Indians, the idea of which is, however, a little different." *Affiches de Paris* (18 December 1771), 203. Graffigny

defined the *quipos* as "cords of cotton or gut, to which other cords of different colors were attached, recalling for them, by knots placed along them, things that they wished to remember," and noted that they "took the place of our art of writing." Françoise de Graffigny, *Lettres d'une Peruvienne* (New York: Modern Language Assn. of America, 1993), 13. See also chapter 7, below.

43. *L'Avantcoureur*, (25 December 1769; no. 52), 821; (21 December 1772; no. 51), 806.

44. Mercier, *Tableau de Paris*, chap. 555: "Le Petit Dunkerque," 2:68. The baronne d'Oberkirch claimed that Le Petit Dunkerque was often crowded enough to require a guard. See Oberkirch, *Mémoires*, 172. Dautresne finds "a spectacular increase in consumption related to New Year's gifts" at the prix fixe store in the Palais Royal, with 412 articles sold between 23 December and 5 January, amounting to 20% of sales for a six-month period. "Magasin à prix fixe," 246.

45. Sargentson, *Merchants and Luxury Markets*, 119–20.

46. Oberkirch, *Mémoires*, 172.

47. Mercier, *Tableau de Paris*, chap. 555: "Le Petit Dunkerque," 2:70.

48. *Mercure de France*, October 1773; quoted in Sargentson, *Merchants and Luxury Markets*, 123.

49. Sargentson, *Merchants and Luxury Markets*, 123; Mercier, *Tableau de Paris*, chap.71: "Cafés," 1:188.

50. McClellan, "Edme Gersaint," 218–19; see also McClellan, "Watteau's Dealer," 440–42.

51. Mercier, *Tableau de Paris*, chap. 337: "Consommation," 1:913.

52. Sargentson, *Merchants and Luxury Markets*, 116.

53. *Recueil des Annonces, affiches et avis divers pour la ville de Bordeaux* (*Affiches de Bordeaux*), 1 January 1778, no. 1; 14 May 1778, no. 20; 24 December 1778, no. 52; see also the ad for Sieur Coutouly *fils* in no. 51 (17 December 1778). The *Affiches de Picardie* carried a similar ad for a furniture dealer in Noyon, as well as notice of a sale of the entire stock of a merchant whose goods were seized for debts, including stationery and other writing supplies. *Annonces, Affiches et Avis Divers de Picardie, Artois, Soissonnois et Pays-Bas François*, 5 March 1774, no. 10; 13 August 1774, no. 33.

54. *Affiches de Provence, feuille hebdomadaire d'Aix*, 13 September 1778, no. 37.

55. *Affiches de Bordeaux*, 14 May 1778, no. 20.

56. Ibid., 30 July 1778, no. 31.

57. *Affiches de Picardie*, 29 January 1774, no. 5, and 26 February 1774, no. 9. The Bureau royale de correspondance générale in Paris also placed a notice in the Amiens paper reminding readers that it was chartered by the king to undertake all sorts of commissions for the public, including "the purchase & sale of merchandise." 21 May 1774, no. 21.

58. Chaudon, *Nouveau manuel épistolaire*, 2:95–96.

59. Dawn Jacobson, *Chinoiserie* (London: Phaidon, 1993), 66–69; see also Maxine Berg, "Asian Luxuries and the Making of the European Consumer Revolution," in *Luxury in the Eighteenth Century*, 228–44; David Porter, "A Wanton Chase in a Foreign Place: Hogarth and the Gendering of Exoticism in the Eighteenth-Century Interior," in *Furnishing the Eighteenth Century: What Furniture Can Tell Us about the European and American Past*, ed. Dena Goodman and Kathryn Norberg (New York: Routledge, 2006), 49–60.

60. Sargentson, *Merchants and Luxury Markets*, 4, 52–56, and chaps. 3 and 4; Verlet, "Le commerce des objets d'art"; Michael Stürmer, "An Economy of Delight: Court Artisans of the Eighteenth Century," *Business History Review* 53 (Winter 1979): 522; Benhamou, "Furniture Production in 18th-Century France," 45–52; John Whitehead, *The French Interior in the Eighteenth Century* (New York: Dutton Studio Books, 1993), 45–47.

61. Michael Finlay, *Western Writing Implements in the Age of the Quill Pen* (Wetheral, Carlisle, Cumbria, UK: Plains Books, 1990), 38–39.

62. Sargentson, *Merchants and Luxury Markets*, 73, and color plate 13; there is also one in the Musée Nissim de Camondo in Paris, inv. CAM 227.

63. *Connaissance des Arts* 72 (February 1958), 3; Sargentson, *Merchants and Luxury Markets*, 52–56, no. 72.

64. *Encyclopédie, ou Dictionnaire raisonné des sciences, des arts et des métiers*, ed. Denis Diderot and Jean le Rond d'Alembert (Paris, 1751–65), 9:861–62; Mercier, *Tableau de Paris*, chap. 76: "De la mode," 1:417.

65. C. H. Wylde, "Mr. J. H. Fitzhenry's Collection of Early French Pâte-Tendre," *Burlington Magazine for Connoisseurs* 7 (June 1905): 196; Danielle Kisluk-Grosheide, "The Reign of Magots and Pagods," *Metropolitan Museum Journal* 37 (2002): 177–97; Olivier Le Fuel, "L'inspiration des écritoires au XVIIIe siècle," *Connaissance des Arts* 72 (February 1958): 35. I am grateful to Aurora Wolfgang for calling this article to my attention.

66. For the Munich version, see Christian Dauterman, *Sèvres Porcelain: Makers and Marks of the Eighteenth Century* (New York: Metropolitan Museum of Art, 1986), 30–31.

67. *L'Avantcoureur*, 20 August 1770, 532–33.

68. Sargentson, *Merchants and Luxury Markets*, 116.

69. Verlet, "Le commerce des objets d'art," 20.

70. Sargentson, *Merchants and Luxury Markets*, 76.

71. See Jeanne Giacomotti, *French Faience*, trans. Diana Imber (New York: Universe Books, 1963), 10–11.

72. For these and other similar examples, see Catherine Arminjon, *Principes d'analyse scientifique: Objects civils domestiques. Vocabulaire* (Paris: Imprimerie Nationale, 1984), 523–44.

73. De Jeze, *État ou tableau de la Ville de Paris considérée relativement au nécessaire, à l'utile, à l'agréable et à l'administration* (Paris, 1759), 1:318–19. See also *Dictionnaire portatif du commerce* (Paris, 1777), 359–65.

74. There are two major collections of trade cards in Parisian repositories, from which the examples below are drawn: BNF, Est Li.4g: Adresses Commerciales; Archives de Paris D43Z: Publicité Commerciale à Paris. Waddesdon Manor also has a rich collection of trade cards, including some for the same merchants represented in the French collections, but sometimes with different designs. The collection can be searched online at http://www.waddesdon.org.uk/plan_your_visit/trade_cards_copyright.html. Often the same text also appears in other advertising venues, such as almanacs or the *affiches*. See Nicolas Petit, *L'éphémère: L'occasionnel et le non livre à la bibliothèque Sainte-Geneviève (XVe–XVIIIe siècles)* (Paris: Klincksieck, 1997), 123–25, 239–41.

75. John Grand-Carteret notes that À la Teste Noire was a popular sign, "taken by I don't know how many marchands-merciers, marchands-épiciers, marchands-confiseurs, marchands-drapiers." Grand-Carteret, *Papeterie & papetiers de l'ancien temps*, 64–66. The daybooks of the mercer Lazare Duvaux note the sale to Mme de Pompadour of a "seal of a *tête de nègre* on a bust, decorated with brilliants and rubies." *Livre-journal de Lazare Duvaux, Marchand-bijoutier ordinaire du Roy, 1748–1758*, ed. Louis Courajod (Paris: F. de Nobele, 1965), vol. 2, transaction no. 2274 (22 November 1755).

76. The various types of letter paper are listed in [Jacques Lacombe], *Encyclopédie méthodique, ou par ordre de matières: Arts et métiers mécaniques* (Paris, 1782–91), 30:555–92.

77. Louis Racine to Mme de Neuville de Saint-Héry, his elder daughter, 4 October 1746, in *Lettres inédites de Jean Racine et de Louis Racine*, ed. Adrien de La Roque (Paris: Hachette, 1862).

78. Racine to Mme de Neuville de Saint-Héry, 1 August 1747, note.

79. Undated letters from Anne-Charlotte de Crussal-Florensac, duchesse d'Aiguillon to Pierre-Louis Moreau de Maupertuis in BNF NAF 10398. These are among several letters she wrote to Maupertuis between 1745, when he moved to Berlin, and his death in 1759. I am grateful to Judith Zinsser for calling these letters to my attention.

80. [Pierre-Joseph Boudier de Villemert and Jean Soret], *La Feuille nécessaire, contenant divers détails sur les sciences, les lettres et les arts* (Paris), 21 May 1759. Boudier de Villemert was the author of *L'Ami des femmes* (1758).

81. Bernard de Bonnard to Sophie Silvestre, 4 December [1783].

82. On fashion plates, see Raymond Gaudriault, *Répertoire de la gravure de mode française des origines à 1815* (Paris: Promodis, 1988).

83. Sarah Lowengard, "Colours and Colour making in the Eighteenth Century," in *Consumers and Luxury: Consumer Culture in Europe 1650–1850*, ed. Maxine Berg and Helen Clifford (Manchester, UK: Manchester University Press, 1999), 103–17, quote 109.

84. Louis-Antoine Caraccioli, *Lettres d'un Indien à Paris, à son ami Glazir, Sur les moeurs françoises, & sur les bizarreries du tems* (Amsterdam and Paris, 1789), 2:274–78; 2:192–93.

85. Pierre Claude Reynard, "Manufacturing Quality in the Pre-Industrial Age: Finding Value in Diversity," *Economic History Review* 53 (2000): 493–516, esp. 494–95. I am grateful to Maxine Berg for calling this article to my attention.

86. Ibid., 504, 505.

87. *Encyclopédie*, 11:860. On ink, see, e.g., *Notices des dix premieres années de l'Almanach sous-verre, des associés, rue du Petit-pont, à Paris, contenant les découvertes, inventions, ou expériences nouvellement faites dans les sciences, les arts, les métiers, l'industrie (1768–1777)* (Paris, n.d); followed by annual *Suites de la Notice* (Paris, 1778–1802), no. 285 (1785); and the virtually identical notice in *Tablettes Royales de renommée, ou de correspondance et d'indication générales des principales fabriques, manufactures, et maisons de commerce, d'épicerie-droguerie . . .* (Paris, 1786).

88. Mimi Hellman, "Furniture, Sociability, and the Work of Leisure in Eighteenth-Century France," *Eighteenth-Century Studies* 32 (Summer 1999): 415–45; see also Pierre Devinoy, *Le meuble léger en France* (Paris: Paul Hartmann, 1952), 19.

89. Raymond Gaudriault, *Filigranes et autres caractéristiques des papiers fabriqués en France au XVIIe et XVIIIe siècles* (Paris: CNRS, 1995), 42; Leonard N. Rosenband, *Papermaking in Eighteenth-Century France: Management, Labor, and Revolution at the Montgolfier Mill, 1761–1805* (Baltimore: Johns Hopkins University Press, 2000), 32.

90. *Suites de la Notice* (1777).

91. Ibid. (1791), no. 142.

92. Joseph Jérôme Le François de Lalande, *Art de faire le papier* (1761 or 1773), in *Descriptions des arts et métiers, faites ou approuvées par messieurs de l'Académie Royale des sciences* (Paris, 1761–88), 80–81. Rosenband agrees: "The smooth grain and robin's-egg-blue tint of Dutch paper posed enormous problems for French manufacturers. It cost them markets, shuttered their mills, and revealed their technological inertia." *Papermaking in Eighteenth-Century France*, 3.

93. "Mémoire du sieur Montgolfier fabricant et propriétaire d'une fabrique à Annonay," quoted in ibid., 36–37. These are the same Montgolfier brothers who invented the hot air balloon.

94. Jean-Baptiste Réveillon, "Exposé justificatif pour le sieur Réveillon, entrepreneur de la Manufacture royale de papiers peints, faubourg St.-Antoine," in *Mémoires du Marquis de Ferrières*, ed. [Saint-Albin] Berville and [François] Barrière (Paris: Baudouin Frères, 1821), 1:432.

95. Gaudriault, *Filigranes*, 50, 52–53 and note. See also Montgolfier listing in *Almanach du dauphin* (1789).

96. *Premier trimestre des tablettes royales de renommée, d'adresse perpétuelle et d'indication des négocians, artistes célèbres et fabricans*

des six corps, arts et métiers de la ville & fauxbourgs de Paris, et autres villes du royaume... pour servir de Supplément & d'Errata au Quatriemestre de la présente Année MDCC LXXV (Paris, 1775), s.v., "Papetiers (Marchands) pour Meubles; Objets relatifs." On industrial espionage, see J. R. Harris, *Industrial Espionage and Technology Transfer: Britain and France in the Eighteenth Century* (Aldershot, UK: Ashgate, 1998).

97. Charles Coulston Gillispie, *The Montgolfier Brothers and the Invention of Aviation, 1783–1784* (Princeton: Princeton University Press, 1983), 18. However, in *Filigranes*, Gaudriault does not mention any Huguenot connection, and the names of eighteenth-century Dutch paper manufacturers whom he lists are all Dutch. On the Dutch papermaking industry, see Jan de Vries and Ad van der Woude, *The First Modern Economy: Success, Failure, and Perseverance of the Dutch Economy, 1500–1815* (Cambridge: Cambridge University Press, 1997), 311–18. They do not mention any Huguenot connection either.

98. J.-N. Barandon and J. Irigoin, "Comment distinguer les papiers fabriqués en Hollande et en Angoumois de 1650 à 1810," in *Avant-texte, texte, après-texte*, ed. Louis Hay and Péter Nagy (Paris: CNRS; Budapest: Akadémiai Kiadó, 1982), 19–21.

99. Other chemicals were used to try to produce the same effect. According to Desmarest, the French and the Germans used Prussian blue, which made the paper pale blue rather than azure. See Gaudriault, *Filigranes*, 42.

100. [Nicolas Desmarest], "Papier (Art de Faire)," in *Encyclopédie méthodique*, 30:525.

101. Gaudriault, *Filigranes*, 52, 42.

102. *Arrêt du Conseil d'état du roi, Qui défend de faire sortir à l'Étranger des matieres propres à la fabrication du Papier & à la formation de la colle: Et fixe les droits que lesdites matieres qui seront apportées de l'Étranger, payeront à leur entrée dans le Royaume* (21 August 1771); *Arrêt du Conseil d'état du roi, Qui fixe les Droits qui seront payés à toutes les entrées du Royaume, sur différentes especes & qualités de Papiers venant de l'Étranger* (21 August 1771); see also Jaubert, *Dictionnaire raisonné*, 3:349–50; *Encyclopédie*, 11:860.

103. *Almanach parisien* (1776), 191.

104. Jaubert, *Dictionnaire raisonné*, 3:347.

105. [André Joseph Panckoucke], *Les Études convenables aux demoiselles* (Paris: Les Libraires Associés, An XI), 1:163.

6. The Writing Desk

1. Annik Pardailhé-Galabrun, *The Birth of Intimacy: Privacy and Domestic Life in Early Modern Paris*, trans. Jocelyn Phelps (Philadelphia: University of Pennsylvania Press, 1991), 63–64; *Dictionnaire de l'Académie française*, 4th ed. (1762) in Project for American and French Research on the Treasury of the French Language (ARTFL), http://humanities.uchicago.edu/orgs/ARTFL (accessed 15 February 2005); see also Roger Chartier, "The Practical Impact of Writing," and Orest Ranum, "The Refuges of Intimacy," in *A History of Private Life*, vol. 3, *Passions of the Renaissance*, ed. Roger Chartier, trans. Arthur Goldhammer (Cambridge: Harvard University Press), 134–44, 210–11.

2. Henry Havard, *Dictionnaire de l'ameublement, et de la décoration depuis le XVIIIe siècle jusqu'à nos jours* (Paris: Quantin, 1887–90), 1:492–93.

3. Much of the research on material culture in the eighteenth century is based on inventories and account books. See, e.g., Lorna Weatherill, *Consumer Behaviour and Material Culture in Britain, 1660–1760* (London: Routledge, 1988); Carole Shammas, *The Pre-Industrial Consumer in England and America* (Oxford: Clarendon Press, 1990); Pardailhé-Galabrun, *Birth of Intimacy*; Natacha Coquery, *L'hôtel aristocratique: Le marché du luxe à Paris au XVIIIe siècle* (Paris: Publications de la Sorbonne, 1998).

4. On bookkeeping practices, see Natacha Coquery, "Fashion, Business, Diffusion: An Upholsterer's Shop in Eighteenth-Century Paris," in *Furnishing the Eighteenth Century: What Furniture Can Tell Us about the European and American Past*, ed. Dena Goodman and Kathryn Norberg (New York: Routledge, 2006), 63–78.

5. All transactions are numbered and listed chronologically in Louis Courajod, ed., *Livre-journal de Lazare Duvaux, Marchand-bijoutier ordinaire du Roy, 1748–1758* (Paris: F. de Nobele, 1965), vol. 2. Mme d'Épinay's purchase of the fire screen is transaction no. 1238 (26 October 1752). For descriptions of other combination fire screen–writing tables, see André Jacob Roubo, *L'Art du menuisier* (Paris, 1769), 741; Havard, *Dictionnaire de l'ameublement*, 4:1192–93. Besides Louis XV's unmarried daughters (Mmes Adélaïde, Louise, Sophie, and Victoire, who were between eleven and twenty-six years old during the period covered by Duvaux's daybooks), the names of only three unmarried women appear among Duvaux's clients: the king's sister, a Mlle La Noix, and Mlle de La Roche-sur-Yonne.

6. *Livre-journal de Lazare Duvaux*, transaction no. 1138 (3 June 1752).

7. Ibid., transaction no. 1147 (16 June 1752); no. 1617 (19 December 1753); no. 1780 (27 May 1754); no. 2492 (24 May 1756).

8. Ibid., transaction no. 650 (22 November 1750); no. 823 (29 May 1751); no. 834 (12 June 1751); no. 1138 (3 June 1752); no. 2189 (3 July 1755); no. 2563 (10 August 1756).

9. Ibid., transaction no. 1138 (3 June 1752); no. 2189 (3 July 1755); no. 804 (8 May 1751).

10. Ibid., transaction no. 650 (22 November 1750); no. 834 (12 June 1751); no. 1894 (18 September 1754).

11. Ibid., transaction no. 981 (17 December 1751).

12. Ibid., transaction no. 2381 (14 January 1756).

13. Coquery, "Fashion, Business, Diffusion," table 4.2 and 72–74.

14. Pierre Verlet, *La maison du XVIIIe siècle en France: Société, décoration, mobilier* (Paris: Baschet, 1966), 193. See also Louis-Sébastien Mercier, *Tableau de Paris*, ed. Jean-Claude Bonnet (Paris: Mercure de France, 1994), chap. 324: "Légères observations," 1:855.

15. *Livre-journal de Lazare Duvaux*, transaction no. 1068 (11 March 1752).

16. Ibid., transaction no. 1972 (5 December 1754); no. 1979 (18 December 1754); no. 2045 (16 January 1755); no. 2051 (19 January 1755).

17. On chairs, see Pardailhé-Galabrun, *Birth of Intimacy*, 100–5. As Daniel Roche has put it: "The eighteenth century was the century of the seat." *A History of Everyday Things: The Birth of Consumption in France, 1600–1800*, trans. Brian Pearce (Cambridge: Cambridge University Press), 188–90.

18. Inventory in Verlet, *La maison du XVIIIe siècle*, 245–46. On cooks, see Sean Takats, "Domestic Expertise: Literacy and Numeracy in the Eighteenth-Century Kitchen," *Proceedings of the Western Society for French History* 32 (2004): 46–64. http://hdl.handle.net/2027/spo .0642292.0032.004.

19. Verlet, *La maison du XVIIIe siècle*, 246.

20. Ibid.

21. Jacques-François Blondel, *De la Distribution des maisons de plaisance, et de la decoration des edifices en general* (Paris, 1737; rpt. Farnborough, UK: Gregg Press, 1967), 1:48.

22. Mercier, *Tableau de Paris*, chap. 165: "Architecture," 1:389–90; see also chap. 89: "Ameublements" ("The magnificence of the nation is entirely in the interior of houses"), 1:228; and chap. 324: "Légères observations," 1:855–56.

23. See Roubo, *Art du menuisier*, 720. On these new values, see Philippe Perrot, "De l'apparat au bien-être: Les avatars d'un superflu nécessaire," in *Du luxe au confort*, ed. J.-P. Goubert (Paris: Belin, 1988), 31–49; Michael Kwass, "Big Hair: A Wig History of Consumption in Eighteenth-Century France," *American Historical Review* 111 (Summer 2006): 631–59; and in England and America, John E. Crowley, *The Invention of Comfort: Sensibilities and Design in Early Modern Britain and Early America* (Baltimore: Johns Hopkins University Press, 2001).

24. Pierre Verlet, *French Furniture of the Eighteenth Century*, trans. Penelope Hunter-Stiebel (Charlottesville: University Press of Virginia, 1991), 11–12. On the distribution of interior space, see Jacques-François Blondel, *L'Homme du monde éclairé par les arts* (Paris [Amsterdam?], 1774; rpt. Geneva: Minkoff, 1973), 38–40.

25. Mimi Hellman, "Furniture, Sociability, and the Work of Leisure in Eighteenth-Century France," *Eighteenth-Century Studies* 32 (Summer 1999): 415–45.

26. Pierre Devinoy, *Le meuble léger en France* (Paris: Paul Hartmann, 1952), 25.

27. John Whitehead, *The French Interior in the Eighteenth Century* (New York: Dutton Studio, 1993), 135.

28. On the theory of gender as performance, see Judith Butler, *Gender Trouble* (New York: Routledge, 1999).

29. Devinoy, *Meuble léger*, 18–19; Verlet, *La maison du XVIIIe siècle*, 162–64, 193–94.

30. The daybooks record several sales of inkstands (usually of cedar, sometimes of tulipwood) to be fitted into the drawer of a table, or just of the silver pots that went into a drawer already fitted with the wooden box. *Livre-journal de Lazare Duvaux*, transaction no. 854 (13 July 1751); no. 884 (10 August 1751); no. 886 (18 August 1751); no. 921 (10 October 1751); no. 981 (17 December 1751); no. 2245 (1 October 1755); no. 2766 (14 April 1757); no. 3188 (26 July 1758).

31. Whitehead, *French Interior*, 126–27, 130.

32. *Encyclopédie méthodique, ou par ordre de matières*, 27: *Arts et métiers mécaniques* [by Jacques Lacombe] (Paris, 1782–91), 301–2; Michael Stürmer, "'Bois des Indes' and the Economics of Luxury Furniture in the Time of David Roentgen," *Burlington Magazine* 120 (December 1978): 800–801.

33. *Dictionnaire du citoyen, ou abregé historique, theorique et pratique du commerce* (Amsterdam, 1762), 1:viii.

34. Alexandre Pradère, *French Furniture Makers: The Art of the Ébéniste from Louis XIV to the Revolution*, trans. Perran Wood (Malibu, CA: J. Paul Getty Museum, 1989), 431. The price of mahogany only came down low enough to bring it into general use in 1770. Stürmer, "'Bois des Indes,'" 800. On mahogany, see also Madeleine Dobie, "Orientalism, Colonialism, and Furniture in Eighteenth-Century France," in *Furnishing the Eighteenth Century*, 13–36.

35. See Pradère, *French Furniture Makers*, 24; Carolyn Sargentson, *Merchants and Luxury Markets: The Marchands Merciers of Eighteenth-Century Paris* (London: Victoria and Albert Museum with the J. Paul Getty Museum, 1996), 25; Whitehead, *French Interior*, 130.

36. Pradère, *French Furniture Makers*, 24–25.

37. Abbé [Pierre] Jaubert, *Dictionnaire raisonné universel des arts et metiers* (Paris, 1773), 3:112; Reed Benhamou, "Furniture Production in 18th-Century France: An Interactive Process," *European Studies Journal* 1 (1984): 46.

38. *L'Avantcoureur, Feuille Hebdomadaire, où sont annoncés les objets particuliers des Sciences, de la Littérature, des arts, des Métiers, de l'Industrie, des Spectacles, & les Nouveautés en tout genre* 28 (13 July 1772).

39. Stürmer, "'Bois des Indes,'" 802; Jaubert, *Dictionnaire raisonné*, 2:88–89, 3:112; Benhamou, "Furniture Production," 46. On color innovation, see Sarah Lowengard, "Colours and Colour Making in the Eighteenth Century," in *Consumers and Luxury: Consumer Culture in Europe 1650–1850*, ed. Maxine Berg and Helen Clifford (Manchester, UK: Manchester University Press, 1999), 103–17.

40. Stürmer, "'Bois des Indes,'" 800–801.

41. For biographical sketches of all the major cabinetmakers, see Pradère, *French Furniture Makers*.

42. Raymonde Monnier, *Le Faubourg Saint Antoine, 1789–1817* (Paris: Société des Études Robespierristes, 1981), 35–47; Steven Kaplan, "Les Corporations, les 'faux ouvriers' et le faubourg Saint-Antoine au XVIIIe siècle," *Annales ESC* (March–April 1988): 353–78.

43. *Almanach parisien en faveur des étrangers et des personnes curieuses* (Paris, 1776), 176; *Almanach du dauphin, ou tableau du vrai mérite des artistes célèbres & d'indication générale, des principaux marchands, négocians, artistes & fabricans du six corps…* (Paris, 1776).

44. Mercier, *Tableau de Paris*, chap. 737: "Faubourg Saint-Antoine," 2:689.

45. Ibid., chap. 733: "Tapissiers," 2:678.

46. Alain Thillay, "La liberté du travail au faubourg Saint-Antoine à l'épreuve des saisies des jurandes parisiennes (1642–1778)," *Revue d'Histoire Moderne et Contemporaine* 44 (October–December 1997): 634–49; Daniel Roche, *France in the Enlightenment*, trans. Arthur Goldhammer (Cambridge: Harvard University Press, 1998), 147–49.

47. The following is based on Anne Droguet, *Nicolas Petit, 1732–1791* (Paris: Éditions de l'Amateur, 2001).

48. Ibid., 37.

49. Ibid., 94. On actresses and courtesans as both consumers and tastemakers, see Kathryn Norberg, "Goddesses of Taste: Courtesans and Their Furniture in Late-Eighteenth-Century Paris," in *Furnishing the Eighteenth Century*, 97–114.

50. Droguet, *Nicolas Petit*, 100, 102.

51. Isabelle Néto, *Catalogue des collections du Musée Cognacq-Jay: Le Mobilier* (Paris: Éditions des musées de la ville de Paris, 2001), 64–65; Rosemarie Stratmann-Döhler, *Jean-François Oeben, 1721–1763* (Paris: Éditions de l'Amateur, 2002), 129; Zelda Eglerm et al., "L'Orient et la mode en Europe au temps des Lumières," in *Modes en miroir: La France et la Hollande au temps des Lumières*, exhibition catalog from *Musée Galliera* (Paris: Paris-Musées, 2005), 62–67.

52. Whitehead, *French Interior*, 188.

53. Michael Sonenscher, *Work and Wages: Natural Law, Politics and the Eighteenth-Century French Trades* (Cambridge: Cambridge University Press, 1989); Maxine Berg, "New Commodities, Luxuries and their Consumers in Eighteenth-Century England," in *Consumers and Luxury*, 78–79.

54. Sargentson, *Merchants and Luxury Markets*, 74.

55. Ibid., 48–49. Both the Metropolitan Museum of Art and the J. Paul Getty Museum have substantial collections of porcelain-mounted furniture. Inkstands in this style can be found at Waddesdon Manor, in the Wallace Collection, and at the Wadsworth Atheneum in Hartford, Connecticut. On sets, and matched porcelain in particular, see Mimi Hellman, "The Joy of Sets: The Uses of Seriality in the French Interior," in *Furnishing the Eighteenth Century*, 129–54.

56. Pradère, *French Furniture Makers*, 343.

57. Roubo, *Art du menuisier*, 720–41.

58. Verlet, *La maison du XVIIIe siècle*, 194–95.

59. Ibid., 193.

60. The eleven known examples are in the following collections: Nissim de Camondo (Paris); Waddesdon Manor, UK (2); Duke of Buccleuch (Boughton House, UK); Bowes Museum (Durham, UK); Metropolitan Museum of Art (4); Huntington Library (San Marino, CA) (2). One is known to have been sold to Mme du Barry in 1768 and another to the comtesse d'Artois. See Sargentson, *Merchants and Luxury Markets*, 49 and n.; Nadine Gasc and Gérard Mabille, *Le Musée Nissim de Camondo* (Paris: Albin Michel, 1991), 39.

61. Néto, *Catalogue des collections/Musée Cognac-Jay*, Inv. J384.

62. Geneviève Souchal, *French Eighteenth-Century Furniture*, trans. Simon Watson-Taylor (New York: G. P. Putnam's Sons, 1961), 67; Pradère, *French Furniture Makers*, 39–40; Whitehead, *French Interior*, 135; Verlet, *La maison du XVIIIe siècle*, 204–5; see also Havard, *Dictionnaire de l'ameublement*, 1:352–53.

63. http://www.vam.ac.uk/collections/index.html (28 December 2007).

64. Roubo, *Art du menuisier*, 739–40.

65. *Livre-journal de Lazare Duvaux*, transaction no. 854 (13 July 1751); no. 2766 (14 April 1757).

66. Néto, *Catalogue des collections/Musée Cognac-Jay*, Inv. J372.

67. *Encyclopédie méthodique*, 29:698. The *Dictionnaire de l'Académie française* defined the *bureau* similarly throughout the eighteenth century, but in the 1798 edition added letter writing to the usage: "*Bureau*, is also a type of table with several drawers and writing slides where papers are kept, and on which one writes. I have put some papers in my *bureau*. I sat down at my *bureau* to write a letter."

68. [Nicolas] Le Camus de Mézières, *Le Génie de l'architecture, ou l'analogie de cet art avec nos sensations* (Paris, 1780), 156–70.

69. Gilian Wilson, Adrian Sassoon, and Charissa Bremer-David, "Acquisitions Made by the Department of Decorative Arts in 1983," *The J. Paul Getty Museum Journal* 12 (1984): 201–7. An identical piece mounted with lacquer panels is in the Victoria and Albert Museum (1049–1882), and a 1786 inventory of the royal château de Bellevue includes a description of a desk of about the same size, mounted with lacquer panels, in the cabinet of Madame Victoire. It is now in the Louvre (OA 10419). See Sargentson, *Merchants and Luxury Markets*, 48–49 and color plates 6 and 7; Daniel Al-couffe, Anne Dion-Tenenbaum, and Amaury Lefébure, *Furniture Collections in the Louvre* (Dijon: Editions Faton, 1993), 1:261.

70. On the exceptional woman, see Geneviève

Fraisse, *Reason's Muse: Sexual Difference and the Birth of Democracy*, trans. Jane Marie Todd (Chicago: University of Chicago Press, 1994); Mary D. Sheriff, *The Exceptional Woman: Élisabeth Vigée-Lebrun and the Cultural Politics of Art* (Chicago: University of Chicago Press, 1996); Judith P. Zinsser, *La Dame d'Esprit: A Biography of the Marquise du Châtelet* (New York: Viking, 2006).

71. Mary Sheriff, "Decorating Knowledge: The Ornamental Book, the Philosophic Image and the Naked Truth," *Art History* 28 (April 2005): 152, 171. For a recent but positive discussion of this theme, see Elise Goodman, *The Portraits of Madame de Pompadour: Celebrating the Femme Savante* (Berkeley: University of California Press, 2000).

72. Pradère, *French Furniture Makers*, 192.

73. Eva Lajer-Burcharth elaborates the erotic reading of this portrait through explicit comparison to Schall's *The Beloved Portrait* (fig. 1.11). "Pompadour's Touch: Difference in Representation," *Representations* 73 (Winter 2001): 60–64.

74. Pierre de Nolhac (1859–1936), elected to the Académie française in 1922; quoted in Jean Leymarie, *The Spirit of the Letter in Painting*, trans. James Emmons (n.p.: Hallmark Cards and Albert Skira, 1961), 64.

75. *Mémoires inédits de Madame la Comtesse de Genlis, sur le dix-huitième siècle et la révolution françoise, depuis 1756 jusqu'à nos jours* (Paris: Ladvocat, 1825), 3:91–93. Genlis fictionalized this anecdote in *Adèle et Théodore*, in which a male character remarks on entering a lady's cabinet: "The first thing that struck me in placing my foot in the cabinet was a bureau covered with papers and books. What, I said, a bureau in a woman's room, and in Madame de Surville's!" Stéphanie-Félicité du Crest de Genlis, *Adèle et Théodore ou lettres sur l'éducation*, ed. Isabelle Brouard-Arends (Rennes: Presses Universitaires de Rennes, 2006), 161.

76. Dena Goodman, "Le spectateur intérieur: Les journaux de Suzanne Necker," trans. Marie Malo, *Littérales* 17 (1995): 91–100; "Suzanne Necker's *Mélanges*: Gender, Writing, and Publicity," in *Going Public: Women and Publishing in Early Modern France*, ed. Elizabeth C. Goldsmith and Dena Goodman (Ithaca: Cornell University Press, 1995), 210–23; Nadine Bérenguier, "Lettres de Suzanne Necker à Antoine Thomas," in *Lettres de femmes: Textes inédits et oubliés du XVIe au XVIIIe siècle*, ed. Elizabeth C. Goldsmith and Colette Winn (Paris: Champion, 2005), 339–77.

77. Albertine Necker de Saussure, "Notice sur le caractère et les écrits de Madame de Staël," in Germaine de Staël-Holstein, *Oeuvres posthumes* (Geneva: Slatkine, 1967), 3:47.

78. Roubo, *Art du menuisier*, 3:720.

79. My database includes pieces identified as *secrétaires* (either *de pente, en abattant, armoire,* or *à cylindre*) from the J. Paul Getty Museum (Los Angeles), the Musée

Cognac-Jay (Paris), the Musée Nissim de Camondo (Paris), and the Louvre (Paris), and those documented in Kjellberg, *Le Mobilier français du XVIIIe siècle,* and Stratmann-Döhler, *Jean-François Oeben.*

80. Two typical bureaux plats in the J. Paul Getty Museum (71.DA.96; 67.DA.10) measure 1.81 and 2.02 meters wide, while a rolltop desk by Bernard Molitor in the same museum (67.DA.9), which has writing slides that extend from both sides to accommodate human secretaries, is also 1.81 meters wide.

81. *Livre-journal de Lazare Duvaux,* transaction no. 40 (19 November 1748); no. 70 (16 December 1748); no. 270 (30 July 1749); no. 692 (26 December 1750); no. 841 (17 June 1751); no. 886 (18 June 1751); no. 1067 (8 March 1752); no. 1107 (21 April 1752); no. 1238 (26 October 1752); no. 1309 (27 December 1752); no. 1314 (28 December 1752); no. 1972 (15 December 1754); no. 2319 (16 December 1755); no. 2662 (22 December 1756); no. 2729 (19 February 1757). Note how many of these purchases were made during the December gift shopping season.

82. *Dictionnaire de l'Académie française* (1798), "Secrétaire," 551; *Encyclopédie,* "Secrétaire," 14:863.

83. For an example of a scribe who became a writer, see *Pierre Prion, scribe: Mémoires d'un écrivain de campagne au XVIIIe siècle,* ed. Emmanuel Le Roy Ladurie and Orest Ranum (Paris: Gallimard-Julliard, 1985). On the erasure of the secretary from the premodern text, see George Hoffmann, *Montaigne's Career* (New York: Oxford University Press, 1998), 39–62.

84. Roland Barthes, "Variations sur l'écriture," in *Oeuvres complètes,* ed. Éric Marty (Paris: Le Seuil, 2002), 4:293.

85. Lesley Smith, "Scriba Femina: Medieval Depictions of Women Writing," in *Women and the Book: Assessing the Visual Evidence,* ed. Lesley Smith and Jane H. M. Taylor, (London: British Library and University of Toronto Press, 1997), 21–44.

86. However, as the case of Bellette Dupuy discussed in chapter 2 demonstrates, illiterate women were still dependent on human secretaries to write for them. Elite women also used secretaries when they were too ill to hold a pen or sit at a desk, which was not infrequently, especially when one includes times around childbirth when women were bedridden. See, e.g., Ferdinando Galliani and Louise d'Épinay, *Correspondance,* vol. 1, *1769–1770,* ed. Daniel Maggetti with Georges Dulac (Paris: Desjonquères, 1992), letters from Épinay dated 29 September 1769, 11 December 1769, 29 October [1770]. Salonnières and women of the royal court also employed secretaries to handle the volume of correspondence in which they engaged as patrons and political players.

87. *Dictionnaire de l'Académie française* (1694; 1762), s.v. "Bureau"; *Encyclopédie,* 2:466.

88. Jürgen Habermas, *The Structural Transformation of*

the *Public Sphere: Inquiry into a Category of Bourgeois Society,* trans. Thomas Burger with Frederick Lawrence (Cambridge: MIT Press, 1989), 17–18.

89. [Louis de Rouvroy, duc de] Saint-Simon, *Mémoires (1691–1701),* ed. Yves Coirault (Paris: Gallimard, 1983), 1:803–4.

90. A "secretaire des dames et messieurs," included in *Le Bijou des dames, Nouveau Costume français: et de la connoisance des diamans, des perles et des parfums les plus précieux; avec tablettes economiques perte et gain; ou Almanach de la toilette et de la coeffure des dames françoises et romaines* (Paris, [1779]), is described as a "faithful and discreet depository, and with a dual use; useful and necessary to Men of Affairs, Businessmen, Travelers, Officers, and those of all stations," in which can be recorded "Losses and Gains, Visits to make, the weekly Agenda, Meetings, Thoughts, Bon mots, stray thoughts—such as Epigrams, Madrigals, conversational witticisms, sallies, addresses, etc."

91. Denis Diderot to Sophie Volland, 8 October 1759, in Diderot, *Correspondance,* ed. Georges Roth (Paris: Minuit, 1955–70), 2:267–68.

92. Diderot to Voland, [5 September 1762], in Diderot, *Correspondance,* 4:136–40.

93. Michel-Jean Sedaine, *Le Philosophe sans le savoir* (Paris, 1766), 3.

94. Mark Ledbury, "Intimate Dramas: Genre Painting and the New Theater in Eighteenth-Century France," in *Intimate Encounters: Love and Domesticity in Eighteenth-Century France,* ed. Richard Rand with Juliette M. Bianco (Princeton: Princeton University Press, 1997), 60–61.

95. Robert Garapon, introduction to Michel-Jean Sedaine, *Le philosophe sans le savoir* (Paris: STFM, 1990), xi; Mark Ledbury, *Sedaine, Greuze and the Boundaries of Genre* (Oxford: Voltaire Foundation, 2000), 102–23. On the *drame,* see Sarah Maza, *The Myth of the French Bourgeoisie: An Essay on the Social Imaginary 1750–1850* (Cambridge: Harvard University Press, 2003), 61–67.

96. See Carolyn Sargentson, "Looking at Furniture Inside Out: Strategies of Secrecy and Security in Eighteenth-Century French Furniture," in *Furnishing the Eighteenth Century,* 205–36.

97. Jean-Baptiste Louvet de Couvray, *Une année de la vie du chevalier de Faublas* (London and Paris, 1787), 533.

98. Joseph-Marie Loaisel de Tréogate, *Ainsi finissent les grandes passions, ou les dernières amours du chevalier de . . .* (Paris, 1788), 216.

99. Ulrich Leben, *Molitor: Ébéniste from the Ancien Régime to the Bourbon Restoration,* trans. William Wheeler (London: Philip Wilson, 1992), 19. When Parisians had a bit of money saved, they tended to buy precisely these sorts of valuables, which could be pawned if necessary and redeemed later, if possible. See Laurence Fontaine, "The Circulation of Luxury Goods in Eighteenth-Century Paris: Social Redistribution and

an Alternative Currency," in *Luxury in the Eighteenth Century: Debates, Desires and Delectable Goods,* ed. Maxine Berg and Elizabeth Eger (Basingstoke, UK: Palgrave Macmillan, 2003), 99.

100. Mercier, *Tableau de Paris,* chap. 859: "Serrurerie," 2:1055. Note the similarity to the sealed letter, whose privacy and integrity were protected from violation only by a thin bit of wax. See Antoine-Joseph-Michel de Servan, "Commentaire sur un passage du livre de M. Necker, ou éclaircissements demandés à messieurs les commis des postes, préposés à décacheter les lettres" (1784), in *Oeuvres choisies de Servan,* ed. X. de Portets (Paris: Didot, 1822), 2:461–509, and my discussion in "Epistolary Property: Michel de Servan and the Plight of Letters on the Eve of the French Revolution," in *Early Modern Conceptions of Property,* ed. John Brewer and Susan Staves (London: Routledge, 1995), 339–64.

101. Antoine-Joseph-Michel de Servan, "Réflexions sur la publication des lettres de Rousseau; et des lettres en général," in *Oeuvres choisies,* 2:407–58, and my discussion in "Epistolary Property," 339–64.

102. Henry René d'Allemagne, *Les Accessoires du costume et du mobilier depuis le treizième jusqu'au milieu du dixneuvième siècle* (Paris: Schemit, 1928), 1:75.

103. [Louise-Florence Pétronille Tardieu d'Esclavelles, marquise d'Épinay], *Histoire de Madame de Montbrillant* (1770), ed. Georges Roth (Paris: Gallimard, 1951), 1:258–59, 263.

104. Ranum, "Refuges of Intimacy," 228.

105. Ruth Plaut Weinreb, *Eagle in a Gauze Cage: Louise d'Épinay, Femme de Lettres* (New York: AMS Press, 1993), 63.

106. Ranum, "Refuges of Intimacy," 207–63.

107. Épinay, *Histoire,* 2:469.

108. Ibid. The character of Mme de Ménil was based on Épinay's sister-in-law, who died in November 1752. See editor's note 1, 2:467.

109. Genlis, *Mémoires,* 3:331.

110. Pierre-Ambroise-François Choderlos de Laclos, *Les Liaisons dangereuses* (Paris: Librairie Générale Française, 1972), 9–10.

111. Edmond Guiraud, *Le Bonheur du jour,* first performed at the Odéon in 1926 and published by him the following year, when it was also made into a silent film directed by Gaston Ravel; José Cabanis, *Le Bonheur du jour* (Paris: Gallimard, 1960); Jean de La Varende, "Le Bonheur-du-jour," in *L'objet aimé* (Paris: Plon, 1967), 25–48; Jacques Almira, "Le Bonheur-du-jour," in *Le marchand d'oublies* (Paris: Gallimard, 1979), 121–71.

7. Coming of Age

1. See, e.g., Julia V. Douthwaite, *Exotic Women: Literary Heroines and Cultural Strategies in Old Regime France* (Philadelphia: University of Pennsylvania Press, 1992), 74–139.

2. Pierre Carlet de Chamblain de Marivaux, *La Vie de Marianne ou, Les aventures de madame la comtesse de* *** (Paris: Julliard, 1965), 23. On the role of reflection in the epistolary novel, see Dena Goodman, "Towards a Critical Vocabulary for Interpretive Fictions of the Eighteenth Century," *Kentucky Romance Quarterly* 31 (1984): 259–68.

3. Joan DeJean, introduction to Françoise de Graffigny, *Letters from a Peruvian Woman*, trans. David Kornacker (New York: Modern Languages Association, 1993), xv. Montpensier quoted in Faith E. Beasley, *Revising Memory: Women's Fiction and Memoirs in Seventeenth-Century France* (New Brunswick, NJ: Rutgers University Press, 1990), 81

4. Graffigny, *Letters from a Peruvian Woman*, 4.

5. Ibid., 17.

6. Ibid., 173.

7. Ibid., 13.

8. Ibid., 79.

9. Ibid., 73–74.

10. Ibid., 80.

11. Ibid., 80–81.

12. Ibid., 170.

13. Ibid. (my translation). On the disappointment of eighteenth-century readers with the ending and their attempts to rewrite it, see Elizabeth J. MacArthur, "Devious Narratives: Refusal of Closure in Two Eighteenth-Century Epistolary Novels," *Eighteenth-Century Studies* 21 (Autumn 1987): 8–10.

14. Graffigny, *Letters from a Peruvian Woman*, 119.

15. Ibid., 121–23.

16. Ibid., 157.

17. Ibid., 51.

18. Walter J. Ong, *Orality and Literacy: The Technologizing of the Word* (London: Methuen, 1982), 105.

19. The high nobility deserted the Marais in the eighteenth century. Natacha Coquery, *L'hôtel aristocratique: Le marché du luxe à Paris au XVIIIe siècle* (Paris: Publications de la Sorbonne, 1998), 191; also Mathieu Marraud, *La noblesse de Paris au XVIIIe siècle* (Paris: Le Seuil, 2000). On the distinctions among the nobility in the eighteenth century, see Guy Chaussinand-Nogaret, *The French Nobility in the Eighteenth Century: From Feudalism to Enlightenment*, trans. William Doyle (Cambridge: Cambridge University Press, 1985).

20. See Geneviève Randon de Malboissière to Adélaïde Méliand, 21 October [1763]; 5 November [1763]; 25 December 1763.

21. A letter that Luppé dates early November 1765 bears the watermark of the Dutch firm, "D & C Blauw."

22. See, e.g., Malboissière to Méliand, 2 May [1765] and 15 May 1765; see also Martine Sonnet, "Le savoir d'une demoiselle de qualité: Geneviève Randon de Malboissière (1746–1766)," *Memorie della Academia delle Scienze di Torino*, 2, *Classe di scienze morali, storiche e filologiche* 24 (2000): 179.

23. Malboissière to Méliand, 27 February [17]64; 14 May [1765].

24. See, e.g., Malboissière to Méliand, 11 August 1765. For Geneviève's other writings, see "Bibliographie des oeuvres de Geneviève de Malboissière," in *Une jeune fille au XVIIIe siècle: Lettres de Geneviève de Malboissière à Adélaïde Méliand 1761–1766*, ed. Comte [Albert Marie Pierre] de Luppé (Paris: Champion, 1925), 347–48.

25. Malboissière to Méliand, 17 November 1763; 19 January 1764; 5 April 1764.

26. Malboissière to Méliand, 30 September 1765; 22 August 1765. On the *toilette* as social practice, see Mimi Hellman, "Furniture, Sociability, and the Work of Leisure in Eighteenth-Century France," *Eighteenth-Century Studies* 32 (Summer 1999): 427; and Carolyn Sargentson, "Looking at Furniture Inside Out: Strategies of Secrecy and Security in Eighteenth-Century French Furniture," in *Furnishing the Eighteenth Century: What Furniture Can Tell Us about the European and American Past*, ed. Dena Goodman and Kathryn Norberg (New York: Routledge, 2006), 223–25.

27. Malboissière to Méliand, [26 August 1762].

28. Malboissière to Méliand, 23 September 1765.

29. Malboissière to Méliand, 16 April 1764; 28 July 1764. On the importance of exchanging objects in constructing friendship and intimacy, see Orest Ranum, "Refuges of Intimacy," in *A History of Private Life*, vol. 3, *Passions of the Renaissance*, ed. Roger Chartier, trans. Arthur Goldhammer (Cambridge: Harvard University Press), 246–52; and Susan M. Stabile, *Memory's Daughters: The Material Culture of Remembrance in Eighteenth-Century America* (Ithaca: Cornell University Press, 2004), 149–50.

30. Malboissière to Méliand, 2 June [1764]; 6 [5] December 1765.

31. E.g., Malboissière to Méliand, [26 August 1762]; 30 December [1763]; 17 May [1765].

32. Malboissière to Méliand, 16 May 1764; Roger Chartier, "The Practical Impact of Writing," in *Passions of the Renaissance*, 134. For the range of Geneviève's reading, see the index of works cited in *Une jeune fille au XVIIIe siècle*, and Martine Sonnet, "Geneviève Randon de Malboissière et ses livres: Lectures et sociabilité culturelle féminines dans le Paris des Lumières," in *Lectrices d'Ancien Régime*, ed. Isabelle Brouard-Arends (Rennes: Presses Universitaires de Rennes, 2003), 131–42. Annik Pardailhé-Galabrun found books in only 51% of the Parisian households she studied for the period 1750–90. Of these 75% possessed fewer than one hundred volumes. *The Birth of Intimacy: Privacy and Domestic Life in Early Modern Paris*, trans. Jocelyn Phelps (Philadelphia: University of Pennsylvania Press, 1991), 175, 185.

33. E.g., Malboissière to Méliand, 21 October [1763]; 11 November [1763]; 14 January 1764.

34. Malboissière to Méliand, 17 November 1763. On the salon, see Dena Goodman, *The Republic of Letters: A Cultural History of the French Enlightenment* (Ithaca: Cornell University Press, 1994), 136–52.

35. Malboissière to Méliand, 13 June 1764.

36. Malboissière to Méliand, 19 January [1764].

37. Malboissière to Méliand, 13 April 1764.

38. Malboissière to Méliand, 8 June [1764].

39. Malboissière to Méliand, 13 June 1764.

40. Malboissière to Méliand, 23 July 1764.

41. Malboissière to Méliand, 6 [September] 1764.

42. On the mirror as a modern furnishing, see Sabine Melchior-Bonnet, *The Mirror: A History*, trans. Katherine H. Jewett (New York: Routledge, 2001), 81; Pardailhé-Galabrun, *Birth of Intimacy*, 164–67, 170–73.

43. Malboissière to Méliand, 25 September 1764.

44. Malboissière to Méliand, 3 October 1764.

45. Malboissière to Méliand, 9 October 1764; 15 October 1764.

46. Malboissière to Méliand, 23 September 1765.

47. Malboissière to Méliand, 11 July 1764.

48. *Journal Encyclopédique*, 1 July 1764, 164–65, quoted in *Une jeune fille au XVIIIe siècle*, 119, n. 1.

49. Malboissière to Méliand, 24 July 1764.

50. Sue Peabody, *"There Are No Slaves in France": The Political Culture of Race and Slavery in the Ancien Régime* (New York: Oxford University Press, 1996).

51. Aphra Behn, *Les Avantures curieuses et intéressantes d'Oronoko, prince afriquain*, trans. P. A. de La Place (The Hague, 1755–56).

52. Aphra Behn, *Oroonoko, or, The Royal Slave. A True History* (London, 1688), 2. La Place reminds the reader of this conceit in his preface to the French translation.

53. Malboissière to Méliand, 11 August 1765; 1 September [17]65; Graffigny, *Letters from a Peruvian Woman*, 49.

54. See, e.g., Malboissière to Méliand, 22–23 October 1764. Like other eighteenth-century letter writers, Geneviève and Adèle also counted on friends and relatives to deliver letters, especially when one of them was away from Paris. See, e.g., 19 September 1764. In Paris Geneviève also used Adèle's services to write to Lucenay, presumably to hide her correspondence with him from her mother. See, e.g., letter of 25 October 1764.

55. On the emancipatory potential of writing, see Chartier, "Practical Impact of Writing," 116–17; Jean Marie Goulemot, "Tensions et contradictions de l'intime dans la pratique des Lumières," *Littérales* 17 (1995): 13–14; and Brigitte Diaz, "L'épistolaire et la connivence féminine: Lettres de Manon Phlipon aux soeurs Cannet (1767–1780)," in *La Lettre au XVIIIe siècle et ses avatars*, ed. Georges Bérubé and Marie-France Silver (Toronto: Le Gref, 1996), esp. 142, 144, 150.

56. Marie-Jeanne Roland, *Mémoires de Madame Roland*, ed. Paul de Roux (Paris: Mercure de France, 1986), 233.

57. In her memoirs Mme Roland claimed that she had written to Sophie "every week, more often twice a week." Roland, *Mémoires*, 248. While it is of course possible that all those letters are lost, it seems more likely that she is remembering the peak of her writing activity (although no doubt there are lost letters as well).

58. Marie-Jeanne Phlipon to Sophie Cannet, 18 October [1770].

59. Phlipon to Cannet, 15 March 1775.

60. Phlipon to Cannet, 3 June 1775; 13 July 1773.

61. Phlipon to Cannet, 16 November 1777.

62. Phlipon to Cannet, 31 March [1775].

63. Roland, *Mémoires*, 248.

64. Phlipon to Cannet, 14 October 1775. Manon's mother had died suddenly on 7 June, after the visit was already planned and only weeks before it took place.

65. Phlipon to Cannet, 5 February 1776. On intimate space and memory, see Ranum, "Refuges of Intimacy," 207; Stabile, *Memory's Daughters*, esp. chap. 1: "The Architecture of Memory."

66. Phlipon to Cannet, 20 December 1771; 17 March 1774.

67. Phlipon to Cannet, [February 1774]; 24 July 1774.

68. Phlipon to Cannet, 8 May 1772.

69. E.g., Phlipon to Cannet, 11 January 1776.

70. Phlipon to Cannet, 24 or 25 February 1772.

71. Phlipon to Cannet, 13 February 1773.

72. Phlipon to Cannet, 23 April 1773.

73. Phlipon to Cannet, 13 February 1773.

74. Phlipon to Cannet, 15–17 May 1775. The poet is Nicolas-Germain Léonard (1744–93), born in Guadeloupe. He published *Idylles morales* in 1766.

75. Phlipon to Cannet, 11 January 1776.

76. Phlipon to Cannet, 3 April 1773; Roland, *Mémoires*, 320.

77. [Cornelius] de Pauw, *Recherches philosophiques sur les Américains; ou Mémoires intéressants pour servir à l'histoire de l'espèce humaine* (Berlin, 1768–69).

78. Phlipon to Sophie and Henriette Cannet, 20 August 1776.

79. Phlipon to Sophie Cannet, 1 September 1776.

80. Phlipon to Sophie and Henriette Cannet, 21 June 1777.

81. Michel de Certeau, *The Practice of Everyday Life*, trans. Steven Rendall (Berkeley: University of California Press, 1984), 174.

82. Phlipon to Sophie Cannet, 25 January 1772.

83. On diary keeping among adolescent girls, see Carroll Smith-Rosenberg, "The Female World of Love and Ritual: Relations between Women in Nineteenth-Century America," in *Disorderly Conduct: Visions of Gender*

in *Victorian America* (Oxford: Oxford University Press, 1985), 53–76; Philippe Lejeune's intervention in the discussion following Béatrice Didier, "Pour une sociologie du journal intime," in *Le journal intime et ses formes littéraires*, ed. V[ictor] del Litto, (Geneva: Droz, 1978), 272; Anne-Vincent Buffault, "L'adolescence inventée," in *L'exercice de l'amitié: Pour une histoire des pratiques amicales aux XVIIIe et XIXe siècles* (Paris: Le Seuil, 1995), 135–82. On the role of the confidante, see Janet Gurkin Altman, *Epistolarity: Approaches to a Form* (Columbus: Ohio State University Press, 1982). Marie-Claire Grassi finds that confidences began to appear in French letters around 1760—around the same time that Rousseau published *Julie*. Grassi, *L'art de la lettre au temps de "La nouvelle Héloïse" et du Romantisme* (Geneva: Slatkine, 1994), 73.

84. In her memoirs Mme Roland maintained that she would leave the finished letter on her desk for a day, unsealed, for her mother to read, before sending it off. *Mémoires*, 262–63. While this may be true, it is also significant that the memoirs were written under the shadow of the guillotine when Mme Roland both wanted to pass on moral teachings to her own daughter and needed to convince her reader of her own moral transparency as a truth-teller.

85. E.g., Phlipon to Sophie Cannet, 30 May 1774; [July 1774].

86. Phlipon to Sophie Cannet, 11 January 1775.

87. Ibid.

88. Malboissière to Méliand, [September 1762]. Manon Phlipon wrote similarly to Sophie Cannet on 26 November 1771.

89. Malboissière to Méliand, 11 October 1764. Manon Phlipon expressed the same sentiments to Sophie Cannet on 21 April 1775.

90. Malboissière to Méliand, 30 April [1765].

91. Diaz, "L'épistolaire et la connivence féminine," 148.

92. Phlipon to Sophie Cannet, 14 October 1775.

93. Phlipon to Sophie Cannet, 24 July 1774.

94. Phlipon to Sophie Cannet, 5 February 1776; see also 24 July 1774, in which she dreams of inhabiting a male body: "If souls existed before bodies, and if they were allowed to choose those which they would like to inhabit, I assure you that mine would not have chosen a weak and inept sex that often remains useless."

95. Phlipon to Sophie Cannet, 1 July 1777.

8. Epistolary Reasoning

1. Denis Diderot, "Sur les femmes," in *Oeuvres complètes* (Paris: Garnier, 1966), 2:252.

2. Merry E. Wiesner, *Women and Gender in Early Modern Europe*, 2nd ed. (Cambridge: Cambridge University Press, 2000), 75–76.

3. See Lieselotte Steinbrügge, *The Moral Sex: Woman's Nature in the French Enlightenment*, trans. Pamela E. Selwyn (New York: Oxford University Press, 1995); Charles Taylor, *Sources of the Self: The Making of Modern Identity* (Cambridge: Harvard University Press, 1989), 292.

4. Mita Choudhury, *Convents and Nuns in Eighteenth-Century French Politics and Culture* (Ithaca: Cornell University Press, 2004), 132; see also Dena Goodman, "Story-Telling in the Republic of Letters: The Rhetorical Context of Diderot's *La Religieuse*," *Nouvelles de la République des Lettres* 1 (1986): 51–70.

5. Denis Diderot, *La Religieuse* (Paris: Armand Colin, 1961), 89.

6. See Olwen Hufton, "Women without Men: Widows and Spinsters in Britain and France in the Eighteenth Century," *Journal of Family History* 9 (Winter 1984): 355–76; Amy M. Froide, "Marital Status as a Category of Difference: Singlewomen and Widows in Early Modern England," in *Singlewomen in the European Past, 1250–1800*, ed. Judith M. Bennett and Amy M. Froide (Philadelphia: University of Pennsylvania Press, 1999), 236–69.

7. Wiesner, *Women and Gender in Early Modern Europe*, 36–41; Dominique Godineau, *Les femmes dans la société française, 16e–18e siècle* (Paris: Armand Colin, 2003), 20–21.

8. Alain Grosrichard, *Structure du sérail: La fiction du despotisme asiatique dans l'Occident classique* (Paris: Le Seuil, 1979); Madeleine Dobie, *Foreign Bodies: Gender, Language, and Culture in French Orientalism* (Stanford: Stanford University Press, 2001).

9. See Taylor, *Sources of the Self*, 289–90; François Lebrun, *La vie conjugale sous l'Ancien Régime* (Paris: Armand Colin, 1975), 21, 22; James F. Traer, *Marriage and the Family in Eighteenth-Century France* (Ithaca: Cornell University Press, 1980), 15–21, 70–78; André Burguière, *Les formes de la culture* (Paris: Le Seuil, 1993), 90–96; Daniel Roche, *France in the Enlightenment*, trans. Arthur Goldhammer (Cambridge: Harvard University Press, 1998), 519–21; Maurice Daumas, *Le mariage amoureux: Histoire du lien conjugal sous l'Ancien Régime* (Paris: Armand Colin, 2004), 259–91; Godineau, *Femmes dans la société française*, 172–73.

10. Charles Louis de Secondat, baron de Montesquieu, *Lettres persanes*, ed. Paul Vernière (Paris: Garnier, 1975), letter 161.

11. Jean-Jacques Rousseau, *Julie, ou la nouvelle Héloïse* (Paris: Garnier-Flammarion, 1967), 140, 146; translation: *Julie, or the New Heloise: Letters of Two Lovers Who Live in a Small Town at the Foot of the Alps*, trans. Philip Stewart and Jean Vaché (Hanover, NH: University Press of New England, 1997), 164, 171.

12. [Jean Baptiste Poquelin] Molière, *L'École des femmes* (1662), act 5, scene 9.

13. Rousseau, *Julie, or the New Heloise*, 158–59.

14. Several historians have cautioned us to avoid

any simple opposition between "interest and emotion," the individual and the family or community, and "individual choice and social constraint" in our understanding of Old Regime marriage. See Roche, *France in the Enlightenment*, 52; Wiesner, *Women and Gender in Early Modern Europe*, 72; Hans Medick and David Warren Sabean, "Interest and Emotion in Family and Kinship Studies: A Critique of Social History and Anthropology," in *Interest and Emotion: Essays on the Study of Family and Kinship*, ed. Hans Medick and David Warren Sabean (Cambridge: Cambridge University Press, 1984), 11; Christine Adams, "A Choice Not to Wed? Unmarried Women in Eighteenth-Century France," *Journal of Social History* 29 (Summer 1996): 883–94.

15. Isabelle de Charrière, *Lettres de Lausanne et autres récits épistolaires* (Paris: Rivages Poche, 2006), 119.

16. Ibid., 163–64.

17. Ibid., 121.

18. Michel de Certeau, *The Practice of Everyday Life*, trans. Steven Rendall (Berkeley: University of California Press, 1984), 34–39.

19. Katharine Ann Jensen, *Writing Love: Letters, Women, and the Novel in France, 1605–1776* (Carbondale: Southern Illinois University Press, 1995), 3.

20. Ibid., 2–3.

21. Godineau, *Femmes dans la société française*, 50; Hufton, "Women without Men," 357; Adams, "Choice Not to Wed?"

22. Natalie Zemon Davis, "Boundaries and the Sense of Self in Sixteenth-Century France," in *Reconstructing Individualism: Autonomy, Individuality, and the Self in Western Thought*, ed. Thomas C. Heller, Morton Sosna, and David E. Wellbery (Stanford: Stanford University Press, 1986), 53–63, quote 53.

23. Maurice Souriau, *Bernardin de Saint-Pierre d'après ces manuscrits* (Paris: Société Française d'Imprimerie et de Librairie, 1905), 18–19.

24. Lieve Spaas, *Lettres de Catherine de Saint-Pierre à son frère Bernardin* (Paris: L'Harmattan, 1996), 29–63; Souriau, *Bernardin de Saint-Pierre*, 2–8, 83. The typical age of marriage for women at this time was not as young as is commonly thought. At twenty-three Catherine was not an "old maid" but in fact just under the mean age of first marriage for women—twenty-four to twenty-five. Moreover, marriage age tended to be higher for urban women such as Catherine than for rural women. See Godineau, *Femmes dans la société française*, 27.

25. Catherine de Saint-Pierre to Bernardin de Saint-Pierre, 9–10 January 1769, 142 (C68–71).

26. Catherine de Saint-Pierre to Bernardin de Saint-Pierre, 15 December 1783, 142 (B12–14).

27. Catherine de Saint-Pierre to Bernardin de Saint-Pierre, 14 October 1766, 142 (C72–74).

28. Catherine de Saint-Pierre to Bernardin de Saint-Pierre, 15 January 1773, 142 (C19–20).

29. Godineau, *Femmes dans la société française*, 32.

30. Catherine de Saint-Pierre to Bernardin de Saint-Pierre, 11 October 1767, 142 (C51–52).

31. Ibid.

32. Ibid. The following year another glassmaker proposed, but he did not even merit consideration. As Catherine reported to Bernardin: "I have learned that he had debts and that he was looking for a wife who, with her fortune, would put him in a better situation. I assured him that I had as much reason to complain about my fortune as he had, since he brought it up." 9 July 1774, 146 (B59–60).

33. Catherine de Saint-Pierre to Bernardin de Saint-Pierre, 1 May [1786], 142 (B3–5).

34. Ibid. "If he does not leave any children to his wife, he wishes that she have ownership of all that he possesses, goods and furnishings, and, in the case that he does leave any [children], he wishes to recognize in the contract a sum of ten thousand livres more or less proportional to his property in order that the children feel that their mother is responsible for their future."

35. On the practice of bringing slaves to France from the colonies to teach them a trade, see Sue Peabody, *"There Are No Slaves in France": The Political Culture of Race and Slavery in the Ancien Régime* (New York: Oxford University Press, 1996).

36. See, e.g., Catherine de Saint-Pierre to Bernardin de Saint-Pierre, 14 October 1766; Spaas, *Lettres de Catherine de Saint-Pierre*, 31–36; and Souriau, *Bernardin de Saint-Pierre*, 2–9.

37. Catherine de Saint-Pierre to Bernardin de Saint-Pierre, 1 May [1786]. Catherine used this same formulation to describe the "young lady" whom Morin married less than a month later. See Catherine de Saint-Pierre to Bernardin de Saint-Pierre, 26 May 1786, 142 (B6–7).

38. Catherine de Saint-Pierre to Bernardin de Saint-Pierre, 13 April 1788, 142 (A3–5).

39. On the gentlemen glassmakers, see Antoine-Gaspard Boucher d'Argis, "Noblesse verrière," in *Encyclopédie, ou Dictionnaire raisonné des sciences, des arts, et des métiers*, ed. Denis Diderot and Jean Le Rond d'Alembert (Paris, 1751–65), 11:178; and Warren C. Scoville, *Capitalism and French Glassmaking, 1640–1789* (Berkeley: University of California Press, 1950), 83–85. Scoville notes both the poverty and the pride of the gentlemen glassmakers, who "refused to marry their daughters to plebeians," despite the fact that they were "generally scorned by peasants and by other nobles." On the Le Vaillant family, to which Catherine's suitor belonged, see A. Milet, *Histoire d'un four à verre de l'ancienne Normandie* (Paris: A. Aubry, 1871); and O[nésime-Jean] Le Vaillant de La Fieffe, *Les Verreries de la Normandie: Les Gentilshommes et artistes verriers normands* (Rouen, 1873; rpt., Brionne: Le Portulan, 1971).

40. Catherine de Saint-Pierre to Bernardin de Saint-Pierre, 15 January 1773.

41. Ibid.

42. Catherine de Saint-Pierre to Bernardin de Saint-Pierre, 11 October 1767.

43. Pierre Bourdieu, "The Forms of Capital," in *Handbook of Theory and Research in the Sociology of Education*, ed. John G. Richardson (Westport, CT: Greenwood Press, 1986), 249.

44. In 1779 Joseph was arrested for treason in Saint-Domingue and held in the Bastille for several years. Bernardin feared that his brother's actions would hurt his own career, and Catherine was concerned about public opinion in Dieppe when Joseph returned there in 1783, "adding to the trials of my status" and claiming he was "in exile." Worse, "he furnishes material for plenty of gossip to which I am more sensitive than he." Catherine de Saint-Pierre to Bernardin de Saint-Pierre, 15 December 1783, 142 (B12–14). See also Catherine de Saint-Pierre to Bernardin de Saint-Pierre, 16 May 1779, 142 (B95–96), in which she wrote of the disgrace of a cousin who had been captured in Scotland. On this episode, see Souriau, *Bernardin de Saint-Pierre*, 185–98.

45. Catherine de Saint-Pierre to Bernardin de Saint-Pierre, 15 January 1773.

46. Wiesner, *Women and Gender in Early Modern Europe*, 77.

47. Cécile Dauphin, "Histoire d'un stéréotype: La vieille fille," in *Madame ou Mademoiselle? Itinéraires de la solitude féminine, XVIIIe–XXe siècle*, ed. Arlette Farge and Christiane Klapisch-Zuber (Paris: Montalba, 1984), 218. The case of the unmarried Lamothe sisters discussed by Christine Adams in "Choice Not to Wed?" supports the idea that there was no shame in remaining single.

48. Catherine de Saint-Pierre to Bernardin de Saint-Pierre, 19 July 1770, 142 (B17–19).

49. Catherine de Saint-Pierre to Bernardin de Saint-Pierre, 15 January 1773.

50. The practice of taking in adult boarders did not become common until the 1720s, when the convents were facing bankruptcy. Over time, the income from these women became "indispensable to the survival of many houses," and, over the course of the century, rates increased six- or sevenfold in some houses. Elizabeth Rapley, *A Social History of the Cloister: Daily Life in the Teaching Monasteries of the Old Regime* (Montreal: McGill–Queen's University Press, 2001), 252–56.

51. Catherine de Saint-Pierre to Bernardin de Saint-Pierre, 22 October 1767, 142 (C77–78); 4 December 1767, 142 (B57–58). Bernardin did send his sister what he could; in the 1780s he managed to secure royal assistance for her through his connections at court. Catherine discusses these gifts in several letters, e.g.,

Catherine de Saint-Pierre to Bernardin de Saint-Pierre, 20 April 1786, 142 (A49–50); 17 December 1786, 142 (A6–7, A51–52); 11 May 1788, 142 (A66–67).

52. Catherine de Saint-Pierre to Bernardin de Saint-Pierre, 9–10 January 1769, 142 (C68–71).

53. Ibid.

54. Catherine de Saint-Pierre to Bernardin de Saint-Pierre, 4 December 1767; 9–10 January 1769; 19 July 1770.

55. Catherine de Saint-Pierre to Bernardin de Saint-Pierre, 15 January 1773.

56. Catherine de Saint-Pierre to Bernardin de Saint-Pierre, 9–10 January 1769.

57. Catherine de Saint-Pierre to Bernardin de Saint-Pierre, 13 April 1788.

58. Ibid.

59. The pension she had to pay was raised periodically, and the privileges she enjoyed just as frequently diminished. The miseries and indignities of her life there formed one of the major themes that run through her letters. See, e.g., Catherine de Saint-Pierre to Bernardin de Saint-Pierre, 19 July 1770; 6 December 1773, 142 (B47–48); 9 March 1783, 142 (C29–31); 20 April 1786; 26 May 1786; 17 December 1786.

60. Catherine de Saint-Pierre to Bernardin de Saint-Pierre, 13 April 1788.

61. Ibid.

62. Catherine de Saint-Pierre to Bernardin de Saint-Pierre, 4 July 1781, 142 (C5–C6).

63. Catherine de Saint-Pierre to Bernardin de Saint-Pierre, 1 May [1786].

64. Catherine de Saint-Pierre to Bernardin de Saint-Pierre, 13 April 1788.

65. Catherine de Saint-Pierre to Bernardin de Saint-Pierre, 15 January 1773.

66. The glassworks would have been in a neighboring forest, where the supply of wood to feed the furnace was plentiful. It may have been in La Verrerie-du-Hellet, a village about 16 km northwest of Saint-Saire in the Forêt du Hellet, where the old glassworks are now a private residence.

67. Catherine de Saint-Pierre to Bernardin de Saint-Pierre, 15 January 1773.

68. Catherine de Saint-Pierre to Bernardin de Saint-Pierre, 1 May [1786].

69. Catherine de Saint-Pierre to Bernardin de Saint-Pierre, 26 May 1786. Catherine herself had evidence of the riskiness of investing in *pacotille*: "We have had some letters from the eldest Godebout, our cousin. Taken prisoner on his word in Scotland, despoiled of all his property, about 150 livres of his own merchandise, his first try at *pacotille* on his own account on the ship where he is second in command." Catherine de Saint-Pierre to Bernardin de Saint-Pierre, 16 May 1779, 142 (B95–96).

70. Catherine de Saint-Pierre to Bernardin de Saint-Pierre, 26 May 1786. Spaas argues that Catherine's letter expresses not only regrets but resentment. She interprets the fact that Catherine told Bernardin of Morin's marriage to a young woman of good family as Catherine's way of saying that Morin was indeed worthy of her. (*Lettres de Catherine de Saint-Pierre*, 133.) I would suggest that Catherine understood that it was her own lack of fortune that made the marriage impossible, or that would at least have made life in such a marriage very difficult and uncertain.

71. Catherine de Saint-Pierre to Bernardin de Saint-Pierre, 13 April 1788.

72. Ibid.

73. Catherine de Saint-Pierre to Bernardin de Saint-Pierre, 19 March 1773, 142 (B20–21); 17 December 1786.

74. Catherine de Saint-Pierre to Bernardin de Saint-Pierre, 15 January 1773.

75. Catherine de Saint-Pierre to Bernardin de Saint-Pierre, 20 April, 1786.

76. Catherine de Saint-Pierre to Bernardin de Saint-Pierre, 1 May [1786].

77. Catherine de Saint-Pierre to Bernardin de Saint-Pierre, 17 December 1786.

78. Ibid.

79. Catherine de Saint-Pierre to Bernardin de Saint-Pierre, 22 December 1788, 142 (A24–26).

80. Marie-Jeanne Phlipon to Sophie Cannet, 20 October 1776.

81. Phlipon to Cannet, [October] 1771.

82. Phlipon to Cannet, 8 November 1771.

83. Phlipon to Cannet, [October] 1771.

84. Phlipon to Cannet, 8 November 1771.

85. Ibid.

86. Phlipon to Cannet, [February 1774].

87. Phlipon to Cannet, 20 February 1773; see also 11 September 1777.

88. Phlipon to Cannet, [February 1774].

89. Phlipon to Cannet, 31 October 1775; and 25 November 1773. La Blancherie's book was published as *Extrait du Journal de mes voyages, ou histoire d'un jeune homme pour servir d'école aux pères et mères* (Paris, 1775). He went on to found the Salon de la Correspondance, where Adélaïde Labille-Guiard showed her work. See Dena Goodman, *The Republic of Letters: A Cultural History of the French Enlightenment* (Ithaca: Cornell University Press, 1994), 242–80; and Laura Auricchio, "Pahin de la Blancherie's Commercial Cabinet of Curiosity (1779–87)," *Eighteenth-Century Studies* 36 (Winter 2002): 47–61.

90. Phlipon to Cannet, 25 November 1773.

91. Phlipon to Cannet, 30 May 1774.

92. Phlipon to Cannet, 5 January, 1776; 13 January 1776.

93. Phlipon to Cannet, 24 January 1776; 15 April 1776.

94. Phlipon to Cannet, 25 June 1776.

95. Phlipon to Cannet, 22 July 1776.

96. Ibid.

97. Phlipon to Cannet, 22 August 1777. Manon developed these thoughts further on 27 August 1777: "M. C. is very well described by the expression that you use in regards to him: he's good husband material; one could expect peaceful days with him. But it must be admitted that when it comes to his mind, his knowledge, and his capacity to raise children, he does not differ at all from the common class [of men]. However, the goodness of his heart will allow a gentle and reasonable wife to exercise considerable authority over him."

98. Phlipon to Cannet, 24 July 1774.

99. Marie-Jeanne Roland, *Mémoires de Madame Roland*, ed. Paul de Roux (Paris: Mercure de France, 1986), 286–87.

100. See, e.g., Phlipon to Cannet, 1 September 1776; 8 October 1776; 2 August 1777.

101. Phlipon to Cannet, 8 October 1776.

102. Ibid.; 23 May 1777; 7 June 1777; 2 August 1777; 16 December 1777; 1 November 1779.

103. Phlipon to Cannet, 11 January 1776.

104. Philippe Godoÿ, introduction to *Lettres d'amour de Madame Roland* (Paris: Mercure de France, 2003), 12. All letters between Phlipon and Roland are from this edition.

105. Phlipon to Cannet, 1 September 1776.

106. Jean-Marie Roland to Marie-Jeanne Phlipon, 22 and 24 April [1779]; Phlipon to Roland, 24 April [1779].

107. Phlipon to Roland, [27 April 1779].

108. Phlipon to Roland, 19 June [1779].

109. Roland, *Mémoires*, 330–33.

110. Jean-Jacques Rousseau, *Émile ou de l'éducation* (Paris: Garnier-Flammarion, 1966), 525, 529; translation: *Émile: or, On Education*, trans. Allan Bloom (New York: Basic Books, 1979), 400, 404.

111. Ibid., 466; translation, 358.

112. Phlipon to Cannet, 29 August 1777.

113. Phlipon to Cannet, 7 May 1778.

114. Phlipon to Cannet, 13 February 1773.

115. Phlipon to Cannet, 20 February 1773.

116. Manon's first mention of Rousseau in her correspondence with Sophie was in a letter of 11 November 1773. She discussed *Émile* at length on 1 August 1774; she first mentioned *Julie* on 31 August 1775; and by 11 January 1776, she was identifying herself as a partisan of Jean-Jacques and defending him to Roland. There are also extensive extracts from the *Discours sur l'inégalité* and a discussion of suicide in response to a letter in *Julie* in her notebooks from 1775, as well as reflections on her pilgrimage to Montmorency that year. Papiers Roland, Bibliothèque nationale de France, NAF 6244;

mf 6057. On the influence of Rousseau on Mme Roland, see Gita May, *De Jean-Jacques Rousseau à Madame Roland: Essai sur la sensibilité préromantique et révolutionnaire* (Geneva: Droz, 1964); Mary Seidman Trouille, *Sexual Politics in the Enlightenment: Women Writers Read Rousseau* (Albany: State University of New York Press, 1997), 163–92; Suellen Diaconoff, *Through the Reading Glass: Women, Books, and Sex in the French Enlightenment* (Albany: State University of New York Press, 2005), 55–76.

117. Phlipon to Cannet, 20 October 1776.

118. Phlipon to Cannet, 5 February 1776. See also 20 August 1776, in which she dreams of cross-dressing to achieve freedom: "I have sometimes wanted to put on breeches, a hat, in order to have the liberty to seek and to see the best of all the talents. We are told that love and devotion have made some people take up this disguise. I swear to you that if I were a little less rational and if circumstances favored me a little more, I have enough ardor to do as much."

119. Phlipon to Cannet, 23 May 1777; see also, 5 September 1777. Nevertheless, when Sophie had declared her intention to take the veil, Manon did everything in her power to dissuade her (17 May 1776). In 1779 Manon retreated temporarily to the convent where she had studied and met Sophie. As Catherine had at the death of her father, she sought refuge with the women who had continued to care about her since her girlhood, entering not as a novice but a boarder. Like the Ursulines in Honfleur, the Filles de la Congrégation in Paris offered this sort of temporary haven to women they cared for as girls when they had nowhere else to turn. Fortunately, Manon was able both to afford the pension she was asked to pay and to sort out in a couple of months her problems with a marriage she sought. Phlipon to Cannet, 1 November 1779; and 27 January 1780.

120. Phlipon to Cannet, 19 September 1777.

121. See Steinbrügge, *Moral Sex*.

122. Traer, *Marriage and the Family*, 22–47; Roche, *France in the Enlightenment*, 522–24; Suzanne Desan, *The Family on Trial in Revolutionary France* (Berkeley: University of California Press, 2004), 26–28.

123. Jean-Jacques Rousseau, *Du Contrat social*, ed. B. de Jouvenel (Geneva: Bourquin, 1947), 200.

124. Carole Pateman, *The Sexual Contract* (Cambridge: Polity Press, 1988). As Pateman notes, Olympe de Gouges proposed a new form of marriage contract in her 1791 *Déclaration des droits de la femme et de la citoyenne*, but it dealt only with issues of property and inheritance.

125. Diderot, "Sur les femmes," 252.

126. Isabelle de Charrière, *Letters of Mistress Henley Published by Her Friend* (1784), trans. Philip Stewart and Jean Vaché (New York: Modern Language Association of America, 1993), 35.

127. Ibid., 13–15.

128. Ibid., 8–9.

129. Roland, *Mémoires*, 333.

9. Marriage, Motherhood, and the Letter-Writing Woman

1. Geneviève Randon de Malboissière to Adélaïde Méliand, [June 1766].

2. Marie-Jeanne Roland, *Mémoires de Madame Roland*, ed. Paul de Roux (Paris: Mercure de France, 1986), 335. Amanda Vickery has argued that motherhood turned women into poor correspondents because it ate up all their time. Amanda Vickery, *The Gentleman's Daughter: Women's Lives in Georgian England* (New Haven: Yale University Press, 1998), 114. Carroll Smith-Rosenberg, however, argues that the friendships maintained through correspondence remained the central bonds of women's lives through marriage and motherhood. Carroll Smith-Rosenberg, "The Female World of Love and Ritual: Relations between Women in Nineteenth-Century America," in *Disorderly Conduct: Visions of Gender in Victorian America* (New York: Oxford University Press, 1985), 53–76.

3. Marie-Jeanne Roland to Sophie Cannet, 16 February 1780.

4. Anne Vincent-Buffault, *L'exercice de l'amitié: Pour une histoire des pratiques amicales aux XVIIIe et XIXe siècles* (Paris: Le Seuil, 1995), 211.

5. La marquise de la Grange, introduction to *Laurette de Malboissière: lettres d'une jeune fille du temps de Louis XV, 1761–1766* (Paris: Librairie Académique Didier et cie, 1866), i.

6. Entry for January 1766 in marquise de la Grange née Méliand, Livre de comptes: dépenses personnelles (1760–81). Papiers Lelièvre de la Grange, AN 341 AP 18.

7. Bernard de Bonnard to Maurice-Jean de Bonnard, 20 October [1777], in AN 352 AP 40.

8. Bernard de Bonnard to Maurice-Jean de Bonnard, 14 May 1780.

9. Bernard de Bonnard to Maurice-Jean de Bonnard, 9 September 1779.

10. Bernard de Bonnard to Maurice-Jean de Bonnard, 22 July 1780.

11. Ibid.

12. Bernard de Bonnard to Maurice-Jean de Bonnard, 28 July 1780.

13. Bernard de Bonnard to Maurice-Jean de Bonnard, 31 July [1780].

14. Bernard de Bonnard to Maurice-Jean de Bonnard, 3 August [1780].

15. AN 352 AP 30.

16. Bernard de Bonnard to Maurice-Jean de Bonnard, 3 September 1780.

17. Ibid.

18. Ibid.

19. Dominique Julia, "Bernard de Bonnard, Gouverneur des princes d'Orléans et son *Journal d'Education* (1778–1782)," *Mélanges de l'École française de Rome, Italie et Méditerranée* 109 (1997): 461. For Bernard's account, see Bernard de Bonnard to Maurice-Jean de Bonnard, 10 January [1782].

20. Julia, "Bernard de Bonnard," 459.

21. Bernard de Bonnard to Maurice-Jean de Bonnard, 10 January [1782]. In fact, one of Bernard's former charges did grow up to be crowned King Louis-Philippe in 1830. On the scandal and the public reaction, see the articles, pamphlets, and letters to the editor, all attacking Genlis, reprinted in [Dominique-Joseph] Garat, *Précis historique de la vie de M. de Bonnard* (Paris, 1787), 97–139.

22. Copy of baptismal record in AN 352 AP 30; Julia, "Bernard de Bonnard," 464. On 25 July 1781, Bernard noted in his journal that he thanked Chartres for agreeing to name his child. The entry for 9 October 1781, reads, in part: "The son is baptized. It cost me two louis. So, he is now in a state of grace before God. When he is [in that state] before Monseigneur and Madame, they will name him." Bernard de Bonnard, *Journal*, AN 352 AP 4.

23. Julia, "Bernard de Bonnard," 462–63. On Harcourt, see Ernest de Ganay, "Vie du duc d'Harcourt," in François-Henri, duc d'Harcourt, *Traité de la décoration des dehors, des jardins et des parcs*, ed. Ernest de Ganay (Paris: Émile-Paul Frères, 1919).

24. Bernard de Bonnard to Sophie Silvestre, 30 June [1782]. Mme Roland, too, corresponded with her husband when he was engaged in business that took him away from her. During these absences she handled his correspondence, serving in general as his secretary. See *Lettres de Madame Roland*, vol. 1, *1780–1787*, ed. Claude Perroud (Paris: Imprimerie Nationale, 1900).

25. Sophie Silvestre to Bernard de Bonnard, 4 July [1782].

26. Silvestre to Bonnard, 6 July [1782].

27. On the discourse of love in similar letters, see Marie-Claire Grassi, "Quand les épouses parlent d'amour . . ." in *Femmes en toutes lettres: Les épistolières du XVIIIe siècle*, ed. Marie-France Silver and Marie-Laure Girou Swiderski (Oxford: Voltaire Foundation, 2000), 229–41.

28. Silvestre to Bonnard, 30 June 1782.

29. Silvestre to Bonnard, 13 April 1783.

30. Bonnard to Silvestre, 14 April [1783]. Bonnard and Philipon de la Madelaine had been brothers in a Masonic lodge in Besançon in the late 1760s and continued to correspond after Bonnard's departure from that city in 1770. See Julia, "Bernard de Bonnard," 409.

31. Silvestre to Bonnard, 14 April 1783; 16 April 1783.

32. Silvestre to Bonnard, 12 November 1782.

33. Bonnard to Silvestre, 16 November 1782.

34. Ibid.

35. Bonnard to Silvestre, 5 November 1782.

36. Bernard de Bonnard to Maurice-Jean de Bonnard, 6 August [1780].

37. Ibid. Maurice-Jean had married recently and his first child, Achilles, was baptized 18 September 1780, just a week after his brother's marriage. Copy of baptismal record in AN 352 AP 30.

38. Dena Goodman, "From Private *Querelle* to Public *Procès*: The Creation of Public Opinion in the Hume/Rousseau Affair," *Eighteenth-Century Studies* 25 (Winter 1991–92): 171–201.

39. Bonnard, *Journal*, entries for 18–21 May 1781. Sophie not only breastfed both her sons but was enthusiastic when others did likewise. See her letter to Bonnard, 1 November 1782. In a long entry in his journal written sometime shortly after the birth of Bonbon in October 1781, Bernard noted the visit of Sophie's grandmother, "who was so strongly opposed to her breastfeeding her child." Not surprisingly, Mme Roland also breastfed her child, Eudora, who was born just four days before Bonbon, on 4 October 1781. Five weeks later, she visited a friend who had just given birth and was appalled at what she saw. "Good God! How bizarre a new mother seems to me, alone, without child. The poor child sucked her fingers and drank cow's milk in a room far away from her mother while she waited for the mercenary who would nurse her. The father was in a big hurry to get the baptism ceremony over with in order to expedite this little creature off to the village." Marie-Jeanne Phlipon to Jean-Marie Roland, 15 November 1781, in *Lettres de Madame Roland*, 1:53. On her own experience of breastfeeding, see Phlipon to Roland, [18 November 1781], in ibid., 57–58.

40. Bonnard, *Journal*, 30 May through 13 July 1781.

41. Bonnard to Silvestre, 18 April [1783].

42. Silvestre to Bonnard, 21 April 1783.

43. Bonnard to Silvestre, 16 April 1783.

44. Jean-Jacques Rousseau, *Julie, ou la nouvelle Héloïse* (Paris: Garnier-Flammarion, 1967), 352–67; translation: *Julie, or the New Heloise: Letters of Two Lovers Who Live in a Small Town at the Foot of the Alps*, trans. Philip Stewart and Jean Vaché (Hanover, NH: University Press of New England, 1997), 386–401; Betsy G. Fryberger, ed., *The Changing Garden: Four Centuries of European and American Art* (Berkeley: University of California Press for the Iris and B. Gerald Cantor Center for Visual Arts at Stanford University, 2003). In the 1770s, the duc d'Harcourt wrote one of the first treatises on what he called "irregular gardens" and designed the garden at Harcourt according to the principles set out there. The English traveler Arthur Young visited it in 1788 because he had been told that it was "the finest English

garden in France" but found it inferior to Ermenon-ville. Harcourt, *Traité de la décoration des dehors*; Arthur Young, *Travels in France during the Years 1787, 1788, 1789*, ed. M[atilda] Betham-Edwards (London: George Bell and Sons, 1924), 118.

45. Bonnard to Silvestre, 30 June 1782. This was the same letter in which Bernard consoled Sophie for his absence by urging her to embrace letter writing.

46. Bonnard to Silvestre, 2 July [1782].

47. Silvestre to Bonnard, 4 July [1782].

48. Silvestre to Bonnard, 6 July [1782].

49. Bonnard to Silvestre, 16 April 1783; Dominique Julia notes the influence of the Latin poet Horace as well as book 4 of *Émile*. See "Bernard de Bonnard," 463–64 and n. 315.

50. Bonnard to Silvestre, 16 April 1783.

51. See Sarah Maza, *Private Lives and Public Affairs: The Causes Célèbres of Prerevolutionary France* (Berkeley: University of California Press, 1993), esp. 68–111.

52. Bonnard to Silvestre, 16 April 1783.

53. Silvestre to Bonnard, [8 April 1783]. On 13 July 1783, Sophie reported an argument she had just had with her father. He was afraid that when he died she would take her share of the inheritance and sink it all into a piece of property, leaving no income for her children, just debts.

54. Bonnard to Silvestre, 11 June 1784.

55. Bonnard to Silvestre, 13 June 1784; Silvestre to Bonnard, 16 June 1784.

56. Bonnard to Silvestre, 16 April 1783.

57. Ibid.

58. Silvestre to Bonnard, 21 April 1783.

59. Ibid.

60. Silvestre to Bonnard, [1 July 1782].

61. Ibid.

62. Silvestre to Bonnard, 6 July [1782].

63. Bonnard to Silvestre, 6 July [1782].

64. Michael Mascuch, *Origins of the Individualist Self: Autobiography and Self-Identity in England, 1591–1791* (Cambridge: Polity Press, 1997), 21.

65. Bonnard to Silvestre, 20 December 1781.

66. Bonnard to Silvestre, 22 [December 1781].

67. Bonnard to Silvestre, 23 December 1781; Silvestre to Bonnard, [23 December 1781].

68. Silvestre to Bonnard, 24 December 1781.

69. Bonnard to Silvestre, 25 December 1781.

70. Bonnard to Silvestre, 26 June [1782].

71. Silvestre to Bonnard, [1 July 1782].

72. Silvestre to Bonnard, 17 July [1782].

73. Silvestre to Bonnard, 26 July [1782].

74. Bonnard to Silvestre, 29 July [1782].

75. Silvestre to Bonnard [22 October 1782]; 27 October [1782]; 1 November 1782. On the journals see Julia, "Bernard de Bonnard," 427–56.

76. Silvestre to Bonnard, 3 November 1782.

77. Ibid.

78. Bonnard to Silvestre, 7 November [1782].

79. Ibid.

80. Silvestre to Bonnard, 12 November 1782.

81. Ibid.

82. Silvestre to Bonnard, 24 June 1783.

83. Silvestre to Bonnard, 4 July 1783.

84. Bonnard to Silvestre, 8 July [1783].

85. Garat, *Précis historique*, 78.

86. Receipts from M. Audet, "Master of Arts from the University of Paris, Former Professor and Member of the Academy of Sciences, Arts, and Literature, Châlons-sur-Marne," AN 352 AP 39.

87. Augustin-François Silvestre to Prefect of Police, 8 Thermidor, An IX, in AN 352 AP 39; E. de Silvestre, *Renseignements sur quelques peintres et graveurs des XVIIe et XVIIIe siècles* (Paris: Mme Vve. Bouchard-Huzard, 1868), 14, 89.

88. AN 352 AP 42. The inventory is dated 22 Brumaire, An VII.

89. A travel pass was issued to Sophie and her two children in Courtacon on 14 Thermidor, An II (1 August 1794), AN 352 AP 42. The portrait is dated to 1794 by the printed address of the shop on "passage honoré," rather than Saint-Honoré, a nod to revolutionary sensibilities during the Terror. See Gabriel Cromer, "Nouvelles précisions; nouveaux documents sur le Physionotrace," *Bulletin de la Société Archéologique & Artistique le Vieux Papier* 29 (October 1928): 289–316. Later, when the address was "Cour Saint-Honoré," Sophie's father had his physionotrace portrait done. The extant prints of both portraits belonged to Sophie's brother, Augustin-François Silvestre, and were struck later, since they both carry legends giving birth and death dates of their subjects. Augustin-François had had his portrait done with the new technology around 1791, according to the artist's account books in the Bibliothèque nationale, but the print still in the family in 1868 is now lost. See Silvestre, *Renseignements sur quelques peintres et graveurs*, 94. On the physionotrace, see also Henry Vivarez, *Un Précurseur de la photographie dans l'art du portrait à bon marché: Le physionotrace* (Lille: Lefebvre-Ducrocq, 1906); René Hennequin, *Avant les photographies: Les portraits au physionotrace, gravés de 1788 à 1830. Catalogue nominatif, biographique et critique* (Troyes: J. L. Paton, 1932).

90. See http://www.polytechnique.fr/institution/eleves.php (accessed 8 June 2008); "Les Auditeurs des cours de Jean-Baptiste Lamarck," http://www.lamarck.cnrs.fr/auditeurs/presentation.php?lang=fr (accessed 8 June 2008). Inscription no. 45 (1797) reads: "Bonnard, born in Paris, age 15–1/2, residing in the Galleries du Louvre, rue des Orties, no. 4."

91. Entry ticket for the date 14 Ventôse, An VI (4 March 1798) in AN 352 AP 39.

92. Death certificates of Anne François Augustin Bonnard, age 14 1/2, (26 Fructidor, An VI); and Anne Charlotte Sophie Silvestre, age 34 (1 Vendémaire, An VII), in AN 352 AP 30. Registration of birth for Augustin-Henry Bonnard in "Reconstitution de l'état civil," Archives de Paris 5Mi 1/59 (misfiled by date under 8 October 1780).

93. See http://www.genea77-shage.org/Mairies/Communes/courtacon.htm (accessed 22 August 2007).

94. AN 352 AP 40; 352 AP 43–44.

95. Silvestre to Bonnard, 6 July [1782].

96. Bonnard, *Journal*, 24 May 1781.

97. Bonnard to Silvestre, 17 October 1782.

98. Bonnard to Silvestre, 16 August 1783.

99. Bonnard to Silvestre, 21 [August 1784]. Sophie's brother Augustin-François Silvestre also embraced and promoted friendship as a value. In 1788 he was one of the founders of the Société philomathique, whose motto was "Friendship and Study." Like Bernard de Bonnard, he was also a Freemason. See Jonathan Mandelbaum, "Science and Friendship: The Société Philomathique de Paris, 1788–1835," *History and Technology* 5 (1988): 179–92.

Conclusion

1. Mary Wollstonecraft, *A Vindication of the Rights of Woman* (Harmondsworth, UK: Penguin, 1975), 81.

2. Ibid., 80–83.

3. Mary Kelley has shown recently that the curriculum of early nineteenth-century American female academies and seminaries (which featured subjects such as writing, modern languages, history, and geography) was more modern than the classical curriculum of the colleges in which young men were educated and the model for their eventual reform. Kelley, *Learning to Stand and Speak: Women, Education, and Public Life in America's Republic* (Chapel Hill: University of North Carolina Press, 2006), chap. 3.

4. Wollstonecraft, *Vindication*, 82.

5. Simone de Beauvoir, *Le deuxième sexe*, vol. 2, *L'expérience vécue* (Paris: Gallimard, 1976), 618.

6. Ibid., 619.

7. Ibid., 620.

8. Ibid., 618.

9. Ibid., 622.

10. Ibid., 631.

11. Ibid., 52.

12. Ibid., 13.

INDEX

Académie française, 118, 119, 121, 122

Adélaïde de France (Madame Adélaïde), 44–46, 179

Adèle et Théodore (Genlis), 64

advertisements: for educators and schools, 68, 88–90, 115–16, 124, 126–27; for epistolary goods, 172–74, 183–93; exoticism and, 185–86, 261; fashion and, 175; *Gersaint's Shop Sign* (Watteau), 163–64, 174–75; novelty and marketing of goods, 223; royal endorsements in, 127–28; shopping and consumption linked to, 169; stationer's trade cards, 185–89; trade card of Edme Gersaint (Boucher), 176–77

affiches, 69, 86, 88, 90, 170

Africa, 260–61

agency: consumption as, 12, 166, 198; privateness as necessary for, 4, 271–72; tactical actions of the other, 277–78; writing as, 198, 272. *See also* subjectivity

Agnew, Jean-Christophe, 12–13

Aiguillon, duchesse d', 190

Alpers, Svetlana, 21

Altman, Janet, 77, 135, 139

Ami des femmes (Boudier de Villemert), 129

Andrews, John, 142, 170

Angélique-Adélaïde de Méliand, marquise de la Grange (Girodet), 308

Annales de l'éducation du sexe (Mouret), 66, 77, 89

architecture, privacy and domestic, 199, 204

Artaud, Jean Baptiste, 134–35

Atlantic world: exoticism and, 260–62; gender and mobility in, 260, 279–80; letters as ties to family, 279, 348n81

authorship, *vs.* writing, 1, 8, 140, 234, 236–37, 333–35, 341n33

autonomy: consumption and, 166, 336; education and, 333; marriage and loss of, 123, 250, 302–4, 306; privacy and, 4, 241, 256, 262, 271–72; relational, 3, 203; writing and, 2–5, 124, 199–200, 207, 247–48, 335. *See also* freedom

Autrèpe, M d', 105, 114

The Bad News (Pierre), 56

Barry, Marie-Jeannette Bécu, Comtesse du, 215

Barthelemy, abbé Louis, 89, 128–30

Barthes, Roland, 237

Batteux, abbé, 89

Baudouin, Pierre-Antoine, 34

Bayer, François, 229

Beaufort, Mlle (school proprietress), 89

Beauharnais, Fanny de, 129

Beaumont, Mme de (client of Lazare Duvaux), 201

Beauvoir, Simone de, 333–37

Beauzée, Nicolas, 124

Behn, Aphra, 261

The Beloved Mother (Greuze), 57–58

The Beloved Portrait (Schall), 35

Bérenguier, Nadine, 75

Bertin, Rose, 312

Bibliothèque des enfans (Dumas), 121

Billiard, Dame (school proprietress), 88, 90

Blakey, Mme (mercer), 175, 179

Blondel, François, 204

the body: civilizing process and control of, 46, 55; desks or writing tables and the female, 205; letters as embodiment of the writer, 9, 100–101, 132, 258; posture or carriage, 46–48, 106, 108, 112–13, 239–40; seal as materialization of the self, 241; writing as discipline of, 105–6

Boilly, Louis-Léopold, 30–31

Boirayon, Mlle (of Annonay), 74, 75, 78–79

Boirayon, Mme (of Annonay), 78–79, 80

Bonnard, Anne François Augustin de, 328

Bonnard, Augustin-Henri de "Bonbon," 135, 313–14, 315, 318, 321–29, 330, 374n39

Bonnard, Bernard de: career of, 310–11, 313, 315, 330; death of, 327; on friendship, 330–31; letters written by, pictured, 190–92, 317; marriage to Sophie Silvestre, 7, 310–13, 330–31; portrait of, 312; Rousseau as influence on, 315–16,

paintings, letter theme in: absent male in, 19, 22–23, 32, 33, 37–38, 41, 47, 57; agency or passivity of subject in, 19–21, 22, 33, 46–48, 59; desks as figures in, 226–27, 241; Dutch genre painting and, 21–25; Epistolary Woman as idealized figure in, 19; eroticization of, 33–37, 41, 57–58, 231–34; fashion depicted in and, 44–46; friendship and, 21, 36–38, 44, 54–55, 330–31; gaze and voyeurism, 41; genre painting conventions in, 15, 19; illegibility of text of letters in, 21, 41; interiority and, 26–28; intimate settings of, 22–23, 27–28, 42, 44, 231–34; love and love letters in, 21–31; maid or messenger figures in, 19, 23–24, 31, 32; male (in)security, 19, 33, 37–41, 58; man-of-letters as subject in, 48–54, 226–27, 229–30; motherhood linked to, 21, 42–43, 46–48, 54–55, 57–59, 308, 329–30; narratives in, 30–31, 36–37, 42–44, 343n19; portraiture and, 19–21, 41–46; pose of sitter in, 19–21, 41–42, 46–54, 53–54, 231–34, 343n31; privacy or confidentiality and, 47; self-restraint and pose in, 46–48; *sensibilité* and, 57, 59; truthfulness and genre of, 44; voyeurism and, 22, 34–36; widows in, 56–57
Palais Royal, 13, 167–69, 175, 199
Panckoucke, André-Joseph, 87, 100–101, 145
Panon Desbassayns, Henry Paulin, 168; education arrangements for children of, 93–99
paper: color of, 186, 190, 194–97, 361n92, 362n99; Dutch, 187, 195–96, 361n92; embellishments on letter-writing, 187, 189; manufacture of, 194–97, 361n92, 362n99; for penmanship practice, 105; varieties and grades of, 185–87. *See also* stationers
paradox, 146–47
Pardailhè-Galabrun, Annik, 199
Pateman, Carole, 304
patronage, 139, 309, 312, 313, 315–16, 330
Paul et Virginie (Saint-Pierre), 5–6, 136–37, 279, 290
Pauw, Cornelius de, 267
penmanship, 31, 102; as art, 205; beauty and aesthetics of, 101, 102, 105–6; copy books as examples of, 106–12; as discipline of the body, 105–6; moral education and, 108; pedagogical theory, 105–6, 114–15; *vs.* writing, 102, 114
pens, 162, 169
periodicals: *affiches* as source of cultural and social news, 90, 170–71; commercial society and, 165–66, 169; education debate, 63–64; the fashion press, 27–28, 105, 164–65, 169, 170, 172, 175, 190, 208; letters published in, 142; poetry published in, 146. *See also* advertisements
Pesselier, Charles-Étienne, 63
Petit, Nicolas, 209–10
Petit Dunkerque, Le, 169, 172–74, 180–81
Petite-Poste dévalisée, La (Artaud), 134–35
Petity, Jean Raymond, abbé de, 113, 114
Philipon de la Madelaine, Louis, 135, 139, 140; on epistolary style, 145
Philosophe sans le savoir, Le (Sedaine), 239
philosophical correspondence, 141, 156
Phlipon, Marie-Jeanne "Manon" (Mme Roland): as autodidact, 152–53, 267–68; on breastfeeding, 374n39; death of, 6; on education as diversion, 66; education of, 66, 67–68, 74, 78, 152–53, 267–68; epistolary friendship with Sophie and Henriette Cannet, 6, 66, 79–80, 85, 145,

149–50, 269–70, 307; extracts in journals of, 152–53; on formal correspondence, 137, 139; on gender restrictions, 369n94, 373n118; on intellectual passion, 268–69; on letter-writing, 163, 265; on marriage, 295–304; on morality, 264–66, 267, 270, 271–72; pride in letters, 157; privacy and developing subjectivity of, 264; Sévigné as model for, 149–50; social and economic situation of, 6, 262–63; on spelling, 127; writing and developing subjectivity of, 5, 15
Pierre, Jean-Baptiste-Marie, 56
Plan d'éducation (Gosselin), 106
playing cards: as impromptu stationery, 252; as teaching tool, 73–74
Pluche, abbé Noël-Antoine, 144–45
Poirer, Simon-Philippe, 215
politics, fashion and, 165–66
Pompadour, Jeanne-Antoinette Poisson, marquise de, 201–2, 236, 361n75; portraits of, 212, 214, 231–34, 344n55
porcelain: French made, 167, 179–80, 215, 221–22; imported, 172 (*See also* pagodes and magots *under this heading*); inkstands, 177–80; lightness as aesthetic value and, 194; *pagodes* and *magots*, 172, 176–78, 215; plaques integrated into writing desks, 200, 207, 215, 217, 218, 221, 222, 230, 231
Portrait of an Architect (Anon.), 230
Portrait of a Woman (Labille-Guiard), 15, 19–21, 28, 41, 44–46, 47, 53–55, 58–59, 181, 329–31
Portrait of a Woman Writing and Her Daughter (Vallyer-Coster), 46–48
Portrait of a Young Actress (Gobert), 56
Portrait of a Young Lady, Beckoning (Santerre), 41, 42
Portrait of Camille Desmoulins, His Wife Lucile, and Their Son Horace Camille (studio of David), 57–58
Portrait of Sir Thomas More (Hans Holbein the Younger), 52–53
Portrait of the Marquis de Vaudreuil (Roslin), 226–27
postal services, 1, 194, 253, 263
posture, 108, 112–13, 239–40
Pradère, Alexandre, 223
précieuses, 118–19, 122, 128, 148, 199
preservation of letters, 156, 252, 309
Prévost, Antoine François, 65
"Prince of Angola," 260–61
Printer's Desk (*bureau typographique*), 71–72, 73, 121
privacy: agency and privateness, 271–72; autonomy and, 4, 241, 256, 262, 271–72; *cabinets* as personal or private space, 7, 199–200, 248, 250–51, 253, 256–60, 262, 264–65, 271–72, 305; desks as personal or private space, 162, 200, 203, 235, 238–44, 240–44, 258; domestic architecture and, 199, 204 (*See also* cabinets … *under this heading*); foreign language and, 257–58; intimate settings in paintings, 226–27; letter writing as private activity, 199, 334–35; seals as mark of, 162, 240–41; secrets and, 238–39; subjectivity and, 251, 253–54, 256–58, 262, 264, 265, 271–72, 334–35. *See also* confidentiality
privateness: domestic space and sociability, 13, 162, 240
Projet pour perfectioner l'ortgrafe des Langues de l'Europe (Saint-Pierre), 121
Promenades de Clarisse (Tournon), 131–32